Feel the
BHAGAVAD GITA

Feel the
BHAGAVAD GITA
A New Interpretation

· →→→ · ←←← ·

VIJAY KUMAR SAXENA

ARCHWAY
PUBLISHING

Archway Publishing books may be ordered through booksellers or by contacting:

Archway Publishing
1663 Liberty Drive
Bloomington, IN 47403
www.archwaypublishing.com
1 (888) 242-5904

Because of the dynamic nature of the Internet, any web addresses or links contained in this book may have changed since publication and may no longer be valid. The views expressed in this work are solely those of the author and do not necessarily reflect the views of the publisher, and the publisher hereby disclaims any responsibility for them.

Any people depicted in stock imagery provided by Thinkstock are models, and such images are being used for illustrative purposes only. Certain stock imagery © Thinkstock.

ISBN: 978-1-4808-2227-6 (sc)
ISBN: 978-1-4808-2228-3 (e)

Library of Congress Control Number: 2015915202

Print information available on the last page.

Archway Publishing rev. date: 2/22/2016

Bliss is now and beyond. Just learn to separate the "truth (never changing)" from the "untruth (ever changing)." This is all the Bhagavad Gita is about.

Table of Contents

i. What does this volume deal with?

Imagine that you are a child of four years. You are walking with your grandfather early in the morning on a lovely track near a river with a lot of foliage and natural beauty. Suddenly a cuckoo coos. You like this cooing and look at your grandfather. Your grandfather also winks at you and smiles back at you. Your grandfather caresses your hair and tells you a beautiful story with an excellent moral lesson. You keep growing and develop an intimate relationship with your grandfather, who plays with you, goes with you and is always at your back and call. Then you grow. Life presents its twists and turns. A strange situation comes very late in life, where you are standing against a group with a gun to save the name and honor of your country. You are about to shoot and then you find suddenly to your horror that the one in your range is none other than your grandfather. Suddenly all those fond memories of childhood crowd your mind. You are at the horns of dilemma. You are not able to press the trigger. Then suddenly someone from your own side comes and understandingly and successfully tells you the invalidity of your emotional change in view of national security, righteousness, ethical, moral and worldly duties explaining at the same time following perennial questions:

- Why does life present conflicting situations like this?
- Why do different negative emotions weave different patterns in life and forcibly dominate our nature?
- What should we go by in this life?
- Why do we behave as we behave?
- What is this secret that I am? Where did I come from? Where will I go finally?
- What is the validity of different stands of the people to judge righteousness and unrighteousness of others?
- Is there a way to live life as naturally as a boat floats in a calm sea, cruising ahead, allowing you to enjoy the winds, the clouds, the expanse of the sea, giving ample opportunity to you to be what you want to be? How do we tune in to rhythm of life? How can we use "The Epitome of Secret Power" within us?
- Is there anything to life better than earning the livelihood and remaining confined to one's family alone?
- How do we maintain in life a separation, balanced in beauty (eternal, inseparable, infinite rhythm of joy) and power (changing pushes and pulls of daily life, swaying the individual all the time)?
- How can we convert our existential living into living with substance, meaning and purpose?
- What is the "Universal Truth" of all the religions?

Yes, this volume deals with these questions. This is essentially about the universal forces, reasons contributing to the composition of human nature and the "Supreme Secret" behind everything animate and inanimate in this universe. This is really what it is about. If you know "This (idam), That (tat) and I (aham)," focused and talked about here in the Bhagavad Gita by Lord Krishna, then there will be nothing remaining to be known or aspired for. The self, that displays, will lose itself in "The Self" that transcends (goes beyond limitations), revealing its true meaning and its true nature.

An insight into the ideas of this volume will help to get to the light of the "Immortal Flame" present within each one of us. This journey into this volume will help to identify "The One" who is felt in the darkness 'within', with closed eyes, but not seen in the light of the day with open eyes. This volume will help the reader to cultivate (to develop a particular skill or quality) the wisdom discriminating the "Never Changing" and "Ever changing."

Each word, each thought and each path of the Bhagavad Gita clarifies that it is only the revelation (making people aware of that, which has been a secret and startling) of the Infinite, which is endlessly new and eternally beautiful in each one of us. The thoughts of "The Infinite" decipher (succeed in giving) the only meaning to the "Self." Intimacy with the details of discussion in this volume will help to realize the "Infinite in the finite" and the "Giver in the gifts." This maturity dawns only when one goes beyond the confinement of the life of self. This volume unfolds the universal secret. None could live or move, if the energy of the "All Pervading Joy" did not fill the sky, earth and millions of stars and innumerable galaxies. In all our actions, in all our thinking and in all our pursuits, the impetus of the "Infinite Energy" guides us and helps us. The "true wholesomeness of a being" comes not from necessity but from "affinity (a strong feeling that you understand and like) of the Infinite." "The Infinite" is the "principle of perfection" that we have in our soul (that part of the person which does not die with death). That is what the Bhagavad Gita stands deals with.

There is nothing wrong in any situation or event. The fault lies in one's own personality within. We all are searching it in the external world. Actually it is within each one of us, lying buried in the layers of consciousness. It is the individual himself or herself or individual's attitude and vision that breathes life, meaning and purpose into events. In the act of seeing the object, seen is inert. "The 'Seer within; The Subject (same within all of us) alone" is sentient (causing the feeling and knowledge that one exist).

Before Lord Krishna starts speaking in the Bhagavad Gita, Arjuna puts forth numerous plausible (reasonable likely to be true) reasons for retreating from the battle field. After this discourse of the Gita, the whole scenario changes for Arjuna. How did Krishna bring about this change in Arjuna? Krishna made Arjuna look at the "Source," which breathes life into life. Truth is that we know Him "Not," and yet we know "Him," beyond all limitations, beneath fathomless layers in the emptiness of our being, ever fresh, ever shining, and ever witnessing. All "My this" and "That Other" are waiting to be reconciled in the "Universal Love." What is to be done for this? Read the Gita. Feel the Gita. Breathe out the Gita. Work out the Gita and the "Ferryman within each one of us," as explained by Lord Krishna in the Gita, will take each one of us across to the "Other shore" in due course … … … … fear not.

Rest assured about one thing. This volume will focus on questions, which have perennially grappled with attention of mankind in all ages – "Who is 'HE', who, within me, validates my existence? Who is 'HE' within me, who sustains me and rather carries me in the critical moments? Who is 'HE' within me, who, without my knowledge, witnesses my each thought, my each action and my whole being inside out?" In this volume, you will learn to sing the 'song of life' from the 'source of life'. Yes, all this is there in this volume.

ii. Relevance of reading the Bhagavad Gita

Why should anyone be interested in spending time about a conversation in the Bhagavad Gita? This conversation is thousands and thousands years old. It is relating to a dispute between cousins over ruler-ship of "kingdom" in north central India. Here focus is on one point. Why should anyone read the Bhagavad Gita at all? Is it to get the magic wand whose touch will fulfill all desires? Is it to fill our "Garbage Can of knowledge" which is finally dumped somewhere for good? Is it to comply with a time beaten tradition about which we do not fully know and mechanically follow? It is not all that.

"Feel the Bhagavad Gita" helps the reader to gain the realization of a "Source of Universal Eternal Energy," whose very thoughts will help to touch in "one's own within" a space or a zone or a chord (which is familiar and true), which pulsates or vibrates with "Eternal Universal Energy." Call it by a general name or a particular name or no name. No name or form has described it fully so far in the history of the world. All names and forms ever used so far only partly describe it or rather refer to it. It is far from defining it precisely. This "Universal Energy Source" can be given any name as we give to our loved ones after we have got used to it i.e. after we get the feel of it as we have the feel of our hands and palms. One purpose of this "Feel the Bhagavad Gita" is to promote awareness (living personal connection) of this "Greatest Source of Energy." Enlivening connection with this "Energy Source" dissolves "**ordinary unconsciousness**" which comes to become integral part of daily life and seeps (allows slowly to flow out) aliveness from life. This aliveness to this connectivity provides all the grand essentials of life i.e. something to do, something to live for, something to love for, something to hope for, something to provide for and something which surpasses everything else. This "Feel the Bhagavad Gita connects us to the "Universal Unfailing Source of Comfort and Inspiration".

It helps one who is exhausted. It helps one who is in turmoil. It helps one who is in despair or utter confusion. It also helps one who is blissfully in oblivion about twists and turns of life, which strike with vengeance in cyclic fashion to shatter the feel good factor of life. It makes each reader (from all walks of life) realize that he or she requires bringing about some difference to live life optimally. It "**evolves**" the readers in all walks of life physically, mentally, emotionally and spiritually. Whatever may be the base of an individual's standing or perception in life, further evolvement may still be geared to be in tune with the "mission of existence" keeping in touch with "**that zone, that space, that chord, that ultimate pulsating reality or truth within**," which is beyond limitation, beyond destruction, beyond description and full with peace, joy and knowledge.

This knowledge is not ordinary knowledge. This knowledge redeems (makes less bad or makes some one free from evil) the past and takes the individual towards highest possible point of perfection in future. It humanizes the human beings and immortalizes (helps to gain freedom from all possible limitations uncovering one's own divinity) the mortals. It is the sovereign remedy for individual's ignorance, sufferings, lack of capacity (physical, mental, emotional and spiritual) and limitations of one's vision. It takes an individual beyond limitations of human knowledge and experience towards "ever continuing peace, ever continuing contentment, and self-effacing joy (joy which refuses to be influenced or affected by one's individual existence and perspective).

"Feel the Bhagavad Gita" helps an individual to identify with that which is not hereditary in an individual, which is not reward of individual efforts alone, but still remains the "True Eternal Potential Within," connecting the individual to the "Universal Eternal Mind," the ground of all that is. The Feel the Bhagavad Gita unfolds that an individual is a delusion. That "Secret" within is the "Reality or Truth." This "Feel the Bhagavad Gita" will take the reader to "a zone of illumination, revelation, knowledge, love and bliss," which the reader has not known thus far in life. To sacredly maintain the universality of the discussion, "**describing words**" have been used along with traditional "words and terms."

One point has to be specially taken care of. It is not enough to be confined to understanding. The focus has to be on awareness, feelings. Understanding ensues when feeling is there. Go for the feel, for the experience of what it is being talked about. Lord Krishna says "***Vasudeva Sarvam***; Vasudeva (The Sovereign Supreme Entity) alone is everywhere." Is this term "Vasudeva" used just to make a mention of an individual who was son of Vasudeva and whose physical presence is no more today? No. That is not the intention. This term is like a "neon light in the dark night" inviting your attention to "The Supreme Eternal energy Source of the Universe," which it represents or which it is. After you have felt it, you can use any name of your choice for it. First feel what Lord Krishna is talking about. Every word that Krishna uses will touch you; will leap at you, if you are able to feel it. This "Feel the Bhagavad Gita" is an attempt to stimulate "that feeling in you; that ever simmering (strong restlessness due to anger, hate and love) hunger for the Truth," which is lying buried under the heap of mundane (ordinary life relating to existential physical self) activities of life, waiting to be explored one day.

In daily life, the feeling "this is mine that is yours" consumes us. We are not able to feel the illumination within. We are not able to shatter the mental blocks. We have to feel the enormity, effectiveness, omnipresence, omnipotence and omniscience of that "Universal Truth." We have to bathe into the "Universal Ocean of unlimited peace, unlimited knowledge and unlimited joy" that is being talked about here. This "Feel the Bhagavad Gita" will bring about a change in level of awareness. When we feel the Bhagavad Gita and get to that "**Zone of Utter and Eternal Magnificence, Unlimited Love, Unlimited Knowledge and unlimited joy**," for which all names and forms are simply insufficient, we get the vision of the creator, which exhorts us to make our contribution to the world for cosmic benefit. All imperfect thoughts, relating to physical afflictions, disease, poverty, unhappiness and miseries relating to "existential-physical-life," pale into insignificance at that level. This "Feel the Bhagavad Gita," will release from the words of Lord Krishna, "that touching experience, that invigorating (more active, more healthy) feeling of undergoing an emotion," which will pull the reader out from the "dead-living" to the "vibrant-living" to serve the purpose of existence meaningfully, joyfully and effectively.

Feel of the "Bhagavad Gita" will make the readers more active, more responsive, more profound and more insightful than anything that they have ever been. It takes the attention of the reader from the "false in you" to the "real in you." Feel of the Bhagavad Gita will be missing till one perceives the "knower within," who dwells behind the "thinker within." The "Deeper self; Real Self; Pure Self; Exclusive Divinity Within" recognizes the spiritual truth, tunes in to it in the language of silence and makes you feel the inner freedom and inner expansion immediately. The Bhagavad Gita will take you beyond limitations of human understanding and experience. It will make you undergo the living experience of how the "Self-Revealing One" stands revealed right within, in the conscious-space, ever afresh and ever smiling in divine splendor.

Reading the Bhagavad Gita will prevent the abatement of interest and enthusiasm in life in misfortune and bereavement. Even the thought of dulling by ashes will not shake the individual. It will prevent slow fading of life's perfect flower, whose essential nature is to smile.

iii. Preparing to feel the Bhagavad Gita

The Bhagavad Gita has got a surprising wealth of ideas. It gives you something to cling to, something on which to build a strong, firm structure of life. It helps you to give direction to your life. This conversation between lord Krishna and Arjuna can give you inner peace, contentment and tranquility, which so many of us are searching but still missing. It can also help you to take life to the "Highest Point of Perfection." The original dialogues are in Sanskrit, which is not in daily use these days. English synonyms are not available for many words, for example, *Sankhya, Dharma, Shraddha* etc. There is one more reason creating difficulty for readers especially in English language. It is not enough to understand the meaning i.e. what Lord Krishna is talking. To feel the Gita, one must know why Lord Krishna is talking as He is talking. There were certain thoughts in the mind of Lord Krishna while he was talking to Arjuna in the battlefield. These thoughts were the life-line of even common people in that era. If one is familiar with these thoughts and terms, the Gita will unfold its beauty, depth and expanse very naturally. That is why, in almost all Indian scriptures including Vedas and Upnishads, these thoughts and related terms have dominated the subject matter. Everyone those days knew these thoughts such as incarnation (manifestation with intense divine powers for cosmic benefit), transmigration (passing into another body after death), "individual as energy field of spirituality in the body in state of delusion" and "Eternal Universal Energy Source of spirituality alone existing as a whole, perceptible by pure intelligence only." The discussion of the Bhagavad Gita took place in the battle field and war was just about to begin. Explanation was given when it was called for by Arjuna. At many places just passing reference was given to the background thoughts such as "soul's journey to its destiny" taking the further details for granted. These thoughts were part of Indian psyche and many of these thoughts were inculcated in the child right in infancy both in the family discussions and at schools (*Gurukuls*). For this reason, Lord has not taken up many points, thoughts and terms in detail. In the discussion of the Bhagavad Gita, Lord is standing in the battle field and war is just about to begin. This concern for the situation has had its impact on the discussion. Even Lord Krishna's treatment of the same subject was different when He talked about this knowledge [*Prakriti* (nature); *Purusha* (eternal existence); projected universe subject to modifications, for it has sprung from disturbance among the gunas or attributes; eternal presence in all beings and steadfast devotion to "IT" for release from all limitations] again with Uddhav, his childhood friend and minister, later in his life. That discourse, the last message of Sri Krishna, is known as "Uddhav Gita." For the modern reader, it becomes difficult to know why Lord Krishna is talking as He is talking and why He is shifting from one issue to another. Arjuna has an agonizing problem. He is in the battle field and war is just about to begin. He is facing a sort of split in his personality. His hand is suddenly shaking and he is not able to hold his bow, Gandiva (name of his bow) seeing his grandfather and reverend teacher ready to fight with him from the opposite camp. His reputation as top notch warrior of that era is at stake. On the other hand, Lord Krishna first smiles (even in this tense situation), with his twinkling eyes doing the talking part. Then strangely (for one, new to abstract discussions) Lord starts talking about something abstract, which is indestructible, eternal and imminent (naturally present everywhere and in everything

5

and being). He does not even say what He is talking about. He simply starts making reference by saying "This or That and later Me and I." Lord knew that Arjuna knew it. Many people, in this era, do not understand the discussion for this reason. Many people, in the beginning, do not know that the subject taken up and talked about by Lord Krishna was the core of ancient Indian thinking and the very root of all the celebrated Indian scriptures (including the Vedas, the Upnishads and the Ramayana) without an exception. It will give the real feel of the Bhagavad Gita, if these formidable important thoughts and terms are selectively discussed first as introduction. The lack of exposure to these thoughts and terms is the reason, why this (Bhagavad Gita), treasure of great "Truth" and enduring ideas, has remained a mystery for many of us in this world especially in English speaking zones due to the unavailability of apt synonyms. The Bhagavad Gita has "ideas that breathe" and "words that burn." If you are able to feel these words and thoughts, they will leap at you. They will knock at the gate of your soul (that part of individual which does not die with death) to give you and press in you hope, faith and confidence. They will catch you. In the Bhagavad Gita, all the ideas and all the words in reality are flowing in one direction only, focusing on one message - "Get that unbounded vision of the 'Truth' within you and live life of boundless height, boundless breath and boundless depth." It will get you to the "pinnacle (most important and successful part) of human experience."

Here an attempt is being made to make you feel the Bhagavad Gita. Feeling is perception by awareness. It is different from mere understanding or intellectual interpretation. When feeling is there, understanding is there, already. Understanding inheres (naturally exist) in feeling. For this reason, an attempt is being made to give first an introduction of selected major thoughts and terms, which have frequently dominated almost all Indian traditions and Indian scriptures. These thoughts and terms have been frequently talked about or touched (for example, journey after death in *lokas* or spheres talked about but not specified due to paucity of time) not fully in the Gita as well. To promote feeling, this attempt has to be participative. Ponder over the following questions and then look at the chart that follows after some discussion:

a) Where do I come from?
b) What is the real purpose of this life?
c) Where do I go after the death?
d) Am I the shadow of "Someone" whom I normally keep out of focus in daily life? Who is this someone?
e) Am I not the one, whom I see in the mirror? Who am I then?

There is a "Divine Play or Continuous Interaction" of "The Eternal Consciousness and the Unconsciousness" within us and around us. Why is it a play? It appears and disappears with startling regularity. Everything in it works with amazing precision. It goes on always all the time at every moment, whether one notices it or not. Ages do not change it. Time does not affect it. This "Eternal Divine Play or Eternal Interaction of consciousness and unconsciousness" goes on always without a break. Lord Krishna had the details of this Divine play (Continuous interaction of consciousness and unconsciousness) in perspective (mental view) while talking to Arjuna in the battle field of Kurukshetra (Mahabharata).The exposure to this Divine Play helps us to understand what we are, what our eternal direction is and how we should get to the final point which optimizes the reach of human efforts. This exposure will also help us to understand, what lord Krishna is talking in the Gita and why he is talking it at a particular moment and in a particular sequence. It will introduce us to the terminology and the basics of the Gita. Above all, the exposure to this Divine Play will provide us a base to intimately feel "The Gita." The basic thoughts of this

"Divine Play; The sequence of interaction and interplay of "the Consciousness and the Unconsciousness" have been summarized in a diagram below with the heading "Cosmic Eternal Flow." Be with the questions given at the start of this paragraph and go through the diagram and comments thereafter:

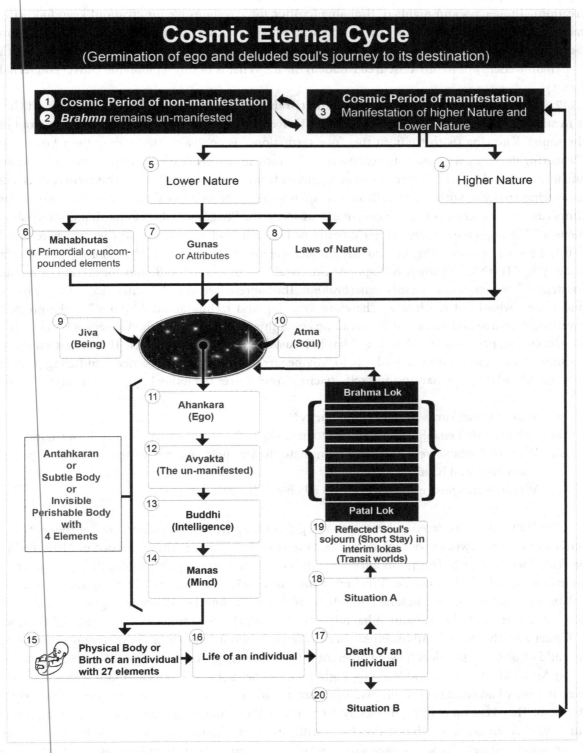

Cosmic Eternal Cycle
(Germination of ego and deluded soul's journey to its destination)

1 Cosmic Period of non-manifestation
2 *Brahmn* remains un-manifested

3 Cosmic Period of manifestation
Manifestation of higher Nature and Lower Nature

5 Lower Nature

4 Higher Nature

6 Mahabhutas or Primordial or uncompounded elements

7 Gunas or Attributes

8 Laws of Nature

9 Jiva (Being)

10 Atma (Soul)

Antahkaran or Subtle Body or Invisible Perishable Body with 4 Elements

11 Ahankara (Ego)

12 Avyakta (The un-manifested)

13 Buddhi (Intelligence)

14 Manas (Mind)

Brahma Lok

Patal Lok

19 Reflected Soul's sojourn (Short Stay) in interim lokas (Transit worlds)

18 Situation A

15 Physical Body or Birth of an individual with 27 elements

16 Life of an individual

17 Death Of an individual

20 Situation B

(The terms used in this flow chart have been extensively used in the Gita-discussion)

1. Cosmic period of manifestation and cosmic period of non-manifestation (*Brahama's* day and Night) - According to Vedic Cosmology, a period of about 432 crores human years is called a *Kalpa*. Each *Kalpa* represents either a day (cosmic period of manifestation; called *prabhava*) or a night (cosmic period of non-manifestation; called *pralaya*) of *Brahama* (cosmic force responsible for creation). These days and nights of Brahama (cosmic force responsible for creation) keep following each other with regularity. During the period of non-manifestation (night of *Brahama*), "The Brahmn (Supreme Universal Eternal Reality)," in un-manifested state, remains like the conscious space, with its dynamic energy or nature obscured (hidden) in "it." What is Brahmn (Supreme Universal Eternal Reality?

2. The Supreme Universal Eternal Reality (Brahmn) - The main purpose of the Bhagwad Gita is to stimulate awareness of Brahmn (Supreme Universal Eternal Reality; God of the Gods; Soul of the souls). Knowing (with feelings) this "one term alone" is equivalent to reading the whole Gita. Measuring its depth, its beauty, its expanse, its relevance, its reverence (great respect and admiration) and its innumerable facets (aspects) will be a journey from head to heart. Feeling this term fully is like measuring an ocean with a tape. Still an attempt is to be made, as it has always been done numerous times earlier. This term, as it is, appears in discussion in the Bhagavad Gita very late but Lord Krishna focuses "The Supreme Reality" either directly or through "indirect connection" everywhere. Lord is using such terms as: "This (*ayam*); Me (*mam*); Me alone (*mam ekam*); Him alone (*Tamev*)" but underlying "Truth" everywhere is "Supreme Universal Eternal Reality (or *Brahmn* or Eternal Universal Existence)." Without knowing this term (*Brahmn*; The Supreme Universal Eternal Reality), one cannot understand who Lord Krishna is. Therefore knowing and feeling about "*Brahmn*" is the greatest investment of time and energy. Simply reading about this term is not enough. Awareness is necessary. Awareness (i.e. perception with feelings) has to be used more than the intellect. The discussion about "*Brahmn*" will be interesting. It will lead to "divine terrain (area under reference)," suffusing (feeling that spreads all over) enchanting and self-effacing. Ponder over the following questions first:

a) Who is it that turns impurity into purity?
b) Who is it that enables an individual to have expanded vision of Un-bounded Awareness?
c) Who is it whose very thoughts culminate (finally help one reach) into unlimited peace, knowledge and bliss?
d) Who is it in whose everlasting joy do all objects have their birth?

The "One" being referred to here, is too large, too deep to be truly understood or measured or limited in the framework of our words. Still an attempt is being made. The discussion of "This Reality or Truth" will always be fruitful in nurturing one's own and others' spiritual growth. It provides one an insight into the "self" and the "Wisdom of the Supreme Consciousness." This discussion in detail will be very fruitful. Dealing in sandal woods always leaves the fingers with some fragrance, come what may. Whom are we talking about? What is the most appropriate way to start this discussion? First, we will start with the three details of experiences, taken at random, happening at different points of time in world's history by people following different beliefs, different customaries and different ceremonies.

i) An incident from World War II – Eight men, in the rubber life rafts and sailing in the ocean, were in pretty bad condition. Their plane, on war mission in the Pacific, had been forced down eight days ago. They kept on drifting helplessly ever since without food and water in the scorching tropic sun, with feet blistered, faces burnt, eyes laden with fatigue and hunger and mouth and bodies parched. Their captain Eddie V. Ricken backer, a man of faith, could not give them strength and understanding that they needed. One of the men had a Bible. They read it, right from the first day, and felt assured that there was "Someone, Somewhere" who knew where they were. Now, on eighth day, they were desperate. There was no sign of a plane or boat anywhere but the wide empty shining expanse of the sea. There was nothing in the sight except the water and water, as far as eye could see. On eighth day, they read the following message from Matthew: "Therefore, take no thought, saying what we shall eat Or what shall we drink? Or, wherewithal shall we be clothed … for your heavenly Father knoweth that ye have need of all these things …?" What happened next was a miracle to the suffering men. It seemed like the direct answer to their prayers. Who can say it was not? A seagull flew in out of nowhere and landed on Ricken Baker's head. He reached up and caught it. They had food. Soon there was a rainstorm and they had drinking water. The experience filled them with awe and astonishment. Who was this "someone, somewhere knowing where they were" or "heavenly father"? When these details appeared in the newspapers, people everywhere were noticeably affected by it and touched by it.

ii) The Bible mentions of a miraculous event. The Israelites in Egypt were slaves and ill treated with extreme cruelties. Moses, a holy man, lead them to escape from Egypt to go out of the country. When the king of Egypt was told that the Israelites had escaped, he got his chariot ready and followed them with an army of six hundred finest soldiers to capture them. Then, the fleeing Israelites came near the red sea. Now the Israelites had the sea before them and enemy-army following them. Desperation (lack of hope) caught them. Then, Moses, the holy man among them, held out his hand over the sea in state of complete surrender remembering the Lord and the "Lord" drove the sea back with a strong east wind. The water was divided and the Israelites went through the sea on the dry ground, with walls of water on both the sides. The Israelites walked through the sea on the dry ground. But, when the Egyptian chariots with their horses and drivers went into the sea, the "Lord" brought the water back and it covered them. Who is this "Lord," who allowed the Israelites to walk on the dry land into the sea with walls of water on both the sides?

iii) The Mahabharta, sage Vyasa's noblest gift to the mankind, mentions a game of dice arranged by the Kauravas to dupe the Pandavas. In this game of dice, Yudhistra, the eldest among the Pandavas, lost everything including his younger brothers. Finally he was cunningly asked to stake Draupadi, the wife of the Pandavas. Yudhistra lost Draupadi as well. Then Duhsasana, on behalf of Kauravas, dragged "queen Draupadi" to the court by force, pulling her hair and least caring about her clothes and femininity (that which is typical of women). In that open court and in the presence of the august assembly, Duhsasana started to pull off her robe (saree, long piece of cloth, which is traditionally worn by ladies to cover the body in India) to remove all the clothes from her body. All earthly aid had failed and in anguish of utter helplessness, Draupdi cried loudly "O Lord of the world, whom I adore and trust, abandon me not in this dire plight; you are my sole refuge. Protect me." Then she almost fainted and evil-minded Duhsasana shamefully kept on pulling Draupadi's robe (saree). Then a miracle happened and everyone there was wonder-struck. As wicked Duhsasana pulled off the robe (saree) of Draupdi, fresh robe (saree) started appearing on her body and this phenomenon continued, till a heap of resplendent robe (saree) was piled up before the assembly and mighty Duhsasana, having the strength of elephants, desisted and sat down in sheer fatigue and disbelief, completely exhausted, unable to pull the robe any more. The assembly trembled at this marvel. Good men in the assembly praised Lord and wept. Who is this "Lord of the world," whom Draupadi addressed in state of utter helplessness?

Still the question remains. Who are we talking about? Many times, we notice that something from the "in-most of our beings," without knowing direction, description and abode, cries in utter despair "Please help me … Tell me what to do." Whom is this cry for? We are talking of "That" only.

9

It is "That" with which we are and without which we are not. It is enough to have faith in saying that it is. It is futile to attempt to describe it. It is unborn, eternal and ancient. It is the all-pervading "Reality," though this "One" is regarded as many. Knowing this, one becomes free from all bondages and comes in state of "Universal Oneness." This "One" is self-existent, eternal and is the base of all the beliefs that "I am." This "One," being discussed, is indivisible, eternal, blissful, knowledge itself, ever-uniform and all-pervasive. This "One" is never born, never dies, neither increases nor decreases nor changes. This "One" remains both as un-manifested and manifested. In manifested form, when the body dies this "One" still remains like the sky in the pitcher. It has no particular form and name. But, being the sovereign lord of the universe, it expresses in all manifestations. An individual is a combination of perishable bodies and spiritual soul. Perishable bodies include physical body (external cover) and finer body (invisible perishable body consisting of mind, intellect, memory and ego). Death is an event in which physical body alone separates and invisible perishable body, with ego enveloping the divine essence within moves forward on journey beyond death. Body (external cover) dies one death. Invincible perishable body undergoes many deaths and births. After a long spiritual journey, divine wisdom (knowledge about the self) dawns. The spell of ego on "Exclusive Divinity" bursts. Ego vanishes and all that remains is divine splendor, "Exclusive Divinity" within. This is real self, the soul and the knower of everything. The qualities and the power of the gross body are borrowed from mind. Finer body (mind, intelligence, memory and ego) borrows its powers and luminosity from the soul standing behind the veil of ego. This finer body (subtle body) relating to an individual, which goes from one body to another body after death of present physical body is called "Individualized soul or Deluded soul." That, which is under the cover of ego or individualized-soul, is soul, Exclusive Divinity or Brahmn. That is what we have been talking about. For our reference in this discussion, we shall call it "Supreme Eternal Universal Reality" or Supreme Being or merely The Supreme.

Where is it? This "Supreme Eternal Universal Energy or Reality or Truth" is everywhere in this universe. The whole universe owes its existence to "the Supreme Being" and yet all the forms of this universe do not contain or express "The Supreme" adequately. "The Absolute Reality" is far above the things in space and time. The Supreme is the source of all phenomena but remains untouched by them. The cosmic process is not the complete manifestation of "The Absolute." No finite process can ever finally and fully expresses "The Absolute," though this world is a living manifestation of the "Supreme." It (being beyond the limitation of the concept of gender) is omnipresent (present everywhere), omnipotent (most powerful) and omniscient (all-knowing). It is the source of all that is. It is also the final and the ultimate destination of all that is. It defies time, words, thoughts and capacity of individual to measure and express. It does not have any form, though it is referred by many names. It suffers from no limitation of caste, creed, sex or any consideration. Its sovereignty is beyond dispute. It is bigger than the biggest and smaller than the smallest. No description of it has ever described it fully so far in this world. Whenever anywhere in this universe, any fit of anxiety or gloominess or emptiness or heaviness or unbearable suffering lays hold upon a being, every being has turned to this "Energy Source." When Christ was being crucified and the pain was intense and unbearable, Jesus cried out with a loud shout "My God! My God! Why did you abandon me?" The reference was to this power by using the word "God." When Draupdi, the wife of Pandavas was being stripped off in open court and her "husbands" could not come to her rescue, she cried out calling "O Krishna: O Lord of the world; God whom I adore and trust, abandon me not in this dire (extremely bad, and terrible) plight; you are my soul refuge; protect me." Reference was again to this "Supreme Divine Energy; *Brahmn*" behind the word 'Krishna'. That "Divine Universal Infinite Energy Source," which Lord Krishna represents in the battlefield in human form, still exists eternally. Physical body of the lord, made up of inert nature and activated for one life time by presence of eternal divine energy, departed after completing the mission of incarnation (manifestation inform with intense divine powers). What is "Brahmn" then in the context of discussion so far? "Brahmn; The Supreme Eternal Universal Truth" is that "Ultimate Reality," by knowing (knowing here means feeling with awareness as firsthand experience) which one goes beyond darkness of ignorance and delusion of death. It is the cause of all causes. It is everywhere in internal world and external world and even beyond that. "Brahmn; the Supreme" manifests in the cosmos but it transcends the cosmos and cannot be confined in limitation of any kind whatsoever.

What does it do? Both real and un-real within a being come from the same source. Therefore "Brahmn: The Supreme Universal Eternal Reality" is just like father and mother. The term used for calling it does not matter. After every ten kilometer one addresses one's mother differently. Some say mom. Some say Bhabi, Some say Baua. Does it matter? It is immaterial how one addresses mother. The terms used for addressing mother may differ due to timings, era, locality, one's culture but mother remains a mother whether it is India or Japan, whether it is today or Mahabharta's time or Biblical time. Terms used do not matter. Brahmn is "Supreme Universal Eternal Reality" with unfathomable power, with unlimited potential and with unlimited knowledge. In daily life also, there are times when life loses its meaning and nothing "known so far in life" seems to be picking up or working and capacity to bear and fight reaches its lowest, stretching an individual to the breaking point of endurance. In these moments of utter desperation, one turns to "this Universal Eternal Energy Source; This substratum (layer under the layer) of one's existence." It has been called by Father, Rama, and Allah in different times by different people. This "Eternal Universal Spirit in all and everywhere" knows the language of heart. The "reality of this reality" does not undergo change ever whether it biblical time, or Ramayana time. This Supreme Reality remains both in un-manifested state or un-manifested state. Existence and non-existence come from this Reality. It is also called "God of gods; Brahmn; Supreme Universal Eternal Existence." Brahmn (The Supreme) is always undivided yet remaining as if divided in all beings. Brahmn (The Supreme Reality) is the sustainer, devourer and the creator, but it does not do anything except just witnessing. Everything is done by its kinetic energy called "Maya or Prakriti," which follows the Supreme like shadow of an individual.

Perceived Gods or Intermediate Gods - All Gods with names, forms and laid down details for worshipping are "Perceived Gods; Intermediate Gods" according to beliefs and traditions. This "God of Gods i.e. Brahmn" responds to all calls in all forms through all Gods. Reference is to this "God of Gods; Brahmn," when the term "God" is used exclusively without any adjective and in singular. When any adjective or name is used, the reference is to "One of the Intermediate Gods" according to one's perceptions, traditions. Supreme Self (Brahmn or God) does not have any particular form. Basically same "Reality" is worshipped in all forms. This is vitally important. Giving the feeling and experience of the joy of being in the "Exclusive Zone of this Reality" is the object of divine knowledge and highest achievement. It may have different aspects but it is one whole. Indians worship the cosmic force responsible for creation of universe as Brahama, cosmic force responsible for sustenance of universe as Vishnu and cosmic force responsible for dissolution as Shiva. This is just like referring to front elevation and right side elevation and left side elevation of the same reality. In whatever form and in whatever way any devotee worships, this "Supreme Reality" responds to the faith in that very form. If reverence is serious, spiritual progress is assured. All forms are the forms of "One Supreme." Giver of all rewards is finally the "Supreme" only either directly or through "Intermediate Gods." It is the same Government (Brahmn) in all space, including all stars and all the planets working through its different officials. To visualize this (Brahmn; the Supreme), one will have to go beyond the thoughts of man-made Governments and also the perceived Gods i.e. result of incapacity to visualize fully, clearly and without limitation. How is this thought to be understood? Imagine that an exceptionally big sculpture (art piece) is placed in the centre. The sculpture is so big that it cannot be seen fully from any point by any one. Now three persons are seeing this sculpture from three different points. Each one will describe the sculptor differently. Description of each one will be correct but not complete and all-acceptable. In this discussion, sculpture is like "Brahmn." Description of each viewer is like "Perceived God or Intermediate God or the God whose description is biased by limitation of viewer." Description of each viewer is correct and at the same time not complete. Same "Reality" is responding to description of all viewers. Brahmn is sum total of all divine descriptions plus all that which remain to be described and that which cannot be described. It is futile to attempt description of the Brahmn with perfection. It is enough to think of "Brahmn" and get immersed totally in that thinking. Those who know the nature of "Brahmn" will accept everybody's description of the Brahmn. They know that "The Supreme Being" alone is being talked about by all in different ways according to individual limitations. They have tolerance due to their knowledge of nature of Brahmn. The intolerance of some people regarding views of others only depicts the incapacity of some to see and feel beyond human limitations and experience.

What is the difference between God and Gods (or Intermediate Gods with names and forms; for example Lord Indira or Lord Varuna)? It is a very relevant question. The term God refers to the unseen, the un-manifested "Supreme, Eternal, Universal Energy Source or Sovereign God or Energy Source which validates existence in all forms." Intermediate Gods are perceived Gods or Cosmic Forces responsible for one or two activities in the cosmic processes of creation, sustenance and dissolution. Intermediate Gods are with names, forms and particular methods of worship and depend on the "Supreme" for sustenance. Gods are the executives who perform specific cosmic functions complying with the will of the "Supreme Self." Fundamentally it is the same "Supreme Self" who rewards and responds through different names and forms called Gods. "The Supreme reality or The Ground of all that is or Brahmn" does not undergo any change ever. It defies changes. It defies time. It is eternal i.e. it has ever continuing existence. All else i.e. Gods or anything else undergoes change or suffers from limitations in one form or the other.

Can one easily get to the realm of the Supreme Being? No. One cannot force access to the realm of the "Supreme Eternal Divine or the Basis of one's own existence within or Brahmn," till one sanctifies (make holy) one's life. For "this," one has to stop the outward habit of mind and cultivate the habit of looking inward i.e. yoga in one form or the other. It is a new term used. What is yoga? Yoga is "dissolution of pain, unconsciousness and lack of co-ordination consciously" in all situations and positions at all levels of existence (i.e. body, mind, intellect, memory and ego) by abiding all disciplines relating to physical body, mind, emotions and spirit. Yoga has special relevance in the context of Brahmn. It (yoga) unites "deluded individual field of divine energy" with "Eternal Universal Field of Energy i.e. it facilitates a river to lose its separate identity in the ever "expanding unfathomable ocean of consciousness, knowledge and bliss." Thus, yoga optimizes coordination of different facets of an individual (i.e. physical body, invisible perishable body and spiritual body).

What is "Brahmn" like? What are its attributes? This "Supreme Universal Eternal Reality or Brahman" in un-manifest form is shadow less, body-less, colorless, pure, indestructible, eternal "Truth." It is omnipresent (present in all everywhere), omnipotent (all-powerful) and omniscient (all-knowing). It is that, from which the things are born. It is that by which the beings (that which exists) live. It is that into which beings enter when they depart. It is father, mother, abode, refuge, friend and ultimate goal of life. The Supreme cannot be disintegrated or broken into pieces. "Man-made rules and mathematics" are not applicable to "The Supreme Self or Brahmn." That is why a scripture says

"That (Brahmn) is full; this (Brahmn) is full; but the full (Brahmn) remains full even after the full has come out of the full." "Supreme-Self or Brahmn" is Sovereign entity. It neither increases nor decreases ever. This "Reality" does not undergo any change. It causes to appear differently through its dynamic energy. It (being beyond consideration of gender) has its own rules beyond human understanding and experience.

How does one, without getting divided, appear as multiple beings? This is a question which often disturbs the people. This "Eternal Infinite Unity or Brahmn" appears as multiplicity. Fact is that "This Unity" is "truth (that which always remains and does not ever undergo change whatsoever" and multiplicity (expression in variety) is a delusion. It is like the sun and the sun rays? The sun is one only. The sunrays are numerous. The sun rays are manifestation of the sun and not the sun. The "Unity" alone remains. The multiplicity goes on changing. One should also not get confused by God and Gods as well. Brahmn alone is permanent. It expresses through all. It is Siva. It is Indra. It is Supreme-Self, Supreme-Ruler. It is Vishnu. It is time. It is fire. It is moon. It alone is that has been or will be. Knowing "IT," one overcomes death. No other path is there for release (mukti). This "One" is without the second, "The Absolute beyond all relativity, beyond space, time and causation." This "One" alone appears in forms innumerable. It manifests itself for restoring righteousness as avtar (incarnation). No one ever knows the origin or end of this "Sovereign Entity" in reality and fullness. The Supreme is the final destination. That is why Kathopnishad (name of a scripture) says "Awake! Arise! Stop not till the goal (Brahmn) is achieved." The Supreme (brahmn) appears both as *Nirguna* (The Supreme Lord without attributes or qualities or forms) and *Saguna* (with attributes, qualities and forms). When the Supreme Lord remains un-manifested, it is called a cosmic period of non-manifestation. When the Supreme Lord manifests its two natures, it is called cosmic period of manifestation. Lord Krishna in the Gita is "Saguna Brahmn." When un-righteousness grows unchecked and threatens the righteousness, "Nirguna Brahmn" expresses as "Saguna Brahmn." When all the desires, which abide in the heart, are cast away, the mortal becomes immortal and individual (he or she) attains the Brahmn (The Supreme Universal Eternal Reality) i.e. gets restored to the original status of immortality (or indestructibility, eternity and immanence i.e. all-pervasive).

What is incarnation (avtar)? Supreme reality is transcendental i.e. beyond all limitations. It is naturally present in all everywhere every moment in every atom of ever thing. This "Supreme Reality" remains manifested and un-manifested as well at the same time. Everything, every being, everywhere represents existence of this "Supreme Truth" alone, but sometimes "this Supreme One," without name and form, conspicuously manifests with obvious and immense divine powers (intense Divinity) to relieve the society of unrighteousness i.e. the Divinity descends in form, breaking all the limitations and super imposing on normal laws, to protect righteousness. It is called Avtar (God-emergent). Lord Krishna in the Gita represents this "Supreme Reality" or "Complete Descent of God or God Emergent." This knowledge is essential for the readers, right in the beginning. This will evoke (produce) the right response in the mind of the reader to the Geeta-discussion. Jesus in Bible represents this "Supreme Reality." Now when the term "Brahmn" is used or Krishna says "I," readers are to understand that the reference is to the "Supreme Reality." By use of the term "Brahmn or the Supreme," discussion is about the "One," who is felt like shinning ray in the darkest secret chamber (full of darkness of lust, anger, hatred pride etc. i.e. whole family of ignorance) of everyone's heart, but appears as manifold in the day light. Reference is to the "Ultimate Cause of origin and also the shelter of repose for the entire world." Reference is to "Pure or un-alloyed Truth, Consciousness and Bliss of the Universe" not subject to change or defilement ever. We all disagree in "Its" descriptions due to our own incapacity to measure the fullness of the Supreme by the finite, but we all, irrespective of cast, creed, location and local beliefs, agree at one point of time or the other in life, that it is there everywhere, in all, every moment. In wider circles, it moves among the stars, galaxies, mountains oceans, deserts. It makes even the pebbles (stones at the bottom of the river) to sing the song of perfection in the language of silence. How can it be fully described by the words of an individual? Thoughts linked with the "Brahmn; the Supreme" are revelation of eternal unfolding of joy. Thus "Supreme" is the "Infinite Possibility of Perfection."

There is a strange order in every nook and corner of the universe. Look at the critical balance in the cell contents in plants and animals, their acidity and alkalinity, chemistry of living and non-living material, temperature, humidity, ratio of matter and antimatter, equilibrium in the pull-and-push of the stars and dance of the atoms and their constituents. Even a slightest change at any stage might not have allowed the universe to remain, as we see it today. Mere thinking about all this fills us with awe (feelings of respect and slight fear). Who is behind all this? It is The Supreme. Albert Einstein, one of the greatest scientists and physicists of the modern era, said " …a spirit is manifest in the laws of the universe." What was he referring to in this statement? He was referring to the evidences of "The Supreme, universally known as Cosmic Awareness or the Soul of the Soul [that eternal and universal part of one in existence that is believed to continue to exist even after death]," pervading the universe in every atom and cell, as butter is latent in the milk. The Gita, intensely emphasizes this point in one way or the other. Develop awareness of the Supreme Reality or Truth. Always, remain linked or connected with this 'Invisible, Eternal, Universal Reality'. Draw from this Energy Source alone. Serve the visible (manifested cosmos) in the perfect state of detachment (i.e. being in it without being of it), surrendering to this "Universal Energy Source." This is the sole message interspersed (something in between) in the Gita everywhere. When all the desires, which abide in the heart, are cast away, the mortal becomes immortal and "Brahmn; the Highest Possible State of Spiritual Perfection, good enough to grant immortality" is experienced. Immortality is a state of deliverance i.e. the state in which one feels one with "One's Pure Eternal Nature."

In the Gita, this "Supreme Universal Energy Source" has been called "*Parmatman* (Supreme Soul); *Brahmn* (The Supreme Universal Eternal Reality); *Ishwarah* (The Powerful Entity controlling everything, everyone, everywhere); God (the being or the Spirit believed to have created the universe)." For the purpose of our discussion in English, we will call it "Supreme Universal Eternal Reality" or simply "Supreme Being" or "Supreme Self" or "Supreme Reality." It is also referred to as "Substratum or the Ground of the visible world" or "The All-Pervading Consciousness" or "The One Cause Behind the Universe" or "The God (without name and form and singular)" or "The Ultimate Reality, which is full by nature and all-pervading like space" or "The Sovereign Self" or "The Mystical Father of All Beings." It can be both "The Manifest" and "The Un-manifest" or "The Visible" and "The Invisible." Since both lower nature (cosmic womb) and higher nature (cosmic seed) come out of the Supreme, it is also called both "The Father and the Mother of the Universe." The Visible is addressed by name and form. The Invisible is the source of all power, knowledge and blessedness. The connectivity to the Invisible is perceived through divine knowledge (divine knowledge or transcendental knowledge or metaphysical knowledge is the true understanding of the creation and the creator) or devotion or action or through amalgam of the three. Then the divine-current (natural inclination or the propensities towards the "Truth") flows from the Invisible to the visible. If there is any limitation anywhere like selfishness or ego, the divine current is impeded. One gets entangled in the cycles of birth and death and one enjoys only limited degree of divine blessedness (divine grace). One, who is free from egoism, becomes an un-impeded channel for the divine current or the power to flow through. One has to draw from "The Invisible" to serve "the Visible" in perfect state of detachment. This is the Brahama Vidya (Divine knowledge) applied to life and conduct. This is the Ultimate message of the Gita. Knowledge, devotion and action are all approaches available but finally one has to intuit [to gain cognizance or understanding through feelings, through awareness rather than thoughts] to get connected to the "Supreme" in the secret chamber of the one's own heart. The very thoughts of the "Brahmn" direct an individual towards spiritual unfolding, inner peace, all-abiding love, higher spiritual joy and true rhythm of the 'Pure Inner Nature'. Only then the individual understands with feelings that he or she is more than himself or herself and that he or she is "One with All." The best way to conclude this discussion is to be with the thoughts of the Brahmn. This repetition is worth going for to gain the initial feeling (connectivity).

"Brahmn or Supreme Eternal Universal Truth" is that "Ultimate Reality," which is beyond darkness, beyond delusion and beyond death. It is the "Supreme Secret" of the universe. It is the "Ultimate source of Eternal Energy" at which all "the individual energy fields" look at for their creation, sustenance and dissolution. It is the root cause of both the real and the unreal. It is "expanded vision of unbounded awareness" in both inner and outer worlds. It is "One-all-pervading "Reality," though this "one" is regarded as many. Very thoughts of "Brahmn; Supreme Reality" turn impurity into purity, darkness into light, ignorance into knowledge and death into immortality. With this, one is. Without this, one is not. Other than this there is nothing that sees. Other than this there is nothing that hears. Other than this there is nothing that understands. This "Great Self" is unborn, un-aging, undying, immortal and fearless. All knots are broken and all karmas (actions) and their effects cease to exist, when "This Divine Truth: this consciousness, knowledge and bliss" is realized, perceived or intuited. Divinity means that it is eternal, indestructible and immanent (present everywhere, every moment and in every atom of everything). The existence of "Brahmn" is felt in the depth of the soul, when sensuous sounds melt in oblivion (forgetfulness), when ceaseless soul-music drowns all discords and when chaos of life subsides in eternal harmony ever flowing on and on in all directions whispering through its existence in everything the divine invitation of immortality. Nothing sounds sweeter than the soundless symphony in the "Exclusive zone of Divinity." "It" exists in all manifestations and beyond the manifestations as well. "Brahmn" is always in and round in the silence of the sea, in the noise of the earth, in the music of the air and beyond all that everywhere. One gains (gain here means intuiting, perceiving and cognizing) "Brahmn" by giving up the individual self. "Brahmn; The Supreme" is eternally waiting to be available, reminding of its presence in the Sun, in the Moon and in the numerous stars in the galaxy maintaining their distance and still always moving in natural rhythm …… . Vague sweetness of the thoughts of "Brahmn; The Supreme" makes the heart ache with intensity of longing initially but when the right moment comes, the perfect sweetness blossoms of its own and at its own pace in the depth of heart of the seeker and the whole creation starts celebrating in unison (speaking same words at the same time). In these moments, one experiences freshness of bareness of soul (zone of exclusive divinity within), inner expansion and blissfulness. Based on firsthand experience, one feels that "The Hidden" has been found and "The un-attainable" has been attained. One feels that it is time to sit quiet and sing "the dedication of life" in "that silence and overflowing leisure." The Emptiness prevailing within breaks out in divine tunes without a purpose. A gust of wind touches you and goes away making you conscious of your experience.

Without attaining "experiential state relating to Supreme Self," the *Jiva* or Individualized soul or deluded soul, will continue to suffer from the awful misery of cycles of birth and death. This Truth (Brahmn; The Supreme Eternal Universal Reality) that is within each one of us is not a subject of discussion. For this we have to become still. We have to feel. We have to experience. We have to increase our sensitivity, purity and forbearance tremendously for that. This again is a subject of a separate book (Live the Bhagavad Gita). Here our concern is to get ready to feel what Lord Krishna has to say in the Bhagavad Gita.

3 Manifestation of Higher Nature and Lower Nature - During the period of non-manifestation (night of Brahama), "The Brahmn (Supreme Universal Eternal Reality)," in un-manifested state, remains like the conscious space, with its dynamic energy or nature obscured (hidden) in "it." After the period of non-manifestation, "Higher Nature and Lower Nature" emerge out of the "Un-manifested Eternal Universal Supreme Reality" heralding (sign that something is to happen) the onset (beginning) of period of manifestation. Higher nature is the "Fundamental Cause, the Truth." Lower nature is the "Shadow of the Truth." When the two natures meet, the "Higher Nature" forgets its divine characteristics (eternity, indestructibility and immanence or present everywhere) and starts identifying with the "Shadow of the Truth" i.e. lower nature. A cloud of ignorance (impact of lower nature) arises from nowhere and envelopes the "Inner Light." A bubble arises in the ocean of divinity, conscious of its separate existence. The flame of light within (Higher nature) starts flickering in the fierce wind of the world. Existence full of miseries starts. "Deluded Eternal Existence within" fears its extinction, forgetting that "Inner Light," "That Star of Immense Beauty" continues shinning even when one feels to have lost contact with it. The deluded self does not know that contact with the "Inner Light" cannot be lost. "That Wondrous Light; That luster of Loveliness; That Ever Fresh Beauty" cannot be extinguished. The deluded self keeps searching and searching, beset with strange longing, without knowing what it has lost, where it has lost it and what it was like that it has lost. Then someone tells the deluded self "You have lost a star of immeasurable divine beauty in the clouds and glare of mortal world, wretched deluded self." Deluded self feels lost, restless and miserable while searching that star in the external world. The wild search goes on and on in all directions like a lost black stallion running wildly in the desert far away from the inhabited world. The deluded self does not know that it has to unlearn a lot. "That Star" is the "Guiding Spirit within," abiding within and working through the deluded self. The deluded self cannot force access to the "Divine Zone" within until it loses the habit of looking outward and starts looking inward. One day the dream of union of the two natures will surely break and one will experience the mute symphony of existence, consciousness and bliss, with peace *dancing,* silence speaking and strange enthralling music of "Intense Inner Connectivity' flowing everywhere in the wind in all directions.

4. Higher Nature – This nature of the "Supreme Universal Lord or Brahmn" validates the existences or brings to life inert nature. It is the efficient cause of creation of the universe. What is it like? It is "Divine Vibratory Force; the Supreme Eternal Energy" which validates or brings alive the inert elements of lower nature (dealt with in detail in the following heading). Higher Nature is "Divine Consciousness" itself. Higher Nature does not permit mixture, adulteration or erosion. It is the divine light of the "Supreme Effulgent Reality" (i.e. "Brahmn; the Supreme").

This "Higher Energy" is called *Para-sakti*, spirit, consciousness (*chetna*). Higher nature is "Excusive Divine Energy; Un-adulterated essence of what is referred to as Universal Truth." It is the effulgence (brightness of the light) of "Brahmn; The Supreme." It is eternal, indestructible and immanent (present everywhere). It is omnipresent (present everywhere), omnipotent (most powerful) and omniscient.

What is the difference in Brahmn (Supreme Self) and Higher Nature? There is no qualitative difference (same divine characteristics of eternity, indestructibility and immanence are there in both) between the two but quantum difference is there. The Supreme is the unimaginable aggregate of the two natures and the Sovereign Universal Master. The Supreme (like One Sun) lights all the multiple beings (each being should be imagined as a field) in the nature. Each being's share of this "Divine Light (Higher Nature) enlivens that being and the perceived individual share of this "divine effulgence (brightness of light)" in a being is referred to as "Soul."

Higher Nature is "Exclusive Divine Essence" (i.e. eternity, indestructibility and immanence).

It remains the same always. It is to "Brahmn" what sunlight is to Sun. Sun remains at it place only. Sunlight brightens the darkness everywhere. Similarly, Brahmn kisses life into inert nature through "Higher Nature." "This Higher Nature or Exclusive Divine Essence" also cannot be fragmented or broken. The space in a room with pitcher is the same as the space of the room with pitcher thrown out of the room. As sunlight cannot be separated from the sun, "Higher Nature or Divine Effulgence" cannot be separated from "Brahmn."

As we know, "Supreme Eternal universal Energy" in un-manifested state is "Brahmn or The Supreme Soul." "Reflected Eternal Universal Energy" in a being (i.e. manifested state) is called soul. During the transition period i.e. from un-manifested state to manifested state this "Eternal Universal Energy" is called Higher Nature. It is hair splitting exercise (i.e. it is not worth it) to go any further in detail about "Brahmn," "Soul" and "Higher Nature."

Higher Nature is the "Life-Element" by which this world is upheld by the "Brahmn; The Supreme." It is through this "Higher Nature" that "The Supreme" awakens or breathes life or imparts (give knowledge to someone) the power to cry or move forward for "Unlimited Fulfillment" the whole animate or inanimate kingdom including even leaf, flower and fruit. Availability of "Higher Nature" is Lord's acceptance to the phenomenon of creation. It is Lord's way of telling the sleeping and inert lower nature - "O! you are still sleeping. Awake! See! ... Your eternal joy lies within you."

5. Lower Nature (Apara Prakriti or phenomenal nature i.e. that nature, which we see, hear and feel in contrast to what the truth is) – Lower nature (Apara Sakti) is inexplicable (too unusual to be explained), incomprehensible, deluding (make someone believe that, which is not true), dynamic energy or power of the "The Supreme Lord" called "Param-Sakti; Mighty power of the Lord." This nature is inert (without power to move). 'Higher Nature' activates the 'Lower Nature'.

Lower Nature is the "Chief Executive In-charge" of the Supreme. The Supreme does not do anything ever. "The Supreme" Simply keeps validating existences and witnessing. Everything is done by lower nature, when it gets activated by the higher nature during cosmic period of manifestation.

Lower nature is defined as the material cause i.e. the material out of which everything is made. Lower nature is the original source of material consisting of three Gunas and eight basic elements (dealt with afterwards), out of which everything in the universe has evolved. Lower nature is referred to as *asat*, (unreal), perishable, body, matter, nature, *Maya*, *Mahat-Brahmn*, field, creation, manifest state. That which creates diversity (or duality) as well as the diversity itself and all that can be seen or known or heard, including the mind, intelligence, memory and ego, is called lower nature or simply Maya.

The moment "Higher nature" and "lower nature" meet, ego (feeling of separateness; that I am) is born (or gets activated). The false identification of the body with the "Spiritual Subject (higher nature; soul; the creative eternal principle)" begins and the sense of "I or My" is produced. Creation starts. Higher nature, which is devoid of attributes, gets deluded (forgets its own pure nature and starts identifying with nature).

This maya or Prakriti or lower nature is sum total of all the insentient (lacking feeling or consciousness) things. It is unconscious and meant to serve by discharging cosmic functions such as creation, sustenance and dissolution. It is the sum total of all the insentient (lacking feeling or consciousness) things and characterized as field. It is incomprehensible by anyone except by Lord. This lower nature or *Maya* (also called simply Prakriti or field) is different from higher nature, which is sentient (with consciousness; knowing and feeling that you exist) by nature. Higher nature is un-manifested nature, while lower nature manifests in the form of diversity.

How do we view the two natures together? "Higher-Nature" observes witnesses and supervises the "Lower Nature." Existence is not possible without either of them. An individual is like a tree. Two birds live on this tree. Both these birds are good friends. One bird is lower nature. It speaks, dances, moves, sings and weeps as well. The other bird is "Higher Nature or Soul or Exclusive Divinity" within the "ego-dominated soul." "The other bird" only keeps listening and witnessing, without any break ever, the restless bird, with serenity and poise. One bird cannot live without the other bird. These two birds are the two natures in an individual always co-existing.

Gross lower Nature, which, as mentioned earlier is inert, has three basic components i.e. i) Five Primordial (un-adulterated elements; elements which are produced by none), ii) three Gunas (attributes) and iii) known and un-known laws of nature. All these components have been taken up in detail in subsequent discussion. All these components remain inactive till "Higher nature" meets the lower nature. This meeting is like the meeting of two lovers (male and female). The touch of "Higher Nature" infuses the "current of life" in lower nature. Lower nature comes alive burning with desire and the three basic components become proactive in process of creation. First reaction of this union is emergence of ego i.e. feeling of separate existence or duality comes in. Higher Nature forgets its divine characteristics. Ego envelops the "Higher Nature" and "Deluded Individual Ego" takes over further process of creation. Under the supervision of ego, "Three basic components of lower nature," mentioned above, exert their influence and change form to cause the outgrowth of 31 elements forming an "individual." Four of these elements (ego, the un-manifested nature (Mahat Brahmn;), intelligence and mind) form subtle body i.e. invisible body subject to decay. Each element of subtle body has been dealt with in detail subsequently. Subtle body undergoes so many births and deaths on the eternal path. The being (one in existence) gets freedom from subtle body when divine knowledge dawns and ego disappears. Remaining 27 outgrown elements form the physical body (five primordial elements, five organs of perception, five organs of actions, five objects of senses, and seven evolutes)." Physical body undergoes only one birth and one death. The elements of physical body have been discussed in detail subsequently at serial number 15 under the heading "birth of an individual.

The "Deluded Individual Ego" or Divine Essence within under the influence of ego is not the real self. Why is it so? Deluded Individual Ego is subject to change. At the dawn of divine knowledge (knowledge of self) ego disappears and the "Divine Essence within" merges with the Supreme as the river merges with the ocean. Divine essence within (Exclusive Divinity within an individual), which remains under the veil of ignorance about its divine characteristics, is the "Real Self" within an individual. It remains either as jiva (deluded self and subtle body) or as individual (deluded self with subtle body and physical body). Deluded self gets rid of spell of ignorance through divine knowledge and reaches its highest level of perfection.

The Gita uses the terms "Truth or Real" and "Untruth or Unreal." Truth here means "That" which defies change or influence of time. It is changeless and eternal. It always remains the same. In the Gita's parlance, "Higher Nature" is "Truth." Higher Nature within the individual self (or ego-dominated self), under the dominance of ego, is "Truth." "The Individual Self or Ego-dominated self" is "untruth or Unreal" because one day ego will disappear at the dawn of divine knowledge. It is enough to remember that from out of Truth (Higher Nature within the individual, called soul hereafter) comes the "Dream Existence" of individual self. Why has it been called a dream existence? It is not real. Like a dream, this individual existence will disappear and "The Universal Divine Bird" within each one of us will fly to its abode beyond the miseries of the world. Each one of us is deluded, living the dream existence. This existence is a dream. These pain and pleasures are dreams. These fortunes and misfortunes are dreams. What is "Truth"? That "Divine Existence" caged within by ego is the real self (the Eternal Existence), the truth. That alone is "Truth." It is always silently witnessing each one of us in an uninterrupted gaze. "The Divine Existence within" at times whispers only through silence without use of words. In the clamor of worldly desires, the "whisper of silence from very deep within" goes unheeded. All that remains is longing, pain and suffering signifying the space between the "Individual Self" and the "Real Self." Days and nights keep following each other. Years after years fly away. "Individual self" keeps living life after life beset with longing but the "silent, divinely winged bird within" only keeps witnessing as if it were saying:

"O bird; O bird, just do not give in. Be a little closer to me, just a little more. There is to be dawn behind those clouds above the hills under the canopy of pathless sky. There we will celebrate our universal oneness."

What have we understood of Lower nature so far? It is subject to decay and change though it is also beginning-less and endless being the part of "The Supreme." It has a) five primordial (uncompounded) elements, b) three attributes gunas and c) known and unknown laws of nature. All these have been taken up in detail in subsequent discussion. When lower nature meets higher nature, it becomes proactive active and there is outgrowth of these elements marking the onset of creation. Creation means change of form of three basic constituents of nature into three bodies i) Spiritual Divine Eternal Element (Higher Nature) which does not change at all and remains enveloped by ego ii) "Subtle body or *Antahkaran* or invisible body" of a being subject to decay. It has four elements a) ego, b) the Un-manifested (**mahad brahmn**) or source of all that is. It is called the womb of the universe; c) intelligence d) mind. Subtle body lives many lives (i.e. undergoes many births and deaths) and continues to be in existence till influence of ego continues in the individual. These four constituents (representing subtle body), which are themselves outgrowth of union of higher Nature and Lower nature play active role in the creation of physical body of an individual, while major part is played by mind. iii) Physical body; it is like the gunny bag in which the individual is seen roaming about with 27 elements (a table is given subsequently showing all the elements) dealt with in detail subsequently.

Thus, union of Higher Nature and lower nature sets in the phenomenon of creation. What does creation mean here? The phenomenon of creation starts with ego enveloping the Higher Nature and bringing Jiva (a being or that which exists) into existence. The phenomenon of creation gets completed when *Jiva* (enveloped deluded soul) becomes an "embodied self" called an individual i.e. one with a deluded soul, a subtle body (an invisible body, which undergoes many deaths and births with 4 elements) and physical body (the body with 27 "consequential elements"; consequential elements means "outgrown elements" after union of lower nature and Higher nature). Physical body dies with death. Real self of an individual is the "Exclusive Divinity," which remains covered by ego. The subtle body and physical body are called in the Gita's parlance "non-self." Exclusive Divinity without a trace of any element of lower nature is called "The Self." The "Exclusive Divinity" enveloped by ego is called "Deluded Self."

In the eternal flow shown above, an event called death appears. What is death? What is the relevance of death? Death is relevant to physical body only. After death the soul (eternal principle under the influence of ego) moves to next body with subtle body (combination of ego, the un-manifested, intelligence and mind). When an individual is able to get rid of subtle bodies (which are also evolutes of nature and the latencies in subconscious mind), the self realizes its own true nature (divinity; eternity, indestructibility and immanence) and gets merged with the supreme or the conscious space within gets merged with the conscious space out everywhere. The higher nature never dies. It cannot be mixed or contaminated ever. It temporarily forgets its nature and when it regains consciousness of true nature it gains freedom from self imposed delusion. The difficulties of a being continue so long as it carries the burden of subtle bodies and the causal body included in it as seed of past impressions and tendencies. The remedy lies in getting established in "the self" through yoga to transcend the two bodies (physical body and subtle body). When an individual dies, it goes to any of the 14 worlds based on its merits and demerits. After having enjoyed or suffered the impact of good or bad actions, the soul again takes birth. If the being has brought to naught its subtle and causal bodies, it gets relieved of the cycles of birth and death and gets merged with the Supreme.

Desire and hatred, pleasure and pain, fame and infamy and life and gain are the result of being in the lower nature. One has to go beyond lower nature to obtain "That; Brahmn" which is the source of all joy.

Now, we can sum up that an individual is a union of the Universal-Infinite (Higher Nature) and Universal-particular (individualized lower nature). As universal-particular, an individual assumes to be a part of the whole. As Universal Infinite, an individual is a "Potential Whole." Highest achievement of an individual is to break the myth of individual self and get restored to "Unity in wholeness" at the end of journey. Greatest possession of an individual is "Inward Eternal Principle," which impels the creative acquisition of qualitative content i.e. spiritual growth of life. Feel about this "Inward Eternal Principle" is divine knowledge. Doubt about this "Inward Eternal Principle" is ignorance.

6. Five Primordial Elements or Uncompounded Gross elements (*Mahabhutas*) are: i) earth, ii) water, iii) air, iv) Fire and v) Ether (*aakash*).

7. Three Attributes (tendencies) of nature (Why we are, as we are) - There are three gunas (attributes or three tendencies) of nature. In a way these are three strands (a strand is a thin piece of thread, wire or hair) making up twisted rope of nature. This rope is extremely powerful. No one can escape it except with the grace of the "Supreme." A particular mix of these three tendencies is the reason why a being behaves as it behaves i.e. these attributes of nature are the causes of behavior of a being. These three tendencies are:

i) *Sattva* – It refers to light of consciousness and directs one towards perfect purity. The result of *sattva* is good action. *Sattva* manifests as humility, guilelessness, self-control, unselfishness, faith, devotion, yearning for liberation and other similar attributes. When *sattva* predominates, an individual feels inclined to renunciation (detachment to fruits of actions) and strives in various ways and means to attain peace and blessedness. Through the cultivation of *sattva*, both rajas and *tamas* are kept under control.

ii) *Rajas* – It refers to tendency of outward movement. It guides towards actions and passions. The result of *rajas* is pain. The principal trait of rajas is energy. The "primal flow of energy" emanates from *rajas*. Its effects are ceaseless activities, lust, anger, avarice (too strong greed), arrogance, egotism, envy, pride, jealousy and so forth. An individual under the influence of rajas remains violently attached to the world. *Rajas* is a source of suffering.

iii) *Tamas* – It refers to inertia (tendency to stay unchanged), heedlessness, indifference and guides one towards darkness and dullness. The result of *tamas* is ignorance. *Tamas* is the veiling power that hides the true nature of a thing and makes it appear as other than what it really is. It results lassitude (tiredness and lack of energy), dullness, inadvertence (without realizing what you are doing) and stupidity. When *tamas* predominates, an individual goes to sleep or remains inactive. It deprives an individual of right judgment and subjects the individual to doubt and uncertainty. It is mother of delusion.

At the universal level, these three tendencies (Cosmic Trinity) are responsible for creation, sustenance and dissolution. The "Cosmic Trinity" reflects the dominance of one of the three modes i.e. a)*Rajas* tendency is known as *Brahma* (creator), ii) *sattva* tendency is known as *Vishnu*, the preserver, iii) *Tamas* is the tendency known as *Shiva*, the destroyer of all negativities.

When the "Higher Nature or Soul or Divine Essence" meets these attributes of nature, it forgets its own divine (eternal, universal immanent) characteristics and it starts using mind, intelligence and body (these are all evolutes of nature activated due to contact of higher nature and lower nature) for egoistic satisfaction.

A being has to rise above three modes (tendencies of nature). It has to become "*trigunatita*" i.e. devoid of all the three modes even *sattva*. Then the soul (the Real Self; the Higher Nature or Truth within a being) gains cognizance of its "Free Incorruptible Universal Nature or Truth." At this stage, *sattva* gets sublimated into light of consciousness. *Rajas* gets sublimated into austerity (*tapas*) and *tamas* gets sublimated into tranquility, rest. This is the highest point of attainment. At this point "veiled soul" gets out of "self created prison" and the mortal gets restored to immortality. This is the highest state of perfection.

Dominant *guna* (attribute; tendency) exerts its influence on the selection of kind of next birth as well. If the embodied one meets with death when *sattva* is dominant, then one goes to the pure worlds of those who know the highest. Meeting death at the time when *rajas* is dominant, one is born among those attached to action. Dying when *tamas* is dominant, one is born in the wombs the deluded.

8. The known and unknown "laws of nature" and the "mystical power" - The lower nature comprises of laws of nature and some events beyond comprehension by human mind. There is an order in universe. Everything seems to be placed, spaced or arranged in relation to each other with a purpose. The seasons change with the same periodicity. The members of the same kind behave in exactly the same manner. The accuracy in the movement of stars and the relative distance maintained in the galaxy is really startling. How does it all come to be? There are laws of nature at work all the time. Some laws have been identified but what we do not know is always much more than what we know. These laws of nature maintain the miraculous order and accuracy in this universe. There are laws like law of gravity, law of procreation, law of pollination etc. There are so many laws beyond understanding. Nobody knows the mystery of black hole, which is an area in space that nothing, not even light, can escape from because gravity is so strong there. These laws of nature are like software in a computer. These laws cannot be seen but the existence of the law is beyond dispute. These laws are at work all the time and systems of nature keep operating due to these laws. These laws automatically come in operation. The honey in bee hive is the result of law of nature only. These laws are for facilitating and maintaining the universe and form an integral part of lower nature or changing nature.

As there are laws of nature beyond understanding, there are events beyond human understanding and experience. As per Bible, Lord Christ was born of a virgin, Mary. Similarly, as per Mahabharta, Karan was born of a virgin called Kunti. As per Bible, Jesus Christ was crucified. His dead body was placed in a tomb of solid rock. Three days later he rose to life. Similarly, in Mahabharta, an attempt was being made to strip off a lady, called Dropadi, in an open court, when a strange phenomenon happened. The sari (a long cloth-covering of a lady) of Dropadi went on increasing to such an extent that even a fully grown warrior, having the strength of elephants, got completely exhausted and found it difficult to continue even pulling the sari. These events from people, following different cultures and different schools of thoughts, are not myths. Scripture are replete with such recorded events. It will be difficult to visualize the capacity of **Maya** (lower nature; changing nature) without considering these events as part of manifested nature. It is relevant to keep this aspect also in view while visualizing the enormity of nature and immensity of its capacity.

9. *Jiva* (being or one who is in existence, whether animate or inanimate or individualized soul) - The moment the lower nature and higher nature meet, "Higher nature" activates the lower nature [Primordial or uncompounded gross elements or *Mahabhutas* + Gunas (Rajas, tamas Sattva) + Known and unknown laws of nature]. First evidence of this union is that ego sprouts (first sign of creation). Jiva (a being, who is in existence) is born (at this stage it is without a body). Ego is feeling of separateness i.e. "I am." "I am" means that there is something other than "what I am." This is called duality. The duality is ignorance. Today "I am" and one day I shall not be. Therefore this notion, that I am, is not truth (Truth does not ever change; Truth is eternal). Higher nature does not ever lose its divine (eternity, indestructibility and immanence or present everywhere) character even when it is enveloped by ego from all sides. It only gets deluded and forgets its divine nature. "Jiva or individualized soul or the deluded self" is born with "soul or higher nature" enveloped within. What is Jiva then? It is the deluded "exclusive Divinity or Higher Nature or soul." It is the also called the Self, Atma or Purusha or knower of the field (field means fully developed Jiva with all the 31 elements), as discussed afterwards.

Jiva = Individualized soul (or deluded soul) or soul enveloped with ego.

It is what we call in English "being i.e. one in egoistic existence." It may be animate or inanimate.

10. *Atma* (Soul) – It is the focal point of discussion in the Gita. The eternal unchanging reality or existence within a being (one in existence) is called soul or *atma*. "The eternal and unchanging existence" with reference to cosmos is called "*Brahmn* or The Supreme Eternal Universal Reality or The Supreme Soul" and with reference to being or individual it is called soul. Soul (*atma*) is to *Brahmn* what wave is to ocean. The Characteristics are the same and the substance is the same. Understanding this "oneness" is wisdom. Getting caught by the idea of duality in this perception is ignorance.

In an individual, "*atma* or soul" always remains surrounded by ego. The Gita-discussion starts when Lord Krishna makes reference to "The indweller in the body," who experiences childhood, youth and old age and then passes on to another body. The Gita-discussion practically ends after Lord Krishna's last advice to Arjuna saying "O son of Bharata, flee unto 'Him' for shelter with all thy Being …." In other words, the Gita starts with discussion about the "Eternal, Unchaging Reality" and the Gita-discussion ends by making reference to the "Eternal Reality." Who is the indweller in the body under reference here? Who Lord Krishna is referring to while saying "..flee unto Him …"? Who is this "Eternal Reality" referred to in the beginning and the end of the Bhagavad Gita? Prime subject matter of discussion in the Gita is soul. What is soul? **Eternal existence with reference to a being (one in existence) is called soul.**

When "Lower Nature" deludes the "Higher Nature," "Deluded Self; Consciousness that I am" comes into existence. That, which deludes us and prevents us from getting into our pure nature, is ego. That which gets deluded is "Higher Nature." That which results is "Deluded Self." The "eternal existence or never changing reality" within the deluded soul or the individualized soul is Higher nature which remains veiled relating to an individual is called soul (atma; the self). It is the "Exclusive Divinity" (i.e. eternity + indestructibility + immanence or presence everywhere) or higher nature within an individual under the veil of ignorance. It is the "Eternal Universal Existence within an individual or a being (one in existence)."

The union of the "Higher nature" and the "Lower nature" marks the onset of the process of creation. Ego envelops the higher nature, encircles it and clouds its effulgence (brightness). The soul (higher nature within relating to an individual) gets deluded by maya (lower nature). Forgetting its divine features it becomes individual soul or deluded soul or *Jiva* or *atma* or knower of the field. Even individual soul or deluded soul has both "exclusive divinity" (deluded within) as well as "lower nature" in the form of ego. "Exclusive Eternal Divinity" (eternity + indestructibility +immanence or present everywhere) or "Higher nature" in an "individual soul" is called "soul." "Exclusive Eternal Divinity or Higher nature" with reference to cosmos is called "Brahmn or Supreme Soul." Qualitatively, we are talking of the same unity (entity) when we are talking about the soul, higher nature or Supreme Soul.

"Eternal Divinity or Higher nature or soul" is the cause of everything animate or inanimate. This eternal divinity or higher nature is "The All-Embracing-Conscious (full of awareness) or Conscious Sameness, devoid of any attributes." It is the "Divine element" which activates the lower nature or causes the things or beings to be. There cannot be conceived or imagined a place or even a point in the universe, where this "Exclusive Divinity" Or Higher nature is not there. As this higher nature is there, lower nature is also there. This gang of lower nature (five primordial elements i.e. earth etc. + Gunas i.e. rajas etc. + Laws of nature i.e. law of gravitation etc.) is also fully active due to proximity of higher nature. Lower nature develops a thought "I am" i.e. one alone is not there or feeling of duality crops in. This thought is like a particular dream in the context of eternal existence. So long as this thought is there or this dream "I am" is there, the existence will be there. Birth and death will be there. Miseries of worldly life will be there. When, in due course, the realization dawns that it is dream only, that it is false notion only, everything will come to a rest. Freedom is experienced. "I am" is individual soul with trace of ego or duality. The eternal "I" behind "I am" is soul. How do we feel what this "I" behind "I am" is?

Let us think of Moon. Moon is one only. A child cries for moon. We put three pots with water on the roof tops. In all the three pots we are able to see reflections of moon. We show it to the child and child starts playing with the image of the moon. After some time we throw away the water in the pots and everything is over. There is one moon only. Similarly there is one "Brahmn; Supreme Self" only. Higher nature is the moon light reflecting the light of moon everywhere far and near on whole earth. Water in the pots is nature creating the delusion (reflection) for the child that moon has been brought down on earth. The image of the moon in the water i.e. reflected moon is like the "individualized soul." The particular ray of moonlight of moon, which reflected in the water, is "soul." Everything is delusion except soul (exclusive divinity). Truth is that one moon is there far away and separate also but still sustaining its association through its rays. That particular ray, which reflected in the water in pots, is still there, after the pots have been taken away from the roof. What is the conclusion?

"Brahmn: The Supreme" is "universal eternal divine conscious" or "divine-sameness" without form and attributes." It is boundless like sky. It is consciousness, knowledge and bliss. It is eternal, indestructible and immanent. It always is. It cannot ever happen that it is not. There is no difference between "Brahmn or The Supreme Self or The Supreme Soul" and "Soul (Atma; the Self)." "Divine knowledge or Divine Light or Divine essence or Divine Effulgence" with reference to universe is "Brahmn" and with reference to a being is soul. "Brahmn: The Supreme Self" can be compared to a vast space in the universe. "The soul or the Self within an individual" can be compared to the room space. This room space is not truth. Truth is space. Room will not be there after its life and then this room-space cannot be identified separately. Therefore, the room-space is a false notion, which will not be there after the life of the room. The space being identified as room-space "was there, is there and will be there" always, as it is. The true nature of "Brahmn; Supreme Self" or the self or soul within an individual is "Eternal Reality" itself. That alone is to be focused, meditated and thought about. Soul cannot be perceived through mind, which is a part of lower nature and destructible. Soul is to be intuited with soul only with torch of pure intelligence. How do we intake the idea that soul is always there while lower-nature (all that is destructible relating to the being) dies or perishes?

One more example can be used. An ocean is there. There comes a mighty wave right from the middle of the ocean. It rises, dances mirthfully high up in the sky and again goes down. What does it mean? Is wave different from ocean? No. A particular phenomenon of rise and fall of water, due to particular reasons of lower nature, at a particular moment, is called a wave. Wave is not the Truth. Only ocean is the "Truth." Similarly each individual, each being is untruth, delusion or play of nature. It will be there as long as false notion "that I am say 'a' " is there (ego is there). This 'a' is a product of changing phenomenon called lower nature. One day existence of 'a' will not be there. One day in "cosmic un-manifested period" even this "lower nature" will become dormant. For this reason, it is all false, cosmic drama. What will remain there always is the "eternal existence" due to which lower nature got activated and then 'a' was there. That is "Brahmn; The Supreme self." What is soul then? As much "assumed higher nature" as is required to sustain the individual self as well as individual body, is soul. The word used is "assumed"; it is all un-truth; it is all ignorance. It is all delusion. One thing should be kept in mind. "Brahmn; The Supreme" cannot be fragmented to find out soul of 'a'. This assumed higher nature relating to 'a' like space of the room is an assumption and not a reality. Soul is inside (due to space within the body) and outside of 'a' invisible to human eye, as air is. This "Exclusive Divinity" within was there before jiva (ego + soul) . It is with the jiva during its term as jiva. It will still be there, as it is, after the term of existence (terms of existence can be many births and deaths) of jiva is over. The soul (the Divine Essence validating everything and every being) is there without "being exclusively of the individual alone." The moon lights so many diverse bodies. It cannot be of one body alone. Lower nature (body and its aggregate including ego, mind, intelligence and memory) is all perishable. We remain busy only with the "aggregate of the perishable parts of self', which we really are not. How much time do we spend thinking about "The soul or the exclusive Divinity or the real Self"? That is the central cause of worry in life. That is the cause of ignorance. We bother too much about "what we are not." We remain blissfully oblivious (forgetful) of what we really are, all our life. That is the tragedy of ignorance in existence. That is what the Bhagavad Gita wants to focus at. We cannot see soul. We experience it.

"The exclusive Divinity or higher nature or soul or Divine Eternal Universal Sameness" is not born, nor does it die. It does not come into being from anything nor does anything come into being from it (manifestation is due to lower nature). It cannot be fragmented. It is one whole. "My soul or your soul" is wrong notion. There is only one "Truth" that shines and everything else shines with it. That which validates the form to be "Unreal" is soul. That which remains "formless and permanent" in the aggregate of "the Unreal" is soul. The same "Truth" with reference to a being is soul and with reference to cosmos is "The Supreme." Due to impact of *maya* (that which changes and deludes) ignorance starts playing the trick. For the wise, there is no difference between the soul and the Supreme. Why is it so? The Divinity (eternity, indestructibility and presence everywhere) is awareness. It is knowledge. It is feeling. It is enlightenment. It cannot be imprisoned. The being due to feeling of separateness suffers. The truth (the Supreme) smiles at its shadow (deluded self) because the one being carried does not understand who is carrying it. Actually there is no physical fragmentation ever. Duality (separate existence) is something that exists in imagination or dream in eternal journey. When one gets up after the spell of slumber (spells of cycles of birth and death) or the sun of divine knowledge dawns and ignorance departs like night at the sunrise, one laughs over the bad dream (worldly existence). One finds that duality is like lurking shadow in the night, which goes away at sun rise. One finds that touch of divinity was never lost. It was the Divinity alone which was sustaining during the spell of slumber (worldly existence). The touch of divine love makes earthly love resplendent. The trees, the stars, white peaks of mountains, the life in the ocean, the flowers, the animal kingdom etc., all appear to be symbols aching with meaning, which cannot be uttered in words but it is felt and it resounds on the orchestra of soul in the wordless sound of silence.

What are the striking features of the soul? Soul is unborn, eternal everlasting and ancient. It suffers no destruction with destruction of the body. Soul (exclusive divinity) cannot be of one body alone. It is smaller than the smallest and greater than the greatest. It is of the nature of divine knowledge or divine light, or conscious space. Soul is ever continuing ever available existence knowledge and bliss. It is boundless like space. The true nature of "Brahmn; Supreme Self" or Soul (Exclusive Divinity assumed to be related to an individual or a being) is "Eternal Universal Reality itself." Soul (Exclusive Divinity) is always there both inside and outside of an individual. "The soul within an individual (assumed notion) and Brahmn with reference to cosmos" is "conscious knowledge" only. Moon is there. Similarly, "Brahmn" is there. Reflected image of moon in water pots on roof top is there. Similarly, individual self or deluded self (that self which has concealed the truth within) is there. One ray, which is "assumed" to be the cause of "Reflected Moon (Individual Self)," is there. Similarly soul is there and the same "Reality" with reference to cosmos is called "Brahmn; The Supreme." This "Divine Reality" was always there before the pots were put on roof top. This Divine Reality was there, while pots were there on the roof top. This Divine Reality will still be there after the pots are removed from the roof. The soul is one only like one moon and it is always there. Diversity or moon-rays are delusion. All are getting divine light of this one Divine Reality for existence or sustenance. The Supreme is one only. It divinely touches all to impart validity of existences to diversities but it is never an individual's monopoly (belonging to one only). Why should one spend so much time and life knowing about soul?

Soul is eternally fulfilled, immovable, eternally established. That is its pure nature. Soul validates creation. It is always uncreated and separate from creation (lower nature). That ray which caused "reflected moon" on the roof top is an integral part of this drama of reflected moon, but this ray has always been there at that point before this drama, in this drama and after this drama as well. Higher nature meets the lower nature. It mingles i.e. both can be still recognized separately. In this meeting or union of the two, higher nature gets covered by ignorance but its existence is always there distinct, effective without dilution of its divine characteristics. Therefore, soul is ever present, untouched by *Maya* (lower nature) but rather enveloped by it. Soul is unclouded and free from clouds of maya always, but gets covered by *Maya* (individual soul or ego-dominated soul only suffers). The soul is pure, unparalleled, formless, support-less, incorporeal (not existing in physical form but as spirit only), desire-less, beyond the pair of opposites, devoid of delusion and of undiminished power. Soul is self-luminous. Lower nature after getting activated by proximity of higher nature brings all the changes. Soul is existence knowledge and bliss. It is boundless like space. Soul is neither doer no enjoyer (doing and enjoying is function of lower nature). Sufferer or enjoyer is ego-dominated soul (jiva). It is "Consciousness; exclusive Divinity" on which the whole universe appears superimposed. The word "appears" has special relevance. This appearance is like dream, which is never a reality. Soul is to be "known with feelings" by soul only i.e. by intuition. Soul is the "Supreme Secret" of the universe. Knowledge of soul restores us to the original divine nature (eternity, indestructibility and immanence). Soul is the final abode. Soul is the doorway to "The Ultimate Freedom or immortality." Realization of the soul means experiencing fullness of soul in which unity and diversity stand merged together forever. It amounts to getting restored to pure nature, blissful and free, far away from the fetters of good and evil qualities and actions of living and dying. This "Highest Consciousness" is identical with Moksha (liberation), which is beyond the limits of human understanding and experience i.e. it requires going beyond limitations.

Where is it in the body? Best answer to this question is another question. Where is it not? Mind is that part of consciousness which perceives and facilitates communication between the internal body and external world. Intelligence is an instrument. It is lower nature. Consciousness is "Brahmn" activating the intelligence. Let us talk of physical body. If consciousness is not there, hand does not work. Hand is instrument (lower nature), Consciousness is the energy activating hand. It can be known by feeling through torch of pure intelligence where there are conscious spaces within the body. What is the conclusion? There is no part or cell of the body where this divine energy is not there. It is inside the body and it is outside the body as well in all the "Conscious Spaces." The exclusive Divine Energy does not allow anything to impact its divine nature. It activates lower nature keeping its separate divine existence. How is it?

Think of the sun. A pot with water inside is kept on the roof top. The sun rays heat the water. The sun is one only. It is far away. Similarly Brahmn is one and it is far away. The sun lights the universe through its rays (higher nature). Some sunrays are there in water (soul or higher nature is there in every part of the body but probability of feeling it is more in the "conscious spaces" within the body). The sunrays heating the water will still be there even tomorrow when water pot is not placed on the roof top i.e. sun rays cannot be exclusively linked with water in the pot. Similarly "MY soul and your soul" is a wrong notion. Divinity is one whole divinizing the universe. The concept of "My soul, your soul and deluded soul" is the result of limitation in thinking. Soul is one whole (like one sun) divinizing the one individual and the whole universe as well. It cannot be any body's monopoly. The "real self" is the soul, the exclusive Divinity and in the context of cosmos same reality is "Brahmn; The Supreme." One should focus on this immanent (present everywhere) and eternal aspects of the soul and all the miseries relating to the "lower nature" will simply vanish like darkness after the sun rise. When the blanket of darkness of ignorance gets removed and one intuits (understanding through feeling) the soul, one will be able to listen to the echo in the inner most chamber of the heart –

"Every direction is His direction; in every manifestation (mountain, tree, plant, animal, being) He is smiling; every step taken is towards "His abode"; He is the sea; He is the river leading to the sea; He is the landing space beyond all, which is finite; He is in the sunshine; He is in the darkness; He is in the night ; He is in the day; The silence of the sea, the noise of the earth and music of the air remind of Him only; The "Highest Reality" has actively to be achieved; the gain of "Truth" is not in the end; It reveals itself through the endless length of achievement … … Where is the end? It is endlessly new beginning always, if the star of "His True Vision" is guiding … …."

When one intuits soul, one finds divine light shinning in every form. When one sees that light, name and form just pale into insignificance. It is divine content, divine essence, which is present everywhere. Very soon consciousness becomes converted into super consciousness. Diversity merges into Unity, "Oneness." *Brahmn veda brahmaive bhavati* i.e. one who knows God becomes God.

11. *Ego (Ahankaar)* is a feeling of separation or mine-ness (i.e. I am). This delusion is the cause of existence and cycles of birth and death. Ego is "cit- jad- granthi; knot of consciousness and matter." Ego is a compound – part of it is reflection of true self and part of it is accidental result (phenomenon) of meeting of higher nature and lower nature. When two natures meet, reflection of higher nature becomes forgetful of its natural divine characteristics (eternity, indestructibility and immanence). Gradually, with detachment and divine knowledge, the conscious part of ego, which is reflection of "True Divine Spiritual Nature," becomes more evident and one begins to feel more and more like the Spirit.

"I or feeling of separateness or ego" is a myth. It cannot remain when divine knowledge dawns. One has to know what ego is and what its limitations are. One effective way to deal with ego is to expand it (ego) so much that one would say "I have cosmic consciousness; I am as large as the whole universe; I feel one with everything." This indicates a very high state of spiritual development, which entitles a being to *moksha* (state of no limitations whatsoever i.e. neither physical, nor mental nor emotional nor spiritual; or *nirvana* i.e. one denies the ego or one comes over ego by being conscious about it and thus one denies what limits an individual). Ego is most dominating and it is the last hurdle in the spiritual development. Beyond ego is the self (*Purusha*; the eternal witness; the Divine; the real self). It is also a reality that cognizance of ego is death of ego. At this point (i.e. when ego dominates no more), body-sense or body-consciousness does not exist and one identifies with one's "True Nature i.e. vast ocean of unending expanse of consciousness with unlimited divine knowledge and bliss." This state (i.e. egoless state of existence) is "Life's Perpetual Spring Unsealed." In this state, stains of worldly life get washed away. Spiritual thirst (that incessant longing) gets quenched and parched spirit gets healed by "The Fullness of the Inexpressible." One awakens (wake up) to see love and joy blossoming all-around in state of charged consciousness.

12. Un-Manifested Nature – This is called *"Mula prakriti"* in Sanskrit. It is the inscrutable (that whose reaction is difficult to be known) primal matter or energy or the *Prakriti* . It veils the *Purusha* (soul; basis of all life and substance) and creates in "Him" the dream of the universe, causing it to become a deluded soul (Divinity under the influence of ignorance) i.e. causing the ego to be there. It is also called *"Mahad Brahmn,"* another name in Sanskrit. It is also known as "Undifferentiated Nature" or inexpressible power of the Lord. It has been called *"Pradhana"* in *Sankhya* philosophy. It is constituted by *rajas* (restlessness), *tamas* (dullness) and *sattva* (peacefulness). It is the source of everything (*Mahat-tattva* onward) and product of nothing. It is called Lord's Maya, difficult to cross. It is like Lord's software to get the "Supreme will" executed. It is also beginning-less and endless. It is integral part of the Lord both as the manifested or un-manifested.

13. Buddhi (Intelligence) – It is that part of subtle body (*antahkaran*) or that aspect of consciousness in which consciousness discriminates between dualities i.e. action or non-action or what ought to be done or what ought not to be done. This is the level of one's existence in which consciousness appraises the information or input and gives the final judgment without ambiguity. Major functions of the *buddhi* are – reasoning, assessment, determination and finally guiding the individual towards ultimate union of the individual self and the universal self. In a normal ego-dominated individual, *buddhi* keeps judging "you are the doer, you are the enjoyer, you are the sufferer …." When *buddhi* gets purified, it knows for certain that the self (soul; *purusha*) exists and that *purusha* (soul) is the real self. Then buddhi starts peeping through the "Self-State; Conscious Space within" and facilitates the final union.

The mind (discussed subsequently) may accept the judgment of intelligence or not. For example, individual's intelligence (*buddhi*) may say "That man is bad; or I do not like him etc." Now mind at times may not abide by "*buddhi* (intellect) and may get swayed by the demands of the senses. This becomes the root cause of the miseries of an individual in spiritual growth. One should ensure that *buddhi* does not become body oriented. The *buddhi* of the individual should always remain aware of the self and its characteristics. *Buddhi* should deny everything that is opposed to the self. Bondage is opposed to the nature of the self. Let it deny bondage outright. The "doer-enjoyer notions" too are opposed to the "self's features." It should be ensured that all these notions are denied repeatedly by the *buddhi*. Whenever the *buddhi* becomes reluctant to deny in this manner, the buddhi should be bathed in the "Self-State." Finally, there comes the stage when contemplation of the "Self" becomes so deep and firm that by its force "doer-enjoyer feeling" sinks and disappears. This process may take time but this is the end to be achieved. What is Lord Krishna doing in the Gita? Lord Krishna is primarily turning Arjuna's buddhi towards the "Sovereign Eternal Universal Existence."

"*Buddhi* (intellect)" puts forth the final judgment. The more it is pure (or devoid of dualities or the opposites i.e. good or bad), the more it directs the individual towards the spiritual growth. When it becomes purest i.e. absolutely devoid of impact of impurities or worldly wisdom, it guides the individual to cognize the "Eternal Presence within, Unlimited Expanse of knowledge within, Unlimited Ocean of bliss within." Then one understands what it means to feel the "life of life" or "soul of the soul" or being "as holy as God (The Sovereign Absolute Reality)" or "the kingdom of the God within" or "Eternal Stability in complete union with the truth within." It is "*buddhi*" alone which makes one realize with feelings that the truth is "all-pervading, infinite, *kaivalya* (one alone), absolute love, absolute consciousness, absolute wisdom and absolute un-selfishness." That eternal truth is "conscious space" within and without (external universe including all objects and space within the objects). "*Buddhi* (pure intellect) helps to realize what it means to feel "That alone exists."

14. *Manas* (Mind) – What is mind? Mind is an instrument of cognition and experience. It is that constituent of "antahkaran; *individual's invisible body which is perishable but it does not die with death of physical body*" or it is that part of consciousness or that field of consciousness, in which consciousness perceives or cognizes (knows or understands with feelings) and facilitates the communication of the internal world and the external world and directs the senses. Mind is the last outgrowth in *Antahkaran* (Subtle body or invisible, perishable individual body, which does not die with death and undergoes several births and deaths). Mind roams about anywhere inside or outside so much so that individual is taken to be in the mind and mind is not confined to the inside of an individual only.

Manas (Mind; this English word does not fully represent manas) is the name given to certain projection or aspect of consciousness. Mind is that aspect of consciousness which reflects or reveals the world. Mind has two properties. It cognizes or reveals the body, senses, objects and world. It is one property. It reveals itself in its purest form. This is the second property. Except that it has got these two aspects, it is difficult to say location or otherwise of the mind. The mind exists throughout the body, inside the body and outside the body. In brief, manifold consciousness is what we call the mind (manifoldness is creation of mind). The mind and the world are truly inseparably, because world's experiences are truly dependent on the mind. One's consciousness of the world begins with the mind and ends with the mind. World-awareness sprouts in an individual when mind is active.

Suppose something is touched by the body. First information of this touch is received by mind and later on it is interpreted by buddhi (intelligence) with the information stored in citta (that part of consciousness which stores the information). Mind is not a gross matter. It cannot be seen or touched. It cannot be measured. It does not require a place for its stay and movement. It can go anywhere anytime.

Ordinarily, one does not see the depth of the mind nor does one see the true expanse of the mind. For this reason, one perceives wrongly. One understands wrongly. One acts or reacts wrongly. These three conditions – lack of full illumination on mind's surface, lack of illumination in its depth and distortion are there because of interference of ego. With ego taken off by awareness and intelligence becoming pure, the whole mind begins to work as one. What does it mean? That which was un-illuminated, that which is called the conscious mind and that which is described as super-conscious mind become, as if it were, one blended together. This is an advanced state. In this state, wherever one looks, one finds the Supreme (the truth, that which Lord Krishna symbolizes) smiling, shining and validating the universe. One finds, through the instrument mind, divine light shining through every form. When one sees that light, "form pales into insignificance." It is the divine content, divine essence that becomes important. After this experience, old impressions no longer continue hold upon the individual. Thus, mind is probably the most essential factor in soul's journey to its "Ultimate Destination." A realized soul is pure consciousness that reflects only through the pure, clear and clean mind.

When the mind is moving, the world is moving. The change is in the mind. That change gets reflected in the world. The soul (spirit inside or pure consciousness inside) inside is steady. All that changes has nothing to do with the soul. The pure consciousness is the eternal observer. Before it, the whole world is playing and world's thoughts are in the mind. In mind one is bound. In mind one is free.

The mind minds everything good, bad and indifferent but one has to "tell the mind how to mind."

Mind moves as guided by the subconscious mind. The mind never becomes impure. Impure thoughts coming close to mind make it feel that it is impure as the crystal reflects the color of the thing placed near it. Pure mind sees things as they are. Prejudiced mind sees what it wants to see. No knowledge is possible with prejudiced mind. One has to become adept in the art of separating the mind from the thoughts. Secret lies in separating the mind from thoughts. The thoughts, urges, modifications in our mind-contents are so devilish, so opaque (not transparent) that when the divine light passes through them, it comes through faintly. One does not see the things properly. One misunderstands according to one's mind. A human being is according to the combination of conscious and the unconscious or sub-conscious layers of the mind (different zones of mind). The whole burden is in the mind. The mind is the tool. The mind is the goal. With mind one gets the knowledge and with mind one communicates. One takes and gives both to the mind. This mind has to be kept free from ignorance, egoism and attachment. The mind expresses at three levels i.e. the thought level first, next at the speech level and then at the action level. First it should be clear that mind is to be made free. One should remain alive to this truth "I am not mind." By the time, mind reaches to the pure ground, it becomes "no mind i.e. impression-less and without thoughts." The words "without thoughts" do not mean that no thoughts are to be there. The thoughts crowd the mind but the thoughts are silenced resolved and integrated by witnessing the thoughts and not associating with the thoughts. Whatever one puts in the mind, one becomes that only. When the mind is pure, that which is behind the mind i.e. real consciousness illumines immediately. There are then no obstacles.

Misery belongs to the mind and can be undone. Others can give pain but not the misery. Misery is one's own making i.e. one yields to the thoughts, one reacts, one retaliates and one becomes a slave to the thoughts. As long as one confines the mind to the body-mind complex, one will always be miserable. Individual's greatest problem is mind and sovereign solution to this problem is detachment (being with something fully still keeping some space somewhere justifying the true identity; divinity does not mix with anything losing its identity completely). Detachment gains a kind of power. The mind becoming pure has the inherent power to flood the light from within to illumine one's entire being.

Mind must be held on to something, because in its natural existential condition mind cannot stay without an impression. Mind must be fed with holy thought, with spiritual thought or spiritual sound symbol or the thought that means something to the individual. The more an individual holds the mind to something, the less the things can come and disturb the individual. At this point one has to take into account what one has in the mind i.e. one's faith, one's conviction, one's belief, one's devotion etc. One has to evolve and purify one's own mind. Nothing foreign can help.

There is nothing in one's mind that happens without one's knowledge, but one does not catch it because one does not hold the mind. One has to keep the mind free of urges and modifications i.e. just looking up at the thoughts that come up without getting caught by the thoughts without developing worry about any thought. It requires one to separate the mind and thoughts and keeping a space between the two or not allowing the mind to go to body level. One has to train the mind to refuse to see, to refuse to hear and to refuse to accept any thought naturally. All traditions, customs and religion cripple the mind and hypnotize it. The "I" without attributes is no "I." When one removes all attributes, all impressions, all identifications, what is left? The pure "I" is all that is left. It does not bind. It is absolutely free. What we need for this is an alert mind. One has to be alert. One has to live with the facts that mind is free and that mind is not the master. The impressions, already in the mind-stuff (the sub-conscious mind) are not the real self. A mind becomes no-mind when it is detached from the impressions from inside and world outside. "The impression-less, quality-less, idea-less, object-less" mind is pure mind. When mind is pure, what is behind the mind i.e. real consciousness illumines immediately. Then what one is left with is pure light. That is why illumination (self-realization) happens, when one makes the mind "no-mind" or pure mind. Purity of heart, purity of mind and purity of consciousness are exactly the same. One has to get detached from all the thoughts to see the world as it is. One attains this state through yoga (sum of all disciplines i.e. physical, mental, emotional and spiritual to unite the individual soul with the supreme soul).

Lord Krishna in the Gita puts enough emphasis on mind. A yogi (one, who is adept in all disciplines relating to physical, mental, emotional and spiritual aspects) is one who controls the mind, analyses the mind, and examines the mind. Every thought, every impulse, every urge, every modification is examined (or watched) thoroughly. Whatever is to be done, one has to be mindful; one has to be alert; one has to be awake to the internal and external world through mind. This is the purpose of the Gita and this also is the purpose of this discussion. **Mind is the door to the "Heart of the Universe"** i.e. the Supreme Being or in the Gita's language *"Parmatma; Vasudeva Sarvam; Mamekam* (Me alone)."

15 Birth of an individual – Who is *Jiva* or being? Who is an individual? How does transition (change form one state to another) from *jiva* to an individual take place? A *jiva* or a being represents "reflected soul" and ego (consciousness of duality). A *jiva* gains consciousness but it requires an existential body. A jiva undergoes numerous births and deaths before it regains truth of its pure nature for achieving liberation. An individual is a jiva which has taken existential form in the womb of mother and it comes out of mother's womb after maturity. Coming out of mother's womb as distinct existential entity is called birth of an individual. Who is an individual? An individual is a jiva or a being, who has grown subtle body and physical body. An individual is a combination of three bodies i.e. i) Spiritual body, ii) Subtle body and iii) Physical body as follows:

a) Reflected Soul or deluded soul or higher nature under the influence of ego or *Jiva* – Reflected Soul or Deluded Soul is the body which emerges due to ignorance or feeling of duality. It is higher nature under the influence of ego. It merges with the Supreme Soul after veil of ignorance or duality gets removed. It does not die with death. Finally it merges with the Supreme Soul after it gains knowledge of its true nature. Till that time comes, it continues going through the cycles of births and deaths.

b) Lower-nature is subject to change. It has got two components i) Subtle body or *antahkaran* (invisible, perishable body which undergoes many births and deaths) and ii) Physical body (which emerges with each birth and dies with each death). Lower nature has got 31 elements as per verse 5 and 6 of 13th chapter of the Bhagavad Gita.

i) Subtle body or *antahkaran* or invisible perishable body, which survives death but undergoes several changes of births and deaths, has got four elements as follows:

1. Ego (discussed earlier)

2. The Un-manifested - It is called *avyaktam* or *mula-prakriti* or energy of the Lord or *Iswara-Sakti*. It is source of everything and not a product of anything whatsoever. It is called Pradhana (term used in Sankhya philosophy of Kapila Muni for this) constituted by sattva, rajas and tamas. It is very powerful and it is cause of all categories mahat-tatva (ego) onwards. The causal body or memories of past lives and past tendencies, has not been mentioned separately in the Gita but the causal body is to be taken as part of this only.

3. Buddhi (Intelligence) – Discussed earlier

4. Manas (mind) – discussed earlier

ii) Physical body – All the 27 elements are as follows:

a) Five gross elements (space, air, fire, water and earth).

b) Five tanmatras (sound potential, touch potential, sight potential, taste potential and smell potential).

c) Five organs of actions (tongue, hands, feet, organ of evacuation and organ of generation).

d) Five organs of perception (hearing, touch, sight, taste and smell).

e) Seven evolutes of mind as follows: i) *Iccha* (passionate longing), ii) aversion (antipathy or animosity or jealousy), iii) pleasure (feeling that arises in the mind by presence of that which is agreeable and disappearance of that which is disagreeable), iv) *dukha* (pain), v) *Sanghata* (aggregate of body and organs or aggregate of 31 elements of lower nature), vi) *chetna* (consciousness or cognizing faculty) and vii) *Dhriti* (Firmness) i.e. that courage which helps an individual to put up with great pain or trouble or steadfastness shown for holding body and organs together when they are exhausted.

Birth of an individual means outgrowth, after union of Higher Nature and lower Nature of 31 elements (4 subtle elements and 27 elements relating to physical body; incase of rebirth outgrowth of 27 elements only) to develop into "physical existential entity" coming out of mother's womb.

In the context of individual, following points should be kept in mind to follow the further discussion: a) Spiritual essence (the exclusive divinity or Real self or atma) enveloped by ego in individual soul (deluded soul or the self) achieves liberation when veil of ignorance or duality is removed, b) subtle body (invisible body or ego, the un-manifested, intelligence and mind) does not die with physical death, it undergoes numerous deaths and births. Birth means the subtle body has grown the 27 elements and comes out of the womb of mother as physical existential entity. Subtle body requires a physical body always to gain physical existential entity. Subtle body undergoes several births and deaths c) Physical body or 27 elements die with death. Death is relevant to physical body alone.

Given below in a table is the summary of constituents of an individual broken up in different categories and elements. It is based on 5th and 6th verses of Chapter 13 of the Bhagavad Gita. It covers the following questions:

i) What is it in a being that dies with death i.e. unreal? ii) What is it in a being that undergoes several births and deaths and is categorized as unreal? iii) What is it in a being that does not die ever i.e. real? iv) What are the different perishable elements of this lower nature? Do the subtle body (invisible perishable nature) and physical body (subject to death) undergo the same numbers of births and deaths?

Table showing different bodies and different elements of an individual

Higher Nature	Lower Nature having 31 elements					
Spiritual Body	Subtle Body having 4 Elements	Physical Body having 27 elements				
Exclusive Divinity not subject to birth and death	i. Ego ii. The un-mani fested iii. Intelligence iv. Mind	Five Primordial Elements	Five organs of perception	Five organs of action	Five objects of senses	Seven Evolutes
		i. Earth ii. Water iii. Fire iv. Air v. Ether or sky	i. Nose for smelling ii. Tongue for taste iii. Eye for sight iv. Skin for touching v. Ear for hearing	i. Legs ii. Hands iii. Tongue iv. Anus v. Genitals	i. Smell Potential ii. Taste Potential iii. Sight Potential iv. Touch Potential v. Sound Potential	i. Desire ii. Aversion iii. Pleasure iv. Pain v. Sanghata (aggregate of 31 elements) vi. Conscious ness vii. Firmness
	Subject to several births and deaths	27 Elements die with deaths				
Self	**Non-Self**					

If the individual is a factory, then ego, the Un-manifested, intelligence are the officers who take part in the decision making relating to this factory. Individualized ego is the overall in charge. Mind is the shop floor manager. It is mind which creates the body with the help of other members of *antahkaran* (subtle body or "invisible, internal and perishable body; this body does not die with physical death; death of this body mean self-realization or restoration to immortality") and finally an individual achieves its final destiny through mind only.

16 Life of an individual animate or inanimate (experience of childhood, youth and old age) – An individual is born with spiritual body ("Exclusive Divinity" alone cannot have physical existential state), subtle body (invisible perishable body which undergoes many births and deaths) and physical body. After birth, individual undergoes the changes like childhood, youth, and old age. Life is the period that an individual spends on this planet earth in a particular form during the course of eternal journey. During life here on earth, an individual gains experiences based on past actions and accumulated tendencies. Experience of each life on earth is different according to one's accumulated merits, demerits, understanding and measure of entitlement for spiritual growth. An individual experiences good, bad or evil experiences in life. Normally we leave life in this world with a feeling of incompleteness. "That feeling of incompleteness, that desire for something" is the reason of next birth. These cycles of birth and death continue till ego dominated soul identifies its true nature and process of transmigration (passing of an individual's soul into another body) stops on gaining living consciousness of "Supreme Truth; the Unchanging One; Universal Secret of the relation of the individual with the universe." What is that in brief? Everything has sprung from "immortal life," which is vibrating with life and this "immortal life" is immense. Focusing this immortal life and bringing it on the central stage in every life is the purpose of this "Feel the Bhagavad Gita."

17. **Death of an individual (Separation and destruction of physical body in soul's journey to its Destination)** – What is death? It was mentioned earlier that an individual is an aggregate of spiritual body (Exclusive Eternal Divinity within), subtle body (invisible, perishable body consisting of ego, the un-manifested, intelligence and mind and geared up to undergo several lives and death) and a physical existential form. Disintegration of this aggregate is called death. Physical body dies in death and spiritual body and subtle body proceed towards further eternal journey in the event of death. Death is a reality which imparts very good lesson in life. An ordinary individual continues to identify with physical body only. It is a wrong notion. At the point of death, one truly recognizes that an individual is not a body alone. Body is only a vehicle (or a gunny bag), which is changed when it is worn-out. In death a part of lower nature (27 elements mentioned above as lower nature) dies and individual soul with subtle body i.e. ego deluded soul, the un-manifested, intelligence and mind, proceed towards onward spiritual journey. Is death really as dreadful as it is presented to be? Death only means that present vehicle (present physical body) has lived its life (i.e. it is worn out) and it is the end of the present physical body (present vehicle). Death enlivens an individual to stark (unpleasantly clear and impossible to avoid) truth. Acceptance of reality of death helps to develop a serene fortitude in the face of disappointments and sufferings. **Death is not a disastrous sundown but rather a spiritual sunrise ushering into un-ending splendors of immortality.** Death accords another chance to renew for the journey of life to come. Each death is a reminder that individual is not physical body. Physical body is only that part of an individual, which goes away in course of life. Death only means that a chapter in the eternal life of an individual is over. Death is like getting out of one train in a very long spiritual journey to catch another train. Birth will be like catching another train. The "Feel the Bhagavad Gita" teaches to live death and seek immortality in death. Death of physical body is renewal into a different body and casting away of worn-out or unusable body. Death of the subtle body is self-realization or merger with the "Self of the Universe: One Supreme alone." The two bodies are virtually one body. Feeling this is wisdom. Failure to feel this is ignorance.

For soul's journey after death, it is necessary to divide the further discussion in two parts a) situation A *and* b) situation B. each situation is discussed below separately.

18. Situation A (Death with limitations of understanding and experience intact) – An individual after death does not have physical body. The composition of individual after death is as follows:

a) Spiritual body (individual soul or deluded soul)

b) Subtle body (antahkaran; invisible body subject to change):

i) Ego, (that feeling, that I am, remains there)

ii) The un-manifested (or hard to know energy of the Lord) is dynamic energy of the Lord.

Its impact in the form of rajas, tamas and sattva influences the jiva (the deluded individual Soul)

iii) Intelligence (the discriminating faculty is in dualities)

iv) Mind (mind is beset with thoughts and thoughts keep interfering the mind)

Next birth is imminent, if subtle body is active i.e. feeling of duality is there, intelligence is clouded, attributes of nature continue to influence the human behavior, past impressions agitate the mind to go for next birth and mind is full with thoughts. The *jiva* (one living entity in existence physically) first goes to any of the *lokas* (Hindu traditions mention 14 worlds or spheres in a universe, detailed in following discussion; Lord makes a passing reference taking for granted that Arjuna knew it, as it was common knowledge those days) and then again goes to world of mortals when the merits are exhausted.

19. Reflected Soul's sojourn (short stay) in interim lokas (transit worlds) - If subtle body or any part of it is dynamic as mentioned at serial no. 17, then the aggregate of spiritual body and subtle body will first go to one of the fourteen *lokas* (transit worlds, which constitute the universe). These are like transit flats where one goes to undergo the impact of good or bad activities that have been done by the individual while having a physical body. These lokas (transit worlds or spheres constituting a universe) are like transit flats where you go to enjoy or suffer the impact of your activities in the past. One does not spiritually evolve in these *lokas*. The individual stays in these *lokas* to either suffer or enjoy the impact of actions in life with previous body. After spending the due time (after merits and demerits are exhausted) in these *lokas* according to one's entitlement, one again goes to the planet earth to be born again in some form and thus the eternal cycle goes on. Hindu tradition enumerates fourteen worlds. Seven upper worlds are known as *Bhuh, Bhuvah, Swah, Mahah, Janah, Tapah* and *Sattyam*. The seven nether worlds are *Atala, Vitala, Sutala, Rasatala, Talatala, Mahatala* and *Patala*.

20. Situation B (Death with no limitation whatsoever) – This is a situation in which the soul recovers from its self forgetfulness, impact or influence of ego. An individual after death does not have physical body and the position of the components of subtle body, is as follows:

a) Spiritual body (In this situation, soul is no more deluded and gets the feel of its divine features through divine knowledge, which gets evolved from within due to yoga-disciplines)

b) Subtle body (antahkaran; invisible body changes as follows):

i) Ego, (It does not trouble any more when one takes cognizance of its presence. It automatically dissolves)

ii) The un-manifested (or hard to know energy or dynamic energy of the Lord does not delude the jiva due to grace of Lord)

iii) Intelligence (the discriminating faculty is not beset by dualities due to divine knowledge)

iv) Mind (mind is not beset with thoughts and thoughts do not keep interfering the mind)

20. **In this state i.e. situation 'B',** there is nothing like individual soul. All ignorance goes away and individual soul merges with the Supreme as the space in the pitchers in the room merges with the space of the room, after the pitchers are thrown out. This phenomenon occurs as naturally and as swiftly as clouds clear in the sky. These are the moments in which the "Self Revealing One" or the Consciousness of the "Infinite" becomes at once direct as light is to the flame. All the conflicts and

contradictions of life are reconciled. Knowledge, love and actions get harmonized. Enjoyment and renunciation becomes equal in goodness. The breach between the finite and the infinite gets filled with love which overflows carrying the message of the Eternal. The formless appears in the form of flowers, fruit and the boundless sky. One feels that one has crossed the bridge leading to "The Immortal Being." One experiences directly effulgence of "One Essence" which manifests in multiplicity of forms, as if it were a reality. This multiplicity is like dream and it is a precursor of forth-coming true state. At this juncture one experiences what it means being lead from unreality to the real, from darkness to the light and from death to the immortality. At this juncture, one experiences that love is the highest bliss that an individual can attain. Through eternal love one knows that one is more than "one self" and that one is "one with all." A seed finishes itself to sprout (coming out as leaves and buds) at this juncture. An individual soul has to annihilate itself (to get rid of its false cover of ignorance) to bring to fore (to place at front) its divine splendor concealed within, its true identity, life of the universe, ever resplendent, endlessly new and eternally beautiful.

The foregoing discussion sums up the thinking of the ancient culture, the Hindu traditions. These thoughts and terms have been extensively referred to in almost all Indian scriptures and in the Bhagavad Gita discussion also. The Lord Krishna does not confine the discussion to these thoughts alone. Lord's treatment of the subject is unique especially theory of action, interpretation of "Dharma," concept of *yajna*, concept of *Lokasamgrah* (cosmic benefit) and lord's concern to direct the individual to the mission of existence (*tameva sharnam gaccha* … ; Flee unto "Him" for shelter with all your being O Bharata) and the three approaches which finally lead to the same truth. The intensity of intake of discussion will tremendously increase, if following major points of all this discussion are kept in view while feeling the Bhagavad Gita:

i) There is an "Ultimate Reality or Truth or Unchanging Essence or The ground of all change." It is consciousness, knowledge and bliss. It is omnipresent, omnipotent and omniscient. It is eternal, indestructible, immovable and immanent (or present everywhere). It does not have one name and one form. According to Hindu traditions, it is called Brahmn or God (in singular). It creates, sustains and dissolves the universe by combination of its lower and higher energies. It manifests in different forms remaining undivided and appearing as if it were divided. This alone exists and nothing can exist without it. At times and according to its own will, it manifests with intense divine powers. At that time, it is called incarnation or *Avtar*. Lord Krishna of the Bhagavad Gita is an avatar (incarnation with supreme and exceptional divine powers) of the Supreme Eternal Universal Reality. Lord Krishna at one point tells Arjuna "The Lord abides in the heart of all beings O Arjuna … .." This is sufficient proof of universal existence that He was referring to. Human form was for certain purposes and this form again changed into the Eternal Universal Un-manifested Existence after achieving the objective. One has to remain conscious of "Eternal Existence within" and then the problem will be no more. The silence will speak and "That Reality" will enchantingly smile through all manifestations.

ii) There is a difference in Jiva (individualized soul or being) and individual (refer to earlier discussion). An individual lives with one physical body. Its physical body dies with death. Jiva undergoes many cycles of births and deaths. All our relations and all our thinking is linked with the individual, which essentially is not true identity. It dies. It goes away into fire and with it goes away all that is covered by "I and mine." Still we keep weeping and worrying for that which we have thrown away so many times in previous eternal journey. We thus read the world wrongly and thus deceive ourselves.

iii) There are two components in that which survives death: i) Deluded Self and ii) Invisible body or lower nature, which any way is to undergo changes. Should we weep or have undue concern for invisible body? No, Invisible body is like a dream created by delusive nature. Should we weep for deluded self?

iv) Answer is no. When divine knowledge dawns, the ego dissolves. The un-manifested nature does not delude anymore. Intelligence does not suffer from dualities and mind is not beset with thoughts. There is only one light, one effulgent truth. It is what an individual is. That is spiritual growth. We seek to eventually unite individual consciousness with the "Consciousness of the Source; the **Universal** Self." The eternal presence is the conscious space within and around. In that space the whole life unfolds. It is the only point of access into the timeless and formless realm of "The Supreme Being." In that direction we have to move and in that direction, Lord exhorts Arjuna to move.

Lord Krishna in the Bhagavad Gita indicates towards the mission of existence. Mission does not change. Targets change. Lord tells various paths which lead to the same "Reality or Truth." It is not easy to walk on these paths. Therefore Lord tells the way to dissolve pain and inconveniences in different situations and positions to optimize one's available inherent resources (physical, mental, emotional and spiritual).

> If one has felt this discussion, then one will understand what the poet Rabindra Nath Tagore is saying in the following words:
> **"Hast thou not heard His silent steps?**
> **He Comes, comes, ever comes … … … …"**

Who the poet is talking about? Was Lord Krishna not referring to the same "Reality" by His presence and words? Time was different. Intensity was different. Context was different.

What is the ultimate outcome of situation B? The myth that "I am" finally shatters. Individual consciousness finally unites with the "Consciousness of the Source; the **Universal** Self." What does it actually mean in terms of reproducible experience? How does one feel when one gets to this point? It is through heightening of our consciousness into love (eternal love) and extending it to all over the world that we attain communion with the "Infinite Eternal Joy." This "Infinite Joy" is "love unlimited, knowledge unlimited and consciousness unlimited." In this "love Unlimited; Love unconditioned" all contradictions of existence dissolve. Motion and rest are in one at this point. Bondage and love are not antagonistic at this point. The finite merges into the "Infinite." This experience is inner happening. Even in war, one is at peace (Lord Krishna smiled at Arjuna even in the fiercest situation in the battle field at the start of the Gita-discussion). One, who uses one's powers in acquisition of knowledge (divine), in fighting evils and dying for gains for cosmic benefit, never suffers. One's own existence becomes a matter of joy. At this point, joy is everywhere in earth's green covering of grass, in the blue serenity of the sky and in reckless exuberance of the spring. This moment is actually a moment of "realization of truth of universal oneness." It is a moment of change of perspective. It is a moment of self-blossoming. It makes sweet, vocal and stirring, **the lifelessness of "dried-up soul life".** In this moment, irresistible current of "Universal Energy" comes like impetuous (tending to do things very quickly) south wind of spring too suffusing (covering and spreading through) with divine fragrance. All one finds is love unlimited overflowing in all direction. From all direction and through all the points of manifestation, same love winks back with a smile, which is living and vibrant and knows no limitations. Something from within, unknowingly yet irresistibly, cries **"this is the smile of the Ever Lasting."**

iv. Major issues focused in the Bhagavad Gita

Narrated above is the setting in which the Gita starts but its purpose is not confined to narrate the details of a war. If it is not war then what else the Bhagavad Gita deals with. It is gospel which narrates how life should be lived fully, why an individual behaves as he or she behaves and what constitutes the ultimate purpose of existence. The impact of attributes of nature [rajas (restlessness), tamas (dullness and inactivity) and sattva (being in peace and joy), which get activated due to union of Higher Nature and Lower Nature, produce the ego, individual-consciousness. The Gita directs individual's attention to integrate the individual self with the Universal Self to achieve spontaneity of love (unbounded love) and unselfish work for cosmic benefit. Submission to misery is not the human way of overcoming loneliness, stress, anxiety and worry. The Gita helps to change perspective of life to gain a new type of relatedness with the world by development of inner spiritual nature. The soul's substantial existence springs from the Divine Intellect [Higher Nature; Exclusive Divinity (Eternity, Indestructibility, presence everywhere all the time); Amalgam of consciousness, knowledge and bliss] and its expression in life is effected by virtue of its vision of the Divine, who is its father, Guru (Ultimate Spiritual Guide) and its ever-present companion in life, death and even beyond. This "Ever Present Eternal Reality" is the indestructible root. An individual is a perishable outgrowth. Whole life one keeps concern with "the body and the body-related" only. The fool (individual) forgets the father (The Exclusive Divinity within) who keeps witnessing sitting right inside. This ignorance is the mother of all the problems. Work, knowledge (divine knowledge) and devotion are the complementary paths that one follows both to seek the goal and also after the goal has been achieved. Mountain can be climbed by any path but the view from the summit is the same. **In the Bhagavad Gita, wisdom (divine wisdom) is personified as being (one entity) whose body is knowledge, breath is consciousness and heart is love. Joy is the realization of truth of oneness, oneness of our soul with world and of the world-soul with the Supreme Lover. This is the focal point of the Gita everywhere and in all the chapters.** Yoga (the amalgam of all the disciplines, physical, mental, emotional and spirit to unite individual consciousness with the "Universal Eternal Infinite Consciousness") is the kingly path that leads from darkness to light, from death to immortality and from the finite to the "Infinity."

v. What is the role of this attempt?

This "Feel the Bhagavad Gita" helps to feel the "Life Ever Continuing" in its aspects of appearing and disappearing. "That" which is past and "that" which is yet to come are hidden in this "Life Ever Continuing." Everything and every being have sprung from this "Life Ever Continuing." Existence is vibrating with this "Life Ever Continuing." This "Life Ever Continuing" is immense. This Life Ever Continuing, this Light and Life of all, who is world-conscious is not only in space but also in the "inner most heart of each being." What is this "Life Ever continuing"? Read this "Feel the Bhagavad Gita" and let Lord Krishna speak to Arjuna about the "Life Ever Continuing." Our egoistic impulses, our selfish desires, obscure our true vision of the soul. That only indicates our own narrow self. When we are conscious of our soul, we perceive the inner being that transcends our ego and has deeper affinity with the "All." Know thou the soul. It is the bridge to the immortal being. After this experiential Truth, one will remain suffused (covered or thoroughly filled) with equanimity both in war and peace. Imagine someone going in the crowd. Suddenly the individual recalls the "smile in balcony" and forgets all the noise and the ordeal of the journey. Similarly, this attempt will help you to focus on the "eternal smile in the chamber of heart" to keep you connected with the main objective.

vi. The background leading to dialogue between Arjuna and Lord Krishna (The Gita)

The Bhagavad Gita is the conversation between Arjuna and Lord Krishna, narrated by Sanjay, minister to the king Dhritrashthra. This conversation occurs in the battle field of Kurukshetra where a terrible war is just about to begin. This conversation and Lord Krishna's exhortations to Arjuna to arise resolved to fight (to restore righteousness in society) cannot be understood till one knows a little the background details in brief or how perpetuated (bad belief continued for a long time) enmity among the princely cousins culminated into war. This conversation occurs in the "Shanti Parva" of Mahabharata, the great epic, narrative of the ancient Indians, who saw the vision of "Great India," one in culture, unified in political life and stretching from the Himalayas to Cape Comorin (now known as kanyakumari). It is not that no effort was made to avoid war. This background must be gone through to understand why Arjuna feels as he feels or why Krishna exhorts him to participate in war to save the society from unrighteousness. In the absence of this background, it is difficult to see Bhisma from the eyes of Arjuna or see Duryodhna from the eyes of Bhima. All these details are available in Mahabharatha, of which the Gita is an extract. Extremely condensed details are available below:

Kuru was the name of a clan (***Kula***) of that time. Kurukshetra was a vast field near their capital Hastinapur (modern Delhi). Dhritrashtra was the blind king of the Kurus. When he became old, he had in his mind to give his throne not to his son Duryodhna (a prince of evil propensities) but to Yudhishthra (noble prince, embodiment of virtues, purity and son of his deceased younger brother Pandu). Duryodhna, from the child hood nurtured enmity against the cousins. He used to feel enraged by the popularity of the Pandvas for their good conduct. He poisoned Bhima (the mightiest of the Pandvas with super human strength), bound him and threw him into the river to drown. He built a palace of wax and highly inflammable material. The idea was to set fire to the palace while the sons of Pandu were asleep in it. The plan was hatched to destroy the Pandavas. With the far-sightedness of Vidura, the Pandvas escaped. Later, the wise, aged and generous Bhisma (the Grandsire, the great uncle of both the Kaurvas and pandavas, who showered love and care to both kauravas and Pandvas in their upbringing) counseled Drona (teacher who taught martial arts to both the Pandvas and Kauravas) and Vidura (the senior of the family) to make peace with the sons of Pandu by giving them half the kingdom. The hotter-headed Duryodhna and Karna (a great warrior and friend of Duryodhna) did not agree to the plan. However, the plan was carried out and the kingdom was divided in two halves. One half was given to Yudhistra and other sons of Pandu. The Pandvas took up residence in the new city called Indraprastha. The Pandvas ruled the city justly and performed the Rajasuya Sacrifice (yajna), which was indispensable for one who sought imperial dominion to become emperor. Duryodhna was inflamed with the prosperity of the Pandvas. He connived (to allow wrong to happen) with Sakuni, brother-in-law of king Dhrithrashtra, who was skilled in the tricks of dice playing. A game of dice was arranged and Yudhisthra was enticed to play this game of dice by a deeply plotted invitation. It may be asked why wise Yudhishthra responded to the invitation. Three answers may be given. Men rush consciously to their ruin impelled by lust, gambling and drinking. Yudhishthra was fond of gambling. The kshetriya tradition made it a matter of lack of etiquette and honor to refuse an invitation to a game of dice. Vyasa had warned yudhishthra that a quarrel would lead to destruction of the race. Yudhishthra did not want to give any occasion for displeasure. In this game of dice, Yudhisthra lost everything including his brothers due to Sakuni. In the end, Sakuni asked Yudhishthra to wager Draupadi, the common wife of the Pandvas. Yudhistra lost even Draupadi. Duryodhna sent brother Duhsasana to fetch queen Draupadi, who was most beautiful lady of that era. Duhsasana caught her by hair and dragged her before the assembly in the open court of the Kurus. He went to the extreme of stripping the clothes of Draupadi in the open court. Having failed to get any response from the husbands and seniors in the assembly, Draupadi cried for help from the "lord of the world." A miracle happened there in the court at that moment. As Draupadi's robes (saree, which the ladies use to cover the body) were stripped away, new robes appeared in their place and Duhsasana, having piled up a great heap of elegant garments, was finally forced to cease exhausted from fatigue. The howling of animals was suddenly heard from the forest and there were bad omens. At this point, Bhima, the second in Pandvas with inhuman physical strength, swore a mighty oath that he would rend the breast of Duhsasana and drink his blood. All the elders in the assembly hung their heads in shame. Dhritarashtra called Yudhisthra and restored their kingdom to them. Duryodhan, on seeing his plans getting frustrated, upbraided his father, King Dhritarashtra and, once again, Yudhishtra was called to play the game of dice. This time the stake was that the defeated party will go with brothers into exile for thirteen years, spending the last year incognito. Again, Sakuni was throwing the dice. Yudhishtra again lost and the Pandavas took to forest. In the period of incognito, Bhima, disguised as cook, killed Kichaca (mighty commander of King Virat's army; the Pandvas stayed incognito at Virat's capital, Matsya, where it happened), who wanted to rape Draupadi, disguised as the attendant to the queen of Virat. After the death of Kichaca, the neighborhood king of Susarman attacked Matsya. King Virat, with the help of disguised Pandvas except Arjuna, went to settle score for the attack. Matsysa was now without commander and king Virat. To take advantage of the opportunity, Duryodhna attacked Matsya. Last day of thirteen years had passed, Arjuna, disguised as eunuch, helped prince Uttara of Matsya and defeated all the Kauravas and seniors put together. When King Virat returned to Matsya, he was informed about the details of victory. He offered his daughter as gift to Arjuna. This girl Uttara was married to Abhimanu. Pandavas left Matsya and settled in the city of Upaplavya, another place in Virat's realm. Here the Pandvas summoned their friends and relatives. A brahaman was sent to Hastinapur with proposals to Duryodhna for peaceful settlement, the settlement being that sons of Dhritarashtra were to accept to return the lands they had taken from the sons of Pandu. The aged Bhisma (uncle of Kauravas and Pandavas) was in favor of the settlement but Karna, a powerful warrior and a great general with the Kaurvas, advocated for war. Then, Dhritrashatra sent his minister Sanjay to speak with great care to conciliate and to avoid war. Yudhishthra was glad to see Sanjay and went to the extent of sending following message to Duryodhna " ...do not covet what belongs to others. We are five. For the five of us give at least give five villages and make peace with us. We shall be content. ... I am prepared and ready for peace as well as war ...." Sanjay returned to Hastinapura and gave a full account of the talks that he had with the Pandvas. Aged Bhishma counseled Dhritarashtra against opposing the combined strength of Arjuna and Krishna. Bhishma warned Dhritrashtra that Arjuna had already humbled Karna and all the kaurvas and seniors put together in attack on Virat's (one king) capital. Duryodhna could not tolerate all this discussion and declared that Pandavas would not get even a needle-point territory. He left the court in excitement. Yudhishtra sought counsel of Lord Krishna. Lord Krishna got ready to again go to Hastinapura to make last ditch of effort to maintain peace. All the seniors in the court and Dhritrashthra tried to bring round Duryodhna without any result. Duryodhna and his friends went to the extent of plotting to seize even Lord Krishna, who laughed at it and disclosed his divinity, which shuddered the king Dhritarashthra and the seniors sitting in the assembly. Any ray of hope of a peaceful settlement had extinguished when Krishna returned. All the possible avenues for peace had been explored without any possibility of settlement. Now, there was to be a war to death. It was destined. Lord Krishna accepted to be the charioteer of Arjuna in the battle field. Both the armies assembled in Kurukshetra and solemnly bound themselves to honor the traditional rules of war. At this Juncture the Bhagavad Gita starts.

All efforts to bring about reconciliation have miserably failed. Both the armies come face to face. This is where the Bhagavad Gita starts. When Arjuna saw men arrayed on both the sides for mutual slaughter, he was deeply agitated and Lord Krishna spoke to him in order to quell (to stop) his agitation and remove his doubts. Krishna's exhortation to Arjuna at this juncture is the "Bhagavad Gita," which is enshrined in millions of hearts as words of the Supreme Being, the God of the Gods, the Absolute Infinite Truth. It is widely acknowledged as one of the supreme treasure of world literature. It is gospel of devotion to duty, without attachment or desire of reward. It has shown the way to life to all men, rich or poor, learned or ignorant, who seek light in the dark-problems of life.

vii. Preface

[A lot has already been written which the people often write in preface. This is a daunting (that which makes others less confident) decision to attempt to write under this heading. In this space, an author intimately and frankly discusses how he initially felt about it and how the volume emerged bit by bit. Somehow it has got going and something has emerged from somewhere of its own. Author is only an instrument. Little do we know that … ." the Bhagavad Gita guides us towards our eternal origin, our far destiny, our purpose of existence beyond false beliefs, false concepts and false ideas."]

I could not understand the Gita in my life time. I am a fellow of the Institute of Cost and Works Accountants and the Gita belongs to a different genre altogether. No one in my family ever read the Gita. I could never make head and tail of it. I purchased the Bhagavad Gita numerous times by different authors and made many attempts and miserably failed always. Actually the terms like "Sankhya," "Dharma" "Brahmn," "Yajna" and "Vyavsayitmika buddhi" always left me disheartened, nonplussed and desperate for something more, which I was never getting. After reading the Bhagavad Gita, I was not getting that touch, that connection, that link, that spark, that marvelous natural communion with "That Something," which was eluding me and which I could never identify or pin point. I could never get the "feel" that I wanted. It was something vague, something too unspecific to be defined or something like my destined star, unknown to me, still uniquely charting my course from far away without my knowledge. I do not know why I was purchasing so many books on the Gita both in Hindi and in English and by different Indian and foreign commentators. Something, within me and definitely unknown to me, made me look at it like a child looking at the galaxy of wide-spread twinkling stars in the dark night, wonderstruck, without making head and tail of it. It (Bhagavad Gita) always attracted me but its presence always disturbed me in my studies, while I was writing books for the professional students on Cost Accounting, Financial Accounting, Management Accounting, Cost Audit and management Audit. This repulsion by its (Bhagavad Gita's) presence was also not ordinary. I would put all the books on the Gita in some remote and obscured corner of my library to avoid them from being in the sight. Its presence will not allow me to concentrate on my other subjects and attempt to read always left me like an athlete gasping for more breath after a long run. One thing was strikingly different. My repulsion for the presence of the Gita could never discourage me from buying the work of new interpreters. I never felt sorry for the volumes about the Gita lying unused. Rather I was feeling amused, at times, for the odd combination i.e. my incapacity to understand the Gita and number of volumes purchased by me for nothing. I could come only to one conclusion. I had some implicit, unexplainable concern for the Gita and it was a riddle for me too. Something, within me and definitely unknown to me and yet beyond my rational thinking, was inviting me through strange language of silence to buy another new book on the Gita. Again I would laugh away the stupidity of buying another Bhagavad Gita without ever feeling sorry in the heart of my heart.

One day I went to attend a talk of Sri Sri Ravi Shankar in Faridabad. He exhorted all present there to read at least one verse daily of the Bhagavad Gita. Somehow this thought appealed me. I started reading and writing one verse (writing means trying to find out how much I could retain and nothing more than that). There was no possibility of any other intention with my limitation about the Gita well known to me. One change I noticed after this very slow intake of the Gita. I started getting interested in the Gita. Very soon a time came when I was reading and writing or rather grappling (because I was trying more and more depth) with one verse only for three or four days continuously enjoying fully, with all my energy at peak at the same time. Now I was gaining my ground in the study of the Bhagavad Gita. I found that I was enjoying the study of the Bhagavad Gita . I lost my interest in all my other subjects. I wanted to feel the Gita. I wanted to breathe the Gita. I found very strange solace in the words spoken by Lord Krishna. I was experiencing strange contentment. There was a time when I removed the Gita volumes from my sight and now the Gita removed all the books from my house including the books written by me. I was interested only in the Gita. Without reading or writing my notes, I was not getting my appetite or sleep. I was reading it more and more and I was getting fascinated by it more and more. New thoughts, new phrases and expanded views relating to the Gita discussion started coming to my mind. I completely finished the Gita up to eighteenth chapter. I was still not satisfied fully. This time I started reading in the reverse order i.e. after 18th chapter I would take up 17th and so on. This time I started preparing fresh detailed notes simultaneously. Things had started happening now. One thing was aptly clear. There is a perennial nobleness and sacredness in the Bhagavad Gita. It is timeless treasure of great thoughts, enduring ideas, reflecting its influence on whole range of human thoughts and human insight. It does not leave you with your choice. It catches you at its will. It forces you to look into the direction of the "Great Secret within," which makes you conscious of inherent power lying untapped but waiting for you to tap it. First time in my life, after grappling for so many long years, I caught the echo of its (Bhagavad Gita's) timeless wisdom and an unclear glimpse of this irresistible, peerless beauty. It was like sun with its thousands of waves coming up in the backdrop of haziness of the winter morning. Somewhere something was taking shape. This time I knew what I was to do. My mission in my attempt was to put light into the shades where beauty was lying concealed behind the veil. I kept on following unknowingly "the silence within me intensely marked by fullness of contentment" under the clutter of daily routine of life. Haltingly, I again came to read the first chapter i.e. the last in reverse order. I felt strange satisfaction, unknown to me earlier. I shared my detailed notes with others. They spoke very encouragingly about it and gave so many suggestions and ideas. Now my notes were taking some shape and the journey had started.

This journey through the Bhagavad Gita, in the end, was as fascinating and enthralling as burdensome it was in the beginning. Now I realize that I was only an instrument. Does the cup know the taste of its content? Does the wave know the purpose of its origin and duration of its existence? Does the lily know why it enchanted with its beauty? I was nothing more than that. I kept on moving with unwavering faith, believing in "The Unseen." The difficulties were obvious due to my limitations and preoccupations. One thing was good. With my earlier background, I was very much used to facing difficulties of this type. I had been through this phase many times earlier.

This interpretation (this volume in your Hand) is with a difference. It has not been written to be a book. That is important. These are very detailed notes prepared for my personal satisfaction, which has always been eluding me while reading the Bhagavad Gita. One thing is assured. Its reading will change the whole perspective of life. There are indeed reasons why the new readers face difficulty in reading the Bhagavad Gita. Therefore, a new heading is being added "Preparing to Feel the Bhagavad Gita." It contains a chart showing "Cosmic Eternal Flow." This chart shows "Germination of ego and deluded soul's journey to its destination." The discussion, following this chart, extensively deals with the thoughts and terms which are a basis of Indo Aryan Culture and the thoughts that the Hindu live by. We find reference to these thoughts and terms even in other ancient Indian scriptures including the Upnishads, the Ramayana and the Gita. The discussion under this heading will help the readers to understand the terms used in the Gita and the thoughts taken for granted in that discussion between Arjuna and Lord Krishna. Now the readers will not only understand what lord Krishna is saying but they will also know why Lord is saying it.

I want to make one thing very clear. I did not write this book. It got written. Rather it got evolved. There was no option for me but to write. Words, phrases, new expanded meanings were coming to my mind. Many a time I used a particular word and I was appalled to see its correct usage after consulting dictionary. Many phrases came to me in my sleep. It was some "grace" forcing me to write, leaving for me no option but to write and at the same time solving all my problems, my current needs as well. All the help kept coming to me from unexpected corners always. It saved me from all the worldly problems to write about the thoughts of the Bhagavad Gita. I can only say that this attempt was destined to be made. It is not at all my making. Yes one thing might have made a difference.

Initially I put a simple question to myself "why should I write on this subject at all?" There is a very beautiful photograph of lord Krishna (teenage Krishna) in my room with naughty piercing eyes, ready to extract meaning out of you, flute in hand, suppressed smile, wearing all the possible ornaments. I do not do any ritual. I thought at least I shall write Krishna, Krishna ten or twelve times in a day. This is sufficient reward for a man like me who never takes Lord's name, even after so richly enjoying Lord's grace. In the heart of my heart, somehow I had profound inkling (right at that moment) that writing "Krishna, Krishna" for years together with regularity can never go waste. A miracle has happened. This is not to support the blind faith. This is to promote the consummate (complete and perfect in every way) faith. I am a commerce man who did not make head and tail of the Bhagavad Gita. Lord Krishna, epitome of peace, joy and happiness says " ...therefore arise, O son of Kunti (Arjuna) resolved upon battle." This is an exhortation to wage war to establish peace and righteousness. I have found myself jumping and pacing with joy, when I started feeling the words of Lord Krishna talking of war to promote peace and righteousness. This is the classical example of how the opposites complement each other. Understanding and feeling the inherent relationship of the opposites is a great lesson of life. Such is the electric effect of the words of Lord Krishna that one feels amazed. They touch you. They play with you. They make you feel happy for no specific reasons. The Sanskrit words will go like dart and hit the heart and make you smile with joy in the middle of the night. Its effect will get you pacing in the room at odd times. Many times you feel that a word is like an ocean (for example Brahmn, Dharma). Even one word of the Gita, if understood in depth and in its entirety with expanded meaning, can change a life. It is not an exaggeration. It is my consummate opinion based on all my thinking ability. I feel like closing my eyes with extreme gratitude while recalling the ecstasy that I have been through in the course of my association with this work. "The Immaculate Matrix of the Universe," called by such names as Maya or lower nature in the Gita, is in action all the time, sometimes confusing you and sometimes working with you to let the things move according to the "Supreme Will."

It is hoped that the discussion will never be a burden. At times the readers may definitely feel that brevity has been sacrificed or rather annihilated. It has been done deliberately. The reason for this is obvious. This discussion has been particularly attempted to feel the Bhagwad Gita and not to translate the Gita, as it has already been translated and even interpreted numerous times earlier. What is the use of reading the Gita, if that awe (feeling of great respect and admiration), that tremor (shaking movement), that pull from within with intensity is not there? What is the use of reading the Gita, if it does not leave you staring in the space with a smile on your face, jumping with joy, pacing in the room? What is the use of reading the Gita, if you do not feel suffused (covered) with contentment with no desire, no complaint with nothing to talk about still so enthusiastic and full with energy? This attempt is for those who want to go to the depth to collect the pearls of wisdom lying buried in the fathomless waves of this ocean called the Bhagavad Gita. It is for those who want to be left with something stirring within when a word or a term of the Gita is spoken about. It is not for those who want to read the Gita by rote (involving repetition). So this is what it is. This book was never meant to be written, it got written. Now I shall deal with: i) What change it has brought about in my perspective and ii) What it contains for the readers.

I have always enjoyed the favor of good luck. I had highest qualification in my commerce line. I retired as Deputy General Manager. I have written many books for professional students preparing of for C.A. and I.C.W.A. Examinations and one of the books happened to be in the 18th edition in the competitive market. People call me a successful man. It is a hollow concept of success. I feel success is different from merely achieving a target. I have just completed this volume in your hand. Today I feel like asking from myself three questions. What is success? What is happiness? What is bliss?

Success, as it is commonly understood, is accomplishment of the objective (target) i.e. achieving something that we have been trying to do with good result. Success has different meaning for different people. First we define what we are going to call success. Then we attain it to call ourselves successful. These days we are in rat race for success especially due to western influences. I have myself seriously read the book "Laws of Success" by Napolean Hill (those days I could not understand the Bhagavad Gita). In western concept of success, we forget one thing very important. All this creation springs from joy. It is maintained and sustained by joy. Towards joy it moves and in joy does it enter. This joy is different from pleasurable feeling of sense satisfaction. This joy is the "state of being in rhythm" with nature. Conventional meaning of success misses one very important component of success. The Success must unite individual's feelings with all-pervasive "Infinite Feeling." One's success should be measured by the extent of one's expanded consciousness. What is the limitation of conventional concept of success? We run short of time to live life. We only exist. We get deprived of beautiful relationships with our fellow beings. We miss them miserably at times. We amass billion dollars and make a great name in the international market. But, we are not able to digest even a bowl of vegetarian soup on the breakfast table. What is the use of conventional success? We daily take ten tablets at least as medicine. We suffer from blood pressure, stress and diabetes. Even at the age of forty, we are not able to sit on the ground for five minutes. How is the reading of this "Feel the Bhagavad Gita" related with all this? We do not know what we are. We do not know where we came from? We do not know where we are going. Our target fixation is not in tune with the "mission of life." For this reason, "this conventional success" becomes good for nothing. It is hollow and empty. In the end we land with miseries in life. We achieve conventional success by giving our very life in exchange. One day we start weeping like Arjuna without knowing the difference between the real and un-real in us. We are in utter depression. Whole life we live without knowing who we live for. We are chasing the shadow without ever focusing the reality within us. If we know the "Beautiful One" within us and start ensuring that everything we do should be a step in the direction of "That Unknown" within us, then everything around us will start smiling at us. Living will become a pleasure. Life will become an eternal song. We will seek "deathlessness" in death. Rest assured about it. This is what this "Feel the Bhagavad Gita" will do. Feeling its discussion will mean that whole life will become a celebration. If we truly know this, we will meet success, wherever we go. This I have experienced. I have stopped writing professional books. What I am doing that I shall discuss in the book "Live the Bhagavad Gita." This "Feel the Bhagavad Gita" is to gain the proper perspective of life. An individual is a composition of "the Divine" (Truth; the eternal essence) and the "Un-divine (untruth subject to death, decay and change)." Due to delusion arising out of ignorance, an individual identifies with the "Un-truth, subject to death, decay and change" and starts suffering. The freedom is achieved when the divine knowledge (knowledge about the self) dawns and ignorance is annihilated. We have to rest assured about it. Now on, the question of success should be put differently with a slight change. Am I living life fully? Am I conscious of who I am? Am I properly identifying and negotiating with the "Un-divine within me subject to death, decay and change"? Is my activity in line with the mission of life? This is very important. Do not worry about the mission of life. Let Lord Krishna tell you about it while "HE" is talking to Arjuna. Rest assured Lord Krishna is supremely aware of the mission of each life. How does this volume help us in success? This "Feel the Bhagavad Gita" tells an individual that real success is that which one gains on one's own "deluded self; ego-dominated self" by intuiting (understanding something by feelings rather than thoughts) with one's "Pure Nature; One's Eternal Existence within." The real success is that one gains on "invisible perishable facets of one's personality" such as mind, intelligence and memory. The real success is that one gains on one's "Un-true Nature" i.e. lust, anger, attachment, hatred, loss of faculty of discrimination by subduing the senses i.e. organs of action, organs of perception and objects of senses. Success is bound to follow the individual, if the interim targets fixed in life are in tune with mission of existence. Gaining perfect love (unbounded love, unconditional love; love of the creator for the creation; realization of joy of yoga of union; the joy of giving ourselves to our true nature) and manifesting our "true nature" through our work is the real success. Success comes from within and not from without (external world). Defining this "true eternal nature within" is the focus of "Feel the Bhagavad Gita" and manifesting the "True nature; The Eternal Truth" is the true success.

Now I come to the next question. What is happiness? Happiness, as we normally see, is the pleasure that we feel when the situations, people and results are according to our expectations. In the reverse situations, we are unhappy. It is also related to our concept of success. Happiness is as deluding in life as success is. We live in the whirlpool of happiness and unhappiness missing, occasionally the rhythm of life. That is the extreme price we pay. What is the reason? We do not know why we behave as we behave. We do not know how nature influences our actions and then charters our destiny through our actions as if an individual were a machine. We become the helpless victims of the circumstances. Are we weak? No. We live life with wrong concept of ourselves, diseased-body, confused mind, inhibited intellect and traumatic memory. Then, we want happiness in the tempest (violent storm) called life. Then we weep. Then we get confused. Our unhappiness is the result of our ignorance of composition of nature and different facets and levels of our existence. This "Feel the Gita" will clear the mist that we have about "the self." We will safely steer through every storm in life, if we just remain connected with the "Beautiful Un-manifested One" within us. We do not know about our strengths i.e. duality-free-intellect, thought-free-mind and disease-free-body and 'eternal existence within us'. This "Feel the Bhagavad Gita will make you conscious about it. Rest assured. Nothing in life is to be feared. It is to be understood and felt. How does "Feel the Bhagavad Gita" help in achieving happiness? This volume introduces you to the most essential quality that one requires for happiness. This is detachment i.e. being in or with something fully but still keeping a space somewhere within distancing from it. It results in total involvement without attachment. Attachment erodes (gradually destroys) one's personality and increases unhappiness in life. Life should always be a cause of joy, celebration or happiness. The Bhagavad Gita boldly emphasizes two points: i) it is attachment that brings misery. In non-attachment lies the only true happiness and ii) Happiness and misery depend on the distribution of the attributes (gunas; qualities). If there is preponderance of sattva (tranquility), individual is happy and if inertia (tamas) or rajas (restlessness) prevail, individual is unhappy.

What is bliss? This is the third question. Bliss is the state of continuing joy where each cell of the body vibrates with energy and makes us move forward to go beyond the limitations of human mind, intellect and self imposed limitations. It is the impact of your connectivity with that personal "zone of inner calm and tranquility," which one just misses without feel of the Bhagavad Gita. It is the glow of immortality. It is the result of unshakeable belief in the "Infinite love and the Infinite power." This is the result of feeling the "Immortality." Do not ever think that you will gain this experience when journey is done or summit is scaled or barriers fall down. That way you will simply keep coming and going into the cycles of birth and death. Immortality is your right. It all depends on how deeply you think about it. Go into the depth of what you have in your hand and see for yourself what happens. Why do we miss such experience as bliss in life? The route available is through our own "Pure field of consciousness," which ultimately is Universal Consciousness. The Universal Consciousness runs the Universe. We miss our own pure consciousness. We miss the Universal Consciousness. We miss the bliss as well while holding its seed right within us always. We get lost in jargons and in "my method or your method," whereas "the Truth" so simply flows before us intermittently all the time. How does this volume help in pursuit for bliss? This "Feel the Bhagavad Gita" emphasizes the importance of intuiting (understanding by feeling and not by thoughts) with one's pure nature. Bliss is a utopian thought (most unrealistic imaginary thought which envisages perfect state with happiness for all) till one realizes by experiencing (by feeling) that fundamentally everything is an "Eternal Universal Energy." This "Eternal Universal Energy" is the innermost self of all that which exists. This "Eternal Universal Energy" is seated in the hearts of all. This "Eternal Universal Energy" is the "Sovereign Ruler; Sovereign Secret and Supreme Sanctity (that which must be respected and preserved without exception)" of the Universe. One attains the highest level of one's existence when one becomes one with "This Root Cause; This Eternal Universal Energy; This Spiritual Eternal Universal Substance" distancing from all available differences in description, interpretation and approach for this "Eternal Universal Reality." Bliss is the joy of realization of the "Truth of Oneness" in the Universe. Gaining firsthand experience of this (bliss) with awareness or feelings is the "Supreme Goal of human life." This incidentally is the focal point of this book "Feel the Bhagavad Gita."

I have dealt with the change that this attempt has brought about in my perspective. What promises does this attempt have for the readers? I have dealt with this aspect in the section that follows i.e. "What does this volume deal with?" It will introduce you with your real self. You will not suffer from depression even after having everything. You will decipher the "Living Principle" within each one of us. You will come to know how "Deluding Principle (Nature or Maya)" works and how you have to find out the way to bring about harmony in different levels of existence in an individual by concentrating on a "point" beyond the range of this "Deluding Principle; Lower nature; *Maya*."

What is the special contribution of this volume? Beautiful Sanskrit words used by the Lord should stimulate or stir or touch something somewhere within the readers even though it is in English. For example in chapter 2, Lord Krishna uses the words "*Padam gacchanti anamayam.*" Lord wants to say that "(the wise with equanimity of mind) verily go to the stainless state beyond all evils." That is all that used Sanskrit words mean. This meaning does not suffice. It leaves the reader wanting something more. Now the questions start coming to the mind. What is this state? What is it like? What does it feel to be in this state? The desire of the reader gets quenched (stop feeling thirsty) if some additional explanation is given as follows:

By use of these words, lord wants to say that divine wisdom (self knowledge) takes an individual beyond the limits of miseries and sufferings. Where does the wise with divine knowledge go? Lord gives a passing reference to the divine abode (permanent home of the Supreme). One reaches this state after gaining equanimity of mind. At this point, one experiences "intense self awareness." No duality exists. No negativity exits. In this charged state, all, that one experiences, is evenness of mind. Actually, this is the state of realization. At this juncture, one experiences intense awareness. "The perishable phenomenon" gets restored to the status of "Imperishable Unchanging Truth ever continuing in everything, everywhere and even beyond it." It is an infallible (never wrong) state where no malady, no affliction, no limitation or no suffering can touch a being (one in existence). "To be in this state" means to be truly united in "knowledge, love and service" with all the beings. In this state, one realizes one's self in the "All-pervading Reality." This is the point at which one sees "action into inaction" and "inaction into action." There are thousand waves on the surface of ocean and at its bottom it is absolute calm and quiet. Getting to this state amounts to getting to the bottom of the self. In every manifestation, lower nature represents action and higher nature represents inaction. It is for us to see whether we are focusing on higher nature (Truth) or on lower nature (untruth). What we see is our choice. At every point of manifestation of divinity, one can gain this experience of getting into state of perfection. One has to set the sight at a particular angle. It is skill. It is culmination of yoga. That is all. At this point, one gains the firsthand experience of feeling that everything has sprung from "Immortal Life." Everything is vibrating with life. Reaching this point, one realizes that this life vibrating within is "Immortal and Immense." We have to search this "Immortal life" in an around, in peace in war, in crowd, in seclusion, in far distances and in the cave of our own heart. All one experiences in these moments is joy unbounded. It is blessedness to be in this state. It is not that this state suddenly emerges from somewhere. It always remains there concealed in veil of ignorance. Truth and untruth always coexist. Untruth cannot prevail without truth in the background. Due to limitations, one only notices untruth and truth keeps witnessing smilingly, waiting to be explored, always immensely reticent and tolerant. Getting into this state requires perfect purity. This is life which is permanent. It knows no decay or diminution (reduction; depreciation). This is the message that Lord wants to convey by using the word "padam anamayam: stainless state beyond all evils." It is a sort of call to dive deep within.

This volume "Feel the Bhagavad Gita" nurtures the mind with great thoughts. Reader will feel the depth, richness and quality of lord's discussion. There are gems of thoughts which are ageless, eternal and immensely effective. This volume will tell us how to live, how to die, how to continue living and dying without ever worrying and how to go beyond life and death into eternity. Many times one single thought will energize the whole mental life of the individual who receives it in its enormity. That is why some terms like "Brahmn" and "Dharam" have been stubbornly dealt with extensively. There is an effort behind it. There is a purpose behind it. There is a promise behind it. Its reading will warm the readers with glow of inspiration, faith and divine sustainability. It will fill the readers with holy rupture (an occasion when something suddenly breaks apart). It will lead the readers safely through the mist of doubt, black darkness of despair beyond the treacherous places of temptation and uncertainty. The thoughts of "Feel the Bhagavad Gita" will guard you giving you the strength, the inspiration and the direction.

Life always presents its twists and turns. There are times when people are desperately in need of faith, hope, courage, peace of mind and standards and ideals, by which to live with abiding belief in the future and in the progress of mankind and cosmos at large. In these moments, this volume will offer something to cling to, something on which to build the strong, firm structure of life. A staggering wealth of ideas and ideals has come down to us from the past in the form of Bhagavad Gita. This is exactly the help that we need today. The terms of Sanskrit have been dealt with in adequate details as far as possible. It is hoped that readers will enjoy Lord Krishna's excellence of expression, depth of discussion and inspirational impact in English as well. It is, as its name signifies, an attempt to feel the Bhagavad Gita. Believe it. A few fragments of boundless height, boundless breath and boundless depth of "Truth" have been gathered in this attempt for sharing with you all.

Some people call the Bhagavad Gita a religious book. What is religion? A particular religion is another approach to interpret the same "Universal Truth" with some bias for certain traditions and specific individual experiences and references. The Bhagavad Gita talks of that which is the subject matter of all the religions. Can the "Supreme One," that the Gita focuses, be confined to any limits laid down? Is it possible? Is "Truth" not more important than the religion that deals with the "Truth" only? Is religion not a means to an end? Will it not be correct to start concentrating right on the "Truth" that all religions are talking about? Will it not be correct to talk about the "Truth" exclusively and not the "discussions" about the Truth. The Bhagavad Gita does exactly that with aplomb (a confident and skillful way). For a while, forget the waves on the surface of the ocean. For a while look at the "ever continuing quietness" at the bottom of the ocean. For a while be confined to that bliss, unforgettable and ever expanding, right at the center of everything. Then one will understand the words of Lord Krishna "*Tam eva sharnam gacch*; flee unto Him alone for shelter." Who is this "tam eva; to him alone" that Lord Krishna is referring to? Understand "That Alone" and then all the differences will subside into joy ever expanding, ever renewing and ever continuing. In the Bhagavad Gita, intention is to help identify and understand the way to live life according to one's true fundamental nature with focus on the mission of one's existence and "cosmic scheme of things." It is for all castes, creeds and religions because it takes you towards the "universal truth of all religions." It helps you to go in the direction of your own "Real Self." Bhagavad Gita is a manual of the art of living life. Its reading is a must for those who, for any reason whatsoever, think that it is not for them. It is most relevant to those who are satisfied with their knowledge. It is most relevant to those who do not have time. It is most relevant to those who are in confusion, danger, darkness, hunger, panic and exhaustion. Rest assured about it. What is the faith, unless it is to believe, what you do not see? Place yourself in the stream of words coming from the mouth of lord Krishna. Place yourself in the full center of that flood. Then you will, without effort, be impelled (make you feel strongly that you must do it) to "The Truth," to "The Right" and to "The Perfect Contentment." Just experience it to believe it.

I spent some time with the great words and thoughts of Lord Krishna in the Bhagwad Gita. I found these words extremely beautiful, immensely effective and good enough to change life. Whatever I could make out of it, I am sharing with you according to my capacity. Your feedback will help to improve further. It will benefit others also. I am happy that Sri Sri Ravi Shanker's one simple advice to read only two lines daily is coming out into the form of a book. This is the grace of the "Divine Soul" and unique celebration of "his advice."

The study of this volume "Feel the Bhagavad Gita" will help to develop the quiet mind. Quiet minds cannot be perplexed and frightened. Quiet minds, with serenity inside, go on in the fortune or the misfortune at their own private pace, like a clock during a thunder storm. Read it to believe it. Then each one of you will feel like saying:

"Why are you cast down, O my soul? Why are you disquieted within me? There is hope, light, knowledge and bliss in the direction shown by Lord Krishna in the Bhagavad Gita. In "That Direction" you go."

Many people have helped me. One name comes ahead of all, His name is Raju. He is an illiterate washer man. He helps me too much in my household work. One day I said "I do not pay you that much. Why do you do so much of work for me?" He was looking at my face with eyes wide open, lips closed with stern silence. After a brief pause, he said "I do not know what you are doing. One thing is sure. You are doing something good. I am an illiterate. I cannot do anything. Let this be my contribution in your work." In my mind, I bowed to his sincerity, simplicity, intensity to do something of enduring value and his capacity and belief to measure the depth of what he was doing not knowing well. Swati Srivastava was another person whom I disturbed very frequently even at very odd times, whenever any good phrase or thought came to me. I am thankful to her for her inordinate and immense patience and intelligence to grab the thoughts. She was always gracefully laughing even when she was in the middle of her household chorus giving food to her children and my call disturbed her all of a sudden like stubborn intruder. Kedar Nath ji is another person with whom I used to discuss my thoughts and plans. He always encouraged me in my efforts and gave me time. Vijay Gupta, my friend from childhood and my driving force, also encouraged me always. I am also grateful to Shri Satish Sinha, who is my neighbor and happens to be senior to me. He has always been scolding me, with his sermons, to be careful about brevity and relevance. His immense concern, for timely completion and qualitative contents of the project, is duly acknowledged. I am extremely grateful to my father late Shri Sham Sunder Lal Saxena and Mother late Shrimati Suraj mukhi for their never-die attitude towards life. May be, they (my parents) are extending their never-die attitude through me in this attempt, which does not at all seem purely mine. I am also very grateful to Anant Narain, C. P Bahri and Dinesh Sinha. Who am I most grateful for? How do I answer this question? "He" does not have one name. "He" does not have one form. "He" does not have one address. "He" weaves words in mind and adds divine music in His messages, which strangely enthrall my heart in silence. I seek time to answer this question but in the meanwhile following words are knocking for expression in my mind:

"O! Nameless, Universal Eternal Reality, let the stream of "my unsaid words" find fulfillment in "Thee." Let me feel that I am no more and "You" alone are stretching yourself through me, speaking in the language of silence, with smile unbroken, mission undisclosed, direction unchartered. This is only your love and grace which is flowing out to be "another stream of words." May my vision of you always remain clear, unwavering, pushing me in continuous movement towards you … … ."

There was time when I was surrounded by dense darkness of ignorance. I was not able to make out head and tail of the Bhagavad Gita. Journey was very difficult. In those moments the earlier attempts made on the Bhagavad Gita were like the lamps on a long lonely pathway. In the light of these lamps I have made my way ahead. I am most thankful to all those who have made attempts on the Bhagavad Gita earlier. They all are too many to be mentioned. It is on their foundation that I started this attempt. I shall like to conclude this discussion with the following thoughts of Swati Srivastava, paraphrased in English words:

"At times I catch the echo of "Thy Voice,"
In my songs, in my actions, in my thoughts,
Then my madness grows with joy …
And I sing again and again,
Not to hear my own voice,
But to catch the echo of "Thy Voice" …
in my songs, in my actions, in my thoughts …"

Lord Krishna in the "Bhagavad Gita" will adequately answer who this one is being referred by "Thy Voice."

A feedback from the readers will immensely help to bring about improvement in future.

V.K. Saxena

प्रथमोऽध्यायः (Chapter 1)

अर्जुनविषादयोगः "Vishad Yoga (Despondency of Arjuna)"

Title of the chapter- The name of this chapter is "*Vishad* (grief) Yoga or Despondency (state of unhappiness and lack of hope) of Arjuna" i.e. two words *Vishad* and *Yoga*. Therefore, first we should discuss two words "Vishad" and "Yoga,"

What is *Vishad* (grief)? It is the feeling of extreme sadness, because someone, whom you love, has died or is about to die. This grief is very relevant for all of us, though it is crippling and heart-piercing. Each one of us faces this situation of grief in life at one point of time or the other. Still, grief is very relevant even for evolution in life.

Grief makes an individual despondent (unhappy and not hopeful). Grief reduces an individual's efficiency, enthusiasm and willingness to live. Life, which is an individual's supreme divine gift, appears too heavy a burden, which clouds an individual's vision of intelligence. At the same time, grief is a very commonplace experience. It raises the question of propriety (correctness or fairness) about what it is to be done and what consequences such action will evoke. Here, from this grief (despondency of Arjuna) comes the wondrous dialogue, which will unfold the secrets about life, deathlessness, duty, non-attachment, the self, love, spiritual practice and inconceivable depths of reality.

Grief and sorrow at times represent the price that one has to pay for birth on earth. Grief and sorrow lose sting, when we see that there is an "Unchanging Essence, the Ground of all Change, the Great Cause, the First Principle or the Ultimate Reality" working as unbounded eternal life. Whatever intellectual or aesthetic satisfaction this dialogue between Lord Krishna and Arjuna gives, its main purpose is to transform life, to find a balance between the conflicting extremes of the worldly existence. On one side, this dialogue is an alluring lullaby to a crying child. On the other side, it is the lasting song of the soul to the entire tormented mankind. This dialogue is bound to make life worth living irrespective of reader's caste, creed and level of understanding.

When we go beyond grief, then only we realize that we all are after some goal. Actually there is "only one goal." The idea that there is a goal other than "this goal" … is wrong. Every goal is finally to contribute to "this goal" to be a worthwhile goal. What is "this goal"? Each one of us is an ocean of "Supreme Peace" and we have to find that peace underneath these layers of grief and sorrow, which are like hovering clouds bound to go away. To get rid of the erroneous idea that we are not peace is all that is required. One has to read this dialogue (the Gita) starting with grief to know completely the "Secret Miracle" of existence. This dialogue starting from grief is not an ordinary dialogue. It will help the readers to recognize themselves. It will describe to the reader what it is like to grow beyond the sense of "separate self" and to live centered in the "Deathless Reality at the core of our being." We are all inseparably linked with each other due to "One stupendous Truth." If we know "That; Stupendous Truth," we will really get to know each other despite of religious, cultural and geographical differences, as horses get to know each other by smell alone. Then we will feel joy and comfort in each other's company, though one is in the east and the other is in the west. Only then the world will become a cosmopolitan family. In the model of life presented in the Gita, every aspect of life is in fact a way of salvation. That is the beauty of the Gita. Lord Krishna is telling Arjuna "Stand up and fight" and through these words he is simultaneously giving him the greatest lesson in non- violence. How can exhortation, in the form of call to fight a war, with weapons, with bloodshed, be called a lesson to practice extreme non-violence?

Grief upsets us but patience and intense maturity is required to understand the subtle reality. Lord Krishna is asking Arjuna to fight a war to restore righteousness through discharge of duty as kshatriya (warrior) with no ill will, with no attachment, with mind and heart surrendered to the Supreme. First Lord Krishna wants Arjuna to concentrate on that "Reality; Truth" right within, which is beyond evil, beyond doubts, beyond limitations, beyond human understanding and experience. Then Lord wants him to discharge his dharma (duty here) to his race, to his heritage, to his society, to his nation and to his own inner self, where purity alone can exist. One understands this only when one is able to realize that the "deepest spiritual awareness" necessarily implies absolute non-violence, identification with the "truth within each one of us." Through grief only, one will go beyond the prism of ignorance to get the feel of "The One," who is the substratum (hidden truth) of the soul and the matter and who always keeps witnessing, each one of us, very silently, very serenely, whatever the situation may happen to be. This grief will finally culminate in the divine knowledge, which will unfold "**ceaseless outbreak of ecstasy within**"

The other word used in the title is yoga, which stands for disciplines **(physical, mental, emotional and spiritual) for union of the individualized-self with the Supreme Self (The Eternal Universal Existence Within)**. How can despondency of Arjuna be yoga? The sorrow for worldly objects (success and material attainments) is to be distinguished from the intense grief and despondency felt by Arjuna for ignorance of truth **(that, which remains the same always)** and dharma. The grief of Arjuna is not for personal gain, prosperity or kingdom. Arjuna is frustrated and unsettled with doubt due to "crisis of conscience **(that part of consciousness which tells you whether you are right or wrong)**." He is ready to give up everything. He yearns to know the truth that transcends the evils of life. He yearns to know dharma to live up to it. This restless state of mind is necessary for all the true seekers. This extreme restlessness of soul makes an individual the deserving candidate to be blessed with divine knowledge **(knowledge about the self; the difference between the real and unreal; the cause of universal oneness; true self of an individual is the self of all beings)**. For this reason, this discourse has been appropriately titled "Arjuna's Vishad (grief) yoga." Blessed are those who undergo this agony for truth and "crisis of dharma" in discharge of daily worldly life. This is a wonderful discussion in which Arjuna keeps asking questions and Lord Krishna keeps on telling him the different paths for freedom (freedom from the world and freedom from the clutches of one's own deluded self, freedom from the impurities and the limitations within an individual).

After discussion of words in the title, a question arises. How is this grief and confrontation in the battle field relevant to the modern reader? Life itself is a battle-field. Each day in life or in heart of each one of us, an incessant (without stopping) battle is going on between good and bad, justice and injustice, right and wrong etc. This is the true state of each human being except the realized souls, who are few and far between (rare). This inner conflict in the heart of each individual (cry of human emotions within) is symbolized by the external conflict between the Kauravas and the Pandavas in the Gita-discussion. Lord Krishna symbolizes the "Universal Eternal Reality; The truth or The Ground Reality of each being." Lord Krishna sides with justice. Lord is against contemporary demonic evil and injustice rampant in the society. Unable to cope with the situation, Arjuna seeks the help of Lord

Krishna to interpret dharma (already explained; duty at that juncture considering the divine dictates and not the man-made rules) in that dubious situation. This is not the unique problem of Arjuna. The whole mankind is searching for truth in the midst of doubts and troubles of life, not only outside in the material world but also within the soul (one's unchanging spiritual existence enveloped in the layers of ego and ignorance). The Gita offers that insight, that freedom releasing light, which a soul searches to bring about unity with the "True Nature of a being or the Truth of a Being or The Ground of a being." The Gita finally brings home the cardinal fact that even war is not a dreadful sin, when it is waged with the support of the awakened moral and spiritual sense, emanating from "All Protecting and All Absorbing Presence Within" to justify the revolt against the sensations and the emotions.

Some brief, about the background, is necessary before the start of the first chapter. There were two clans of a royal family in northern India. One clan is the Pandvas (the good guys). Pandvas represent virtues. They are led by Arjuna, the hero of the Gita and his four brothers. Opposing them are the forces of the Kaurvas (the bad guys), their evil cousins, the hundred sons of the blind and the weak-minded king Dhritarashtra. This is an era, in which un-righteousness is rampant. An attempt has been made to strip off a lady (from the Pandvas side) in the open court in broad day light, in the presence of all the seniors. Poison is given to a prince. A house of wax is built to burn the Pandavas alive. Pandavas have been vehemently (showing strong feelings) denied the bare princely rights and all sincere and successive attempts to restore peace have failed due to arrogance and stubbornness of Duryodhana, the main bad character, the eldest brother of Kauravas and son of king, Dhritarahtra. All efforts to bring about reconciliation have miserably failed. There is no recourse left now but war. Finally both the armies have come face to face to fight unto death in the field of Kurukshetra.

Chapter is about to start. A few names will frequently appear in this ensuing discussion. Dhritrashtra is the blind and weak-minded king, the father of Kaurvas (bad guys), unmindful of righteousness (*dharma*, morally good and fair). The blind king is listening to the happenings in the battle field (Kurukshetra) through his charioteer Sanjay. Saint Vyasa gives a special blessing to Sanjay that, though he will be sitting in the palace with the king, he will be able to see and hear everything going on in the battle field of Kurukshetra. Arjuna, son of Pratha or Kunti, is the hero of the Bhagavad Gita. He is a blameless knight and a powerful warrior noted particularly for his skill as an archer. Lord Krishna, the charioteer of Arjuna, is the divine incarnation, God himself, having all the powers to do and undo things. Lord Krishna and Arjuna have been intimately associated with each other (Arjuna did not know before this confrontation, that Lord Krishna was actually the Supreme Being, the God himself). Before coming to the battle field, Lord Krishna has accepted to be charioteer of Arjuna. Lord Krishna is avtar (incarnation) of Vishnu or the Supreme Spirit and speaks most of the line of the Bhagavad Gita. He is related to the Pandavas by marriage, being brother of Kunti, mother of sons of Pandu, and hence he is their uncle.

The king Dhritrashtra is sitting in the palace anxious to know about the happenings at the battle field. First chapter begins with a question from Dhrtarashtra.

1. Dhritarashtra, the blind king, asks Sanjay about the battle.

Dhritarashtra's query – 1

धृतराष्ट्र उवाच ।
धर्मक्षेत्रे कुरुक्षेत्रे समवेता युयुत्सवः ।
मामकाः पाण्डवाश्चैव किमकुर्वत सञ्जय ॥ १-१ ॥

dhrtarastra uvaca

dharma-ksetre kuru-ksetre samaveta yuyutsavah
mamakah pandavas caiva kim akurvata sanjaya 1.1

dhrtarastrah—Dhrtarastra, the blind king of Hastinapur, unduly attached to his children (bad guys); *uvaca*--said; *dharma-ksetre*—on the holy plain; *kuru-ksetre*--in the place named Kuruksetra; *samavetah*--assembled; *yuyutsavah*--desiring to fight; *mamakah*--my people (sons); *pandavah*--the sons of Pandu; *ca*--and; *eva*—also; *kim* --what; *akurvata*--did do; *sanjaya*--O Sanjaya.

Dhritarashtra said:

"On the field of Kurukshetra, the field of righteousness, gathered together eager for battle, what did they, O Sanjay, my people and the Pandvas, do?"   II 1.1 II

It is most appropriate that the Gita starts with the word "Dharmakshetre" i.e. field, where *Dharma* evolves or develops by gradually changing. What is *dharma*? It is one of the most important terms used in the Gita like Brahmn and atma. It is used both as noun and as adjective. Since this term is extensively used in the Gita and has far reaching meaning, it is essential to deal with it in detail both as noun and as an adjective.

First this term is dealt with as noun. Dharma is an auspicious word. There is no synonym for this word in the English language. It is not a simple word. This word is of profound importance. If one truly and effectively understands this word (*Dharma*) alone in its entirety, one will meaningfully understand the whole purpose of the Gita. The Supreme Eternal Universal Reality manifests differently (or incarnates) again and again to save Dharma (righteousness) only

Dharma is the "divine code of conduct" with a particular reference to natural attributes (rajas, tamas and sttava; refer to chart in introduction) of being, associated circumstances and related factors. *Dharma* means "righteousness as per law of nature or righteousness as per divine dictates." It is the ultimate purpose as per providence (a force that people believe controls our life) that is inherently working in a being, whether it is explicitly cognized or not. It is one's inherent commitment to one's true nature irrespective of whether it is properly deciphered or not. Its proper interpretation requires extreme spiritual purity and one's absolute commitment to find one's true nature. Deciphering of Dharma may present difficulty. Appearance of a seed may contradict its true nature. If a seed is subjected to chemical analysis, one may find in it carbon, proteins and good many things but not the idea of sprouting a tree. When the tree begins to shape, we say with certainty that the seed, allowed to rot in the ground, has fulfilled its *Dharma*. *Dharma* is universal and not man-made. A judgment is given in a court based on laws made by human beings. *Dharma* is experienced in the inner chamber of a being in soul-touched communication in silence with one's own self. Highest achievement of a being is to identify and fulfill one's *Dharma*. Freedom of a being is in attainment of its *Dharma*. *Dharma* is essence of nature. Dharma is like searching the real meaning of one's self.

Dharma is assessment of righteousness considering peculiar combination of an individual's gunas (*sattva, rajas and tamas* i.e. attributes of nature), cultural and social upbringing (cumulative impact of surrounding nature or environment and social traditions), individual heritage (not individual's prerogative again but nature's response to past actions and tendencies of the individual), individual's spiritual maturity (intellectual blossoming of an individual with reference to divine knowledge) and objective of individual existence not as per man-made rules but as per interpretation of divine dictates or law of nature. *Dharma* is the inner most nature, the essence, the implicit "Truth" of all things not as man expects but as nature demands. *Dharma* is that which works in each one of us steering our life towards the ultimate purpose of existence. When any wrong is done, we say that *Dharma* is violated. What does it mean? It means that "wrong-done" is a lie to true nature. When there are no qualms (feelings of doubt and worry) about *Dharma*, it means that life is in tune with one's true nature. *Dharma* is that which upholds the individual, upholds the individual's conscience (that part of consciousness, which tells whether or not what individual is doing is morally right or wrong) and precludes the individual's down fall on the spiritual path. *Dharma* is not man-made. *Dharma* is universal. One does not require education or man-made input for interpretation of *Dharma*. *Dharma* stands for interpretation as per law of nature (not man-made laws), which takes into account many visible and invisible factors and considerations. For interpretation of *Dharma*, one needs intense purity, sensitivity, and total belief in divine participation and divine inference and interference. That is why interpretation of dharma does not require a man-made language. It whispers even to animals, plants and beasts. The interpretation of dharma is felt by a being through silence in the inner most and invisible chamber of one's existence. The Supreme Universal Reality, the Ground of every being (here Lord Krishna) is the embodiment of *dharma*. Reverence for Dharma is the worship of the Lord. The main aim of the Gita and its teachings is to direct an individual to determine its dharma. Dharma helps to interpret righteousness through sensitivity and awareness based on soul-touched wisdom. Lord incarnates from time to time to establish dharma. *Dharma* protects those, who protect *Dharma*.

The meaning of the term Dharma changes, when some adjective is used with it. Then Dharma is interpreted in the light of adjective used. One word Dharamkshetre is used here. It means field, where Dharma evolves. Similarly another word Svadharma is also used in the Gita. It means duty of an individual considering individual's peculiar composition of attributes (i.e. feverish, lazy and peaceful and contended), heritage, one's cultural and social upbringing and one's social and moral obligations and commitments to other individuals and society at large. Dharma does not change, as it is universal. Dharma of an Indian and an Italian as a human being will remain the same. Its interpretation changes according to the interpreter and the adjective. Dharma does not require a man-made language. Recently there was a picture in the news paper. A big monkey was coming out of the inferno with small, newly born puppy in hands. Puppy's mother had died and monkey was risking his life to save the life of the puppy. Who was guiding the monkey to save the puppy in the inferno? It was Dharma. It speaks to animates and in-animates in language of silence.

In this verse, *Kurukshetra* has been called *dharmakshetra*. Why? It is a field that has been used for evolving *dharma* from time immemorial. This is the field where a lot of work has been done to harmonize human activities with spiritual existence. This is a field where even by mutual conflict development is advanced and cosmic purpose is served. In former *yugas*, Brahma, Indra and Agni (the intermediate Gods with names and forms: different executives of the Supreme for different purposes; Supreme Self is always addressed in singular without name and form) performed tapas (self-purifying exercises) in this sacred place. Emperor Kuru, the ancestors of the Kauravas and the Pandvas ploughed land and so it is called Kurukshetra. Lord Indira (Intermediate God; executive force of the Supreme for a particular cosmic function) offered a boon to Kuru that anyone who performed tapas (exercises to evolve spiritually) or left his or her mortal body in Kurukshetra would ascend to higher realms of existence (refer to fourteen *lokas* mentioned in the chart in introduction). Many great and holy persons have performed meritorious acts of dharma in Kurukashetra. That is why it is called Dharamkshetra. Lord Krishna, the protector of Dharma, is actively present in this field called Kurukashetra. That may be another reason why it has been called the Dharamkshetra.

Two armies of conflicting cousins (the Pandvas and the Kaurvas) have come face to face in the battle field of kurukshetra to fight unto death. Kurukshetra is a land of the Kurus, a leading clan of that period. Kurukshetra is a vast field near Hastinapur, in the neighborhood of modern Delhi.

Dhritarashtra is raising this question to Sanjay, his minister and charioteer, who is blessed with divine vision for reporting him the events of war, sitting in the palace.

The use of the word "*mamakah*," in this verse, is very significant. It means "my people." It means that the king is suffering from the sense of "mine-ness" i.e. bias for his own children. It shows that the king has more attachment with his own sons than the Pandvas, whereas both the Pandava and the Kauravas were brought up together in his care as members of a family. This undue attachment for own children arises from *ahamkara* (ego), which is the root of all evils. The use of this word shows selfishness on the part of Dhritarashtra and hence the Kaurvas. Love for power and domination, which is the main cause of war between the cousins, emanated from this trait of the Kauravas. Thus right in the beginning we get to know what type of group the kauravas is and why they are considered the bad guys. Actually the conflict between the Kaurvas and the Pandvas represents the conflict between two great movements within each being, the upward and the downward, the divine and the demonic, the *dharma* (righteousness), which helps to grow spiritually and *adharma* (un-righteousness) which drags an individual down deeper into entanglement with the matter.

The two words "*Dharamkshetre kurukshetrey*" used at the beginning of this verse are very significant. Srimati Ahalya Bai Holkar of Indore was a pious and devout lady. She once heard the greatness of the Gita from the court *Pandit* (one well versed in the scriptures and the methodology of traditional worship) and desired him to read the Gita to her. No sooner did the *Pandit* read out the first quarter of the first verse, she bade him to stop. The Pandit was astounded and looked at her in bewildered gaze. She then explained herself "well, sir, you read in the chapter dealing with greatness of the Gita that one verse, half of it, a quarter of it, will serve to liberate one from samsara (worldly existence confining an individual to the thoughts of "my and mind"), the ever-revolving cycles of birth and death. This quarter on the first verse well serves that purpose. Where then is the need to proceed any further?" Then she expounded that portion of the verse as she understood it "*kshetre kshetre dharmam kuru*" i.e. in every field (kshetra; considering that each individual is a field) or whatever you are, do righteous deeds. This only shows that if even one word of the Gita is properly understood, assimilated and internalized, it will suffice to lead an individual to the "highest; the Universal Eternal Source of all that is." Everywhere the Gita's focus is the same i.e. how the individual should conduct in baffling situations and how the individual should connect to the Divine (The Supreme Eternal Source of Energy and the Ground of everything).

What is the sum and substance of the first verse? The blind King Dhritarashtra, whose mental perception has got clouded due to greed, attachment with his children and lack of discrimination, asks from this charioteer the news of war.

2. Sanjay replies to the question raised by king Dhritarashtra.

सञ्जय उवाच ।
दृष्ट्वा तु पाण्डवानीकं व्यूढं दुर्योधनस्तदा ।
आचार्यमुपसंगम्य राजा वचनमब्रवीत् ॥ १- २ ॥

sanjaya uvaca drstva tu pandavanikam vyudham duryodhanas tada
acaryam upasangamya raja vacanam abravit 1.2

sanjayah—Sanjaya (minister of Dhrtrashtra); *uvaca*--said; *drstva*—having seen; *tu*--indeed; *pandava-anikam*--the army of the Pandavas; *vyudham*—drawn up for the battle; *duryodhanah*—Duryodhana (the wicked son of king Drtrashtra); *tada*--then; *acaryam*--the teacher (Drona, supposed to be the master in divine knowledge by caste but he is master in use of contemporary weapons used in war); *upasangamya*--approaching nearby; *raja*--the king; *vacanam*--words; *abravit*--spoke.

Sanjay said:

"Having surveyed the Pandva forces arrayed in the battle order, Duryodhana approached his teacher, Drona and spoke these words." II 2 II

Duryodhna is the dirty fighter, as the name suggests. He is the eldest son of blind king Drtarashtra and the instigator of the event that led to the battle of Kurukshetra. His primary aim is to deny Yudhisthira, the eldest of the Pandvas princes, the throne of Hastinapur and to rule in his place. In the battle field, when the forces are taking positions, he goes to Drona.

Drona is a great warrior and teacher of archery for both the Pandvas and the Kauravas. He is Brahman (a high caste) by birth and father of Asvatthaman (one, who has strength of a horse). Drona is highly respected like grand sire and uncle, Bhisma. These two are the highly respected elders in the Mahabharta war.

This discussion will be enjoyed only when one keenly observes what is said and why it is said. Actually the Gita appears as a portion of the Mahabharata. This discussion cannot be understood and felt fully, till the background details, not specified here in discussion, are made known simultaneously. Overlooking Bhishma, the illustrious commander-in-chief of the Kaurvas, Duryodhna exhorts Drona to survey the opposing army of the Pandvas right in the beginning. Is it because Duryodhna has no confidence in Bhishma or is it because Drona is greater than Bhishma? There are reasons for this. Bhishma, the grand sire and the uncle, is a noble and righteous warrior rather indisputably the greatest of the warriors assembled there. At the outset, Bhishma has made three things very clear to Duryodhana. He will not slay the Pandvas. He will not strike a blow to sikhandin (son of Drupada, a reincarnation of Amba, who had refused to marry Vicitravirya – now a powerful warrior, a female in earlier birth and whom Bhishma still regarded a female) however hard the later might strike him. He will definitely destroy the rest of the Pandva forces to "repay for his loyalty to the throne." On the other hand, Drona has not committed himself like Bhishma though he is also partially attached to the Pandavas for their characters and deeds. Actually Duryodhna is a great diplomat. It is due to his diplomacy that he goes to Drona, the teacher, instead of Bhishma, the commander-in-chief. Duryodhna wants quick results by fair or foul means without caring the least for righteousness and hierarchy (system of having control over the people in the rank below).

This verse beautifully presents contrast between Duryodhna and Arjuna. Duyodhna saw the Pandva army arrayed in special formation in the battle field. He (Duryodhana) does not feel the qualm (worry, whether you are right or wrong) of conscience like a righteous man. He runs to the teacher (Drona) as a frightened child runs to the parents, disregarding hierarchy by not going to Bhishma, commander-in-chief with due respect. He starts his diplomacy. Later, when Arjuna similarly sees the arrayed armies, his reaction is going to be different and for this reason Arjuna has been blessed with the divine message of the Gita, the immortalizing nectar in the form of divine knowledge.

3. Duryodhana specifically invites attention of Drona on Dhristadumana, commander-in chief of the Pandavs and son of Drupada, old friend and the arch enemy of Drona. In this verse, Sanjay repeats the words spoken by Duryodhana to Dronacharya, his teacher of warfare.

पश्यैतां पाण्डुपुत्राणामाचार्य महतीं चमूम् ।
व्यूढां द्रुपदपुत्रेण तव शिष्येण धीमता ॥ १- ३ ॥

pasyaitam pandu-putranam acarya mahatim camum
vyudham drupada-putrena tava sisyena dhimata 1.3

pasya--behold; *etam*--this; *pandu-putranam*-- the sons of Pandu; *acarya*--O teacher; *mahatim*--great; *camum*--army; *vyudham*—arranged for battle; *drupada-putrena*--by the son of Drupada; *tava*--your; *sisyena*--disciple; *dhi-mata*--wise.

"O teacher (Guruji)! Behold the great Pandava army, formed in the battle order by your wise disciple, son of Drupada (Dhrishtadumana; he, whose splendor is bold))." II 3 II

In the second verse, it becomes obvious that Duryodhana ignores the hierarchy by going to Drona, the teacher instead of Bhishma, the commander-in chief of the Kauravas. Every word in the third verse has been chosen by Duryodhana to incite Drona against Dhrishtadumana. Dhristaduman is commander-in chief of Pandva's army. He is son of Drupada, a disciple of Drona and is a man of intelligence. Each word used by Duryodhana to describe Dhrishtadymana is significant. Some background story is necessary to understand the feelings between Drona and Dhrishtaduman. Actually, the Gita is an extract from the epic Mahabharata. When it is read as a separate book, background details, which are not available in the Gita, become necessary to understand the meaning and context of the statement.

Drona and Drupada had been boyhood friends and fellow disciples. Later Drupada became king of Panchala while Drona remained poor. Later, when Drona approached Drupada for help, the king Drupada, insulted Drona, the poor Brahamin. Drona was deeply hurt but he calmly accepted the insult and went to Hastinapur, where he became the teacher of warfare of the Pandva and the Kaurava princes. After their education was complete, Drona desired that Drupda should be captured and brought alive to him by way of Gurudakshina (offering to the teacher by way of gratitude with reverence). Arjuna succeeded in capturing Drupada, whom he threw at Drona's feet. Drona repaid him his insult with interest and set him free. Drupada felt utterly humiliated and wanted to take revenge from Drona. He performed, *Putrameshthi*, a sacrificial ceremony to beget children or yajna as it is called in Sanskrit and engendered Dhrishtadyumana. Drupada then requested Drona to teach Dhrishtaduman, archery. Drona was in dilemma but he accepted to initiate Dhristadumana into mysteries of art of war taking into account his reputation now. Thus, Dhristadumana became the disciple of Drona but enmity was always there due to disgrace of king Drupada. Now by talking straight to Drona to survey the arrayed armies, Duryodhana wants to bring his attention to Dhristadumana, the commander in chief of the Pandavas, who was primarily born to take revenge from Drona. This was an attempt to incite Drona against his pupil and to recall to his memory (Drona's memory) past history of rivalry in a few significantly chosen words. What is the reason? If commander is conquered, the army is easily routed.

In this way, Duryodhana flings the words of insolence at his teacher, as a scorpion stings its savior. Actually Duryodhana wants to say that Drona has made a mistake in choosing to teach science of war to Dhrishtadumana, who is disciple of Drona, ready to fight against his own teacher.

4, 5 and 6. Thus, Duryodhana pointed out to the battle formation of the Pandava army. This particular Battle formation was known as "Vajra Vyuha" in the science of war those days. Duryodhana now proceeds to mention in next three verses the names of the principal warriors on the Pandva side.

अत्र शूरा महेष्वासा भीमार्जुनसमा युधि ।
युयुधानो विराटश्च द्रुपदश्च महारथः ॥ १- ४ ॥
धृष्टकेतुश्चेकितानः काशिराजश्च वीर्यवान् ।
पुरुजित्कुन्तिभोजश्च शैब्यश्च नरपुंगवः ॥ १- ५ ॥
युधामन्युश्च विक्रान्त उत्तमौजाश्च वीर्यवान् ।
सौभद्रो द्रौपदेयाश्च सर्व एव महारथाः ॥ १- ६ ॥

atra sura mahesvasa bhimarjuna-sama yudhi
yuyudhano viratas ca drupadas ca maha-rathah 1.4

atra--here; *surah*--heroes; *maha-isu-asah*--mighty archers; *bhima-arjuna*--Bhima and Arjuna; *samah*--equal; *yudhi*--in the fight; *yuyudhanah*—Yuyudhana (other name of satyaki, Arjuna's disciple); *viratah*—Virata (King of Matsya); *ca*--also; *drupadah*—Drupad (king of Panchala); *ca*--also; *maha-rathah*--great fighter; (Duryodhana mentions here the names of main warriors form the Pandava side)

dhrstaketus cekitanah kasirajas ca viryavan
purujit kuntibhojas ca saibyas ca nara-pungavah 1.5

dhrstaketuh—Dhrstaketu (King of cedi); *cekitanah*—Cekitana (a Yadava hero belonging to the clan of Vrsnis); *kasirajah*—Kasiraja (King of Kasi); *ca*--also; *virya-van*--very powerful; *purujit*--Purujit; *kuntibhojah*—Kuntibhoja (Purjit and Kuntibhoja were brothers of Kunti, mother of the Pandvas) ; *ca*--and; *saibyah*—Saiby (father in law of righteous king Yudhishtra, eldest of the Pandavas); *ca*--and; *nara-pungavah*—the best of men.

yudhamanyus ca vikranta uttamaujas ca viryavan
saubhadro draupadeyas ca sarva eva maha-rathah 1.6

yudhamanyuh—Yudhamanyu (other name of satyaki, Arjuna's disciple); *ca*--and; *vikrantah*--mighty; *uttamaujah*—Uttamauja (Yudhmanu and Uttamaja were the two princes of Panchala); *ca*--and; *virya-van*--very powerful; *saubhadrah*--the son of Subhadra; *draupadeyah*--the sons of Draupadi (five); *ca*--and; *sarve*--all; *eva*-even; *maha-rathah*--great chariot fighters

"There are in this army heroes wielding mighty bows and equal in military prowess to Bhima an Arjuna – Yuyudhana, Virata and maharathi (warrior chief) Drupada; Dhretaketu, Cekitana and the valiant king of Kasi and Purujit, Kuntibhoja and Saibya, the best of men, and mighty Yudhamanu and valiant Uttamanuja, Abimanyu, the son of Subhadra and the five sons of Draupadi – all of them *Maharathis* (warrior chief). II 4, 5 and 6II

A brief about each hero mentioned in this verse is given below. A description of this relationship will give an idea about the response that their presence might have evoked in the battle field.

Yuyudhana (anxious to fight) was the other name of Satyaki (he, whose name is truth). He was kinsman of Krishna and king of Vrsni tribe. He was very much attached to Lord Krishna. He was a powerful warrior and an *"atirathi"* i.e. he could fight with any number of warriors single-handedly. He survived the Mahabharatha war and he met his death in the feud that followed among the *Yadavas* (Lord Krishna's clan) near Lord Krishna's departure from this world.

Virata (ruling widely) is the king of Matsya at whose court the Pandva Princes had taken refuge in disguise during the thirteenth year of their exile. His daughter, Uttara, was given in marriage to Arjuna's son Abhimanyu. Virata and his three sons Uttara, Sveta and Sankha, were killed in the Mahabharatha war.

Drupada was son of king Prsat of Panchala. King Prasat and Sage Bharadvaja were great friends. For this reason, Draupada passed a certain period of his early days in the hermitage of Sage Bharadvaja, where an intimacy was formed between him and Drona, son of Sage Bharadvaja. On demise of Prsat, Draupada became the king of Panchala. Drona on one occasion went to see him and addressed him as friend. This was resented by Drupada and Drona felt wounded at heart. After the education of

Pandavas in warfare was competed, Drona, the teacher, realized the preceptor's fee by having Drupada vanquished in battle by Arjuna in repayment of the insult he had suffered at Drupda's hands. Drona appropriated half of Draupda's kingdom. Vanquished in battle, Draupda re-established his friendship with Drona only as a matter of show, nursing a grudge against him in the core of heart. With the help of a couple of Brahamarishis, named Yaja and Upayaja, he performed a sacrificial ceremony (yajna) with the motive of obtaining a son, who would kill Drona. From the altar of that sacrificial ceremony (yajna) sprang up both Dhrstadumana and Krsna. This Krsna later became known in history by the names Draupadi and Yajnaseni. The Padavas married her, after Arjuna won her hand in the open trial of skill in archery. Drupada was a Maharathi (warrior chiefs). In Mahabharata war, he was killed by Drona in an open fight.

Dhrshtaketu (he whose brightness is bold) was the son of Sisupala, king of Cedis. He was killed by Drona in Mahabharatha war.

Cekitana was a yadav hero belonging to the clan of Vrsnis. He was a *Maharathi* (warrior chief) as a fighter and possessed great prowess. He was one of the seven commanders of the seven *Aksauhini* army of the Pandava. He met his death while fighting Duryodhana in Mahabharatha war.

The king of Kasi (Varanasi) was also a great hero and a Maharathi (warrior chief). His name appears in Karna-Parva of Mahabaratha as Abhibu.

Purujit and Kuntibhoja were both brothers of Kunti (the mother of the Pandavas) and maternal uncles of the Pandavas. Both of them met their ends while fighting with Drona in the Mahabharatha war.

Saibya was the father-in-law of the righteous king Yudhishtra. His daughter Devika was given in marriage to Yudhishtra. He was not only hero and powerful fighter, but was also great as man of character. That is why he has been called the 'best of men'.

Yudhamanyu and Uttamanuja were two brothers, who were princes of the Panchala territory. In the formation of the battle array, they were posted to guard the wheels of Arjuna's chariot. They were both great fighters and heroes possessed of immense strength and therefore two attributes 'mighty' and 'valiant' have been added to their names. They both met their deaths at the hands of Asvatthama while they were asleep at night.

Abhimanyu was Arjuna's son, born of Subhadra, second wife of Arjuna and sister of Lord Krishna. He was married to Uttara, the daughter of Virata, King of Matsya. Abhimanyu received his training from his father Arjuna and Krishna's eldest son Pradyumana. He was a fighter of uncommon merit. On a particular day in the course of the Mahabharata war, Dronacharya adopted the military formation of Cakravyuha (array of the wheel) of such exceptional strength that even the foremost Pandva warriors like Yudhishtra, Bhima, Nakula, Sehdeva, Virata, Drupada and Dhrstadyumana failed to enter it. Jayadratha from Kaurava army was made to safeguard the entry point. Arjuna, who knew to break this particular military formation, was engaged in fighting elsewhere deliberately. On that day the young hero Abhimanyu broke into the military formation called "Cakravyuha" of the Kauravas single-handed and gave an exhibition of his exceptional military prowess by killing innumerable fighters on the side of the enemy. But Drona, Kripacharya, Karna, Asvatthama, Bradbala and Krtavarma- these six Maharathis of the Kaurava army, in contravention of the rules of war, surrounded the young hero, Abhimanyu, who in that state dispatched single-handed many fighters to their doom. In the end, Abhimanyu was killed by a strike on head with a club by Dushasana's son, Lakshamana. King Parikshit was son of Abhimanyu.

The names of the five sons of Draupadi were Prativindhya, Srutasoma, Srutkarma, Satanika and Srutsena from the five Padavas were also present in the battle field and they were killed by Asvatthama at the dead of the night.

All these chief fighters in the Pandava army were exceptionally well versed in scriptures and in the science of arms. They were all Maharathis i.e. capable of commanding ten thousand bowmen together. Separate and detailed description of almost all these fighters is available in the Udyogya Parva of the Mahabharata.

7. Having named some of the foremost heroes of the Pandava army, Duryodhana now mentions the names of the warriors on his side.

अस्माकं तु विशिष्टा ये तान्निबोध द्विजोत्तम ।
नायका मम सैन्यस्य संज्ञार्थ तान्ब्रवीमि ते ॥ १- ७ ॥

asmakam tu visista ye tan nibodha dvijottama
nayaka mama sainyasya samjnartham tan bravimi te 1.7

asmakam--ours; *tu*-also; *visistah*--especially powerful; *ye*--those; *tan*--them; *nibodha*--just take note, be informed; *dvija-uttama*--the best of the twice born (those with ceremonious sacred thread are called twice born) ; *nayakah*—the leaders; *mama*--my; *sainyasya*--of the army; *samjna-artham*--for information; *tan*--them; *bravimi*--I am speaking, mentioning; *te*--thee.

"Know also, O Best among the twice born, the leaders of my army, those who are most distinguished among us. I shall speak of them to you for your information." II 7 II

The word "tu" has been used in this verse in the sense of also. The idea is to depict the intention of Duryodhana. He wants to say that not only in Pandava army but in his own army also, there are many great heroes and fighters. Drona is very senior commander well acquainted with all those present there. He has taught the art of warfare to both the Pandavas and the Kauravas. He knew all the names already. Still Duryodhana is introducing them. By this introduction, he is actually hiding the fear and uncertainty, which seems to have arisen in his own mind.

Duryodhana addresses Drona as the "best among the twice-born." "Dvija or twice-born" means one, who has undergone the "sacred thread ceremony." Sacred thread ceremony is very common and important ceremony among traditional upper castes among the Hindus. Initiation into the life of spirit is the aim of education to evolve the individual. We all are born into the world of nature by providential will. That is our first birth and natural birth. By sacred thread ceremony an individual is initiated into the life of spirit. Thus second birth, by sacred thread ceremony, is into the world of spirit. After this ceremony, one has to observe certain conditions as well. An individual is born as child of nature. Then the individual grows into spiritual manhood. Finally the individual again becomes a child (as innocent as child) after attaining perfection.

Duryoodhana is very wicked person. He is focusing on Drona's being a Brahmin. These words can be taken as Duryodhana's censure to his teacher in a subtle and concealed manner. His reprimand may mean to say "However capable you may be in teaching the art of warfare, you are after all a Brahamin, used to peaceful life and a bit too timid by nature. It may be too much to expect you to be courageous in this war with the Pandvas. Still there is no need to worry. We too have mighty warriors on our side."

8 and 9. Now in next two verses, Duryodhana mentions the names of the principal warriors on his side showering praise on the heroes of his side.

भवान्भीष्मश्च कर्णश्च कृपश्च समितिञ्जयः ।
अश्वत्थामा विकर्णश्च सौमदत्तिस्तथैव च ॥ १- ८ ॥
अन्ये च बहवः शूरा मदर्थे त्यक्तजीविताः ।
नानाशस्त्रप्रहरणाः सर्वे युद्धविशारदाः ॥ १- ९ ॥

bhavan bhismas ca karnas ca krpas ca samitim-jayah
asvatthama vikarnas ca saumadattis tathaiva ca 1.8

bhavan--yourself; *bhismah*--Grandfather Bhisma (he looked after both the Kaurvas and the Pandvas in childhood; greatest of the warriors, respected by all, a model character); *ca*--also; *karnah*—Karna (Karna was son of Kunti fighting from the side of Kaurvas, begotten of the Sun-god, a great friend of Duryodhana, a great warrior); *ca*--and; *krpah*—Krpa (a great scholar, who taught archery to the Kaurvas and the Pandvas before Dronacharya) ; *ca*--and; *samitim-jayah*-- victorious in war; *asvatthama*—Asvatthama (son of teacher Drona, a great warrior); *vikarnah*—Vikarna (one of the hundred sons of Dhrtarashtra; *ca*--as well as; *saumadattih*--the son of Somadatta; *tatha*--and as; *eva*--even; *ca*--and.

anye ca bahavah sura mad-arthe tyakta-jivitah
nana-sastra-praharanah sarve yuddha-visaradah 1,9

anye--many others; *ca*--also; *bahavah*--many; *surah*--heroes; *mad-arthe*--for my sake; *tyakta-jivitah*--prepared to give up their lives; *nana*--many; *sastra*--weapons; *praharanah*—armed with various weapons and missiles; *sarve*--all of them; *yuddha*--battle; *visaradah*—well skilled in battle.

"(They are) Thyself, Bhishma, Karna, the victorious in fight, Asvatthama, Vikarna, Saumadatti and Jayadrath and there are other heroes well trained in warfare, who equipped with manifold weapons and missiles, are ready to lay down their lives for my sake." II 8 and 9 II

In these two verses, *Duryodhna* recounts the names of the principal warriors of the *Kaurava* army:

Dronacharya – Duryodhana began with the world "yourself." He began like this so that Drona might be highly pleased with him. He taught the art of warfare to both the Pandava and the Kaurava princes. Acarya (teacher) Drona was the son of Maharishi Bharadvaja. He obtained knowledge of all forms of arms and missiles with their secrets from Maharishi Agnivesya and Sri Parasurama. He was exceptionally bold *athirathi* (one who could fight with ten thousands warriors single-handedly). He was fully aware of the *Brahamastra*, *Agneyastra* and other wonderful weapons of war. Drona carried on a fearful fight as commander-in-chief of the Kaurava army for five days but in the end hearing the false news of the death of his son, he renounced his arms and sat down in the posture of yoga. At this stage, Dhrstadyumana struck him with a sharp weapon, which separated his head from the trunk.

Bhishma, grand sire, was the eldest son of king Santanu. He was born of Bhagirathi, the spirit of river Ganga. He was incarnation of the ninth Vasu, a celestial named "Dyu." His original name was Devaratta. In his prime youth, he took a vow of life-long celibacy and renunciation of claim to the throne in order to facilitate his father's marriage with Satyavati, in answer to the demand of Satyavati's foster-father. Due to the terrible nature of his vow, he became famous as Bhishma (the terrible). For the happiness of his father he wholly abandoned without the least hesitation the happiness of possessing a wife and a kingdom. Bhishma's father, Santanu was extremely happy with his son and gave him a boon that even death will be powerless to kill him without his consent. He was a life-long celibate, the very embodiment of flaming energy and a master of scriptures and science of warfare. He made a promise to Duryodhana that though he would refrain from killing the five Pandvas, he would in the course of fight slaughter with his own hand ten thousand warriors every day. Holding the post of commander-in-chief of the Kaurava army he carried on a fearful fight for ten days. Even while lying on the bed of arrows in the battle fields, he enlightened all by the store of his knowledge and then when the sun started on the northern course he gave up his body of his own sweet will. Bhishma was the most memorable character of the Mahabharata.

Karna, the great warrior from the Kaurava side, perhaps derived his name from the fact that he was born wearing a pair of earrings. Karna was the eldest son of Kunti, the mother of the Pandvas, begotten of Sun-God when Kunti was a maiden. He was left afloat in a box in a river as an infant. One man, called Adhiratha, a suta (charioteer by caste), picked up the box and took it home. Karna was nursed and brought up by Radha, the wife of Adhiratha, as their own child. As he was born with natural gold armor and earrings, he was given the name "Vasesena." Karna received his training in arms from Dronacharya and Parasurama. He had good knowledge of scriptures and he was master in the science of warfare. He was a match for Arjuna in the knowledge of arms and as fighter in the battle-field. Duryodhana crowned him as the king of the Angas (territory corresponding to modern Bhagalpur in Bihar). He was bosom friend of Duryodhana. His devotion to Duryodhana was very deep so much so that he refused to give up the cause of Duryodhana even though he was approached by his mother Kunti and Bhagvan Krishna to join the Pandavas in the Mahabharata war at Kurukshetra. His spirit of charity was incomparable. He was a regular worshipper of Sun-God. He used to give away with pleasure whatever was asked from him, by whoever it may be, at the time of worship. One day, in Arjuna's interest, Indira, the king of the celestials, assumed the form of Brahmin and begged him to make a gift of natural armor and earrings attached to his body. With great delight, that very moment, Karna tore his armor and earrings from his body and gave them away, well knowing why he was being deceived. In exchange, Lord Indira gave him a missile, which was infallible in its effect when hurled against a fighter in the face to face combat. Karna killed Bhishma's son Ghatotkatch with this missile during the war. After the death of Dronacharya, Karna remained commander-in- chief for two days. Karna always nursed grudge against Arjuna. He met his death in fight with Arjuna only in the battle field.

Kripacharya was a warrior and teacher of warriors. He was son of Maharishi Saradvan of the family of sage Gotama. He was experienced master of the science of archery. He had a sister named Kripi. He was brought up by the king Santanu out of pity (kripa). For this reason he got the name of kripa and his sister got the name of Kripi. He was good scholar of scriptures. Before the advent of Dronacharya, he used to impart the instructions in archery to the Kauravas, the Pandvas and the Yadvas. He remained alive even after the Mahabhrata war. It was Kripacahrya, who gave knowledge of arms to king Parikshat.

Asvatthama (he, who had strength of a horse) was the son of Drona by Kripa's sister Kripi. He was great expert in military science. He was considered a Maharathi (one who could fight with ten thousand soldiers single-handedly). He received the training in arms from his father Dronacharya.

Vikarna was the third of the hundred sons of Dhritarashtra. He was extremely virtuous soul, great hero and a *Maharathi*. At the time of Draupadi's persecution in the kaurava court, Darupadi asked from the assembled people whether she had been actually lost to the Pandavas as stake in the gamble, except Vidarana there appeared none to open the mouth against the persecution of Draupadi. Vikarna got up in the court and declared in scathing terms, upholding both justice and righteousness, that it was a great injustice not to answer the question raised by Draupadi. Without reservation, Vikarna said that in his opinion Draupadi had not been won by the Kauravas as a stake in the game.

Bhurisrava was son of Somdatta and was grandson of King Santanu's elder brother, Bahlika. He was cousin brother of Bhishma. He too was a virtuous soul, an expert in the art of warfare, a great hero and a *Maharathi*. He performed a lot of sacrifices (*yajna*) giving away huge riches as sacrificial fees. He met his death at hands of Satyaki in the Mahabharata war.

By concluding his remark thus, Duryodhana wanted to assure the Acharya that this special mention of some names did not exhaust the list of great warriors from the side of Kauravas. There were still many, ready to lay down their life for his sake. They were all well skilled well accomplished in the art of war. They were all armed with diverse weapons and missiles, ready to fight till their very last breath.

10. First Duryodhana praises the prowess of the great warriors on his side and then he proceeds to compare the two armies declaring in the end that his army was more powerful and more superior to the Pandava army.

अपर्याप्तं तदस्माकं बलं भीष्माभिरक्षितम् ।
पर्याप्तं त्विदमेतेषां बलं भीमाभिरक्षितम् ॥ १- १० ॥

aparyaptam tad asmakam balam bhismabhiraksitam
paryaptam tv idam etesam balam bhimabhiraksitam 1.10

aparyaptam—unlimited; *tat*--that; *asmakam*-- ours; *balam*--strength; *bhisma*--by Grandfather Bhisma; *abhiraksitam* — marshalled by; *paryaptam*--limited; *tu*--while; *idam*-- these; *etesam*- their (of the Pandavas); *balam*--strength; *bhima*—Bhima (brother of Arjuna); *abhiraksitam*— marshalled by .

"Multitudinous is our army marshaled by Bhishma but meager is the army of theirs marshaled by Bhima." II 10 II

The egoistic people resort to self aggrandizement (increase in power, size and importance) when the days of destruction draw near. This happened to Ravana also in the epic the Ramayana. This happens because they are blind and insensitive to the reality before them. Righteousness and rationalization was not the consideration of Duyodhana. He was hell bent to vanquish the Pandavas. He was harboring fear within. For this reason he used controversial words i.e. unlimited for the Kaurava army and limited for Pandava army. Duryodhana is right in estimating the valour of Bhishma superior to that of Bhima, who was his sworn enemy. But Duryodhana spells ruin to himself by depicting the Bhima's army as limited or meager or good enough to be decimated by the Kaurava army, which, Duryodhana considers, unlimited i.e. much more than required to match with the Pandava army. Duryodhana is forgetting that the strength of an army depends on training, team-spirit, adherence to righteousness and **the divine grace.** The Pandava army is well-knit and is equal to any eventuality with Lord Krishna on their side. The Kaurava army is promiscuous (made of many different parts) and placed together pell-mell (rushing very quickly uncontrolled). The boastful words of Duryodhana stand self condemned.

Duryodhana expresses some satisfaction over the kaurava army being marshaled by Bhishma. Actually the ethical excellence of Bhishma remains beyond the ken (knowledge) of worldly-minded Duryodhana. Bhishma is divinely gifted and invincible man. He consented to wage war wholeheartedly for Kauravas as the price for the loyalty he had for the throne of Hastinapur. At the heart of his heart, Bhishma knew that dharma (righteousness, as per law of nature and not as per man-made standards) alone was going to triumph in the end. He was always true to his words. He knowingly chose to champion the cause of the wicked only to prove that no power on earth or in heaven could make adharma (unrighteousness) victorious. Bhishma was not tainted even though he sided with the wicked, because he was supremely above selfishness. By his life, Bhishma truly justified the tenet "BE active in this world but do not be of the world."

Duryodhana is an egoistic man. Ego's main function is to maintain the delusions of the body and material world. For this reason, he says that his forces protected by Bhishma are unlimited (i.e. much more than required limit or invincible) and the forces of the Pandavas marshaled by Bhima are limited (i.e. easy to conquer). Ego intoxicates an individual and blinds individual's vision of intelligence. Duryodhana is ignoring completely adherence to righteousness and grace of the Supreme, which finally bring crowning glory to an individual's efforts and existence.

11. After declaring the Kaurava army, protected by Bhishma as unconquerable, Duryodhana now in this proceeds to exhort all generals Including Dronacharya to guard Bhishma in particular from all sides.

अयनेषु च सर्वेषु यथाभागमवस्थिताः ।
भीष्ममेवाभिरक्षन्तु भवन्तः सर्व एव हि ॥ १- ११ ॥

ayanesu ca sarvesu yatha-bhagam avasthitah
bhismam evabhiraksantu bhavantah sarva eva hi 1,11

ayanesu--in the arrays (of the army); *ca*--also; *sarvesu*--everywhere; *yatha-bhagam*--as they are differently arranged or according to division; *avasthitah*—being stationed; *bhismam*--unto Grandfather Bhisma; *eva*-- even; *abhiraksantu*—supported or protected by ; *bhavantah*-- you; *sarve*-- all; *eva*-- even; *hi*-- indeed.

Bhishma was the commander-in-chief and the most powerful hero of the Kaurava army with a history of valor in the past, far and wide. Duryodhana too knew this fact very well. What is the reason that Duryodhana is so particularly concerned about safety of Bhishma? There is a reason for this.

Bhishma had already told Duryodhana that Drupada's son Shikhandi had taken birth as female and subsequently became a male through sex-transformation. Because he was born as female, Bhishma regarded Shikhandi as female. Bhishma had pledged that he would never face a eunuch in a battle field according to canons of chivalry followed by a kshetriya fighter. If the Pandvas placed Shikhandi in front, Bhishma would not face him and so Bhishma's power would be partially neutralized. In Mahabharata (Bhishma 15.14-20) it is mentioned that in previous occasion while reviewing the army, Duryodhana had cautioned Duhsasana and other warriors by explaining this danger in detail. Duryodhna wanted to ensure that Shikhandi should not get the opportunity to come in front of Bhishma. If Bhishma could be saved from Shikhandi there was nothing else for the Kauravas to fear about. But, it was for this reason that Duryodhana was unduly concerned about the protection of Bhishma. Words used reflect the mind, the speaker, wholesome or unwholesome. The words used by Duryodhana and his manner of expression before Dronacharya express the inner doubt and insecurity of Duryodhana's mind.

12. After describing how Duryodhana praised the principal warriors of Kaurava army and more particularly his commander-in-chief Bhishma, Sanjay now proceeds to narrate the subsequent events on the battle field including sounding of conches.

तस्य सञ्जनयन्हर्षं कुरुवृद्धः पितामहः ।
सिंहनादं विनद्योच्चैः शङ्खं दध्मौ प्रतापवान् ॥ १- १२ ॥

tasya sanjanayan harsam kuru-vrddhah pitamahah
simha-nadam vinadyoccaih sankham dadhmau pratapavan 1.12

tasya—his (Duryodhan's); *sanjanayan*--increasing; *harsam*--cheerfulness; *kuru-vrddhah*--the grandsire of the Kuru dynasty (Bhisma); *pitamahah*--the grandfather; *simha-nadam*--roaring sound, like a lion; *vinadya*—having sounded; *uccaih*--very loudly; *sankham*--conch shell; *dadhmau*--blew; *pratapa-van*--the glorious.

"In order to embolden him (Duryodhana), Bhishma, the mighty grandsire, the oldest of the Kuru dynasty, now raised a lion's roar and blew his conch." II 12 II

There was no substance in the indiscreet (careless) remarks of unimaginative Duryodhana, who was only dampening the war zeal of his own people. The grand old warrior (Bhishma) noticed Duryodhana standing near Dronacharya, somewhat startled and anxious at the sight of the Pandava army. The ever watchful commander-in-chief, Bhishma, took notice of this deteriorating situation and came to prompt rescue. Bhishma roared like a lion and blew his conch with great force to delight Duryodhana's heart and to proclaim, as commander-in-chief, the commencement of the fight.

The adjectives used in this verse are very relevant. Sanjay has used the word "*pratapvan*; glorious" for Bhishma. It is very appropriate adjective for Bhishma. Bhishma had defeated the mighty warriors like Parusaram and others in war-encounters. Bhishma had also been called the eldest of the Kauravas. Bhishma, with the exception of Bahilika, was the oldest member of the Kaurava race in the battle field. Blowing of the conch was the indication that the battle was about to start. By roaring like a lion or by uttering the terrible war cry, Bhishma declared emphatically his level of confidence. This act, calculated to infuse courage and enthusiasm in the mind of Duryodhana, at this critical juncture, amounted, according to the codes of warfare, aggression (threatening behavior) by the Kaurvas.

13. Following Bhishma, other heroes in the kaurava army started blowing conches, trumpets, playing various musical instruments of martial music making tumultuous noise.

ततः शङ्खाश्च भेर्यश्च पणवानकगोमुखाः ।
सहसैवाभ्यहन्यन्त स शब्दस्तुमुलोऽभवत् ॥ १- १३ ॥

tatah sankhas ca bheryas ca panavanaka-gomukhah
sahasaivabhyahanyanta sa sabdas tumulo abhavat 1.13

tatah—thereafter or then; *sankhah*--conch shells; *ca*--also; *bheryah*—kettledrums or bugles; *ca*--and; *panava-anaka*--trumpets and drums; *go-mukhah*- cow-horns; *sahasa*--all of a sudden; *eva*—quitw suddenly; *abhyahanyanta*--being simultaneously sounded; *sah*--that; *sabdah*--combined sound; *tumulah*--tumultuous; *abhavat*-- was.

"Then suddenly blared forth conches, kettledrums, tabors, trumpets and cow-horns and tremendous was that noise." II 13 II

This verse refers to the uproar created by the Kaurava army. When Bhishma blew the conch, the whole Kaurava army roused in action. Everyone in the Kaurava army got flooded with hope and encouragement. Suddenly in all sections of the army, conches, trumpets and other instruments of the martial music, belonging to different commanders, were sounded. The sound of these instruments made a terrible noise and reverberated in the entire region of the sky.

In verse 1, king Dhrtarashtra asked from his charioteer, Sanjay as to what his sons and the Pandvas, eager to fight, did after having assembled in the holy field of Kurukshetra. Up to this verse,

Sanjay described about the principal fighters from both the sides. Now in the next five verses, Sanjay focuses on Pandva army.

14. Lord Krishna and Arjuna blew their conchs.

तततः श्वेतैर्हयैर्युक्ते महति स्यन्दने स्थितौ ।
माधवः पाण्डवश्चैव दिव्यौ शङ्खौ प्रदध्मतुः ॥ १- १४ ॥

*tatah svetair hayair yukte mahati syandane sthitau
madhavah pandavas caiva divyau sankhau pradadhmatuh 1.14*

tatah--then; *svetaih*—(with) white; *hayaih*--horses; *yukte*—being yoked; *mahati*—magnificient;; *syandane*—in the chariot; *sthitau*--seated; *madhavah*--Krsna (the husband of the goddess of fortune; distinct physical manifestation of the supreme); *pandavah*--Arjuna (the son of Pandu, greatest archer of the era); *ca*--also; *eva*-- also; *divyau*-- divine; *sankhau*--conch shells; *pradadhmatuh*—sounded or blew.

"Then seated in their magnificent chariot, yoked with white horses, Madhava (Lord Krishna) and Pandava (son of Pandava or Arjuna) blew their divine conchs." II 14 II

Madhava is one of the thousand names of Vishnu (preserving phase or sustenance aspect of the Supreme Universal Eternal Reality with name and form). Here it refers to Lord Krishna, the embodied aspect of Vishnu.

Pandava means son of Pandu. Any of the five brothers can be called Pandava. Here this title Pandav has been used for Arjuna.

Lord Krishna and Arjuna first appear here in the Gita sitting in a chariot. In Hindu mythology, the chariot is compared with human body. Four horses are four Vedas or four Purusharthas i.e. i) dharma (righteousness), artha (wealth), kama (desire) moksha (liberation). Arjuna represents jiva and Krishna represents the Supreme Eternal Universal Reality or God. Both the jiva and the Lord are sitting in the chariot of the body. This is how the Hindus compare the body with a chariot. In this description of the chariot, focus should be on the "Soul of the Soul," represented by lord Krishna here. If this thought gets ingrained in the mind, then one will stop identifying with the body. Duality will vanquish. The distinction between the real and unreal will become clear.

Arjuna's chariot was not an ordinary chariot. It was very large and excellent in every way. It was covered all over with plate of gold. It looked exceptionally beautiful and was very strongly built. It had flags on all sides with small tinkling bells attached to them. It had very large and strong wheels attached to it. It had a high flag containing the emblem of moon and stars glittering on it. Sri Hanuman was posted on it. This flag was as variegated as rainbow in clouds. Though it was so large and widely extended, it was very light and it could not be stopped by any obstruction. Four celestial horses were harnessed to this chariot, all white, very beautiful, well decorated, well trained, strong and nimble (able to move quickly with light neat movements). These horses were taken from the hundred celestial horses received as gift from the Gandharva king Citratha. There was a peculiarity about these horses. Any number of these horses might be killed in action and yet their number would ever remain the hundred and could not be reduced. These horses could go anywhere on earth and heaven. This was also true of the chariot (Mahabharat. Udyoga., 56), which was a gift to Arjuna from the Fire-God as mark of pleasure after the burning of Khandava forest.

Sitting in the glorious chariot, Lord Krishna and the great warrior Arjuna heard the tumultuous noise of the war cry of the Kaurava army especially the blowing of the conch by Bhishma. It was an announcement of the beginning of war. Lord Krishna and Arjuna too blew their conch to announce the commencement of the fight. The conches used by Lord Krishna and Arjuna were not ordinary conches. They were extraordinary conches brilliant to look at and uncommon in character. For this reason these conches have been called celestial conches.

On the Kaurava's side Bhishma was the principal hero. For this reason, he blew the conch first. On the Pandva's side, Lord Krishna was the first to blow the conch. What does it indicate? Lord Krishna was the main force from the Pandava side. All others were instruments in his hands to be used for restoring righteousness.

15 to 18. These four verses describe the conchs used by the warriors of the Pandava army.

पाञ्चजन्यं हृषीकेशो देवदत्तं धनञ्जयः ।
पौण्ड्रं दध्मौ महाशङ्खं भीमकर्मा वृकोदरः ॥ १- १५ ॥
अनन्तविजयं राजा कुन्तीपुत्रो युधिष्ठिरः ।
नकुलः सहदेवश्च सुघोषमणिपुष्पकौ ॥ १- १६ ॥
काश्यश्च परमेष्वासः शिखण्डी च महारथः ।
धृष्टद्युम्नो विराटश्च सात्यकिश्चापराजितः ॥ १- १७ ॥
द्रुपदो द्रौपदेयाश्च सर्वशः पृथिवीपते ।
सौभद्रश्च महाबाहुः शङ्खान्दध्मुः पृथक्पृथक् ॥ १- १८ ॥

pancajanyam hrsikeso devadattam dhananjayah
paundram dadhmau maha-sankham bhima-karma vrkodarah 1.15

pancajanyam—(the conch shell named) Pancajanya; *hrsika-isah*--Hrsikesa (Krsna, the Lord who directs the senses of the devotees); *devadattam*-- (the conch shell named) Devadatta; *dhanam-jayah*--Dhananjaya (Arjuna, the winner of wealth); *paundram*— (the conch shell) named Paundra; *dadhmau*--blew; *maha-sankham*-- great conch shell; *bhima-karma*—doer of herculean tasks; *vrka-udarah*--the voracious eater or having the belly of wolf (Bhima).

anantavijayam raja kunti-putro yudhisthirah
nakulah sahadevas ca sughosa-manipuspakau 1.16
kasyas ca paramesv-asah sikhandi ca maha-rathah
dhrstadyumno viratas ca satyakis caparajitah 1.17
drupado draupadeyas ca sarvasah prthivi-pate
saubhadras ca maha-bahuh sankhan dadhmuh prthak prthak 1.18

1.16-1.18 *ananta-vijayam*-- (the conch named) Ananta-vijaya; *raja*--the king; *kunti-putrah*--the son of Kunti; *yudhisthirah*—Yudhisthira, known to be the most righteous personality and eldest of the Pandavas; *nakulah*—Nakula (one of the Pandavas, fourth son of Pandu from madri and not Kunti); *sahadevah*—Sahadeva ((one of the Pandavas, fifth son of Pandu from madri and not Kunti); *ca*--and; *sughosa-manipuspakau*—(the conches named) Sughosa and Manipuspaka; *kasyah*--the King of Kasi (Varanasi); *ca*--and; *parama-isu-asah*—an excellent archer; *sikhandi*—Sikhandi (arch enemy of Bhishma, Amba, a female in previous birth, Bhishma had told Duryodhna that he would not fight with Shikhandi as he was female in previous birth); *ca*--also; *maha-rathah*—a great chariot warrior; *dhrstadyumnah*--Dhrstadyumna (the son of King Drupada); *viratah*--Virata (the king, who gave shelter to the Pandavas while they were in disguise); *ca*--also; *satyakih*--Satyaki (the same as

Yuyudhana, the charioteer of Lord Krsna); *ca*--and; *aparajitah*--who were never vanquished before; *drupadah*--Drupada, the King of Pancala; *draupadeyah*--the sons of Draupadi; *ca*--also; *sarvasah*--all; *prthivi-pate*--O Lord of the earth; *saubhadrah*--the son of Subhadra (Abhimanyu); *ca*--also; *maha-bahuh*--mighty-armed; *sankhan*--conch shells; *dadhmuh*--blew; *prthak prthak*--separately.

"Sri Krishna blew his conch Panchjanyam; Arjuna, his own called Devadutta; while Bhima, of terrible deeds and ravenous hunger, blew his mighty conch named Paundram." II 15 II

"King Yudhisthira, son of Kunti, blew his conch, named Anantvijay; while Nakula and Sahadeva blew their conchs known as Sughosa and Manipuspaka respectively." II 16 II

"And the excellent archer, the king of Kasi and Shikhandi, the Maharathi (great chariot warrior), Dhrshtadumana and Virata; and invincible Satyaki, Draupada as well as the five sons of Draupadi and mighty armed Abhimanyu, son of Subhadra, all of them, O Lord of the earth, severally blew their respective conchs from all sides." II 17, 18 II

The names used by Sanjay are very appropriate.

Sanjay addresses Sri Krishna as Hrisikesha i.e. controller or ruler of sense-organs. This also means repository of joy, happiness and power accompanied with amenities of life. For this reason one of the names of Lord Krishna is Hrisikesa. Lord Krishna killed a demon Panchjanya by name. This demon possessed the shape of a conch. Sri Krishna took him for his conch. This is how Lord Krishna's conch came to be known as Panchjanya.

Sanjay calls Arjuna as Dhananjay. When the Pandvas performed Rajsuya Yajna (sacrificial ceremony), Arjuna conquered a number of kingdoms and brought untold riches in the fold of the Pandavas. That is why Arjuna was known as Dhananjaya.

Arjuna used to blow the conch Devdutta. He obtained this conch from Indira, the king of heaven, when Arjuna went there to fight the demon Nivatakavacas and others (Maha. Vana.174.5). The sound of this conch was so loud and clear that the soldiers in enemy rank used to get terrified by it.

Bhima was the second among the Pandava brothers. He had exceptional physical health and immense hunger. He used to do so terrible deeds that his deeds evoked terror in the heart of those who either heard him or saw him. For this reason, he came to be known as "Bhima of terrible deeds." He was ferocious eater and he had extraordinary power to digest large quantity of foods. For this reason, he came to be known as "Vrikodara." Vrika means wolf and vrikodara means one with wolf-belly. Bhima was capable of digesting anything. He had a conch, whose sound reverberated up to long distance. It was called Paundram or mighty conch.

Five Pandavas were the five sons of Pandu. Yudhishtra (one, who is steady in the battle), Bhima and Arjuna were born of his first wife Kunti. Bhima and Arjuna's names were mentioned in verse 15. Verse 16 starts mentioning Yudhishtra as son of Kunti. Nakula and Sehdeva were born of Madri, the second wife of Pandu. In the verse 16, Sanjay mentions about Nakula and sehdeva only just to show that yudhishtra, Bhima, Arjuna and Nakula and Sehdeva (all the Pandavas) were not the sons of the same mother. At the time of war, Yudhishtra had no kingdom but they had conquered all the kings at the time of Rajasuya Yajna (sacrifice). For this reason, Yudhishtra assumed the position of an emperor. Sanjay knew that after the war, Yudhishtra would again regain the sovereignty. Yudhishtra had all the apparent signs of a king. For this reason, Sanjay calls him king in this verse. Yudhishtra blew the conch, Anantayijay, Nakula and sehdeva blew their conchs Sughosha and Manipuspaka.

King of Kasi was a supreme archer. Kasi is modern Benaras.

Shikhandi and Dhrstadumana, both were sons of Drupada. Shikhandi was the elder brother and Drshtadumana was junior to him. In the beginning, Drupada had no issue. He worshipped Shiva with the motive of obtaining a successor. Lord Shiva, pleased with his worship asked him to take a boon. Drupada submitted his desire for a child. Lord Shiva said that he would get a daughter. Drupada replied that he wanted a son and not a daughter. Lord Shiva assured him that the girl will subsequently get transformed as a son. As a result of the boon, a daughter was born to Drpada. Drupada had full faith in the words of lord Shiva. He announced it as the birth of a son. The daughter was given a boy's name Shikhandi. The girl was dressed as boy and was given the education and training of a prince. After sometime the Shikhandi was married to the daughter of Hiranyavarma, king of Dasarnas. When the daughter of Hiranyavarma came to live with her husband, she discovered that Shikhandi was a woman. She was very sad and went to her father. Hiranyavarma was raged and declared war on King Drupada. Shikhandi was very upset with the plight and left the palace to end life in the forest. There Shikhandi met with a yaksha, with supernatural power. Yaksha, out of pity gave his manhood to Shikhandi for a stipulated period accepting his femininity in exchange. Shikhandi came back from the forest as a man. Due to curse of Kubera, the Yaksha remained a woman all his life and Shikhandi had not to return his manhood. Bhima was aware of this history of Shikhandi and therefore always refused to publicly declare him (Shikhandi) as adversary (counting opponent) of the Kauravas. Shikahndi was a great hero and a *Maharathi*. Taking cover of Shikhandi Arjuna struck Bhishma on the last day of Bhishma's plight. The other two heroes mentioned in this verse have already been introduced to the readers.

Thus, in the verses 15 to 18, Sanjay describes how, following the lead of Lord Krishna and Arjuna, all heroes in the Pandava army blew their conchs from their respective positions.

19. Sanjay in this verse describes the effect produced by that immense sound.

स घोषो धार्तराष्ट्राणां हृदयानि व्यदारयत् ।
नभश्च पृथिवीं चैव तुमुलोऽभ्यनुनादयन् ॥ १- १९ ॥

sa ghoso dhartarastranam hrdayani vyadarayat
nabhas ca prthivim caiva tumulo abhyanunadayan 1.19

sah--that; *ghosah*-- uproar; *dhartarastranam*--of the sons of Dhrtarastra; *hrdayani*--hearts; *vyadarayat*- shattered or rent ; *nabhah*--the sky; *ca*--also; *prthivim*-- earth; *ca*--also; *eva*-- also; *tumulah*--uproarious; *abhyanunadayan*--by resounding

"The tumultuous uproar resounding through earth and sky rent the heart of the Dhritarastra's sons." II 19 II

There is one point to be noted in this verse. Though the sound of the conchs and military music of Kaurava army was also tumultuous, yet it did not become a source of agitation to the Pandavas and their army. This is due to the difference in being in conformity with the righteousness (**dharma**) or being against the righteousness i.e. being with the divine will or against the divine will. Socrates was not disturbed, when he was drinking poison from the cup at the time of his death. This is the marked impact of being with the righteousness. The Pandavas and their army were not agitated as they were fighting for justice i.e. for them war was to restore righteousness. The Kauravas knew in the hearts of hearts that they were on the side of un-righteousness. For this reason, their inner poise was missing due to crisis of conscience and they felt agitated by the uproar of the Pandavas and discerning eye of Sanjay noticed the trace of this subtle underlying weakness.

20. Hitherto, Sanjay was answering the question of king Dhritrashtra raised in verse 1 of this chapter. Now Sanjay is about to start reproducing the conversation between Arjuna and Sri Krishna, which is known as "The Bhagwad Gita."

अथ व्यवस्थितान्दृष्ट्वा धार्तराष्ट्रान् कपिध्वजः ।
प्रवृत्ते शस्त्रसम्पाते धनुरुद्यम्य पाण्डवः ॥ १- २० ॥
हृषीकेशं तदा वाक्यमिदमाह महीपते । **(21 first half)**

atha vyavasthitan drstva dhartarastran kapi-dhvajah
pravrtte sastra-sampate dhanur udyamya pandavah
hrsikesam tada vakyam idam aha mahi-pate 1.20

atha-- now; *vyavasthitan*—standing arrayed; *drstva*-- seeing; *dhartarastran*--the sons of Dhrtarastra; *kapi-dhvajah*--one whose flag is marked with Hanuman; *pravrtte*-- about to begin; *sastra-sampate*—discharge of weapons; *dhanuh*--bow; *udyamya*--after taking up; *pandavah*--the son of Pandu (Arjuna); *hrsikesam*-- to Lord Krsna; *tada*-- then; *vakyam*--words; *idam*--this; *aha*--said; *mahi-pate*—O Lord of the earth.

"Now, O Lord of the Earth (Mahipate), seeing Kaurava army (Dhritrashtra's party) arrayed in battle-order and discharge of weapons about to begin, Pandava (Arjuna), whose ensign was monkey, took up his bow and said the following to Krishna." II 20 II

Sanjay has used the word "Kapidwaj" i.e. one whose flag had the crest (a special picture used as sign) of Lord Hanuman. Reference is to Arjuna. This has a background. Once, Bhima reached the Kadali forests. There, he happened to meet Lord Hanuman of Ramayana's era. The monkey-God was pleased with Bhima and promised him that in Mahabharata war he would sit on the banner of Arjuna's chariot and sitting there he would make such a roar that it would terrify the enemy. All the positive forces help the one who treads the path of righteousness (dharma). Sanjay is particularly inviting attention of Dhritrashtra to this episode to remind him that Pandvas enjoyed favor of Monkey-God (Hanuman). In other words, Sanjay wants to remind Dhritarastra that victory of one who enjoyed the favor of Lord Hanuman was certain. The faithful minster is doing possible best by trying to pass on the impending danger by subtle descriptions. It is Dhritrashtra's fate that he was not able to decipher the subtle message. Some, with scientific back ground and having antipathy (strong dislike) for faith without reasons, find it strange as to why the warriors of that caliber followed faith indiscriminately. **Faith is the greatest force ever evidenced in human history**. Nothing works like faith. It works when nothing else works. In the matter of faith, one has to transcend the limits of human experience and understanding. In the Gita also, at one point, Lord clarifies that the "The Supreme Universal Eternal Energy Source" responds to the seeker in the form in which the seeker seeks. That "Eternal and Infinite Energy Source" serves both in form and without form. The relevance is of intensity, hunger and extreme restlessness for the "Supreme Objective of Human Existence."

Sanjay has used the words very carefully and aptly. Sanjay says that Arjuna used the following words to Hrsikesam i.e. to one who is lord of the organs. What is the purpose of using this particular name here? Sanjay wants to remind Dhritarashtra, the blind king, that the "Internal controller of all," as the Impeller of all the organs, is helping Arjuna. The minister has passed on the subtle message (a sort of implied warning) but the king, blinded with selfishness and undue attachment, did not pay any heed to the subtle message of the words used by the minister or charioteer. Sanjay was nor routinely using the names. He was trying to pass a subtle message which his king did not perhaps value to understand owing to his insensitivity, undue attachment and worldly wisdom. Divine wisdom, as opposed to the worldly wisdom, makes one alive to the truth likely to be faced after death.

Sanjay wanted to pass on another message by using the words "pravrtte sastresampate" i.e. the commencement, of discharging (or using) the weapons, had been announced by blowing the conchs.

Most of the warriors there were full with the enthusiasm and thrill of anticipated war. They were now ready to start using the weapons. Arjuna was of different mould. He noticed that the critical moment had come. This moment was to change the whole scheme of his life. This moment was to have impact on his patriotism, his reverence for teachers and seniors and his values of life. This realization pushed Arjuna into the moment of self realization (introspection). He also lifted his bow, like others, but he spoke the following words to Lord Krishna.

21 & 22, Arjuna requests Sri Krishna to place the chariot in between the two armies.

अर्जुन उवाच ।
सेनयोरुभयोर्मध्ये रथं स्थापय मेऽच्युत ॥ १- २१ ॥ (2ⁿᵈ **half**)
यावदेतान्निरीक्षेऽहं योद्धुकामानवस्थितान् ।
कैर्मया सह योद्धव्यमस्मिन् रणसमुद्यमे ॥ १- २२ ॥

arjuna uvaca
senayor ubhayor madhye ratham sthapaya me 'cyuta
yavad etan nirikse 'ham yoddhu-kaman avasthitan 1.21&22
kair maya saha yoddhavyam asmin rana-samudyame

arjunah--Arjuna; *uvaca*--said; *senayoh*--of the armies; *ubhayoh*--of both the parties; *madhye*--in the middle; *ratham*--the chariot; *sthapaya*--please keep; *me*--my; *acyuta*--O infallible changeless, Krishna; *yavat*-- while; *etan*--these; *nirikse*--may look; *aham*--I; *yoddhu-kaman*--desiring to fight; *avasthitan*-arrayed or standing on the battlefield; *kaih*--with whom; *maya*--by me; *saha*--with; *yoddhavyam*—must be fought; *asmin*--in this; *rana*--strife; *samudyame*--in this attempt.

Arjuna said:

"O Achutya. Place my chariot between the two armies so that I may behold those who stand here desirous to fight and know with whom I must wage this war." II 21 & 22 II

As a matter of fact Arjuna had already got, through the spies, full information about the strength of Kaurava army and its prominent chief. It was anyway the second hand information. There could have been additions and abstentions in the information that he had. For this reason, Arjuna decided to survey the enemy's ranks. It was prudent on the part of Arjuna to reassess his position as well as the position of enemy before the exact start of the war.

Arjuna addresses Lord Krishna as *Achutya*. It is not an ordinary name or title. It means "the faultless; the immovable" i.e. one who never slips down from the lofty state of "Supreme Self." It also means imperishable one or one who has not fallen. It was another name of Lord Krishna. The use of this name for Sri Krishna speaks the amount of reverence his presence commanded from all, around him. He is not only the God in man, who unveils in the world of knowledge and in the spells of meditation, but he is also the God in man who moves along with his seeker in the battle field, in the midst of hurtling shafts, taking all the risks, jumping himself and saving his seeker. He is one, who moves the world of action and for whom the whole humanity works struggles and labors. In the period of desperation and in the depths of heart, "HE" shines like the star filling the life of the seeker with reason to live for, to struggle for and to fight for. "The secret and the supreme master of works, sacrifice and devotion" remains always faultless (*achutya*; immovable), ever smiling, unperturbed and serene even in the battle field with tumultuous noise and severely dangerous missiles about to let lose.

23. Arjuna emphasizes the desire to see the warriors in the opposite camp.

योत्स्यमानानवेक्षेऽहं य एतेऽत्र समागताः ।
धार्तराष्ट्रस्य दुर्बुद्धेर्युद्धे प्रियचिकीर्षवः ॥ १- २३ ॥

yotsyamanan avekse aham ya ete 'tra samagatah
dhartarastrasya durbuddher yuddhe priya-cikirsavah 1.23

yotsyamanan--those who will be fighting; *avekse*--let me see; *aham*--I; *ye*--who; *ete*--those; *atra*—here (in this Kurukshetra); *samagatah*--assembled; *dhartarastrasya*--the son of Dhrtarastra (Duryodhana); *durbuddheh*--evil-minded; *yuddhe*--in the fight; *priya*--well; *cikirsavah*—wishing to please

"For I desire to observe those who have assembled here to fight, wishing to please in battle the evil minded Duryodhana (the son of Dritarashtra). II 23 II

Arjuna calls Duryodhana evil-minded (durbuddher). Actually, he is recalling how Duryodhana conspired against the Pandavas and humiliated them time and again. It was decided that on the completion of thirteenth year in exile, the kingdom of Pandvas would be returned to them. During the period of these thirteen years the Kauravas were to keep the kingdom as trust. Duryodhana, with the evil intention of wrongfully appropriating the kingdom, altogether denied this condition. Duryodhana always practiced many forms of persecution (subjecting someone cruelly) against the Pandvas but the last wrong action (denial of kingsom after exile of thirteen years became wholly intolerable. All attempts to reconcile the dispute failed miserably due to Duryodhana. Remebering this evil intention of Duryodhana, Arjuan speaks of him in this verse as evil minded.

Duryodhana's evil-mindedness was known to all. Still some people assembled to uphold his cause and help him in the fight. This was a bit disturbing to Arjuna and actually it was this fact which unsettled Arjuna a bit at that juncture. The mind and intellect of those who gathered there was as vitiated as that of Duryodhana. Thus, by trying to advance the cause of Duryodhana, some people were causing injury to Arjuna, who always supported righteousness. Arjuna wanted to see with his own eyes those warriors who supported Duryodhana and thus unrighteousness. Arjuna always firmly believed that those who desired victory conquered not so much by might and prowess as by truth, compassion, piety and virtue. It was his firm belief. Arjuna was not able to understand how people with fairness, with belief in justice could go against his stand. He wanted to see those people himself. Actually, Arjuna was taking this as a challenge. He wanted to teach supporters of Duryodhana that it did not pay to side with wrong and unrighteousness. The poverty of virtues and insensitivity did not allow the people (supporting Duryodhana) to realize that finally victory (reward for purity, righteousness and humility) was to be where Krishna (Consciousness of the Divine) was. Arjuna wanted to see those who did not understand this simple truth.

24 & 25. Sanjay narrates what Lord did thereafter.

सञ्जय उवाच ।
एवमुक्तो हृषीकेशो गुडाकेशेन भारत ।
सेनयोरुभयोर्मध्ये स्थापयित्वा रथोत्तमम् ॥ १- २४ ॥
भीष्मद्रोणप्रमुखतः सर्वेषां च महीक्षिताम् ।
उवाच पार्थ पश्यैतान्समवेतान्कुरूनिति ॥ १- २५ ॥

sanjaya uvaca
evam ukto hrsikeso gudakesena bharata
senayor ubhayor madhye sthapayitva rathottamam 1.24

sanjayah--Sanjaya; *uvaca*--said; *evam*--thus; *uktah*--addressed; *hrsikesah*--Lord Krsna; *gudakesena*--by Arjuna (conqueror of sleep); *bharata*--O descendant of Bharata (king Dhrttashtra); *senayoh*--of armies; *ubhayoh*--of both; *madhye*--in the middle; *sthapayitva-* having stationed; *ratha-uttamam*--the finest chariot.

bhisma-drona-pramukhatah sarvesam ca mahi-ksitam
uvaca partha pasyaitan samavetan kurun iti 1.25

bhisma--Grandfather Bhisma; *drona*--the teacher Drona; *pramukhatah*--in front of; *sarvesam*—of all; *ca*--also; *mahi-ksitam*—rulers of the earth; *uvaca*--said; *partha*--O *Partha* (son of Prtha); *pasya*--behold; *etan*-- these; *samavetan*--assembled; *kurun*--all the members of the Kuru dynasty; *iti*--thus.

"Thus requested by Gudakesa (Arjuna), Hrishikesa (Krishna), O Bharata (King Dhritarastra), having placed his chariot in between two armies, facing Bhishma, Drona and all the rulers of earth, said "O Parth (son of Pritha or Arjuna), behold these Kurus gathered together."

After the request of Arjuna, Lord Krishna stationed the magnificent chariot in between the two armies facing, Bhishma, Drona and the other kings. Then Krishna asked Arjuna to behold the Kurus gathered together.

The divine Charioteer brought Arjuna in the middle of the army to face the stark (simple and severe in appearance) reality directly. Arjuna now had the clear view of Bhishma, the grand sire, who was with him throughout his upbringing in childhood. He had the clear view of Drona, the reverend teacher, who encouraged him always very intimately to excel in archery. Now, with the chariot placed in the middle of the two armies, he had for the first time clear view of all other kings and warriors in rival camp ready to fight against the Pandvas.

We all human beings nurture dreams. When these dreams crumble before the reality, we feel extremely hurt, disjointed (not well connected together) and upset. Hitherto everything has been normal. Arjuma has come to the battle field ready to fight. Now for the first time he is facing Bhishma and Drona as enemies. He has always revered, adored and experienced a strong feeling of respect for these two personalities. Now, he has to kill them to win the war. This very fact strikes a blow at the very centre of Arjuna, as emotional being (as human being) to create for him "sensational and emotional crisis." This blow of Arjuna is often experienced by those who are sincere enough to identify the "law of being and law of action with the Divine" i.e. they expect to see righteousness to triumph in all worldly phenomena. There is a "Spiritual Treasure" hidden within each one of us, but all cannot listen to the pangs for this very special "Spiritual Treasure." For some, like Arjuna, it (this hidden call within) becomes too intense to be ignored.

Certain names have been used in this verse. The name Gudakesa has two meanings i.e. one with curly hair; it also means one who has mastered or conquered his sleep. Arjuna has curly hair and he has conquered the sleep. For this reason this name has been used for Arjuna. The name, Hrsikesah, appeared earlier as well. It means Lord of senses. It has been used for Sri Krishna. The term, Bharat, has been used for Dhritarashtra, king of Bharata.

26, 27 & 28 (with first half of the verse) Sanjay describes what happens thereafter.

तत्रापश्यत्स्थितान्पार्थः पितॄनथ पितामहान् ।
आचार्यान्मातुलान्भ्रातॄन्पुत्रान्पौत्रान्सखींस्तथा ॥ १- २६ ॥
श्वशुरान्सुहृदश्चैव सेनयोरुभयोरपि ।
तान्समीक्ष्य स कौन्तेयः सर्वान्बन्धूनवस्थितान् ॥ १- २७ ॥

74

कृपया परयाविष्टो विषीदन्निदमब्रवीत् । (ist half of 28th)

tatrapasyat sthitan parthah pitrn atha pitamahan
acaryan matulan bhratrn putran pautran sakhims tatha
svasuran suhrdas caiva senayor ubhayor api 1.26

tatra--there; *apasyat*-- saw; *sthitan*--standing; *parthah*--Arjuna; *pitrn*--fathers; *atha*--also; *pitamahan*--grandfathers; *acaryan*--teachers; *matulan*--maternal uncles; *bhratrn*--brothers; *putran*--sons; *pautran*--grandsons; *sakhin*--friends; *tatha*--too; *svasuran*--fathers-in-law; *suhrdah*--well-wishers; *ca*--also; *eva*--also; *senayoh*-- in armies; *ubhayoh*--of both parties; *api*--also..

tan samiksya sa kaunteyah sarvan bandhun avasthitan
krpaya parayavisto visidann idam abravit 1.27

tan-- those; *samiksya*—having seen; *sah*--he; *kaunteyah*--the son of Kunti (Arjuna); *sarvan*--all kinds of; *bandhun*--relatives; *avasthitan*—standing (arrayed); *krpaya*--by pity; *paraya*-- deep; *avistah*—filled or overwhelmed by; *visidan*-- sorrowfully; *idam*--thus; *abravit*-- said.

arjuna uvaca
drstvemam sva-janam krsna yuyutsum samupasthitam
sidanti mama gatrani mukham ca parisusyati 1.28

arjunah--Arjuna; *uvaca*--said; *drstva*—having seen; *imam*--all these; *sva-janam*--kinsmen; *krsna*--O Krsna; *yuyutsum*—eager to fight; *samupasthitam*-- arrayed; *sidanti*-- fail; *mama*--my; *gatrani*--limbs of the body; *mukham*--mouth; *ca*--also; *parisusyati*—is parching.

"There Arjuna saw standing fathers, sons, grandfathers, teachers, uncles, brothers, sons and grandsons, companions and also father-in laws from both the armies. When son of Kunti (Arjuna) saw all these kinsmen thus standing arrayed (i.e. in war position), he (Arjuna), invaded by great pity, spoke thus in sadness and dejection." II 26, 27 and 28 (1st half) II

Arjuna sees his very own people standing against him ready to take life and give life. Who were they all?

Fathers : Bhurisrava and others,
Grand fathers : Bhishma and others.
Teachers : Drona and others
Uncles : Saibya and others
Brothers : Duryodhana and others
Sons : Lakshmana and others
Grandsons : The sons of Lakshmana and others
Friends : Aswatthama and others
Father-in-law : Drupda and others
Well-wishers : Kritvarma and others

Arjuna surveyed both the armies and saw therein his own near and dear ones (*svajanam*). He saw them arrayed for the battle. Now for the first time, he got the grip of the naked truth of the situation. It meant that all of them would meet their inevitable doom in the impending holocaust (a situation in which there is great destruction and a lot of people die). This sight filled Arjuna with a new response and resignation, which he was not used to. He was overtaken by a sentiment, which was reverse of his militant nature. He experienced a sneaky cowardliness born of excessive feeling of fellowship and tenderness for the relatives. Sanjay has used the word deep compassion (strong feeling of sympathy). Under the influence of this sentiment, .Arjuna forgot his own inherent nature, the manliness of a *kshetriya* (warrior). He felt sorrow (vishad). For this reason this chapter has been called "vishad yoga; Arjuna's dispassion."

In many battles it happens. You fight with your own people. This holds good especially in civil war. This was a different kind of war. This was a war in a family – same family with the Kauravas on one side and the Padavas on the other side. All their comrades, teachers and seniors were standing in the opposite army. They were all the same people with whom he had grown. He had fond memories of childhood with Bhishma (grand sire) and with his teacher Drona, who always bestowed upon Arjuna his best care. Now they were standing in the opposite camp ready to kill or be killed. Arjuna experienced intense agony within, which was the result of cry of emotions. A crisis rapidly brew [something unpleasant likely to happen; a premonition (a strange and unexplainable feeling) of something bad about to occur] in the mind of Arjuna. It was a strange moment unknown to Arjuna, thus far in life. Stout-heartedness gave way to soft-heartedness. Manliness gave way to effeminacy. The known warrior of the world, who entered the field to teach a lesson to the wicked, developed the attitude of kinsmen towards those, who were his arch enemies, truly deserving to be punished as per his patient thinking thus far. This Change in attitude marks the absence of discrimination and dominance of emotions for action, for material objects for life itself. **At times, there are reasons, which reasons do not know.**

Arjuna was overcome with pity, compassion and kindness. Pity is normally a noble quality but it loses it divine virtue when an individual is called upon "*Dharma*" to fight to restore righteousness. What was it that caused this change? Arjuna was overtaken by feeling of "I and mine" i.e. my relatives, my teachers, my friends. At that moment Arjuna's pity was a sign of mental weakness, a negation of "Dharma." He forgot that he came to battle field after due deliberation to wage a war. "This weakness for mine" is a mental disease which made even heroes like Arjuna, a warrior of first rank, to sink into desperation in that critical situation. In that mental turmoil, Arjuna, filled with pity, spoke sorrowfully to Sri Krishna.

28 (second half) to 31 (first half) Arjun's words describe how he feels in that colossally depressive state of mind.

अर्जुन उवाच ।
दृष्ट्वेमं स्वजनं कृष्ण युयुत्सुं समुपस्थितम् ॥ १- २८ ॥
सीदन्ति मम गात्राणि मुखं च परिशुष्यति ।
वेपथुश्च शरीरे मे रोमहर्षश्च जायते ॥ १- २९ ॥
गाण्डीवं संसते हस्तात्त्वक्चैव परिदह्यते ।
न च शक्नोम्यवस्थातुं भ्रमतीव च मे मनः ॥ १- ३० ॥
निमित्तानि च पश्यामि विपरीतानि केशव । (**1st half of 31st verse**)

arjuna uvaca
drstvemam sva-janam krsna yuyutsum samupasthitam
sidanti mama gatrani mukham ca parisusyati 1.28

arjunah--Arjuna; *uvaca*--said; *drstva*—having seen; *imam*--all these; *sva-janam*--kinsmen; *krsna*--O Krsna; *yuyutsum*—eager to fight; *samupasthitam*-- arrayed; *sidanti*-- fail; *mama*--my; *gatrani*--limbs of the body; *mukham*--mouth; *ca*--also; *parisusyati*—is parching.

> *vepathus ca sarire me roma-harsas ca jayate*
> *gandivam sramsate hastat tvak caiva paridahyate 1.29*

vepathuh--trembling of the body or shivering; *ca*--also; *sarire*--on the body; *me*--my; *roma-harsah*--standing of the hair on end; *ca*--also; *jayate*-- arise; *gandivam*—name of the bow of Arjuna; *sramsate*--is slipping; *hastat*--from the hands; *tvak*--skin; *ca*--also; *eva*—also; *paridahyate*—burning all over.

> *na ca saknomy avasthatum bhramativa ca me manah*
> *nimittani ca pasyami viparitani kesava 1.30*

na--nor; *ca*--also; *saknomi*--am I able; *avasthatum*—to stand; *bhramati*-- whirling; *iva*--as; *ca*--and; *me*--my; *manah*--mind; *nimittani*-- omens; *ca*-- and; *pasyami*--I foresee; *viparitani*—adverse or just the opposite; *kesava*--O killer of the demon Kesi (Lord Krishna).

Arjuna said:

"O Krishna, at the sight of these kinsmen arrayed and eager for battle ..." II 28 (second half) II

"...my limbs quail (tremble or fail), my mouth parches (goes dry), my body quivers and my hair stand on end ... ."

II 29 II

"...The bow, Gandiva, slips from my hand; my skin burns all over; I am unable to stand steady; my mind is reeling ... ..."

II 30 II

"...and O kesava, I see adverse omen ... ." II 31 (first half) II

From verse 28th (second half) to 31st (first half), words used by Arjuna give picturesque description of the violent, sensational and physical crisis (rather nervous breaks down) that Arjuna is in, seeing the relatives in the opposite camp, ready for the battle. Arjuna is in a very difficult situation. He is highly worked up in his nerves. Seeing his own people, arrayed for the battle, ready for the bloodshed, ready to sacrifice their lives, their material achievements, their dreams, their own people, Arjuna's limbs collapse; his mouth is parched; his body shakes; his hair stands on end; his bow, Gandiva, with which he has established his superiority in archery all over the world, is getting out of his grip and all his body is burning. These changes are unknown to Arjuna, who has been a known warrior throughout his life. What is the reason of these physical changes unknown to Arjuna earlier? It is not peculiar to Arjuna alone. In the life of each one of us there comes a time when we are at the cross road of right and wrong. An individual's life seems to be slipping out of hands and individual becomes a spectacle of helplessness, whatever his or her material, physical powers and prowess (skill of doing something) may have been in life. Why should this plight, this unmanliness, this unbecoming weakness overpower an individual at a critical juncture in life? Individual becomes a spectacle of helplessness and experiences creeping within a dreadful and strange heaviness, which sweeps away, for the time being, individual's rationality, discrimination and resolve.

There is nothing wrong in the situation. The fault lies within one's own personality. The events, the situations do not themselves determine or influence the character and behavior of the individual.

It is something within an individual which breathes life, meaning and purpose into events and situations. There is something "unbelievably unique" within an individual, which remains most obscured within. It is not the result of individual's making. The mother-nature teaches even beasts to know their friends. It is the call from individual's within to recognize one's true nature. It makes an individual sink into the whirlpool of dismay and despondency to search for the right course of action. This happens, when the truth within and unknown to our own selves desists the garb of falsehood that we carelessly bear in life. It is the spiritual hunger within an individual, which is not the result of individual's achievement or efforts. It is the true nature his being, of which individual often remains ignorant. This "spiritual unrest" raises itself against ignorance and makes an individual to weep and wail, like a child vehemently, restless for the light in the dark room. It is a moment of high tide in an individual's life. If harnessed properly, it (spiritual restlessness) takes the individual to the height of spiritual evolution. If it is missed, individual's life gets smeared with tears, sufferings and sorrow. Blessed are those who get this spiritual restlessness, which finally culminates into spiritual awakening. There is no perfection, except the "Absolute Truth," which some impurity does not pollute. To do away with impurity in life, individual worldly achievements are not enough. For this, one requires spiritual awakening. The moments, for this blessedness, for this spiritual awakening, come uncalled for, unexpectedly in disguise of extreme restlessness of the soul, as it happens to Arjuna in this situation, in the battle field, at the time of confrontation with the enemy-forces. One is always at pains when this "immortal longing within" knocks one's wisdom. Why does it happen? It is our "joy of the infinite in us" that gives us our joy in ourselves. Our ignorance of the "joy of the Infinite in us" is the cause of this "spiritual dilemma" that we experience in life. This is all that this Bhagavad Gita, this dialogue between Sri Krishna and Arjuna, is about. This grief of Arjuna (vishad) is the ground, from which the sapling of spiritual awareness will sprout by the grace of his charioteer Sri Krishna. This intolerable sadness (vishad) is experience of those, who are due for the vision of "Truth or Reality."

Arjuna finally tells Sri Krishna that he sees bad omens. Omen is the sign of what will happen in future. It can be either good or bad. What are these bad omens like? An untimely, eclipse, shaking of the earth are all inauspicious omens. Even the known virtuous people, with upright characters like Bhishma and Drona, have ignored the call of conscience and ganged together to oppose the Pandavas. Arjuna sees this as bad omen and instinctively infers that the result of the war will not be happy one. Arjuna's attention to omens indicates his mental weakness, instability and lack of balance and discrimination in judgment.

31 (second half of the verse) & 32. After describing his condition in the state of dejection in the above words, Arjuna now proceeds to give his reasons against the very war, which he came to fight in the battle field.

न च श्रेयोऽनुपश्यामि हत्वा स्वजनमाहवे ॥ १- ३१ ॥
न काङ्क्षे विजयं कृष्ण न च राज्यं सुखानि च ।
किं नो राज्येन गोविन्द किं भोगैर्जीवितेन वा ॥ १- ३२ ॥

na ca sreyo 'nupasyami hatva sva-janam ahave 1.31
na kankse vijayam krsna na ca rajyam sukhani ca kim no rajyena govinda kim
bhogair jivitena va 1.32

na--nor; *ca*--also; *sreyah*--good; *anupasyami*--do I foresee; *hatva*--by killing; *sva-janam*--own kinsmen; *ahave*--in the fight; *na*--nor; *kankse*--do I desire; *vijayam*--victory; *krsna*--O Krsna; *na*--nor;

ca--also; *rajyam*--kingdom; *sukhani*--happiness thereof; *ca*--also. *kim*--what use; *nah*--to us; *rajyena*--is the kingdom; *govinda*--O Krishna; *kim*--what; *bhogaih*—by pleasures; *jivitena*--by living; *va*—either

"...I do not foresee any good ensuing from the slaughter of kinsmen in the battle" II 31 second half II

"O Krishna, I do not covet (hanker for) victory, nor kingdom nor pleasures. O Govinda, of what avail to us is kingdom or enjoyment or even life?" II 32 II

Arjuna, the known warrior of that era, came to battle field to fight, to restore righteousness when all the initiatives for reconciliation have failed. It was a well deliberated decision of not one man but a group consisting of Lord Krishna as well. Arjuna already knew before coming to the battle field the heroes of the kaurava army and his relationship with them. Nothing has changed externally. Primarily the same people whom he knew to be there were there. Arjuna is stressing the word 'savajnam' i.e. his own people, kinsmen. It is not so much slaughter but slaughter of own people, which is causing distress and anxiety to Arjuna. Initially when we talk of the war, we remain mechanically aware of war and its statistics and data and remain unduly enthusiastic about it. It takes some time for the truth of the situation to start showing its effects or seep (gradually flow through the holes) into the emotional system of a being. When we get the grip of the situation, we get a kick from inside to realize that enemies are also human beings, with sons, fathers, mothers and individual lives with their longings and aspirations. Then we ask whether war is worth the sacrifice and the waste necessary for it.

Now seeing these people right before him, ready to fight, a distinct change has overcome Arjuna. Now he says that he does not want victory, kingdom, royal pleasures and enjoyments. What is this change? What is it called? Why is this "distinct change" so effective that even a warrior, like Arjuna, is vulnerable to weakness, unmanliness?

This is a commonplace experience. This change makes ineffective **reasons, resolve and determination.** It does not come from outside. It comes from within, from inner depths of the **soul (eternal existence within a being),** from individual's secret chamber of Divinity. This change heralds (sign that something is going to happen) spiritual awakening. It is called renunciation. **Renunciation** does necessarily mean going to Himalayas or any other secluded places. It means developing detachment **(emotional distance)** or **dispassion (not being influenced by the emotions)** without abandoning the participation and present association and intensity for the objective. Principle of renunciation is simple i.e. "be in it without being of it." Renunciation means "assuming a feeling of apparently looking resignation or poise" without the least sacrifice of the concern for the accomplishment of objective. Feverishness goes away. Undue attachment goes away but "true association requiring internal absorption within" remains fresh, lively and inspiring forever. Arjuna is leaning towards renunciation without knowing specifically, being a warrior, what renunciation is. **Renunciation is precursor of spiritual evolution.** Extreme grief or light of wisdom (divine knowledge) teaches self-detachment – detachment from petty details of life i.e. what looks bad is not to be ignored and avoided. We have to make way to the good through the bad patch that we are in. This is possible when the focus is on the ultimate goal and not the mass of the intermediate details bothering attention. This is true renunciation. We must never forget "our connection with divinity" even if it means actual, brutal fighting with the un-righteousness. This is what Sri Krishna is finally going to tell Arjuna in this "dialogue," called Bhagavad Gita.

It is a common belief that divine knowledge or the supreme knowledge (or the knowledge of *atma* or soul) is taught to those who possess the quality of renunciation. Arjuna did not have renunciation. He was a warrior with a pure heart. The mixture of his honesty and internal turmoil has heralded a situation, which makes him fit to receive the grace of the supreme knowledge. Therefore, the auspicious moment has come for Arjuna for the revelation of supreme wisdom. Whenever the fire of renunciation burns bright in the heart of an individual, a teacher comes from somewhere to teach divine wisdom. Here Lord Krishna is there right before Arjuna to unfold for him the divine secrets relating to the "Truth," uncreated by the mortal hand. In order to abide by the "Higher Principle; Inexhaustible Source of All Blessedness" within, one has to ensure that one does not allow oneself to be moved by passing conditions (pain. misery and death of self or the relatives) i.e. one has to ensure that one does not get unnerved.

33 & 34. In these two verses Arjuna puts forth his reasons for not coveting (to have strong desire for something belonging to someone else) kingdom and other pleasures gained through the bloodshed of kith and kin.

येषामर्थे काङ्क्षितं नो राज्यं भोगाः सुखानि च ।
त इमेऽवस्थिता युद्धे प्राणांस्त्यक्त्वा धनानि च ॥ १- ३३ ॥
आचार्याः पितरः पुत्रास्तथैव च पितामहाः ।
मातुलाः श्वशुराः पौत्राः श्यालाः सम्बन्धिनस्तथा ॥ १- ३४ ॥

yesam arthe kanksitam no rajyam bhogah sukhani ca
ta ime 'vasthita yuddhe pranams tyaktva dhanani ca 1.33
acaryah pitarah putras tathaiva ca pitamahah1. matulah svasurah pautrah
syalah sambandhinas tatha 1.34

yesam--for whom; *arthe*-- sake; *kanksitam*--desired; *nah*--our; *rajyam*--kingdom; *bhogah*--material enjoyment; *sukhani*-- pleasures; *ca*-- and; *te*—they; *ime*--these; *avasthitah*-- standing; *yuddhe*--in this battlefield; *pranan*--lives; *tyaktva*--giving up; *dhanani*--riches; *ca*-- and; *acaryah*--teachers; *pitarah*--fathers; *putrah*--sons; *tatha*-- thus; *eva*-- also; *ca*-- and; *pitamahah*--grandfathers; *matulah*--maternal uncles; *svasurah*--fathers-in-law; *pautrah*--grandsons; *syalah*--brothers-in-law; *sambandhinah*--relatives; *tatha*--as well as;

"Those, for whose sake we desire kingdom, enjoyments and pleasures, stand here in the battle field renouncing (or staking or risking) their lives and riches ... ..." II 1.33 II

"...Teachers, fathers, sons, and also grandfathers, uncles and father-in-law, grandsons and brothers-in-law and (other) kinsmen or relatives." II 1.34 II

Arjuna has mentioned in earlier verses that he does not want victory, kingdom and royal pleasures. In these verses, Arjuna gives arguments to support his statement. It is a common feeling from worldly angle that enjoyment becomes complete when it is shared with near and dear ones. But, if the near and dear ones are killed, securing enjoyment becomes irrelevant or pointless. Arjuna elaborates in verse 34 who these near and dear ones are i.e. teachers, fathers, sons, grandfathers, grandsons, brothers-in-law and other relatives. All these relatives are already there standing in the battle field, ready to fight, having made up their mind to abandon their wealth and life even.

These words are not from Arjuna, the known warrior, but from Arjuna, in the whirlpool of emotions. When there is emotional distraught, one justifies living a coward in one's own esteem. This is what Arjuna is doing. He feels that those, who are objects of reverence and love and without whom one will not like to live, should not be slaughtered. Arjuna's words may reveal depth and meaning for those who are in the clutches of grief. These words are based on reasons apparent to eye but these words do not appeal on moral and ethical ground. In emotional turmoil, Arjuna has forgotten basic reason why he came to the battle field. He came to the battle field to restore righteousness in the society after getting disappointed in efforts to bring about reconciliation. This point becomes clear in the earlier details of Mahabharata not available here (The Gita is an extract from Mahabharata). These words simply give vent to Arjuna's sudden and abrupt feelings of despondency, disappointment and dismay.

35. Now, in this verse, Arjuna expresses his unwillingness to kill his enemies for any reason whatsoever.

एतान्न हन्तुमिच्छामि घ्नतोऽपि मधुसूदन ।
अपि त्रैलोक्यराज्यस्य हेतोः किं नु महीकृते ॥ १- ३५ ॥

etan na hantum icchami ghnato 'pi madhusudana
api trailokya-rajyasya hetoh kim nu mahi-krte 1.35

etan--all these; *na*--not; *hantum*—to kill; *icchami*—(do I) wish; *ghnatah*—if they kill me; *api*--even; *madhusudana*--O killer of the demon Madhu (Krisnna); *api*--even if; *trai-lokya*--of the three worlds; *rajyasya*--of the kingdoms; *hetoh*--in exchange; *kim*--what to speak of; *nu*-- then; *mahi-krte*--for the sake of the earth;

"O Slayer of Madhu, demon (i.e. O Sri Krishna)! Though they (enemies) kill me, these (enemies) I would not consent to kill, even for the kingdom (sovereignty) of the three worlds, let alone for this earthly kingdom." II 35 II

This verse contains emotional outburst of Arjuna. Emotional outbursts always conceal truth under the words (or cover) of magnanimity and righteousness. He has come to the battle field to fight but his words in this verse speak of change in his mind. He knows that the people in the opposite army may kill him for kingdom. He says that he will not kill them for the kingdom of the three words (the three words refer to the Vedic idea of earth, heaven and atmosphere or *antariksha*), what to talk of the kingdom of earth.

Arjuna calls Sri Krishna "*Madhusudana*" i.e. killer of the demon, Madhu. Madhu (demon) had stolen the three Vedas from Brahama (Intermediate God or Phase of the Supreme in form of Brahama, responsible for cosmic function of creation). Lord Krishna killed him for recovering the Vedas. Bhishma and Drona were not demons and they had not stolen the Vedas. Therefore, Lord should not urge him to un-Vedic war. That is the import (hidden meaning) Arjuna's statement.

From the words used by Arjuna, it is clear that he is in a definite mood to withdraw from the battle field due to emotional considerations. When a sudden change upsurges (increases) like this, one tries to conceal truth under the garb of magnanimity and righteousness. Arjuna expresses his magnanimity by saying that he would not kill his enemies even for the kingdom of three words, let alone the kingdom of the earth. Arjuna is covering his emotional weakness by display of his magnanimity, without talking at all about what he came for in the battle field. All moral and ethical reasons, well deliberated and discussed in the minutest details by the group of the Pandavas in the presence of Sri Krishna relating to the decision to come to the battle field, have been abruptly ignored by Arjuna. Why? His emotional outrage is not permitting Arjuna to look at the issue dispassionately. He is overemphasizing the reasons which conveniently support the view to retreat from the battlefield. It is not the case of Arjuna alone. In weak emotional moment, an individual, instinctively feels inclined, to sidetrack the matters of, prudence, conscience and righteousness.

There is one more reason indicating that Arjuna is emotionally disturbed and he is not in the right frame of mind due to his emotional onslaught. An individual, for whom the kingdom of three worlds do not matter, will be a man of true renunciation with a smile on his lips, with a twinkle in his eyes and with a gesture of a man, free from the confinement of the life of the- self. Arjuna is distraught (upset and worried).

36. In this verse, Arjuna has put forth his reasons why he should not kill his enemies.

निहत्य धार्तराष्ट्रान्नः का प्रीतिः स्याज्जनार्दन ।
पापमेवाश्रयेदस्मान्हत्वैतानाततायिनः ॥ १- ३६ ॥

nihatya dhartarastran nah ka pritih syaj janardana
papam evasrayed asman hatvaitan atatayinah 1.36

nihatya—having slain; *dhartarastran*--the sons of Dhrtarastra; *nah*—to us; *ka*--what; *pritih*--pleasure; *syat*--will there be; *janardana*--O maintainer of all living entities (Krishna); *papam*- vices (those acts which cause suffering to soul and force rebirth) ; *eva*--only; *asrayet*—will take hold of; *asman*- to us; *hatva*--having killed; *etan*--all these; *atatayinah*—felcon or aggressors

"O *Janardan* (Krishna)! What pleasures shall we derive by killing these sons of Dhritarashtra? Sin only will accrue to us by slaying these desperadoes (those, who do dangerous and criminal things without caring for themselves and other people)." II 36 II

"*Janardan*" is another name of Lord Krishna. *Janardan* means a person, who is worshipped by people for prosperity and emancipation (freeing from limitations and restrictions). Sri Krishna is known for these traits. To feel this verse, words 'sin' and '*atatayinah*', used by Arjuna, should be properly understood.

Sin - Arjuna says that killing these relatives and seniors in the Kaurava army will be a sin. What is sin? Sin is that whose impact torments the individualized soul or deluded soul and necessitates rebirth as normal course. It is an offence (physical, emotional, moral and spiritual) against God (the Supreme Eternal Universal Energy), religion or moral law. Is there any other way to explain sin? Sin is that which causes sufferings and pain to *jiva* or "assumed individualized soul" (ego with exclusive divinity or soul covered in it; it is the last part of the subtle body to be perished; no influence can be exerted on exclusive divinity or soul; hurt is caused to perishable body only; refer to chart under the heading "Cosmic Eternal Flow "in introduction for the term *jiva*). A sin results in gross moral turpitude (immoral behavior; wickedness) and necessitates rebirth to undergo the matching impact (the price one receives at any later point of time) for the sin. This is ancient Indian thinking: "as you sow, so shall you reap."

Atatayinah -Arjuna has used the word *atatayinah* i.e. those who have committed felony or those who are desperadoes. Felony is an act of committing serious crime such as murder or rape. There is a general principle of behavior not to kill in retaliation for another sin. Some proponents of good behavior go the extent of saying "conquer the anger of others by non-anger; conquer evil-doers by saintliness; conquer the miser by gifts, conquer the falsehood by truth." Now Arjuna is in dilemma. He has to make a choice between two extremes i.e. i) One should not injure and ii) one should kill a felon (one who is guilty of serious crime).

Arjuna is being guided by social customs and customary-morality. He is completely ignorant of perception of individual truth within. He is forgetting at the spur of these moments that the Pandavas have always been good guys, obedient, tolerant with immense reverence for the seniors, for dharma (righteousness) and for values of life. Still Duryodhana and his henchmen poisoned Bhima, defrauded the Pandavas in the game of dice, sent the Pandavas to house of wax, attempted to strip off Draupadi (wife of the Pandavas) in the open the court and finally refused them the princely rights even after agreed exile of thirteen years. Here, all possible limits of tolerance have been crossed. It is a situation showing complete collapse of useful, intellectual and moral values ever laid down by a man for a man (i.e. in scriptures). Only one thing remains. Fighter's personal notes of love, sympathy or concern should not at any time intercept the royal dispensation (special permission from an authority) emitting from the "Infinite Universal and Eternal Source"* within the fighter. The problem is that Arjuna does not at all know about it (Infinite Universal and Eternal Source within an individual). He is standing baffled, in his new discomfiture, before Lord Krishna at the cross roads of righteousness and unrighteousness.

37. There is another extreme as well. Arjuna, ignorant of "the ultimate Truth; Reality," also knows that the individual who destroys his own race and family is the greatest sinner. For this reason, he continues upholding and elucidating his point of view up to the end of this chapter. In this verse, Arjuna discusses the evils likely to follow by destruction of one's race.

तस्मान्नार्हा वयं हन्तुं धार्तराष्ट्रान्स्वबान्धवान् ।
स्वजनं हि कथं हत्वा सुखिनः स्याम माधव ॥ १- ३७ ॥

tasman narha vayam hantum dhartarastran sva-bandhavan
sva-janam hi katham hatva sukhinah syama madhava 37

tasmat--therefore; *na*--not; *arhah*--justified; *vayam*--we; *hantum*- to kill; *dhartarastran*--the sons of Dhrtarastra; *sva-bandhavan*—our relatives; *sva-janam*-- our kinsmen; *hi*-- indeed; *katham*--how; *hatva*—having killed; *sukhinah*--happy; *syama*—may (we) be; *madhava*--O Krishna, husband of the goddess of fortune.

"Therefore, we should not kill the sons of Dhritarashtra, our kinsmen; for, how can we, O Madhava (Krishna), be happy having killed our own people." II 1.37 II

A small child is extremely possessive of its toys. With age, child grows in wisdom and toy does not remain the limit of child's attention. Arjuna is obsessed with the limiting thoughts of 'I and mine'. It is obvious from his often repeated words such as 'our relations', 'our kinsmen', '*svabandhava*', *svajanam*'. These thoughts of "I and mine" emanate due to ego (that which does not allow us to be our pure nature), which is the greatest barrier on the path of self-realization (realization of Truth within or getting the vision of Eternal Life of the Universe)**. These thoughts, expressed by Arjuna and emanating from ego, do not allow us to remain in the "spiritual depth of our being" and we remain away from the life that radiates power and brightness of true joy of living, of being alive. Due to ego, an individual remains confined to the thoughts of mind-body-complex. The teachings of Lord Krishna in this dialogue "The Bhagavad Gita" focus on this subject alone. These thoughts of the Gita awaken us to the **"Holy Eternal Presence"** within each one of us. Then we abide by the existence of "This Holy Eternal Presence" every hour in our work and play and in due course we become the instruments of this "Eternal Universal presence" in all our thoughts, words and deeds. The knowledge, which Arjuna is about to receive from lord Krishna, fills the life of an individual (here Arjuna) with "Divine Radiance." Then Arjuna will understand the way out of his present difficulty. When someone's misbehavior does not respond to the sound advice or reason persistently and stubbornly, as is in the case of Duryodhana here, it calls for a powerful treatment of resistance, protest so much so that even violence is justified to be used to vanquish the causes perpetrating violence. Then, Arjuna will

---

* main subject of discussion in the Gita
** main subject of discussion in the Gita

understand why even a battle is meritorious for a Kshetriya (one from the warrior-clan). Now Arjuna is questioning Lord Krishna and in the end of this discussion (i.e. the Bhagavad Gita) he will seek pardon of the Lord for this questioning even. Arjuna is talking about happiness. Lasting happiness does not depend on the situations, the events and the people. It depends on the feel of the presence of "The Great Spirit of the Universe; the Universal Oneness," symbolized by Lord Krishna here in the Gita, within, in the depth and silence of the self. The divine discourse of Lord Krishna is just about to begin to focus an individual's attention to "**The bright and shinning Super Structure of the self arising from the indeterminate depths and darkness within**," too obvious to be concealed, still so far away.

38 and 39. In these two verses, Arjuna puts forth an argument, apparently very convincing based on worldly wisdom but lacking based on standard (criterion) of awareness.

यद्यप्येते न पश्यन्ति लोभोपहतचेतसः ।
कुलक्षयकृतं दोषं मित्रद्रोहे च पातकम् ॥ १- ३८ ॥
कथं न ज्ञेयमस्माभिः पापादस्मान्निवर्तितुम् ।
कुलक्षयकृतं दोषं प्रपश्यद्भिर्जनार्दन ॥ १- ३९ ॥

yady apy ete na pasyanti lobhopahata-cetasah
kula-ksaya-krtam dosam mitra-drohe ca patakam 38
katham na jneyam asmabhih papad asman nivartitum
kula-ksaya-krtam dosam prapasyadbhir janardana 39

yadi-- though; *api*--even; *ete*-- these; *na*--not; *pasyanti*--see; *lobha*--greed; *upahata*--overpowered; *cetasah*-- intelligence; *kula-ksaya*--in killing the family; *krtam*—act of; *dosam*-- evil; *mitra-drohe*-(involved) in treason to (one's) friends; *ca*--also; *patakam*--sin; *katham*--why; *na*-- not; *jneyam*--know this; *asmabhih*--by us; *papat*- sins; *asmat*—from this; *nivartitum*—turning away; *kula-ksaya*--the destruction of a dynasty; *krtam*--by so doing; *dosam*--crime; *prapasyadbhih*—clearly seeing; *janardana*--O Krishna.

"Though these men (the Kaurvas), whose minds are overpowered (clouded) by greed, do not see the evil in the destruction of families and the sin in hostility to friends, why should not we, O janardan (Krishna), who realize the evil of race-destruction (destruction of family and society), draw back from such a sin." II 1.38 and 1.39 II

Here Arjuna is using the word evil. What is evil? Evil is that force which causes the wicked and bad things to happen. One such evil is greed i.e. strong desire for more wealth, possession, power etc. than a person needs. Those (like Duryodhana), whose understanding has been clouded by greed, see no guilt in the extermination of family and no crime in hostility to friends. Why does it happen? Those, obsessed with greed, become bereft of their own "light of wisdom within," which focuses attention on the detachment from the petty details of life (more wealth, more possession and more power). These people truly fail to see (due to their helplessness, due to their blindness to inner and innate wisdom) "**That in life**," which makes life more beautiful, more fruitful more meaningful, keeping into vision overall mission of life. The greedy people (like Duryodhna with their spiritual wisdom blocked by greed)) cannot understand that he who gives up always finds something of the higher value, which alone is relevant for mission of human life (focused by Lord Krishna in the Gita later in discussion with Arjuna). What is the reason for insensitivity to this awareness of "inner sense of sanctity"? One penetrates to inner depth of being when there is cession of turbulence and unrest caused by greed (this point will again be focused by Lord Krishna in the discussion later in other chapters). Arjuna takes the stand that the Pandvas are not greedy. Why should not they (the Pandavas) have the wisdom to turn away from the sin (of killing the relatives)? Arjuna is taking a different stand. Yes, the war will lead to slaughter in society, break-up of families resulting in so many widows and so many orphans and immense miseries to the innocents. These are wanton (causing harm or damage deliberately and for no acceptable reason) effects of war. Ignorance of law is no excuse but at the same time wanton (deliberately harming) sinful conduct is a grave crime unworthy of the Pandavas, who are relatively wiser. A blind man can fall in a pit. A man, who can see, should avoid falling in the pit. According to Arjuna, the kauravs will commit the sin ignorantly (i.e. blinded by passions and unconscious of the guilt), but by indulging in war the Pandavas will commit the sin knowingly. The knower of the self (as Arjuna thinks) should not do the same thing which is being done by those bereft of the self. Lord is listening to Arjuna's high sounding words based on worldly wisdom, high on pitch but wanting in soul-suffusing impact. Lord will start replying in next chapter after listening to Arjuna completely.

40. In this verse, Arjuna speaks of the evil that will follow the destruction of the race. Arjuna puts forth another argument to support why he should retreat (move away) from the battle field.

कुलक्षये प्रणश्यन्ति कुलधर्माः सनातनाः ।
धर्मे नष्टे कुलं कृत्स्नमधर्मोऽभिभवत्युत ॥ १- ४० ॥

kula-ksaye pranasyantikula-dharmah sanatanah
dharme naste kulam krtsnam adharmo 'bhibhavaty uta

kula-ksaye--in the destruction of the family; *pranasyanti*—perish; *kula-dharmah*--the family rites (as per traditions); *sanatanah*--eternal; *dharme*-- spirituality; *naste*--being destroyed; *kulam*--family; *krtsnam*—the whole family; *adharmah*-- impiety; *abhibhavati*--overcomes; *uta*- indeed

"In the annihilation (or extermination) of a family, time-honored and ancient customs and traditions of the family are lost (or uprooted). When dharma (righteousness as per law of nature) decays, vice (evil or criminal activities involving sex and drugs) becomes rampant in the race or sin takes hold of entire family."

This verse particularly focuses on "*kuldharma*" and the losses accruing (becoming due) for deviating from "*Kuldharma*." What is "*Kuldharma*"? "*Kuldharma*" are the time-honored (ages-old) rites, duties, customs and traditions befitting a family. These are not the practices recently introduced in the family in a hurry. These beneficial and up-lifting traditions represent the "distilled wisdom and experience" of so many generations gone by. They (time-honored traditions in the form of immemorial religious rites, customs, gatherings, celebrations and rituals) nurture the roots of the families with virtues of life. These "family traditions" are handed down from generation to generation to help maintain the high standard of the conduct of the family. Finally, these family traditions become the cause for maintenance of family morality, character of family, social law and even law of nation. With destruction of families, these family traditions get destroyed. How does it happen? The family loses its venerable seniors responsible for nurturing the family traditions and family values. When the knowledge of ages-old customs and traditions disappear with the venerable seniors, the remnants of struggling women and children lose this knowledge. Righteousness (dharma) decays and vice becomes rampant in the race. These surviving unfortunate women and children, bereft of ages-old family traditions, become unruly and wayward like a "restive steed" (strong horse unable to keep still) without control of bridle. Gradually the members of the bereaved family throw off every form of restraint. Sin extends its sway over the family as a matter of course. This is what is meant by the words "sin takes hold of the entire family" i.e. the whole family yields to lawlessness and irreligion (typical domain of unrighteousness).

41. In this verse, Arjuna proceeds to show what happens when the entire family comes under the sway of sin.

अधर्माभिभवात्कृष्ण प्रदुष्यन्ति कुलस्त्रियः ।
स्त्रीषु दुष्टासु वार्ष्णेय जायते वर्णसङ्करः ॥ १- ४१ ॥

adharmabhibhavat krsna pradusyanti kula-striyah
strisu dustasu varsneya jayate varna-sankarah

adharma-- impiety; *abhibhavat*—the prevalence of; *krsna*--O Krishna; *pradusyanti*--become corrupt; *kula-striyah*--family ladies; *strisu*--of the womanhood; *dustasu*—(being) corrupt; *varsneya*--O descendant of Vrsni (Krishna); *jayate*-- arises; *varna-sankarah*--unwanted progeny(caste-mixture).

"When *adharma* (unrighteousness; impiety or lack of respect for religion, right values and family traditions) holds sway over the family, O Krishna, the women of the family become unchaste; and with women becoming unchaste (polluted) due to degradation of womanhood, O Varshneya, varna-admixture (unwanted progeny i.e. child born may have not characteristic of family-varna)ensues." II 1-41 II

Arjuna is giving another argument to support his stand using the word "*varanasamkarah*." There is no English synonym for this word. It is made up of two words "*varan*" and "*samkarah*."

"***Varna***" - In ancient India, the society was divided in four categories based on "varna." "Varna" is different from caste. Caste is recognized based on heritage. Varna is based on the natural propensities i.e. different mixtures of sattva (tendency to abide by righteousness), rajas (feverishness; tearing hurry for the objective) and tamas (dullness and inactivity. The seniors in the family used to work hard to inculcate in the child "family values" relating to their "varna." The Gita supports categorization of society based on natural propensities of the varna. The society was classified in four varnas or grades as follows: i) brahamins i.e. those showing naturally abundance of unmixed sattva, control of mind, ii) Kshetriya i.e. those showing abundance of rajas mixed with sattva having tendency to save other even at the cost of risking themselves. iii) Vaisya i.e. showing abundance of rajas with tamas and having tendencies to go for agriculture and cow-rearing, iv) Sudra i.e. those having dominance of tamas mixed with rajas. The purpose was to help individuals to identify best jobs according to their natural flair (ability). The people were at liberty to work hard to change their "varna" for the better. Valmiki was a kshetriya but in the end he was declared a "Brahma-Rishi" - a saint knowing brahma-vidya. Ravana was a brahamin but he was declared as demon (rakshasha). Varna is different from present caste system and varna is based on the natural propensities of an individual i.e. law abiding or restless to impose on others and too dull to take right actions or decisions. A society suffers when inherent individual characteristics are ignored and caste system, based on heritage and insensitive to inherent merits and demerits, is imposed.

Samkarah – It stands for confusion. If there is a question mark about the chastity of a mother, then the varna of the child may not be pure. It may be a mixture, having traces of more than one varna i.e. purity of varna may be under confusion. Therefore, "varan-samkarah" i.e. ad-mixture of two varnas ensues due to cross breeding in two varnas.

Arjuna is saying that, after the destruction of a family and with the seniors of the family gone, the remnant women and children get bereft of the family values. In this situation, the women of the family, in the absence of the cover of seniors, may get unchaste. With women getting corrupted, varna-admixture (degradation of purity of varna) ensues. Impiety (lack of respect for religion, God and true values of life) ensues and varna-admixture heralds the degradation of the society. The point raised will be clear if one pauses to find out why a black stallion is considered a "horse, best for races." Why is it that a mule does not come anywhere near a black stallion for consideration for races?

42. In this verse, Arjuna states the affect of varna-admixture (intermingling of varnas i.e. categorization based on natural propensities of individual in different proportions of sattva, rajas and tamas).

सङ्करो नरकायैव कुलघ्नानां कुलस्य च ।
पतन्ति पितरो ह्येषां लुप्तपिण्डोदकक्रियाः ॥ १- ४२ ॥

sankaro narakayaiva kula-ghnanam kulasya ca
patanti pitaro hy esam lupta-pindodaka-kriyah 1.42

sankarah--such unwanted children of mixed caste; *narakaya*--for hellish life; *eva*--certainly; *kula-ghnanam*--of those who are killers of the family; *kulasya*--of the family; *ca*--also; *patanti*--fall down; *pitarah*--forefathers; *hi*--certainly; *esam*--of them; *lupta*--stopped; *pinda*--offerings; *udaka*--water; *kriyah*--performances

"*Varanasamkarah* (confusion of *varnas* or categorization based on natural propensities i.e. rajas, tamas, sattva and their admixture) leads to hell both the family and those who have destroyed the family; the forefathers of these families fall (down to hell), deprived of the offerings of *pindas* (rice balls) and water." II 1.42 II

In this verse, the important words used by Arjuna are i) patanti and ii) Pindodakakriyah. First, these two terms are discussed:

i) **Patanti** (fall down) – Arjuna says that in the absence of the (scripturally prescribed; time tested and laid down in scriptures or holy books) ritual (explained hereafter) the ancestors fall down to hell. The Gita makes mention of fourteen *lokas* [transit planes where one (the subtle body) goes after death; for further details refer to the chart in the introduction]. All these *lokas* are temporary places to experience the matching effect of past actions. One comes back to earth to resume the spiritual journey after sojourn to these transit lokas. Seven of these *lokas* show ascend in spiritual path and seven of these *lokas* show descend in the spiritual path. Arjuna wants to say that in the absence of ceremonial offerings with reverence and gratitude the ancestors fall on the spiritual path. The lowest of this spiritual path is hell. Why does it happen? The ancestors do not get the offerings with reverence and gratitude from their descendents. The descendents do not perform the ceremonies because of lack of knowledge about the family values and practices which get discontinued due to decline of families. The use of this word "patanti" indicates that in spiritual journey of ancestors spiritual descend ensues instead of spiritual ascend.

ii) **Pindodakakriyah** – In India, it is considered the duty (according to our scriptural command or holy books) of a surviving male member of Hindu family to perform "Pindodakakriya" both at the time of death as well as in the specific period called "Shraddha." When this ritual is performed, balls of rice and water are offered to the ancestors with reverence and gratitude. In other societies also some ceremony like this is performed to ceremoniously remember and express gratitude to members. Arjunas says that when the families get destroyed and seniors are not there to look after the family traditions and values, the remnants of surviving women and children do not perform these practices as they remain bereft of the knowledge and spiritual richness of performing these ceremonies. Two important ingredient of this ceremony are i) shraddha i.e. mixture of reverence, gratitude and memory and ii) tarpan i.e. ceremonious offerings in a particular manner with recitation of some prescribed holy sanctified words.

Arjuna says that, due to "varna-pollution," both the family and the slayers of the families are lead to degradation in spiritual growth. Ancestors do not get offerings of rice balls and water. This is not something small for orthodox Hindu family. It marks the destruction of the eternal laws of the race and the moral laws of the family. The reason is simple. There is a very strong belief among the orthodox Hindus that the deceased ancestors require these offerings for their welfare. This ceremonious offering of rice balls and water to the deceased ancestor, involving shraddha (reverence and gratitude) and tarpan (offerings in scriptural manner), are utterly important and are a cause of immense concern to the orthodox Hindu families even today.

Arjuna is suffering from anguish (mental suffering and unhappiness). He considers that the slaughter of the seniors, relatives and friends is an act of *adharma* (unrighteousness i.e. fundamentally wrong being against the nature of the fabric or values of society), which will create evil (by depriving the surviving women and children of their seniors), sustain evil (by adding the gap of ignorance) and make the society suffer from evil (in the form of wickedness and cruelty).

Arjuna came to the battle field determined to annihilate the enemies after due deliberation of the issues relating to war. What is the reason of this sudden change? This is a very relevant and important point here requiring pause and consideration. When there is a lack of spiritual wisdom (knowledge about the "Ultimate Truth', about the distinction between the "Real' and unreal, about the "Unity" in diversity), we see the things in a wrong way. For one who sees with the spiritual eye (Divine wisdom), there are no evil forces. When one learns higher dependence (dependence on the "Eternal Universal Existence within," there is no more anguish of mind and no more rebellion. Then, virtue and vice, sin and merit, praise and censure, light and darkness, life and death appear naturally composed in the "Eternal Unity," about which Lord Krishna is going to tell Arjuna in the coming discussion.

43 and 44. Arjuna continues narrating the deep rooted consequences of "*Varna*-Pollution" in these two verses as well.

दोषैरेतैः कुलघ्नानां वर्णसङ्करकारकैः ।
उत्साद्यन्ते जातिधर्माः कुलधर्माश्च शाश्वताः ॥ १- ४३ ॥
उत्सन्नकुलधर्माणां मनुष्याणां जनार्दन ।
नरके नियतं वासो भवतीत्यनुशुश्रुम ॥ १- ४४ ॥

dosair etaih kula-ghnanam varna-sankara-karakaih
utsadyante jati-dharmah kula-dharmas ca sasvatah 1.43

dosaih--by evil deeds; *etaih*--all these; *kula-ghnanam*--of the destroyer of the family; *varna-sankara-- karakaih*—causing intermingling of castes; *utsadyante*—are destroyed; *jati-dharmah*-practices based on traditions in castes (for example a kshetriya must fight to restore righteousness to ensure judiciousness in society); *kula-dharmah*-- family rites based on traditions (like offering rice balls with water to the ancestors); *ca*--also; *sasvatah*--eternal.

utsanna-kula-dharmanam manusyanam janardana
narake aniyatam vaso bhavatity anususruma 1.44

utsanna—spoiled or destruction of;- *kuldharmanam*-- family rites based on traditions ; *manusyanam*--of the men; *janardana*--O Krishna; *narake*--in hell (lowest category of lokas; refer to 14 lokas in chart in introduction); *aniyatam*—for unknown period; *vasah*—dwelling; *bhavati*--is; *iti*--thus; *anususruma*- we have heard.

"By the evil deeds of those who destroy the family, leading to confusion of purity of varna (or pollution of varna i.e. natural composition of order in society based on various degrees of attributes like sattva, rajas and tamas), eternal laws (family virtues) of the race (like a Kshetriya should always fight with all the might to restore righteousness) and moral laws of the family (i.e. commitment to practices like "shraddha" and performance of family traditions and ceremonies) are devastated." II 1.43 II

"We have heard, O Janardana (Krishna), that it is inevitable for those men whose religious activities have been destroyed, to dwell in hell for an unknown period of time." II 1.44 II

Arjuna is extremely concerned about the varna-admixture (pollution of varna). It is necessary to understand why Arjuna is giving so much emphasis to "varna-pollution." Varna these days is usually translated as caste but the existing caste system, based on heritage and not attributes of nature, is very different from the ancient social classification of 'Chaturvarna' (Brhamin, kshetriya, vaishya and Sudra). In the days of Arjuna, 'varna-admixture' was considered a sin. In the present era, people take it very lightly and inter-caste marriages have become very common. For those, who hanker for bodily comfort and sensuous pleasures, Arjuna's stand may appear too farfetched. There has been significant degradation in values of life from spiritual point of view. Rampant and very strong desire for sex (not including liking or love) is the result of this change. Some present day scientists recommend intermingling of breeds. It is slightly strange that these enlightened minds try to preserve the purity of breed among the **race-horses and the blood-hounds**, but perhaps this purity of blood is not desirable for men. In Arjuna's days, intermingling of blood was considered a sin. According to thinking in Arjuna's time, intermingling of blood shatters the ideals enshrined in immemorial traditions. It disturbs the social equilibrium and brings chaos in the world. What is the reason? The pure consciousness becomes covered by its eternal enemy (lust), which is never satisfied and which burns like fire. Those, whose sacred rites and rituals are destroyed are compelled to live in hell for unknown period of time. Inner purity cannot be safeguarded if individual's heart is soiled by the worldly reasons and heated by the fever of life.

Arjuna's condition is very peculiar. Sometimes we close our doors and nothing can penetrate. We become barren and dry inside. Self-consciousness (my people, my thoughts, my traditions, my ancestors) dries our hearts and binds it to the finite. Everything becomes parched within. When a man is out of rhythm (**tuning with the "fundamental original nature," about which Arjuna will learn from Lord Krishna**), whatever he undertakes, cannot be in rhythm with the universe. People, who fasten themselves to small things, deprive themselves of bigger things in life. **Those, who lose their life for the sake of "Truth," find life**. This is what Lord will tell Arjuna in the Gita. When the bigger thing comes, lesser thing is wiped out.

45. In this verse, Arjuna gets overwhelmed by his own description of disastrous consequences of fighting a war.

अहो बत महत्पापं कर्तुं व्यवसिता वयम् ।
यद्राज्यसुखलोभेन हन्तुं स्वजनमुद्यताः ॥ १- ४५ ॥

aho bata mahat papam kartum vyavasita vayam
yad rajya-sukha-lobhena hantum sva-janam udyatah

aho- bata-- alas; *mahat*--great; *papam*—that sin, which creates intense suffering to the righteousness within (individualized eternal existence or soul within); *kartum*--to do; *vyavasitah*-- prepared; *vayam*--we; *yat*-- that; *rajya*--kingdom; *sukha-lobhena*--driven by greed for royal happiness; *hantum*--to kill; *sva-janam*—our own kinsmen; *udyatah*-- prepared.

"Alas! We are ready to commit a great sin by attempting the wholesale massacre of our kinsmen because of greed for the pleasures of the kingdom II 1.45 II

In the thirty eighth verse of this chapter, Arjuna says that Duryodhana and his companions, with mind blinded with greed, do not perceive the evil of destruction of their clan. They are not guided by righteousness. For this reason they are prepared to wage a war. Pandavas are able to discriminate between righteousness and unrighteousness. They are also prepared to wage war. It is very shocking and surprising for Arjuna. He expresses his shock by use of the word "*Aho.*" Arjuna finds it surprising that they (the Pandvas including Lord Krishna) have also decided to commit the sin by waging this war, even having known its horrifying consequences. He feels that Pandavas are involved in committing a great sin. They are prepared to kill their kinsmen driven by the desire to enjoy royal happiness of owning a kingdom. So, the sight of kinsmen, in the opposite camp ready to fight, has filled Arjuna with a new response and resignation. He is reacting to the situation with his own sincerity and firmness. He is slowly moving towards the climax of his sudden dispassion and new yearning (strong emotional desire).

46. Based on the discussion so far, Arjuna is in surprise and sorrow. Arjuna has also given the arguments to support the change in his stand. In this verse, Arjuna comes to a definite decision.

यदि मामप्रतीकारमशस्त्रं शस्त्रपाणयः ।
धार्तराष्ट्रा रणे हन्युस्तन्मे क्षेमतरं भवेत् ॥ १- ४६ ॥

yadi mam apratikaram asastram sastra-panayah
dhartarastra rane hanyus tan me ksemataram bhavet 1.46

yadi- if; *mam*-unto me; *apratikaram*- unresisting; *asastram*-- unarmed; *sastra-panayah*- with weapons in hand; *dhartarastrah*--the sons of Dhrtarastra; *rane*--in the battlefield; *hanyuh*- (should) slayl; *tat*-that; *me*-of me; *ksema-taram*--better; *bhavet*-would be.

"It would be better for me, if the sons of Dhritarashtra (the Kauravas), with weapons in hand, were to kill me, un-resistant, unarmed in the battle field." II 1-46 II

Arjuna has finally come out openly. He will not kill his enemies, even though his enemies kill him, finding him un-resisting and unarmed. Thus, in this verse, Arjuna's lack of hope and lack of happiness i.e. despondency reaches its highest point. Arjuna has given his decision, but it is not the decision of a man who is in "rhythm with his inner self." That unshakable confidence, which one reflects while working in the "ordered state of mind," being unified with oneself, is not visible by the statements of Arjuna. History is a witness that virtuous people have faced death with poise and composure (Socrates, one of the wisest men of the world, drank poison without expressing least disturbance or uneasiness, showing his extreme balance of mind even at the hour of death). Where does this balanced state of mind come from? For this we need to go within. Arjuna, like all of us, seem to think, feel and seek more outwardly than inwardly. That is the reason he is distressed in mind and body. That boisterous attitude (the attitude that should make others feel better, more positive and more confident), expected from world's known warrior, is obviously missing here. Arjuna, the mighty warrior, came to the battle field ready to fight. Now, he sees his intimate relatives, teachers and friends in both the armies ready to fight and sacrifice their lives. Grief and pity overcomes Arjuna. Remorse (feeling of being extremely sorry) seizes (forcibly takes control) him. He fails in strength. His mind is bewildered and finally he gives up his determination to fight. He seems to be at war with his own self, with his own new decision, which he has supported with arguments. Worldly people will support the arguments of Arjuna, because these arguments are based on the feeling of attachment and affection for the family. He has taken the decision not to fight. Now at least he should be happy showing the serenity of decision well taken. What is the reason of his lack of involvement even in this decision (Next verse says that he casts aside his bow and arrow and takes his seat in chariot overwhelmed with sorrow)?

Far beyond the victory of war, far beyond the royal pump and show and far beyond the attachment for the family, there reigns within each one of us a "supreme spiritual treasure," which, when realized, will alone crown the human life eternally. This is the foremost truth, which Pandu's son (Arjuna) has ignored all along in the discussion so far in this first chapter. Intellectual reasoning will not take an individual to this "Supreme Spiritual Treasure" within. For the awareness of this, an individual must have "finer intelligence of a higher order." This particular awareness is life's achievement. For the awareness of "this Higher Order" within, one will have to be full of finer feelings, free from self-assertion and petty limiting considerations like anger, envy, avarice etc. After this, we require blending our individual selves with this "Great Power of Higher Order" within us. For this, we need a spiritual guide, who teaches how to lose outward-looking habit of mind and cultivate the habit of looking inwardly. Here Lord Krishna is there to tell Arjuna the nitty-gritty of the art of tuning in to the perfect unison, to the "Divine Grace within." This is the sovereign remedy for the selfishness, egotism and attachment, with which Arjuna and almost all of us are suffering. Lord Krishna's words will make us conscious of that "reservoir of highest abiding joy unifying all enjoyments."

47. Arjuna finally expressed his decision not to fight. In this verse Sanjay describes what he did afterwards.

सञ्जय उवाच ।
एवमुक्त्वार्जुनः सङ्ख्ये रथोपस्थ उपाविशत् ।
विसृज्य सशरं चापं शोकसंविग्नमानसः ॥ १- ४७ ॥

sanjaya uvaca
evam uktvarjunah sankhye rathopastha upavisat
visrjya sa-saram capam soka-samvigna-manasah 1,47

sanjayah--Sanjaya; *uvaca*--said; *evam*--thus; *uktva*—having said; *arjunah*--Arjuna; *sankhye*--in the battlefield; *rathopastha*—on the seat of chariot; *upavisat*-- sat down; *visrjya*—having cast away; *sa-saram*-- with arrows; *capam*--the bow; *soka--samvigna-- manasah*-- with a mind distressed with sorrow.

Sanjay said:

"Having thus spoken on the battlefield, Arjuna, with his mind overwhelmed with sorrow, sank down on the seat of his chariot, casting aside his bow and arrows." II 1-47 II

Arjuna is having a nervous breakdown. The language used in the last verses, clearly expresses this situation. Body is shivering. Mind is whirling. Doubt is mounting (increasing). He sits down or rather sinks on the seat in the chariot. Normally, when they fight in the chariot they stand up. That is the custom of those days. He has thrown away the bow and arrows. This is at least the complete negation of the purpose of his presence in the battle field. His mind is completely immersed in grief and dejection. He has talked of non-violence. Many people will initially support the arguments of Arjuna. Is there virtue (attitude showing high moral standard) in Arjuna's words? Is virtue a weakness? Is virtue psychic breakdown? Arjuna cannot pass judgment about the situation with grief stricken mind. We should never let our mind grow turbulent or be shaken by agitation. When we limit ourselves to one sided vision (Arjuna is overemphasizing presence of relatives and seniors in the battlefield, completely ignoring "eternal existence" within each one of us, of which each one of us mostly remains ignorant like Arjuna), everything becomes distorted and we are weakened. We all are a part of great "Immensity," an "Unbounded Spirit of the Universe." We should not have any weakness or doubt about it. These unexpected changes, which Arjuna is undergoing, creep in life due to lack of awareness of that "All-abiding Spirit." What should be done? Lord will answer in the next chapters in detail. In brief, we should express the awareness of "The Infinite" in our thoughts, words and action. Then we cannot be moved by any passing condition of life like Arjuna. So long as we keep a firm grasp on this "awareness of eternal immensity," we shall always maintain our balance and be at peace. The whole discussion in the Gita focuses on developing the 'inward relationship' with this "All-loving Father, Mother or Truth of the Universe." Lord's discourse in the Gita will change Arjuna's (mankind's) emptiness into fullness, anxiety into peace and this decision not to fight into a resolve to fight to the finish in order to justify commitment to the "Providential Will; will of the 'Force' that some people believe, controls our life and the things that happen to us." In the end, after getting convinced, Arjuna will himself say that his delusion is destroyed, that he has gained knowledge and that his confusion is dispelled. This Gita will help us to realize that we cannot be truly living, if our consciousness is cut off from the "Source" or is at variance with the "Source." An individual, like Arjuna, ignorant of the spiritual nature, has to be restored to it for evolution. The fight (duel or the struggle between right and wrong, good and bad) takes place (or is experienced) every moment in the innermost recesses of an individual or the life of an individual. In most of the cases, life is out of rhythm or sync (or working at the same time and speed as the original nature), like life of Arjuna at this moment, if the connection with the "Source" is missing. Lord in the next chapter will offer the sovereign remedy to Arjuna (or to humanity at large).

ॐ तत्सदिति श्रीमद्भगवद्गीतासूपनिषत्सु
ब्रह्मविद्यायां योगशास्त्रे श्रीकृष्णार्जुनसंवादे
अर्जुनविषादयोगो नाम प्रथमोऽध्यायः ॥ १ ॥

In the Upnishad of the Bhagavad Gita, the science of "The Absolute; The Eternal," the scripture of yoga and the dialogue between Sri Krishna and Arjuna, this is the first chapter entitled "The Depression of Arjuna"

Some words used in this concluding remark are dealt with below:

Upnishad means discussion between a teacher and pupil sitting for transfer of divine knowledge from the former to the latter.

Brahamvidya means science relating to "the Absolute or The Eternal." It is the science of God i.e. how this universe (this exuberant play of infinite possibilities) goes on. Who Is he, who compels or impels this whole universal drama of creating, sustaining and dissolution? The purpose of Brahmn-vidya is to understand the true nature of this "Underlying Truth or Reality." This logical investigation is necessary for attaining divine wisdom as light is necessary to see the world.

Bhagavadgita means "the Lord's song" or "the song celestial"

Yogasastra means scripture of yoga. It is called scripture of yoga because it leads to the union of the "egoistic self (the particular)" with the "Universal Self (the Universal)" after true understanding the true nature of universe, God (The Supreme), *nishkama-karma* (action without attachment to fruit thereof), *lokasngraha* (for cosmic benefit) and bhakti (devotion).

"**Krishna Arjuna samvade**" means it is dialogue between Sri Krishna and Arjuna.

Arjuna's Visad yoga i.e. this chapter ends with Arjuna's grief. It is also called yoga. This debilitating (making body and mind weak) grief is like darkness around the soul (that eternal consciousness within which survives death). After one transcends (goes beyond) grief, one gains self- knowledge which facilitates self realization. For this reason, it has been called Arjuma's *Visad Yoga*.

Sum and substance of the chapter

An individual is the centre of a number of conflicting impulses, tendencies. For this reason, individual gets divided within and does not know what path to follow. The first chapter illustrates how Arjuna, the known warrior of that era, becomes a victim of debilitating (making mind and body weak) tendencies. He is seized with despair due to his egoistic tendencies. Arjuna came to participate in war after due deliberations. Now he wants to abandon war, which involves killing of teachers, senior members of the family and relatives. He ignores even this fact that he is a Kshetriya (a warrior) and it is his bounden (morally correct) duty to fight this righteous war. As a result of all this inner conflict, Arjuna suffers from total paralysis of his personality, his will. He throws away bow and arrow in sheer dejection. Arjuna's grief and delusion is caused by his undue attachment and fear of separation (due to deatha) from grandfathers, preceptors, sons, kinsmen, friends, well wishers etc. He proposes to abstain from fighting. He is ready to lead the life of a mendicant, living by begging. All persons, whose minds get swayed by grief, delusion and other evil influences, abandon their bounden duty and resort to the "dharma (duty here)" of others, which is prohibited. Thus, this chapter concludes at dejection and despondency of Arjuna, which later becomes cause of Lord's blessings to Arjuna in the form of divine knowledge.

द्वितीयोऽध्यायः (Chapter 2)

साङ्ख्ययोग {Sankhya (Self-knowledge)-Yoga}

Meaning of the chapter heading – This chapter contains the structure on which the whole Gita-discussion is based. In this chapter one gets the whole philosophical contents of the Gita. Therefore, in some ways, this is the most important chapter of the Bhagavad Gita. First, some general aspects of the chapter will be discussed.

The name of this chapter raises three questions in mind. What is Sankhya? What is yoga? What is Sankhya-yoga? In ordinary language Sankhya means relating to number or statistics. This meaning is not sufficient to understand the Bhagavad Gita. For the purpose of understanding the Bhagavad Gita, it will be enough to say that Sankhya means "self-knowledge" i.e. who I am. What is the truth in me? What is the untruth in me? It leads to another good question. What is truth? Truth is eternal existence. It defies (refuses to obey) change and influence of time. It is the basic ground or source of all i.e. it remains unaffected by past, present and future. *Sankhya* means identifying the components of truth and untruth relevant to "self." If we know the "truth within," we will abide by the truth and we will get relieved of untruth, whose dominance brings innumerable miseries in life. That speaks of relevance of "Sankhya" in life.

Now, what is yoga? Yoga is combination of all disciplines (physical, mental, emotional and spiritual) to unite an individual to individual's true nature (The Real Self, The Ever Continuing Self, The Indestructible Self or The Eternal Existence) within each one of us. Yoga results in the control of urges, modifications and tendencies of mind to set in the process of unification. Yoga facilitates unification of diversity into unity. Diversification is the false notion. To do away with this false notion, yoga enlivens one's awareness to feel that only "One" alone exists and expresses itself into diversity. Rest all is untruth. The moment one experiences that "never ending, never-exhausting, ever-renewing expanse of one's blessedness, peace and contentment," yoga's function has reached its climax.

An attempt to unite with the "real self within" through "self-knowledge" along with various disciplines of yoga is "Sankhya-yoga." Self-Knowledge has dominance in "Sankhya-yoga" and various disciplines, as already mentioned, include all other physical, mental, emotional and spiritual disciplines to understand the truth (eternal, indestructible reality) of one's being i.e. the truth of what one is.

How this chapter is connected with the previous chapter and the plight of Arjuna- In the first chapter, Arjuna requests Lord Krishna to bring the chariot in the middle of the two armies to be able to see those who assembled there to fight in order to appease the evil-minded son of Dhritrashtra. Lord Krishna accordingly places the chariot in the middle of the two armies, right in front of Bhishma, Drona and other seniors. Arjuna had grown seeing Bhisma (grandsire), Drona (teacher) and respecting them. On seeing them, whom he adored, in the opposite camps ready to fight along with others, utter grief (visada) overcomes Arjuna. Arjuna feels bewildered, depressed and utterly shaken. He gives vent to his feelings of despondency, disappointment and dismay. He has come to the battle field prepared to fight against the Kaurvas. A sudden change seizes this bull among the men, this known warrior of that era. His body trembles, mouth goes dry, Gandiva (bow) slips and his intelligence is completely shaken. He suffers from the physical shrinking of nerves and emotional shrinking of the heart from the thought of destruction of Dhritarastrians (son of king Dhrirtarastra). Arjuna has come to the battle field to kill the enemies. Now, he thinks that life will be empty without them (Kauravas). He suffers from self-indulgence (focus on the "egoistic self" alone) and his own valiant personality gets lapsed into un-heroic weakness, which is unbecoming of a warrior of his stature. Horror overtakes him. It is very pertinent to understand here, what this horror is due to. Earlier in life, horror has been unknown to him. Rather his presence has been a cause of horror to the people. He is a warrior to the core. Somewhere, deep within him, something, unknown to his basic nature, is silently working against his will. It is emotionalizing him, compelling him (driving him) against his heroic nature and pushing him towards the weak thoughts of retreating from the battle field. Arjuna is not confident of his new stand as well. To conceal his inner split, he supports his new stand by the web (net) of worldly wisdom. In fact, he is appalled (shocked) by his own behavior. This compassion, consideration and pity gripping Arjuna is unknown to his basic characteristics. He gives forth a number of arguments explaining why he feels like abandoning the war and retreating from Kurukshetra (battlefield). In the end, the greatest among the warriors of that time, whose name used to be a terror in the opposite camp, is shivering with tears in his eyes. Arjuna, has reached a point of desperation, where thoughts of committing a sin and his sincerity to uphold the values he has learnt (from the point of view of morality and worldly wisdom) intensely conflict and he requires a way out of his present predicament (difficult and unpleasant situation).

What is all this sudden change of Arjuna due to? It is very much like our own experience in life at one point of time or the other. When flame of faith (in the deepest recesses within an individual), that sheds light upon life's straight and narrow path, moves here and there and there appears turbulence and unrest within and all around, one stands in the dark spell in life, puzzled, helpless, exposed to vagaries (unexpected events). Arjuna is suffering from "crisis of conscience."

What is conscience? What is consciousness? It is relevant to know all this. Conscience is that level within, beyond human intelligence (worldly-related, ego-related intelligence) and ego, which is akin to divine component within. What is Divine Component? Divine component in a being (eternal spiritual existence) is the "Divine Capacity" available to each one of us, validating our existence and helping us to gain awareness, aliveness and realization of our pure nature. It is eternal, indestructible and immanent i.e. present everywhere. How do we connect conscience and Divine Capacity? We do it by consciousness. What is consciousness? It is awareness i.e. that by which we see without eyes, hear without ears, walk without legs and get to know the secrets unknown to us but within us. It marks the presence of the Divinity but it alone is not the Divinity; Consciousness is the most obvious evidence of existence of Divinity. "The universal Eternal Divinity" has besides consciousness knowledge and bliss. Conscience stimulates awareness to differentiate between righteousness and unrighteousness. In this situation, a sudden change has gripped Arjuna totally. He came to the battle field to fight with the enemies. Now he is in a state of confusion. He is talking of avoiding war but somewhere within him something is pulling him from this stand as well. He is speaking something without being sure whether "not-fighting" will be the correct decision. He is apparently in doubt whether even this new development in him is correct. Has this decision to come to the battle field been taken in a day or in a hurry? It is a decision well deliberated at different levels by different people in Pandva's group including Lord Krishna. Last ditch effort to avoid war (massacre or ruthless killing) was taken by sending Krishna as a messenger. Even this effort failed. Now he is talking about compassion, about avoiding massacre, about feeding on alms. Is there anything new in the battle field, which he is not able to anticipate? Arjuna is talking in a language unknown to him and his nature. He is also giving plausible (likely to be true) reason, looking convincing from worldly point of view, for avoiding war at any cost whatsoever. He is so overwhelmed with emotions that (in this chapter) he surrenders to Krishna for guidance to be able to choose between righteousness and unrighteousness in that state of utter confusion.

A peep (quick look) into Arjuna's predicament - The Bhagavad Gita cannot be understood or rather really felt, till we identify Arjuna's predicament or mental condition i.e. why Arjuna came to wage a war, why he finds himself in the present hopeless state. Arjuna is really not sure of his changed stand i.e. avoiding war. How is Arjuna's predicament relevant to us? Arjuna did not come there to settle a personal grudge against anyone. Arjuna came to wage a war against those who were collectively responsible for outrageously attempting to strip off a woman in an open court in the presence of all the seniors and wise people. He came to wage a war against those who were deceiving others in the name of a game. Those against Arjuna were so blind by their sinful gains that they ganged themselves together and refused to give as much land as the tip of a needle what to talk of adequate princely rights. Arjuna came to wage a war to restore righteousness in the society where unrighteousness was mounting. He was fully aware of the imminent massacre before coming to the battle field. At the spur of that moment in the battle field, seeing all his people ready to fight to finish, he forgot all about it. He forgot that he came for a noble cause bigger than an individual's desire. Emotions overpowered his conscience. A change unknown to his basic nature gripped him and he became victim of imbalance, uncertainty and doubt. He was not himself sure of the correctness or appropriateness of his newly found worldly wisdom. He was not in a position to hold his own Gandiva (bow) even. Obviously he was in utter confusion. He experienced a strange resistance coming from somewhere from some corner in his own self. It is a new development not known to him. In that moment of utter confusion, he becomes a disciple of Lord Krishna and seeks refuge in him for guidance for right course of action. What Arjuna (like each one of us) seeks is a "basis in life and not just the suggestion to fight or not," which will bring spiritual solace (feeling of emotional comfort), courage, resourcefulness and release him from the vice (tool that holds objects) like grip of one's own self. All of us feel the same way in life at one point of time or the other.

Relevance of Arjuna's condition - Arjuna, here in the Gita, represents a sincere common individual and unmatched warrior of that era. Kindled in him is a new response of dejection and resignation, while he is in a battle field and heinous war is about to begin. Arjuna's condition symbolizes human life and action. There comes a time in every life, when an individual abruptly and unknowingly extends beyond individual self (egoistic-self) whom he or she is familiar with. The individual becomes a new different self abruptly. The individual starts doing things that he or she is not accustomed to do. The experience of the change, the experience of unaccustomed activity, the experience of being on unfamiliar ground, the experience of doing things differently is frightening to the individual. It always was. It always is. It always will be. One faces a dilemma. It becomes difficult to choose between right and wrong. The individual yearns to know the truth that survives all changes, goes to the Guru or the Master. This happens because an individual does not know well what an individual is. An individual does not know that besides physical aspect there are other various dimensions (associated intangibles) of an individual i.e. mental, emotional and spiritual. An individual does not know underlying reasons of behavioral pattern. An individual suffers without knowing that there is a war going on among one's own levels of existence. In this chapter, due to Arjuna's surrender, Lord blesses him with divine wisdom (that wisdom which helps an individual to go beyond human understanding and human experience), which suffices all, in all situations, in present, past and future.

Arjuna's submission to Lord Krishna and then Krishna's clarifications of fundamental truth in life - Important point is that Arjuna submits to Lord as a disciple. Krishna first smiles at him and then, in his reproachful (expressing blame and criticism) words, lashes out at the at the anxiety- state-neurosis (a mental illness in which a person suffers from strong feelings of fear and worry) in Arjuna, the known warrior of that era and now a weakling (a person who is not physically and mentally strong). Lord Krishna has been silent so far but now in this chapter HE bursts forth in eloquence (expression which explains well with feelings). Every word of Krishna is a chosen missile. Every word is a pounding-hammer-stroke that can flat any victim. Every word pierces into ignorance guiding towards the divine truth. Lord Krishna explains to Arjuna the fundamental distinction between the temporary material body and the "eternal spiritual existence within" i.e. first know who you really are. Then Lord explains process of transmigration (i.e. why a soul passes after death into another body undergoing pains and pathos again and again), nature of selfless service (a service dedicated for a "Greater Cause" leads to everlasting peace and happiness here and hereafter) and the characteristics of a self-realized person. Lord Krishna's call to rise and resolve to fight is not just a call for war but a divine call to an individual to discard melancholy, dejection and helplessness in the face of life's challenges. It is a call to transcend or to go beyond human limitations (i.e. human understanding and human experience). The game of life should be played with pointed determination without attachments to the results and awareness of the "Eternal Existence within." The Gita elaborates three basic approaches i.e. Karma-yoga (action-dominated approach with focus on the realization of the Supreme Truth), Jnana-yoga (Divine-knowledge dominated approach with focus on the realization of the Supreme Truth) and Bhakti-yoga (Devotion-for-the-Supreme dominated approach with focus on the realization of the Supreme Truth). In the second chapter, karam-yoga and jnana-yoga have been clearly discussed with a glimpse of Bhakti-yoga.

This dialogue, started in the preceding chapter, goes on between Arjuna and Lord Krishna in the battle field. In the palace of Dhritarastra, Sanjay, the trusted counselor, is narrating the detailed events to the king. This second chapter starts with the statement of Sanjay after Arjuna's decision not to fight.

1. Sanjay describes to the king the pitiable condition of Arjuna in grief.

सञ्जय उवाच ।
तं तथा कृपयाविष्टमश्रुपूर्णाकुलेक्षणम् ।
विषीदन्तमिदं वाक्यमुवाच मधुसूदनः ॥ २ - १ ॥

sanjaya uvaca
tam tatha krpayavistam asru-purnakuleksanam
visidantam idam vakyam uvaca madhusudanah 2.1

sanjayah uvaca--Sanjaya said; *tam*—to him (Arjuna); *tatha*--thus; *krpaya*--by compassion; *avistam*--overcome; *asru-purna--akula--iksanam*—with eyes filled with tears and agitted; *visidantam*--sorrowing; *idam*--this; *vakyam*--words; *uvaca*--said; *madhu-sudanah*--the killer of Madhu (Krishna).

Sanjay said:

"To him (Arjuna), who was overwhelmed with compassion and who was despondent with eyes full of tears and agitated, Madhusudana (killer of demon Madhu; Lord Krishna) spoke these words." II 1 II

Sanjay says that Arjuna was overwhelmed with pity. Normally pity is a positive or divine feeling of sympathy and sadness caused by suffering and troubles being experienced by others. A sensitive individual should have sympathy with others. Pity generates out of compassion by those who observe others with love, wisdom, calmness, consideration and strength. Pity brings individual in a mood where an individual helps and heals the other individual. He alone, who is the master of his senses, can extend compassion to the distressed and seek to allay (to make a feeling less strong) their sorrows. Arjuna's pity is different. It is a form of self-indulgence. It is the physical shrinking of nerves from the act of slaughter. It is the emotional shrinking of heart from the destruction which is about to ensue. It is a result of pure focus on physical existence alone. It is the reflection of lack of awareness of spiritual existence of a being. Arjuna here at this moment is not concerned about righteousness or unrighteousness. Arjuna is afraid of the emptiness that one experiences after losing someone for good. Arjuna has got invaded by the self-indulgent pity, which has pushed, him into un-heroic weakness. The one who was capable of having pity on others has come into a pitiable situation. This Arjuna is in the dire need of redemption from distress. This Arjuna (overwhelmed with distress) cannot show mercy to others. This condition of Arjuna is complete negation of purpose for which he came to the battle field i.e. to relieve the society of those: i) who dared to strip a woman in the open court; ii) who treacherously deceived others in name of a game iii) and who refused to even negotiate the issue to give princely rights to the rightful princes of the family). It was not compassion and pity but "weakness in disguise" that seized Arjuna at that moment in the battle field. Arjuna was talking of peace, non-violence and compassion. These virtues are for the braves and not for the psychic wreck that mighty-Arjuna became at that moment. He was not sure of his newly-found wisdom. He was talking about avoiding war. Now having come there in the battle field to fight, he is saying that war would lead to decay in society, break-up of family, adverse impact on widows and the coming generations.

Arjunas words are deceiving and in the beginning appeal to those who do not have the back ground information of purpose of war and efforts made by the Pandvas to avoid confrontation for war. Many readers, especially foreigners may say "Arjuna is better than Krishna. He is against war. He wants peace." Those who do not have back ground information (the Gita is an extract of Mahabharta and does not give background information about Arjuna and Krishna) go to the extent of saying that Krishna is egging Arjuna on to war. Actually Arjuna is not concerned about restoring lasting peace in the society. He wants an escape from the present situation. Running away from the problems will not solve the problem. One has to face the problem boldly or the problem will keep chasing. No problem will be solved till the reasons contributing the problem are done away with. Lord Krishna wants to restore righteousness in the society. He is telling Arjuna to do his duty (duty for the society and not for the individual self, duty according to divine code of conduct and duty according to his natural abilities and established family traditions). It is a very beautiful scene indeed. The one, who does not know about peace, is talking about avoiding war. The One who knows just everything everywhere is smiling on the "dancing display of ignorance" before epitome of wisdom.

Arjuna was a known warrior of that era. Fear was unknown to him. He himself was a cause of fear for his enemies. What is it that seizes Arjuna at this particular junction? Something deep from somewhere within him is pulling him from this new stand as well. He is evidently confused unsure of the "alien words" that he is talking about. He is shivering. Even gandiva (bow) is coming out of his trembling hands. He is sincere to the core. Therefore he becomes disciple of Lord Krishna. He beseeches Krishna to guide him out of this predicament. One thing is sure. Arjuna is definitely unsure of what he is talking. If he had firmly believed what he is talking, he must not have become the "psychic wreck" that he appears to be based on his statements and lack of confidence displayed by him.

2. This verse contains the first words that came out of the Lord in response to Arjuna's plight.

श्रीभगवानुवाच ।
कुतस्त्वा कश्मलमिदं विषमे समुपस्थितम् ।
अनार्यजुष्टमस्वर्ग्यमकीर्तिकरमर्जुन ॥ २- २ ॥

sri-bhagavan uvaca
kutas tva kasmalam idam visame samupasthitam
anarya-justam asvargyam akirti-karam arjuna 2.2

sri-bhagavan uvaca—Distinct manifestation (incarnation) of the Supreme Reality (lord Krishna) said; *kutah*--wherefrom; *tva*--unto you; *kasmalam*-- dejection; *idam*—this (lamentation); *visame*--in this hour of crisis; *samupasthitam*-- comes; *anarya-justam*-unworthy (un-aryan like); *asvargyam*--that which does not lead to higher planes (refer to *lokas* in the chart in introduction); *akirti--karam*--disgraceful; *arjuna*--O Arjuna.

The blessed Lord (or Bhagvan i.e. one who knows the origin and destruction, gain and loss and state of enlightenment and ignorance of all creatures) said:

"How has this dejection come to you at this juncture? This is not fit for an Aryan (people of noble mind and deed). It is disgraceful and it does not lead one to heaven, O Arjuna!" II 2 II

By his words and actions, Arjuna has presented himself as a weakling (one who is not strong) who allows to be overpowered by circumstances or outer happenings. Lord has been silent up till now. Now lord Krishna bursts into eloquence (intensely expressive speech) and every word spoken by Him is a chosen missile, a pounding, a hammer stroke that can flatten any victim. The objective is to pull Arjuna or inspire Arjuna to get out of this hopeless mental state. Lord specifically uses three beautiful words:

i) Anaryajustam (unworthy or un-aryan like) – The most appropriate translation of this Sanskrit word should be "ignoble" i.e. not good or that which should make you feel shame. Arya means a gentleman and enlightened person having divine awareness or sensitivity. There is a very beautiful line in Rig Veda – "krinavanto visvamaryam; make every human being an aryan'. Arjuna's present condition is not Aryan-like. Aryan are those who follow the path of righteousness, who follow the path of light, who are bold and try to find a solution in a determined manner i.e. resolutely. Getting carried away by the passion and losing the self poise is "un-aryan" way of life. In those days, people used to feel pride in calling themselves Aryan. By use of this word, Lord wants Arjuna to carefully examine his thoughts, feelings and reasons for behaving in that particular manner. This is necessary to help him strive and attain the level of the wise by determined efforts.

ii) Asvargam (heaven-excluding) - What is heaven? It is a place or region where you are very happy. According to Indian traditional thinking, a soul goes to any of the 14 regions, if it has not gained absolute freedom (mukti) and one of these regions is heaven where one feels very comfortable and satisfied. According to Indian philosophy, heaven is not the final abode of the Supreme. One comes back again from heaven, after one has received the due for good actions done by the individual. Lord wants to say that this behavior of Arjuna is not compatible to entitle him for entry in heaven what to talk of final absolute liberation.

iii) Akiritikaram (an act which forfeits one of glory) – In short, Lord wants to tell Arjuna that his behavior will bring infamy. This is not the sort of behavior that one will expect from one who has gained eminence like Arjuna. Rather it is the behavior that is to be shunned by those who desire liberation, heaven and fame.

In simple words Lord is telling Arjuna: "My dear Arjuna, how has this perilous (dangerous) condition come upon you? It is not befitting to a man who is so brave and noble. It will not lead you to fame and honor. It is disgraceful."

These words contain both the advice as well as the command to set the things right. Lord is reminding Arjuna about the juncture (particular point or stage in an activity) as well. An all-out effort to negotiate the issues has failed. War has been proclaimed (publicly declared). The onslaught (the strong and violent attack of the enemy) is about to start and Arjuna is talking now of avoiding the war or running away from the war. Arjuna's weakness (a common phenomenon with the human beings except the enlightened) will remain uncovered till every word of the Lord is felt.

3. After telling Arjuna some words of warning in the preceding words, now Lord Krishna gives Arjuna some advice in this verse.

क्लैब्यं मा स्म गमः पार्थ नैतत्त्वय्युपपद्यते ।
क्षुद्रं हृदयदौर्बल्यं त्यक्त्वोत्तिष्ठ परन्तप ॥ २- ३ ॥

klaibyam ma sma gamah partha naitat tvayy upapadyate
ksudram hrdaya-daurbalyam tyaktvottistha parantapa 2.3

klaibyam—impotence or unmanliness; *ma--sma—gamah-* yield not; *partha*--O son of Prtha (Arjuna); *na--*not; *etat-* this; *tvayi--* in you; *upadyate--*is befitting; *ksudram--* mean; *hrdaya--*heart; *daurbalyam--*weakness; *tyaktva*—having abandoned; *uttistha*—stand up; *param-tapa--*O scorghers of enemies.

"O Parth (Arjuna; son of Pritha or Kunti or Arjuna's mother)! Yield not to unmanliness (the state of impotence). It does not befit you. O Parantap (scorcher of foes)! Arise, giving up the faintheartedness." II 2.3 II

Arjuna's emotions have overpowered him at the critical juncture (the war is just about to begin). Lord knows that Arjuna is an exceptionally good warrior. Therefore, Lord wants to stabilize Arjuna. For this purpose, Lord has used appropriate words, combining concern and righteous indignation, as follows:

i) **Klaibyam ma smagamah Parth** [O Parth (Arjuna)! Yield not to unmanliness] - Lord is reminding Arjuna that he belongs to an illustrious, royal family, being son of Pritha (Kunti). By these words, Lord wants to cheer up Arjuna a little expressing his concern as well and recalling Arjuna's mother name at the same time. The word "*kailabhyam*" means state of impotence, unmanliness or state of lack of vitality and vigor.

ii) **nai 'tat tvayy upapadyate** (It does not befit you) – lord is reminding Arjuna that his behavior is not befitting (considering his lineage, valor and personal reputation).

iii) **Kshudram, hrdaya daurbalyam tyaktvo uttistha** Parantap (O Parantap! Arise giving up faintheartedness) – Lord is telling Arjuna that his attitude is mean. *Kshudram* also means petty, because it leads to pettiness or it is easy to get over. Another word used is "*hrdaya daurbalyam*." It means "weakness of heart." Arjuna was sitting, broken and sunk, in his chariot. Therefore, Lord asks him to stand up (face up to your problems). Appreciating a person increases his or her strength. Therefore, Lord calls him Parantap i.e. one who scorches his enemies. Lord is reminding him of his great reputation as the scorcher of enemies. This is a reminder that this behavior of Arjuna will tarnish his reputation of being a terror to the enemies.

Lord is dealing with Arjuna psychologically. Lord has given initial tonic (appreciation for his valor and righteous indignation for his unbecoming behavior) to Arjuna to feel normal. This helps him to get composed and feel strengthened. In verses 2 and 3, Lord is trying to buck up (make someone more cheerful) Arjuna. Strength is life. Weakness is death. Lord wants Arjuna to recall his innate strength, the strength that comes from one's inside.

4. Arjuna declines to fight with the reverend (deserving respect) ones.

अर्जुन उवाच ।
कथं भीष्ममहं सङ्ख्ये द्रोणं च मधुसूदन ।
इषुभिः प्रतियोत्स्यामि पूजार्हावरिसूदन ॥ २- ४ ॥

arjuna uvaca
katham bhismam aham sankhye dronam ca madhusudana
isubhih pratiyotsyami pujarhav ari-sudana 2.4

arjunah uvaca--Arjuna said; *katham*--how; *bhismam*--unto Bhisma (gransire); *aham*--I; *sankhye*--in the fight; *dronam*--unto Drona; *ca*--also; *madhu-sudana*--O killer of Madhu; *isubhih*--with arrows; *pratiyotsyami*--shall fight (counterattack); *puja-arhau*—worthy to be worshipped; *ari-sudana*--O destroyer of enemies.

Arjuna said:

"O slayer of Madhu (Krishna), O slayer of foes, how can I shoot in battle arrows at men like Bhisma and Drona, who are worthy of being worshipped by me?" II 2-4 II

Lord Krishna says in preceding verses that it will be faint-heartedness and cowardice to avoid war at that juncture. Arjuna raises this question to reply Krishna. According to Arjuna faint-heartedness and cowardice are not the reasons for shrinking from fight. By this question, Arjuna asserts that fight means that he will have to use arrows against those whom he should worship with flowers. It should be kept in mind that Lord Krishna knew it already. That is why he places Arjuna's chariot in front of Bhisma and Drona and said to Arjuna deliberately "Behold, O Partha, the assembled Kurus." Lord already had the inkling of Arjuna's response. Arjuna had immense respect for his seniors. Arjuna particularly used two adjectives for Lord Krishna as follows:

i) Slayer of Madhu – Lord Krishna has killed demons like Madhu. By addressing like this, Arjuna wants to say that Krishna has killed demons and not the teachers yet.

ii) Slayer of foes – Lord Krishna killed numerous enemies in his life. By addressing like this, Arjuna wants to say that Krishna has killed only his foes and not friends, well-wishers and teachers.

Bhisma is great-grand father. Drona is Arjuna's teacher. Arjuna presents his difficulties to Lord Krishna i.e. how he can use sharp weapons against those who are worthy of being worshipped.

5. In this verse, Arjuna continues giving his arguments for his inclination not to fight.

गुरूनहत्वा हि महानुभावान श्रेयो भोक्तुं भैक्ष्यमपीह लोके ।
हत्वार्थकामांस्तु गुरूनिहैव भुञ्जीय भोगान् रुधिरप्रदिग्धान् ॥ २- ५ ॥

gurun ahatva hi mahanubhavan sreyo bhoktum bhaiksyam apiha loke
hatvartha-kamams tu gurun ihaiva bhunjiya bhogan rudhira-pradigdhan 2.5

gurun--the teachers; *ahatva*—insteas of slaying; *hi*--indeed; *maha-anubhavan*—most noble souls; *sreyah*-- it is better; *bhoktum*—to eat; *bhaiksyam*--begging; *api*--even; *iha*—here (in this life); *loke*--in this world; *hatva*—having slain; *artha*--*kaman*— wealth and desires; *tu*-- indeed; *gurun*--superiors;

iha—here (in this world); *eva*-- also; *bhunjiya*--has to enjoy; *bhogan*--enjoyments; *rudhira*--blood; *pradigdhan*--tainted with.

"It would, indeed, be better, to live on alms in this world than to slay these high-souled gurus (teachers), because by killing them I would enjoy wealth and pleasures stained with their blood." II 5 II

Arjuna is justifying the change (not to fight) overcoming him by giving various arguments as follows:

i) ***gurun ahatva hi mahanubhavan sreyo bhoktum bhaiksyam api ihi loke*** (it is indeed far better to eat beggar's bread in this world than to slay slay these great-souled masters) –

Lord has deliberately stopped the chariot in front of Bhisma and Drona, because Arjuna was very much attached to both of them. Arjuna's reaction cannot be understood without a bit of knowledge about these two personalities. Arjuna was a darling of both of them since childhood. Bhisma was the very embodiment of continence (practice of controlling your desire for sex or conserving vital energy; there is no parallel to Bhisma, most reverend personality, in the world in this respect). His self-denial and lifelong austerity stands matchless even now. The preceptor Drona is versatile genius and a man of right conduct. Arjuna owes his skill in archery to this teacher. Arjuna has always been holding these people of merit in high veneration. "To treat them suddenly as ruthless enemies" has become well-nigh (almost) impossible to the sincere fellow like Arjuna. Arjuna sees them now face to face, ready to fight and, for the first time, feels **the weight of the reality and the dire consequences thereof.** In this emotionally charged state, Arjuna feels that begging for living in this world will be better than slaying these honored teachers (Both were teachers in respective fields); Bhisma taught the values of life and family traditions and Drona taught the archery to Arjuna).

ii) ***hatva arthkamams tu gurun ih aiva bhunjiya bhogan*** rudhirapradigdhan (By killing these respectable teachers, I shall be enjoying here the pleasures of wealth and desirable things drenched in their blood) - Arjuna has got emotionalized. He feels that by slaying these teachers, he would only enjoy world-delights smeared in blood of respected seniors. Arjuna has used the word "rudhrapradigdhan," which means stained in blood. This thought brings to mind the blood stained pages of history, the woes of women, the cries of children, the tales of calamity and different hues of oppression and injustice in its myriad form. All these descriptions make one realize that no one delights in the blood stained conquests. Arjuna has used another important word here i.e. 'arthkamastu'. He wants to say that these people are respectable even though they are attached to desire and wealth.

Arjuna's reaction is very common. It happens when one gets overpowered by emotions. According to "Shanti Parva" in Mahabharta, even Yudhistra, the senior most brother among Padvas, also got emotionalized on seeing Bhisma, Drona and Salya and walked towards the opposite side unarmed to touch the feet of Bhisma, Drona and Salya and also to request them to come to his side. The seniors could not accept Yudhistra's request, as they were under obligations of Kaurvas. They were all getting salary and food from Kaurvas and for this reason they were ready to die for Kaurvas. This explains that in this world "desire and wealth" cause extreme bondage.

Arjuna is placing undue emphasis on the seniors being his teachers. He is forgetting that, **according to Hindu scriptures**, a teacher, who is out for his own gain or who upholds adharma (un-righteousness), deserves to be fought, and, if necessary, killed.

6. In this verse also, Arjuna continues presenting the reasons for change in his stand.

न चैतद्विद्मः कतरन्नो गरीयो यद्वा जयेम यदि वा नो जयेयुः ।
यानेव हत्वा न जिजीविषामस्तेऽवस्थिताः प्रमुखे धार्तराष्ट्राः ॥ २- ६ ॥

na caitad vidmah kataran no gariyo yad va jayema yadi va no jayeyuh
yan eva hatva na jijivisamas te 'vasthitah pramukhe dhartarastrah 2.6

na--not; *ca*--and; *etat*--this; *vidmah*--(we) know; *katarat*--which; *nah*—for us; *gariyah*--better; *yat*-- that; *va*-- or; *jayema*—we should conquer; *yadi*--if; *va*--or; *nah*--us; *jayeyuh*—they should conquer; *yan*--those; *eva*-- even; *hatva*—having slain; *na*-- not; *jijivisamah*—we wish to live; *te*--those; *avasthitah*—(are) standing; *pramukhe*--in face; *dhartarastrah*--the sons of Dhrtarastra

"Nor do we know which is better for us i.e. whether they conquer us or we conquer them; before us stand the sons of Dhritrastrah, whom having slain, we should not care to live." II 2-6 II

Arjuna is on the horns of dilemma i.e. he is unable to choose between the two unpleasant choices. What is precisely Arjuna's dilemma? He does not know whether Pandavas will win or Kaurvas will win. He does not know whether he should fight or refuse to fight. If he runs away from the battle field, he does not do justice to duty expected of a kshatriya (warrior-clan). Arjuna raises two points in this verse:

i) *yadva jayema yadi va no jayeyuh* (whether we will win or they will win) – Arjuna finds it difficult to forecast the probable final result of the war i.e. whether the Pandvas will win or the Kaurvas will win. Arjuna finds enemy equally formidable. The point raised only indicates the doubtful mental state of Arjuna. It was not in his nature to doubt. He had faced in disguise alone (protecting small son of Virat) all the Kaurvas, Bhisma, Drona, Karna put together, when the Kaurvas attacked kingdom of king Virat in his absence for grabbing Virat's cattle-wealth. It only means that there is something amiss (wrong) with Arjuna.

ii) *Yan eva hatva na jijitvisamas te avasthitah pramukhe dhartarastrah* (Those very sons of Dharrastrah, killing whom we do not wish to live, stand in the enemy ranks) – By this statement Arjuna means to say that even if the success of Pandvas is guaranteed, it will mean the slaughter of the whole family i.e. in either case the happiness cannot be dreamt of. In other words, Arjuna is indicating the futility of war at this juncture when the war is just about to begin.

One learns very good lesson from this verse. There is always uncertainty in life on every step. One cannot ever be sure of final outcome i.e. uncertainty has to be faced. How is this uncertainty to be faced? A righteous war has to be fought regardless of victory or defeat. Again that inner connectivity with the "eternal existence" within becomes relevant. In the perfect symphony, no one note is final, yet each note reflects or connects with the Infinite. It will make a difference, if, instead of raising doubt, one starts asking "Does my note in singing reach the singer of the "Eternal Melodies?." Where is the harp-string or note in singing, which touches "the Master"? We should ask instead of doubting.

7. Arjuna's confusion reaches its climax and in this verse he surrenders to Lord Krishna for guidance.

कार्पण्यदोषोपहतस्वभावः पृच्छामि त्वां धर्मसम्मूढचेताः ।
यच्छ्रेयः स्यान्निश्चितं ब्रूहि तन्मे शिष्यस्तेऽहं शाधि मां त्वां प्रपन्नम् ॥ २- ७ ॥

karpanya-dosopahata-svabhavah prcchami tvam dharma-sammudha-cetah
yac chreyah syan niscitam bruhi tan me sisyas te 'ham sadhi mam tvam
prapannam 2.7

karpanya--miserly; *dosa*--weakness; *upahata*--being inflicted by; *sva-bhavah*--characteristics; *prcchami*--I ask; *tvam*--unto You; *dharma*--*sammudha*--*cetah*—with a mind in confusion about duty based on righteousness as per divine will; *yat*--which; *sreyah*--good; *syat*--may be; *niscitam*--decisively; *bruhi*—tell say; *tat*--that; *me*--unto me; *sisyah*--disciple; *te*--Your; *aham*--I am; *sadhi*—teach or just instruct; *mam*--me; *tvam*--unto You; *prapannam*—taken refuge or surrendered.

"My inborn nature has been overwhelmed by bane (something that troubles) of faintheartedness and I am confused as regards my Dharma (or *svadharma* i.e. duty in particular circumstances); so i am asking you; tell me what will prove beneficial to me. I am your disciple; teach me who has surrendered to you." II 2-7 II

In this verse, Arjuna is explaining his position more clearly than he did at the end of chapter number one. Now Arjuna is conceding (accepting) that all is not well with him. Hitherto, Arjuna was not calling a spade a spade i.e. he did not speak the truth. He was experiencing a sort of uncertainty and fear somewhere within. That is why he was trembling. Even Gandiva was getting out of his grip. He lacked conviction (very strong belief or opinion). When Lord asked him to stand up and get rid of faintheartedness in preceding verses, he found confidence to speak. Now he is accepting the truth and coming out with it very clearly as follows:

i) *Karpanyadosopahat svbhavah* (nature overpowered with faintheartedness) – Now arjuna is accepting that his nature (full of valor) appears (to him) to have been weighed down by feeble-mindedness i.e. he is unable to think clearly and decide what to do. He is accepting that "poorness of spirit" seems to have smitten away his true heroic nature. This is what he was trying to conceal up till now.

ii) **Dharmsammudha cetah** [with (my) understanding confused about duty] – Actually word "*Dharma*" means divine code of conduct as per law of nature. It is identification of righteousness as per law of nature at the level of consciousness i.e. beyond level of intelligence or "individual discriminating faculty of an individual." "*Dharma*" is not man-made. It is universal and it is felt by divine grace in silence at the level of consciousness. Awareness of "*Dharma*" is a feeling and it does not necessarily come in words. It is interpretation of righteousness as per law of nature as per "divine providence; a force that controls the universe." It is experienced by an individual in the form of a feeling. It is interpretation of righteousness based on individual experience very deep within. "*Dharma*" does not need words or a particular language. An individual following "*Dharma*" does not shake. The interpretation of "Dharma" by someone in "human form" is religion and religion may suffer from human bias. "Dharma" is free from any limitation being righteousness as per law of nature. An individual following Dharma becomes embodiment of conviction (strong belief). What one requires for "dharma" is truthfulness and sincerity. Arjuna accepts here that he is not in a position to discriminate between righteousness and unrighteousness. This is the real difficulty of Arjuna. This is what made the hero shake like an ordinary individual. One who is having this difficulty and abides by it is rather a lucky man. The realization of this difficulty is a mark of divine grace for spiritual progress.

iii) *Yac chreyah syat nischitam bruhi tan me* (I entreat you, say definitely what is good for me) - **The good is different from the pleasant.** It is of great importance to understand this in life. The good takes one towards liberation (mukti). The pleasant binds one to the cycles of birth and death. The pleasant takes towards the world. The good takes towards the Divinity (eternity, immortality, immanence or present everywhere). Whenever there is a choice between the good and the pleasant, one should choose the good and not the pleasant. This is what Arjuna is doing now. He has got an inkling of his weakness. He now finds himself at the cross-roads between the good and the pleasant. Arjuna has used a beautiful Sanskrit word "sreyas" which means that which promises the good. Learning, culture, wealth, wife, children, kingdom are all sources of enjoyment in this world. They come in the category of "preyas" and not "sreyas or the good." They are of no good when one suffers from agony of "catastrophe (terrible event in which there is a loss of destruction and many people die)," crisis of conscience or when one is conscience–stricken i.e. when one feels guilty at a level of awareness beyond intelligence. Now Arjuna is gaining composure. He is realizing his limitation. He is requesting Lord to guide him towards the good and not the pleasant. This frame of mind is pre-requisite to the attainment of the spiritual enlightenment.

v) *Sisyas te aham sadhi mam tvam prapanni* (I am your disciple and seek refuge in you) – Now Arjuna has surrendered. Arjuna is following the Vedic precept "Go and seek the knowledge of '*Dharma*' from a guru." Arjuna becomes Krishna's disciple. He asks Krishna to teach him his duty which represents adherence to righteousness as per law of nature or which is according to providential (force that governs the universe) will. The entire Gita is the result of this prayer, the answer to this request of Arjuna. There is one thing very significant here. Now Arjuna does not want knowledge. **The man of action (Arjuna) wants to know the law of action, "dharma"** i.e. how one should adhere to "righteous action in conformity with providential (force that governs the universe) will." It is very beautiful. Arjuna does not want success. He does not want to know the secret of life or the world. He wants to know dharma, the law, the one vast rule of living in the divine and acting from the awareness of that consciousness. Dharma is not "disinterested performance of duty alone." One turns towards "dharma" when: i) one experiences concept of duty ending in the collapse of intellectual and moral considerations and ii) existence in the world loses its meaning, purpose and direction. Dharma means deciphering divine life and listening to the "Supreme" in the indescribable experience at the level of conscience. Dharma means taking refuge in the Supreme alone at the level of consciousness and operating from there for welfare of the world. It is blessedness to yearn for 'Dharma' in life.

Almost all confront doubts in life at one point of time or the other. One should feel it. One should not shy away from it. The consciousness of imperfection means that soul is alive. So long as consciousness or awareness of doubt is there, one can improve as the living body heals. This condition should be termed as crisis of contrition (when one feels sorry for something bad that one has done). This is a commonplace experience. This struggle with darkness (the effect of ignorance) continues until light (divine knowledge) fills one's whole being i.e. enlightenment happens. What should one do? One should do what Arjuna is doing. Put the doubts at the altar i.e. before the spiritual master. The only solution for this condition (crisis of contrition) is divine knowledge which comes from a spiritual master (who has directly experienced this divine current) only. This higher guidance always comes when one surrenders everything to the divine which a spiritual master or Guru represents. Everybody cannot surrender. Unless one is strong, one cannot surrender. Arjuna has surrendered. Surrender is the start of the spiritual journey. Surrender means being conscious about one's limitation and committing to abide by the wisdom of spiritual master without reservation. For this reason greatest care is to be exercised in selecting a Guru (spiritual master).

8. Arjuna fully expresses his mind to Krishna.

न हि प्रपश्यामि ममापनुद्याद् यच्छोकमुच्छोषणमिन्द्रियाणाम् ।
अवाप्य भूमावसपत्नमृद्धं राज्यं सुराणामपि चाधिपत्यम् ॥ २- ८ ॥

na hi prapasyami mamapanudyad yac chokam ucchosanam indriyanam
avapya bhumav asapatnam rddham rajyam suranam api cadhipatyam 2.8

na-no; *hi*--indeed; *prapasyami*--I see; *mama*--my; *apanudyat*—would remove; *yat*--that; *sokam*--grief; *ucchosanam*--drying up; *indriyanam*--of the senses; *avapya*—having obtained; *bhumau*--on the earth; *asapatnam*-- unrivalled; *rddham*--prosperous; *rajyam*--dominion; *suranam*—over the Gods (refer to God an Gods in introduction); *api*--even; *ca*--and; *adhipatyam*—lordship or supremacy.

"I do not see anything that will remove the grief that parches my senses; even I should gain unrivalled prosperous monarchy on earth or even sovereignty over the celestials (related to sky or heaven) or Gods in heaven." II 2-8 II

Arjuna has lost his poise. Enjoyment neither in this world nor in any other world is a remover of sorrow. An individual becomes a slave to enjoyment during its existence and gets separated from it during its cessation. For this type of "inner crisis" one needs divine wisdom only. Arjuna finds no remedy to his inner turmoil. He admits that the prosperous kingdom of earth and the sovereignty even over the celestial bodies cannot relieve him of his grief. One thing is very important here. Arjuna is showing dispassion towards enjoyment. This is actually a qualification which takes an individual towards the highest good. Initially Arjuna put forth different type of arguments. He was trying to hide away depression and conflict within him by saying that the living and the departed will be adversely affected if war was waged. Now he is unfolding his real condition to the benign (kind, gentle and not causing any harm) protector without reservation. This will earn him the grace of the Lord.

This must be noted that grief of Arjuna is the result of egotism and ignorance of the "Truth; the Supreme Eternal Existence," which is the cause of all that is. He is suffering due to excessive concerns for the life of his seniors and relatives. He is not at all concerned or even aware of the love for the mankind.

9. Now Sanjay explains what happened after Arjuna finished speaking.

सञ्जय उवाच ।
एवमुक्त्वा हृषीकेशं गुडाकेशः परन्तप ।
न योत्स्य इति गोविन्दमुक्त्वा तूष्णीं बभूव ह ॥ २- ९ ॥

sanjaya uvaca
evam uktva hrsikesam gudakesah parantapah
na yotsya iti govindam uktva tusnim babhuva ha 2.9

sanjayah uvaca--Sanjaya said; *evam*--thus; *uktva*—having spoken; *hrsikesam*--unto (Krishna), the master of the senses; *gudakesah*—conqueror of sleep (Arjuna), the master at curbing ignorance; *parantapah*--the chastiser of the enemies; *na yotsye*--I shall not fight; *iti*--thus; *govindam*—unto the giver of pleasure (Krishna); *uktva*—having said; *tusnim*--silent; *babhuva ha*-- became.

Sanjay said:

"After having spoken thus to Hrishikesa (Lord of the senses or Krishna), Gudakesha (the conqueror of sleep), Parantap (the destroyer of the foes or Arjuna) said to Govinda (Krishna) "I will not fight" and became silent." II2-9 II

This verse is self-explanatory. Arjuna refused to fight and became silent. Two adjectives, used by Sanjay in this verse, are very good:

i) **Gudakesha** - This adjective has been used by Sanjay for Arjuna i.e. Arjuna is one who has conquered sleep. This shows that Arjuna is not an ordinary warrior. He is widely known for his control and discipline.

ii) **Govinda** – This adjective has been used for Lord Krishna. It means that Krishna is like "cow-herd" or "shepherd." Arjuna is like a cow, which is on the path stubbornly refusing to move and Krishna will take it along the path.

This verse has to be properly understood both as to its meaning and context. Arjuna understands his weakness and he still accepts surrendering to it (weakness). He lapses into silence to justify his defiance (refusal to obey) on ethical and rational ground. Actually, Arjuna, at this juncture, is a victim of his egoistic being. He is in the influence of his revolting ignorance and un-chastened (un-apologetic) emotions. This is commonplace experience. Only higher knowledge or divine wisdom can transcend these egoistic motives of action. One feels bound by one's own weaknesses and somehow one continues with it as well. At the same time, one thing is very clear. He has surrendered without reservation and he is begging for guidance from Lord Krishna to get rid of this emotional turmoil, which has almost crippled him.

He has asked the teacher to advise him but he has given his own decision before the teacher has spoken any word. This only makes the task of a teacher more difficult. One thing is good. Arjuna has gone into silence and voice of truth can be heard only in silence.

10. Sanjay continues speaking in this verse.

तमुवाच हृषीकेशः प्रहसन्निव भारत ।
सेनयोरुभयोर्मध्ये विषीदन्तमिदं वचः ॥ २- १० ॥

tam uvaca hrsikesah prahasann iva bharata
senayor ubhayor madhye visidantam, idam vacah 2.10

tam-- to him; *uvaca*--said; *hrsikesah*--the master of the senses, Krishna; *prahasan*--smiling; *iva*—as it were; *bharata*--O Dhrtarastra, descendant of Bharata; *senayoh*--of the armies; *ubhayoh*--of both parties; *madhye*—in the middle; *visidantam*—despondent; *idam*--this; *vacah*--words.

"O Bhartha (King Dhritarashtra)! To him (for Arjuna) thus depressed in the middle of two armies, Hrishikesa (Lord Krishna), smiling as it were, spoke these words." II2-10 II

It was a very precarious (not safe or dangerous) situation. They were standing between the two armies and war was about to start. Lord Krishna has got tremendous control over the situation. He is not confused like Arjuna. First he smiles. That shows his tremendous control. That is the reflection of yoga, the various disciplines (physical, mental, emotional and spiritual), which restore a being to his or her original nature. That shows that He is the master and he is in command of the situation. The first reflection of yoga is that one is not unnerved by the changing situation even if they take alarming proportions. This type of spontaneous smile is not possible for an individual who is distressed. For one who is master of yoga, this smile comes from within. This smile is the reflection of peace at the core within. This smile is the harbinger of the divine knowledge, the sovereign remedy of all the evils of the mundane existence. Only Krishna, the Lord of Yoga can smile like that in that utterly grim situation. Arjuna is depressed. Lord is smiling. That is the difference between the wise and the ignorant. This is how the brave and the expert deal with a situation. This shows Krishna's composure, knowledge confidence and intuitive ability to perceive a situation.

11. Lord Krishna starts imparting divine knowledge (the Gita's philosophy; central thoughts of the Gita; knowledge relating to the self) to Arjuna from this verse.

श्रीभगवानुवाच ।
अशोच्यानन्वशोचस्त्वं प्रज्ञावादांश्च भाषसे ।
गतासूनगतासूंश्च नानुशोचन्ति पण्डिताः ॥ २- ११ ॥

sri-bhagavan uvaca
asocyan anvasocas tvam prajna-vadams ca bhasase
gatasun agatasums ca nanusocanti panditah 2.11

sri-bhagavan uvaca—the blessed Lord (Krishna) said; *asocyan*—those who should not be grieved for; *anvasocah*--you are lamenting grieving over; *tvam*--you; *prajna-vadan*—words of wisdom; *ca*--and; *bhasase*—you speak; *gatasun*—the dead; *agatasun*—the living; *ca*--and; *na*--; *anusocanti*—grieve not; *panditah*--the wise.

Blessed Lord said:

"You grieve for those who should not be grieved for; yet you spell words of wisdom. The wise grieve neither for the living nor for the dead." II 2-11 II

Arjuna refused to fight. He gave a lot of arguments to justify his stand such as sin of killing the kinsmen (svajanam; close relatives) for greed of kingdom, the impact of war on the living, the dead and on the coming generations and possibility of vice becoming rampant after war. Now from this verse Lord Krishna starts answering Arjuna as follows:

i) ***Asocyan anvasocas tvam prajnavadams ca bhasase*** (You grieve for those who should not be grieved for) - According to Lord Krishna, Arjuna is grieving for those who should not be grieved for? Arjuna's main concern was for Bhishma (Great-grand father who imparted to Arjuna values of life; Bhishma too had particular affection for Arjuna) and Drona (one, who taught Arjuna archery; Arjuna was a darling of Drona as well).From a worldly point of view, Arjuna's behavior is reasonable. How is Lord Krishna saying that Bhishma and Drona should not be grieved for? No one, with worldly knowledge alone, will be able to understand the meaning and basis of Lord's remark. Actually Lord's remark is based on "general Aryan culture" in which Arjuna was educated and brought up. This remark is based on more intimate knowledge or deeper truth of our being. This remark emanates from the basic ideas about the nature and meaning of existence and reality. The source of this remark is the fundamental or core thinking of Hinduism. This is what one grows with in India. One may not be able to spell out what it is but one grows with it somehow even when one is in infancy in mother's lap listening to mother's tales, discussions and rituals. In India, one cannot altogether remain away from this thinking. This is the philosophic, moral and ethical basis of our culture. What is it?

Each being has two dimensions i.e. physical dimension and spiritual dimension. Our physical dimension undergoes changes. It is ever changing. Spiritual dimension does not change. An individual basically is a spiritual being in a physical dimension.

Arjuna's grief is due to lack of true wisdom relating to spiritual dimension. Arjuna is identifying his uncle and teachers etc, based on their body, mind, senses and ego i.e. based on their physical beings, which alone are affected by old age, death, pleasure, pain, hunger thirst, desire and disappointment. Arjuna says "If I kill them … …." How can he (Arjuna) kill that which cannot be killed? Arjuna gave his comments based on physical dimensions of beings i.e. bodies of Bhisma and Drona. Arjuna is confining his concern to bodies (forms and names known as Bhisma and Drona). Lord's comment is based on spiritual dimension of beings. Of the two (physical dimension or the spiritual dimension), spiritual dimension is of substance, relevance and continuing in nature. Physical dimension keeps changing and getting destroyed. Arjuna is grieving for those (physical dimensions or forms and names known as Bhisma and Drona) who should not be grieved for? Of the truth (undying reality in a being) and untruth (that which keeps on changing and dying), one should go for the truth (which always stays) and not the untruth (which always goes away). Arjuna is concerned about the physical bodies, which have to die anyway.

Both Bhishma and Drona were matured individualities having insight into the mystery of life and death. They both deserved respect. They both knew the real reasons for war (relieving society of growing unrighteousness; attempt was made to strip off a woman in an open court; the princes were denied their due; attempts were made on the life of princes; Virat's kingdom was attacked in his absence without provocation for the greed of animal wealth). They were pure souls. They knew they were on wrong side. They knew that their death was imminent in the war. Still they refused to fight from the side of Pandvas, whom they loved. They came to battlefield to sacrifice themselves for Duryodhna for the Kauravas were paying for their existence. They came to battlefield to redeem themselves of their indebtedness to Kauravas. Arjuna lacked true wisdom. He did not at all consider this higher aspect of individualities (or spiritual bodies) known as Bhishma and Drona. He only thought of their physical bodies which they themselves came to sacrifice in order to be free from indebtedness to Kauravas.

Arjuna is looking at the lower dimensions of the individualities (i.e. forms and names known as Bhishma and Drona) ignoring the higher dimensions relating to the same personalities (i.e. those undying dimensions of these personalities which made them appear in the battlefield to be killed knowingly). That is why Lord says "You are grieving for those who should not be grieved for. Yet you are using the words of wisdom." By this statement, Lord replied to the falsification in the arguments given by Arjuna. He came to war knowing pretty well already everything (every word) that he spoke. Actually he got unduly emotionalized and lost his poise. This is not expected of a role model in a society, who has come to the battlefield to relieve the society of those who were hell-bent (determined to do something that others do not approve of) upon perpetuating unrighteousness.

ii) *Gatasun agatasums ca na anusocanti panditah* (the wise grieve neither for the living nor for the dead) - Lord has used the term "*Panditah*." Here it refers to those wise people who know the mystery of life and death. Death is relevant to physical dimension only, which is perishable and changing in nature. Death means separation of spiritual dimension from the five primordial elements (earth, water, fire, air and sky). As we change old vehicle, the spiritual dimension within changes physical vehicle (physical body) through death. For the wise, it is as simple as that. The "reality of a being or the continuing entity in a being" is spiritual dimension, which forever remains the same. The wise i.e. those who know the mystery of life and death grieve neither for the living nor for the dead. Why is it so? Physical dimension has to end anyway. Whatever begins has to end somewhere. Why should one unduly weep and wail for it? Nothing whatsoever can ever happen to spiritual dimension. Our thinking, our concern, all our tears and all our wisdom are of no avail, so far as spiritual dimension is concerned. Destiny (i.e. fate or the course of events to be followed based on the "Cosmic intelligence; divine logic; that force which ensures order or destruction in the universe") will take its course. Arjuna forgot about the eternal component within each being. He forgot that our relations in the present life are the result of past actions. When a body dies, all relations end here. Nothing of the physical dimension goes beyond death. When one takes another body, again new relations crop up like new leave in the spring season. Arjuna is grieving because he is treating the impermanent as the permanent. Those who know this difference between the real and unreal or truth and untruth or self (spiritual dimension in a being) and not-self (physical dimension in a being) grieve neither for the living nor for the dead. For them, the living is temporary phenomenon and the death is an event relating to physical body, which goes away for good never to come back. This awareness of truth and untruth in a being precludes (to make something impossible) an individual from developing uncalled for infatuation (unreasonably strong feeling of love that develops only for a short time) with the living. Arjuna is victim of his failure to decipher between real and unreal and love (unlimited love; love without limitations) and infatuation. Lord is bringing Arjuna's attention to distinction between the self (enveloped in ego in individualized-self or jiva) and the body.

12. Each one in existence has eternal element (divine component within).

न त्वेवाहं जातु नासं न त्वं नेमे जनाधिपाः ।
न चैव न भविष्यामः सर्वे वयमतः परम् ॥ २- १२ ॥

*na tv evaham jatu nasam na tvam neme janadhipah
na caiva na bhavisyamah sarve vayam atah param 2.12*

na--not; *tu*--indeed; *eva*-- alsocertainly; *aham*--I; *jatu*—at any time; *na*--not; *asam*—was; *na*--not; *tvam*--yourself; *na*--not; *ime*--these; *jana-adhipah*—rulers of men; *na*--not; *ca*--and; *eva*-- also; *na*--not; *bhavisyamah*—shall be; *sarve*--all; *vayam*--we; *atah param*--hereafter.

"There was never a time when these monarchs, you and I did not exist; nor shall we cease to be in future." II 2-12 II

This one verse expresses the sum total of all that divine knowledge is. In preceding verse, it was brought out that each being has two dimensions i.e. physical dimension and spiritual dimension. Arjuna was focusing on the physical dimensions i.e. forms and names known as Bhishma and Drona. Lord is focusing on the spiritual dimension in this verse. Each being has an eternal element (divine component) which always has been, which is and which will always be. It means that Krishna, Arjuna and all the kings were always there in the past. They are still there. They will never cease to be. What does it mean? How is one to accept it? What is the basis for this?

This statement of Lord Krishna is based on postulate (a statement that is accepted as truth and forms the basis of a theory; it is believed to be true but not proven). This is not the statement of an individual. This is based on the universal truth which has been passed on from time immemorial in different stages to different recipients. In yore (gone by days), our *rishis* (those adept in yoga and divine wisdom) experimented with truth in life and experienced with awareness this universal truth. All our Vedas, Upnishads and ancient scriptures only confirmed this truth. What is this? This is known as "Sanatan dharma; Eternal Righteousness."

One visual presentation of it, in the form of a flow chart, is given in introduction under the heading "Cosmic Eternal Flow" along with notes dealing with it in detail. There is a "Supreme Universal Eternal Energy," which is eternal, indestructible pervading everywhere in everything. It manifests in all beings and validates all existences. This universal energy only validates. It does not do anything. This universal energy is accompanied by a kinetic energy, a sort of inbuilt divine software to carry on the functions of generation, preservation and destruction in the universe. Birth is the result of process of generation, existence as a being is the result of process of preservation and death is a result of process of destruction. When a fraction of Supreme Energy merges with this Kinetic Energy (Divine Software; lower nature), ego emerges and an individualized self (divinity enveloped with ego or some impressions due to connection with that kinetic energy or nature) comes into existence.

Anything that exists has two aspects i.e. i) divinity (i.e. that divine essence, which is immortal, eternal and immanent) within; it is the spiritual dimension of a being; it is always free from the limitations of time or past, present and future; it is beyond death and destruction. This divine component remains "as a separate being under the cover of ego"; If ego is not there, then the divine component merges with the Supreme Energy and exists in Supreme as indistinguishable part of it. In brief, it always remains (unaffected by past, present and future); ii) the individualized self with soul or Atma veiled under it i.e. divine component + ego + impression due to contact with kinetic energy. This individualized self gets individual intelligence as gift from contact with the divine component; being (one who exits) with a body develops into an individual. All these thoughts are implicit in the term "Sanatan Dharma; eternal Righteousness."

Lord says in this verse "Never was there a time when I was not, nor thou nor these lords of men (kings) …" One initially finds it difficult to assimilate these thoughts. The Supreme Reality is eternal, universal and immanent i.e. present everywhere. It expresses into multitudinous entities of universe through "Higher nature (refer to point no. 13 under the heading "Preparing to feel the Bhagwad Gita)." The Eternal Supreme is one only. It is always there as "Un-manifested Supreme Universal Eternal Self" and also perceived to be manifested as individual self or deluded self. The individualized-self changes physical bodies, undergoing births and deaths. "The eternal existence," perceived to be relating to the individual, always remains. It merges in the Supreme Reality at the end of "dream-like worldly existence" at the dawn of divine knowledge, as the space within a pitcher merges with room space, after the pitcher is broken. Formlessness gains forms when it is viewed with reference to time and cause and effect relationship. When one transcends (looks beyond time, cause, effect, life of habits or any so called limitation) the view beyond these limitations, there is no form. There is only "formlessness, eternal unfolding of joy, eternal perfection, eternal love-unlimited." The statement of the lord is based on this premise that the "Truth within or Eternal Existence within an entity" never dies or always remains. One cannot "feel" this aspect (this impact of transcendence beyond limitations) of an individual, till one is alive to the "Spiritual Dimension" in a being. Arjuna was ignorant of this aspect.

Arjuna is worried about the possible death of Bhishma and Drona because he is obsessed with physical dimension only. He is not aware of the spiritual dimensions or divine components of Bhishma and Drona in them. Only bodies of Bhishma and Drona can be destroyed in the war. But these bodies (being physical dimension) will be destroyed anyway one day. That is the meaning of Lord's statement. Arjuna is grieving for the perishable bodies of Bhishma and Drona, which should not be grieved for. Bodies will definitely get destroyed one day. The divine components of Bhishma and Drona will always remain either as part of their individual selves (selves with ego) or as indistinguishable and integral part of the Supreme Universal Energy.

Arjuna, Lord Krishna and even the relatives, will not cease to be after war i.e. "the divine components within all will continue to exist" either in the present body or in any other body or as integral indistinguishable part of the Supreme Eternal Energy. Svetasvatara Upnishad proclaims *"We are all amrtasya putra (children of immortality)."* We will always remain either as self in a being covered under the ignorance or as integral, indistinguishable part of the Supreme i.e. spiritual dimension of a being cannot be done away with. Arjuna grief is due to ignorance of this "divine dimension of a being."

What is the message of this verse? Lord wants to bring attention of Arjuna to "life after death" or the perpetual existence of our divine components either in selves (i.e. divinity with ego and impressions) or as indistinguishable integral part of the Supreme. Each one of us has "**that something deathless**" within. The perspective of an individual immediately undergoes changes when immortality aspect is taken in view. What is Arjuna wailing or grieving for? It is for the bodies of Bhisma, Drona and others, which are "destined" to be destroyed one day. That is precisely what Lord is telling Arjuna. Before we set our hearts too much upon anything in this world, it is expected of us, being human beings, to examine whether we are aware of the "deathlessness" within each one of us. This very awareness of "deathlessness within" enlivens us or changes our perspective and makes us fearless.

There is one thing very beautiful, behind the scene here at this juncture. It has been focused in

Mahabharata not here. The Gita is the dialogue in the battle field. Arjuna is worried about Bhishma and Drona. But, Bhishma and Drona are not worried knowing pretty well the imminent defeat of kaurvas and their own death, as Lord Krishna (the embodiment of the Supreme Being) was with Arjuna. This fearlessness emanates (comes) naturally from awareness of deathlessness within. Awareness within of this deathlessness is the central message of this verse. They have come to sacrifice their lives to redeem themselves of indebtedness to Kaurvas. Why is it so? They both (bhishma and Drona) are like sages. They know the mystery of life and death and the way to prepare for fullness of eternal life. They had the divine knowledge. That is why they are not afraid of death. They have deliberately come to die to free themselves from indebtedness to Kaurvas, who provided for sustenance of their existences. Lord Krishna has started imparting on Arjuna divine knowledge (mystery of truth and untruth on every step in everything and every being) from this verse only. It makes a difference to be aware of "eternal origin existence and far-destiny."

13. In the preceding verse, Lord told Arjuna about the awareness of deathlessness within. What is this deathlessness within? Lord elaborates further in this verse.

देहिनोऽस्मिन्यथा देहे कौमारं यौवनं जरा ।
तथा देहान्तरप्राप्तिर्धीरस्तत्र न मुह्यति ॥ २- १३ ॥

dehino 'smin yatha dehe kaumaram yauvanam jara
tatha dehantara-praptir dhiras tatra na muhyati 2.13

dehinah--of the embodied (soul; individualizes eternal existence; refer to discussion in introduction); *asmin*--in this; *yatha*--as; *dehe*--in the body; *kaumaram*-- childhood; *yauvanam*--youth; *jara*--old age; *tatha*--similarly; *deha-antara--praptih*—the attaining of another body; *dhirah*--the firm; *tatra*--thereupon; *na*--not; *muhyati*-- grieves.

"As the indweller within (the soul within the body with divine component) experiences childhood, youth and old age in the body, similarly "the indweller or soul within the body with divine component" passes to another body. This indweller or soul within the body, which is of steadfast wisdom (divine component is the store house of divine wisdom), is not deluded (confused). It (soul) undergoes change of body as naturally as it witnesses childhood, youth and old age)." II 2-13 II

Understanding this statement of the Lord requires exposure to some background, which both Krishna and Arjuna have taken for granted, as everybody those days knew these thoughts. What is this indweller within? What is soul? What is individualized soul? What is body? What is the connection of indweller, soul, body and the director (Supreme Witness behind all this)? What is this drama (cosmic play; birth, limited existence of indweller in the body and death and repetition of whole cycle once again) all about? These are the questions that our "Indo Aryan philosophy of life and death" deal with. These facts, arising out of these questions, are about the "basic truths" of life, which our rishis, ones adept in yoga and divine knowledge, after experimenting with truth in the utter state of purity and holy ambience, experienced at the level of awareness. Our Vedas, Upnishads and ancient Indian literature, primarily focus on these questions. All through this discussion in the battle field called the Bhagavad Gita, Lord Krishna awakened Arjuna to these facts and the utterly dejected prince was capitulated into the pristine glory of a warrior committed to annihilate unrighteousness in the society. To get the real-intake (feel) of the Gita, first the truths coming out of these questions should be assimilated (understood so much that it can be used).

These thoughts have been dealt with in detail in the symbolic flow chart under the heading "Cosmic

Eternal Flow" in introduction. It is taken up in brief here also. There is one Supreme Eternal Universal Divine Energy. It is not mere energy. Energy does not possess intelligence. It possesses intelligence. It is superior to energies like heat, magnetism, electricity etc. It is called Supreme Consciousness or *Parameswar* or Supreme self or source of all that is. It is beyond caste, creed and religion and even Gods. It (Supreme Self) facilitates functions through Gods (perceived Divinities based on traditions and beliefs). It responds to Gods and religions. It does not have a form or name. It alone exists. It exists either without name and form or through multitudinous varieties in the universe. This alone is "Truth; that which eternally remains." Rest all is untruth or subject to decay and death.

It has a shadow like constant companion Nature (Higher Nature and Lower Nature). Higher Nature is exclusive divine essence i.e. eternal existence. Lower Nature is its software, its kinetic energy. Lower Nature is combination of five primordial elements + three gunas + seen and unseen laws of nature. When the Supreme Eternal Consciousness meets lower nature, ego (feeling of I and mine or feeling of separateness) is born. Ego is the feeling of separateness i.e. I am. This is called individual self or *jiva* (i.e. soul or *atma veiled within* under ego). Individual Self (*jiva*) is combination of divine component (exclusive divinity or soul) and ego. Individual Self has two dimensions i.e. i) divinity within which is eternal and indestructible (exclusive divinity or real self or soul or Atma) and II) ego, cause of ignorance. The divinity (self or real self or atma) impels "the individual self" towards spiritual growth or realization of divine nature or truth i.e. "That divine component" which is not affected by time. Ego pulls "the self or soul or *atma*" towards the world of sufferings towards cycles of birth and death.

After the individual self (egoistic self or *jiva* or being) comes into existence, a group of four evolutes i.e. ego, the un-manifested nature, intelligence and mind work together to form a subtle body or invisible perishable body (four elements), which undergoes so many births and deaths. This subtle body guides the mind to develop 27 elements (refer to the chart in introduction) representing physical body. Physical body lasts for one birth and death. Thus an individual comes into existence with i) veiled eternal existence or soul within (this spiritual body is eternal), ii) subtle body which lasts for several births and deaths and iii) physical body which undergoes only one birth and death.

If an individual is to be considered a factory, then soul (eternal existence within) is the owner or real self. Individualized soul (soul and ego) is the director who runs the factory with ego, un-manifested nature, and intelligence as the senior officers. Mind is the shop floor-in-charge, who gets the work done by 27 elements (Refer to chart in introduction). The soul impels the individual for freedom from ego. Ego pulls the individual towards the world of miseries. This cosmic drama starts with individualized self and ends when the "Real Self or soul" gets out of the clutches of ego.

What is the difference between "Supreme Soul or *Parmatama*" and soul or *Atma*? "Supreme Eternal Universal Divine Reality or Supreme Divine or *Isshwar or Paarmatm*" has sovereignty over nature, gods, castes and religion or anything else in this universe. It exists either without form or with form [i.e. as individualized divinity within the soul of a being (anything that is in existence)]. Exclusive Divinity with reference to cosmos is called "Supreme Soul" and with reference to individual it is called Soul or atma. There is only one soul. With reference to cosmos it is called the Supreme Soul and with reference to individual it is called soul or atma.

When a being is able to get rid of ego and past impressions, the individualized divinity merges in Supreme Being. What is the meaning of merges in the "Supreme Being"? If the being (that which is in existence), after getting rid of ego and past impression dies, "he or she or it" becomes indistinguishable and integral part of the "Supreme Being" or its separate existence is lost. If the being, after getting rid of ego and past impressions still continues in the body, he or she becomes a "liberated individual" i.e. an individual who exists not for self but for world welfare like Sriramakrisna or king Janak. For liberated souls still in the body [i.e. after realization of truth], duality ends and their existence remains for the purpose of *loksangraha* (welfare of the universe).

Now it will be easy to understand and visualize the statement of the Lord. Reference in this verse is to the indweller in the body (soul or exclusive divinity). This indweller within, under the veil of ego, oversees different stages of life i.e. childhood, youth and old age. Everything changes but indweller remains the same. Body is constantly changing. Skin is changing. Blood is changing. Bones are changing. Who is this 'I' in an individual? It is not the physical body. It is the soul, whose divine component (exclusive divinity) remains veiled within the subtle body. This veiled soul witnesses the changes of childhood, youth and old age. Similarly it also witnesses the change over from one body to another body. Childhood passes away. Youth and old age also passes away. Similarly subtle body passes from one body to another body. This is the routine that goes on till the soul gets freedom from ego with divine knowledge. Knowing this routine of soul, the wise do not feel perplexed. They know that death is relevant to physical body alone.

Lord wants to tell Arjuna that death of physical body is a routine of soul's journey towards its final destiny. Death is relevant to body and not the soul (real self), who never dies. Only body dies. Body is impermanent or untruth i.e. a combination of nature which is bound to undergo changes or perish, come what may. The wise [i.e. the one, who have knowledge about the identity of self (or soul or exclusive Divinity or about the truth within] do not grieve at all for the death, which is inevitable to body. Arjuna is grieving about the possible death of Bhishma and Drona. Real self is soul (exclusive Divinity not even individualized soul). How can death occur to souls of Bhishma and Drona? It is not possible. Lord wants to bring the attention of Arjuma on the immortality of the soul. Those who know this (difference between truth and untruth) look at the element of deathless (divinity within) even in death. Such people create fear even for the fear. One such personality in that battle field is of Bhishma.

In this verse Lord Krishna is bringing attention of Arjuna to fundamental facts. Each one of us has got two dimensions i.e. i) perishable bodies including a) subtle body with 4 elements (ego, un-manifested nature, intelligence and mind; this body undergoes several births and deaths and b) physical body with 27 elements; it dies with death (refer to the chart "Cosmic Eternal Flow"; when we see in the mirror we see physical body carrying invisible body within it; physical body is perishable and in the Gita's parlance it is not called self; it is called "non-self" and ii) the real self or atma, which remains under the veil of ego; with divine knowledge this exclusive divinity (soul) transcends all limitations and thereby reveals its own truth and meaning; this is called real self, soul or exclusive divinity; it is eternal.

Arjuna is looking at the scenario from physical dimension alone and that is why he is worried. Arjuna is looking at the "non-selves (physical dimensions)" of Bhisma and Drona and not the true self, the immortal soul, the **"One Universal Root"** from which all the multitudinous variety in universe sprouts. There is one Sun only and there are innumerable rays. Each form in the universe is like one ray of the Sun. Focus of the verse is on immortality of the soul (exclusive eternal existence), which alone is truth. The knower of this distinction of truth and untruth (self and non-self) is called a *dhira* i.e. one who is calm and wise and who sees the real truth (divine component) of the soul of a being beyond materiality, emotions, physical desires and ignorant nature. Grief results from the ignorance of true nature of death.

14. In this verse Lord tells Arjuna about the experiences of the body in the form of feelings.

मात्रास्पर्शास्तु कौन्तेय शीतोष्णसुखदुःखदाः ।
आगमापायिनोऽनित्यास्तांस्तितिक्षस्व भारत ॥ २- १४ ॥

matra-sparsas tu kaunteya sitosna-sukha-duhkha-dah
agamapayino 'nityas tams titiksasva bharata 2.14

matra--sparsah—contact of the sense with the object; *tu*-- indeed; *kaunteya*--O son of Kunti (Arjuna); *sitausna--sukha--duhkha-dah*—producers of cold and heat, pleasure and pain; *agama-- apayinah*—with beginning and end; *anityah*-- impermanent; *tan*-- them; *titiksasva*--just try to tolerate or bear; *bharata*--O descendant of the Bharata dynasty (Arjuna).

"O Son of Kunti (Arjuna)! The 'contacts of senses with their objects (i.e. material touch owing to physical dimension)' creates feelings of heat and cold, pain and pleasure. They come and go and do not last forever, O descendent of Bharat." II 2- 14 II

Lord has used a beautiful word "*matrasparsas.*" It means contacts between the senses and sense objects. That, by which things are measured or by which knowledge of things is obtained, is called "*matra*" in Sanskrit. Here this term is intended to mean all senses including mind. Another word is 'sparsha' i.e. contact. Thus the compound word "*matrasparsas*" means contact of senses and mind with sense-objects. How does it happen? This contact happens through "*tanmatras*" i.e. medium through which senses experience the sense objects. Senses experience sense objects through sound, touch, color, taste, smell and also thoughts in this situation (for mind is also perishable being product of nature and its medium is thought).

The sensory system of an individual comes in contact with the sense objects through "tanmatras i.e. through respective mediums of communication" i.e. sound, touch, color, taste and smell. In other words, eyes see. Ears hear. Skin recognizes the touch. Tongue tastes. Nose smells and so on. The hub of the discussion is that senses and sense objects contact each other and inter-act each other or influence each other. This interaction of senses and sense objects gives rise to the experiences of dualities i.e. heat and cold, pain and pleasure, love and hatred, joy and grief etc. This is a sort of game that goes on. It takes two to play a game. Here it is between the senses and sense objects. The game cannot continue if the pairs of opposites like pain and pleasure are altogether eliminated. Cessation of pain brings pleasure and cessation of pleasure results in pain. Pain is born in the womb of pleasure. Peace is born in the womb of war. What is the fundamental reason of pain and pleasure? The experience of dualities (pain and pleasure, joy and happiness) arise due to contact with worldly objects i.e. objects having materiality. This happens because the individual (i.e. being with body and soul) does not see the "divinity within the soul" or immortality of the soul. Grief results from the non-perception of the soul or from ignorance of true nature of soul. Individual ignores nectar (divinity within the soul) and chooses the poison (ordeals of transmigration or cycles of birth and death) instead. What one does not see is the finite nature (nature with limitations) of both senses and sense objects and the fleeting (lasting for a short time) nature of experiences arising from their mutual contacts. Pleasure comes after pain and pain is again followed by pleasure. Reflecting on this, one must endure. "These results of contacts of senses with sense-objects in the form of pleasure and pain" will come and go (*agama-apayino*). It is nature of such contacts. What is Arjuna expected to do then? Lord has used a beautiful word here "titiksha" i.e. forbearance or calm endurance in pleasure and pain and heat and cold or in dualities. Titiksha (forbearance) is an essential attribute for spiritual growth or deliverance (moksha or absolute freedom). Arjuna is grieving because he is looking at the physical dimension only unmindful of the spiritual dimension (souls of Bhisma and Drona are immortal).

By saying "*tan titiksha* i.e. forbear with them (or dualities) like pain and pleasure." The dualities of mind (pain and pleasure etc.) are modifications of mind, perceptions of mind and modifications of mind are temporary, fleeting or changing in nature. Therefore, Lord is telling Arjuna what he should do in the present situations. By using this word "*titiksha*," Lord is saying "what cannot be cured must be endured" remaining mindful of the ultimate nature of dualities. "*Titiksha* i.e. capacity to withstand the non-sense of life with equanimity or balanced-mind" is an important capacity of an individual. This "*titiksha* or bearing of all sufferings without anxiety and without the intention to react" matures the mind or seasons the mind or prepares the mind or makes the mind ready for higher spiritual journey. Titiksha is immensely useful when one faces crisis of action, disharmony of the mind with the intelligence and discrepancy between choice of one or the other alternative. It is through the mind and senses that we feel pain and pleasure and for this "*titiksha*" has been offered as an alternative here.

In this verse, Lord addresses Arjuan as Bharta i.e. descendent of Bharata, who was the bravest of the brave and had infinite capacity to endure. This word has been used to compose (to make him feel or look calm) Arjuna. At the same time it is a reminder to Arjuna that ignorance is not befitting to the one who is descendent of Bharata. By addressing Arjuna like this, Lord wants him to feel settled mentally so that he is able to take further spiritual knowledge.

15. The one who keeps equanimity (calmness in reacting to things or situations) is fit for immortality (i.e. freedom from all possible limitations especially cycles of birth and death).

यं हि न व्यथयन्त्येते पुरुषं पुरुषर्षभ ।
समदुःखसुखं धीरं सोऽमृतत्वाय कल्पते ॥ २- १५ ॥

yam hi na vyathayanty ete purusam purusarsabha
sama-duhkha-sukham dhiram so 'mrtatvaya kalpate 2.15

yam--whom; *hi*-- surely; *na*--not; *vyathayanti*—afflict not; *ete*-- these; *purusam*-- man; *purusa-rsabha*--O chief among men; *sama*-- *duhkha*--*sukham*—same in pleasure and pain; *dhiram*-- firm; *sah*--he; *amrtatvaya*--for immortality; *kalpate*--is fit.

"O Chief of men (Arjuna) the indweller in the body, who is not tormented by these (experiences of dualities, like joy and happiness, arising from contact of senses with the sense-objects) and maintains equanimity in pain and pleasure, is fit for immortality." II 2-15 II

In Sanskrit "*puri*" is called city. This body is considered a city. Who is the indweller in this city? Soul (exclusive divinity; eternal existence; atma) is the indweller in the body. For this reason, soul is also called "Purusah; indweller in the body." That indweller in the body, who is not perturbed by the experiences of dualities such as joy and happiness, is able to maintain calmness in reacting to different situations and things. One has to get it firmly established at the level of consciousness that changing seasons bring with them dualities i.e. excess of heat and cold. Likewise, pleasurable or painful, befall us as a result of past actions (lord will take up in detail). The indweller, who is able to maintain equanimity under the oppsites is fit for immortality. What is immortality?

Immortality means freedom from all limitations. It is that last stage of moving up in spiritual growth where a being ceases to live as mind-informed body and finally lives as a spirit in the spirit ever-continuing. Death i.e. separation of physical body and spirit (subtle body; refer to chart in introduction), is not a prerequisite for immortality. Ashtavakra, Janak, Budha, Ramakrishna lived after attaining immortality. It is a "**particular attitude or say state**" reflected by living awareness of divine consciousness embodying truth, peace and bliss. It is ultimate experience within at the core of our being or at the center of our being. It is not actually an end. It is a beginning of a being to be eternally alive to what it really is whether it is in form or not in form. It is also called '*moksha*'. '*Moksha*' or liberation or 'amrtava' is considered the great ultimate goal of human existence. It is the outcome of true spiritual enlightenment. It can be had when one undergoes necessary **'sadhna' (resolutely preparing physically, mentally, emotionally and spiritually for receiving grace for realization of ultimate truth)**. Haste and hurry is to be avoided. Delusion is to be kept at bay for immortality or eternal life. Inner friction has to be overcome by right reflection, introspection and *vichar* (thought). One has to consciously take note of the dualities (pain and pleasure, joy and sorrow etc.) which the whole multitudinous variety of nature repeatedly stimulates and preserves in the mental plane of a being. This eternal life is different from survival through cycles of birth and death which all the beings anyway go through. It is transcendence (going beyond) to life and death. It is either merger (i.e. becoming indistinguishable and integral part of the Supreme) or allowing the existence exclusively for the divine purpose. One goes beyond human experience and knowledge after gaining immortality. One becomes an exclusive (not available for purpose other than divine) instrument of the Supreme. Here it is to be kept in mind that the divinity within is always immortal. "That divinity" gets entangled in limitations due to ego. The word "Immortality" used here means freedom from cycles of birth and death, freedom from the influence of ego, freedom from all that binds the divine component within. If one has living awareness of the immortality of the soul and destructibility of the body, there is no cause for grief then. For this reason, Lord said in the 11th verse of this chapter that the wise grieve neither for the dead nor for the living. In this verse, Lord has elucidated the same view. To be subjected to the grief and sorrow, to be disturbed by these disturbances in the discharge of nitya-karma (obligatory duties of the daily routine and routine required for the day for the chosen objective) means that avidya (ignorance of divine knowledge) is still there. That is what Arjuna's problem is.

In this verse, special attention is to be given to the word "sama duhkha sukham; bearing both pain and pleasure with the same calmness." It is very important and this thought has been repeatedly emphasized in the Gita. One has to treat sukha (pleasure) and dukha (pain) alike or equally. Immediately one may say "is it possible? They are opposites," it is our vision about them (pain and pleasure or any other duality) which requires adjustment. Whenever one faces a duality, "the vision of equanimity" has to be occasioned, displayed tested and reinforced. What is vision of equanimity? "The Vision of equanimity" results when one calmly reacts to things situations and people keeping sharp focus on their essential changing nature and one's own spiritual immortality. How is this state to be attained? First response should be to sublimate sukha (pleasure). When this is accomplished the heaviness about pain-related factors reduces. Most important is to face the opposites evenly. Against pleasure (sukha), it will be a process of moderating the alluring note. Against the backdrop of pain or sufferings it will be process of moderating distaste. In the course of time, one shifts attention from alternatives of pain and pleasure to the practice and pursuit of evenness towards them. Pain and sorrows are like waves on the surface of lake (in this case lake is mind). Wave is only formation of water in water by water. Wave is rising water only, which will get dissolved in the water-body again. This attitude brings drastic change in response, attention and sublimation process and the individual proceeds towards immortality. The whole focus in the Gita is on giving the even response (samatava) to opposites in the multiple ways. Samatva (evenness in responding to the opposites) in responding to contrasting situations is a great concept. It is discussed again and again in different ways. When one goes deep in the practice of samatva (evenness in responding to the opposites) and matures in it, one proceeds towards Sanyasa (renunciation; to be discussed later in detail) which is the finale of spiritual life. Samatva (evenness in responding to the opposites) is the pinnacle of spiritual vision and a key note to the seeker of spirituality and it is essential to gain relief from grief that Arjuna is suffering from.

Lord is giving emphasis to another word "dhiram; wise" in this verse. Who is a wise individual? A wise individual is one to whom the pain and pleasures and other opposites or the dualities have become equal. A wise individual is one who knows that things must be borne until they are conquered or until one is able to receive all material happenings of the world, whether joyful or sorrowful, with the same calm evenness or equality (i.e. soul-touched calmness, which comes only from direct perception or awareness, i.e. understanding with feelings, of the soul). This is to tell Arjuna to be wise because grieving is not the trait of a warrior known in the world for fearlessness and commitment to protect righteousness. This is the same thought which Lord referred to by saying earlier "the wise grieve neither for the living nor for the dead."

There is no point in repeating like a parrot "soul is immortal; body is subject to destruction." Do we really know it? If it is so then why do we get unduly carried away like Arjuna by the inevitable contrasting experiences in the journey in this world? That is knowledge, which exerts its influence on individual's attitude towards existence. It is necessary to "live the wisdom in this verse." Lord has taken up key issues. Life should be lived with final purpose (immortality; discussed above) of human existence in view i.e. long range view of life. May be that in giving we get, in pardoning we are pardoned and in death we achieve immortality. Again it is a matter of dealing with the contrasts in which the points raised by the Lord are very important. This review enlivens us in the inertia of ignorance.

What are the important lessons in this verse? Arjuna should be a wise man to whom pain and pleasures are alike, who is not tormented by the contrasting experiences in the course of journey in this world and who has gained mental maturity to be entitled (deserving one) for immortality. How can there be grief for such a man?

16. Lord is gradually exposing Arjuna to Divine knowledge (i.e. who am I? where do I come from? where do I go? What is the ultimate end of this journey?). The purpose is to broaden his mental perspective to explore the distinction between the truth or untruth or real and unreal in every happening, everything and every being. Lord made a passing reference of soul in 13th verse. Now Lord is unfolding further this secret gradually.

नासतो विद्यते भावो नाभावो विद्यते सतः ।
उभयोरपि दृष्टोऽन्तस्त्वनयोस्तत्त्वदर्शिभिः ॥ २- १६ ॥

nasato vidyate bhavo nabhavo vidyate satah
ubhayor api drsto 'ntas tv anayos tattva-darsibhih 2.16

na--not; *asatah*-- of the unreal; *vidyate*-- is; *bhavah*-being (one in existence); *na*--not; *abhavah*—non-being (not in existence); *vidyate*--there is; *satah*--of the truth or real or eternal; *ubhayoh*--of the two; *api*-- also; *drstah*—(has been) seen; *antah*—final truth; *tu*—indeed but; *anayoh*--of theses; *tattva*--truth; *darsibhih*--by the seers (knowers of the truth)..

"There is no existence of the asat (unreal or untruth i.e. the visible world including physical body or even subtle body) and there is no non-existence of sat (real or truth i.e. soul with divine component). The reality of the two is indeed certainly seen by the seers of truth." II 2-16 II

This is a very famous verse of the Gita and actually from this verse the Lord starts discussing the truth and untruth of everything, every situation and every being that is. This knowledge, this awareness makes available even, for the commoners, the nectar of immortality. The words used by the Lord are meaningful and beautiful as follows:

i) **na asato vidyatey bhavo** (the untruth has no existence) – Lord starts the discussion in this verse by use of two words "sat and asat." What is sat (truth or real)? What is asat (untruth or unreal)? Every being (being means that which is in existence) is a combination of sat and asat. Sat (truth) is that which defies (or remains unaffected by) the influence of time (past, present and future). For this reason it is said that sat (truth) is indestructible and ever present. Sat (truth) is never changing. It ever remains the same in all states. It is not sat (truth) if it ever changes. What does sat refer to in this verse? The sat refers to the soul i.e. divine component or eternal existence or Higher Nature within a being.

Asat (untruth) is that which changes with the changes, with the time, with the environment. It never remains the same. What does asat (untruth) refer to in this verse? In this verse, asat (untruth) refers to nature within a being. What is nature? Nature is a combination in a being represented by five primordial elements, three gunas and known and unknown laws. Nature is ever dynamic. It is never static. It always keeps changing. In a being, physical body including subtle body (mind and intellect etc.) is represented by lower nature nature (asat).

Lord says that there is no bhava (no being, no existence) of untruth. What does it mean? Our body is perishable. It is not the truth (the reality) of a being. It keeps on changing. A soul deluded in the company of subtle body passes through so many bodies in spiritual journey. Body represents untruth in the body i.e. body is not real. Its reality is delusion. It dies. It is perishable. It is always changing. It is untruth. In spiritual parlance body is delusion and not the reality. Body will not remain. Similarly the dualities also keep changing. Heat and cold and their objects (causes, for whom or due to whom the feelings of pain and pleasure arise) are temporary. We get unduly attracted or attached by the asat (untruth). We see breathtakingly beautiful scenery with river flowing, trees swinging in the backdrop of small hills and silence enchanting in its wordless language. We get unduly attracted (carried away) or attached to it. Was it there like this five hundred years back? Will it be there in this beautiful state five hundred years hence? Answer is no. Therefore, this natural beauty is unreal and untruth while seemingly it is real and true (not false). Why is Lord talking about truth and untruth? What is the relevance of this discussion?

Arjuna is grieved about the physical presence (combination of elements of nature subject to decay) and possible absence of physical existence of Bhisma and Drona. These bodies will die anyway. Like dream bodies appear, vanish and reappear. For the seeker of truth it (physical existence or non-existence) is not worth grieving for. Why? Unreal is conditioned by the cause (i.e. nature which itself is changing being a cause). The untruth relating to a being (body, mind and intelligence) undergoes change, when the impact of cause (nature) changes. Arjuna is grieving for that which is bound to change the physical existence (untruth) relating to Bhisma and Drona.

ii) **na bhavo vidyate satah** (there is no non-existence for the truth or real) – There is no "non-existence" for the truth i.e. truth always remains. Why is it so? Truth means real, the absolute reality. Absolute reality is not conditioned by causality. Perception of series of causes and effects (father, mother, son, wife and wealth) is an illusion. This drama of relationships has been witnessed many times by the soul (the truth of a being) in spiritual journey. The reality (soul in a being) is that with regard to which our consciousness never fails. Our consciousness fails with regard to untruth. I make three statements based on my perception at different points of my age "I am a child (at the age of ten); I am young man (at the age of thirty); I am an old man (at the age of eighty five)." It means I have been a child and childhood passes away. That means childhood is not my truth. Then, based on the same analogy, I can say "I am neither a child, nor a youth and nor an old man of eighty five. All these are changes relating to me." This is a very profound statement of mine relating to my existence because this statement is based on my knowledge of awareness called consciousness. I am not even consciousness.

My consciousness is the result of my association with that which validates my existence. What is it that validates my existence? Who am I then? I am that "something," which has witnessed me as a child, as a youth and as an old man of eighty five. This "something" will witness me transmigrating (going from one body to another) as well. What is this something? It is my soul (my truth, my reality i.e. who I am), which has been witness to all changes relating to my existence. This soul is the truth of each being. Body is not the truth. Body including mind and intellect is unreal, a passing show of the world. It veils the unchanging reality "soul of a being." Then who is a being? Each being (that which is in existence) is a soul (truth) in the body (untruth) with divinity covered under the veil of ignorance. This truth is so simple that on account of its simplicity very few people realize it.

iii) ***ubhayor api drstah antah tu anayoh tattvadarsibhih*** [the truth about both (soul is the reality that survives; body is not the reality that survives) has been realized or perceived by tattvadarsihih] - Who is a ***tattvadarsibhih*** (knower of the knower of the truth)? Knower of the truth is one who has "realized the soul" and in the end becomes aware of the one "Imperishable Self" (Supreme Universal Eternal Reality), by whom this entire universe has been extended. What is the meaning of the words "realization of the soul" used in the earlier sentence? In introduction, a chart under the heading "Cosmic Eternal Flow) is given with some notes dealing with this issue in detail. This knowledge about the self and non-self within a being has been taken for granted both by Krishna and Arjuna being wise men of that era. The Individualized Soul relating to "an individual being" is that in which ego along with past impressions conceal the divine truth i.e. divine truth remains under a sort of veil (cover) of ego and memories of past actions. Self realization means relieving the divine component of ego (one cover) and past impressions (second cover) discussed above. How this exercise of relieving the divine component of its coverings (divine component remains unmixed always; ego and past impressions cover it) is done, is the subject matter, having prime focus in all the discussions, in the Gita. Has there been anyone who can be put in this category of "tattvadarsibhih (knower of truth)"? Yes. Ashtavakra, Janak, Buddha, Ramakrisna paramhans and numerous Rishis (those who scaled the heights and matured in spirituality like Vashistha) have been the knower of truth.

What is the important message of this wonderful verse? "Each being (one in existence)" is a composition of truth and untruth. Truth or soul with divine component within survives all possible limitations and retains its pristine characteristics (eternity, indestructibility and presence everywhere) always. It ever remains un-mixed. Non-existence is not relevant to truth. Untruth (body, mind and soul) is only a delusion, a cloud that has covered the ray of sun (Divine). It is perishable. In spiritual journey, it (untruth or body, mind and soul) is like cloud hovering in the sky and bound to go away after a short while. "Truth within i.e. soul" is bound to outlive this darkness of ignorance. The shift of focus from untruth (body, mind and soul) to truth (soul with immortal, eternal divinity within) leads to revelation (surprising facts about someone or something) of the Infinite, which is endlessly new and eternally beautiful in us and all around us.

This (Infinite) gives the only meaning to "ourselves" i.e. all in "One" and "one" in all. Arjuna is grieving. His focus is on the "untruth" i.e. physical existence of Bhisma, Drona and numerous others. Lord is telling Arjuna eternal truths which have perennially (always all the time) helped, since time immemorial, to outlive grief and sufferings, which will go away anyway. In spiritual journey, ignorance (cause of delusion, which is what Arjuna is suffering from) is like bubble in the water whose existence lacks relevance, meaning and substance. We read the world wrong and say that it deceives us. "The world" rushes over the whimsical impulses of the heart making the music of sadness and lack of hope. That is what Arjuna is doing. Lord Krishna wants Arjuna's attention to be shifted to "That," which alone is which survives everything and which knows no destruction. The term "non-existent" is not relevant to "That."

17. What is the nature of "That," which was referred to as "sat; truth in contrast to asat; untruth" by Lord Krishna in the previous verse? Lord narrates the characteristics of "That" in this verse.

अविनाशि तु तद्विद्धि येन सर्वमिदं ततम् ।
विनाशमव्ययस्यास्य न कश्चित्कर्तुमर्हति ॥ २- १७ ॥

avinasi tu tad viddhi yena sarvam idam tatam
vinasam avyayasyasya na kascit kartum arhati 2.17

avinasi- -imperishable or indestructible *tu--* indeed; *tat--*that; *viddhi--*know; *yena--*by whom; *sarvam--*all; *idam--*this; *tatam—*is pervaded; *vinasam--*destruction; *avyayasya—asya* of the imperishable; *na-* not; *kascit--* anyone; *kartum--*to do; *arhati--*is able.

"Know that, by which all this universe is pervaded, to be verily indestructible. No one can destroy the indestructible (atma or soul or exclusive divinity within)." II 2-17 II

These words of Lord Krishna are very emphatic and contain some deep message of lasting value to human beings. Lord is for the first time introducing the universality of that "something or exclusive divinity or soul." Lord is gradually shifting Arjuna's attention from physical dimension (bodies of Bhisma, Drona and others) to something, very subtle, rather "some entity or soul with divinity," which perhaps cannot be described like something tangible, which eyes can see and hands can touch. Lord is referring to "that something within a being or soul" by description in different ways i.e. eternal existence versus no existence in verse 12 and truth versus untruth in verse 16. That something or soul is eternal. That something or soul is truth. How else, Lord is to refer to that? After all Lord is talking about the "non-material spiritual substance." Now Lord reveals more about that something or soul as follows in following words:

i) **avinasi tu tat viddhi** (know that to be indestructible) – Lord is directing Arjuna's attention to "some entity," which lord wants to be known as indestructible. It means "That something or soul" is not perishable. So Lord has added one more attribute to the list of eternity and truth, which he mentioned indirectly earlier. Lord is giving clues to recognize "That" which one cannot see by eyes and touch by hands.

ii) *yena sarvam idam tatam* [by whom this (whole universe) is pervaded] - Lord is directing Arjuna's attention to that by which this (whole universe) is pervaded. What is the meaning of this? When a feeling, idea, smell or something pervades a place or anything, it spreads every part of it. It means that "That something or soul" is very pervasive (rather exists everywhere in every atom of the universe). How is it to be understood? Even in an atom (the smallest part of an element), electrons keep moving around the nucleus. This is the evidence of all-pervasiveness of "That i.e. soul" about which Lord Krishna is referring here. The divinity (eternity, indestructibility and characteristic of being present everywhere) of the soul is all pervasive. This idea of all-pervasiveness becomes difficult to understand in the beginning.

To have the feel of all-pervasiveness, it will be necessary to approach this discussion differently. What is the most apparent and fundamental evidence of presence of soul in the body? It is consciousness i.e. capacity to feel with awareness. Consciousness is subtler than the space (the most subtle or *suksma* of the five elements) and for this reason it pervades in the space present in the body thoroughly i.e. in every nook and corner of it. Consciousness has supra-subtle nature. Therefore, it goes beyond body.

It fills the whole universe permeating the entire range of objects and elements. Therefore, soul, due to consciousness being most subtle (*sarva-suksma*), is all-pervading (*sarva vyapaka*). Therefore, any reference to soul takes us to its source, which is *caitanya* or consciousness, which is *sarva-vyapaka* (all-pervading). By referring to all-pervasiveness, Lord wants to add universality to soul (i.e. Universal Oneness manifesting through all, still keeping the wholeness of the whole and the part as well; this thought has been dealt with in detail in introduction under the heading "Cosmic Eternal Flow" and its subsequent discussion).

Lord wants Arjuna to see beyond physical dimension (i.e. bodies of Bhisma and Drona and others) to all pervasiveness of soul, which cannot be destroyed. Reference to soul is not an ordinary reference. Soul is "That" by which the whole universe is pervaded. Every moving and unmoving object in this universe is pervaded by the self (divine consciousness or *caitanya* i.e. the nucleus of the soul). In *Brhadaranyaka Upnishad, Yajnavalkya* says "O *Matreyi*! This atma (soul) is to be seen, heard, thought about and finally meditated upon." This is the focal point of all the Gita-discussion.

iii) ***vinasam avyayasya asya na kascit kartum aarhati*** (no one is capable of putting an end to this "Imperishable One" – First it is necessary to feel what is being discussed. Suppose I make a statement - "I am an old man wearing a torn suit." It is necessary to consider this statement both from i) the perspective of an ordinary man and ii) from the perspective of a man having Gita-gyan. Now who is "I" in this statement? From the perspective of an ordinary man, the discussion is about the body of an old man wearing a torn suit. Even a photograph of an old man can be taken. The Gita does not take the body as the "I" of this old man. The body is perishable. It will not survive death. The real "I" of the old man is represented by the soul of this old man, which validates the existence of this body of the old man. That soul cannot be seen. No photograph of this can be taken but that entity (soul) of the old man is the "Reality of this old man," which survives death i.e. soul of this old man cannot be destroyed ever. What does Lord Krishna want to say by these words? There, within each individual, is a self (divinity covered by ego and further covered by past impressions), which is the "Real Self" or soul (or whose presence keeps the body alive) of that individual. It cannot be destroyed. The miseries of this world arise because the individual keeps the whole focus of existence on this body or the body-related. "The one," with whose association the body is and without whose association the body is not, normally remains out of the focus of an ordinary individual.

The precise message of this verse is about the "soul," the real self within an individual or the truth of an individual. The soul is indestructible and all-pervasive (present everywhere). Soul is eternal, indestructible existence within an individual. What is the relevance of this seemingly out of context (from an ordinary point of view) discussion at this juncture when a fierce battle is just about to start? The discussion is not touching Arjuna's dilemma i.e. whether he should fight or not. This discussion about the soul at this juncture is most relevant. Nothing can get the individual out of the dungeon (dark underground prison) of depression in which Arjuna is. The moment the attention shifts to the "Immortality" the whole perspective of the individual changes. The fear of death recedes. In spiritual journey, the soul changes body numerous times and, with every change, the event of death is experienced by the body at the time of separation of soul from the present body. When one knows that the death cannot destroy the "Real Self" within, one becomes fearless. One transcends one's inescapable limitation. This realization takes time, but this realization is necessary. Arjuna is in distress because he is not looking at the "indestructible and all-pervasive reality" within Bhisma, Drona and others. When we say that an individual has within "the silence of the sea, the noise of the earth and the music of the air," the reference is to the soul only. When one realizes this "thus far not realized Reality within," the conflicts within break out in the form of exuberance (full of energy and excitement) of soul and the individual surges towards the destined end of the human pursuit.

18. In this verse Lord tells two more very important characteristics of soul i.e. incomprehensible and ever remains the same.

अन्तवन्त इमे देहा नित्यस्योक्ताः शरीरिणः ।
अनाशिनोऽप्रमेयस्य तस्माद्युध्यस्व भारत ॥ २- १८ ॥

antavanta ime deha nityasyoktah saririnah
anasino 'prameyasya tasmad yudhyasva bharata 2.18

anta-vantah—having an end i.e. perishable; *ime*--these; *dehah*—(material) bodies; *nityasya*--eternal in existence or everlasting; *uktah*-- is so said; *saririnah*--the embodied soul (individualized eternal existence); *anasinah*—of the indetructible; *aprameyasya*—of the immeasurable; *tasmat*--therefore; *yudhyasva*--fight; *bharata*--O descendant of Bharata (Arjuna).

"The bodies of the indweller (i.e. soul, which dwells in the present body under the cover of ego or ignorance of its divine characteristics), who is eternal. Indestructible and Incomprehensible (being immeasurable and incapable of being proved), are said to have an end. Fight, therefore, O Bharata." II 2-18 II

Lord Krishna is telling Arjuna the various characteristics of the soul to help him to feel with awareness of the indweller in the bodies. At the same time attention is being brought to the bodies of the indweller? Reference to the soul is in singular (indweller). Reference to bodies is in plural – dehas. Now two questions arise in the mind. What are these bodies (deha; plural)? Are these bodies indestructible like soul? Both Lord Krishna and Arjuna knew the answer, as it was a common topic those days. Answer has been taken for granted in this discussion of the Bhagavad Gita. Bodies have not been discussed further. For further details, refer to the chart "Cosmic Eternal Flow" in introduction giving special attention to discussion on i) subtle body (with four elements; it is invisible perishable body which undergoes many deaths and births), and ii) physical body with 27 elements and it lasts for one birth and death. Both the bodies are perishable (at one point of the time or the other) and therefore both these bodies taken together are called "non- self" relating to the individual. Both these bodies of the soul (eternal existence within) are perishable. Soul (the real self) is the spiritual body which does not die. It is eternal, indestructible and immanent. Ordinary people like Arjuna remain confined to physical body alone and suffer. Those who are evolving spiritually know about the subtle body as well. Very few people get to feel the spiritual body (exclusive divinity) and at that point the 'Immortality in the individual" imparts its own quality of permanence i.e. the mortal becomes immortal. With this background we should feel the further discussion under this verse.

All the characteristics used for soul are unique and none of these can be used for anyone else in the universe. The words used by the Lord are as follows:

i) *antavanta ime deha nityasyo uktah sararinah anasino aprameyasya* (these bodies of the embodied, who is eternal, indestructible, incomprehensible, are said to have an end) – Who is *saririnah* (the embodied) in the bodies? The one, who has put on the bodies like pieces of clothing, is soul. The focus of the discussion is on soul. The characteristics of the bodies and the "soul within" are different. These bodies (physical bodies and subtle bodies) of the individual are perishable. The soul is indestructible (not perishable), ever anew eternally (always remains as it is) and incomprehensible. Why is it incomprehensible? Soul does not require any proof to be proved because it is self proven.

It cannot be grasped through *tark* (logical reasoning). For proof, it will have to be put in limitations but it is beyond all limitations. For this reason, it is not easily comprehensible to senses, mind and intelligence. It can be intuited with faith, sadhna (regular practice to commit to discipline with dedication) and guidance of a spiritual master.

In this verse, bodies are in plural. Soul (the one who is the root cause of the embodied self or deluded self) has been used in singular. This reiterates another truth. There is "one supreme soul" in the universe. This one soul reflects in multitudinous bodies. The spot light of Lord's discussion is on ancient Indian philosophy that there is only "One Supreme Soul" (Supreme Eternal Universal Reality) and concept of pluralities of soul is a delusion. How is it? There is only one sun but its numerous rays light the whole space and things around in all direction. A ray has definitely got the characteristic of the sun i.e. it too lights and dispels the darkness. But ray is not the reality. Ray is the reflection of the sun though it lights darkness as sun lights. This comparison should be properly understood. There is only "One Supreme Soul." Each individual soul or "the individual self" is ego illumined by the light of the Supreme Divine which is not in reality separate but due to ignorance it considers itself separate and continues on spiritual path purifying itself of all impurities in the form of ignorance. Finally a day comes when realization dawns that there is no existence separate from the Supreme. The mist of ignorance disappears and the ray starts shining as ever before singing the providential glory. "**The Space within the covering of this body-aggregate**" merges with the space outside. One experiences the highest joy of losing "egoistic-self" and uniting with the "Universal Ever-Alive Principle" perpetually flowing and shinning immaculately in its divine splendor. To know our soul apart from the individual self (body-aggregate) is the first step towards the realization of "Supreme Deliverance" (the state of being rescued from danger, evil and pain). The purpose of using these adjectives and the purpose of using "soul in singular and bodies in plural" is to tell Arjuna that all these beings (including bodies of Bhisma, Drona and others) seemingly looking separate due to maya (nature) but carrying within the reflection of divine purity, cannot be destroyed. Arjuna is worried as his view is confined to physical existence only. Bhisma and Drona know that they will die. Still they are not worried. They know the divine secret.

Lord wants Arjuna to know the real and unreal within an individual. The Real (soul) cannot die. The unreal [i.e. physical body (for one birth and death) and subtle body (for several births and deaths] die at different points of time. Living in this knowledge makes an individual fearless and worthy of absolute freedom (moksha).

ii) *tasmat yudhyasva bharata* (**therefore fight, O Arjuna**) – Lord Krishna is asking Arjuna to fight. Does He want Arjuna to go for mass murder? Answer is emphatic no. Lord wants Arjuna to relieve the society of the "brutes in human form i.e. Kaurvas" who were degrading mother earth (attempting to strip off a woman in open court etc.) by their presence. Lord wants Arjuna to behave like a warrior. A warrior, considering the social order of those days, means fighting for winning or sacrificing life for restoring righteousness. The truth, the reality cannot die. Death is relevant to body, which will die anyway. The warriors, for the right cause for restoring righteousness in the society, immortalize themselves and seek deathlessness in death.

The message is simple. Death is relevant to bodies. Soul is indestructible, eternal and does not require proof. It is beyond logical reasoning. By referencing soul in singular and bodies in plural, Lord has pointed out one more truth. There is only One Supreme Soul, which is immortal. The bodies of the embodied soul i.e. physical body and subtle body (this explanation has been taken for granted in the Gita and this discussion in detail are available in introduction) are destined to perish. If it is so, what is the reason to worry about to Arjuna? By doing duty for the right cause (here in case of Arjuna it is fighting), one gets a chance to be alive to "That Perpetual Surprise and Delight within," which is "Life of life," which is ever anew. It takes the mortal being towards immortality. Lord is guiding Arjuna in that direction only. "That Limitless Inner Perceiving Substance" is evidently not within sensory perception. It is different from the body-aggregate. Arjuna has to understand it. When the vision is taken beyond the visible and also beyond the perceptible, the first impasse (a deadlock where people involved do not agree what to do) in solving the problem of grief is overcome. This is precisely what Lord Krishna is doing i.e. taking Arjuna from darkness and hollowness of grief to the light of "Immortality."

This verse has a few more peculiarities - Lord in this verse has clarified: i) unity of the soul (word *saririnah* i.e. one (singular) indweller in the bodies (subtle body and physical body of the individual), ii) the same soul (singular) exists in all body-aggregates in all forms, as one moon shines everywhere in all receptacles through its reflections, iii) Supreme Self or soul is indestructible (*anasino*) and iv) all these bodies (*eme dehas* i.e. physical body and subtle body) and different body aggregates in different forms are having an end (antavantah). The great sentences such as "He (the supreme Self) is one and only God; Infinite-all pervading Reality, though one, is regarded as many; wise men call this one God by several names; superior to the *Mahat* (cosmic intelligence) is the Ayakta (divinity within) and superior to the Avyakta is Purusha (used for parmatama; Supreme Self) and superior to Purusha is nothing)" are all based on the knowledge gleamed (inherently shinning) in this verse.

19. In this verse Lord tells Arjuna another characteristic of soul (the self; the atma; the truth of a being) i.e. it is a non-doer. It can neither slay nor can it be slain.

य एनं वेत्ति हन्तारं यश्चैनं मन्यते हतम् ।
उभौ तौ न विजानीतो नायं हन्ति न हन्यते ॥ २- १९ ॥

ya enam vetti hantaram yas cainam manyate hatam
ubhau tau na vijanito nayam hanti na hanyate 2.19

yah—he who; *enam*—this (soul, individualized eternal existence); *vetti*--knows; *hantaram*--the killer; *yah*--anyone; *ca*--also; *enam*--this; *manyate*--thinks; *hatam*--killed; *ubhau*--both of them; *tau*—those ; *na*--not; *vijanitah*-- know; *na*--not; *ayam*--this; *hanti*--kills; *na*--not; *hanyate*-- is killed.

"The one who thinks that "This (the self of a being or soul or atma)" is a slayer, and the one who thinks that "This (again soul)" is slain, both are ignorant. This (self of an individual or atma) neither slays nor is it slain." II 2-19 II

It is necessary to particularly note the way in which Lord refers to "Atma or Soul or Self" in this discussion. Soul is beyond any limitations. It cannot be categorized as male or female. Why is it so? Soul is "That" which encompasses or envelopes the manifestation of the divinity and creates the misconception of separate entity due to ego. The process of formation of "aggregate body of a being" starts by ego with "divinity" in and "individual intelligence" along with. It is a state much before formation of body or sex determination. It is also possible that a body of a soul in this birth is male and in next birth it is female. Therefore a soul is intrinsically neither a male nor a female. Therefore, most suitable pronouns for soul are "this, that or it."

In the beginning of this discussion Arjuna used the words "killing or slaying" while referencing the kinsmen. In this verse, Lord is replying the point raised by Arjuna. Is it possible to kill or slay the self (or the soul or the atma) relating to a being? Lord is unfolding a universal secret to Arjuna by saying that the self (atma or soul) cannot kill any one nor can it be killed by any one. Use of such words as killing or slaying with reference to soul is ignorance i.e. the one using these words does not know the intrinsic nature or basic nature of soul (the self). Why is it that the self (soul) can neither slay nor can it be slain? It is indestructible. Why and how is it indestructible?

I) **na ayam hanti na hanyate** (this neither slays nor gets slain) – The soul or the self is basically the **"reflection of divine awareness"** concealed under the layers of ego and past impressions. Its emergence is due to ego and its onward journey is due to past memories and impressions. So long as the ego and impressions of the past continue, deluded-soul or individualized-soul keeps changing the bodies and the 'eternal existence' perceived to be related to the individualized-soul remains concealed under the dense layer of ignorance. Finally the moment comes, when ego and past impressions vanish. The **"conscious space within the deluded self" merges with the "space all around the self." Duality ends.** The fact is that **"exclusive divinity within or the soul always remains"** either as deluded-self within an individual enveloped under ego and past impressions or as one with the Supreme. **How does anyone become one with the Supreme?** Think of an empty room. It is all space within the room. Now place an earthen pitcher in the centre of a room. Now some of the space of the room is occupied by this pitcher. A being is like the earthen pitcher occupying the divinity. Now break the earthen pitcher. Space within the pitcher merges with the space outside. The total space of the room before the pitcher and after the pitcher remains the same. Characteristics-wise, space within the pitcher is the same as the space outside the pitcher. As space within the pitcher cannot be destroyed, the divinity (soul) within the deluded-soul cannot be destroyed. Similarly, it is water before the wave and after wave also it is water. Therefore, like space or water, soul is indestructible. Reflection of Supreme universal self is death as well as immortality. **This knowledge results in an awakening within, good enough to illumine darkness of death.** When only that, which is perceivable through senses, becomes subject to birth and death, what is, then, the reason for grief? That indestructible soul cannot be slain, should be sufficient cause for poise, equanimity of mind and a conviction that all is well. Arjuna is lacking it.

But Lord tells another characteristic (of soul) as well. Lord says "it (soul) slays not." What does it mean? Lord is highlighting another divine characteristic. Supreme Universal self just remains. It does not do anything. Everything is done by nature (five primordial elements + three gunas + known and unknown laws of nature). By its (divinity within soul) presence all existences get validated. With it, everything is. Without it, there is nothing. Being immutable (that which is impossible to change), the self (atma or soul) is neither the agent nor the object of action of slaying. Those, who say that *atma* slays, do not understand the real nature of the self (soul). Arjuna is afraid of killing the relative. Is it possible to kill? A being is composed of five elements. Death only disintegrates the five elements. All the five elements still ever remain in some different form after death. "Truth of a being (soul)" always remains, after the space within merges with the space outside. It is eternal. Coverings of the truth (disintegrated body, mind complex), in different forms, also remain. Death, therefore, in reality, is a delusion. All changes, whatever they are, are due to nature (the kinetic energy of the Supreme). Truth is that soul neither slays nor gets slain. "Limited intelligence within an individual" knows facts alone and not the truth behind the facts. Human mind has the power in its subconscious zone to comprehend the truth. Arjunas is not aware of this aspect of reality. For this reason he is in grief. Krishna, Bhishma and Drona, as Mahabharta reveals, are not in grief.

What is, in nut shell, the message of the verse? The thoughts of killing or getting killed are delusion (Arjuna is in delusion). The soul is indestructible at the same time it is non-doer. The Supreme Being is innate goodness (divinity in the soul) in all. Everything has sprung from this "innate goodness or immortal life or divinity within the deluded soul or conscious universal principle." Everything is vibrating with consciousness, the conclusive evidence of life in existence. This "everything around (nature)" will change but the "immortal life within, the divinity within, the reality or truth within does not change. What do we see when we see the Supreme One or the one covered under the bodies? This is our ethical basis (basis of the essence of ancient indo Aryan Culture). Lord first wants to invoke Arjuna's awareness towards this "**Conscious Universal Principle within and in all everywhere.**" Lord wants Arjuna to connect to this "Eternal Universal Principle" through action. Action for Arjuna at this juncture is fighting a war to restore righteousness. "Thoughts of slaying and getting slain," which are not relevant to soul, are confusing the mind of Arjuna. Through this knowledge, Lord wants Arjuna to be awakened to the truth (soul) within and not the coverings (bodies).

A question may arise in the mind here at this point. Why is Lord Krishna talking about philosophy and lofty spiritual heights of Vedanta, when they are standing in the battle field and a fierce war is just about to start? It is true that Arjuna's problem is a worldly problem and social problem. It has been the consummate (complete and perfect in every way) belief of the people of this land (Bhararat; India) that soul (the Infinite Eternal Ultimate Cause of everything; Eternal Universal Existence) is far greater fact and reality than what the body may seem to be. Whenever a subject of human life and compulsions are taken for deeper study, thinkers of India cannot help moving into sublime realm of the spirit. For them, spirit is not a heavenly concept or a speculative indulgence. Spirit (soul) is the fulcrum and the pivot of the human personality. According to ancient Indo Aryan thinking, the body is the perceived object dependent on the perceiver while the soul shines ever as the independent perceiver.

20. In the preceding verse Lord says that the soul cannot be killed by anybody. One natural question arises in the mind as to how it is that soul cannot be killed. In answer to this, Lord explains in this verse six characteristics of the soul bringing out that soul is not subject to any modification (change; even the event of death is a change in spiritual journey) relevant to the body.

न जायते म्रियते वा कदाचिन्नायं भूत्वा भविता वा न भूयः ।
अजो नित्यः शाश्वतोऽयं पुराणो न हन्यते हन्यमाने शरीरे ॥ २-२० ॥

na jayate mriyate va kadacin nayam bhutva bhavita va na bhuyah
ajo nityah sasvato 'yam purano na hanyate hanyamane sarire 2.20

na--not; *jayate*--takes birth; *mriyate*-- dies; *va*--either; *kadacit*--at any time (past, present or future); *na*--not; *ayam*—this (self); *bhutva*—having been; *bhavita*--will be; *va*--or; *na*--not; *bhuyah*—(any more); *ajah*--unborn; *nityah*--eternal; *sasvatah*-- changeless; *ayam*--this; *puranah*--the oldest or ancient; *na*--not; *hanyate*--is killed; *hanyamane*--being killed; *sarire*--by the body

"This (i.e. soul, which is the subject of discussion in these verses) is neither born nor does it die. Coming to be (i.e. becoming) and ceasing to be do not take place in it. It (soul) is unborn, eternal, constant, and ancient. It (soul) is not slain when body is slain." II 2-20 II

That this (or soul) cannot be killed, has been sufficiently emphasized, in discussion thus far, by the Lord but it is not easy to accept this at the level of awareness by any individual. What is to be done then? Lord in this verse informs six innate (that characteristic, which one has at the time of birth) characteristics of "divinity within the soul." What is the relevance of this wording "Divinity within" the soul? This is a very important and very relevant question. Divinity obscured under the layers of ignorance and past impressions is soul. Divinity without any fold of limitations like ignorance and past impressions is the Supreme Self. For this reason, soul means "The Supreme Being within a being under the layers of ignorance and past impressions." Therefore, the characteristics being summarized below are the characteristics of the "Supreme Being" equally applicable to divinity within a soul. For this reason, after nearly completing the Gita-discussion in 18th chapter (verse 61), Lord tells Arjuna "The Lord dwells in the heart of all beings, O Arjuna, causing all by His illusive power to revolve as if mounted on a machine." Lord's prime emphasis in the Gita-discussion is to shift the attention from "mortality of an individual" to "the immortality concealed (or obscured or difficult to be seen and understood) within each being." The purpose is to drive away Arjuna's diffidence (not having much confidence ... seeing the grandfather and teacher), fear and doubt. What are the six characteristics of Divinity within the soul? Lord replies in this verse in following words:

i) *Na jayate* (it is not born) – It (soul) is not born. What is the meaning of it? This statement (soul is not born) emphasizes the distinction of body and soul. The relevance of birth is for body and not for soul. Soul is "Divinity" concealed under the cover of ignorance and past impressions. With adjuncts or annexure or covering around the Divinity gone, the space within a being is as good as space outside. The space is simply space. It only validates the existence i.e. nature comes alive in the presence of the divinity (conscious space). Without divinity, nature is inert. There is one more point to it. Initially an individual asks where the "individual divinity" goes away. It does not go anywhere. It always remains as it is. Change is in the perception of the individual. It can be explained in a different way also. Suppose an empty room is there. You put five pitchers in it duly numbered as 1 to 5. Each pitcher contains some space. Total space in the room is not reduced by putting the pitchers. The space before the pitchers and after the pitchers is the same. Now you break all the pitchers and throw away all the residual material. Can you now identify the particular space occupied by the pitchers? Does the total space in the room increase or decrease without pitchers or with pitchers? Is it possible to identify the space occupied by pitcher number 1 or 2 or 3 etc.? In this analogy (comparison), the pitcher represents body of a being. Space within the pitcher symbolizes the divinity within, referred to as the soul, which validates individualized soul's (jiva's) existence. Space outside the pitchers in the universe symbolically represents the Supreme. Formation of pitcher is like birth of a being. Space within the pitcher was already there. Does the space in the pitchers in the room get birth with the formation of pitchers? It was already there before the formation of pitchers. It will still remain there always. On the same analogy, it is said that there is no birth of a soul (space within the pitcher). Now think that another new pitcher, brought from outside, is placed in the room. How does one explain the space within the 8th pitcher? Is it a new space or the space occupied by pitcher number, say, 1 in the room? How does one explain this? Total space of the room is still the same. It means mathematics does not apply here. There is no addition or subtraction in the space of the universe due to birth of new souls or liberation of old souls, as the space in the room remains the same before the pitchers and after the pitchers. Tags of name and forms are relevant to bodies and not the space within the soul of a particular individual. Space is always independent of form and name. Now the thought becomes clear. There is one Universal Supreme Self. It is "eternal, indestructible and unlimited." The thought that this is "my space or my divinity within the soul" is a delusion. It reflects ignorance or ego. Ego starts the whole drama. When divine knowledge dawns then one awakens from slumber feeling that "existence in limitations" is a wretched dream and not the reality. The real one was ever there. It was never born. It is there and it will be there always.

ii) *na miryate* [(it) never dies] – There is no death for soul. What does it mean? Individualized Soul's existence is primarily due to divinity within, without which nature's elements (Primordial elements, attributes and laws of nature) do not get activated. When divinity departs from the "body–mind–intelligence–aggregate," there is no existence of the body. The five primordial elements, of which the body is made of, get disintegrated the moment that "Divine Essence" that infuses life (consciousness) in the inert primordial elements, departs from the body. Actually, death is relevant to the body and not to the soul. Suppose an individual is in a jungle. Now he comes to a point where river has to be crossed. The individual has to go to other end. Now individual uses a log of wood to cross the river. After getting to the "other shore" the individual throws away the log and proceeds towards its destination. In this analogy, individual represents soul. Log of wood used to go across the river is body. Throwing away of the wood-log is like death of the body. Soul is like the traveler who has proceeded towards the destination after the log of wood (present body) is cast aside. Divinity enveloped within the soul never dies. It keeps moving ahead either in a body or in universe like space outside the individual body. For the knower of the soul, there is no death. Death, birth and immortality are the different events in the universal drama. There is no birth and no death for a liberated individual. This is the objective, which the Upnishad has in view, when it proclaims (publicly or officially tells) "Know *thine* own soul or in other words, realize the One great principle of unity or divine truth, that there is in each being." Where does this awakening come from? It (this knowledge, this awakening) descends in our own being, when we are conscious of our soul i.e. when we perceive the inner being that transcends our ego and has deeper affinity with "The All." The death loses its stings when one experiences the true nature of one's being and realizes that he or she is more than himself or herself and that he or she is one with "The All."

iii) *va kadachit ayam bhutva bhavita va na bhuyah* (it is not that once having been it ceases to be) – Special attention is required on these words "once having been …." It has already been said that the soul does not have birth. Then what is the meaning of "once having been … …"? Lord is making a special reference to the "proclaimed indo Aryan thoughts relating to existence of universe contained in the scriptures." Every eon (kalpa; extremely long period of time) of manifestation is followed by eon of non-manifestation. When the eon of manifestation starts, universe is formed by twin make up of both the nature and spirit (the divinity within the self or enlightened space within the self of the being or splendor of the Supreme *Purusha*). Someone has beautifully described it as "all are parts of a stupendous whole, whose body is nature validated by divinity covered within the soul." With the eon of manifestation, multitudinous varieties of nature and even Gods like Brahma and others emerge out of the "Stupendous Whole; *Purshottama*; Universal Eternal Supreme Self," unless liberated from limits of human experience and thoughts. A soul, till it is liberated (made free from all possible limitations of experience and thoughts) will continue to be in indifferent bodies till the end of eon of manifestation and it will again emerge after the eon of non-manifestation. In simple words, it never happens that soul is existent at one time (one eon) and non-existent at another (next eon of manifestation) till it is liberated. This is the idea conveyed by the words "having once come into being." This does not contradict with the statement that there is no birth and death for the soul.

Never it was that "this ancient and still ever anew i.e. soul or self or Purusha" was not there. Never it will be that "It" is not there (the emphasis is on invalidity of birth and death relating to soul). Lord is using different words and expressions to reinforce this conviction (very strong belief and opinion) that for the "divine one within or the real one within or the self," there is no birth and death. When does this thought of "self immortality" become an integral part of human psyche or as natural or conscious feeling to a being as breath is to the body i.e. something going in, invigorating and touching the whole inner area form nose or mouth to at least the navel? This happens with the realization with awareness (and not with intellect alone) that the body undergoes six types of modifications (*bhavas or vicharas*) i.e. to be born, to exist, to change, to grow, to decay and to perish. These six modifications do not apply to the soul, whose characteristics are different and dealt with in the same verse a little afterwards. True awareness of the message of these words (understanding the meaning with feelings) takes an individual beyond the "conscious of the self" to "cosmic consciousness." For this one has to stay with these thoughts. One has live with or meditate on these expressions "no birth, no death, no becoming, no withering away, ever continuing, ever anew." Just doing is not enough. The realization of these expressions or their true import or meaning comes alive (intellectual understanding is inadequate) only when one approaches with yoga (i.e. after gaining proficiency in all disciplines relating of body, mind, emotions and spirit necessary to gain awareness of Universal, Eternal, Indestructible One Truth). Knowing this verse means knowing the "One," which is within, which is his or her truth, which is his or her soul and which is the bridge to immortality. This amounts to knowing with awareness the physical existence and spiritual life and beauty.

iii) *ajo, nitya, sasvato ayam purano na hanyate hnayamane sarire* ["this divinity enveloped within the soul" is unborn, eternal, constant and ancient; it is not killed when body is slain.] - The emphasis of these words is to bring round the truth that six modifications relevant to body are not relevant to soul as follows.

a) *Ajo* (not born) – Soul is not born. It has always been there. It is there. It will always be there either within the soul covered by ego or as an integral, indistinguishable part of the "Supreme Consciousness." This aspect is as difficult to be assimilated as simple it appears in the beginning. Mastering this aspect alone is enough. One comes to realize it when one realizes the "Truth" which comprehends the multiplicity. Living awareness of this just one aspect (the result of *sadhna* or all efforts for purifying the self worthiness of divine grace) opens up the individual to panorama of horizon leading to the "Infinite." True assimilation of this aspect means gaining true awareness of what it means to be relieved of all possible distractions and limitations and getting centered on one unity in the soul, mysterious, resplendent, ineffable and resonant with divine music.

b) *nittyah* (eternal) – It means that soul continues to be forever having no end.

c) *sasvatah* (unchanging) – Exclusive Divinity within or the soul is unchanging. Everything else changes. Why does it not change? The divinity within the soul has divine characteristics (eternity, indestructibility, immanence, unchanging). The divinity within gets obscured by nature but it can never be made bereft of its divine characteristics.

d) *puranah* (ancient) – Ancient means it has been in existence for a very long period of time. (It may be there up to the end of an eon of manifestation and it may continue to be after the end of eon of non-manifestation). It explains how ancient it is always.

e) *na hanyate hanyamane sarire* (it is not killed when body gets destroyed) – Lord is emphasizing one single thought. Soul is different from body. Lord is emphasizing this thought so much that it becomes the pivot of our awareness. One should learn to live with this awareness. Perhaps perfect life is life lived with living awareness of this thought. Body dies. Soul does not die. Why should Arjuna worry then when the souls (that part of individuality which is sentient i.e. which can see and feel through senses) of Bhisma, Drona and others will not be destroyed by death of their bodies (that part of their individualities which cannot see and feel through senses). An individual is composed of the sentient and the insentient. The insentient dies and is reborn. The sentient (that which is able to see and feel things) is always resplendent, ever fresh and it does not become inert.

This verse is a gold-mine of knowledge which can surely relieve an individual of grief due to delusion and ignorance. Message in brief is simple. All the attributes of "the insentient" (i.e. bodies which cannot see and feel through the senses) like birth and death etc. do not touch or apply to the self (the soul). The sentient (soul which can see and feel through senses) is unborn and eternal. The self (soul) is not slain when body is slain. Lord's focus is on the infinite in an individual. When one knows one's true nature as the immortal and infinite atman (soul) i.e. one is deathless, ever pure, unborn, a new surge of fearlessness is experienced in attitude and in dealings with others. Then one works and thinks with the intuition of soul-consciousness, which naturally and totally realizes its unity with the "Supreme One" i.e. one remains in soul-soaked consciousness. Mists disappear (Krishna, Bhishma and Drona were not worried at all knowing pretty well their destined end). Contradictions subside. Knowledge, love and actions get harmonized. Pleasure and pain become one in beauty. Enjoyment and renunciation equal in goodness. "The formless" starts manifesting in the forms of fruit, flower, animal, friend and foe with unbounded beauty and perfection, common in all. Feeling "the richness of this perception" is joy unbounded, knowledge unrestricted and peace unfathomed (measured) within. The complete assimilation of the knowledge of this verse is enough to help an individual to gain that spiritual vision which is the vision of whole truth. This knowledge will point out that our sin is not mere actions. Our greatest sin is to take for granted that we are finite, that our individual-self (body-mind-intelligence complex) is the ultimate truth and that we are not all essentially one but exist each for his or her own separate individual existence. Let the history of one's life in actions be written in the light of this awareness. That is what lord Krishna wants to convey to Arjuna, who is confined to mirage (dream or hope or wish that cannot come true) of body-consciousness (death of near and dear ones).

21. Arjuna was afraid of action of killing the relatives. Lord, in this verse, further tells the "secrets of the soul" to explain that what Arjuna is thinking is not actually killing though it appears to be so. Nothing can bring an end to the eternal existence within. Can "the divine essence of a being" be killed? That one can kill is also misunderstanding, if one takes one's thinking beyond body consciousness.

वेदाविनाशिनं नित्यं य एनमजमव्ययम् ।
कथं स पुरुषः पार्थ कं घातयति हन्ति कम् ॥ २-२१ ॥

vedavinasinam nityam ya enam ajam avyayam
katham sa purusah partha kam ghatayati hanti kam 2.21

veda-- knows; *avinasinam*--indestructible; *nityam*—always or eternal; *yah*--one who; *enam*--this (soul); *ajam*--unborn; *avyayam*--immutable; *katham*--how; *sah*--he; *purusah*--person; *partha*--O Partha (Arjuna); *kam*--whom; *ghatayati*—causes to be slain; *hanti*--kills; *kam*—whom.

"The one who knows that this (the self or *purusha* or soul or divine essence of a being) as indestructible, eternal, unborn and changeless, how can he or she, O Partha, slay or cause to be slain?" II 2-21 II

Lord is emphasizing the thoughts repeatedly to bring round to Arjuna of the message of divinity within. That soul is indestructible, eternal, unborn and changeless has already been mentioned by the Lord in earlier verses as well. These four characteristics point out the uniqueness of the soul. "The divinity within, the essence of purity within or the truth within" is indestructible, eternal, unborn and changeless. These four characteristics, point towards a very special unique characteristic of the soul (*atma*) i.e. action-less-ness. The soul is action-less. It is free from ego (that is why it is eternal). The divinity within is free from feeling of doer-ship. Slaying and causing to slay are actions. Soul does not do anything except for validating the existences. It just is and it just remains validating all with its presence. How can it slay or how can it be slain? How can it become a cause to action like killing? The question itself is the answer i.e. soul cannot kill nor can it cause to be killed.

What are the most important words of this verse?

"How can it kill or cause someone to kill it?" are the most important words of this verse? How is it that the one enlightened about the divinity within cannot kill? How does it come to be? The one who is enlightened knows that there is one universal Being which manifest through all? The divinity within an individual is not small or big. The space within the being and out beyond the being is the same. Space of a being is not like one small branch of a tree. The tree remains with one branch less after a branch is take away from the tree. The idea of fragmentation is not applicable to the Supreme Divinity. It remains the same whether in beings or beyond the beings, like the space in a room with pitchers and without pitchers. What is an individual? It is not body. It is the soul (atma or the self). It is not anything that perishes. Even the "Supreme Being or *Paramatama*" cannot kill or extinguish the divinity (the self or the soul within) because it is the same Divinity inside and outside. This has to be very carefully felt. Extinguishment of the "individual divinity or soul" will mean that "The whole cannot remain The Whole." The thought of extinguishment of soul contradicts the universal accepted characteristic that soul is eternal. This thought that it is "my soul" and it is "your soul" is ignorance. The moon, reflected in three pots in a moon-lit night, does not mean four moons. There is only one moon always. Similarly, there is only "One Reality or One Truth," which manifests in all. Therefore, it is true that one knowing the truth of soul (*atma*) cannot kill or cause to kill. Killing or causing to kill is not the characteristics of the soul, which is ever eternal, indestructible, unborn and unchanging. Soul (or Supreme Being within) simply validates. It has been. It is and it will always be. What is the reason for grief then? The grief is due to this feeling: "I cause the slaying of these selves. I slay these." This feeling "I slay" has its basis in ignorance about the true nature of the self (atma), which just cannot be slain. That is what Arjuna is suffering from.

There is no dream anymore, when an individual dreaming wakes up. Similarly there is no grief when "the self" gets awakened all **by the self, in the self and for self**. When an individual becomes aware of the self, he or she becomes aware of others around (divinity around in the nook and corner of the universe and beyond). This awakening of the self and that of the others things around are the two twin aspects of the same wakeful state. The accomplishment of this feeling in "all consuming totality and intensity" is enlightenment. From our dream state, we wake up due to biological and psychological reasons. From ignorance, we wake up by divine knowledge (soul does not kill nor cause to be killed; the truth within, the divine substance within, the true-self within is beyond destruction, decay or extinction). So that is what it is. Arjuna is afraid of killing. Lord is saying "Is anyone capable of killing the reality or truth or real self in any being?."

This knowledge, that neither the "Real-Self" can kill nor it can be killed, is not ordinary knowledge. There stays alive in this knowledge redress (correction or balance) to all the problems of life. When this knowledge reigns supreme in the psyche of a being, no disharmony (result of grief, doubt, misunderstanding, uncalled for intense desire to subject someone to be indiscriminately used for personal satisfaction and fear) can intimidate the mind.

These four words used by the lord "indestructible, eternal, unborn and changeless" are not ordinary words. Understanding their meaning alone is not enough. When one meditates on these words, relating to the self and all others and their ripple effect, it starts dawning to an individual what Lord is talking about. The soul is only one. Bodies, it permeates, are many. Moon is one. Its reflections in pots are many. Slowly one overcomes the idea of differences and plurality of the soul. Even if all the bodies assembled in the Kurukshetra are killed, "Single, Indestructible, All-pervading soul" would not stand to lose the least. Why? For the 'real self within' there is no death (see the four word used by the Lord). Lord wants to say "Let this truth be the vision and strength for you, O Arjuna. What are you grieving for? You cannot kill the real-self who is immortal and who is in all." That Supreme Reality is the string that runs through all the beings in the universe or seeming plurality of the souls.

What is the additional and single message of this verse? Arjuna is thinking that he can kill. Is it possible to extinguish (or kill) the reality within (the soul; the divinity within; the reflection of the

Supreme Being with in an individual)? That Supreme Reality within (the soul; *atma*) is invulnerable (cannot be harmed or damaged due to attack or criticism). "Living life with this awareness" is a great strength. It is extreme assurance for an individual to assimilate that "the real Self" can neither kill nor can it be killed. This message cannot be understood with awareness, with feelings, till one probes the truth (fundamental nature) of one's soul, the ground spirituality or exclusive divinity within. Getting to this stage requires a lot of *sadhna* (practical applications of disciplines of yoga to unite with the spiritual immortal foundation within) which will be taken up in detail in the next volume "Live the Bhagavad *Gita*." Till that time comes, one has to suffice (make do or satisfy with) with the faith within. The wind is blowing out there over the sea (… nature), while the forest is seeking to hear its own voice within (… soul).

The relevance of this profound and deep message of this verse - This is how the world exists, keeping always nature and soul together. The living is different from mere existence. But the divine knowledge discussed in this verse exposes one to that other side of existence whose direction is towards the "Infinite." Then, one seeks not to get but to be. One, who truly apprehends this (divine secret; the true import of the four words used by the Lord and discussed above), neither kills nor cause be killed. The more an individual progresses in this divine knowledge (the truth indicated in this verse), the more it becomes difficult for the individual to establish separateness (ego).

Lord is telling Arjuna path of knowledge. Knowledge does not feel. It makes the seeker to feel. Knowledge is language of head and not heart. Feeling is language of heart. Lord says "It" and then uses four adjectives dealt with above. Where is Lord taking Arjuna by this path of knowledge? How should Arjuna feel about "It" that Lord is talking about? Assimilation of this message (impact of words used in the verse) requires being clear about the truth - "From love, world is born; by love it is sustained; towards the love it moves and into the love it enters." Lord is asking Arjuna to fight because of his love for the duty, love for the righteousness and love for the commitment. Lord wants the "love of Arjuna to be in motion" by the act of fighting for restoring righteousness in society. Lord is helping Arjuna to get ready to fight by making him realize first the truth of oneness (indestructibility of the soul; separateness is a delusion), oneness of our soul with the world and the manifestation of the "world- soul" in each being (numerous reflections of the moon through rays, while the moon is only one). There perhaps remains little to be known after assimilating the latent meaning, the ripple effect and expanding relevance of the words used by the lord in this verse. The opposition of "is and is not," representing the dilemma of Arjuna, is mind's view of existence. It finds its end in the realization of the soul. That is what the Lord is doing by taking Arjuna's attention temporarily from the battle field to the realm of knowledge so that Arjuna does what he does best (fighting for restoring the righteousness) for the self and the society at large.

22. In this verse Lord uses a simile to explain that this body is like a worn-out garment for the soul.

वासांसि जीर्णानि यथा विहाय नवानि गृह्णाति नरोऽपराणि ।
तथा शरीराणि विहाय जीर्णान्यन्यानि संयाति नवानि देही ॥ २- २२ ॥

vasamsi jirnani yatha vihaya navani grhnati naro 'parani
tatha sarirani vihaya jirnany anyani samyati navani dehi 2.22

vasamsi-- clothes; *jirnani*--old and worn out; *yatha*--as; *vihaya*—having cast away; *navani*—new (clothes); *grhnati*—puts on or wearst; *narah*-- man; *aparani*--other; *tatha*--in the same way; *sarirani*--bodies; *vihaya*—having cast away; *jirnani*—worn-out clothes; *anyani*-- others; *samyati*—enters; *navani*--news; *dehi*--the embodied one (i.e. soul)

"Just as a man casts off his worn-out clothes and puts on new clothes, similarly, the embodied self (soul or atma or Exclusive Divinity within) casts off worn-out bodies and enters into new physical bodies." II 2-22 II

This verse beautifully describes the true relationship between the body and the soul. This knowledge drives away the undue attachment with the bodies or relieves an individual of body-consciousness. For this purpose Lord uses a simile. What does an individual do when the clothes that he or she wears are worn-out? The individual casts away the worn-out clothes and puts on new clothes. Similarly, the soul uses a new body when the old body gets worn-out. What is more important of the two, clothes or the one who wears the clothes? Soul is the one, who wears the body. That is why, after wearing the body, it is called the embodied-self. The soul changes the worn-out raiment (clothing) for the new. This thought can be explained by another example as well. A snake develops a new skin within and then casts off the slough (a layer of the dead skin).

Here also Lord Krishna is trying to establish through a simile that soul is different from body. The "real self" is the soul and not the body. When the clothes are removed the individual still remains. Similarly when the body is cast away, soul takes another body. What is body then? Body is the medium for the soul to exist in this world of materiality. Highlighting "body-different" character of the soul is the supreme point of this verse. Imagine an individual going on a journey in a car. On the way, car gets damaged and becomes unusable. What will the individual do? The individual will take another other car leaving the damaged car to proceed towards the destination. The body is like the old car. Soul represents the individual going somewhere on a journey. It is very important to assimilate the "body-different characteristic of the soul." Apart from body-aggregate, there is something (soul) central within which keeps its identity unaltered. It (soul) is the witness of all actions, sensations, thoughts and understanding. Lord Krishna's focus is on that only. By *vivek* (divine intelligence here or intelligence soaked in divine knowledge) only that reality can be grasped. It is wrong to think that an individual is what body is. This message is the purpose of this simile.

For soul, body is like the clothes that we wear and change. When an ordinary individual considers that body is the self, the whole problem arises. If someone is sitting in a car and car gets damaged, then car is damaged and not the one sitting in the car. The one sitting in the car will take another car. An ordinary man thinks that damage to car (or death to body) is the death of the self sitting in the car. That is why an ordinary man is in problems. Arjuna is feeling panicky about the bodies of Bhishma, Drona and others not knowing that souls (real selves; the truth) of all these individuals cannot be killed. It is soul's routine to change the worn-out body.

The "Real One within or soul" is always there witnessing in mute silence and communicating at times in "flashes of gladness" about the "Unbounded Ocean of joy with resplendent (very bright and shining) light" right within lying unexplored, untouched, unpolluted while the clamor (loud noise) in the air is about the thundering high tide (body related afflictions and problems; as well as death of the body) in the sea. Is it worthwhile to cry for the stained clothes while the wearer remains hale and hearty after some bad experience (life here)? That is what Lord wants to tell Arjun by this simile. Lord wants to convey to Arjuna, "You are weeping over the loss of dress or body unmindful of 'the eternal life within or soul' which is deathless."

23. In this verse Lord points out that the four primordial elements cannot destroy the soul.

नैनं छिन्दन्ति शस्त्राणि नैनं दहति पावकः ।
न चैनं क्लेदयन्त्यापो न शोषयति मारुतः ॥ २- २३ ॥

nainam chindanti sastrani nainam dahati pavakah
na cainam kledayanty apo na sosayati marutah 2..23

na--not; *enam*--this (soul); *chindanti*—cannot be cut (to pieces); *sastrani*-- weapons; *na*--not; *enam*-this (soul) ; *dahati*--burns; *pavakah*--fire; *na*--not; *ca*--and; *enam*— this (soul); *kledayanti*-- wet; *apah*--water; *na*--not; *sosayati*--dries; *marutah*—wind.

"Weapons cannot cut it nor can fire burn it; water cannot wet it nor can wind dry it." II2-23 II

Actually Arjuna's grief was due to the apprehension (anxiety that you will have to deal with something unpleasant and bad) that he would be required to kill his elders in the battle field by hurling destructive weapons at them. Lord wants to put this misapprehension to rest. For this reason, lord is establishing the immortality (deathlessness) of soul by pointing out the unique features of soul and the inability of the four primordial elements to destroy the soul.

There are five primordial elements i.e. earth, fire, water, air and ether (radio waves travel through the ether and it is also called upper part of sky or *akash*). *Askash* is action-less. Therefore, Lord has mentioned only four primordial elements in this verse.

No weapon can cut the soul. A weapon can cut the body and kill the body but it cannot cut (or destroy) the soul, which is, as already mentioned, indestructible. Weapons are made up of earth-element. They cannot even touch the soul. How can they hurt the soul? Nothing made-up of earth-element can destroy the soul.

The fire cannot consume the soul or change its form. The soul is changeless. No destructive fire-missile can do any harm to the soul. Fire can burn the body but the soul cannot be burnt. Arjuna may have the fear that, if Bhishma etc. are killed in the battle and cremated, the selves in Bhishma and others will feel the burning. Lord is particularly clarifying this point. The self (the soul; the real self; the truth of the being) has no form. Fire cannot consume it or change its form. The soul is changeless. The fire, even if blazing greatly, cannot reduce the soul to ashes.

Varunastra (weapon of water) can be applied to destroy or dissolve the body, but soul cannot be dissolved by the water. Arjuna need not think that after the copses are burnt, the ashes are thrown into the water (Ganges etc) and the soul in the ashes will get wet. Soul has no parts. Water cannot enter it and soak it.

Vayu-astra (weapons of air) may dry up the body. The air cannot dry up the soul. Arjuna need not think that the subsequent winds, blowing over the cremation ground, will wither away the soul within the dead bodies. The soul has no moisture in it. It cannot be dried away from the wind. The wind, even when it blows tempestuously, cannot dry up the soul.

What is the focal point of discussion in this verse? The soul is indestructible, changeless and deathless. In this verse, Lord describes the inability of weapon of any kind to destroy the self. Even the well known destroyers i.e. earth, water, fire and air can do no harm to the soul. All the four elements such as earth etc. are validated or get activated by the presence of the soul. They become inert without presence of the soul. They cannot impair soul, the source of their power. The soul is all-pervading, while the four elements such as earth etc. are the pervaded ones. It is not possible for pervaded (that, which pervades, spread through every part) ones to destroy the all-pervading one.

The soul is super mundane (ordinary) with divine features [eternal, indestructible, immanent (naturally present everywhere), ancient, immutable (never changing)]. It is sheer ignorance to lament the loss to the soul which can suffer no loss ever, whatever may be the circumstances. **Arjuna is grieving over the anticipated losses to the body unmindful of the inner truth that "from the 'Everlasting Joy' do all the objects have their birth."** Lord is saying all this to Arjuna to remind him the futility of grieving over the loss of body while each one of us is rich like a king by having the soul (Divinity) within. It is a routine for an individual to change a worn-out shirt. Similarly it is a routine for the soul to change the worn-out body. Autumn makes the tree leave-less. Spring brings new leaves. It is a routine of nature. What is the point if the tree weeps about the loss of leaves due to arrival of the autumn? A flower blooms and fades away but the one (soul) which witnesses both the blooming and withering away of flowers is always there still continuing. Arjuna is full of grief in anticipation of physical death of "Bhishma, Drona and others" unmindful of "Substance of immortality (soul)" in each one of them. In sadness of all things, we hear the "crooning (singing or speaking in a soft gentle voice) of Eternal Mother." What does it mean? Due to grief of Arjuna, it has become possible to hear the song of immortality of soul. In all these verses, one message prominently comes out. An individual's body-aggregate is not the highest truth. There in each one of us is "That (soul)" which is universal, immortal, eternal and the highest truth. Nothing whatsoever can destroy it. This knowledge is a joy to us. This knowledge (divine knowledge) is our channels of our relation with the things out side. This knowledge is widening the limit of our self.

When there is so much talk about the "deathlessness of soul," a thought may come to mind. A murderer may say "Why is murder as horrible and heinous as it has been made to be, when the "Real One, soul" survives the murder? Murder is horrible and heinous and it will become clear when lord talks about Dharm (righteousness as per law of nature) in the latter part of this discourse.

24. In the preceding verse Lord tells Arjuna that the four primordial elements (earth, fire etc,) cannot hurt the soul. In this verse lord explains why these primordial elements cannot do any harm to the soul further mentioning four more characteristics.

अच्छेद्योऽयमदाह्योऽयमक्लेद्योऽशोष्य एव च ।
नित्यः सर्वगतः स्थाणुरचलोऽयं सनातनः ॥ २- २४ ॥

acchedyo ayam adahyo ayam akledyo 'sosya eva ca
nityah sarva-gatah sthanur acalo 'yam sanatanah 2.24

acchedyah--unbreakable; *ayam*--this soul; *adahyah*--cannot be burned; *ayam*--this soul; *akledyah*--insoluble; *asosyah*--cannot be dried; *eva*--certainly; *ca*--and; *nityah*--everlasting; *sarva-gatah*--all-pervading; *sthanuh*--stable; *acalah*--immovable; *ayam*—this (soul); *sanatanah*-- everlasting.

"This soul is un-cleavable (incapable of being cut into separate parts), incombustible and neither can be wetted nor dried; it (soul) is eternal, all-pervading, stable constant; it is forever and forever (everlasting)." II 2-24 II

There is a lot of repetition in this verse. Lord Krishna is trying to impress upon Arjuna the same basic thought that an individual is not body-mind-complex. Within this complex, there is something of ever lasting value (soul). This doctrine (belief) of the self (*atma* or soul) is not an easy subject. It is a very mystical (magical power which the people do not understand) and confusing subject especially for the beginners. For this reason Lord Krishna, again and again, introduces and describes the same thing in different words so that in some way or the other truth may be grasped by Arjuna. Repetition is called for and is justified as well because this knowledge is utterly important and has the effect of vanishing the grief and fear of an individual.

This (soul or *atma*) cannot be cut. Therefore, weapons cannot cut it. This (soul or *atma*) cannot be burnt. Therefore, fire cannot burn it. It cannot be moistened. Therefore, water cannot moisten it. It cannot be dried up. Therefore, air does not dry it. The effects stated in the preceding verse have to be successively (coming or following one after another) connected with the causes stated in the present verse.

The latter part of the verse states the reasons why it cannot be cut, why it cannot be burnt, why it cannot be moistened and why it cannot be dried up. It has divine features as follows:

It (soul or *atma*) is nityah (eternal) i.e. devoid of two alternatives of before and after. It is not a product which can be cut. Since it is eternal, it cannot be cut.

It is *sarvagatah* (all-pervading). Like akash (ether) soul is everywhere. How can it be burnt then? This character of the soul also dismisses the idea that self can be acquired. It always has been. It is and it will always be there, as explained earlier. This trait of the soul also speaks of its universality, its unborn-character and its in-born connectivity with the world outside. It is for this unique feature that world is called "one family."

This (soul or *atma*) is sthanuh (stable), change-less. That is why it is omnipresent. Mathematics does not apply to atman. It does not gain by addition or loses by subtraction. Mathematics applies to worldly things. Think of a tree. Break the branch of a tree. Now tree's wholeness is broken. Tree is one branch less. This feature does not apply to the soul. It maintains its wholeness. Change is not the characteristic of the soul. For this reason it cannot be moistened, capable of being destroyed by water. Atma is stable. It does not shake or even vibrate. Its presence causes vibration because the nature within a being becomes alive.

This (soul or *atma*) is acalah (immovable). Soul does not go anywhere. It always is everywhere. That it comes and goes is delusion. How is it that it (soul or *atma*) does not go anywhere? Recall the earlier discussion of space in a room. Bring a pitcher and place it in the room. Total space of the room is not reduced while the pitcher has occupied some space. No throw away the pitcher. The space of the room is not increased while the space of the pitcher is not there now. Recall that mathematics does not apply to soul. Diversity of the souls is like rays of the sun having all the characteristic of the sun while the sun always is one, always brightening and never sets in. Setting of sun is our delusion. Factually, sun never sets in. Soul is one. It is immovable. It does not go anywhere. Due to delusion we consider each ray separately. Sun is one, immovable. Similarly, soul is one immovable. Its reflection in a being, due to lack of divine knowledge, is mistaken as separate entity. Soul is reflection of the "Supreme Being" in a being validating the existence of the being. Soul does not move. Being effulgent as the ray of sun is, it validates (as ray lights the darkness) and infuses consciousness in a being. Like sun it is immovable. The concept of soul cannot be understood without thought of the "Supreme Being." The Supreme is sun. The soul is ray of sun, resplendent light of the sun. A particular ray of sun will always remain at a particular point and at a particular angle, immovable. The thoughts of change and variety are due to our perceptions based on worldly knowledge. There is no movement in the soul. This is the point to be remembered.

It (soul or *atma*) is sanatan (ancient) i.e. it is primeval or one belonging to the earlier period in the existence of the universe. The sun is also primeval. Its ray at a particular point and at a particular angle is also as old as sun is. For this reason also, "*Sanatan Dharma*" (ever present divine code of conduct) is "*atma-dharma.*" Those who have assimilated this "*atma-dharma*" become either liberated (free from birth and death or merged in the Supreme i.e. as the space in the pitcher becomes the part of the space of the room) or liberated individuals (stay in this world for cosmic benefit but free from all limitations of human understanding and experience). Lord is telling Arjuna "*atma-dharma*" by all these characteristics of the soul. Arjuan should understand that the souls of Bhishma and Drona are not 100 or 200 hundred years old only. The souls may be as old as creation. This very knowledge should convey to Arjuna that the subject of death of bodies is not a matter to be grieved about by the "knower of the self."

These discussions can be fully assimilated only when we know the concept of soul and the Supreme as one. Sun cannot be without sun rays. A wave in an ocean is ocean's water only temporarily in different form. All the features discussed so far are divine features. That is why *Sruti* (part of Vedas, divine knowledge) mention – "The Omnipresent inhabits the earth but is within it. The Omnipresent inhabits the water but is within it. The Omnipresent inhabits the light but is within it. The Omnipresent inhabits the air but is within it." The "Omnipresent," who is inner controller of all, is not subject to their actions. A weapon cuts what is not in the weapon. "This One," being the giver of existence and manifestation of weapon, is their mover and indwelling self. How can weapon etc. make it (soul) an object of their actions? Who is the One, who validates the existence of a being? This "self or *atma* or soul" only validates the existence of a being.

In this verse also Lord is throwing light on the glory of *atman* (soul) to cure Arjuna of the despondency (unhappiness and lack of hope) meaninglessly assumed by him due to lack of divine knowledge. When an individual begins to have extended view (i.e. there is a spiritual dimension to an individuality besides physical dimension) of his or her true nature, true self (soul and through soul the supreme; like the sun and the sun rays), then he or she realizes that he or she is much more than at present he or she seems to be. The individual begins to get conscious of his or her fundamental nature essentially different from physical existence. The individual grows aware of "that," which he or she is yet to be to grow to the full stature spiritually. The "state not experienced by the individual" so far becomes more real than that under his or her direct experience presently. Lord is gradually broadening the perspective of Arjuna by giving him knowledge of those facets (a particular part or aspect of something) of life, which Arjuna does not know about i.e. spiritual existence within a being, its queer (strange or unusual such as being all-pervasive, ever the same or devoid of two alternatives before and after) characteristics. Lord is awakening Arjuna to the divinity within (soul or *atma*).

25. The soul is not capable of being confined to limits of words. Lord wants Arjuna to be soul-conscious. For this reason, three negative attributes have been described by the lord in this verse.

अव्यक्तोऽयमचिन्त्योऽयमविकार्योऽयमुच्यते ।
तस्मादेवं विदित्वैनं नानुशोचितुमर्हसि ॥ २- २५ ॥

avyakto ayam acintyo ayam avikaryo ayam ucyate
tasmad evam viditvainam nanusocitum arhasi 2.25

avyaktah—un-manifested; *ayam*--this (soul); *acintyah*--unthinkable; *ayam*--this (soul); *avikaryah*-- unchangeable; *ayam*--this (soul); *ucyate*--is said; *tasmat*--therefore; *evam*-- this; *viditva*—having known; *enam*--this (soul); *na*--not; *anusocitum*—to grieve; *arhasi*—(you) ought

"This (*atman* or soul) is said to be un-manifested, unthinkable and immutable; therefore, knowing it as such, you should not grieve." II 2- 25 II

Nobody knows how to teach about this soul. Still Lord wants Arjuna to be soul-conscious. Situation is precarious (not safe; dangerous). Therefore, Lord is making reference to soul in a very peculiar way in this verse using negative adjectives as follows:

i) ***Ucyate*** (is said) – Lord is saying here something or referring to some features that have already been stated somewhere. The soul has been said to be, as summarized by the Lord here, in Vedas. Veda is the treatise (long and serious writing on a subject) on divine knowledge (knowledge about the self, the Supreme or the Ultimate Truth). It means that these features of atman (soul), which Lord is about to summarize herein this verse, are said to be there in Vedas (the four ancient sacred Hindu scripture or the book of divine knowledge).

ii) *Avyakto ayam* [This (soul or *atma*) is un-manifested or does not show clearly] – The soul is beyond the changes of body-mind-aggregate. It is not manifested like body, a physical entity, which can be touched and seen. At the same time it is greater than all the manifestations. It cannot be analyzed by intelligence as it is beyond human experience and understanding. It does not change, as everything in life changes, because it is changeless. Yet it is that, which, "all these individually or together" try to figure out. It (soul) is ear of the ear, eye of the eye, speech of the speech and breath of the breath. What cannot be expressed through speech and whereby speech is expressed, is soul. That, which cannot be breathed and whereby the breath goes on, is soul. It enables the eye to see, the ear to hear and the mind to contemplate. In brief, that which sees without eye, hears without ears, walks without legs, speaks without tongue, is soul. It is that, which is but it cannot be perceived like things having form. Since it cannot be perceived by any of the senses, it is called un-manifested entity within. It (soul or atman) is not a thing. It is eternal consciousness. It knows all the secrets. It is "The Awareness within." It is the life behind all the organs. It makes everything work without doing anything because it is action-less. It is life of life.

ii) *Acintyo ayam* [this (soul or atma) is unthinkable] – It (soul or *atma*) is inconceivable i.e. it is impossible to imagine it. Imagination requires at least two parameters i.e. thought and form. The soul is beyond thought and it is formless. Therefore, it is unthinkable, as it cannot be confined by the parameters of imagination. Mind cannot conceptualize it by a piece of thought. It is, therefore, inconceivable. Brhadaranyaka Upnishad mentions that "It (or *atman)"* is beyond the scope of term and concept. Still some word is to be used to refer to it. We use the word "atman." It is witness of every event. Every "yes" and "no" is watched by the eternal self. It has got strong foundation in experience in your own self. Suppose fire is there and it is not visible to eye. Then based on smoke one can infer that fire is there. In case of soul, even this type of inference is not possible. Therefore, soul is unthinkable.

iii) *Avikaryo ayam* [This (soul or *atma*) is changeless] – This (which is referred to as soul or *atma*) is changeless. Many of our organs (like mind, intelligence and memory), though imperceptible (unable to be seen or felt), are seen to be objects, that are inferred from noticing their effects. How else do we know the existence of memory? Whatever is changeable, such as eye etc. is taken to exist on the ground that its effects cannot be explained in any other way. It becomes an object inferable (suggested indirectly) from noticing its effects. But this One (soul or *atma*) is neither changeable not transformable. It is sovereign knowledge, which is beyond understanding (by intellect) but it can be intuitively [using feelings, rather awareness, than facts] experienced. It is "that" which eternally remains as it is without change like the sun-ray falling on earth on a particular point at a particular time at a particular angle.

There is definite repetitiveness of either meaning or words in these verses. It is deliberate. In the beginning, when we think about the soul, it is hard to know what we are thinking (i.e. soul is inscrutable). For this reason, Lord Krishna is raising this topic again and again and explains the same object again and again so that somehow "the self (soul or *atma*)" may come under the range of feelings of the concerned individual. Even this much intuitive exposure to soul is enough to bring cessation to cycles of death and birth of the one, who strives.

iv) *tasmad evam viditva enam na anusociati arhasi* [Therefore, having known it (soul or *atma*) as such, you should not grieve] - Having known this (soul) as such (as it has been described by different adjectives used by the Lord), it is not fit to grieve for the supposed destruction of the un-manifested, the inconceivable and the immutable i.e. soul or *atma*. The root cause of man's sorrow is ignorance of

One's real nature. Due to ignorance an individual starts identifying with the body and mind complex. The divine knowledge (knowledge of eternity, indestructibility, immanence and immutability of the soul) dispels darkness of ignorance. Now Arjuna knows the true nature of the self (soul or *atma*). Therefore, it is not befitting to bewail or grieve for the bodies of the kith and kin (at this juncture when war is just about to start). Lord is exhorting Arjuna to know the truth in the light of discussion so far and transcend sorrow and delusion.

Lord is making Arjuna realize that there is no point in grieving over the bodies of kith and kin. Things are what they are and we have to know them rather experience them, if we have to deal with them. Lord wants Arjuna to be thoroughly exposed to the divine knowledge. This knowledge is one of the channels of our relations with things outside us. When we know the divine characteristics, as mentioned by Lord Krishna in this verse also, and experience them within us, we make the factors outside our selves our own. We start looking at the things with a wider perspective. Suffering is a part of living. We suffer pain, because somewhere we are in conflict with the universal law. An all out solution of our sufferings lies in realizing the truth, the immortality within and around. This exposure to the divinity within us, awakens "**The Holy Giant**" (uncovers the self or *atma*) in us and this is sufficient reason to catapult (to throw suddenly and violently) us on the path of divinity. Lord's prime focus is to ensure that sight of body is not confused with perception of the self within (soul or atma). The "Supreme Self; Eternal, Universal Reality" is one. Bodies, it permeates, are many. It is necessary to overcome the idea of plurality of souls, which is result of inability to grasp the truth. "Supreme Self, One Single Whole, One eternal Unity" reflects in all souls, as one sun reflects in numerous rays. "That divine reflection within all, that awakened space within all, that ocean of bliss and knowledge within all" is the divinity within all, concealed under the layers of ignorance. Supreme Self is like the sun (One only) and individual souls are like numerous sunrays, products of our ignorance. This divinity within, with ignorance and memories of the past, is referred to as the self (individualized soul i.e. divine reflection plus ignorance and past memories). Through each "sun-ray" same sun is visible. Similarly, through each soul, same truth, same supreme is visible. Who is a friend? Who is an enemy? The fundamental truth of all is the same. Differences of opinions are vagaries of thinking, distorted perception of same "Reality." With this vision, all beings (friends, foes and relatives) are extensions of the same Reality. Nothing except "One" exists. Everything exists as This (Supreme Reality) exists. When one gets established in this thinking, death loses stings.

26. Now in this verse, Lord justifies his stand inversely (completely opposite of earlier stand) based on materialistic stand point i.e. Lord is now arguing from a different and lower point of view.

अथ चैनं नित्यजातं नित्यं वा मन्यसे मृतम् ।
तथापि त्वं महाबाहो नैवं शोचितुमर्हसि ॥ २- २६ ॥

atha cainam nitya-jatam nityam va manyase mrtam
tathapi tvam maha-baho nainam socitum arhasi 2.26

atha-- now; *ca*--and; *enam*--this (soul); *nitya-jatam*-- constantly born; *nityam*-- constatnly; *va*-- or; *manyase*—you regard; *mrtam*--dead; *tatha api*—even then; *tvam*--you; *maha-baho*--O mighty-armed one (Arjuna); *na*--not; *enam*—this (sou); *socitum*--to grieve; *arhasi*— (you) ought.

"Even if you think of it (soul) as being constantly born and constantly dying, even then, O mighty-armed, you should not grieve." II 2-26 II

Lord has told Arjuna about the divine characteristics of the soul in earlier discussion. Lord now in this verse reverts (goes back) from his authoritarian and mystic (spiritual matters with powers which people do not understand) teaching to rationalistic arguments based on common man's understanding bereft (without any hope) of divine knowledge. If Arjuna thinks that soul is born regularly and dies regularly, even then there is no reason to lament. Why is it so? Those who die will be born again and those who are born will die again. If this continuity in the form of life and death is law of nature and it simply cannot be changed, then there is no option but to accept the inevitable. Why should Arjuna then grieve in killing seniors, teachers and kinsmen? Death, according to new arguments, is inevitable for those who are born and birth is inevitable for those who die. Therefore, as a matter of fact, there will be no extinction or utter destruction of teachers and kinsmen, as Arjuna fears. If death and birth is taken as natural law of soul, then let the natural law prevail. What is there in the form of loss or disadvantage? In that case also, taking for granted (admitting something as true without being sure), like an ordinary man, that there is birth and death for soul, will it not be good to let the continuity go on unhindered? Why has Lord changed the line of arguments in this verse? Theoretical affirmation of the immortality of the soul may still be difficult to be grasped by Arjuna with feelings, with awareness, despite of all the above explanations. For this reason, Lord in this verse gives practical reason, which the common man without divine knowledge may follow.

The Lord is calling Arjuna mighty-armed i.e. Arjuna is having great physical energy and strength. Arjuna is very dear to Lord. Lord wants to endow him with the divine knowledge, which is not easy to grasp. Therefore, the Lord appreciates Arjuna's strong points and uses suitable adjectives after every now and then to bring him (Arjuna) in receptive mood.

27. Lord continues with the cogent (strongly and cleverly expressed in a way that influences what the people believe) argument started in the previous verse i.e. even if it is taken for granted that soul regularly takes birth and dies, grieving for the death is not justified.

जातस्य हि ध्रुवो मृत्युर्ध्रुवं जन्म मृतस्य च ।
तस्मादपरिहार्येऽर्थे न त्वं शोचितुमर्हसि ॥ २- २७ ॥

jatasya hi dhruvo mrtyur dhruvam janma mrtasya ca
tasmad apariharye 'rthe na tvam socitum arhasi 2.27

jatasya—of the born i.e. one who has taken his birth; *hi*--for; *dhruvah*—(is) certain; *mrtyuh*--death; *dhruvam*-- certain; *janma*--birth; *mrtasya*--of the dead; *ca*--and; *tasmat*--therefore; *apariharye*—inevitable or unavoidable; *arthe*--in the matter of; *na*--not; *tvam*--you; *socitum*—to grieve; *arhasi*—(you) ought.

"For, to the one who is born, death is certain and certain one is about the birth for the one who has died. You should not therefore lament over the inevitable." II 2-27 II

Even if it is taken for granted that the soul is subject to birth and death, death is certain for one who is born and birth is certain for one who has died. Even based on worldly arguments (soul is subject to birth and death), birth and death are inevitable events in the continuity of the soul. Accepting the inevitable (the event of death which has to be necessarily faced by all) should not be a cause of Arjuna's grief. It is one way of putting the things. If there is life, there will be death as well. Accepting this (birth and death) as law of nature, which cannot be interfered with by human beings, has a greater bearing upon the happiness of life than any other factor. Developing the right mind set, somehow, towards the intriguing events and realities (birth, death, soul and the Supreme i.e. grand essentials of life) is the ultimate purpose of the Lord. Others have done it (Bhishma and Drona came to battle

141

field prepared to die). why can't Arjuna do it? It is a matter of daily experience that everything that is born, dies sooner or later and new forms spring up from the dead remains of old ones. Fountain of "this wisdom" makes the still water of life play. In nut shell, Arjuna's sorrow, about the possible death of seniors, teachers and relatives, is an ignorant grieving because the dead ones have neither gone out of existence nor suffered any painful or terrible change of condition. Arjuna has to just look beyond the apparent (which can be seen by senses) to the "Reality" within.

In this world of becoming, everything changes and becomes something else. The realization of this fact brings in a human being poise, proportion and peace. Death is certain for the one who is born. Lord Buddha explained it very beautifully. Once, a mother lost her son. She was inconsolable (so sad that it was impossible for anyone to comfort her). Lord Buddha asked her to go into the town to bring a little mustard seed from any house where no one till then had died. The mother went and found that there was no house where death had not occurred. This is a law of nature that one, who has taken birth, will pass away. Through birth we come. Through death we go away. By one way we come. By another way we go away. What is there to weep for? What is there to be worried for? Weeping for death is inconsequential.

28. The discussion in verses 26 and 27 was based on the assumption that soul is subject to birth and death. In this verse, Lord mentions the simple law of nature relating to events called birth and death and indirectly hints towards the soul again.

अव्यक्तादीनि भूतानि व्यक्तमध्यानि भारत ।
अव्यक्तनिधनान्येव तत्र का परिदेवना ॥ २- २८ ॥

avyaktadini bhutani vyakta-madhyani bharata
avyakta-nidhanany eva tatra ka paridevana 2.28

avyakta-adini--in the beginning un-manifested; *bhutani*—all beings (that are created); *vyakta*--manifested; *madhyani*--in the middle state; *bharata*--O descendant of Bharata (Arjuna); *avyakta*—un-manifested; *nidhanani*—in the end; *eva*--also; *tatra*--therefore; *ka*--what; *paridevana*—lamentation or grief.

"Beings are all, O Bharata (Arjuna), un-manifested in the beginning, manifested in the middle and un-manifested in their end. What is there to be worried about?" II 2-28 II

Let the truth be known. This is the intention of the Lord. There is a beautiful expression of the same truth in the Sanatsujatiya Section of the Santi Parva of the Mahabharata "we come from the un-seen and go back to the unseen." That is our everyday experience. There is past. There is future and in between there is the present. Birth and death are mysteries and midway one assumes form. What precedes birth or follows death, no one knows. All creatures appear only for a short time and then disappear. What is there to be grieved about it? **Death is not that bad. Fountain of death makes the still water of life play.**

How does this appearance and disappearance before and after the existence happen? That is the secret, supreme secret. Lord is tangentially (only indirectly and related to the subject) bringing this issue again and again to make Arjuna aware of it. This life is a union of the nature and the "Exclusive Divine Essence, or Truth or Reality (no name and form can define it fully)," which is the ultimate source or validating cause of all existences. This physical body is a combination of five primordial elements (nature). Appearance of form (birth) is the result of presence of the Divinity (eternity, indestructibility and presence everywhere) in the cover of aggregate of ego, past impressions, five primordial elements and attributes of nature. With death these five elements disintegrate. Physical body separates from subtle body and the soul veiled within. There is no life visible in the body after death. This body appears only in the middle state. All the relationships in the form of son, daughter, wife, father, mother, and teacher are formed through this body due to attachment and delusion. Planks (long narrow flat piece of wood) on the surface of a running river float (move quickly on water), unite and separate. Pilgrims unite and separate in the public inn and also in a railway compartment. Similarly, relationships in the forms of fathers, mothers, husbands, wives, sons, daughters etc. arise due to body. With death we separate from them all. This world is a public inn. People unite and separate as a matter of course. One who truly understands this inevitable phenomenon of the nature of bodies, appearing and disappearing, will not grieve. This is a very difficult subject but it is also a profound truth. Extreme subtlety (quality of noticing and understanding based on very small details) is required to comprehend even a bit of it. Lamenting over or getting glued up to the loss of temporarily-looking relations serves no purpose. Arjuna is in a very peculiar predicament. Life has no longer any meaning for him at this stage. He requires a method for managing his way through and out of his grief. Lord Krishna is therefore telling him a sure method, a philosophy, a fundamental reality and a truth, which has perennially helped all to bear with due acceptance the burden of grief. Feeling this secret of soul at the level of perception and then deliberately picking up again with faith, which is an inevitable consequence of this awareness, makes an individual victorious in achieving the mission of life. Birth is not the supreme truth nor is death the supreme truth. In spiritual journey, appearance and disappearance are like dreams which appear and pass away or like waves in the ocean which appear and then disappear. The "knower of the truth of the soul" does not grieve for all this. One, enriched with divine knowledge, takes it differently. Then even this darkness in death may unfold into "**the eternal dawn," glittering with the gold of divine truth**. Death is the inevitable change in the eternal journey, which just cannot be negotiated. There should be no lamentations for death.

29. The heterodox (not following the usual or accepted beliefs and opinions) argument dealt with in preceding verses (i.e. soul is subject to birth and death; basis of discussion between verses 26 to 27) winds up here. From this verse, Lord again returns to orthodox method of enquiry, which requires constant attempts to "understand while feelings at the level of awareness." Without these earnest efforts to feel with awareness, the Gita-reading gets reduced to parrot-reading. Lord again reverts to discussion on soul and how one feels while thinking about soul.

आश्चर्यवत्पश्यति कश्चिदेनमाश्चर्यवद्वदति तथैव चान्यः ।
आश्चर्यवच्चैनमन्यः शृणोति श्रुत्वाप्येनं वेद न चैव कश्चित् ॥ २- २९ ॥

ascarya-vat pasyati kascid enam ascarya-vad vadati tathaiva canyah
ascarya-vac cainam anyah srnoti srutvapy enam veda na caiva kascit 2.29

ascarya-vat—as a wonder; *pasyati*--sees; *kascit*—some one; *enam*--this (soul); *ascarya-vat*—as awonder; *vadati*—speaks of; *tatha*--so; *eva*--also; *ca*--and; *anyah*--another; *ascarya-vat*—as a wonder; *ca*--and; *enam*--this (soul); *anyah*--another; *srnoti*--hears; *srutva*--having heard; *api*--even; *enam*--this (soul); *veda*--do know; *na*--not; *ca*--and; *eva*--also; *kascit*--anyone.

"One beholds this (the self) as wonder; another mentions of it (the self) as marvelous (amazing); again another hears of it as strange; while none knows it even after hearing of it." II 2-29 II

Lord is again talking about this (the self or soul). Some see this truth (the self or *atma*) as wonder. Some speak and hear about it as wonder. This (the self or the soul or *atma*) is a tremendous mystery, "imprisoned splendor." It (the self) is imprisoned in each one of us. Very few understand it. It (the self or *atma*) is always there but it does not allow you to notice and discover it. Even Kathopnishad says "it does not manifest." We cannot see it. We cannot understand it but we can intuitively (based on feelings rather than knowledge) realize it. That is exactly what we do in the spiritual span of life. If one is able to intuit (know with feelings) with this (soul or *atma*), all hatred, all doubts, all misunderstandings, all limitations, all short comings of narrow vision will disappear like the fog after the sun shine. This great mystery (the self or the *atma*) is so near to us but it is still so far away from our understanding. One may have all the richness (abundance of resources in worldly terms) but still one may not feel free. But, with the knowledge of your true nature (nature of the self or atma), one really feels free in the true sense of the world. We have heard a lot "Let it (the self or atma) come out; let it manifest." How do we do it? That is a million dollar question. When we probe deep into our own nature, the secret within, the self, the *atma*, the wonder that we see outside becomes less and with efforts "greater nature within our own; the self or *atma*" becomes revealed to us.

The knowledge of this "wondrous self; the atma" cannot be achieved through senses. The self is beyond the realm of the senses. It is truly "wondrous self." Why is it that the soul is considered a wonder? What is it that makes soul so wonderful? Every trait of soul mentioned in earlier discussion is unique and startling. An individual has three bodies (covers) i.e. physical body (which we can see and touch; changes continuously; non intelligent), subtle body (*sukshma sarira*; composed of very fine elements; no shock can destroy it; can endure for eons and eons; consists of mind, intellect, the un-manifested and ego; the causal body i.e. the past impressions and tendencies in seed form are taken to be the part of the "Un-manifested Nature" for this discussion and brevity) and none of these individually is the "knower." Knower is behind them all. In Sanskrit this knower is called *Atman* (soul of the individual or the real self). Soul is the ruler of all these instruments, the master of the house. The faculty of egoism, the faculty of intellect and the faculty of cognition, the organs, the instruments, the body, all of them depend for sustenance on the validation by soul. It is the soul which validates or manifests all of these. Are there many souls? The thought of plurality of souls is ignorance and manifests only imperfect state of understanding of "Cause of all the causes." In the context of an individual, it is called the self (atma or soul). In the context of universe it is called Brahamn (Parmatama; Supreme Etenal Universal Self; the God)). As sun manifests through numerous rays, Universal Eternal Self (Parmatama; the God) manifests through numerous souls. Imagine a mass of fire and an infinite numbers of sparks flying out. Similarly from the Supreme Eternal Universal Self all this universe of soul has come out. Soul (with Unmixed Divine Purity enveloped within) is the divine light within covered under the layer of ignorance i.e. divinity enveloped in limitations. Supreme Universal Self is divinity without any limitations. When the soul breaks the shackles of ignorance, it shines brightly without limitations and individual light mixes with the light out in the universe. As the space within mixes with the space outside, the individual soul loses its identity in the "Supreme." The infinite is one and not many. That "One Infinite" is reflecting through thousands and thousands of mirrors appearing to be so many different souls as the Sun is reflecting through different rays. This "One-Infinite" has two aspects i.e. immanent aspect (naturally present in every form) and transcendental aspect (or beyond human understanding and experience). The whole universe shrinks and expands. This whole universe will goes back to "Cause of causes; transcendental aspect of the Supreme reality" and again its material will come together and take forms like the wave that goes down, rises again and takes shape. The acts of going back to "Cause of causes" and coming out again are all truly wondrous phenomena. Why is Lord laying so much stress on soul-awareness and wonders associated to it? Eternal peace belongs to those, who perceive eternity existing within everybody as *atma* (the self; soul). The one, who sees "One in all and all in "One," sees the "One" everywhere (this is the most wonderful aspect of this knowledge; wonder of the wonders). To fully understand this (this divine knowledge) and to experience the "oneness" of the "Supreme Universal Eternal Reality; transcendental aspect) and the individual soul (the immanent aspect i.e. it is naturally present in all forms), is the highest achievement and the only goal of human birth. When an individual realizes that the Supreme Soul is all-pervading and is none other than one's own self "bereft of all impurities collected over numerous lives in past," the individual attains immortality, knowledge and bliss. In these moments of realization one finds oneself wonderstruck. Words do not come out. Illusion turns into illumination of joy. Only smile communicates the feeling of bliss inside. Desires evaporate. A desire to envelope all in love surges. One thinks only in the larger interest of the cosmos. The purpose of this discussion is to tell what the people do not know and what "wonder" they miss by not being aware of the divinity within.

This verse beautifully describes the four stages (hearing, thinking meditating and seeing) of this "most tremendous and wondrous of all mysteries; Cause of all causes." Lord stresses the word wonder and then adds that none understands it. The indirect reference is to the immanent (naturally present in every form; soul or *Purusha*) and transcendental aspects (beyond human understanding and experience) of the Supreme Self (*Parmatama*). Being stuck up with this wonder is eternal union with the life and joy of the "Supreme Master." It shadows the solitude and deepens the effect of the touch of the "One" who sustains in birth, in death and even beyond that.

30. The basic discussion (Self-knowledge) about existence of the Supreme Soul in all the bodies, started in 11th verse concludes here in 30th verse. Arjuna's grief was due to body-consciousness i.e. body is the self. Lord tells Arjuna that the self (atman; the reflection of the Divine self within; the Consciousness within) is the "Real Self" within an individual. This knowledge (sum and substance of the knowledge expounded in verse 11th to 30th) brings freedom from all limitations such as cycles of birth and death.

देही नित्यमवध्योऽयं देहे सर्वस्य भारत ।
तस्मात्सर्वाणि भूतानि न त्वं शोचितुमर्हसि ॥ २- ३० ॥

dehi nityam avadhyo ayam dehe sarvasya bharata
tasmat sarvani bhutani na tvam socitum arhasi 2.30

dehi—indweller or the owner of the material body or the soul; *nityam*-- always; *avadhyah*--cannot be killed or destroued; *ayam*--this (soul); *dehe*--in the bodies; *sarvasya*--of all; *bharata*--O descendant of Bharata (Arjuna); *tasmat*--therefore; *sarvani*--all; *bhutani*--living entities (that are born) or creatures; *na*--not; *tvam*--yourself; *socitum*—to grieve; *arhasi*— (you) ought.

"The Indweller in the bodies [the soul; atman; reflected (individual) soul] of all is ever indestructible or invulnerable (i.e. it cannot be hurt physically and emotionally), O Bharata (Arjuna). Therefore, you should not grieve for any being." II 2-30 II

The soul within an individual is indestructible i.e. "truth; eternal existence" of Bhishma, Drona and others will not be destroyed with death of physical bodies. Therefore there is no point in grieving for any creature. Lord seems capable of filling an atom with ocean. The words used are extremely meaningful and one starts feeling staggered when on thinking one becomes aware of the full meaning as is clear from the following:

dehi nityam avadhyo ayam dehe sarvasya, **O Bharat** (O Arjuna, indweller in the bodies of all is ever indestructible) – More important than apparent meaning is the inherent meaning of these words. Lord has used singular for the indweller and plural for the bodies of all. What is the inherent meaning of the lord by this? There is only "One Truth; One Reality" (Supreme Universal Eternal Reality; Brahman; the God; *Parmatman*) without a second. This "One Truth and One Reality" manifests through all beings. This "One Reality; One Truth" exists both as formless and in forms. How does it happen? Nature is inert. Its movement results from the presence of "The Divine." There is only "One Self" who exists. This all-pervading Reality is regarded as many due to ignorance. This One Supreme Self (Brahman; *Parmataman*; Supreme Universal Eternal Self) is the self (atman; divinity within covered in the layers of ignorance) of everybody i.e. every being in this universe. The Omnipresent, omniscient and omnipotent God (The Supreme Self; Brahmn) associated with maya (nature – five primordial elements, three attributes and known and unknown laws of nature) exists in all as the "reflected self or the individualized soul of an individual." This establishes the essential distinction between the self (*atma*) and Supreme Universal Reality (*Parmataman*; the God without name and form and with name and form as well). The soul [*atma* or reflected (individual) self] has all the divine characteristics (eternity, indestructibility, immanence or present everywhere) of the Supreme beings. Lord's knowledge is not understood by intelligence. It has to be intuited (perceived with feelings). The real self of a being is not body but the soul which is consciousness, bliss and non-duality in nature. This feature of non duality establishes that Supreme exists in each being under the cover of ignorance. So, "That reality; That Truth" with reference to an individual is called "the individual self; the Atma (in contrast the Supreme is called Parmatama); Divinity under the cover of ignorance" and with reference to cosmos it is called "Universal Eternal Supreme Self." The difference is due to perception and arises due to ignorance. The state of perceiving no distinction between the souls (perceived divinity under cover or limitations) and the single "the Supreme Universal Eternal Reality" is highest state of enlightenment. The Moon is one. It is being reflected in multitudinous rays as many. When we realize it there is no grief. One discovers deathlessness in death. Then what is it that one has to do? One has to control and attempt more and more on the purification of mind so that it may reflect more and more on the "Light of the Self." This is what Lord is doing i.e. shifting Arjuna's mind from physical dimension to the "the Spiritual essence within," which is also the gateway to "Light of All the Lights; All-Pervading One." Lord is removing the "darkness of ignorance" opening our eyes to "The Truth and the Reality" which is the same as 'The Formless (i.e. Supreme Universal Reality) or as "reflected (individual) realities or souls" (i.e. in forms). When this conviction, that an individual is a compound of the "Reality" which is immortal and the body which is mortal, becomes an integral part of a being's psyche, there is no grief. The "Truth and Reality" is really not affected by body and mind. The body and mind merely hide its (truth's) glory as clouds hide the sun. This discussion touches the heart with a flash of gladness. Then the seeker moves forward towards the "spiritual vision," which is the vision of the whole truth. This causes highest delight to a being (jiva), because it reveals to a being "the deepest harmony" that exists between the seeker and the surroundings.

A relook at related aspects of Sankhya (Self-knowledge) or the contents of verse 11 to verse 30

The discussion contained in the verses from 11th to 30th is called **Sankhya** [self-knowledge i.e. how reflection of the "Supreme Eternal Universal Reality: Supreme **Purusha; Paramatma**" in every aspect of nature (**maya**) makes inert (without power to move or act) nature take on the appearance of consciousness]. This term Sankhya has been used for the first time in verse 39 only when Lord Krishna is concluding the discussion on Sankhya (self-knowledge). This is the most secret knowledge and at the same time most important as well for living the Gita and not merely reciting or parroting it. One should live with this conviction, which is the greatest mystery of the Universe. It is as follows:

i) There is "One Supreme Universal Eternal Self; *Parmataman; Brahmna*" which exists both as "One formless; Nirguna" and in forms (Saguna);

ii) "One Reality or One Truth" reflects in all beings as one sun reflects in all numerous rays. The concept of plurality of soul is an illusion. It is the product of mind under the influence of ego. "THAT ONE" alone exists through all.

iii) This Truth is eternal, indestructible, immanent (present everywhere and in everything) and immutable (unchanging). It is the "Ultimate Secret." It is unfathomable (immeasurable) energy field which is the "Sole Cause" of everything everywhere. To become conscious of this "Universal Power" is to become a live wire.

This secret has got three aspects i.e. i) transcendental (beyond human mind and experience) aspect, ii) Immanent aspect (present everywhere and in everything thing) and iii) mystic aspect (present everywhere as providential or universal software).

i) Transcendental aspect - In this aspect it (Supreme Universal Eternal Reality) is in un-manifested form. It is consciousness, knowledge and bliss. In this form it is called "The God (It is always referred to in singular)." It is the sole reason, which validates the existence of all that is. This power alone exists either in "Un-manifested form" or in manifested form i.e. as creation. It is unborn, eternal, permanent and primeval (present at the time of creation as well). It is beyond caste, creed, concept, faith and limits of countries. It is the Supreme Master, Lord of Lords. It is omnipresent (present everywhere), omnipotent (most powerful) and omniscient (knower of everything). It is the same for the whole universe. It is indestructible, immanent (present everywhere and in everything) and immutable (unchanging). It does not kill nor can it be killed by any one. The same Supreme Being exists in all, in all bodies without exception. With reference to universe, it is called "The God (always in singular)" (The Supreme Being; The Supreme Brahman; The Supreme Soul; The *parmatman; Param Purush*, The Exalted Being; The Primeval being; The God of Gods; The Ultimate Source of Cosmic Energy; The Sovereign Knowledge). Weapons do not cut it. Fire does not burn it. Water does not make it wet. It is always there whether you believe it or not or understand it or not. When there is nothing (cosmic period of non-manifestation running into unimaginable number of years), it is there. Whenever reference is made to eternity or immanence (present everywhere) in transcendental (beyond limitation of human understanding and experience) aspect, this is to emphasize that the Supreme Universal Eternal Reality is limitless. Lord Krishna after some discussion shows Arjuna the transcendental cosmic form with divine eye and even then Arjuna could not see the beginning and end of that vision. It was so big that Arjuna got horrified and started trembling. This aspect always remains un-manifested and incomprehensible because the Supreme Being is subject to none. No rules and regulations are binding on this aspect. Based on this aspect, the Supreme Being is called "the Sovereign Lord; Lord of Lords; The Infinite." In our discussion we will use the term "Supreme Self or Supreme Being or Supreme Soul" for making a reference to this aspect. This Supreme Being remains both as un-manifested and manifested. It (Supreme Being; gender is not relevant to this aspect) always manifests as combination of two aspects i.e. Higher Nature and Lower Nature. Feeling it with awareness is beyond human knowledge and experience. One has to consciously overcome limitations of human understanding and human experience to feel it. That is why it is called the transcendental aspect of self-knowledge.

ii) Immanent aspect – At the time of creation the same "Supreme Soul" manifests in all beings.

That is why Lord, in verse 2.30, says "The indweller (dehi; singular) in all bodies (dehe;plural) is eternal and un-killable (not liable to destruction)." "Understanding how one exists in all" presents difficulties in initial stages and definitely requires some aid in gaining comprehension. Recall the two attributes of the Supreme Being in transcendental aspect i.e. indestructible and immanent (present in everything and being everywhere). Whenever there is creation, "The Un-manifested Supreme Universal Self" extends its two aspects i) Higher nature and ii) lower Nature (Refer to the chart in introduction for further details). Note the word "extends and not creates." This can be explained by an example. Suppose a ball is there. At one time, only half of the view of the ball is possible. We write on one half "A" and leave the other half blank. Now we hold the blank portion. The side with A is not available. We now show the side with marking "A." Now side with marking 'A' is in view and blank side is not in view. Ball is the same. Similarly at the time of creation the Supreme Universal Self extends its two aspects i.e. Higher Nature and Lower Nature. Truth or Reality is the same.

Lower Nature has been dealt with in detail in introduction. Here it should suffice that nature is the mystical power or dynamic energy or software or executive director of the Supreme Universal Reality. In verse 2.25 Lord says the Supreme Soul is *avikaryah* i.e. it is Unchanging. It does not do anything. All the activities of the cosmos i.e. creation, sustenance and destruction are carried out by nature. What is the function of the Lord then? It validates everything by its presence. It activates nature which remains inert without divine presence. Nature is too big. It is also beginning-less and deathless. It is combination of five primordial elements, three gunas (sattva, rajas and tamas) and Mahat (Cosmic intelligence i.e. known and unknown laws of nature). The presence of Lord is there in everything everywhere as "Reflected Individual Reality or Individualized Soul."

When lower nature and higher nature (Refer to chart in introduction for further details) meet, two things happen simultaneously. Ego (consciousness about separate existence i.e. "i-am-feeling") is born. Mahat (cosmic intelligence) under the influence of ego joins this combination as individual intelligence. These two create mind i.e. a medium, an individual zone of consciousness for cognizing and facilitating transmission between internal world and external world. Since nature is involved actively, all five primordial elements and other components of nature (refer to chart in introduction) are available at service. Ego, un-manifested Nature, and intelligence keep guiding the mind. The mind gets loaded with certain relevant impression of past tendencies (vasanas), for which "matching experience" has not been lived so far to off-set them. Mind also gets company of individual intelligence (that part of consciousness which discriminates). Now the seed for the production of an individual (i.e. addition of physical body) is ready and it develops further into an individual (Subtle body plus physical body and "exclusive divinity" concealed within).

Self realization (or perceiving the individual aspects and cosmic aspect of eternal existence at the level of consciousness) is the state in which an individual's *antahkaran* (combination of ego, *avyakta* or the un-manifested, intelligence and mind) becomes conscious of the divine presence within the "Reflected individual self; Individualized Soul; Deluded Soul; Jiva." Mind becomes no-mind with all its impressions gone. Intelligence perceives no duality. Divine knowledge makes ego conscious of its invalidity. Past impression and tendencies do not haunt and disturb. One starts perceiving that the same "Supreme Soul" as conscious-space (soul) exists in all beings as "Reflected Individual Reality; Deluded Self; Individualized Soul." Exclusive Divinity or soul is the Real Self or Truth without cover of ignorance. A liberated soul, i.e. soul without any trace of nature, is as good as effective and as expansive as the Supreme universal Reality (Brahmn).

Multiplicity of souls is a wrong concept. For self-realization, one has to overcome the concept of duality. Same Universal Self exists through all everywhere. How is it? The Supreme Universal Self is not anything solid which has to be fragmented so that each soul gets its appropriate share or content. It is "Consciousness, Knowledge and bliss." Suppose five open containers are placed on the roof top. In each container, reflection of moon is there. Each ray has the characteristic of luminosity of moon light. Now it does not mean that there are five moons on the roof. There is only one moon with its rays all over. Similarly there is only one "Supreme Universal Eternal Reality" which is eternal, indestructible, all-pervasive without beginning and end. It is of the nature of knowledge, awareness and unlimited joy. There is no place, where it is not there. There cannot be a place without divine presence. Everywhere according to divine potential, a being (living being or non-living being) comes out. Each being is different based on peculiar combination of attributes (sattva, rajas and tamas), primordial elements and extent of consciousness. A being remains there as a being so long as combination of divinity (divine spiritual essence) and nature (ego, ignorance and its associates) is there. When a being cognizes its divine nature, it becomes liberated from limitations i.e. birth and death are no more relevant for it. The "Truth" in each being, after gaining full awareness of its divine nature, regains the knowledge of its divine characteristics, which it has been missing due to ignorance. So, what is soul? It is that (Real Self), which validates the "Reflected Individual Reality or Jiva) and remains under the cover of ego (Refer to the chart in introduction for further details). Actually this "Reflected Individual Self" under the veil of ignorance is also not reality. It is illusion. It is the limitation which the Supreme Being puts on through nature to set in motion the processes of creation, sustenance and destruction. Thus soul ("Divine Content or "Real Self") within symbolizes the "immanent (present everywhere)" aspect of the Supreme i.e. Supreme is there in every being everywhere even in every cell and atom. Sankhya knowledge emphasizes this "immanent; present everywhere" aspect of the Supreme Being.

iii) **The Mystic aspect** – This is symbolized by the term nature [five primordial elements, three gunas or attributes and known and unknown laws of nature (as Mahat i.e. Cosmic Intelligence)]. A passing reference of this aspect was also made during the discussion of immanent aspect. Nature (here lower nature) is the software of the Lord or the "Executive Director of "The Supreme Universal Eternal Reality." It is most powerful. It is subject to none except the "Supreme Being." It is impossible to cross this formidable Maya (lower nature) without the grace of the Lord. It is also beginning-less and endless. It also always remains either in manifested form or in dormant state within the Supreme in the "Cosmic Period of non-manifestation (refer to chart in introduction, if required)."

What is the sum and substance of the "Sankhya (Self- knowledge)"? Lord is prompting Arjuna to focus on the "Supreme Universal Eternal Reality" which exists through all beings as indweller or soul (the real self; divinity in exclusion) concealed in the "Reflected Individual Reality or deluded soul or individualized soul or jiva." This indweller alone is truth. This indweller alone is to be thought about. This indweller alone is the object of existence. This is the bull's eye that one has to focus upon as the supreme reward of existence. Nothing else matter. "That one alone exists" is truth. Duality is delusion. Arjuna's grief is due to impact of nature, which is sure to go away with divine knowledge (eternity, indestructibility and immanence present everywhere in everything). For this reason, Lord keeps telling Arjuna, in the whole Gita, about the three aspects (i.e. transcendental, immanent and mystic aspects dealt with above) and three ways (path of action, path of knowledge and path of devotion). That is all the Gita is about. The most essential feature of the Gita is to focus towards one's purest nature, "Divinity without veil of nature; Divinity in Exclusion; Divinity sometimes dancing as mighty wave and sometimes mirthfully expanding as silence beneath the unfathomable depths of ocean." This point of prime focus of the Gita is so formidably important that in the end while concluding the

Gita the Lord once again reminds Arjuna by two important statements i) The Lord* (the Supreme Universal Eternal Reality; *Ishwarah*, as Lord calls this "Reality" at a latter stage) is seated in the hearts of all beings … ii) Seek refuge in HIM, O Bharta (Arjuna). By His grace you will gain Supreme peace and Eternal Abode.

31. In this verse Lord reminds Arjuna of his *svadharma*.

स्वधर्ममपि चावेक्ष्य न विकम्पितुमर्हसि ।
धर्म्याद्धि युद्धाच्छ्रेयोऽन्यत्क्षत्रियस्य न विद्यते ॥ २- ३१ ॥

sva-dharmam api caveksya na vikampitum arhasi
dharmyad dhi yuddhac chreyo 'nyat ksatriyasya na vidyate 2.31

sva-dharmam--one's own duty (considered after all tangible and intangible factors); *api*--also; *ca-* and; *aveksya*—looking at; *na*--not; *vikampitum*—to waver; *arhasi*--you (ought); *dharmyat*—than righteousness (arrived at in soul-touched wisdom after consideration of all relevant factors, written or spoken); *hi*--indeed; *yuddhat*--than war; *sreyah*-- higher; *anyat*-- other; *ksatriyasya*--of a *ksatriya* (warrior-caste) ; *na*--not; *vidyate*-- is.

"From the point of view of your "svadharma," (refer to explanation below), it is not fit for you to waver. For a kshetriya (caste of Arjuna), there is nothing more auspicious than a just war." II 2-31 II

In this verse Lord is giving worldly reasons for fighting the war. Arjuna is a kshetriya by caste. The protection of righteousness by accepting a war is the social duty of a kshetriya. Lord asks Arjuna to consider his "Svadharma" in finally deciding what to do.

Svadharma is a very peculiar Sanskrit word with no English synonym. It means considering

---

* Whom does the Lord (Krishna) refer to by using the word "Ishwarah; The God" in the above statement? Lord Krishna here refers to that "Supreme Eternal Universal Self; The Absolute Universal Self," whom lord Krishna represents in human form. Lord Krishna is incarnation (The act of the God coming to earth in human form) of the "Supreme Eternal Universal Self; The God of the Gods." The word "Lord; **Ishwarah**" used by Lord Krishna, in the above quoted statement, requires explanation. For this Supreme Universal Eternal Reality (Lord or *Ishwara*), we have to enter the inmost self of our existence. Then we become aware that there is one spirit (Universal Divine Energy) in us and in all. The whole nature serves and manifests this "Supreme Divine Energy." This Supreme Divine energy is the Soul of our souls (the soul is one; beings are innumerable like sun and sunrays). This life is a movement of rhythm of "That Divine Existence." This mind is a sheath of "divine consciousness with limitations." Actually, our sense-instruments, our emotions, our delight, our sufferings, our actions, our freedom and our limitations are all essentially influenced by "Divine Will." Our achievements are only reflection of "Divine Power" at work. Our best knowledge is partial manifestation of "Divine Knowledge." Our "ultimate salvation" lies in realizing that behind all that happens or does not happen, lies the will of "The Supreme Master; Supreme Soul of the Universe." To live continuously, consciously and integrally in this awareness is the best way to escape from ego. The continuous awareness of this "Divine Reality" i.e. to feel unbreakable continuity and association with that "Supreme Eternal Reality" at all times is the only way to break out of maya (nature), most illusory impasse (a situation in which no progress can be made) for any being in the pursuit of self-realization. The greatest yoga is to take break from all the perplexities and difficulties of life and take refuge in this "Indwelling Supreme Lord of nature." This is why Lord's focus in Sankhya (Self-knowledge between verse 11 and verse 30) is on "Supreme Universal soul" existing through all beings. But this turning to "The Lord of the Universe" is to be with our whole being, with life, body, senses, mind, heart and understanding, with whole dedicated knowledge and action in every way of our conscious selves and our peculiar nature based on our gunas (attributes). "Divine Light; Divine Love; Divine Power" takes hold of us (ourselves; our instruments), when this happens. Then "Divinity" leads us all, beyond the limits of our understanding and experience, to the "Supreme Peace, Spiritual Freedom and ever renewing joy" of our immortal and eternal status. Now Lord has told Arjuna the "Final Destination" [Supreme Eternal Being present in all under the garb of ignorance; to uncover this ignorance and be aware of the Truth (Divine nature)}. To be aware of this quintessential (most important aim of life] knowledge is this Sankhya (this self knowledge between verse 11 and verse 30). In the rest of the Gita, Lord will discuss various aspects and routes to get to this destination. That is what the Bhagavad Gita and self knowledge is all about.

duty based on an individual's peculiar temperament in view of mix of three attributes i.e. sattva (seed of divine intelligence), rajas (seed of energy) and *tamas* (seed of inertia or non-action or ignorance), cultural upbringing and heritage. Viewed from this angle, Arjuna's grief and retraction (pulling back from waging a war) is not justified. Being a *kshetriya*, his duties are i) not to retreat from battle-field, ii) protection of his people and iii) serving the brahamins. Considering the issue from point of view of *svadharma*, he is a renowned warrior. He is a *kshetriya*. It is his duty to save his people by accepting the war. War, as it is, is not a good option. But at times, for the sake of upholding righteousness and abiding the social order, a war is the only option or last resort. For Arjuna, war is an option in line with his social order, the law of his life (he is a warrior) and law of his being (he is rajas-dominated individual: this attribute is not conducive to asceticism or renunciation). There is nothing more auspicious than a righteous war for an individual of his background. There is no greater merit than doing one's own *Dharma (svadharma)* and no greater evil than forgetting and neglecting it.

32. In this verse also, Lord Krishna continues to convince Arjuna to wage war for restoring righteousness.

यदृच्छया चोपपन्नं स्वर्गद्वारमपावृतम् ।
सुखिनः क्षत्रियाः पार्थ लभन्ते युद्धमीदृशम् ॥ २- ३२ ॥

yadrcchaya copapannam svarga-dvaram apavrtam
sukhinah ksatriyah partha labhante yuddham idrsam 2.32

yadrcchaya—of itself; *ca*--and; *upapannam*—come; *svarga*--heavenly planet (highest *lokas* of the 14 *lokas* mentioned in chart in the introduction); *dvaram*--door; *apavrtam*--wide open; *sukhinah*--happy; *ksatriyah*--the members of the royal order of warrior-caste; *partha*--O son of Prtha (Arjuna); *labhante*-- obtain; *yuddham*--war; *idrsam*-- such.

"Happy are the kshetriyas (ones belonging to the caste of Arjuna), O Partha (Arjuna), who get such an unsolicited opportunity for war, which offers an open gateway to heaven." II 2-32 II

It has always been a conviction (strong belief) of that era that the warriors of "Kshatriya category" must fight a righteous war for the eradication of un-righteousness and protection of society. If there is victory in the end, they will attain fame and kingdom. In case of defeat, they will attain "svargadvaram; gate of heaven." What is this "svarga; heaven"? Heaven is some region (pleasant, happy place) believed to be the home of the God (kingdom of God) where good people go after death. By this statement, Lord turns aside (or responds to) Arjuna's undue emphasis on the sin of committing murder of kinsmen in the war. This doubt was expressed by Arjuna in the beginning of the Gita. Arjuna's argument was that the death of kindred ones (those with family relationship) will empty his life of causes and objects of living. Lord is touching the same point. What is the true object of kshatriya's life, his true happiness? A kshatriya essentially does not clamor (demands loudly) for self-pleasing domestic happiness or life of comfort and peace with friends and relatives. To fight for restoration of righteousness (i.e. fair and acceptable worldly and morally as well) is the true object of life of a kshetritya. A true kshatriya does not seek shallow victory. His true happiness lies in seeking hero's existence. A kshatriya therefore feels happy for fighting a righteous war i.e. his aim is not murder and slaughter to amass wealth. His prime focus is always on righteousness which culminates by continuously struggling in between right and wrong and justice at the conscious level within. War remains a last option to be exercised when justice is denied and righteousness is vanquished (defeated). In Mahabharta also, the option of war was resorted to when all other options had failed. A kshetriya fights not for just visible goals (winning a kingdom or self glorification) but for that, which his conscience considers worthy of fighting for on moral ground. Arjuna did not seek war. It has come by itself by chance. Pandvas wanted to avoid war knowing its consequences. Therefore, now Arjuna should accept it acting like a true ksatriya. That is what Lord Krishna wants to convey in this verse. Arjuna should feel happy for having gained this awaited opportunity of waging a righteous war.

According to the ancient Indian thinking, there are only two types of men who can pierce the constellation of sun and reach sphere of Brahmn (Supreme Self); the one is ***sanyasin*** who is steeped in yoga and the other is the warrior who falls in the battle field while fighting.

33. In this verse also, Lord Krishna continues to reply point raised by Arjuna at the beginning of the dialogue.

अथ चेत्त्वमिमं धर्म्यं संग्रामं न करिष्यसि ।
ततः स्वधर्मं कीर्तिं च हित्वा पापमवाप्स्यसि ॥ २- ३३ ॥

atha cet tvam imam dharmyam sangramam na karisyasi
tatah sva-dharmam kirtim ca hitva papam avapsyasi 2.33

atha--but; *cet*--if; *tvam*--you; *imam*--this; *dharmyam*—righteous duty (arrived at after considering all relevant factors, written or spoken, in soul-touched wisdom); *sangramam*- war-fare; *na*--not; *karisyasi*—will do; *tatah*--then; *sva-dharmam*--your righteous duty; *kirtim*--reputation; *ca*--and; *hitva*—having abandoned; *papam*--sin; *avapsyasi*-- shall incur.

"If you will not wage this righteous warfare abandoning your duty and honor, you will incur sin." II 2-33 II

Arjuna at the start of this dialogue made a very bold statement, which can win favor of any ordinary man i.e. "Sin will certainly accrue to us by killing these felons (those who have committed serious crimes), O! Madhusudana (krishna), and even while we die by them (in battle), I do not want to kill them." It appears to be a very plausible (reasonable and likely to be true) statement from an ordinary point of view but it conceals the righteousness invisible to the naked eye but inherent form moral angle.

It has been called a righteous war. Why is it so? This war was not being waged to snatch the kingdom or wealth of others. It was being waged to relieve the society of those who were hell-bent to strip off a lady in the open court in the presence of even all known righteous people (Bhishma etc.). This war was being waged to teach a lesson to the spoilt prince (Duryodhna) who did not think necessary to give even princely rights to other members of the clan and ganged up even people with good judgment (Karna) to participate in the war. Duryodhna was adversely using his influence and official machinery to harm the selected few. When there is a conflict between the morals and political economy, one should not transgress (cross) the Dharma-sastra (moral ground). Righteousness (moral ground) was openly ignored by the Kaurvas who were after visible results regulated by artha-sastra (economic angle alone). This was the primary bone of contention that triggered war. When there exists uncertainty between right and wrong, justice and injustice, the force that protects and the force that violates and oppresses, the champions and standard-torch-bearer have to come forward to shed even blood to turn the events to restore the righteousness in society i.e. justice to all as per law of nature. This struggle, this violence, this terrible nature of work for the just ends is called "righteous war."

In this verse Lord gives a mild warning to Arjuna i.e. by not fighting the righteous war he was likely to forfeit his own duty and honor. Arjuna was not an ordinary warrior. He was known worldwide for his archery. He rather used to be talk of the town. He fought even with Mahadeva (Lord Shiva)

who got pleased with his skill and gave him a boon. Arjuna's real earning was his fame for bravery and rightful conduct towards his seniors (Drona and Bhishma etc.). By running away from the battle field, Arjuna was likely to lose reputation, which others could have earned in many lives.

Arjuna's enemies were not going to let him go off the field. There was every possibility or likelihood that the wicked people would kill him in the war even if he decided not to kill. Thus, he was to earn only demerits by retreating from his original stand to fight. Thus by not waging the war at that juncture, Arjuna was likely to lose life as well as the merits earned over a long period of time.

Arjuna talked about incurring sin by waging the war against the relatives, seniors and teachers. What is sin? It is that act which creates ordeal, suffocation, helplessness, intense suffering and repentance to "individualized soul or *jiva* or deluded self" (nothing happens to exclusive divinity concealed within). It is an act of offence against a religious or moral law. It is of two-fold nature: i) sin of commission i.e. doing something wrong or forbidden such as theft, adultery etc. and ii) sins of omissions such as not respecting or maintaining parents and elders, not punishing the undesirables or the dangerous elements in the family or society . The evil called sin yields or results intense pain and suffering even after a long time when it becomes due for "matching experience" based on law of morality (this is the thinking as per scriptures). Based on the logic put forth by Lord Krishna in these verses, the sin was not in fighting the war. The sin was in running way from the war based on law of morality and social expectations from a well known 'kshetriaya'. As per accepted ancient Indian thinking, pain from a sin is experienced even in subsequent life when "matching experience" becomes due for past actions after thorough considerations of all merits and demerits. If Arjuna abstains from the fight, he will incur the sin of neglecting his duty, a violation of Dharma (duty or righteousness as per law of nature). Lord Krishna warns him that he will be hurled into hell (region or place believed to be the home of devils and where bad people go after death), if he does not fight the righteous war.

Lord has clarified that sin arises from the act of desisting from battle, which is forbidden by scriptures (i.e. traditionally accepted and documented moral values and facts). This sin will also forfeit merits and fame earned by Arjuna.

34. In the next three verses as well, Lord Krishna continues about the consequences of not waging a war.

अकीर्तिं चापि भूतानि कथयिष्यन्ति तेऽव्ययाम् ।
सम्भावितस्य चाकीर्तिर्मरणादतिरिच्यते ॥ २- ३४ ॥

*akirtim capi bhutani kathayisyanti te 'vyayam
sambhavitasya cakirtir maranad atiricyate 2.34*

akirtim—infamy, dishonor ; *ca*—and; *api*— also; *bhutani*—all beings or all people; *kathayisyanti*-- will speak; *te*--of you; *avyayam*—ever lasting; *sambhavitasya*--for a respectable man; *ca*--and; *akirtih*- -ill -fame; *maranat*--than death; *atiricyate*--becomes more than or exceeds.

"People will ever speak of your unending infamy. To the honored, infamy is surely worse than death." II 2-34 II

In war, there always remains a possibility of death. The characteristic of an ordinary man is to preserve life somehow. For avoiding death even infamy has to be tolerated by people who cling to life at the cost of dishonor. For a righteous man like Arjuna, who is very famous as well, the infamy ((state of being well known for evil things or wrong reasons) is worse than death. Lord is bringing Arjuna's attention to his good fame. He has confronted even Lord Shiva. It will be difficult for Arjuna to bear the humiliation and resulting pain from the infamy (Arjuna was never like that; he was a true kshetriya). In Shantiparva of Mahabharta, it is given that for a king dharma-sastra (i.e. moral duties) is more important than artha-sastra (i.e. economic advantage). A king should never retreat from a battle field. Arjuna has always been a hero. He knows well to safeguard life and to sacrifice it as well for a great cause. It is indeed bad for a hero to cringe (to move back due to fear) before the enemy for life after losing honor and fame. Lord, is telling Arjuna what he (Arjuna) is going to face, if he decides to run away from the battle field or retreat at that juncture. So, it is a sort of warning to Arjuna that his infamy will be proclaimed all over the world for all the time to come. All the heroic people think that death is better than dishonor. For them, ignominy (public shame and loss of honor) is unbearable.

35. Another warning to Arjuna.

भयाद्रणादुपरतं मंस्यन्ते त्वां महारथाः ।
येषां च त्वं बहुमतो भूत्वा यास्यसि लाघवम् ॥ २- ३५ ॥

bhayad ranad uparatam mamsyante tvam maha-rathah
yesam ca tvam bahu-mato bhutva yasyasi laghavam 2.35

bhayat—from fear; *ranat*--from the battlefield; *uparatam*-- withdrawn; *mamsyante*—will think; *tvam*--you; *maha-rathah*--the great chariot warrior; *yesam*--of whom; *ca*--and; *tvam*--you; *bahu-matah*--in great estimation; *bhutva*—having been; *yasyasi*--will receive; *laghavam*--decreased in value or smallness.

"The great chariot-warriors will view you as one fled from the war out of fear. You, who were highly esteemed by them, will be lightly held." II 2-35 II

In this verse, the term 'great chariot-warriors' has been used for Drona and Bhishma etc. They were very senior and both of them loved Arjuna dearly. In this situation, a warrior like Arjuna may think to justify himself "Let the indifferent people defame me. But the great chariot-riders, Bhishma, Drona and others, will eulogize me because of my being compassionate." To do away the possibility of this type of thinking, Lord gives another warning. Bhishma and Drona etc. will think of him as having run away from the battle field out of fear. Thus, Arjuna was likely to earn the contempt of those who have held him in high esteem (held with great honor and respect). Lord wants to make it clear to Arjuna that his avoidance of battle will never be construed (taken to mean) an act of mercy and consideration but as one of the cowardice or weak-heartedness caused by fear.

36. In this verse, Lord warns Arjuna against the possible adverse comments of his sworn enemies (that have strong hatred for each other).

अवाच्यवादांश्च बहून्वदिष्यन्ति तवाहिताः ।
निन्दन्तस्तव सामर्थ्यं ततो दुःखतरं नु किम् ॥ २- ३६ ॥

avacya-vadams ca bahun vadisyanti tavahitah
nindantas tava samarthyam tato duhkhataram nu kim 2,36

avacya—vadan—words that are improper to be spoken or unbecoming words; *ca*—and; *bahun*—many; *vadisyanti*—will say; *tava*—your; *ahitah*—enemies; *nindantah*- caviling or disparaging or criticizing remarks; *tava*—your; *samarthyam*—might or ability; *tatah*—thereafter; *duhkha-taram*—more painful; *nu*— indeed; *kim*—what.

"Many of your enemies will use unseemly (vile) words disparaging your strength. Could anything be sadder than that?" II 2-36 II

Duryodhna and others were arch enemies of the Pandvas. Arjuna's name used to create shudder in the hearts of his enemies. Arjuna's martial appearance in the battle field damped the war-zeal of his enemies. If Arjuna beats a retreat at this juncture, his enemies will ridicule him. They will not understand the concern that Arjuna is having for them despite of enmity. They will slander (false spoken statement intended to damage the good opinion that the people have) Arjuna using unbearable words. They will indulge in insolent (rude showing lack of respect) jokes, using indecent language. In other words, Arjuna will have to bear the sorrow caused by belittling of his prowess by the enemies. Their (enemies') fear of Arjuna will turn into ridicule. There is no greater sorrow than being subject to calumny (false statements). In other words, at that juncture, there was no alternative to waging the war that has been declared. Lord is making all efforts to make Arjuna conscious of direction in which his moral and social standards point him to go (These remarks of the Lord should be seen in contrast to the central teaching of the Gita that one should be indifferent to praise and blame; For life as a whole, that is the correct philosophy, but in short run when war, already declared, is about to begin, Arjuna has to decide the immediate action to be taken). Both moral and social standards demand Arjuna to wage war at this juncture.

37. Now in this verse, lord finally exhorts Arjuna to take action.

हतो वा प्राप्स्यसि स्वर्गं जित्वा वा भोक्ष्यसे महीम् ।
तस्मादुत्तिष्ठ कौन्तेय युद्धाय कृतनिश्चयः ॥ २- ३७ ॥

hato va prapsyasi svargam jitva va bhoksyase mahim
tasmad uttistha kaunteya yuddhaya krta-niscayah 2.37

88 *hatah*--being killed; *va*-- or; *prapsyasi*--you will gain; *svargam*--the heaven (highest loka; refer to chart in introduction); *jitva*--by conquering; *va*--or; *bhoksyase*--you enjoy; *mahim*--the world; *tasmat*--therefore; *uttistha*-- stand up; *kaunteya*--O son of Kunti (Arjuna); *yuddhaya*-- for fight (to do away with perpetrators of unrighteousness, which was the main consideration before coming to battle field); *krta*--determined; *niscayah*- resolved.

"You will go to heaven, if killed or you will enjoy the kingdom of earth if victorious. Therefore, get up with a determination to fight, O Son of Kunti (mother of Arjuna)." II 2-37 II

Lord has already told Arjuna that it is a righteous war. Its purpose is to do away the unrighteousness perpetrated by the Kaurvas and their associates in the society. They were committing crimes that even today will make the onlooker shudder (stripping off a lady in the open court in broad day light in the presence of whole assembly). Lord has told Arjuna both moral and worldly reasons of waging this war in detail in the preceding verses. There was no option left now but to wage the war, because the war had already been declared and it was just about to start. Now in this verse Lord exhorts (to try hard to persuade) Arjuna to takes action finally. The issue has been well deliberated in the preceding verses. All the options are open now. If Arjuna dies in the battle field, as this one possibility always remains there in a war, then he will enjoy heaven (i.e. beautiful, pleasant and enjoyable region or place, where God is believed live and where good people are believed to go when they die). If Arjuna is victorious in the war finally, then he will enjoy the kingdom of earth i.e. he will enjoy the sovereign earthly bliss. Therefore, lord tells Arjuna to get up with determination to fight (not for slaughtering the people for material gains but to restore righteousness in the society).

In this verse also Lord replies one point raised by Arjuna. In verse 2.6, Arjuna says " …nor do we know whether we shall conquer them or they will conquer us." Lord has now told Arjuna the end result of both eventualities of war i.e. in death he (Arjuna) will attain heaven and in victory he will enjoy the kingdom of earth. Therefore Lord asks Arjuna to fight (the righteous war; which is the only alternative left now because all other possibilities have already been discussed, explored and discarded on being found lacking). This exhortation of the Lord to fight is sometime discussed and interpreted wrongly by some people. They ignore that it is a righteous war. It is not a war to amass wealth. It is a war to protect the call of conscience, rule of moral and social laws. It is a war to protect "Dharma; interpretation of righteousness as per law of nature." The war has already been declared, conches have been blown and it is just about to start after a while. This exhortation to fight is not instigation to fight. It is a favor to an individual to save him from "self-destruction due to ignorance." It is a well thought of guidance given to Arjuna because he admitted that he did not know what his duty was under those very confusing circumstances. This advice was given by the Lord because he (Arjuna) took refuge in the Lord. Lord is exhorting Arjuna to fight (to restore righteousness). Some people, due to ignorance, say that Lord has instigated Arjuna to fight. This amounts to ignorance of facts. Lord has told Arjuna "His" considered opinion. Arjuna has to fight with the resolution to either conquer them (enemies) or die in the attempt.

38. In the preceding verse Lord Krishna asked Arjuna to get ready to fight against the enemies. In this verse, Lord tells him how he has to get ready for this eventuality i.e. what his attitude should be.

सुखदुःखे समे कृत्वा लाभालाभौ जयाजयौ ।
ततो युद्धाय युज्यस्व नैवं पापमवाप्स्यसि ॥ २- ३८ ॥

sukha-duhkhe same krtva labhalabhau jayajayau
tato yuddhaya yujyasva naivam papam avapsyasi 2,38

sukha—in pleasure; *duhkhe*--in pain or distress; *same*-- alike; *krtva*—having made; *labha-alabhau*--both in gain and; *jaya-ajayau*--both in defeat and victory; *tatah*--thereafter; *yuddhaya*--for battle; *yujyasva*—engage thou; *na*--not; *evam*-- thus; *papam*--sin; *avapsyasi*--you shall incur.

"Treating pleasure and pain, gain and loss and victory and defeat alike, engage yourself in your duty. By doing your duty this way, you will not incur sin." II 2-38 II

This verse contains very important message to help anyone to face any situation of life even today. For best outcome one has to remain in mental state of equanimity (mental calmness with which one reacts with patience and forbearance in difficult times). The wise wholeheartedly welcome pleasure and pain and joy and sorrow without being discouraged. Only two types of people are happy in this world i.e. those who are completely ignorant and those who are truly wise. All others are unhappy because they get swayed (to move slowly from one side to another) by emotions. The whole social, economic and spiritual make-up of the world is based on the central and dominating idea of pleasure, gain and victory. Due to these thoughts (pleasure, gain and victory), we harbor (keep bad thoughts) the thoughts of fear and undue concern. Thoughts of fear drive us to exploit others we start incurring sins. Therefore, Lord has given the advice to treat the opposites equally.

Lord says that following this advice (i.e. being in the state of equanimity, calmness, away from duality), Arjuna will avoid incurring sins. Why is it so? Desire (kama) and anger (krodha) are the emotions that bring about sins. By being indifferent to gain and loss, victory and defeat, pleasure and pain, one feel naturally inclined to eschew (avoid) lust and anger. Keeping the mind off the opposites, one is able to free the mind from evil thoughts. This is the whole Dharma (maintenance of righteousness as per law of nature). Therefore, one should not allow the mind to get colored (influenced) by these contrasting emotions. This is the basic thought. Rest is sound and show (play of nature) which can be handled effectively, if basic are taken care of.

This verse contains a very important lesson. One should not allow mind to be influenced by contrasting emotions. Best course is to remain in the state of equanimity without yielding to restless desire for change, without being at the mercy of emotional ups and downs. Lord's emphasis is on being in the state of equanimity (equal-mindedness in all situations) in this verse. Where does this equanimity come from? This comes from firm belief in "Eternal existence within." When we have this treasure (i.e. firm belief in eternal existence), sorrows of the world (loss of property, name, honor, children and wife) do not disturb. One attains this state of equanimity only when one discovers the true end of life and commits to it with utter commitment i.e. application of sankhya-knowledge (self-knowledge0 discussed by the Lord in verses 11 to 30.

39. The discourse (serious conversation) of lord about "*Sankhya*" is over. Now Lord imparts about "karam-yoga."

एषा तेऽभिहिता साङ्ख्ये बुद्धिर्योगे त्विमां शृणु ।
बुद्ध्या युक्तो यया पार्थ कर्मबन्धं प्रहास्यसि ॥ २- ३९ ॥

esa te abhihita sankhye buddhir yoge tv imam srnu
buddhya yukto yaya partha karma-bandham prahasyasi 2.39

esa—this (whatever has been talked about so far by Krishna); *te*--unto you; *abhihita*--described; *sankhye*- (self-knowledge); *buddhih*--intelligence; *yoge*—in the yoga; *tu*-- indeed; *imam*--this; *srnu*-- just hear; *buddhya*-- with intelligence; *yuktah*-- induced; *yaya*--by which; *partha*--O son of Prtha (Arjuna); *karma-bandham*—bondage or shackles of action; *prahasyasi*--you can be released from or you shall cast off.

"This (equanimity; even-mindedness; or spirit of equal-mindedness for dualities explained in verse 38) has been taught to you in wisdom of Sankhya (jnana-yoga) now listen to it according to wisdom of yoga (or yoga mode or path of yoga or how work can lead to spiritual realization), endowed with which, O Arjuna, you shall cast off the bonds of actions." II 2.39 II

Lord has told Arjuna self-liberating wisdom of Sankhya [nature of One Supreme soul which exists in all bodies and its two aspects the transcendent (beyond human knowledge and experience) and immanent (present in everything everywhere) aspect of the Supreme Self]. This knowledge is capable of achieving equanimity (equal-mindedness) referred to in verse 38.

Traditional *Sankhya* vs. the Gita's version of *Sankhya* - This *Sankhya* (self- knowledge), preached in the Gita, is different from the *Sankhya* philosophy of sage kapila. The *Sankhya* of the Gita has gone beyond the *Sankhya* of sage Kapila. The *Sankhya* of Kapila is of the opinion that highest duty of everyone in this world is to give up worldly life and take up sanyas (renunciation; abandoning action, which binds). The *Sankhya* of the Gita expects the seeker to transcend all limitations (impressions and dualities of mind) and attain the state of equanimity (equal-mindedness in all situations i.e. spiritual freedom) to have union with "eternally continuing joy, knowledge and awareness."

Lord Krishna is not confined to the traditional concept in the Gita. Traditionally speaking, *Sankhya* means focus on Purusha (self; atma; exclusive divinity) and nature (non-self). As per traditional version of concept of Sankhya, liberation is achieved when buddhi (intelligence) discriminates the purusha (self) and prakriti (non-self). The Sankhya concept of the Bhagavad Gita stresses on the reality of the "Supreme Self" as sovereign Lord of all and stresses on the transcendence i.e. going beyond human limits of understanding and experience. The Gita focuses on the intuition (idea of truth on feeling and not facts alone) of "Eternal and Unchanging One" and this must become an inward experience i.e. an integral part of psyche by self-searching. Thus the Gita's concept of Sankhya goes beyond mere discrimination of self and non-self. It focuses on intelligent knowledge of things and "prime or ultimate cause of the things" and internalization of this knowledge i.e. internal discipline or internal absorption of this knowledge of the self (sankhya). Now in this verse, Lord proceeds to tell Arjuna use of intelligent knowledge of Sankhya in external discipline of action or path of work (i.e. practice of this knowledge in action). Use of this knowledge (Sankhya) in discipline of action will relieve from bondage or impurity caused by action. Up till this verse, lord told Arjuna "Pure science (of self knowledge)." Now Lord wants to tell Arjuna the applied science.

Lord tells Arjuna that attaining equanimity through Sankhya has been taught already (from verse 11th to verse 30th). Now Lord asks Arjuna to listen how same equanimity (equal-mindedness in dualities or contrasting situations; spiritual liberation) can be attained through wisdom of yoga (or through "intelligence disciplined in yoga"; yoga-buddhi). In this verse, Lord calls it "buddhiryoga" and in verse 3.3 Lord refers to it as karam-yoga (path of action under the guidance of purified or disciplined intelligence).

Why is Lord teaching Arjuna another technique (Buddhiryoga path of action under the guidance of purified or disciplined intelligence), when Arjuna has already heard the path of Sankya (jnana-yoga)? For discharging a function one has to know both theory and practical as well. For spiritual maturity, one must know the Supreme and its two aspects i.e. transcendental (beyond human understanding and experience or un-manifested aspect of the Supreme) aspect and immanent aspect (the Supreme is in all as soul). But this knowledge (Sankhya) becomes dry. The dominant thought of "Sankhya" is that this world is false (mitthya). Soul alone is real. That means we have to learn to live in "the unreal world" thinking always about a "Reality" which is yet to unfold itself to us. First we are being taught that world is unreal and yet we have to work out our way to "the Supreme" in this very world. As a matter of fact we are being taught in Sankhya to live in the world and our work has to show absolute unconcern (renunciation) for the world. Sankhya philosophy makes an individual self-centered and unconcerned about others. Sankhya philosophy separates a seeker more and more from world of action an emotion. The seeker starts withdrawing into realm of abstractions. There are two major limitations of traditional Sankhya approach for which the new approach in the Gita offers solution i.e. i) desire of results is the motive and ii) one works for the result. These two factors cause bondage to a living being.

Lord Krishna in the Gita offers now "buddhi-yoga i.e. buddhi (intelligence) must be disciplined to attain insight, constancy and equal mindedness in dualities while working, while doing actions right here in this world." The essence of new approach is the "karam-yoga" i.e. buddhi (intelligence, which is higher than mind) should guide the mind to be united with the purified buddhi (disciplined, cultivated, pointed intelligence) and not with the senses. A disciplined, cultivated intelligence knows the difference between nature (always dynamic never static) and purusha (the individualized self i.e. reflected individual divinity under the veil of ego, mind and past impressions). What is the change that happens with this new approach? Buddhi (intelligence i.e. one which knows the discrimination between real and unreal) becomes the driver in the chariot called body. This chariot (body) is drawn by the horses called senses. These horses (senses, which so swiftly go here and there) are controlled by the rein called mind. Who is there travelling in this chariot? The one travelling in this chariot is "the self; soul' exclusive divinity," who is superior to buddhi (intelligence) but is a passive witness, a validating reality, whose sovereign presence certifies that a being is.

The word yoga in exclusion means all disciplines (physical, mental, emotional and spiritual) used to take off impact of all nature (gunas; mind with impressions of different experiences in the past) so that one perceives the true nature of one's self (divinity as embodiment of truth, consciousness and bliss). Here in this verse, yoga does not mean Patanjali-yoga. Here, the word used is "Buddhiryoga" i.e. that intelligence, which has been subjected to various disciplines to make it sharp, sensitive, perceptive, one pointed, with far vision, qualified enough to be called "self–liberating intelligence." This type of intelligence, cultivated through various disciplines, casts away the bondages of works (actions). Why is it so? The work done under the guidance of such intelligence is not done with attachment for fruit of action but it is done as an offering to the Supreme for cosmic-benefit. This mode of doing work casts away the bondage (capturing tendencies) of works or actions done.

Lord has concluded discussion on *Sankhya* (*jnana-yoga*) and the discussion on *buddhir-yoga* (karam-yog i.e. working under guidance of disciplined or cultured intelligence) is about to be started. What is the difference between wisdom and intelligence? Intelligence is the high level discriminating faculty i.e. ability to understand and think clearly, quickly without trace of ambiguity. It is a tool that one employs to manage (why, how, where and whether to act or not to act) the different actions in life. Wisdom is the maturity (outcome of association or experience) that one gains after applying the knowledge and acting according to one's intelligence. Wisdom is just like the crop that you get after putting the seeds and tendering (gently and careful loving) them over the time. Wisdom is abstract in nature (based on general ideas or principles) i.e. what sankha (jnana-yoga) is about. Buddhiryoga (karam-yoga or action in accordance with purified, cultured intelligence) is related to practical employment of wisdom in action (i.e. in daily life) through the medium of intelligence. *Sankhya-yoga,* implemented traditionally (i.e. with stress on sanyas or abandonment of action), leads to boredom. *Buddhiryoga* (path of action under the guidance of pure buddhi) gives direction to action through disciplined buddhi (intelligence) keeping in view the ultimate purpose of life based on Sankhya (jnana-yoga). Buddhiryoga (the path of action without attachment to fruit of action and doing action in spirit of surrender to the Supreme i.e. under the guidance of cultured intelligence) gives emphasis on disciplining the intelligence that guides the senses through mind. Buddhiryoga (path of action under the guidance of cultured intelligence) is the practical workout of "**inward experience; vision of ultimate purpose of life**" through *Sankhya* (jnana-yoga; knowledge of the Supreme and its two aspects, the Self and the nature). In "*buddhiryoga*" emphasis is not as much on external karma as it is on "*Yoga-buddhi*; the intelligence engrossed in the awakening or awareness due to proximity of soul or soul-touched intelligence."

This verse makes a mention of two paths i.e. Sankhya (Self-knowledge/jnana-yoga) and buddhiryoga (path of action under the guidance of disciplined or cultivated or nurtured intelligence) intelligence. These are not discordant paths (seemingly strange and lacking harmony). While the first system helps to get the grip of the intuition of "The Ever Unchanging Existing in All" and the other requires a through workout in yoga, various disciplines for uniting the mind to pure buddhi (to become buddhi-yukta, united with pure intelligence nurtured in Sankhya). When buddhi (individual intelligence) is lit up by the consciousness of the self (resplendent truth obscured in the soul or the Cosmic Intelligence or Mahat), it becomes a "master light of life" like ray of a light house in the darkness of night to a ship lost very away in the ocean. The guidance of such nurtured intelligence is always in harmony with cosmic purpose and the "Divine Will." The individual intelligence becomes pure intelligence only when it gets clear of obscuring and capturing tendencies of working in this world for its benefit. Then the intelligence is not distorted by the impressions of the actions performed. The individual intelligence, then, always gets transformed anew, sparkling and clear and reflects the true nature of the "Supreme Being" like crystal clear mirror without just any spot. Actions performed under such intelligence are not of capturing nature. One casts way all the bondages (limitations) and work is done without attachment to the results for cosmic benefit as an offering to the Lord within. Purified intelligence means thoughts of the Supreme reflects in it and, with divine thoughts within, the intelligence cannot go astray or one will get saved from the influence of nature. The Gita's most special contribution is its unique "Path of action" i.e. there is no need to run away from the creation to the caves of mountains for the "Creator," who lives in the creation all the time in every aspect of it, in it and around it. It is due to Creator's presence that the entire creation comes alive. Therefore, be in this world with 100% active participation for the world with full consciousness all the time about the "The Wordless, Nameless, Formless, Universal, Eternal Reality" keeping in view its two aspects i.e. nature and the self. That is the message of this verse. Like *Sankhya* (self-knowledge), karam-yoga is the full fledged intelligence-based approach. This "yoga-buddhi" is the intelligence baked in the awareness of soul. It is "*samattva-buddhi*" i.e. the intelligence which remains in state of equanimity against mind's responses to host of interactions in daily life. It sublimates (directs) the individual's vital energies towards the objective of existence, which is not a subject of mind but a concern of the soul.

In this verse, Lord has beautifully used two terms "*Sankhya-yoga*; Self-knowledge" and "*Buddhiryoga*; yoga of knowledge." What is the difference in these two terms? *Sankhya-yoga* is intuitive knowledge about the attributes and nature of "Divine Eternal existence" at the level of conscience through awareness. Ascending to the level of "*Sankhya*; Self-knowledge" through individual intelligence and cosmic intelligence is "*Buddhiryoga*; intelligence faculty steeped in yoga." Sankhya (self-knowledge) may be a result of divine grace or it may result from Bhakti yoga (gaining absorption in the Supreme through devotion) as well. But *Buddhir yoga*, necessitates use of intelligence (both individual and cosmic) for self-knowledge. *Sankhya* is the "ultimate wisdom," while *Buddhir-yoga* is one approach for attaining this.

40. In this verse, Lord tells Arjuna that there is no loss in following buddhiryoga (the path of action under the guidance of disciplined intelligence).

नेहाभिक्रमनाशोऽस्ति प्रत्यवायो न विद्यते ।
स्वल्पमप्यस्य धर्मस्य त्रायते महतो भयात् ॥ २- ४० ॥

nehabhikrama-naso asti pratyavayo na vidyate
svalpam apy asya dharmasya trayate mahato bhayat 2.40

na--not; *iha*--in this; *abhikram-nasah*—loss of effort; *asti*--is; *pratyavayah*- diminution or production of contrary results; *na*--not; *vidyate*--is; *svalpam*—very little; *api*--even; *asya*--this *dharmasya*-- of this discipline; *trayate*-- protects *mahatah*—(from) very great; *bhayat*--danger.

"In this (**buddhiryoga**; path of action under the guidance of disciplined intelligence), there is no loss of effort and there is no contrary result. The practice of even a little of this dharma (path of action under the guidance of intelligence) protects one from great fear." II 2- 40 II

Lord is talking in this verse about "buddhiryoga; path of action under the guidance of disciplined intelligence." Lord says there is no loss of effort in this path. What does it mean? If the construction of a house is not completed the work done so far becomes waste. If the crop raised is not harvested, there will be a lot of wastage. Anything, started but not taken to its logical end, often results in some amount of wastage. Partial practice of "path of action under the guidance of disciplined intelligence" does not suffer from this kind of disadvantages.

It is necessary to recall once again the nature of "buddhiryoga; path of action under the guidance of disciplined intelligence." "Karam-yoga; path of action" is an attitude of mind. A particular way of thinking precedes the action in "Karam-yoga." It is a way of doing work with a particular state of mind. Form of action does not fully convey whether the "path of karam-yoga" was followed. The background thoughts or the attitude of mind or the state of intelligence prompting the mind to work out the way through sense-organs truly determine whether "path of action under the guidance of disciplined intelligence" was followed. In this approach, the focus is on disciplined intelligence, which guides mind and the mind in turn guides the sense-organs. Actions are only physical reflection of the thoughts of the medium called intelligence i.e. the driver of the coach called the body.

The efforts made in "buddhiryoga" do not go waste. Why is it so? "Buddhiryoga" is a particular form of discipline i.e. the practice of obeying rule of thinking in a particular manner or keeping intelligence free of all external influences so much so that it reflects the divine presence within. It requires practice, time and follow-up. It cannot be done in one day. The efforts made in the beginning to start it do not go waste if it is left mid-way. Why is it so? Action of starting is over but its impression in the mind and the experience undergone always exists in mental realm somewhere. These impressions on the mind are long lasting and subsist in memory. For this reason nothing goes waste in starting "buddhiryoga; path of action under the guidance of disciplined intelligence."

"Buddhiryoga" is a very high level state, which presumes i) that efforts to discipline the intelligence have been made faithfully, ii) that actions are done without attachment to results of actions and iii) that the action are done as offering to "The Supreme" for cosmic benefit. Nothing done in this direction goes waste and everything done remains as experience of impression in sub-conscious mind. How can any thing worldly wipe off the impression of the "divine glow" in intelligence (disciplined buddhi)? Divinity never changes its character (eternity, indestructibility and immanence or prevailing everywhere). Any thought in the divine direction (towards self) is an investment. It appears to have been lost, but it is never lost and may get revived any time in future based on stored impressions.

"Buddhiryoga" does not have contrary results. Many activities exert adverse effects on discontinuance. If we open a shop and discontinue it after a little while, some loss is imminent. This does not hold well about "budddhiryoga." There is no loss in this (buddhiryoga). The work, done for cosmic benefit without attachment of results thereof, is bound to do well to the one who has started it. The background disciplined intelligence and lack of personal attachment spiritually uplifts the seeker and breaks free him from the bonds of actions. When work is done in this mode, one is not influenced by capturing propensities of actions. There are many rituals, especially in the "karam-kanda; detailed rituals of Vedas," which, if not carried out scrupulously, will result adversely. There is nothing of this sort in "buddhiryoga." Actually, "buddhiryoga" is an effort to control your attitude, your propensities, your way of looking and interacting with the things, situations and people. You do not have to depend on anything external. Therefore, there is no possibility of loss of effort in "buddhiryoga; path of action under the guidance of disciplined intelligence i.e. intelligence which has been nurtured and cultivated."

Even a little practice of "buddhiryoga" protects one from great fear. What is fear and what is the 'great fear'? Fear means feeling frightened or worried that something bad (uncertain, unpleasant or unfavorable or adverse to what you are attached to) is going to happen. The "great fear" is the fear of death i.e. the event of separation of body and soul (the self; reflected individual divinity under the veil of ignorance; the Truth or Reality within). The disciplined intelligence is the result of the background information of Sankhya i.e. the Supreme and its two aspects, the nature and the self. When in the 'individual intelligence' the knowledge starts dawning that "the 'Nameless Reality's benign presence is always there in inner most being," the game of "eternal love" starts. After the cognizance of eternal love at the level of intelligence, all actions in life become services of eternal love. The compatible signals are passed on to the mind (from the driver of the coach of life) to subjugate the sense organs accordingly. Then the troubles and tribulations of life become trials triumphantly borne to prove the strength of eternal love. Then even excruciating situations become like the streets where one searches one's eternal love unmindful of physical discomforts. In the realm of pure intellect, only the thoughts of the "Supreme" dominate and tales of tribulations become journey of love where one is determined to go from starvation to starvation, from trouble to trouble and from fear to fear getting only one feeble constant message from within "**Get me across to the other shore.**" Where is the ground for fear to appear in a situation like that? Only one message rings loud even at the far end at the semblance of meeting point of earth and sky "**Take me across to the other shore.**" In a situation like this, the fear vanishes. The death loses its stings. One continuously feels the "Everlasting Presence of the Ever Shinning Truth" not at a distance, but within, right within, in the inmost sacred corner of the self. When one is just about to meet the "Eternal Lover" just nearby somewhere, can the fear exist? Lord says that even a little practice of this "Dharma" saves from the bondages of works. What is the meaning of the term "Dharma" here? Here the word Dharma means this philosophy of "buddhiryoga." It means that intelligence should be disciplined so much that all the worldly impacts, effects of dualities, all the doubts and concerns are taken off the intelligence by yoga (various disciplines to connect the mind to purified intelligence and not to the whims and fancy of sense organs). Mind should follow the buddhi and should remain at rest without depressing and depreciating thoughts. Mind should be so guided by the intelligence that the actions are in line with "Dharma" (i.e. in accordance with one's natural propensities, social customs and heritage). In this verse, focus is on discriminative faculty i.e. the luminous point in humans system where reasons, imagination and will are integrated and mind is directed towards those actions, which are in harmony with "**inherent, eternal divine richness**" being reflected in intelligence. How do we recognize this intelligence? It is a state in which the difference between the finite and the infinite gets filled with love. Every moment carries the message of "The Eternal." The unclear soft but resolute echo from within gradually gains the shade of awareness under which one paves way for life. The wisdom seems to be coming from the void (space where nothing exists) of silence, contentment, peace and happiness. "The Formless" smiles in the whole creation, in the flowers, in the plants and in the animals. We see the union of the Supreme will with our will and our love with the love everlasting. This divine richness sublimates and refines the "disciplined intelligence; yoga-buddhi" and helps it to guide the mind towards the activities, which relieve the existence of limitations of birth and death, two dreadful events of existence and cause of fear and miseries.

This verse concludes with a beautiful note of assurance. If a seeker once sets out on this path, no step is lost. Every movement will be a gain. No obstacle can discourage a seeker's growth. What is the basis of all these assurances? Lord has himself clarified by use of the words "a little of this dharma." What is this? Reference is to purified intelligence with self knowledge in the background. Dualities do not disturb. Constant memory of the foot marks of "The Eternal Traveler" keep guiding, keeping the heart of the seeker full with peace, contentment and joy.

41. In this verse, Lord tells Arjuna about Vyavasayatimika (unified, resolute, one pointed) intelligence.

व्यवसायात्मिका बुद्धिरेकेह कुरुनन्दन ।
बहुशाखा ह्यनन्ताश्च बुद्धयोऽव्यवसायिनाम् ॥ २- ४१ ॥

vyavasayatmika buddhir ekeha kuru-nandana
bahu-sakha hy anantas ca buddhayo 'vyavasayinam 2.41

vyavasaya-atmika—one pointed and resolute or determined; *buddhih*--intelligence; *eka*-- single; *iha*-- here; *kuru-nandana*--O delighter of Kuru race; *bahu-sakhah*—many branched; *hi*--indeed; *anantah*—unlimited or endless; *ca*-- and; *buddhayah*- thoughts; *avyavasayinam*--of the irresolute

"In this, O Joy of the Kuru (Arjuna), there is only one-pointed "vyavasayatmikta intelligence; deterministic and resolute intelligence" but the thoughts of the undecided are many branched and endless." II 2-41 II

Lord has started imparting knowledge of "Buddhiryoga; path of action under the guidance of disciplined intelligence." By using the words "in this," Lord is referring to the new approach that he has started talking about in preceding verse. The focus in this verse is on one-pointed "vyavasayatmika buddih; deterministic, resolute intelligence."

What is vyavasayaktmika buddhi? This intelligence is deterministic, one-pointed and resolute in nature. It is discriminating and deciding as well. There are no earthly hankerings in this and it leads to firmness in mind. This world is full of objects and the irresolute (i.e. those not having this type of intelligence) run after from one object to another. The intelligence of the irresolute is discursive (i.e. moving from one point to another without any fixed structure) in nature. The discriminating, one pointed and deteminitic intelligence decides both the direction and use of thoughts as well as direction and use of actions. So this particular type of intelligence involves process of thinking, judgment and perceptive choice of the inner divine force. How is it?

The intelligence becomes pure only when it starts becoming aware of the proximity (nearness) of the inner universal eternal force and this purity is possible through yoga-buddhi or intelligence nurtured and cultivated by all disciplines with awareness of "eternal existence within." This cultured, cultivated, disciplined intelligence with awareness of proximity of divine presence (or enlightened soul) becomes 'unified intelligence', which results in concentration of mind i.e. ability to direct all efforts and attention on one point only. This concentration is not an ordinary achievement. It is epitome (perfect example) of human virtue. When sunbeams are focused on one point, their power of heat and light get intensified. Arjuna was in a position to shoot his arrow successfully at the target within the grove due to concentration only. The one-pointed devotion of the gopis (cowherd maidens) of Vrandavan and srimati Radha Rani supports this point. The gopis (cowherd maidens of vrandavan) breathed in and breathed out in the pangs of separation with tears trickling in the eyes all the times. Even the flowers, birds, bowers, desolate places with fond memories and that very bank of Yamuna pricked like thorns during the period of utter loneliness after Krishna left Vrandavan. What was the single thought in the minds of these maidens? It was Krishna alone for them everywhere in their hearts, in the creation and beyond the creation as well. This type of one pointed determination brings about the difference. Those who are of irresolute intelligence do not determinedly follow one course of action. They attempt so many activities and projects at the same time fretting away their vital energies. The successful completion of any venture or project or trade requires one pointed intelligence.

In verse 39, Lord started to talk about 'buddhir-yoga' i.e. use of "disciplined intelligence free from all external influences" to guide in path of action. Now Lord is talking about one-pointed intelligence or deterministic intelligence (vyavsayitmika Buddhi). What is the relevance of this new term? Actually, "disciplined intelligence free from all external influences" is required on path of action. One-pointed intelligence used in karam-yoga gets transformed into yoga-buddhi, the final instrument for self-realization. Even a common trader, a student and a monstrous individual planning to create mayhem in the society may have one-pointed determination. Thus there is a difference in one pointed intelligence and yoga-buddhi. Yoga-buddhi is matured (rather baked) in the light of awareness of the soul remaining one pointed at the same time. One has to start karam-yoga with one-pointed intelligence to finally get individual intelligence transformed into "Yoga-buddhi"

Yoga-buddhi (disciplined intelligence) is entrenched in the memory of the proximity of soul alone and it directs the mind only to the activities which relieve the mind of the impact of phenomena of creation, conservation and dissolution, birth and life, consciousness and unconsciousness, intellectual knowledge and ignorance, action and inaction and happiness and sufferings. Yoga-buddhi follows "the inner light; light of consciousness; reflection of the Supreme in the self" and takes the mind towards unchanging immobility. Yoga-buddhi directs the mind towards the liberation of the soul from nature and her works. Yoga buddhi takes its root from the essence of Sankhya. It is fixed, one pointed and homogeneous in nature.

Lord is talking about buddhir-yoga (verse 39) while mentioning one-pointed intelligence or *vyavsyitmika Buddhi* (verse 41). How does "this intelligence," starting as one-pointed intelligence and maturing into yoga-buddhi, happen to be as it is described? Started as one pointed, it is soaked in the light of awareness of the divine presence within due to knowledge of Sankhya. Think where this power is coming from. In Sankhya (Self-knowledge), Lord is talking about the "Universal Eternal Reality which is everywhere both in form and without form" as prime focus. Then Lord simultaneously explains that the same Supreme Force exists in a being i.e. ultimate Source, by and large, is the same. Sankhya-Yoga (Self-knowledge) talks about the Supreme and its various facets. "Budhiryoga; path of action under the guidance of disciplined intelligence" is starting with thoughts of the presence of "The Supreme" within. For Yoga-buddhi in the path of action, one has to start with one-pointed intelligence with thoughts of the Supreme in the background due to knowledge of Sankhya. In contrast, thoughts of the irresolute are many branched and endless.

42. In next these three verses Lord explains the behavior of the Unwise i.e. those lacking discrimination.

यामिमां पुष्पितां वाचं प्रवदन्त्यविपश्चितः ।
वेदवादरताः पार्थ नान्यदस्तीति वादिनः ॥ २- ४२ ॥

yam imam puspitam vacam pravadanty avipascitah
veda-vada-ratah partha nanyad astiti vadinah 2.42

yam- which; *imam*-- this; *puspitam*--flowery; *vacam*-speech; *pravadanti*-- utter; *avipascitah*—the un-wise; *veda-vada-ratah*-- taking pleasure in eulogizing words of the Vedas; *partha*--O son of Prtha (Arjuna); *na*--not; *anyat*-other; *asti*-- is; *iti*--thus; *vadinah*-- saying

"O son of Pratha (Arjuna), some people lacking wisdom take pleasure in repeating the flowery language of the Vedas and saying "there is nothing else." II 42 II

There are some unwise people who lack in discrimination. They lay a great emphasis on the "**karam-kand** (ritualistic portion)" of the Vedas. These portions provide specific rites (such as **Agnihotra, Darsa-Purna-Masa,** *Jyotistoma* etc,) for attainment of specific fruits. These people extol (praise very much) these actions and reward unduly. These rites mention such pleasures as arise from drinking nectar, sporting with **Urvasi (heavenly damsel)**, fragrance of **Parijata, aiswarya** (rulership over the Gods). These people remain highly enamored of these Vedic passages prescribing ways for the attainment of heavenly enjoyments. These people hold that there is nothing beyond the heavenly enjoyments. These flowery utterances of the Vedas relating to karam-kand (ritualistic practices) are like "Palas-tree" blossoming with beautiful red flowers, which are not followed by fruits (ultimate self-realization remains eluding by following ritualistic practices).

There are two main divisions of the Vedas- i) **Karam-kand** (section dealing with actions or rituals) and ii) **Jnana- Kand** (section dealing with knowledge). The **Karam-kand** includes **Brahmanas** and **Samhitas. The Jnana-Khand** comprises the **Arankyas** and the **Upnishads.** This portion deals with Supreme Universal Eternal Reality (Brahman) and its various facets.

Life in heaven is of transitory (continuing for a short while) nature. After the accumulated impact of good actions gets exhausted, one has to come back to the earth-plane. Liberation [**Mukti** i.e. freedom from all limitations, bondages, sufferings and infirmities (weaknesses) of human nature] can be attained only by self-knowledge and not by thousand and one sacrifices (yajnas).

It is important to note here that Lord Krishna has assigned a comparatively lower position to the doctrine of the **Mimansakas** relating to performance of Vedic sacrifices for obtaining heaven, power and lordship (**aiswarya**). These rituals are not in a position to lead the seeker to self realization, which relieves the individual from cycles of birth and death. The one who asks for a boon is not a devotee but a bargainer with the Lord or an individual who trades for profit. Those who lay undue emphasis to "karam-kand" of the Vedas remain engrossed in eulogizing (speaking highly of) utterances of the Vedas (**veda vad ratah**). They hold that there is nothing higher than celestial joy of heaven, to attain which they keep performing elaborate rites and ceremonies, inextricably involving themselves in the cycles of birth and death.

What is the main point of this verse? It distinguishes the ritualistic practices mentioned in the karam-kand of the Vedas from true action (the action that adds value to main purpose of life) from the Gita's point of view. Vedic ritualistic practices are directed to the acquisition of the material reward. The Gita propagates (spreads the message) to work without attachment to results of action. According to the Gita, work is to be done for cosmic benefit as an offering to the Supreme. The Gita's path of action requires a complete shift of attitude and expects an individual to make whole life a sacrifice (offering in a yajna) offered with true devotion. Karam-kand of the Vedas is not the whole teaching of the Vedas. The "buddiryoga" (started from verse 39) leads an individual towards total release.

43 In this verse Lord tells what happens to those attached to pleasure and lordship (**aiswarya**).

कामात्मानः स्वर्गपरा जन्मकर्मफलप्रदाम् ।
क्रियाविशेषबहुलां भोगैश्वर्यगतिं प्रति ॥ २- ४३ ॥

kamatmanah svarga-para janma-karma-phala-pradam
kriya-visesa-bahulam bhogaisvarya-gatim prati 2.43

kama-atmanah--desirous of sense gratification; *svarga-parah*—with heaven as their highest goal; *janma-karma-phala-pradam*-- leading to (new) birth as the result of their work; *kriya-visesa*—exuberant or pompous with various specific actions or ceremonies; *bahulam*--various; *bhoga-aisvarya-gatim-prati*—for the attainment of pleasure and lordship.

"(Those who are unwise and lack discrimination) are full of desires. (They) keep heaven as their goal. (Their speeches and activities) lead to cycles of birth and death. (Their actions include) specialized rites for attainment of power and enjoyment." II 2-43 II

The individuals, lacking discrimination, are full of desires. They are full of desires because their minds are full of hundred desirable things such as wealth, power, longevity of fame, progeny (children) etc.

These unwise individuals, lacking discrimination, make efforts to attain heaven. Heaven is considered to be a place where God is believed to live and where good people are believed to go after death. These people are "svargapara" i.e. they take heaven as the highest goal. What are the thoughts associated in the minds of these people. They keep thinking about the joy of drinking nectar, sporting with Urvashi (a dancing angel) and enjoying the fragrance of Parijata (celestial flower). These people remain in the erroneous idea that apart from heaven there is no other goal. These people are not able to bear any talk of liberation (*mukti* form all limitations, bondages and infirmities of human nature) due to absence of discrimination and dispassion in their attitude.

Since all the activities of these unwise people are desire-prompted, they are always bound in the cycles of birth and death. They are especially busy in performing numerous rites (*kriya visesa bahulam*) promising worldly pleasures and lordship (bhoga and *aisvarya*).

This verse mentions the limitations of going for the heavenly pleasures in life. These heavenly pleasures are short-lived and fleeting (lasting for a short time) in nature. Having enjoyed the life in heaven, one has to come back to earth-plane i.e. they are not able to get free from cycles of birth and death.

This verse explains that going for activities that do not "add value" to the objective of life are not worth going for. One who asks for gifts and boons is not a devotee but a bargainer or a trader. Prahalad, one of the most famous devotees, tells the Lord in Bhagvatam "O Lord, the greatest bestow-er of boons, if you insist on my asking for a boon, then give me a boon that desires may not spring in my heart." This is the message of this verse. Desire-prompted actions cannot be the part of karam-yoga.

This is the message of this verse. Desire-prompted actions cannot be the part of karam-yoga.

44. In this verse, lord tells about those who are attached to pleasure and lordship (*aisvarya*).

भोगैश्वर्यप्रसक्तानां तयापहृतचेतसाम् ।
व्यवसायात्मिका बुद्धिः समाधौ न विधीयते ॥ २- ४४ ॥

bhogaisvarya-prasaktanam tayapahrta-cetasam
vyavasayatmika buddhih samadhau na vidhiyate 2.44

bhoga-aisvarya--prasaktanam—of the people deeply attached to pleasure and lordship; *taya*--by that *apahrta-cetasam*—whose minds are drawn away; *vyavasaya-atmika*—one pointed and resolute; *buddhih*-- intellect; *samadhau*—spell of absorption (self-forgetfulness and immersion) in the thought of the supreme; *na*--not; *vidhiyate*—takes place.

"(Those unwise people) who are attached to pleasure, power and lordship and whose minds get carried away by worldly desires cannot have one-pointed intelligence (vyavsayatmika buddhi) and Samadhi (super-conscious state charged with awareness of the proximity of soul in which an individual gets focused on the true nature of the self or the light of the soul)." II 2-44 II

Those unwise people, who are attached to pleasure and power, often get misled by worldly attractions and ritualistic practices laid down in the "karam-kand" of the Vedas. They cannot have one-pointed intelligence (vyavsaytmika buddhi) i.e. that intelligence which can take them to the highest spiritual realization. What is the reason? The intelligence of the irresolute is often discursive (moving from one point to another). It is not able to guide the mind towards the true objective of life, realization of the true nature of the self.

One-pointed intelligence is not anything ordinary. One-pointed intelligence alone can guide a mind to collect the needed facts for the mission of life. The world is ready to give up all the secrets if one knows how to give the necessary blow. The strength and force for that necessary blow comes when one-pointed intelligence prompts the mind, with the whole will of the being to tame all the evil tendencies within to bring them under control. This one-pointed intelligence (*vyavsyitmika buddhi*) is required in all situations of life by all i.e. students, traders and even monsters planning to annihilate the society. When one-pointed intelligence is used to make service the whole purpose of life (i.e. actions for cosmic benefit), it culminates or mature into yoga-buddhi, the soul-touched intelligence aware of the divine presence within. Arjuna was able to shoot the eye of the bird in bower due to concentration. When the Gopies (cow-herd maidens of Vrandavan) and Shrimati Radha Rani were suffering from the pangs of separation and even the flowers, the birds, the bowers, deserted places with fond memories and even the desolate bank of Yamuna were pricking like thorns, what was one thought that they were thinking about? It was Krishna alone for them in the whole creation, in its sustenance and even beyond that. One-pointed intelligence through service to the cosmos invites the divine grace to culminate the individual intelligence into Yoga-buddhi [intelligence, cultured in all disciplines, matured in the awareness of the self and free from all limitations and infirmities of human nature, ready to guide (or catapult) the individual into the exclusive realm of the "Divinity (eternity, indestructibility and immanence i.e. present everywhere all the time],"

The irresolute, lacking discrimination, are not able to go into "Samadhi [… a state within, far beyond the zone of movement of mind, where you directly perceive the proximity of the divinity within, in the form of awareness; you enter a sort of realm within you with no name, no form and no definition; You are surprised that you are not there in your present form, mind and thoughts; you find that you are an energy full with awareness and everything around you has come alive, intensely alive; You find that you are supremely relaxed, contended and at peace with awareness at peak; you are feeling the tranquility and light of the pure consciousness within; you experience an identification with the divine ground; you are in touch with the expanse of shore-less ocean going on and on without an end; there is light and light, a strange light, enthralling light, suffusing light, engulfing light as far as you can identify; you are filled with the truth that you are and there is just nothing else; salt doll becomes one with the ocean; an assurance stirs within you affirming "This is it; That I am"; a realization dawns that you are That Eternal Presence; knowledge is there, light is there, bliss is there but 'no end' is there; you are full with knowledge which is filled with truth, consciousness and bliss …]."

What, then, is the brief message of this verse? Those, whose minds are swayed (moved from one side to another) by worldly desires and who hanker (secretly want) for enjoyments in heaven, cannot have even-mindedness. They cannot have the experience of being in the exclusive domain of tranquility of the soul, the ultimate object of life, the unique spectacle (very impressive show) of fullness of self-awakening.

The focus in this verse is on "vyavsyitmika buddhi; one pointed, deterministic intelligence … with soul touched wisdom i.*e. impact* of **Sankhya**." Without this it is difficult to go into state of "Samahi."

45. In this Verse, Lord tells Arjuna what he should do.

त्रैगुण्यविषया वेदा निस्त्रैगुण्यो भवार्जुन ।
निर्द्वन्द्वो नित्यसत्त्वस्थो निर्योगक्षेम आत्मवान् ॥ २- ४५ ॥

trai-gunya-visaya veda nistraigunyo bhavarjuna
nirdvandvo nitya-sattva-stho niryoga-ksema atmavan 2.45

trai-gunya--visayah—deal with three attributes of nature (sat, rajas and tamas; refer to discussion in introduction on the subject matter); *vedah*--Vedic literatures; *nistraigunyah*—without these three attributes; *bhava*--be; *arjuna*--O Arjuna; *nirdvandvah*--free from the pains of opposites; *nitya-sattva-sthah*--ever remaining in *sattva* (goodness); *niryoga-ksemah*--free from (the thought of) acquisition and preservation; *atma-van*--established in the self (eternal existence within or soul).

"The action of the three attributes of nature (sattva, rajas and tamas) is the subject matter of the Vedas; be you free from this three-fold nature; be free from dualities (the pair of opposites), ever-balanced; be free from thoughts of acquisition and preservation and be possessed of the self." II 2-45 II

The Vedas deal with three attributes of nature i.e. **sattva** (seed of calmness, serenity, contentment, light and positivity), **rajas** (seed of greed, feverishness, intense endeavor, longing, unrest, the undertaking of activities). These gunas are the reasons why an individual behaves as it behaves. All the attributes are inherent in a being (one in existence) in a unique ratio. That is the reason of difference in behavior. No two-persons behave exactly in the same manner. This is a subject of great importance and it has been extensively discussed in the Vedas. After telling this importance of gunas, Lord uses five words in this verse telling Arjuna about what he should do.

Nistraigunyo bhav (be free from these attributes) – By use of these words, Lord advises Arjuna to transcend (go beyond) these three gunas. To be prakriti-bound (to continue to remain influenced by these attributes) is not the goal of human existence. All the emotions such as anger, hatred, love (with limitation, conditions, specifications) etc., contributing to our mundane (not exciting or interesting or ordinary) state, are the results of these attributes of nature. The Gunas and their effects alone impact the working of the whole universe. Even the "Brahmloka (heaven)" representing the highest ritualistic promise, is within the range of gunas only. One has to comeback from the heaven after the impact of the accumulated good actions in the past is exhausted. For the highest state of self-realization (eternally continuing divine state), one has to transcend (go beyond) gunas. For this reason, Lord asks Arjuna to be free from the influence of these attributes of nature.

Nirdvando (be free from dualities) – Dualities mean pair of the opposites i.e. cold and heat, pleasure and pain, profit and loss etc. A duality represents two sides of the same coin. One side follows the other side. Being aware of this reality is wisdom. One should not get unduly affected or attached to one side of the duality. This teaches an individual to be moderate. We face **dvandas** (pair of the opposites) in all walks of life i.e. day and night, good and bad, morality and immorality, sin and virtue, heaven and hell, past life and future life, prosperity and adversity and so on. If one side has come the other side is bound to follow. There is no point in getting unduly affected by one side of **a dvanda.** Lord exhorts Arjuna to wisely and sternly remain indifferent to the opposites. What is the meaning? One should show forbearance (quality of being patient and sympathetic) in facing the opposites. A yogic practitioner should keep these opposites at a distance in life and focus attention to something beyond these opposites. This will help the seeker to save his or her vital energies from getting dissipated in the opposites. By this proposed diversion of attention, the vital energies will be utilized for the main objective of life. This attitude of not getting unduly influenced by the opposites makes spiritual life easy and comfortable. This requires only an orientation (direction in which something faces) of attitude, a habit of seeing the sunny-side or remaining focused on the prime objective instead of interfering considerations. This will bring inward sublimation and refinement in an individual.

Nityasatvastho (be established in the eternal existence within) – Lord has already asked Arjuna to be free from the effect of three gunas. Therefore, word sattva here has not been used as attribute of nature. Here Lord is asking Arjuna to remain poised in unwavering sattva (one's divine character, one's true nature, "Eternal Truth within"). Ritualistic practices confine a being (one who is in existence) to birth and death. For higher, qualitative and spiritual enrichment of life, focus has to be on "Supreme Eternal Universal Reality." The Gopis of Vrindavan really practiced (rather lived) this state of "nittyasatvastho; to be established in the eternal existence within," after Krishna left Vrindavan for Mathura. They saw Krishna (the eternal Reality in body, incarnation) within (in the breath going in and out and in the conscious space within), in creation (flowers, bowers, deserted places with fond memories and desolate bank of Yamuna) and beyond this creation (as eternal being responsible for creation, sustenance and dissolution). "Nityasatvastho; to remain established in the Eternal Truth" is the highest state of spiritual achievement. If this state is achieved, one will remain calm, poised, contended, focused, free from all limitations. This state culminates divine grace, which itself takes care of everything. This state means remaining constantly connected with the "Eternal, Imperishable, Omniscient (knowing everything) Supreme Being" somewhere within. This state is a prelude (introductory exercise) to become an integral part of the "Divine Perfection." It amounts to remaining in soul-touched awareness of the proximity of the soul and then doing everything for cosmic benefit as an offering without attachment for the results.

Niryogaksema (free from thoughts of acquisition and possession) – This term requires to be clarified. *Yoga* in Sanskrit stands for addition. Here it stands for seeking to acquire needful earthly things. *Ksema* stands for keeping carefully the things procured. Majority, in worldly life, keeps craving for acquisition and possession. For a spiritual aspirant, acquisition and possession are distractions. When we crave for acquisition and possession, we become poor spiritually. What do we need acquisition and possession for? Once we are possessed of the self (the "Core Divinity" within), we are in possession of everything and, yet, we do not stop working for the cosmic benefit. *Niryogaksema* (being free from thoughts of acquisition and possession) adds innate spiritual strength in day to day working. "Living and striving and still remaining without domination of thoughts of acquisition and possession" is one of the unique thoughts of the Gita. Tempering makes metal as hard as required by heating it and then putting it in cold water. Similarly "*niryogaksema*" strengthens the spiritual character of a seeker of truth. This attitude connects the individual to unlimited reservoir of innate spiritual strength within and helps a being in gaining superiority over the influence of three gunas. When we escape the acquisition and possession, we experience a sort of emptiness in earthly terms initially, but we get connected to, thus far, untapped spiritual energies within. The whole nature starts supporting when we use these high ideals or perfect spiritual standards.

Atmavan (be possessed of the self) – First it is necessary to understand the meaning of the self. This self is not the physical body or the subtle body or the causal body (the three guna remain in the germ state, which is the cause of rebirth). Beyond the five sheaths [annamayakosha (material particles); pranamayakosha (vital force); manomayakosha (mental thoughts); vijnanamayakosha (knowledge) and anandmayakosha (bliss)], there is "One," who is self-existent, who is base of the belief that "I am," who is the witness of the three states of consciousness, who is separate from the five sheaths, who sees everything but none sees it and who enlightens the intellect but whom nothing can enlighten. That is our real self. It is "**indivisible, eternal, blissful knowledge**" – perceived by disciplined and awakened intelligence only and engaged by whom all senses work. We can call it, for the sake of present discussion, "Reflected individual Divinity." The term "Reflected Individual Divinity" presumes the existence of ignorance and delusion in the seeker. When this ignorance and delusion goes away, the small amount of water in the wave mixes in the ocean, extinguishing its "assumed existence." Then, one finds only "One Supreme Spirit" manifesting in all, in full splendor, eternally. "That Divine Zone within; that conscious space within" is where Lord wants Arjuna to get established. That is the idea of being "Atmavan; be possessed of the self." An "atmavan; self-possessed individual" is "self-disciplining and self-orienting (self-trained) individual." Lord is now talking about "Karam-yoga under the guidance of the disciplined intelligence," but actually it is a direction to remain connected to the essence of "Sankhya; Self-Knowledge." The focus of the Gita everywhere is on one focal point "Supreme Eternal Universal Reality; Brahman." Lord exhorts Arjuna to get possessed of the self, that "Supreme Reality," that cause of all that is.

If these five words of the Lord are understood and implemented in letter and spirit, there is no need for anything else. The whole divine knowledge seems to have been compressed and condensed in simple five words for implementation. This is graciousness of the Lord to whole mankind through Arjuna. What is common in all these five words? One should live life fully with an attitude of renunciation (to hold from getting immersed) for phenomenal (unusual and impressive) existence in worldly life.

46. Lord tells Arjuna about the limitation of Vedic knowledge for a self-realized (who has known the self) individual.

यावानर्थ उदपाने सर्वतः सम्प्लुतोदके ।
तावान्सर्वेषु वेदेषु ब्राह्मणस्य विजानतः ॥ २- ४६ ॥

yavan artha udapane sarvatah samplutodake
tavan sarvaeshu vedeshu bramanasya vijanatah 2.46

yavan- as much; *artha-*use; *udapane-* in a reservoir; *sarvatah-*everywhere; *samplutodake-* being flooded; *tavan-*so much (use); *sarvaeshu-*in all; *vedeshu-*in the Vedas; b*ramanasya-* one who has realized the Supreme or who is enlightened; *vijanatah-* the illumined.

"To an enlightened Brahamina (a spiritual individual who has realized self) all the Vedas are of so much use as a reservoir is when there is flood everywhere." II 2-46 II

For those with illumined consciousness, the knowledge of Vedas is of little use. A scripture (holy book of a particular religion) is like a finite pond which derives its water from the "Infinite Ocean Of Truth." These scriptures (Vedas etc.) become unnecessary after enlightenment, after the mystery of the self is realized by the individual with awareness. An individual does not need a reservoir when water is flooded on all sides. This is not to criticize the Vedas. The Vedas are the necessary means but not the end. The Vedas are required for guidance on spiritual path. After the goal is reached, the Vedas have served their purpose.

On spiritual path, mere scholarship is not sufficient. After the initial stage, one requires spiritual inclination and practices and not the books. The scholarly individuals, lacking spiritual inclination and practices (sadhna), become like vultures who soar high in the sky but they keep their eyes always on the carcass (dead bodies of animals) lying on the ground. Books have limited use on spiritual path. After initial introduction, success in spiritual path depends on individual urge and spiritual practices only. Yoga-sadhna (spiritual practices relating to various disciplines) provides the personal fullness, inner-enrichment and exalted state of self- sufficiency on spiritual path and not the books. Lord is not criticizing Vedas. Lord is highlighting importance of sadhna (spiritual practices), which alone comes to rescue in the final stages of spiritual pursuit. An individual with divine wisdom realizes the "Truth" everywhere and in everything all the time without needing books. When there is water everywhere, no one needs a well.

What is the message of this verse in brief? For those, who have illumined consciousness (*brahamin* having knowledge of Vedas with awakened consciousness), adherence to ritual observation (especially *karam-kand* of vedas) is of little value. There is no need of a well in a place where there is flood.

47. In this verse, Lord propounds (suggests) the doctrine of "karam-yoga" to Arjuna.

कर्मण्येवाधिकारस्ते मा फलेषु कदाचन ।
मा कर्मफलहेतुर्भूर्मा ते सङ्गोऽस्त्वकर्मणि ॥ २- ४७ ॥

karmany evadhikaras te ma phalesu kadacana
ma karma-phala-hetur bhur ma te sango 'stv akarmani 2.47

karmani—in work; *eva*-- only; *adhikarah*--right; *te*--of you; *ma*--never; *phalesu*--in the fruits; *kadacana*--at any time; *ma*--never; *karma-phala*--in the result of the work; *hetuh*--cause; *bhuh*--become; *ma*--not; *te*--of you; *sangah*--attachment; *astu*—let (there) be; *akarmani*--in not doing.

"To work alone, you have the right and not to the fruits of action. Do not be impelled (strong or unduly impressed) by the fruits of action, nor let thy attachment be to inaction." II 2-47 II

These are oft-repeated, famous lines of the Gita, containing its original and unique message. Lord explains in this verse the spirit or attitude and various considerations required for doing an action. Lord is talking about four tenets of "path of action," which are often misunderstood and misdirected:

i) *Karmanyevadhikaraste* (You have 'adhikara' for respective action only) – What is an action? Here all activities, whether physical or mental, are to be included in the term "action." What is **adhikara**? While translating, we take 'right' as the only meaning of it. The word 'adhikara' here means ability, privilege, prerogative, choice, rightful claim, authority, suitability, control. This word "**adhikar**" used here is a spiritual concept to ascertain one's own suitability for the activity.

There are all types of actions. Some actions take you from your lower nature to higher nature and some actions take you from the conscious-Divine to the apparent Un-divine. Lord says that your focus should be on actions alone. What does it mean? Two aspects are implicit in Lord's advice to Arjuna. Action selected should be such that divinely conscious individual can do it i.e. soul-touched wisdom inside or consciousness inside can approve of it. Many terrorist annihilate humanity in the name of religion. They are guided by some misinterpreted word written somewhere. They are not guided by their soul-touched wisdom, their own innate experience or "living-feeling" within. They do not even see the action from victim's point of view. Therefore, one has to ascertain whether the activity selected is in accordance with "yoga-buddhi" i.e. intensely awakened intelligence due to yoga with *sankhya* knowledge in the background. Then one will gain the authority to do the activity i.e. "conscious inner freedom or volition to do something." This is the first aspect of selection of activity. Secondly, one has to understand whether work being done is in accordance with one's peculiar combination of gunas (attributes of nature). One's suitability to selected activity based on gunas (attributes) is very important consideration to ensure that no conflict with one's own nature is allowed. Everyone should pause to ascertain one's suitability for the objective based on one's attributes. In the absence of this type of review, Arjuna started talking like a jnani (the wise man), even though he was a rajas (passion)-dominated individual.

When an activity has been viewed from these two points of view, then one will be in a position to ascertain whether one has the authority, deservingness or suitability to do the work or whether it is one's prerogative (right due to various reasons) to do that work. Arjuna failed on both the points. He obvious did not have yoga-buddhi. The review like this amounts to ascertaining one's own deservingness, suitability to undertake that activity. If this type of review has not been undertaken, one's conflict with one's own nature will creep in, bringing down one's own efficiency. This part (review of the activity from these two points of view) cannot be done in a hurry. It requires reflection, introspection and meditation also to appraise its ultimate impact on the cosmos and the world, to which we belong to. When a self searching on the above mentioned lines has been done, one develops the "karam-nishtha (natural affinity or belief or immovable faith or natural alignment with the activity)" for the activity. After developing this "karam-nishtha" only, one starts doing work not for results but for activity alone.

ii) ma phaleshu kadachan [(right) is never to fruits of action] – In this phase of the verse Lord wants to say "Do not let the fruits of your work be your motive." Most of us do the work for the fruits, results and not for activity alone or due to "*karam-nistha.*" What is *karam-nishtha*? It is natural alignment or inner connectivity with the activity and not the results thereof. If there is attachment to fruits or results, "Karam-nistha" (natural belief, spiritual bond, affinity) with the activity will not be there and work will not be done for the sake of work alone. Work-done for results or fruits creates bondages and becomes the cause of birth and death.

iii) **Ma karam phala hetur bhuh** (Do not work always looking for what it is going to come out of it) – This third part of the verse states that one should not focus on the results or fruits alone. Here Lord Krishna advises Arjuna not to become one of those for whom the external cause becomes the reason for doing the work. In our daily life, we notice that in most of the cases, external-results that work promises, motivates us to work. Thus Lord has unfolded the secret of winning by showing the pathway to gain supreme efficiency in action, whether it is war or hazard of daily experience. Two thoughts from this verse always remain alive in mental realm a) abandon attachment and b) make yoga a way of life.

iv) *Na te sango astu akarmani* (neither let there be in you any attachment to inactivity) – Traditional and old spiritual thinking required avoiding action to avoid bondage caused by action. The Gita opposes this view. Its command is that attachment or focus on results of action should be given up and not the work. To avoid action is to give up to laziness. It is tamas (the seed of delusion and ignorance). It is the negation of spiritual growth. It is rather negation of the divinity within. **"Tamasic-inaction"** is the first enemy of spiritual progress. It should be first understood that no one can live without doing at least some work (for sustenance of life). Why is it so? This is all due to peculiar combination of three gunas (attributes of nature in us). Action is necessary so long as life is. Here Lord introduces "niskama-karam (i.e. action without focus on the results thereof) for "karam-nistha; natural affinity, spiritual preponderance (natural disposition) to do that activity. Work having this character (niskama-karam) spiritually uplifts an individual and changes him or her from the unconscious self to the "Conscious Divine."

This verse, if properly understood, opens the gates to the higher dimension in a being. It connects the individual to the core spiritual potential within through the medium of work. Lord introduces us here to four-step approach of "karam-yoga": i) to work alone you have the right (you gain the understanding or appropriateness of your right to work when work has been seen in broad perspective summarized above), ii) be not attached to the fruits or results thereof, iii) be not running after the results of the work and iv) do not remain inactive.

This verse helps to gain awareness of the positive aspect of the subject of work. "To work on to either enjoy or to suffer" means reducing the great human life to an animal life. We have to see the "value addition of work in terms of cosmos," with which we are inextricably related. We have to see whether the activity has backing of our "Spiritual Existence." We have to see how our activity exerts its influence on the cosmos. The cosmos is also the expansion of our self. One can be aware of this with yoga-buddhi alone. At the same time, we have to ensure that we do not give in to inaction. On working on these lines, we will understand that work should not be done for perishable external results alone. This concept of "karam-yoga" integrates body, mind, intelligence and spiritual "Reality within" and this will bring lasting and crowning fulfillment to human effort.

By this verse, Lord has told Arjuna not to choose the jnan-nistha (wisdom-pursuit; Arjuna was talking words of wisdom in initial stages) straightaway. Lord advises Arjuna the path of "karam-nistha; natural (i.e. from guna's point of view) and spiritual alignment with the activity," for this path alone suits his rajasic (passion-driven)-nature. Arjuna has to ensure that his mind does not suffer from any torment or addiction caused by the action (bondages of action). At the same time Lord warns that under no circumstances inaction has to become one's refuge. The individual lives for an idea, for a purpose, for the country and for the good of humanity, when that individual identifies the action on these parameters (i.e. from guna's point of view as well as from comprehensive view of life's purpose and spiritual strength within). To live life of goodness is to live life of all. In the context of duty (action willingly acknowledged as obligation), these terms "good, pain and death" will have different interpretation. Pleasure may be shunned. Pain may be negotiated with patience and death itself may be made welcome as giving a higher value to the life. Correct interpretation of path of action will give extended and expansive meaning of life. Salvation is possible by the path of action as well, if action has been well understood and duly discharged according to this verse.

48. In this verse, Lord exhorts (persuades) Arjuna to get established in state of yoga.

योगस्थः कुरु कर्माणि सङ्गं त्यक्त्वा धनञ्जय ।
सिद्ध्यसिद्ध्योः समो भूत्वा समत्वं योग उच्यते ॥ २- ४८ ॥

yoga-sthah kuru karmani sangam tyaktva dhananjaya
siddhy-asiddhyoh samo bhutva samatvam yoga ucyate 2.48

yoga-sthah--steadfast in *yoga; kuru*--perform; *karmani*--your duties; *sangam*--attachment; *tyaktva*--having abandoned; *dhananjaya*--O Dhananjaya (Arjuna); *siddhi-asiddhyoh*--success and failure; *samah*--the same; *bhutva*--having become; *samatvam*--evenness of mind; *yogah*--yoga; *ucyate*--is called.

"O Dhanajay (Arjuna), (you) perform your actions keeping yourself established in yoga, abandoning attachment and remaining unconcerned about success and failure. This equanimity (state of evenness of mind) is known as yoga." II 2-48 II

In this verse Lord suggests Arjuna to perform his actions keeping himself established in the state of yoga. What is "Yoga." Yoga means getting perfection in all the disciplines (physical, mental, emotional and spiritual) to unite one's self with the "Universal Eternal Spiritual Reality." Is this unification a physical exercise? Answer is no. It is a sort of merger, as a river merges into the sea for good. Its separate existence extinguishes. This unification or merger is a mental state of realization in which one cognizes with one's awareness that "the Supreme, Universal, Infinite, Eternal Reality" exists in all beings. One universal or spiritual essence exists in all. This state cannot be achieved till one directs the mind with "Yoga-buddhi; disciplined and one-pointed intelligence soaked in knowledge of Sankhya." This "yoga-buddhi" helps to control the urges, modifications and tendencies arising in the realm of mind and one gains the mental state of equanimity. Mind like much disciplined pet follows the instruction of "yoga-buddhi." Two conclusions come out of this discussion. Yoga leads to the state of equanimity (mental state, in which there are no urges, no modifications, no impulses and no tendencies). In state of yoga, mind is in perfect balance, equal serenity, not running about in different directions under the thousands impulses. Yoga, therefore, is control of mind's stuff i.e. urges modifications, impulses and tendencies. Therefore, Lord's first advice for implementing karam-yoga is to be steadfast (faithful and very loyal), in composure, in the state of yoga-consciousness.

It should be recalled that Lord is talking about "Buddhiryoga" from verse 39. It is this attitude (buddhiryoga), in which Arjuna should work to achieve most effective results. When disciplined, one pointed buddhi enriched by self knowledge guides the mind; mind gets relieved of its usual stuff (urges, modifications and tendencies).

After explaining the various phases of Karam-yoga in preceding verse, Lord exhorts Arjuna to get established in yoga. How is Arjuna to go about to implement the thought of Karam-yoga? Lord gives three detailed instructions in this verse:

i) *Sangam tyakatva* **(Give up attachment, O Arjuna)** - The action of an ordinary individual (obsession with the results) is always distressed by choice between relative good and evil. What is the result? Life's vital energy and time (time span allotted to an individual is life) gets dissipated before getting utilized for the objective (mission of existence; deciphering everlasting joy, from which all objects have their birth ; focal point). An ordinary individual remains thinking about the results. This attachment with the results does not allow focus. Therefore Lord asks Arjuna to give up attachment. How is this attachment to go? Yoga-buddhi will help here. Yoga-buddhi will guide the individual towards action not for results but for "karam-nishta; Natural affinity with the action being in conformity with 'attitude of gunas' and the "spiritual strength." This "karam-nistha" will save the individual from the dilemma of results. One should work for the sake of work alone, with perfect serenity, indifferent to results. This particular advice cannot be implemented without following "Karam-nistha; the natural affinity or loyalty to do action based on gunas (svadharma) and the spiritual strength within, which is global (including the whole world) in nature and considers the impact of actions in terms of cosmic benefit." It essentially does not mean indifference to actions or performance of action. It requires a mental attitude, an orientation (training) of mind by way of yoga-introspection. What is this "giving up of attachment like"? It is like being a good judge. When the judge considers a murder case, he is unattached to either side and takes evenly a conviction or an acquittal, necessitated by the evidences.

ii) *Siddhy assiddhyo samo bhutva* (in state of equanimity i.e. having become equal in success and failure)- What is *siddhy*? It is accomplishment of the activity. *Assiddhy* is failure in the accomplishment of the activity. When work is done with "karam-nistha" i.e. due to natural flair to do the work or the work is considered self-accepted obligation for inner involvement, then the whole focus is on discharge of activity. Results of the activity do not motivate to do the work. Activity itself motivates because activity is linked with inner spiritual existence within. This inner involvement arises due to *lokasangraha* (overall cosmic benefit). Selection of such an activity is itself a reward and thereafter there is no fear of failure. Neither, there is any elation of success of activity. The thoughts of success and failure intrude the mind and disturb, when work is done with "irresolute intelligence." These thoughts are in form of hope, fear, anger, grief, transient (fleeting, for a short while) joy. Again this equanimity comes by yoga-buddhi alone. When work is done with awareness that there is "One in all" and work is made as an offering to the One, there is no fear of failure or anxiety about success. Yoga of "disciplined intelligence," referred to earlier, results in this attitude of equanimity for success and failure. It helps the individual to work with diligence and devotion i.e. wholesomely without getting deluded by anything else (i.e. elation of success and fear of failure).

iii) *Samatvam yoga ucyate* (yoga is equanimity, balanced mental attitude under the circumstances existing to imbalance the mind) – Every experience generates mental impulses. Sometime it is a small impulse and sometime it is a big impulse. A human being at times becomes a shuttle-cock on the river bed. Every wave pushes it in different direction. Is a human being to be as helpless as a shuttle-cock on the river bed, being tossed by the waves? A human being is a conscious being. A human being has the capacity to keep the mind in balance when so many reasons are there to unbalance it. This is the true measure of greatness of a human being. Intellectual growth, creative growth and spiritual growth requires prior stabilization of psychic impulses. Doing this (i.e. controlling the urges, modification and tendencies of mind) is yoga. The result is calmness, balance, serenity, an inherent "even-minded-ess" to accept any eventuality gracefully as providential dictate. This calmness generates an inner freedom which unleashes the inner potential of a being good enough to transform an ordinary being into spiritual being. Where does this state come from? When "*sama*" (mental disciplines) and "*dama*"(physical disciplines) of "Ashtanga-yoga" of sage Patanjali have been made an integral part of life. This part of the verse lays emphasis on handling the mind. In normal life, we handle the activity. We do not handle our mind first. First, mind has to be controlled through yoga-buddhi and then mind will control the other organs of action and perception.

This verse explains how one has to go about the implementation of "karam-yoga" by taking care of the four aspects mentioned by the Lord. Action can be done by just any one. Action in karam-yoga requires self-searching, introspection, discipline, devotion, dedication and commitment. First one should gain the awareness of one's spiritual existence through yoga-buddhi. One should feel one's identity with universal being. In the light of this awareness action to be done should be identified to develop karam-nistha, natural affinity with work itself. Then activity should be performed without getting influenced by waves of monetary elation, depression, pride and despondency in sate of equanimity. What will happen due to this karam-yoga? Heart will be full with love, established in the natural state of a being. Mind will be empty, not responding to the natural psychic impulses. Physical organs of performance (actions) will be 100 % busy. One should work steadfastly in yoga, free from attachment and equally disposed to negotiate with success and failure. One gets equally disposed to negotiate (to discuss to reach an agreement) with success and failure due to focus on Karam-nistha and not the results. This equal mindedness for success and failure does not ever cause laxity (not careful about standards of accomplishments) in performance of activity due to "karam-nistha; natural affinity (strong feeling that you like or close connection) with work."

This verse emphasizes a sure way to efficiency – In this wonderful verse 48, Lord Krishna tells humanity through Arjuna most beautiful approach to gain highest efficiency possible in life and work. In west, people very restlessly crave for secret to efficiency. Here Lord unfolds that secret magnificently and too simply. First step is to control the mind and bring it in the state of equanimity. Abandon attachment, anger, fear and undue concern for any consideration. Become even minded both for success and failure. Avoid depression in failure and elation in success. Gaining this state of equanimity provides an internal balance i.e. soothing experience of tranquility within. For this reason, it has been described as yoga. This is the state in which optimum coordination of mind, body and soul happens. It leads to highest achievement of human endeavor in both war and mundane daily experiences. The relevance of this wisdom particularly arises, when decision has already been taken and the stage of executing the plan has come. Remember that war had been declared and Arjuna expressed reluctance to wage war. It is here that Lord said "Stop attachment. Be in equanimity. That is the best mental state to achieve the highest level of performance." Thus Lord has unfolded the secret of winning by showing the pathway to gain supreme efficiency in action, whether it is war or hazard of daily experience. Two thoughts from this verse always remain alive in mental realm a) abandon attachment and b) make yoga a way of life.

49. In this verse, Lord tells Arjuna how the mind of a yogi (one who is established in state of yoga) works.

दूरेण ह्यवरं कर्म बुद्धियोगाद्धनञ्जय ।
बुद्धौ शरणमन्विच्छ कृपणाः फलहेतवः ॥ २- ४९ ॥

durena hy avaram karma buddhi-yogad dhananjaya
buddhau saranam anviccha krpanah phala-hetavah 2.49

durena- by far; *hi*—indeed; *avaram*-- inferior; *karma*-- action; *buddhi-yogat*—than the yoga of intelligence i.e. submersion with the Supreme induced by intelligence (pure); *dhananjaya*--O conqueror of wealth (Arjuna); *buddhau*--in wisdom induced by intelligence (divine); *saranam*-- refuge; *anviccha*-- seek; *krpanah*--the misers or wretched (are); *phala-hetavah*- seekers after fruits.

"Far inferior, O Dhananjay (Winner of wealth i.e. Arjuna), indeed is work (i.e. work done with attachment with results) to budhiryoga [i.e. work done in a state of equanimity where yoga-budhi (disciplined intelligence) is guiding the mind]. Take refuge in intelligence (disciplined and awakened by yoga and established in the awareness of the proximity of soul). They are poor and wretched souls, who make fruits of work the object of their thoughts and activities." II 2-49 II

Work done for selfish motives is far inferior to that done with yoga buddhi (disciplined, soul-centered, focused intelligence). This word buddhiryoga should not be taken to mean jnana-yoga (Sankhya; self-knowledge). By buddhiryoga, Lord here means work done with "disciplined, soul touched, one pointed intelligence." That is why Lord immediately after this asks Arjuna to take refuge in intelligence (yoga-buddhi). Then Lord says that those who work only for fruits or results are *krpana* (miser).

It is relevant here to consider Lord's description of the word *krpana* (miserable or wretched or annoying person for whom you feel sympathy). An individual, who focuses merely on the results while doing work, is a *krpana* (miserable or wretched). What has to be done to avoid this narrowness of mind, this habit of going for petty allurements? One has to get rid of *phala-buddhi* (that is that intelligence which seeks objectives or results alone). One has to imbibe yoga-buddhi (disciplined intelligence that works with awareness of divinity within). A miser individual frequently suffers from bitter disappointment and change of mood. The work done by them binds them because their attachment happens to be with results and they remain confined to the cycles of birth and death. They are miserable and unfortunate for one more reason. They are not able to experience the joy and contentment of doing the work for *lokasangraha* (cosmic benefit) i.e. another dimension that Lord will discuss afterwards. "The work done for lokasangraha (cosmic benefit)" helps an individual to experience bliss of soul (result of expansion within), which is of self-releasing nature.

Lord asks Arjuna to take refuge in intelligence (yoga-buddhi; equipoise state of mind; that state of mind which balances different influences i.e. mental and emotional influences). "Phal-hetavah" is the word used by the Lord in this verse to represent those who thirst for rewards. Intelligence is a faculty of reason, judgment and discrimination. It amounts to refining psychic energy and helps an individual to identify and comply with one's original divine nature. Without refinement of this higher-level energy within, one lives only at a relatively lower level of one's existence. But this "yoga-buddhi' is not a mean achievement. It is a result of regular and rigorous "*sadhna*" (work done consistently for improving proficiency in various disciplines i.e. physical, mental, emotional and spiritual), *seva* (service rendered without self-interest for cosmic benefit) and a lot of heart-churning and soul searching.

What does Lord tell in brief in this verse? Lord makes three bold statements in this verse. "Far lower than yoga of wisdom" (state in which yoga-buddhi, disciplined and one-pointed intelligence, guides mind towards action for cosmic benefit) is action propelled by desire to satisfy self. One should seek refuge in wisdom, disciplined by sadhna (work-outs laid down for various disciplines) and soaked in the awareness of divinity within. Wretched are those who work only for desire-prompted actions.

Lord uses three very beautiful words in this verse i.e. "budddhau sarnam anviccha; seek refuge in state of mind which balances between different influences, especially mental and emotional influences." Under this mental state mind keeps appropriate balance (evenness) in different influences. This state unlocks the secret sealed door within an individual. It induces harmony in factors influencing the activity, seeker and circumstances. Once decision has been taken to do something there should be no demand for fruits and no seeking of reward. The state of equanimity slowly generates constant progression in divine consciousness, calmness, strength and bliss. The joy of service and joy of inner growth come to become sufficient recompense for the seeker in this mental state. The seeker in this state starts becoming an instrument and not the doer. For this reason Lord asks Arjuna to take refuge in state of mind, which balances the impact of influencing factors.

This verse emphasizes the best attitude to work with – There can be right attitude to work. There can be wrong attitude to do the work. Lord Krishna has given the best attitude to work i.e. work should be performed in mental attitude called "Buddhi yoga." Under this attitude, attention is free from fruit of action and dualities. This approach further optimizes the results when work is done as offering to "The Divine." Buddhi-yoga leads to a state of mind which balances the influences of different factors (seeker, sought and the circumstances). What does it mean? It is not a small statement. In a way Lord is giving caution to take care. This can happen, when we are receptive to "Nature's Guidance System." Nature guides us through the feelings of expansion and contraction. When we feel expansion within, we should take action. We should move forward and enjoy the process of achievement. When we feel contracted we should stop. We should take a break, rest, reflect and enjoy the process of coming back to our own self. How do we recognize the state of contraction? In this state we feel upset, angry, anxious, tense, irritable, shut down, disconnected, unhappy and depressed. Generally contraction feels uncomfortable. How do we recognize the state of expansion? In this state we feel satisfied, turned on, enthusiastic, ready for anything, open, connected, loving, generous, kind and compassionate i.e. all those wonderful things that feel good. We should utilize the work situation to expand our mind and heart and to manifest the tremendous possibilities lying within. Therefore, main points of "Nature's" sayings are "Take it easy; be kind to yourself; step back and take another look." The state of equanimity will be easy to be observed, if we have improved our sensitivity to "Nature's Guidance System."

50. Now after explaining "buddhiryoga, which was started in 39th verse" in sufficient details, Lord in this verse again exhorts Arjuna to do all actions established in this "yoga" to avoid fluctuations in mind (Arjuna came to battle field, ready to fight and started talking about 'not fighting' in emotional state not justified by the poised mind).

बुद्धियुक्तो जहातीह उभे सुकृतदुष्कृते ।
तस्माद्योगाय युज्यस्व योगः कर्मसु कौशलम् ॥ २- ५० ॥

buddhi-yukto jahatiha ubhe sukrta-duskrte
tasmad yogaya yujyasva yogah karmasu kausalam2.50

buddhi-yuktah-- endowed with wisdom (result of divine-intelligence); *jahati*- casts off; *iha*--in this life; *ubhe*--both; *sukrta-duskrte*-- good and evil deeds; *tasmat*--therefore; *yogaya*—to yoga (all disciplines, physical, mental, emotional and spiritual for union with the Supreme); *yujyasva*—devote thyself; *yogah- karmasu-- kausalam*—yoga engenders skill in action.

"The one, who has yoked (joined two together) with intelligence (i.e. one whose intelligence is soaked in the divine universal energy within and thus whose mind is free from natural oscillating (to keep moving regularly) impulses of the mind, casts off in this life (**iha** i.e. in this world) both the good actions and the bad actions; therefore strive to be in yoga; Yoga engenders (to cause a situation or feeling) efficiency (skill i.e. ability to do something well and cleverly with minimum loss of resources because you have learnt and practiced it)." II 2-50 II

This is a very famous verse and contains three important messages as follows:

i) **Buddhi yukto jahati both sukrta and duskrta** [(one) united with yoga-buddhi derives freedom from good deeds and bad deeds] – The word good "**buddhi-yukto** i.e. one yoked with or established in intelligence; or one who is integrated well with equanimity in intelligence" has been discussed in sufficient details. Lord says that one, with **yoga-buddhi**, frees oneself from the good deeds and the bad deeds. What is this the good and the Bad? When persons, things and circumstances are in conformity with our expectations, we experience a sort of pleasurable feeling and use the word good for them. We consider everything else as bad. For self-realization, we have to go beyond this zone where we feel good or bad. The one, who follows **yoga-buddhi**, frees oneself from the good and bad because both the good and the bad deeds are of capturing nature and bind an individual to cycles of birth and death. What is the reason? The one, who follows the **yoga-buddhi**, follows a higher law, beyond good and bad, established in the freedom of the divine-self within. Such an individual goes beyond actions with conflicting dualities. That soul-touched wisdom is always guiding such an individual. Such an individual remains fixed in equanimity the state free from likes and dislikes attachment and aversion (strong dislike).

ii) **Tasmad yogaya yujasva** (therefore devote yourself to yoga) - What will happen? First effect will be yoga-buddhi, which will properly guide the mind without disturbing impulses about dualities. An individual with yoga-buddhi is able to give detached performance. Detached performance adds to efficiency (ratio of per unit of output to per unit of input; simply speaking relationship of output and input expressed in numbers explaining how much greater or otherwise output is to input). How is it? An individual with yoga-buddhi rises to a status higher than ethical standards (connected with the principles of right and wrong) i.e. laid down principles of right and wrong always have some amount of bias for human intervention and interpretation. Use of words "**Yoga-buddhi**" means that decision for the action has been deliberated in the light of awareness of soul-touched wisdom. The soul is a zone of exclusive divine-purity, equanimity, contentment and bliss, beyond possibility of bias (tendency to accord one person or group more favorably than others) due to human intervention and interpretation. Therefore, Lord gives a clarion call (strong and direct call) to Arjuna to devote to yoga, disciplinary workouts, laid down for physical, mental, emotional and spiritual improvement, uniting the self to the Supreme Self.

iii) yogah karamsu kausalam (Yoga engenders, creates or causes efficiency i.e. yoga causes improvement in relationship of output to input; i.e. ratio of per unit of output expressed as per unit of input) – Yoga causes extreme dexterity (ability to be very quick and skilful) in doing one's actions. In this state, one does not doubt, desists or fears. One courageously goes forward in action whatever it is, not for results but for karam-nistha (natural affinity with action due to compatibility to gunas and commitment to inner divine existence). Yoga-budhi generates efficiency, confidence, perception, effectiveness and results in a sort of immunity from doubts and dualities. It brings about a unique excellence and skill for doing actions. Yogic-buddhi empowers an individual to take up any venture, meet any eventuality and reconciles with any outcome anytime. Enriched by yoga-buddhi, an individual moves forward and forward, unmindful of the consequences but extremely focused on the awareness of the divinity within and interpreting and manifesting the inner connectivity with divine existence in terms of actions. This particular state of efficiency comes only when action is in accordance with "righteousness as per law of nature" and "svabhava" (compatibility of action to one's unique combination of gunas, attributes of nature).

Constant inner perspective about the pursuit, purpose and "the lasting reality within" is yoga. One has to remain in this state abandoning attachment for the results, material pursuits. This state ensures optimum results of efforts made or input sacrificed (this input may be in form of material, actions or emotions). The limited time span allotted to an individual is life and this limitation presents the greatest challenges to use life's resources optimally for life's mission, which is self-realization. What is the uniqueness of this approach? The uniqueness of this approach involves combining mind, heart and spiritual awareness. It centers on how one should set one's inner potential to work to push an individual beyond the limitations of human experience and limitations. Yoga is the only way. It help's an individual to become an instrument of divine graciousness for the benefit of cosmos, creator's own creation. Productive efficiency or work efficiency or behavioral (inter-active) efficiency is finally the reflection (or manifestation) of inner personal outlook or character-efficiency. If one possesses one's self, everything else will be taken care of. That art of getting truly the grip of one's own hidden self, one's own communion, one's own guidance, one's own inherent faculties, is yoga, which has been eulogized (praised) and also focused in this verse.

Lord has beautifully used the word efficiency saying "yogah Karamsu kaushalam" i.e. Yoga engenders efficiency. What is efficiency? In common language, efficiency means optimum output per unit of input with least sacrifice of resources. This efficiency may result from abused utilization of resources as well. For example, efficiency can be managed by exploiting the labor and beating them to the bones. Will it match Lord's Krishna's concept of efficiency? Lord's concept of efficiency will take into account, besides output, poise, inner rhythm, purpose of output and impact of output on environment. Efficiency nurtured through yoga will have different impact. Even to be efficiently selfish, one has to recognize the truth and one has to curb one's immediate impulses.

51. In this verse, Lord explains what happens when an individual works with yoga-buddhi (one-pointed intelligence enriched in the awareness about the divine existence within).

कर्मजं बुद्धियुक्ता हि फलं त्यक्त्वा मनीषिणः ।
जन्मबन्धविनिर्मुक्ताः पदं गच्छन्त्यनामयम् ॥ २- ५१ ॥

karma-jam buddhi-yukta hi phalam tyaktva manisinah
janma-bandha-vinirmuktah padam gacchanty anamayam 2,51

karma-jam—action- born; *buddhi-yuktah*—possessed of knowledge; *hi--* indeed; *phalam*—the fruit; *tyaktva*—having abandoned; *manisinah*—the wise; *janma-bandha--vinirmuktah*—one freed from fetters of birth; *padam*—the abode; *gacchanti--* go; *anamayam*—beyond evil or without miseries.

"The wise (manisinah; or sages, wise in spirituality and not in worldly matters alone), in yoga-buddhi (with one-pointed intelligence enriched in awareness about the divine existence within), having abandoned fruits of actions (i.e. attachment) and freed from fetters (something, which restricts the freedom) of birth, verily go to the stainless state, which is beyond all evils." II 2-51 II

Lord makes two statements here in this verse as follows:

i) Karmjam budhiyukta hi phalam tyaktva manisinah [only the wise (introspective) people who are having yoga-buddhi (one-pointed intelligence, established in the awareness of the proximity of the Divinity within) are able to abandon (renounce or keep themselves away) from attachment to fruits or results of their actions.] – What is the root cause of afflictions and sufferings in this world? All these afflictions and sufferings are due to hankering for the results. Lord has used the word manisinah i.e. those people who introspect, ruminate (think for a long time about the self) are included in this category. The people in this category do a lot of *manan* (deep thinking) and think a lot about the self within, nature of the world, about the actions and their consequences on self and others and about the bondage and freedom. Actions alone do not contribute to one's spiritual maturity. Spiritual maturity or spiritual vision requires depth and it comes only when yoga-buddhi guides mind and gets established in the awareness of the proximity of the Divinity within. Only wise people with yoga-buddhi (one-pointed intelligence, deeply rooted in the knowledge of the self) are able to renounce (publicly say that you will no longer keep the attachment to) the results of action.

ii) *Janma bandha vinirmuktah padam gacchanty anamayam* [(those, who have gained freedom from fetters of birth verily go to the stainless state or the perfect status (brahmi sthiti i.e. a state in which one remains established in the self, free from afflictions, maladies and sufferings of this worldly existence dominated by desire-satisfaction) – The worldly actions are normally desire-prompted actions, which lead to bondage of birth. One, adept in yoga is able to gain yoga-buddhi to manage the actions in such a way that the bondage-producing actions become freedom producing actions. Lack of attachment to the results and committing the actions to the Universal Divine Force strengthens the resolve of an individual and takes the individual beyond the zone of sufferings, stress and sorrow to a highest state of perfection. This state has been described by the Lord as "padam gacchanty anamayam; go to this place or abode beyond all evils." Normally, in life, we do actions for results. First we grapple with uncertainty before results. Then we get lost in enjoyment of results and then again take birth to gain the matching results of those actions which have not yielded results. This cycle of birth and death goes on and on. When the wisdom dawns about the awareness of the aim of human birth, then we stop hankering for results and seek the union with one who is "Unbounded Eternal Awareness," where consciousness prevails, bliss prevails and knowledge prevails. In this state, there is no desire, no afflictions and no sufferings. This is moksha (liberation). In this state the splendor of the Divinity allows to bare open its eternal expanse of beauty. Eternal knowledge whispers in the wordless language of silence. Supreme state of contentment prevails. This is a state of inner integration where harmony reigns in all corners, in all walks of life. For this reason, Lord has used the word *anamayam* i.e. state beyond all evils. In verse 47, it was stated that desire for results is the cause of rebirth. By abandoning fruits of actions, rebirth is automatically ended. The desire for fruit is bondage. Relinquishing fruits of action is liberation, the highest status of perfection.

How does result seeking individual become established in perfect state of utter harmony, considered to be the highest human achievement? This can be explained by an analogy (a comparison). This human life is like a tree, on which two birds remain. One bird is very restless, ever active, ever curious, ever chirping, ever trying to go near the other bird. This is represented by "non-self i.e. physical body, subtle body (mind, intelligence etc.) and causal body (peculiar impression of combination of three gunas)." Combination of these bodies is "non-self" i.e. that self which is undergoing changes due to changes around. The other bird is represented by the "Divine Existence within." The first bird is ever active and keeps looking at the other bird which is simply a witness, supremely relaxed and continuously watching the first bird (non-self). The ever active bird keeps going on nearer to the first bird and then finally one day the first bird (non-self) realizes that its existence is a delusion. It is not a reality. The silent bird (the Divinity within) alone exists waiting for the first bird (Non-Self) to get out of its self imposed delusion and recognize its real identity (the real self, the pure self, the ever shinning Divinity within). This awakening, this realization is the highest state. We all are like first bird (non-self). We realize our "Eternal Existence within," when the wisdom dawns. That is the point when we gain freedom from fetter (that which stops) of birth and get restored to our natural state of equanimity, knowledge and bliss. That is the moment of utter freedom. This is called the divine abode [*padam anamayam* (beyond all evils) are the words used by the Lord in the verse] i.e. a mental status of "Supreme Self Awareness," where you yourself consciously realize "That I am." This is the state of realization where perishable phenomenon gets restored to status of "Imperishable Unchanging Truth ever continuing in everything, everywhere and even beyond it." It is an infallible (never wrong) state where no malady, no affliction, no limitation or no suffering can touch a human being. To be in this state (*padam annayam*; abode beyond all evils) i.e. to be truly united in knowledge, love and service with all beings means to realize one's self in the "All-pervading Reality." At this point, one perceives that everything has sprung from "Immortal Life" and is vibrating with life and this life is "Immense." It is blessedness to be in "padam anayam; abode beyond evils."

Padam gacchanty anamyam [(The wise, as mentioned above) go to the blissful state or the immortal abode] – The stress in this verse is on these three words. This state is beyond sorrows diseases, afflictions and evils. The individual soul in this state finds itself in enthralling peace. Lasting bliss submerges it. Limitlessness is reached at this point. Silence speaks. Eternity unfolds. The secret reveals. There is nothing beyond to ascend or aspire for. Pinnacle of perfection is reached. In that self-effacing state, one feels the resounding, vibrating presence of the "Absolute Truth" or amalgam of the "*Sat, Chit and anand.*" One finally finds oneself suffused with the bliss, immersed in one's own glory. One undergoes a feeling or a sort of echo coming from deep within to go on and on in the same mode uninterrupted. What is Sri Sri Ravishankar talking about in the following lines?

> "… … Beyond the heaven is my abode,
> Come to me, come to me,
> Do not get stuck up (by heaven, by charming faces, by angels … .),
> Do not stop, walk through them all and pass through them all,
> Come to me, come to me, Come to me … …"

This reassuring resounding within only keeps an individual cruising towards the blissful state and immortal abode … . "*Padam gacchanti annamyam.*"

52. In this verse also, Lord tells Arjuna what happens when an individual reaches the blissful, supreme state, free from blemishes (that mark which reduces the beauty).

यदा ते मोहकलिलं बुद्धिर्व्यतितरिष्यति ।
तदा गन्तासि निर्वेदं श्रोतव्यस्य श्रुतस्य च ॥ २- ५२ ॥

yada te moha-kalilam buddhir vyatitarisyati
tada gantasi nirvedam srotavyasya srutasya ca 2.52

yada--when; *te*--your; *moha- kalilam*—mire or dense forest of delusion; *buddhih*-- intelligence; *vyatitarisyati*—crosses beyond; *tada*—then; *ganta asi*--you shall attain; *nirvedam*—to indifference; *srotavyasya*—what has to be heard; *srutasya*—what has been heard already; *ca*--also.

"When your intelligence (one-pointed, disciplined, cultured and focused at the divinity within) crosses the mire of delusion, then you gain indifference to things heard and yet to be heard." II2-52 II

This verse is also in two parts as follows:

1) **yada te moha kalilam buddhir vyattatarisyati** [when the "pure intelligence" goes beyond the mire of delusion) – What is this mire (muddy area) of delusion? An individual's incapacity to understand the distinction between the **Atma** (soul) and the **Parmatman** (the Supreme Reality), the real and the unreal, being and becoming, marked by delusion, duality and such emotions as anger hatred and avarice are represented by the words "*moha kalilam.*" The identification of self with the "non-self (aggregate of physical, subtle and causal bodies is also covered by these words)" and attachment for the body, family, kinsmen, and objects are also covered by the words "moha kalilam; muddy area of delusion." An individual's sense of discrimination is confounded (feel annoyed) by "moha kalilam" described above. All attention and actions towards the worldly life lead an individual away from the universal aim of escaping the bondage to miserable and sorrowful birth. With yoga-buddhi (one-pointed, disciplined intelligence, steeped in self knowledge) one is able to bypass this zone of "fatal attractions (sensual pleasures)" and capturing tendencies i.e. **moha kalilum**.

Moha kalilum (Mire, i.e. to be stuck up in the deep mud, of delusion) – Delusion is false belief. It may be for one's role in life, for one's near and dear ones or for situation in life. Delusion disrupts true perspective. Undue attachment for dear ones has produced delusion in the mind of Arjuna. It has rendered him incapable of performing his duties. Delusion is like glass with blemishes, which prevents a clear view. This delusion arises from such reasons as infatuations, ego, anger, jealousy, greed and flattery. It helps to know these perpetrators of delusion. These are incidentally the enemies to be faces before realizing the "eternal-life-presence" or the "Universal Gateway."

ii) **tada gantasi nirvedam srotavyasya srutasya ca** (then you gain indifference to what has been heard and yet to be heard) - Here lord has three important words "nirvedam srotavyasya srutasya; indifferent to what is heard and yet to be heard." After going beyond mire (muddy area) of delusion, one becomes indifferent to what has been heard and what is yet to be heard. The two words "*srotvyasaya*" (what has been heard) and "*srutasya*" (what is yet to be heard) require emphasis in discussion. This has reference to such things as karam-kand (ritualistic practices laid down for stated results) of Vedas, traditional notions of morality like sin of killing kinsmen, even if they deserved to be killed. This may also include the supreme duty of offering **pindas** (flour balls offered to the memory of the dead) and moral opinion against fighting one's own guru etc. Failure to abide by all these things, stated here, cause a lot of heaviness on the mind of an ordinary individual. One follows all these things and feels concerned about all these things, because one has heard about these things. Only one thing remains there. The implementation about these things is not backed by self conviction. However, when the individual follows yoga-buddhi (one pointed intelligence disciplined in the light of awareness of the proximity of the "Universal Divinity (divine essence which is immortal, indestructible and immanent or present everywhere) within," one is not disturbed by all these considerations, which are followed, because they are heard. One gains an outlook of renunciation (detached with the results but highly committed to perform the action as an offering to the Supreme due to spiritual conviction (spiritual affinity, spiritual connection within) for the cosmic benefit. The turbidity of delusion (full of mud or meaning confusion here so that you cannot see due to false beliefs) such as non-discrimination, deep-rooted ignorance in the form of notions like "I am such or this is mine or I have done this" do not disturb the mind. One gains **nirvedam** (renunciation) a state full of detachment to results and self-spiritual-commitment. After attaining this detachment, one does not face the maladies (something wrong or illness), which afflict the mind and life of suffering humanity.

Lord has expounded (explained or talked in detail) to Arjuna a very beautiful message. One should not allow one's mind to be perturbed on the basis of "things heard or yet to be heard." This disturbance, so common in worldly life, is uncalled for. What should one do in the light of this verse? **Catch the wordless message of the "sound of silence" within at the point where you are supremely relaxed, charged with awareness, intensely alive, far away from feverishness and full with bliss, with your vision capable of covering past, present and future equally.** This amounts to gaining "*yoga-buddhi* or interpretation in the light of spiritual connectivity." When one is in "*yoga-buddhi*," one cannot commit any wrong. Actions are backed by awareness of the proximity of the Divinity within. Actions get relieved of capturing tendencies. Action is performed without attachment with results as offering to the supreme for cosmic benefit. What is, then, the most important formidable consideration in doing an action? **This is awareness of the divine proximity within.** This was the focal point in sankhya (Self-knowledge). This is the focal point here too i.e. in karam-yoga, because without this "self awareness of the divine proximity within," the divine guidance, that irrepressible conviction of doing only in accordance to righteousness as per law of nature, that ultimate source of unknown divine energy, will be missing. What is the final lesson? One should work in the light of self awareness [i.e. yoga-buddhi; intelligence, one-pointed, disciplined and steeped (thinking and learning for a long time) in self-knowledge] and not on what has been heard or what is yet to be heard. Lord's focus, even in this discussion on karam-yoga, is on the self, the divine essence, the implicit truth of all things, which transcends itself and reveals its own meaning. The awareness alone, in the form of yoga-buddhi, helps the individual to go beyond the zone of "*moha kalilum*; muddy area of delusion."

What is the central message of the verse? Right thinking will bridle the horse (mind), which itself, of its own accord, takes us here and there and everywhere dissipating the vital energy of life and vital resource (life-span). For knowing the one, whose only definition is "self-awareness," development of the proper attitude is necessary.

53. In this verse, Lord is telling the way to the exalted state (yoga-buddhi) referred to in preceding verse.

श्रुतिविप्रतिपन्ना ते यदा स्थास्यति निश्चला ।
समाधावचला बुद्धिस्तदा योगमवाप्स्यसि ॥ २- ५३ ॥

sruti-vipratipanna te yada sthasyati niscala
samadhav acala buddhis tada yoga m avapsyasi 2.53

sruti-- vipratipanna—perplexed by what you have heard; *te*--your; *yada*--when; *sthasyati*—shall stand; *niscala*-- immovable; *samadhau*—a state of absorption in the thoughts of Supreme Reality or Truth; *acala*-- steady; *buddhih*--intelligence; *tada*-- then; *yogam*—state of self-realization after perfecting in yoga (disciplines for union with the Supreme); *avapsyasi*—(you) will achieve.

"When your intellect, bewildered by what you have heard (karam-kand of Vedas), has become poised and firmly fixed in equilibrium, then you shall get into yoga." II 2-53 II

First it is necessary to discuss two words used in this verse:

i) *Srutiviparatipanna* (perplexed with what you have heard)- Sruti is a general terms used for Vedas and Upnishads. First part of Vedas, known as "sruti (known of revelation)" is chiefly made up of hymns and instructions regarding rites and ceremonies. Second part is known as knowledge. It is made up of the Upnishads. Upnishads are concerned about the highest aspect of the "Sacred Truth" or "God." A lot of rituals in Vedas are for the worldly pleasures i.e. it may be a boon for getting a son. An ordinary individual of present era, with a lot of stress of daily life, finds it confusing and difficult to assimilate and relate it with the prime objective of human life i.e. who I am. What does it feel to know who I am? Is it possible to come face to face and be one with the "Real One or The Supreme Inside"? The statement laid down for getting only a son may not be in tune with the statements for realization of "The Supreme Reality," which speaks without words, hears without ears and walks without legs. One gets confused in assimilating the different impact of different statements. Such a distracted confused and wavering has been referred to in this verse as "*srutivipatipanna*."

ii) *Samadhi* (a state in which one attains freedom from modifications of mind and gets established in one's own self in superconscious state) – This is another important word used by the Lord in this discussion. True test of *Samadhi* is expulsion of (or rather freedom from) all desires i.e. one so disciplines that desires or modifications of mind do not disturb. In this state desires face inability to get to the mind. Steadfast equilibrium of the mind is termed *Samadhi*. The altercations, storms and stress of external life do not disturb the mind in *samadhi*. Mind gets drawn inward when acting outwardly. This is the end of yoga. When this culmination is reached, all strivings cease and novice in yoga becomes an adept in yoga. There are two types of *Samadhi* i.e. *Savikalpa Samadhi* and *Nirvikapla Samadhi*. *Savikalpa Samadhi* is a kind of spiritual absorption in which persists awareness of the knower, the known and the knowledge. *Nirvikalpa Samadhi* has three levels. In first level one awakes from the *Nirvikalpa Samadhi* by one's own self. In the second stage, one is awakened by others. In last stage one does not awake at all. An individual becomes a sage, a prophet and a saint in smadhi. An individual gets illumined in Samadhi.

There is so much discussion about "yoga-buddhi" in the preceding verses. Where does it come from? Yoga-buddhi is awakening of pure intelligence (a grace of Mahat or Cosmic Intelligence) and it dawns when one has become adept in yoga (all disciplines i.e. physical, mental, emotional and spiritual) to unite the self with the Supreme Self (**Parmatama**). The message of this verse is discussed in three parts as follows:

i) *srutivipratopanna te yada sthasyati nischala* [(when your) intellect, bewildered by what you have heard, gets established in the self) – An individual's mind is naturally disturbed by the conflicting ideas coming from hearing this and hearing that. For example, karam-kanda of Vedas lays down rituals, which lead to specified results. A new seeker naturally feels attraction but these rituals are not enough to procure freedom from cycles of birth and death. Still, a time comes when the mind becomes steady, overcoming all distractions of hearing this and hearing that.

ii) *Samdhavachla buddhi* (steady intelligence becomes immovable or established in the awareness of proximity of divine existence within) - When the condition stated in point number one is satisfied i.e. when basic delusion is shed, buddhi (intelligence) becomes quite indifferent to whatever it has been exposed to or whatever it is yet to come across. At this moment there is nothing in the form of influence to make intelligence agitated or perplexed. This is the point when an individual enters the transcendent (beyond human experience and knowledge) state of Samadhi [absorption in the core-self; transcending ego and getting the grip of deeper affinity with all; prelude to freedom of soul; precursor to living relationship with surroundings and becoming one with the "All"]. What is, then, the most important formidable consideration in doing an action? This is awareness of the divine proximity within. This was the focal point in Sankhya (Self-knowledge). This is the focal point here too i.e. in karam-yoga, because without this "self awareness of the divine proximity within," the divine guidance, that irrepressible conviction of doing only in accordance to righteousness as per law of nature, that ultimate source of unknown divine energy, will be missing. "This Divine Clarity or Samadhi" puts to rest yearning for "The Self." By sacrificing and surrendering all (absolutely all; leaving touch with nothing, un-divine) to "The Higher Spiritual Universal Ground," comes "Samadhi."

Major stress in these words is on "Samadhi." Samadhi is not loss of consciousness. It is highest form of consciousness. Under Samadhi, the object with which mind is in communion is divine self. The method to be followed is "Buddhir-yoga" i.e. intelligence, cultured, refined and dedicated to "the self; the unending expanse of divinity within; all-feeling being in the soul."

iii) *Tada yogam vapsyasi* (Then one attains yoga) – These are very beautiful words. What is yoga? Does it merely mean control on mental, urges, modifications and tendencies? Various disciplines (physical, mental, emotional and spiritual) are used to gain this objective of controlling urges, modifications and tendencies of mind. These are all means of gaining cessation of mental impressions to attain the "state of yoga; final Unity with Divine Eternal Nature, That Infinite Universal Consciousness." Yoga means getting to the highest state of excellence and awareness where one loses one's own "Reflected Individual Divinity; distorted version of "one's own Truth" in the light of ego and goes into "The Sublime, Supreme, Infinite, Eternal Reality or Truth." That feeling of separateness, that peculiar impact of ego, that false awareness, that I am, goes away for good. Getting into this state means gaining "Immortality." There is no relapse (to start becoming bad again) after this state into worldliness. Death loses its sting and relevance. Even if one remains alive after this, one becomes "Jeevan-mukata or Self-liberated living entity or One having attained freedom from all possible limitation." This is the ultimate state of fruition of yoga-sadhna (practice all laid-down disciplines) to gain oneness with "The Supreme Truth; The Immortal Self." Buddhi (awakened, disciplined, one pointed and steeped into divine proximity) helps the individual to go beyond the zone of *"moha kalilum*; muddy area of delusion."

54. Arjuna's spiritual curiosity gets inflamed by the Lord's ultimate words about Samadhi and Yoga, having deep meaning, depth and impact. Emboldened, he asks a question from the Lord:

अर्जुन उवाच ।
स्थितप्रज्ञस्य का भाषा समाधिस्थस्य केशव ।
स्थितधीः किं प्रभाषेत किमासीत व्रजेत किम् ॥ २- ५४ ॥

arjuna uvaca
sthita-prajnasya ka bhasa samadhi-sthasya kesava
sthita-dhih kim prabhaseta kim asita vrajeta kim 2.54

arjunah uvaca--Arjuna said; *sthita-prajnasya*--of one who is situated in fixed Krsna consciousness; *ka*--what; *bhasa*--language; *samadhi-sthasya*--of one situated in trance; *kesava*--O Krsna; *sthita-dhih*--one fixed in Krsna consciousness; *kim*--what; *prabhaseta*--speak; *kim*--how; *asita*--does remain; *vrajeta*--walks; *kim*--how.

Arjuna said:

"O Kesava (Krishna)! What is the description of the person established in the super conscious state (sthitaprjanasya)? How does an individual steeped in "*Samadhi*" speak? How does he sit and move?" II 2-54 II

After hearing the words Samadhi (state of merger with the Divinity within) and Yoga (irreversible state of merger with the Supreme Consciousness) in verse 53, Arjuna feels anxious to know about the characteristics of individual of steady wisdom, individual of self-realization, the jeevanmukta (one liberated from all limitations while remaining alive). "*Samadhi*" is a state of absolute stability, strength, intense awareness and infinite compassion and consideration. Here the word used is "sthitaprajnasya" i.e. one who has steady wisdom and is absorbed in the awareness of the Divine consciousness. Outwardly such an individual may look similar to others but there is always tremendous difference inside. When an individual and a foolish person work together, there is similarity at bodily level but dissimilarity at intellectual level. "*Sthiti*" means steady and "*prajna*" means wisdom (not worldly wisdom but divinely directed). In brief, "steady wisdom" means settled knowledge of one's identity of the self (one's true divine nature, one's truth) by direct experience or with awareness.. Arjuna asks for outward, physical, practical and discernible signs of an individual with steady (disciplined, cultured, divinely-directed) wisdom established in the state of awareness of Divine proximity (nearness) i.e. how such an individual sits (or regulates the external organs to control the mind emerged from the state of Samadhi), speaks (or how he appreciates or despises other beings) or walks (it may be arrogant or amicable). The verbs in this verse are used in potential mood i.e. conveying the sense of probability. Arjuna calls Krishna Kesava i.e. killer of demon Kesav. Krishna is physical symbol of inner controller of all. He has himself been through all moods and therefore Lord Krishna is most suitable to speak on these matters. Arjuna makes a diligent enquiry because ardent practice is required to achieve the ideal (being in divine wisdom and remaining established in Supreme awareness of Divine Consciousness). Arjuna's question is focused to know the discernible signs or distinguishing marks of individuals established in steady intelligence (divinely disposed, focused intelligence).

55. In the next 18 verses, Lord explains the characteristics of "sthitaprjnan; one established in divine wisdom."

श्रीभगवानुवाच ।
प्रजहाति यदा कामान्सर्वान्पार्थ मनोगतान् ।
आत्मन्येवात्मना तुष्टः स्थितप्रज्ञस्तदोच्यते ॥ २- ५५ ॥

sri-bhagavan uvaca
prajahati yada kaman sarvan partha mano-gatan
atmany evatmana tustah sthita-prajnas tadocyate 2.55

sri-bhagavan uvaca—the blessed Lord Krishna said; *prajahati*—casts off or gives up; *yada*--when; *kaman*—intense desires (for sense gratification); *sarvan*--of all varieties; *partha*--O son of Prtha (Arjuna); *manah-gatan*—belonging to mind; *atmani*--in the self (soul with cover of ignorance); *eva*--only; *atmana*-- by the pure joy of the self (exclusive eternal existence within soul; indweller of the soul, who can only be experienced); *tustah*--satisfied; *sthita-prajnah*— one with steady (un-moving) wisdom; *tada*-- then; *ucyate*-- is clled.

"When an individual casts off (or abandons) all the desire of mind, O Partha (Arjuna), and is satisfied in the self by the self, then the individual is said to be one stable in wisdom." II 2-55 II

Negatively stated, this state (established in divine wisdom) means freedom from all desires, the mother or cause of all sufferings, afflictions and cravings. Positively stated, it is the state in which one is focused on the "Divine existence within and everywhere, all-around in everything and even beyond." It is an exercise of collecting itself (different dimensions of existence i.e. physical, mental, emotional and spiritual) and then concentrating or pouring every bit of "this combined collection of different aspects of one's existence" on the awareness of the divine existence within. Lord makes this statement in three parts as follows:

i) *prajahatih yada Kaman sarvan partha manogatan* [(when an individual) puts away all the desires of mind, O Partha (Arjuna) – Arjuna's question is to know how an individual established in divine intelligence behaves. Lord starts answering the question. What is the first condition to be complied with? First condition is expulsion of all desires. The inability of the desires to get to the mind takes you to the inner state where the all-out freedom comes from. Mind is the only instrument or raft which will take us afar to that "Other Shore," beyond the zone of common human experience and understanding, which is called the abode of the Supreme. The first condition is to keep the mind away from attractions and repulsions, sunshine, storm and stress of external worldly existence.

ii) *Atmany eva atmana tustah* (satisfied by the self in the self) – These are very beautiful words and tell about the highest form of worship. First let us understand what the self is. An individual is a combined collection of different aspects of its existence (i.e. body, breath, mind, intelligence, memory and the self). One has to keep away from everything which makes one being part of one's existence and falls in the category of perishable. One will find that the self (atma or soul or the seventh level) alone remains. Then one has to go still further. First, there is "Reflected Individual divinity" loaded with the layers of ignorance and past memories. Even ignorance and past memories are not permanent. Even these two have to be removed, while one washes the pearl lying in the mud. What will happen? Then one will see the divine splendor of the Divinity. This is the focal point. One has to be in this zone in which one gets absorbed in feeling awareness about the Divinity exclusively. It is enchanting, absorbing and enthralling experience. This is what is meant by feeling satisfied in the Self by the Self. One is completely charged with awareness. One comes face to face with the Truth. No thought can reach the individual. One feels utterly enthralled and supremely satisfied. Every bit of the self is full with bliss. One remains smiling. One feels that there is nothing except 'This Awareness'. One get awakened to the reality "That I am." There remains no shred of ego (I, me and mine) anywhere within, in the vast unfathomable void. One continues in this awareness only, for good, for all the time to come. This state comes when one draws inwardly even while acting outwardly. One's connectivity remains with the "Universal Divinity" even when one is gazing out at the external things, participating outwardly. Breathing in and breathing out is mechanical routine which goes on without affecting one's connectivity with divine consciousness. These are the moments when one opens the inner doors of the "shrine within." One lights the candle of awareness and then in that inner, unending expanse of silence one find oneself face to face with the Supreme Truth. Heaven is born within. One meets one's eternal love. A realization grows with a flash of gladness, culminating in soft whisper … **"I am in your heart, my dear."** This is what one feels when one is satisfied by the self in the self. Undergoing the experience of being satisfied by the self in the self is the precondition. Then one will be aware of the bliss of realization of truth of "Oneness," oneness of soul with the world and through the world with the "Supreme Lover."

iii) *sthita prajanas tado ucyate* (then one is said to be established in the steady wisdom) – When one's wisdom enables one to gain above mentioned experience, one is said to be established in divine wisdom.

These are very beautiful lines. Lord is telling Arjuna the way to the most exalted state of human experience. "This awakening within" feels like stretching for "Unlimited Fulfillment." One has to feel satisfied by the self in the self and experience the miracle within. The sum-total of all the pleasures of the world are worthless for the sage of steady wisdom who is satisfied by the self in the self. Being satisfied by the self in the self is the "Ultimate Spiritual Experience" called "Self-Realization."

56. In this verse Lord tells Arjuna about the mental status of a sage of "steady wisdom; **sthitaprjana**."

दुःखेष्वनुद्विग्नमनाः सुखेषु विगतस्पृहः ।
वीतरागभयक्रोधः स्थितधीमुनिरुच्यते ॥ २- ५६

duhkhesv anudvigna-manah sukhesu vigata-sprhah
vita-raga-bhaya-krodhah sthita-dhir munir ucyate 2.56

duhkhesu--in adversity; *anudvigna-manah*-- of unshaken mind; *sukhesu*—in pleasure; *vigata-sprhah*--without hankering i.e. whose thirst for pleasure has altogether has disappeared; *vita*--free from; *raga*—attachment i.e. insatiable desire to continue pleasure; *bhaya*--fear; *krodhah*--anger; *sthita-dhih*—(one) whose intelligence is steady; *munih*--a sage; *ucyate*--is called.

"(One), whose mind is not perturbed in the midst of sorrow, who does not crave for happiness and who is free from attachment, fear and anger, is called a sage of steady wisdom." II 2-56 II

In state of "sthitaprjana; divinely disposed focused intelligence" alone, the self can be realized fully directly. In this verse, Lord continues enumerating the hall-marks of the individual of steady wisdom as follows:

i) *dukhesu anudvignamanah* (not shaken by adversity) – The mind of a sage of steady wisdom is not distressed in adverse circumstances or adversity i.e. such an individual is not affected by the three types of afflictions: i) *adhyatmika* (arising from diseases and disorders in one's own body), ii) *adhidaivika* (arising from natural calamities such as thunder, lightning storm or flood etc.) and iii) *adhibhautika* (arising from being victim of living beings such as scorpions, cobras, tigers etc.).

ii) *sukhesu vigataspraha* (without hankering or craving for the pleasures) - Such an individual keeps away from craving for pleasures. What is pleasure? Pleasure means an experience of temporary (fleeting) happiness with the place, person or the outcome of event. An individual established in wisdom does not crave for pleasures. Why is it so? Such an individual knows about the difference between pleasure and bliss. Bliss is a continuous state of spiritual happiness. Bliss leads to perfection and contentment. Pleasure leads to dissatisfaction and disappointment. Keeping the eventual outcome in view and being wise, an individual refrains from craving for pleasures.

iii) *vita raga, bhaya, krodhah* (keeps free from longing, fear and anger) – These are the negative traits of character. An individual becomes victim of these negative traits when there is no control on the urges, modifications and tendencies of mind. Steady intelligence is "divinely disposed, focused intelligence," which truly guides the mind towards righteousness as per law of nature. Due to poised intelligence, one is able to keep away from these negative traits. 'These negative traits', arising due to *rajas* (longing for feverishness) and *tamas* (ignorance and inaction), drive an individual to act or interact. All these negative traits arise due to desire. An individual, established in poised and focused intelligence, knows pretty well that desire cannot be the real motivation for action or inaction. Therefore, an individual established in divinely disposed and focused intelligence, goes for either sublimating the negative characteristics (i.e. if one has to be angry, one should be angry with one's own insufficient spiritual growth) or keeping away from these characteristics. Finally, these *dukha* (sorrow)-producing events and situations are not able to ruffle the mind and dislodge the individual from deeper mooring (place where a boat or ship is moored to be kept at one place) bestowed upon being "Sthitaprajna."

iv) **sthitadhir munir ucyate** [(an individual showing above mentioned characteristics) is called muni (or sage] - First Lord mentions the characteristics, discussed above. Then it is confirmed that such an individual is called a **muni** (sage). Who is a **muni**? A **muni** (sage) is an individual, committed to spiritual growth after having gained self mastery and conquest over desire and passion. A **muni** (sage) is not tossed, lost and broken by worldly joys and sorrows. The main focus of a **muni** remains on beholding the ever effulgent (bright), calm, beauteous expanse of soul within, where spiritual colors, tunes and fragrance pour, in endless cascades (flow), in the abounding bliss, in rhythmic measures, in the "Infinite and Eternal Universal Fountain of Joy."

The three marks of "**Sthitaprajna** (one established in intelligence drawn inwardly towards calm, beauteous stretch of 'Unbounded Consciousness', the cause of all)" narrated by the Lord are: i) unshaken in adversities, ii) not hankering towards pleasures and iii) free from attachment, fear (without duality there is no fear and **shitaprajna** goes for "universal oneness") and anger.

57. In this verse, lord tells Arjuna how an individual established in "yoga-buddhi; immersed (to become completely involved) in divinely disposed or inwardly focused wisdom" conducts (behaves) with the outside world.

यः सर्वत्रानभिस्नेहस्तत्तत्प्राप्य शुभाशुभम् ।
नाभिनन्दति न द्वेष्टि तस्य प्रज्ञा प्रतिष्ठिता ॥ २- ५७ ॥

yah sarvatranabhisnehas tat tat prapya subhasubham
nabhinandati na dvesti tasya prajna pratisthita 2.57

yah—(one) who; *sarvatra*--everywhere; *anabhisnehah*--without attachment; *tat*--that; *tat*--that; *prapya*—having obtained; *subha*--good; *asubham*--evil; *na*--not; *abhinandati*-- rejoices; *na*—not; *dvesti*—envies or hates; *tasya*--his; *prajna*—perfect (divine) knowledge; *pratisthita*- (is) fixed.

"One, who is everywhere without attachment, who neither rejoices nor hates anything on meeting good or bad, is an individual of steady wisdom." II 2-57 II

The three characteristics pointed out by the Lord in this verse are as follows:

I) *yah sarvatra anabhisnehah tat-tat prapya subha subham* (such an individual is unattached everywhere though visited by good and evil.) – This world is full of mixture of good and evil. The people who are attached are bound to experience both joy and sorrow. Such people oscillate between impulsive happiness and woe (great sadness). An individual, with wisdom, transcends (goes beyond) these limitations and utters neither words of praise nor those of censure (criticism). These words in this verse are implied answer to the question of Arjuna as to how a "**sthitaprajna**; one- established in wisdom" speaks. These words indicate towards an attitude of "accepting the inevitable" actively without murmur, excitement, pain or revolt. Reaction i.e. impulsive response to the situation is avoided and action is taken in a poised manner without affection on any side. Lord has used the word "*anabhisnehah*" which refers to a mental modification in which an individual has no attachment [no love (strong bond of caring, liking and attraction)]; no **sneha** (a feeling more than caring but lighter than love in intensity] for either of the probable outcome of action or situation. The individual in this category does not care even for one's own life, let alone relatives, possession, name and fame. For this reasons, individual in this category does not develop predilection (unusual liking), likes and dislikes or, in other words, does not immediately reflect emotions in facing good (auspicious) or bad (inauspicious) situations and people.

ii) **na abhinandati na dvesti** (does not rejoice and does not hate) - Since a "sthitaprajna" is having conscious control over the feelings, ego, senses and discrimination, an individual in this category does not over-rejoices or hates. Such an individual is quiescent (being there but not doing anything) in mind, mind is quiescent in intelligence and intelligence is quiescent in "Divine Felicity (happiness) and Self-Knowledge" within. Reason is simple. The individual, in this category, makes way through nature, observing it but not subjecting to it and especially not desiring anything that objective life can offer. The individual in this category seeks the satisfaction of the soul and not the senses. Due to yoga-buddhi (pure-soul wisdom), the focus of "sthitaprajna, one disciplined and divinely focused" remains on renunciation (abandonment) of desire, a natural withdrawal from satisfaction of senses and in seeking consummation (the point at which something is complete or perfect) in the "Joy of the Infinite ever flowing within."

Sorrows and pleasures are our reactions to situations, people and events. The focus of this verse is on how the individual of steady and settled intelligence (sthitiprajna) should react. **A seed patiently remains true to its nature in solitary silence and bears with fortitude awaiting the divine grace.** Finally it finds its fulfillment in the form of a fruit. Coming to be alive is an opportunity given and one should feel that one is born to be successful only. The element of ignorance involves in denying and delaying it. That is all. With the above mentioned interpretation in view, one's response to experiences of sorrows and pleasures will automatically undergo a sea change. One should water the roots and not the leaves. That is the idea. One should concentrate on the underlying causes of sorrows and pleasures. Sorrows are bound to be there. Pleasures are bound to be there. Pain is bound to be there. Life is to be like that only. One has to adjust the understanding, the approach and reaction appropriately with the thoughts of the Gita in the background. **The world cannot hinder us if we do not allow ourselves to be hindered by our reactions to sorrows and pleasures.** This is the sun and substance of this verse.

This verse is the answer given by the Lord to Arjuna's query: "How does a sage of wisdom conduct in this world? What is this that brings about this change in "Sthitaprajna"? The life of a "sthitaprajna; one disciplined and divinely focused within" is a life of offering, life of worship (strong feeling of love and respect for the Divine). The life-stream of such an individual touches the "Deep Divine Flow Within" and this world of forms comes to its nest to repose in "The ever continuing beauty, ever continuing joy and ever continuing knowledge beyond all forms."

58. In this verse, Lord explains how a "Sthitaprajna; one disciplined and focused within" sits.

यदा संहरते चायं कूर्मोऽङ्गानीव सर्वशः ।
इन्द्रियाणीन्द्रियार्थेभ्यस्तस्य प्रज्ञा प्रतिष्ठिता ॥ २- ५८ ॥

yada samharate cayam kurmo 'nganiva sarvasah
indriyanindriyarthebhyas tasya prajna pratisthita 2,58

yada--when; *samharate*-- withdraws ; *ca*--and; *ayam*-- this; *kurmah*--tortoise; *angani*--limbs; *iva*--like; *sarvasah*-- everywhere; *indriyani*—the senses; *indriya-arthebhyah*--from the sense objects; *tasya*--his; *prajna*—intelligence (steeped in divine wisdom); *pratisthita*—(is) steadied or gets fixed up.

A tortoise puts out its limbs when necessary and withdraws them into its shell at will. Using this smiley, Lord says: "When an individual withdraws its senses from respective objects of enjoyments like tortoise, which draws in its limbs into the shell, then the intelligence of such an individual gets (or sits) firmly founded in wisdom." II2-58 II

In this verse, Lord tells Arjuna about a very important discipline of inducing the mind (the head of all the senses) with the awareness "not to mind anything." Imagine a dog is sitting in the middle of the night and there is a soft tap somewhere. What will happen? The dog will very attentively and simultaneously look in the direction from where the voice has come. The same is the condition of mind. Withholding (rather minding) this out-going tendency of mind to respond to any provocation, is what Lord is telling in this verse. Sage Patanjali has called it "*Pratyahara*; retracting; keeping awareness on the out-going tendency of mind or telling the mind "never mind, hold on." This is a very positive trait of protecting the individual self by positive thinking and self control. It does not mean imposition. It simply means inducing the mind to hold on to something sacred, spiritual, divine so that mind is not unnecessarily dragged. Why do we want to spare the mind? With mind alone, one can experience the "Truth." Mind is the mirror in which one sees the "Truth; Divine Reality." Senses also can be controlled by mind only.

This withdrawal of senses (which is through mind only) from sense-objects, talked about in this verse, is very important for a perfect sage (*sthitaprajna*). This withdrawal has to be active when one is alive and the senses are in full vigor. If an individual lives a life of self-control withdrawing the five senses, as a tortoise when it senses danger draws itself into its shell, then the concerned individual will be ready to behold all, undisturbed by fear of birth and death, un-swayed by the rhythm of earthly day and night. One starts resting in the divinely-lit solitude of "Exclusively Pure Infinite Soul." Discipline of life is more precious than life itself, for its through discipline itself that life finds out its direction, purpose, meaning and value. If one neglects to lead a disciplined life, one loses forever the advantage of human birth. Self control unfolds to an individual an awareness of the "Truth of the Self." Lack of this discipline, discussed by the Lord in this verse, pushes an individual into deep depths of darkness. It is necessary to put an end to rushing out of the senses to seize and enjoy sense-objects. The best way to do this is to take those senses to quiescence (not developing or doing anything) in the mind. One who becomes adept in this discipline becomes a "*sthitaprajna*; one disciplined and divinely focused in the quiescence (not moving, not doing anything) of the soul."

Seeking the Shield of divinity to gain sense control – Final focus of this verse is on control of senses. Self-control takes one to the highest possible level of perfection achievable by a being. Its want will push one into utter darkness.The Gita does not advise to banish all sensory temptations. The individual should consciously gain freedom from sensory intrusion. How this is to be done has been picturesquely described by comparison with a tortoise. All sense addicts find later at one point of time or the other that they are disillusioned and dissatisfied. They come to realize later that they are seeking happiness in foreign territory hostile to soul bliss. A tortoise withdraws its limbs within armor of its shell to protect from harm outside. Similarly an individual has to gain the knowledge of using the mind and life force at will continuously. One has to learn to withdraw the mind (controller of senses) from the gravitational zone of the material world. This is the first step. Second step to control the senses is to unite the mind and life energy with the intoxicating joy of inner bliss caused by inner communion with the soul. This communion with the soul is the armor (like shell of the tortoise) to protect the individual from all sides. One should understand what this armor mentioned here is like. In advanced stages of yoga one consciously withdraws life force upward through the spinal centers. In this process, one dissolves the grosser into the successively finer manifestation while continuously reciting "*Aum Aum Aum*." This continuous vibration of "*Aum Aum Aum*" finally melts into cosmic consciousness. Even recalling this armor or experience is a joy for those, who have gone into state of deep meditation. By going into armor or experience, one gets the shield of the divinity. One has to taste to believe it. Same thought is expressed by Kashmiri poetess, Lal Ded (1320-1392) in her "*Vakya*; sentence" in words paraphrased below:

"Let good and bad come to me.
My ears shall not hear nor do eyes see.
When the inner call comes up in the mind,
My lamp will be lighted even by the lamp of adversity.

59. In this verse Lord glorifies the fasting (abstinence for food).

विषया विनिवर्तन्ते निराहारस्य देहिनः ।
रसवर्जं रसोऽप्यस्य परं दृष्ट्वा निवर्तते ॥ २- ५९ ॥

visaya vinivartante niraharasya dehinah
rasa-varjam raso 'py asya param drstva nivartate 2.59

visayah—objects of senses; *vinivartante*—(are) turned away; *niraharasya*—abstinent (deliberate restrictions); *dehinah*- of the man ; *rasa-varjam*—leaving the longing; *rasah*—(loving taste) ; *api*—even ; *asya*--his; *param*—the Supreme; *drstva*—having seen; *nivartate*—turns away.

"If one abstains from food (or in-take of senses), the objects of senses (forms, sound, food etc.) cease to affect but the affection itself for the senses (for example taste for food) or rasa or longing remains. This longing also ceases when one intuits (to know with feelings rather than facts) "The Supreme Drstva, seeing whom one gains unbounded vision to witness one and all and each level of each being simultaneously." II2-58 II

Lord is gradually telling Arjuna, the greatest truth very simply. Fasting and similar discipline is one of the means towards self-restraining or taming the senses or reducing the natural restlessness for the sense objects, but it is not all. If physical fasting is not accompanied by mental fasting, it will lead the individual to hypocrisy and disaster. One should get rid of the memory of the sense-enjoyments as well. This memory keeps lying within obscured (hidden). This resident, silent longing of the sense-experiences also goes away when one intuits (to know with feelings rather than facts) with the "Effulgent (full of brightness or light), Infinite and Eternal Reality." Lord is telling in this verse the difference between the internal abstinence and the outer abstinence. We all nurture a tendency. We may reject the object but desire for the object (longing or mental memory of the object) still continues or remains. These remnants (small parts of something that remain) of the sense objects also go away when one intuits with the Supreme Universal Reality. The message is simple. It is not enough to gain freedom from the tyranny of the body. One must free oneself from the tyranny of desire (residual longing, mental involvement with the thoughts of sense-objects). The message has been given by the Lord as follows in very beautiful words:

i) **visaya vinivartante niraharasya dehinah** (sense-objects drop out or fall away from an abstinent, embodied individual) – What does it mean? An embodied individual may say "I shall not eat today. I shall observe fast." The individual may not eat or even see the food but he or she may suffer from the longing for the food or thinking about the taste of favorite items for the day long. This applies to every sensory craving. By taking away the sense-objects from front, an individual does not become self-controlled person. This is not abstinence (i.e. deliberate act of choosing or deciding or not allowing yourself food, alcoholic drink, sex etc. for moral and spiritual development).

Lord has used the word "nirahara." Its antonym is "aahar." "Aahar" is that the use of which or consumption of which satisfies the senses. All the things in the world, the use of which or the consumption of which satisfy senses sometimes, somewhere, are covered by the word "visayas; things." Visayas are food (in-take) for senses. One craves for "visayas" for satisfaction of senses. When one gets so disciplined in life that the individual makes the senses turn inward i.e. senses do not jump towards sense objects but turn inward for that "much-talked about soul-touched happiness," one becomes "nirahari" i.e. one who observes abstinence in the form of turning the sense-objects away. Soon the abstinence matures and the attachment for sense objects recedes. The hunger for sense-objects only recedes but that "inherent interest; seed of longing" in sense-objects remains in human system, may be, in memory zone. That is why many saints talk jokingly among their private company about the sense-objects which they avoid in practical life.

ii) *rasasvarjam* (leaving the longing) – One may remove the **visayas** (sense-objects) from the sight, but **rasam** (longing for the taste) still persists i.e. memory of the residual effect of satisfying the thirst or hunger for that sense-object remains in the memory-zone. One gains full freedom when cravings also go. If craving is still there, it will create new challenges, new temptations, and possibility of getting flared up anytime. What does Lord want to say? One gains absolute freedom, when the craving for the sense-object is gone from the zone of consciousness, called memory i.e. even mental craving has to be uprooted.

iii) *param drasta nivartate* [(longings, discussed above) turn away having seen the "Supreme"] – These three words used here describe the ultimate purpose of all that Lord has talked about so far through sankhya-yoga and buddhir yoga. What is the ultimate purpose of Sankhya-yoga or buddhiryoga? There is only one purpose of human existence. It is that highest state of realization, where disciplined and divine intelligence turns the tamed-mind towards "The Supreme" having unbounded vision, capable of witnessing inside and outside and each level of existence of every being of the universe simultaneously. What happens hereafter cannot be done perfectly even by intelligence and discipline. One gets into the zone of "Universal Oneness." One gains that vision of the Supreme Being (Universal Eternal Infinite Reality (Truth). No one can see "The Supreme Being; The Formless" with the mortal eyes. Divine Vision is required to see the nature of the "Supreme Being, The Supreme Eternal Secret." This vision cannot be earned in any way i.e. knowledge, action or meditation. It is always a grace dependent on the mercy of "The Supreme" alone. By this grace, one realizes the Self. By this grace alone one gets free from the bondage of birth and death. All perceived Divinities (i.e. gods and Goddesses with names and forms and the rituals) can fulfill the desire of the devotee but none except the "Supreme being; Eternal Universal Reality)"can relieve the individual from cycles of birth and death. All the paths mentioned in the Gita finally take one to state of Samadhi but final "union with the Truth" is not possible without grace of "The Supreme Being," who gives the "Divine Vision; the unbounded expanse of vision" to be aware of the Supreme Truth. Who is this "Supreme Being" mentioned in this verse, seeing whom the subtle mental impressions, called **vasanas** or **ragas**, disappear?

Getting the "Divine Vision" of the Supreme Being, experiencing the self-realization or merging in the "Supreme-Oneness" refers to the same state. The "Supreme; One, seeing whom all subtle impression, hidden in different level of consciousness, disappear" is that supreme knowledge, that Awareness of Divine Consciousness and Bliss which is beginning-less and endless. It cannot be described by words. It can be only experienced by pure intelligence. It is basis (source) of all. It is self existent different from the manifested and the un-manifested. How is it different from the un-manifested? Anything

193

else, if un-manifested will not be there, but it evidences its presence even when it is un-manifested. It sees without eyes, walks without legs and communicates without language. "**The Supreme**" is God of All Gods (perceived Divinities with name and form and described by someone). "**The Supreme**" is both the self (being reflected individual divinities in all) and non-self (being there without identifiable apparent existence). There is no past, present and future for it. Every religion is a manual effort (either in thinking or in hearing) to describe it. It is beyond all casts, religions, genders or limitations. When awareness of this Supreme is there, one is able to have desire-less contact with the objects and un-sensuous use of senses. A strange soul-felicity (full of bliss, knowledge and consciousness) is experienced, untouched by any passion, pure, spotless. It is the "Divine Inhabitant" within both the manifested and the un-manifested. It is both the "flame and the offering," "Supreme Truth and the Origin," "the Equilibrium and the Absolute Fitness in harmony." The Supreme is not negative annihilation of the self but it is a state of merging the individual reality (ego) into "Vast Reality of One Infinite Impersonal Existence with Divine Love charged with Awareness." This "Supreme" is the abiding strength, the living principle, the true indivisible blissfulness, the non-dual Reality. It is the "Truth" of that, which comprehends multiplicity. "This Supreme" is one, awareness of whose presence makes one feel "I am That; I am *Brahman* (Supreme Universal Eternal Reality)." It opens up the whole horizon and leads us to "The Infinite" becoming both the subject and object in one (it is highest state of realization). It is One Eternal Being who manifests one divine essence in all. It is this reality which leads all from unreality to the real, from darkness to the light and from death to the immortality. "A being is" means its (of the Infinite and Eternal) touch is there. Lord Krishna in the Gita symbolizes "This Supreme" i.e. "One who enables to have Unbounded Cosmic Vision," a "Witness of Past, Present and Future"; "an Entity Capable of witnessing all the levels of existences of all the beings in the Universe simultaneously." This "Supreme Being" is the focal point of both the *Sankhya-Yoga* and the *Buddhir-Yoga*, discussed by the Lord. If the Gita is to be viewed as a divine river, eternally moving forward and flowing, then "This Supreme One," who witnesses all without being witnessed, is the final point towards which this river flows. There remains nothing to be seen and known beyond this "Supreme Being," who is "One in all and All in One." Awareness of "This Supreme Being" means perfect repose in the truth, perfect activity in the goodness and perfect union in the love (eternal, unlimited and for all). The revelation of "This Supreme" means an experience of being endlessly new, eternally beautiful and gaining the meaning of the self, the real self. If an individual becomes aware of own truth by fully apprehending in this life "The Supreme," life achieves its crowning glory and becomes an arrow that has completely penetrated its target. Failure to apprehend "This Supreme" means passing from starvation to starvation, from trouble to trouble and from fear to fear. The one, who knows or who has intuited (known by feelings and not facts) with the "This Supreme Truth, the all-Consciousness, and the Infinite," hidden in the depth of the soul, in the inner sky of consciousness, enjoys, with the divine vision, all objects of desire in unbreakable-union with "The all-knowing or The Supreme." What does it mean? Mortal being gains "Immortality" after being face to face with "This Supreme Being."

60. In this verse, Lord explains the ferocity, vehement insistence of the senses.

यततो ह्यपि कौन्तेय पुरुषस्य विपश्चितः ।
इन्द्रियाणि प्रमाथीनि हरन्ति प्रसभं मनः ॥ २- ६० ॥

yatato hy api kaunteya purusasya vipascitah
indriyani pramathini haranti prasabham manah 2.60

yatatah—of the striving; *hi*-- indeed; *api*-- even; *kaunteya*--O son of Kunti (Arjuna); *purusasya*--of the man; *vipascitah*--full of discriminating knowledge i.e. of the wise; *indriyani*--the senses; *pramathini*-- turbulent; *haranti*- carry away; *prasabham*--by force; *manah*--the mind.

"The turbulent (excited) senses, O son of Kunti (Arjuna), impetuously (done quickly without thinking carefully) carry away the mind of even a wise man by force even though he may strive for perfection (and be ever so discerning)." II 2-60 II

This verse is a sort of warning (a word of caution) to the new aspirants. The first challenge that a new aspirant faces is to bring the senses under control. The use of the word control is not very appropriate. One should gain freedom on allowing intrusion of senses. The senses are like horses. If one keeps the horses under perfect control, one will reach the destination. If one is riding on a wild horse, newly harnessed, it may be risky to life as well. The senses are dangerous also because they agitate the mind and carry the mind away by force, even when the man is wide awake and is trying best to control them. This self-discipline or self-control is never easy. All intelligent people know that self-control must be exercised but nothing is more common than advice to control the senses. Even after all these warnings, a sage, a man of clear, wise, discerning soul, who earnestly makes conscious efforts to acquire self-mastery suddenly finds himself hurriedly carried away by the vehement insistence of the senses. What is the reason for this? The subduing of senses depends on the vision of the self. If the vision of the self is towards the individual self under the influence of ego, ferocity of senses will be horrible. If the individual vision is in the direction of "Param drstva; seeing whom one gains Divine vision to see one and all and each level of existence of each being simultaneously i.e. one becomes '*antaryami*' or one knowing the inner secrets of all," the hold of senses will start receding. If one swings between these two extremes, firm devotion to "*yoga- buddhi*, **disciplined intelligence, focused due to awareness of divine proximity within, that luminous, free reality of the soul**" becomes difficult. The senses drag away the mind of even a wise man. That is the nature and competence of sensory energy. We can say that we have within us both i) call of ignorance and ii) call of Divine. The dictates of senses are call of ignorance. The dictates of senses dupe an individual very treacherously. Initially they come begging for an entry in human system alluringly, but suddenly at times they attack all of a sudden like thunderbolt from within at the middle of night and blow away at sixes and sevens an individual's resolve to adhere to righteousness and knowledge. Lord wants to pass on a caution about the management of sensory energy on these lines.

Towards the sealed garden within each one of us – Nobody asks to leave aside the sensory system or cripple the sensory system. It should not happen that we are going to control a sensory object and sensory object catches us by neck. Swami Vivekananda always said "Work like a master and not like a slave." A very strong will is required to move out of this valley of death, which is our physical world. An untrained will becomes an enemy and a trained will becomes a powerful ally. It will carry us to the point of realization of the "Supreme," which is like beautiful garden obscured within us. It is a garden of soul. With each lesson, with each effort, this garden grows. With efforts for sense-control, we should seek the "Divine Grace." Then this garden within each one of us will become a tranquil paradise, where afflictions and miseries do not exist. This is a point of peace unrestricted. This is as well a point of no return. This is akin to "**exploring that sealed garden of the soul right within us.**" Our life flourishes when it gets connected to the source. Infuse life with that which can be relied upon and trusted. Let us hurry. Time is short. Garden is calling in language of silence

"Come, come, come … …." Same thought is expressed by Kashmiri poetess, Lal Ded (1320-1392) in her "*Vakya*; sentence" in words paraphrased below:

"Think not to kill the greed and to contemplate
The self is difficult of attainment,
"HE" is near you, seek not far,
The void gets merged into the void."

61. In this verse, Lord tells Arjuna how "sthitaprjana; one disciplined and divinely focused in the quiescence (not moving, not doing anything) of the soul" sits.

तानि सर्वाणि संयम्य युक्त आसीत मत्परः ।
वशे हि यस्येन्द्रियाणि तस्य प्रज्ञा प्रतिष्ठिता ॥ २- ६१ ॥

tani sarvani samyamya yukta asita mat-parah
vase hi yasyendriyani tasya prajna pratisthita 2.61

tani—them (those senses); *sarvani*--all; *samyamya*—having restrained; *yuktah*-- joined; *asita*--should sit down (for meditation); *mat-parah*—intent on me i.e. devoting one's heart and soul to Me; *vase*—under control; *hi*-- indeed; *yasya*--whose; *indriyani*--senses; *tasya*--his; *prajna*—intelligence (steeped in divine knowledge); *pratisthita*—(is) steadied or fixed.

"Having restrained them all (i.e. senses), the one in the state of "sthitaprajna; disciplined and immersed in the quiescence (not moving and doing anything) of the divine proximity" should sit focused on "Me" as the supreme goal. One whose senses are under control is an individual of steady wisdom." II 2-61 II

In this explains how a spiritual aspirant shoul proceed to get intelligence established in soul felicity (happiness) as follows:

i) **Tani sarvani samyam** (Discipline all the sensory energy within) – Lord has used the word "*sarvani*" i.e. all the senses have to be disciplined. Even if one is left out. It is enough to destroy the discipline. So, first of all, the spiritual aspirant should control the senses. These senses are very powerful as they have behind them the force of habits of countless births. Unless this habit, which becomes our second nature, is destroyed by control (by constant persuasion and practice with awareness), turbulent senses will not be governable and mind will continue to be carried away by force of old habits. Some amount of diligence is to be definitely exercised in subduing the senses.

ii) **Yuktah asita matparah** (sit, firm in yoga and wholly devoted to "Me") – Now Lord is coming out with a secret. Control of senses represents psychic energy. This energy flow cannot be stopped. It has to be given a direction. How is this psychic energy to be sublimated? Lord is giving a suggestion "sit devoted to ME, firm in yoga." Where has this "ME" suddenly come from?

Lord started speaking on "**Sankhya**; Self-knowledge" and there the pronouns "that" or "this" were used and reference was for the "Supreme Eternal Universal Being" who exists in all bodies. The focus was on the "Supreme Soul" through the soul. Then Lord talked about "**Buddhiryoga**" i.e. those who unite their intelligence and will with "The Divine" reach the status beyond misery (**Brahmisthiti**), in which there are none of the maladies which afflict the mind and life of suffering humanity. Now Lord is saying "sit, devoted to 'ME', firm in yoga." Actually, "this and that" in **Sankya**-discussion, "Divine" in the **Buddhir**-Yoga and "ME," here, refer to the same "Universal Eternal Reality or Truth."

That Supreme Eternal Universal Energy does not have a form and name. But, whenever righteousness declines and un-righteousness grows, this "source of all that is" incarnates (the Divine descends into the human form) to remove chaos and bring order in the society. In un-manifested form, "The Divine" remains as invisible, un-smell-able, untouchable, quality-less, devoid of parts, unborn, eternal, permanent and action-less. The assumption of human form by the "Divine Reality" does not take away form or add to the integrity or wholeness of the Divine. According to the Bhagvata (A scripture, primarily about the life of Krishna) " ...at midnight, in the thickest darkness, "The Dweller" in every heart revealed Himself in divine Devki, for the Lord is self hidden in the hearts of all beings." This is to tell that Lord Krishna is the incarnation (descent of the Divine in human form) of the "Supreme Universal Eternal Reality," "The Infinite" manifested in human form. The Divine exists in all but manifests in some forms conspicuously to lift the world from out of its rut and set it on new tracks. For the first time in this verse, Lord Krishna manifests that 'He' represents the Divine Reality (or incarnation of the Supreme). This word "Matparah; intent on Me" focuses on this point.

This is the first verse in the Gita in which Lord introduces to Arjuna as the "Supreme Self in human form; *avtar*." Hither to, all references to "The Supreme Reality" were made in the third person. Now Lord is telling Arjuna "**remain in this life controlling the psychic and sensory energies, devoted to ME.**" It means "That of Sankhya," "Param Drstva of Buddhiyoga" and "ME, Krishna in human form" refer to the same Divine Reality. For proper assimilation of discussion in the Gita, this awareness is essential. Time and again, reference will be made to this reality in first person (as ME) or third person (that, in 18th chapter, Lord says "Tamev sarnam gachch ... take refuge in 'That' alone"). The assimilation of the Gita's message starts when one accepts this aspect. "This Supreme Reality," referred to by any pronoun or in any way or through any specific God even, resides in the heart of every being. HE is the enjoyer of all sacrifices. HE stirs our hearts to devotion and grants our prayers. HE is the source and sustainer of all values, righteousness as per law of nature. The word "*matparah*" meaning developing superior fondness for wisdom and hence knower also, makes mind fully receptive or sensitized both to the self and others as well. The spiritual seeker starts gaining purity and allied attunements for spiritual orientation. It develops a natural tendency for physical and sensory regulation and control. This brings about great change. The beings intuit with the Supreme through prayers. The Supreme Being, through lower nature and higher nature (these terms will be dealt with by the Lord later), carries on the cosmic functions of creation, sustenance and dissolution. Even in Bible, creation is the act of father (the Supreme here). The incarnation is that of the son, Christ. The end of the world is brought about by the "Holy Ghost" (nature here). After accepting divine presence everywhere an in all, one starts understanding and becoming an integral part of universal drama of creation, sustenance and dissolution. "*Matparah*; sit focused on ME" brings about required mental orientation in the seeker. This is rather central message of the Gita, focal point.

This is just to tell what the Lord means by use of word "ME." The reference is to the Supreme Reality, the main "**Subject of Love**," whom Lord Krishna represented by Krishna *avtar* (**incarnation**). It is necessary here to pause over the main theme of the words "be devoted to me; i.e. the 'Truth' behind Krishna or the image of Krishna or the form or the formless." **One has to remain "connected to the Divinity" whatever the situation may be.** That is the idea of using the words "That or This or The Supreme or Me" in this chapter. Words "*aasita matparah*" may also be taken to mean "I am no other than He" (Supreme Universal Eternal Reality). Knowledge will ultimately makes one a knower. This can happen only when one has deep, unflinching fondness for the Knower. Self-discipline gets the instruments (physical body and subtle body) ready but that "**away from ordinary element, divine favor or spiritual favor**" comes only through Divine grace. Divine grace comes when you look at the Divine, surrender to the Divine, focus on Divine, depend on Divine, keep faith on the Divine. This superior fondness for the Supreme (through *Matparah*; be devoted to me) develops vivek (divine wisdom, here) **vairgya** (renunciation) for intelligence and mind.

iii) ***tasya prajana pratisthita*** [(his or her) wisdom is well established] – It has already been made amply clear by the Lord that we have to have the psychic control and sensory control. Is it enough? Human efforts alone are not enough to gain the state of perfection (state of merger of individual space of consciousness with the Supreme Universal Consciousness). There is every chance of falling down and down and getting lost, if one is to depend on one's own potential alone.

What is the message of the verse in brief? One should subjugate the senses focusing on "the Form or the Formless i.e. ME or the Universal Force behind Krishna." The use of these words may also mean that self-discipline is easy when one follows vision of the "Highest." Caution has been given. Self-efforts alone are not sufficient. One has to keep "**Divine-Connectivity**" intact focusing the Divine. By use of words "***Matparah***," Lord has made it clear that "Divine Connectivity" can be established both through the Form or the Formless [earlier Lord was using this (***idam***) and that (***tat***) or satisfied in the self by the self (***atmany iva atmana tustah***) or One whose sight enables one to behold the unbounded universal vision (***Param drstva***)].

Self discipline is not a matter of will and emotions alone. Self-discipline becomes easy with the "vision of the Highest." Every effort (physical or mental) should be made with this vision at the center of heart. This is the central message of the Gita as well.

62. In verse 61, Lord told Arjuna to subjugate the senses with intelligence firmly fixed on the "Supreme." In this verse Lord tells Arjuna what happens if the senses are not controlled.

ध्यायतो विषयान्पुंसः सङ्गस्तेषूपजायते ।
सङ्गात्सञ्जायते कामः कामात्क्रोधोऽभिजायते ॥ २- ६२ ॥

dhyayato visayan pumsah sangas tesupajayate
sangat sanjayate kamah kamat krodho 'bhijayate 2.62

dhyayatah—while thinking or contemplating; *visayan*--sense objects; *pumsah*--of a man; *sangah*--attachment; *tesu*--in them (sense objects); *upajayate*—arises or develops; *sangat*—from attachment; *sanjayate*—is born or develops; *kamah*--desire; *kamat*--from desire; *krodhah*--anger; *abhijayate*-- arises.

"One develops attachment to sense-objects by thinking about the sense objects. From attachment comes desire (to possess) and from desire anger arises." II 2-62 II

This is a very beautiful verse. Lord narrates in this verse how downward trend sets in as follows:

i) dhayato visayanpunsah (Thinking of sense objects)- Contemplation of sense objects is the first step in downward process of an individual. One thinks about the sense objects over and over again. This is the phase in which an individual develops the fondness for the sense-objects by mentally thinking about the sense-objects (a form, an object or image or sound) again and again. Desire for sense-objects constitutes impurity of mind and these (desires) have their source in constant contemplation of enjoyments. The remedy lies in not allowing the mind to be diverted towards the sense-objects but fixing the mind on the Divinity [***Matparah*** (intent on ME); Lord or the Truth that Lord represents; the Form or the Formless].

ii) ***sangah tesu upjayete*** (one develops attachment to sense objects) – Mind develops attachment for sense-objects. Initially one starts liking but a little afterward one starts getting glued to the thoughts of sense-objects.

iii) sangat samjayate kamah (from attachment comes desire) – From attachment springs desire. A feeling, "I must have it," develops in the mind with intensity. Desire may prove to be as resistless as the most powerful external forces. It can both lift an individual to glory, if checked, or hurl the individual to disgrace, if unchecked.

iv) kamat krodho upjayate (anger comes from desire) – What is anger? It is obstructed desire, temporary insanity. This is a state in which soul is obscured in passion. When desire is not fulfilled for any reason, anger is the result. Anger is a feeling that whatever has happened is bad and unfair. It utterly devastates the spiritual progress, shatters internal perception. If anyone puts any obstruction in the way of obtaining the objects, the victim of anger starts arguing, quarreling and hating him. Anger only results in mounting hostility.

This verse beautifully describes that lust and anger are two vital factors which lower the individual and make him or her either sub-human or inhuman. Therefore, wise individuals should take precaution not to allow the mind to brood upon worldly pleasures.

A peepal-seed gets into a crack in the wall. It sprouts there rents (cracks) the wall even at its foundation. Similarly, an evil thought first germinates in mind, develops in its own way and then brings about the wreck of that individual ultimately. A thought can make or mar an individual.

Reservoir of Untapped power – There is a vast reservoir of untapped power waiting to be used within all of us. **No one can use this potential until one learns to manage anger. Anger directly attacks the point where your creativity or balance in life originates**. Your inner speech and your silent thoughts and feelings are experienced in the reactions of others. You have to ensure that this beautiful inner garden is not devastated by the tornado of anger. Avoiding anger is not the solution. In this respect this world is like a jungle. All carnivorous and herbivorous animals together live in a jungle. Therefore anger should be managed. That is the correct word. Anger has to be managed. The Bible says " Do not let the sun go down on your anger." The advice is psychologically sound. Anger can accumulate to the exploding point. Do not let it explode you. Anger generates emotional energy. Harness it constructively. Relate it to life's final target. If it does not contribute to that, ignore it and keep moving in the direction of your choice (your Reservoir of Untapped Power within you) being in tune with your inner rhythm. One should keep these thoughts while dealing mental, emotional, physical and behavioral aspects at the same time. Thus this verse contains a beautiful lesson.

63. in this verse Lord concludes (or takes to logical conclusion) the point raised in the preceding verse.

क्रोधाद्भवति सम्मोहः सम्मोहात्स्मृतिविभ्रमः ।
स्मृतिभ्रंशाद् बुद्धिनाशो बुद्धिनाशात्प्रणश्यति ॥ २- ६३ ॥

krodhad bhavati sammohah sammohat smrti-vibhramah
smrti-bhramsad buddhi-naso buddhi-nasat pranasyati 2.63

krodhat--from anger; *bhavati*-- comes; *sammohah*—delusion or perfect illusion; *sammohat*--from delusion; *smrti*--of memory; *vibhramah*-- loss; *smrti-bhramsat*—from loss of memory; *buddhi-nasah*-- loss of intelligence or discriminating faculty; *buddhi-nasat*- from destruction of intelligence (discriminating faculty); *pranasyati*—(individual) perishes.

"From anger proceeds delusion (bewilderment); from bewilderment comes loss of memory; by loss of memory intelligence is destroyed; from destruction of intelligence one perishes." II 2-63 II

Anger is that fire in whose smoke one's soul gets obscured. Intelligence and one's determination to do something find it difficult to remain seated in the divine splendor of calm observing soul. It develops into false belief about oneself and doubts about the eternal existence.This situation leads to loss of memory. Loss of memory results in destruction of intelligence. It is intelligence which discriminates and warns the mind. When one's intelligence is destroyed, one perishes.

Lord has used a beautiful word "buddhinasa; destruction of intelligence." What does it mean? It means failure to discriminate between the right and the wrong. Intelligence is the faculty to learn, understand, discern and think about the people, things and situations. It is intelligence which gives an internal alarm and forewarns. Without this faculty, one cannot gain self-mastery. An individual surely gets carried away by the senses, if this faculty is not working properly.

One perishes. It means one becomes unfit for all the worthwhile human goals. Anyone, who has become unfit for worthwhile human goal, is verily referred to as dead. Therefore, it has been said that one perishes.

What is the message of the verse? External control alone is not enough. One should control the mind i.e. the tendency to respond to stimulus of thoughts. These two verses (62 and 63), graphically present psychological stages, through which a "slave to sense enjoyment" passes. By this description, one comes to know who the enemies are, how they work, how they tempt, how they subdue and how finally they destroy. Therefore, Lord suggests exercising self-control. Self-control (un-sensuous use of senses or appropriate use of senses) is different from crippling the senses. Senses are one's instruments. Senses should always be kept in readiness to be used appropriately. To hate the senses is as wrong as to love them. A pet dog in a palace and a street dog behave differently. An individual should use the senses. Senses should not start using the individual. Self-control does not mean grappling with mind and senses all the time. This discussion should not be taken to mean a forced isolation from the world and destruction of sense-life but it should induce inward withdrawal, an awakened attitude towards conscious of final outcome. Most important point is the inward contemplation and focus on the divine proximity within. If this aspect is taken care of, the mind will get fixed in inward contemplation **(that eternal journey, that silence which, whispers in mute language, that dim splendor, that all-effacing, soul-touched peace within)** and not the ephemeral (popular and important for only a short time) world. Let the new seekers be assured that it is not a journey into boredom. Those three words of preceding verse **"Yukta asita matparah; sit firmly in yoga wholly given up to Me"** contain in seed-form the whole gist of the highest secret yet to be cracked by the seeker. Let these three words be like the light of the light-house to a ship, long lost, famished with fatigue and hunger in the sea with nothing to guide but water and water everywhere in all directions. It will itself save from destruction of intelligence and loss of self for the highest goal of human existence (self-realization; merger in the Supreme; Nirvana).

64. In this verse Lord tells what will happen to the mind withdrawn from senses.

रागद्वेषविमुक्तैस्तु विषयानिन्द्रियैश्चरन् ।
आत्मवश्यैर्विधेयात्मा प्रसादमधिगच्छति ॥ २- ६४ ॥

raga-dvesa-vimuktais tu visayan indriyais caran
atma-vasyair vidheyatma prasadam adhigacchati 2.64

raga—continuing desire; *dvesa*-- repulsion; *vimuktaih*—free from (raga and dvesa); *tu*--but; *visayan*-- sense objects; *indriyaih*—with the senses; *caran*-- moving; *atma-vasyaih*—self-restrained; *vidheya-atma*—self-controlled; *prasadam*-- the favor of or mercy of the Divine (in form of peace); *adhigacchati*--attains.

"But the self-controlled individual, free from attraction and repulsion, moving among objects with senses under restraint, attains a state where a clear, happy, calm tranquility settles upon the individual." II 2-64 II

In verses 62 and 63, Lord tells what happens when an individual lacks control of senses. One perishes finally. In this verse, Lord presents a contrasting picture as follows:

i) ragadvesaviyuktaistu visayan indriyaiscaran (but an individual of disciplined mind moves among the sense-objects with senses under control) – When an individual wields control over mind and the senses, he or she is not the victim to dualities or likes and dislikes. The discussion is about the disciplined individual focused on the self. Such an individual does not have selfish aims or aspirations and is not disturbed by the touches of outward things.

ii)atmavasyaih vidheyatma (self-restrained, self controlled) – What is the difference between self-restrained and self-controlled? The one, who has had self control, is ready for self-realization. This means that the individual has achieved some amount of proficiency in restraining the senses. Initially one uses one's senses and sense objects for sustaining the life with sufficient caution that purity and peace of mind is not disturbed. Gradually it becomes a way of life. After the poisonous fangs of a serpent are pulled out, the serpent is harmless. One gains self control, after one becomes well versed in restraining the senses. Attraction repulsion (*raga and dvesa*) get eliminated. Senses start behaving like tamed horses. What is the underlying thought of these words? Focus should be on conscious management of senses (i.e. appropriate use of senses should be based on final outcome, life's mission and consciousness of eternal existence in view).

iii) prasadam adhigacchati (one attains serenity, purity of mind and fitness for realizing the Supreme soul) – What does one gain after self-restraint and self- control? What is this "prasadam" which finally one gets as a reward? **It is soul-touched serenity and peace that surpasses understanding.** This clear expanse of tranquility is the source of soul's felicity (bliss of the soul). This peace and understanding is not ordinary experience of this ephemeral (temporary for a short time) world. This peace is unique. It is beyond human understanding and experience. This soul touched serenity and peace helps an individual to gain that "**unbounded divine vision of the Supreme Reality,**" that turns the mortal into the immortal. One gains unity with "Oneness of the whole i.e. universal oneness." At this point, grief loses power to touch the tranquil soul (soul focused on Divine proximity within). One is calm, desire-less and griefless with no suffering at all (in this mental realm suffering is simply not possible).

What is the message of this verse? An individual, rescued from distractions, finds unity (*Prasadam*; left- over after ceremony of sharing with the Divine) in the soul. This '*prasadam*' is of the nature of vision of purity (Truth), unbounded awareness and bliss, unique to worldly existence. Then, the consciousness of the Infinite becomes as direct and natural to such an individual as light is to the flame. All conflicts and contradictions of life get reconciled. Knowledge, love and action get harmonized. Pleasure and pain become one in beauty. Enjoyment and renunciation become equal in goodness. Every moment carries the message of the Eternal, as the air caresses (way of showing affection) all the time. The formless appears and appeals to us in the form of the flower, the fruit and the animal, just in all forms. **Divine- love** makes earthly life resplendent. All this happens, when one attains soul- felicity (happiness), the *prasadam* (that, which one gets as left over after the ceremony of worshiping, offering and sharing with the Divine is over). This happens, when soul draws her heavy curtain of self (ego) aside, when her veil (ignorance born of ego) is lifted and she comes face to face with the eternal lover (The Supreme). This is the ultimate reward of disciplining the mind, desiring nothing, demanding nothing, doing nothing, being nothing and being jealous to none. Divine love (unlimited, un-sensuous, intensity to care, share and bear for all eternally) overflows in all directions.

65. In this verse, Lord tells Arjuna what happens when the Divinity bestows its **prasadam** (eternal, soul-touched bliss, grace).

प्रसादे सर्वदुःखानां हानिरस्योपजायते ।
प्रसन्नचेतसो ह्याशु बुद्धिः पर्यवतिष्ठते ॥ २- ६५ ॥

prasade sarva-duhkhanam hanir asyopajayate
prasanna-cetaso hy asu buddhih paryavatisthate 2.65

prasade- favor of the Supreme (in the form of peace or placidity of mind); *sarva--* all; *duhkhanam—* (of) all pains and miseries; *hanih--*destruction; *asya-* of him; *upajayate--* arises; *prasanna-cetasah-* the tranquil-minded; *hi--*because; *asu--* soon; *buddhih--*intelligence; *pari--* *avatisthate—*becomes steady or established.

"When an individual attains this tranquility, all sorrows get destroyed; the intellect, awakened by divine tranquility, soon gets anchored in serenity or gets wholly established." II 2-65 II

By the discussion so far, it becomes amply clear that attachment to body and mind is the main reason of sorrow. When sorrow stops, peace and serenity come in life. When the mind is freed from impure impulses, the aim of spiritual life is achieved. In a clean mirror, reflection is without blemishes. Similarly, the self shines in the purity of mind. Sage Vasishta states in "Yoga-Vasishta" that purity of mind arising from deep knowledge of soul (i.e. awakening arising out of focus on divine proximity within) is liberation (moksha; freedom from all possible limitations). For this reason, all those who desire liberation should keep the mind pure by constant focus on the self. It results in two advantages i) elimination of all sorrows and sufferings, ii) mind firmly rests in the soul-felicity (happiness). Stress is on following two points in this verse;

i) Sarva dukhanam (all sufferings) - All worldly sufferings have been put in three categories i) adhyatmika i.e. sufferings in the struggle for spiritual development, ii) adibhautika- means those sufferings and afflictions which are relating to body and mind (physical or subtle), iii) adidaivika- means relating to nature such as famine or tsunami etc. An individual is saved from all these sufferings when the individual contemplates on the nature of self and remains divinely focused.

ii)*prasannacetso hyasu buddhi paryavatisthate* (the intellect of an individual with tranquil mind becomes steady) – Again, Lord is focusing on the same thought. An individual's abiding happiness is not in getting but it is in recognizing one's true, spiritual nature (**Infinite Truth**). Once our soul recognizes the ultimate object of reposing in the "Supreme Consciousness," all the movements acquire a purpose, new meaning and new joy. The Supreme is known by this joy alone. This joy is knowledge in completeness. This joy stands for knowing by all our being. Normal knowledge sets us apart from the things to be known. This knowledge, which is **blossoming of divine love,** knows its object by fusion (joining the separate things). This is the point where the intelligence gets established. What does it mean? This is the state in which time and space cease to rule and this is the point where links of evolution are merged into unity. This state of happiness is everlasting abode of the soul in which the revelation of the Supreme finds completion. In this state of bliss, one sees the Supreme in the inner sky of consciousness. The union gets accomplished. With steadiness of intellect and inner focus one realizes that the **"Eternal Nameless and Formless Presence" is ever here in innermost being.** These two verses (64 and 65) guide us to live in this world, to work in this world and to enjoy bliss in this world at various levels.

66. Yoga is a science of self-culture. In this verse, Lord explains what happens when yoga is not practiced.

नास्ति बुद्धिरयुक्तस्य न चायुक्तस्य भावना ।
न चाभावयतः शान्तिरशान्तस्य कुतः सुखम् ॥ २- ६६ ॥

nasti buddhir ayuktasya na cayuktasya bhavana
na cabhavayatah santir asantasya kutah sukham 2.66

na- not; *asti*- is; *buddhih*—intelligence or discriminating faulty; *ayuktasya*--of one who has not been able to get connected within or unsteady-one; *na*--not; *ca*--and; *ayuktasya*- (for the unsteady; *bhavana*—thought (fixed on the supreme) in happiness; *na*--not; *ca*--and; *abhavayatah*—of the un-meditative; *santih*—peace (not absence of noise but soul touching experience of contentment while contemplating on the Supreme); *asantasya*—(for) the un-peaceful; *kutah*--where is; *sukham*--happiness.

"For one, who has not harmonized in yoga (i.e. those who are unsteady, fickle-minded, uncontrolled), there is no intelligence; nor has he or she meditation; to the un-meditative, there is no peace; how can one without peace have happiness?" II 2-66 II

In these lines, one gets profound depth of psychology step by step. Narration is very beautiful. It is not all dogmatic (ideas that people will accept without questions) discussion. It requires self examination, self-searching to get to the truth of it. One can examine one's own reaction on every part of the verse as follows:

i) **nasti buddhih ayuktasya** (for the one not harmonized in yoga, there is no intelligence) – What is the meaning of buddih (intelligence) here? Here in this verse buddih means 'yoga-buddhi' i.e. intelligence which is disciplined and focused in the divine proximity within. This divine intelligence helps an individual to achieve **"Unbounded Cosmic Vision."** This vision sees the divinity within, around and beyond. One cannot have this buddhi (intelligence), till one has gained a particular level of proficiency in various disciplines (physical, mental, emotional and spiritual) soaked (completely wet) in divine consciousness of "eternal Existence within." Actually, this buddhi (intelligence), referred to in this verse, is culmination (reaching the highest point) of mastery in all disciplines. It is not possible for those who have yet to achieve stable life and realize the true freedom within. This buddhi (intelligence) comes when one attains discipline at sensory level and intelligence is yoked (united) with the soul, the self. This buddhi (intelligence) starts getting pulsation of soul i.e. starts perceiving proximity of soul. For the one, lacking perfection in various disciplines (physical, mental, emotional and spiritual), this intelligence is not possible.

ii) **na ca ayuktasya bhavna** (without this sensory discipline, no meditation is possible)- This meditation, that Lord is referring here, is not simple exercise of emptying thoughts to relax the mind. This word "bhavana; meditation," used here, means diving within and feeling the "space of consciousness within" which radiates joy, light and peace. At this point, one is able to catch with awareness the radiation from spiritual dimension of the human personality. This "bhavana; meditation," talked about by the Lord here, stabilizes the human system and gets it ready to take glimmering glimpse of something beyond the sensory level. This stage is not a process of the mind. It is discipline of the mind. This word "bhavana," used by the Lord, unfolds from within the "Pure Conscious State." Actually this is the ultimate goal of meditation. One simply cannot reach this point without proficiency in yoga (various disciplines to unite the individual consciousness with "Infinite Universal Consciousness"). Jesus said "Enter into thy closet and shut the door." Closet means not a place but in your own mind. What Lord Krishna has referred to here by use this word "*bhavana*," is a still more advanced stage of this discipline.

iii) **na ca abhavyatah santir** (without that '*bhavana*; meditaion' there is no "santir; peace") – Without meditative state of mind, referred to here, there is no *santir* (peace). What is this peace? This peace is not lack of noise or disturbances. This peace is the tranquility, which has as its source in soul's felicity. This is that stage in which one sees "luminosity of one's own true being." This is the state in which one experiences calm, desire-less, griefless unity of intelligence with self poise and self knowledge. Without "bhavan; meditation dealt with above" this peace is not possible. This experience is the reversal of the whole view, experience, knowledge, values and emotional attachment of the earth bound creatures. This experience helps to go beyond (to transcend human understanding and experience). This experience (meditation) takes beyond into that "zone of soul-touched peace."

iv) **asantasya kutah sukaham** (for the un-peaceful, how can there be peace) - To the individual without peace, how can there be happiness? What is **sukham** (happiness)? In normal language, happiness means experience of pleasure in a situation in which thing, individual or situation is in accordance with your expectations. This is not the meaning of happiness here. Here, happiness means blissfulness of the soul. This bliss, which Lord is referring to, is one's perception in "Divine Union with One's Source." One gains this blissfulness of the soul when one disciplines and purifies one's consciousness by moral perfection. When there is no multiplicity, no dualism, there is bliss (ananda; soul-touched happiness). It (this bliss; sukaham) is permanent state unlike ephemeral (popular or important for a short time) happiness in mundane (ordinary) worldly experiences. Budha called it compassion. Jesus called it love, Krishna called it loving consciousness. This "sukham," mentioned by the Lord here, is the experience that one gains when one is blessed with unity with "Universal Loving Consciousness." It is a spiritual experience. When this experience is gained, the universe melts away in "**Cosmic Whole**." This "sukaham; bliss of the soul" is not to be compared with happiness that we feel when we get a desired object in this world. This bliss cannot be gained without peace. This bliss brings total contentment. One needs nothing after this. One, who has this, is free from all fears.

What is the message? In this verse, Lord has laid down a sequence in which an aspirant should proceed. First focus should be on yoga. Then one should go for disciplined and focused intelligence. Then one should go for diving within and feeling that "Conscious Space," which leads to bliss of the soul finally. At this point, individual love merges with the "**Love Everlasting**." Everything all-around starts merging into "**Universal whole**." Blossoming of the self happens through an experience of bliss (**sukaham**; ananda). There remains nothing to be achieved hereafter

67. Lord beautifully explains in this verse what happens to an undisciplined mind.

इन्द्रियाणां हि चरतां यन्मनोऽनुविधीयते ।
तदस्य हरति प्रज्ञां वायुर्नावमिवाम्भसि ॥ २- ६७ ॥

indriyanam hi caratam yan mano 'nuvidhiyate
tad asya harati prajnam vayur navam ivambhasi 2.67

indriyanam—senses ; *hi*- for ; *caratam*- wandering or roving (in sense objects); *yat*--that; *manah*--mind; *anuvidhiyate*— yields or follows; *tat*--that; *asya*-- his; *harati*- carries away or -takes away; *prajnam*—discriminating-intelligence; *vayuh*--wind; *navam*--a boat; *iva*--like; *ambhasi*—in the water.

"When the mind runs after the roving (moving from one place to another without a particular purpose or keep looking in different directions) senses, it carries away the intelligence, as the wind carries away a ship on the water." II 2-67 II

A ship without rudder (a piece of wood or metal at the back of ship or aircraft, used for controlling its direction), is at the mercy of strong winds. No one knows where it (ship or boat) will be shoved (pushed) by the strong winds. Same thing holds good about the senses involuntarily drawn to sense-objects. If mind is not disciplined, it will be lead astray by the wild (left in natural and free conditions without control) senses. A rudderless ship does not reach its destination. Similarly, if the mind follows the wild senses, it renders its discrimination ineffective. When intelligence is rendered ineffective, it (intelligence) cannot discern (to notice and understand something only after looking at it or thinking about it carefully) and forewarn. Mind, instead of being led by the intelligence, carries it away like the ship by the wind in the sea. It becomes a tragedy. What is this tragedy? One experiences a wild fire in one's heart in the form of desire. From desire one stumbles to possession. In possession one languishes (forced to stay and suffer) from desire. This is the tragedy of human life. What is the way out? Lord has already talked about it. One should follow disciplined intelligence focused on the self. Intelligence should lead. It should not be allowed to be lead by the mind, ever restless like the wind. It will mean developing awareness within higher and higher till it starts perceiving the divine proximity, the eternal source of guidance, which knows no wrong and cruises (to travel in a ship or boat) the seeker towards "**One Essence in a multiplicity of Forms.**"

68. In this verse, lord explains how the senses are to be handled for spiritual evolution.

तस्माद्यस्य महाबाहो निगृहीतानि सर्वशः ।
इन्द्रियाणीन्द्रियार्थेभ्यस्तस्य प्रज्ञा प्रतिष्ठिता ॥ २- ६८ ॥

tasmad yasya maha-baho nigrhitani sarvasah
indriyanindriyarthebhyas tasya prajna pratisthita 2.68

tasmat--therefore; *yasya*—whose; *maha-baho*--O mighty-armed one (Arjua); *nigrhitani*-- (are) restrained; *sarvasah*-- completely; *indriyani*--the senses; *indriya-arthebhyah*—(from) sense objects; *tasya*--his; *prajna*—discriminating-intelligence; *pratisthita*—(is) steadied or fixed.

"Therefore, O Mighty-armed (Arjuna), one, who has completely restrained the excitement of the senses by the sense-objects, sits with intelligence firmly established (in awareness of the divine proximity within or calmness of self-knowledge)." II 2-68 II

The wick that contacts a flame gets lit. Similarly, the unruffled mind that intuits with the soul gets illumined. This is possible only through sense-control (or rather management of senses) as highlighted by the Lord in the discussion below:

i) *tasmad yasya, mahabaho, nigrihitani sarvasah indriyani indriyarthebyas* (Therefore, O Arjuna, whose senses are completely restrained from sense-objects) - It becomes amply clear from the discussion so far that sense-control is essential for spiritual evolvement. This point is not properly understood by some individuals. Some individuals, considering the senses as obstacle in spiritual pursuit, make the senses ineffective for good. Many people damage their eyes so that they may not see the sense objects. Similarly some people harm the senses for good to make them ineffective. Damaging the senses is not sense-control. Our senses are like our horses that will carry our vehicle up to the point of destination. The very purpose of having the senses is lost if senses are rendered incapable to contact sense-objects. Senses have always to be kept in state of readiness to follow the command. This is different from being dragged by the sense towards the sense objects. This is actually the management of senses. Control of senses depicts success. Lack of control on senses shows weakness. Here one question is very pertinent. What is the difference between sense-control and sense indulgence? Deciding factor here is attitude. Perceiving with covetousness is sin, while viewing them as object of adoration is virtue. **Looking at the body of an individual with lustful eyes is sin, while viewing it as temple of divinity is virtue.** All the senses should be sublimated (i.e. energy of senses should be directed) and sense objects should be sanctified (made holy by identifying universal essence in them) so that divinity is reflected in and through them all. Sri Ramakrishna perfected his sense of sight so that all women folk including street walkers were to him embodiments of the Divine Mother. That is the message of the Lord by sense-control (employment of awakened intelligence in use of senses). This type of sense-control enables an individual to intuit (know with feelings), in silence, with the **"Voice of the Eternal Master."** It makes the atoms in the body to leap forward in a rush for the feel of **"The Permanent"** in all that is impermanent. For the Supreme, there is no need to seek something extra or to manufacture anything new. All that is required is sense-control (employment of awakened intelligence in use of senses) and not the sense-indulgence (indiscriminate doing something or using something for pleasure).

ii) *Tasya prajna pratisthita* [that individual's wisdom is steady (not moving, firmly held] - The individual who complies with the requirement of the first half of this verse is taken to be steady (i.e. not-moving). In other words, sense control (employment of awakened discrimination in use of senses) is essential for intelligence, which is established, not moving. That intelligence is well established means that intelligence is founded in calmness of proximity of soul or bliss of self-knowledge. What is the meaning of the words "prajna pratisthta; wisdom becomes steady"? It means that all momentary impulses of the heart find their completion in love (love without limitations and conditions or unrestricted love ever flowing). All petty details of life reveal an "Infinite Purpose." All deeds unite themselves in an internal harmony. "Attainment of this stage" means getting to the bridge leading to the "Immortal Being."

An individual's intelligence gets established only when senses are restrained from sense-objects. Earlier also in verse 61, Lord talked about sense-control. From this discussion, it becomes clear that Lord wants Arjuna to go in a particular direction where sense-control (management of senses) is necessary? How is this sense-control or management of senses to be brought about? For moral excellence, physical fitness, mental equilibrium and spiritual awareness, one has to know the "Ashtang-yoga" of Patanjali. A very brief discussion, which is of paramount importance to experience the Gita discussion, is given below to convey to the readers how one has to go step by step to bring about management of senses (only restriction and control is not required one has to make the senses celebrate nearness to divinity). Sage Patanjali has given eight limbs of "Ashtang-yoga; eight practical limbs of yoga" (i.e. what all has to be done to have the highest spiritual experience) to know one's own ground, one's own true nature, one's own self. These eight limbs are as follows:

i) *Yama* (i.e. Thou shall not do or moral principles of right and wrong)- Five principles to be followed in *Yama* are: a) *ahimsa* (i.e. Thou shall not hurt anybody including your own self); b) *Satyam* (Thou shall not lie); c) *Asteya* (Thou shall not steal or covet other's wealth); d) *Brahmcharya* (continence or Thou shall not waste your energy) and e) *Aparigraha* (Not receiving favors i.e. thou shall not be obliged to anybody). One hurts one's own conscience by not following principles laid down in *Yama*.

ii) *Niyam* (Thou shall do) – It contains five commandments: a) Sauch (purity, cleanliness - internal, external, mental and physical); b) *Santosha* (contentment; it is a state of mind; there is no end to our requirements); c) *tapah* (mortification; avoid too much fasting; too much eating; too much running; avoid all extremes; austerities have to be moderate); be your own judge and do not let down your mind; d) *svadhyaya* (study; it can be done by hearing, reading and observing; focus should be on thinking, contemplation and assimilation) and e) *Ishvarapranidhani* (Worship of Divinity either with form or without form).

iii) *Asanas* (posture is that which in which one is steady, pleasant and comfortable) – Exercise regularly. If you do not use your limbs, you lose your limbs. *Asanas* are necessary to keep body in free and flexible condition. Head, neck and spine must be erect and steady. Patanjali says "sthira sukham asanam; Posture should be steady and comfortable." The seat should be neither high nor low. Neck, head and body must be straight. What is the purpose of various asanas, the postures? In right posture, mind becomes one's mind. Otherwise one belongs to the mind. In right posture, mind is free. One can lift the mind away from body consciousness. In right asana (posture), one is free from body consciousness. When the body is in good condition, healthy condition, stable condition and comfortable condition, one can make the mind move up from physical plane to mental plane and from mental plane to spiritual plane.

iv) *Pranayam* – Prana is the vital force (cosmic energy; power in us." Prana is not breath. Breath is one effect of prana. Breathing exercises called pranayam bring about regulation of breathing, rhythmic action of prana. It has three phases i.e. a) inhaling very slowly feeling it, b) exhaling has to be still slower feeling it again and iii) holding (outside and inside). It can be done in four steps as follows; Step 1- Breathe in (in one nostril) or inhale feeling it (up to the count of say 4) and holding the other nostril with the thumb; Step 2 – hold inside (up to the count of say 4); Step 3 – Breathe out (in the other nostril) or exhale feeling it (say up to the count of say 6 or 8) holding the first nostril by the thumb; Step – 4 hold out side (up to the count of say 2). Next cycle will be initiated by the other nostril. These four steps becomes one cycle and then this cycle has to be repeated regularly. Time duration is to be followed according to the instruction of spiritual master. Pranayam is a purifying process. We fill the whole being with that force (prana) and hold it for some time inside. Then slowly we release it again holding it for sometime outside. Pranayam exerts tremendous effect on the body. By rhythmic movement of prana, one automatically draws mind to this process. Unconsciously, mind is taken away from the rest of the thoughts. Without any effort on our part, when we breathe in and out, sitting quietly, we discover that our mind has come to that level, not restless, not eager to runaway but watching the breathing in and out. When we are able to bring about this situation consciously, we can consciously bring the mind to any topic any thought any impression or any idea or ideal. In other words, Pranayam tames the mind like a disciplined pet, which keeps watching lost (lost, because it is without its usual urges and modifications) and amused (amused, because it feels soothed by slow inhaling and exhaling). All we do is inhaling (puraka), exhaling (rechaka), stopping in and stopping out (kumbhaka). Pranayam sets in the process of meditation as understood by this word 'meditation' in English. Actually Dhyanam, described by sage Patanjali and discussed below at chronological order, happens at 7th stage of "Ashtang-yoga."

v) *Pratyahara* - After this stage, one practices not putting the mind on anything but remaining detached (pratyahara). Not putting the mind on anything is negative way of telling about pratyahara. Positively speaking, pratyahara means telling the mind "Let it go. Watch it and then slowly and slowly a stage comes when mind is watching the mind. Aahar means food. What is the food of the mind? Thoughts are the food of mind. Telling no to the food of the mind is pratyahara. When internal thoughts influence the mind, do not allow the mind to go there is Pratyahara ("let it go; just watch" tendency). The term "Kriya-Yoga" contains these five steps.

vi) **Dharna** - After gaining proficiency in pratyahara, one goes for holding the mind on to some particular phase, point, object, idea, symbol and thought (called dharna). Now, one goes to the next stage called Dharna. "One-pointed-ness" requires efforts. At this stage, one has to bring the mind to silence all the tendencies, all modifications, all urges, all thoughts, all imaginations and mind does not runaway. One pours the mental energy at one point. One point bears the whole mental energy. That is called dharna. Dharna results into concentration i.e. concentration is the result of dhrana or holding the mind to something. Dharna is pouring mental energy (or say holding the mind) to something sublime, something holy, something spiritual. Mind is already in one's control. Then, dharna comes. It is like telling the mind "mind this." **Dharna** is getting to the deep depth or undisturbed layer or level of consciousness called mind (i.e. extreme keenness within) or pouring the essence that mind is on to something, as mentioned above. Feeding the mind (that part of consciousness which perceives the external stimulae and passes the instructions to senses) to mind something is Dharna. It creates psychic energy that results in concentration (ability to direct consciousness to one point; it is not process; it is result, ability). In Dharna one goes into the object, holds on to it. In natural state, mind jumps to all stimulous like dog in the absolute silence in the night. When the mind is turned this way, one gets to a stage where mind is gone. It is a "no mind situation." Actually, mind does not go anywhere. Mind gets relieved of its natural urges, modifications and tendencies. A great psychic power is generated in mind in this phase. What do we get as a reward from this phase? It is concentration (ability to direct consciousness to one point)

vii) **Dhyanam** - After holding on to something (i.e. dharna), one goes to next phase called "Dhyanam." Dhyana means to continue unbroken flow of ability to hold on in the object selected in Dharna. In Dharna (i.e. in holding on to something), one experiences concentration as a result. Now continuing with this concentration in the object so much that a fusion (joining two or more things in one) of mind and the object happens, is Dhyan. At this stage, there is "no mind i.e. no mental impulses." Only object remains there or joy remains there. Dhyana is not what we mean by meditation in English. Dhyana means fusion i.e. to fuse the mind in that unbroken continuation of concentration with the object. **What is the difference between Dharna and Dhyana?** Dharna resulted in concentration. Dhyana means continuation of the unbroken flow of this concentration and achieving fusion of mind and the object. What do we get after this phase, Dhyana? It is fusion (joining two or more things as one) of mind with the object and immense happiness.

viii) **Samadhi** - Now after the fusion of mind and the object, unified mind (unified consciousness) goes to transcendental realm (area of awareness beyond human experience and understanding) through the last phase, called "Samadhi; culmination (highest point happening); perfect absorption of thought into Supreme Spirit." When the mind gets relieved of mind's functioning (ideas, thoughts and impressions), it becomes pure mind. If one can hold it and continue holding it, it reaches the highest state of consciousness. Mind becomes one pure consciousness. The pure mind and the pure self are the same. This "no-mind i.e. mind without mind's functioning" has the capacity to unfold from within the light of Truth or Light of Pure Consciousness. It is Samadhi. It is fusion. It means culmination i.e. reaching the highest point. When the mind loses its mental activities (ideas, thoughts, and impulses) and reflects the light within, this state (i.e. after fusion with the space behind the object or reaching the culmination, highest point) is called Samadhi. This is the point where one experiences "I am that (The Absolute; The Supreme Universal Self; The Brahman; I and my father are one; the point where the salt doll melts in the ocean)." Different words are used to describe this state. The meaning of "their meaning" is the same. One enters into an ocean where there is no bound. In "no-mind" experience, one attains the "The Cosmic Consciousness Level; seeing all as One Whole." It is a mystical experience.

It is not imagination. It is a conscious or intuitive experience. It is a state in which "Divine Mystery" unfolds itself. This stage comes when one loses name and form. In this state one goes very deep to "One's own Ground; one's own pure consciousness." After this stage one is able to see this pure consciousness in everything and every being, everywhere. This is the stage in which pure mind enters into pure consciousness, becomes one with it and sees only pure consciousness everywhere. This is the state for which the Christ said "The kingdom of Heaven is within you, seek ye first the kingdom of God." Those (Christ; Moses; Mohammad; Buddha; Krishna), who taught about it used different words to give meaning. But the meaning of 'their meaning' is the same everywhere. This is the point where one experiences All-pervasive spirit, All-inclusive Spirit; Supreme Universal Eternal Reality.

All these terms (used in above discussion of 'Ashtang Yoga of Patanjali') should not be confused with English words meditation (translation of dhyan) and concentration (ability to direct consciousness to one point, which is result of Dharna). Here various phases (eight phases) of "**Ashtang-Yoga**" are being discussed in detail. For getting the feel of these stages, one should keep aside the English words meditation and concentration. Meditation starts a little from pranayam and culminates in Dhyanam (four phases). Concentration is the result that we gain in the phase "Dharna; i,e, hold on to something."

This (Ashtang-yoga) is in itself a subject and one requires a Spiritual Master for teaching "Ashtang-Yoga." A discussion on sense-control cannot be complete without reference to "Ashtang yoga." Yoga has to be worked out by effort, diligence and determination in different steps. One can read the Gita a number of times. One can understand it and teach the Gita as well. Still one cannot live the Gita (or gain firsthand experience or living awareness of **Matparah** (ME), Prasadam adhi gacchati (purity of spirit), Param drsta) without being perfect in Ashtang-yoga. Each phase (or limb of Ashtang-yoga) has to be given exclusive attention putting one's whole soul into it to the exclusion of all else. Then one will feel with vibrating awareness what the Lord means when Lord uses the words "Prasadam adhigacchati; Param drsta; Matparah etc." Till that perfection is achieved in different limbs of yoga, all the terms used will remain a jargon of theoretical importance with much ado about nothing. With perfection in ashtang-yoga, one will start intuiting. One will, with awareness, feel the change happening at experiential level. It (Ashtang-Yoga) is actually the "GO-Mukh (origin point)" from which "Ganges" of the capacity to implement the Gita flows. For this reason, a little feel of the words used has been given to help those who want to live the Gita or experience the Gita-terms and thoughts).

Lord Krishna is telling the principal features of the individual, who has his intelligence established, who keeps spiritual eye open to the "Ultimate Truth," who has heightened awareness, who perceives the soul by soul and who meets "Eternal Spirit" in all objects.

69. In this verse, Lord tells Arjuna that an individual of established intelligence, due to heightened awareness, develops sense of true values and rejects the false values of the mob.

या निशा सर्वभूतानां तस्यां जागर्ति संयमी ।
यस्यां जाग्रति भूतानि सा निशा पश्यतो मुनेः ॥ २- ६९ ॥

ya nisa sarva-bhutanam tasyam jagarti samyami
yasyam jagrati bhutani sa nisa pasyato muneh 2.69

ya--which; *nisa*—(is) night; *sarva*--all; *bhutanam*—beings or living entities; *tasyam*--in that; *jagarti*--wakeful; *samyami*--the self-controlled; *yasyam*--in which; *jagrati*--awake; *bhutani*--all beings; *sa*--that is; *nisa*--night; *pasyatah*-- (of the) seeing or introspecting; *muneh*--sage.

"What is night to all beings, therein, self-controlled one is awake; where all beings are awake; that is the night for sage who sees." II 2-69 II

Day and night are realities of perception on physical plane. A man is able to see in broad day light. Owls and tigers are not able to see in broad day. This Sanskrit word "*nisa*" means night or the period in which the people sleep. The word "*Muni*" has been used for an individual, who is self-controlled, who has developed sense for true values who perceives Divinity all around. The words used are as follows:

i) *Ya nisa sarva bhutanam* - that aspect of reality which is treated as darkness or night by all beings.

ii) *tasyam jagrati samyami* – During the period called night for all beings, a self-controlled sage keeps awake.

iii) *yasyam jagrati bhutani sa nisa pasyato muneh* – In that aspect of reality, in which beings see plenty of light, a self-awakened sage sees darkness.

A **paradox** – This verse presents a beautiful paradox. It shows how the perception of a *muni* is different from the perception of an ordinary man. A *muni* is one who is able to see beyond what just eyes are able to see. A muni is disciplined and is alive to the beauty of the reality within or *atma* (soul). A muni realizes atma (soul). He is able to see its grandeur, its reality, its expanse, its irresistibility and its permanent effect. A muni (an accomplished sage) does not run after wealth and power. However, this view does not match with the view of an ordinary man. An ordinary man does not find interest in the higher thinking or soul-based thinking. An ordinary man is extremely attracted by the glitter of the sense-objects. For a yogi, sense objects are like dark nights. What is the reason? A muni is wakeful (or alive) to the nature of reality to which an ordinary man is asleep or indifferent. While an ordinary man is alive to the glitter of the worldly objects as day light, for a muni it is like darkness of the night. In darkness of night, nothing is visible to eye. Similarly, a sage has no attraction whatsoever in the glitter of the sense objects. What is the reason? A muni (an accomplished sage) does not go on the upper layers of the things. He seeks to go to the bottom of the reality. He goes for the substance or the enduring feature of the reality or truth in the worldly objects. A muni (accomplished sage) does not see substance in the worldly objects and therefore finds the "impermanence of the worldly objects" as dark nights. A muni (an accomplished sage) sees in the light of the soul. He is self-realized and awakened person. He goes for the intrinsic worth and not for the looks. A muni sees nothing but darkness in the worldly objects due to their mere show and lack of substance. A muni is more cognizant of the inner world where one can walk and talk and remain in the blissful relationship with the "One" in the "**Inner castle of peace in the Individual**," of which mother Teresa also spoke. For one alive (or fully sensitive) to richness inside of one's self, the worldly activities appear to be dull, lifeless and colorless like darkness of night. An obvious reason is there for this. A muni remains anchored in that, which alone is changeless in this changing world. Within each of us, there is a "**Temple of Stillness**" that permits no intrusion of worldly turmoil. A muni knows this. An ordinary man does not even understand this owing to preoccupation in the temptations of worldly affairs.

In a way, Lord is reminding even in this verse that nothing on earth can equal the joy of sweet, pure and loving relationship between an individual and its soul. Of course, only awakened one with steady wisdom can understand this. To understand this, an ordinary individual will have to keep an uncluttered place within, where it can daily go quietly to be with the soul like a muni (sage). A routine of devotion, contemplation and meditation helps an ordinary man to tread the path of illumination adopted by a yogi. The result is miraculous. Frustration, unhappiness and heart-aches of mundane life start melting in the inner glory of "atman (soul)" and get changed into joy, cheerfulness, purposefulness, courage strength and love continuing with the self and with all others in the world. When this difference of perspectives of an ordinary man and a "*muni*" get eliminated, an ordinary man gets elevated for the entitlement to be a yogi. This contrast can be explained further relatively. A muni (an accomplished sage) goes to bed early and gets up early morning to comply with his discipline and daily routine of devotion, contemplation and "**communication with the self in the wordless language of silence.**" An ordinary man keeps awake till late night (seeing T.V. and gossiping idly) and sleeps till late in the day. This change in routine also brings about change in attitude as well. A yogi (an awakened person, who is alive to the secret of life all around) has a positive attitude. An ordinary man always remains rundown, agitated with negative attitude. A yogi sees possibility even in situation of utter despair. An awakened sage sees the reflection of the sublime beauty of the Supreme in even routine things of life. It becomes a second nature of a yogi to look at the sunny side of the things. A worldly man is a pessimist and looks at the future with a perspective dimly obscured with uncertainty and risk. A yogi is a giver. He knows well that it is in giving that we get. The ordinary man is a materialist. He often amasses snatches, grabs and dupes (to trick and deceive) others ignoring the final consequences not yet apparent.

Different perceptions due to different dispositions – This verse highlights one very important point. This world opens up different vistas (far view of beautiful scenery or the possibility of new experiences) to different people in accordance with their innate dispositions. A gambler is full of enthusiasm for gambling. He finds gambling as bright as day. He feels stimulated at the idea of gambling while everything else seems to him enshrouded with darkness. A learned man sees well into the literary world unmindful of everything else. Similarly saint (a Brahman-jnani or knower of the Supreme) feels at odd both in gambling and literature. He only wants to go deep within himself and there he feels a presence that fascinates him with joy of elevated thoughts. Difference in perceptions is due to difference in dispositions. A saint and a worldly man perceive this world differently.

A night, a spell for contemplation, solitude and quietude - Lord Krishna says "that in which all beings are awake is night to the sage." This reference to the night is for a particular reason. Night is the spell in which people take rest and calm their frayed nerves. For the ordinary people, day is the time for mundane activities. The ordinary people often remain busy during the day with material pursuits. A sage is not interested in material pursuit and for him day is the spell of taking rest i.e. what ordinary people do at night. During the night there is silence. The quietude of night creates conducive atmosphere for the yogi to contemplate on the Divine thoughts. The night for one is the day for the other and the day for the one is night for the other. One (ordinary individual) is confined to the world with focus on the "individual self and those closely related to the self." The other one (yogi) is also in the world but for permanent welfare of the world only.

In brief, according to the attainments (experience or level of awareness), beings are attuned to different planes of existence. An ordinary man works in the day and seeks rest in the night. For a sage, the day is the period of rest (there is disturbance during the day for a sage) and in night a sage keeps awake for reflection, contemplation and meditation.

A yogi (one with awakened intelligence and focus on the eternal existence within) sees things in reality piercing the clouds woven of desire, anger and delusion. The stars, the heaven and "the resplendent truth within" are seen only when the glaring light of the day goes and darkness comes. A perfect sage focuses on true values and rejects false values of the mob so much so that at times a yogi starts treading the path all alone when no one in the mob supports but "**his or her sense of true values**" bids to move ahead all alone (*ekla chalo, ekla chalo, ekla chalo re* …). People with this strong conviction (i.e. yogi in the Gita's parlance; people like Buddha and Maharishi Ramana) make the difference in society and finally attain the highest perfection in the form of self-realization. They (*yogis*) eternally shine in incessant, natural self-abidance.

70. In this verse lord explains how an individual feels when there is fullness within.

आपूर्यमाणमचलप्रतिष्ठं समुद्रमापः प्रविशन्ति यद्वत् ।
तद्वत्कामा यं प्रविशन्ति सर्वे स शान्तिमाप्नोति न कामकामी ॥ २- ७०

apuryamanam acala-pratistham samudram apah pravisanti yadvat
tadvat kama yam pravisanti sarve sa santim apnoti na kama-kami 2.70

apuryamanam— brimming or filled from all sides; *acala-pratistham*-- undisturbed (from its position); *samudram*--the ocean; *apah*--water; *pravisanti*--enter; *yadvat*--as; *tadvat*--so; *kamah*--desires; *yam*--whom; *pravisanti*--enter; *sarve*--all; *sah*--that person; *santim*--peace; *apnoti*--achieves; *na*--not; *kama-kami*--one who desires to fulfill desires.

"He, unto whom all desires enter, as water enters into the sea, which, though ever being filled is ever motionless, attains peace and not he who hankers for desires." II 2-70 II

This verse unfolds as follows:

i) *apurymanam acalapratistham samudram apah pravisanti yadavat* – Ocean always remains full to the brim. Even then the water of the rivers enters into it. It still remains unshaken. This is a simile. The idea is to say that only "the big one, the calm one, the deep one like ocean" can remain unmoved by the provocations.

ii) *tadavat kama yam pravisanti sarve sa santim apnoti na kamamami* – In this way a person, who is not perturbed by influx of desires (being ever filled still ever motionless), in whom all the desire merge like rivers in the ocean, he alone attains peace and not the one who desires the sense objects.

How does the vicious cycle of desires affect? - Think of a river in flood. Torrents of water carry away logs of wood, big trees and other objects in its path. Similarly, all current desires sway away the mind of a materialistic individual. An individual with materialistic bend of mind falls prey to this and that. Glitter of just anything disturbs the mind of such a person, because control on senses is not there. These desires, whether filled or unfilled, finally lead to dissatisfaction or misery. Fulfillment of desire does not ever lead to continuing peace. It leads to momentary physical satisfaction and not the lasting peace of mind. In contrast to this, the mind of a yogi is like an ocean. An ocean, though full, receives the water of all the rivers of the world without being disturbed. The yogi with equanimity of mind is not disturbed by the current desires. A yogi knows the truth. Human desires are endless. To satisfy the human desires is like drinking the salty water of the ocean. This salty water never quenches the thirst. It rather increases the thirst. It is like extinguishing fire in something like gasoline. It will only explode. Trying to fulfill material desires is like adding more wood to the fire. Tendency to fall a prey to the allurement of sense-objects breeds a vicious cycle. One desire gives rise to another desire. Today you may buy curtains. Then you find that upholstery does not match with the curtains. Then you may find that color of the drawing room does not exactly match with the inside setting. This way the desires go on multiplying without end. To add fuel to the fire, the products are being advertised aggressively. This also stokes the fire of desire further. This does not happen with the individual with steady mind, who has reached the stage of infinite bliss. The peace and harmony so urgently sought by all cannot be had from material things or any other outer experience. Sometimes watching a beautiful sunset or going to mountains or seaside may provide us with temporary serenity. But, even the most inspiring setting will not give us peace, if we are inharmonious in our within. An ordinary man having longing for materialistic satisfaction does not know the secret of bringing harmony within. There are, on the contrary, individuals in whom the desires cannot disturb the individuals. They may fulfill or may not fulfill the desires. These people often have a way of dealing with desires. They do not let their mind feel disturbed by the desires. Desires have a tendency to disturb. The expected response is to deal with desires calmly with serenity in an unruffled manner. A desire for desires lacks this poise and suffers from misery eventually.

Harmony is necessary for peace – The foregoing discussion, in this verse, talks of harmony and peace. Harmony is the pleasant effect made by different things that positively form a whole. The word peace refers to inner calmness, felicity of soul, complete lack of worry and problems. Peace is to virtues what good manure is for the crops. It is in peace that we start looking beyond the boundaries of life and death. It is in peace that we search the sublime Supreme Soul in the deep core of our hearts. It is in peace that we traverse within us to realize the "Reality" engulfed in light and brilliance beyond the description in words. This peace comes in the share of only those who control the desires and not in share of those, who hanker for desires. Thus indirect focus is on discipline. When we discipline our response to desires, then alone we become aware of "**Great Eternal River of Peace and Love and Bliss**" constantly flowing within fulfilling us forever and making us feel anew always. This discipline of bringing harmony in outer life leads to an inner harmony which connects us to the Supreme Reality within all of us. Whenever we are filled with upsetting emotions, hurt feelings and restless desires, we should pause to find out where the wrong is. We should get to the root. Somewhere our response to our desires requires improvement. Know it. This will provide the solution. This is where the remedy lies, whereas we search it in all corners of the world with load of medicines and series of sufferings. The "**Nameless Unknown**" is the source of something known to us. Harmony is the direction. Peace is the gateway.

What does this peace feel like? In this verse, Lord Krishna refers to tranquility, peace. What is it like? How does one feel in this spell? It is a difficult question. It is really difficult to answer these questions exactly with precision. All the individual experiences will be different. However, based on the experiences of others, an effort is made to give an idea how some people felt in this state (This is just for introduction for an exposure of what others have felt. It cannot be an exhaustive list or a conclusive list; this is how some people have mentioned about this elusive peace):

i) In the spell proceeding to this state, one invariably finds rocklike faith.

ii) You not only know with mind, but you also feel it and see it with inner experience.

iii) In this state, there is no demand for fruit, no seeking of reward.

iv) There is no attempt to make reserve or hide doubts, confusion and revolts. There is self openness, releasing of the self or blooming of the self. Billows (a wave or moving cloud or mass of something like smoke) of love envelope you.

v) One feels the experience of "Truth" descending, expanding, and followed by constant rejection of falsehood.

vi) One feels in touch with Supreme Knowledge, Immutable (never changing) Peace.

vii) An Inexpressible Glory uncovers itself, suffused with ineffable splendor and opens the glad tidings.

viii) Suddenly you hear that a musical instrument is being played. You find that you are in an extremely soothing magical spell, lost.

ix) All of a sudden you notice that all the directions are filled with beautiful notes of the flute being played at a far distance somewhere dispersing the melodious secret of the "Unknown." Silence whispers. Even darkness appears to be smiling. Unknown secrets start unfolding.

x) Sometime you hear irresistibly sweet, resonant voice calling from somewhere within you

"Come, Come Come … … …." You have no option but to keep moving in that unknown direction, lost, because everything else in existence has come to a standstill. Hypnotized or working like a robot, you only follow the call coming from within you.

xi) Some feel a soft voice whispering to them … … "Beyond the boundaries of life and death, "The Supreme" stands there in deep core of your heart engulfed in light.

> Same thought is expressed by Kashmiri poetess, Lal Ded (1320-1392) in her
> "Vakya; sentence" in words paraphrased below:
> "With a loving heart, search within this very body,
> This body is the abode of the "Supreme Self,
> Greed and delusion dispelled, this very body,
> Will acquire grace and hallo of illumination … …"

71. Lord in this verse tells Arjuna the necessary conditions to achieve divine peace.

विहाय कामान्यः सर्वान्पुमांश्चरति निःस्पृहः ।
निर्ममो निरहङ्कारः स शान्तिमधिगच्छति ॥ २- ७१ ॥

vihaya kaman yah sarvan pumams carati nihsprhah
nirmamo nirahankarah sa santim adhigacchati 2.71

vihaya—after abandoning or giving up; *kaman*—all desires for sense gratification; *yah*--that (person); *sarvan*--all; *puman*-- a person; *carati*—moves about; *nihsprh*—free from longings; *nirmamah*—without sense of proprietorship; *nirahankarah*--without false ego; *sah*--all; *santim*—to perfect peace (not absence of noise but charged expanse of stillness within with unending contentment, awareness and joy of the proximity of the soul) ; *adhigacchati*--attains.

"That individual, who, abandoning all desires, moves about, without longing for possession and sense of "I and Mine," attains peace." II 2-71 II

Lord Krishna, in this verse, is describing the attributes of an individual who attains peace. Three attributes have been talked about as follows:

i) *Vihaya Kaman yah sarvan* – (That person), who abandons all desires.

iii) *pumams carati nisprhah* – ((That person), who moves about free from longings.

iii) *nir mamonir ahmkaram* – (That person), who is devoid of false ego (i.e. who is without the sense of "I, My and Mine") and pride.

iv) *sah santim adhigacchati* – That person attains peace.

In verse 54, Arjuna asked the description of the person with steady wisdom or realized person. In verse 55, Lord answered this question. In verse 70, Lord again started to explain this concept further. Spotlight is on how an individual becomes entitled for peace. We all want peace i.e. feeling of calmness with soul's felicity (happiness), lacking worries and problems. This peace eludes most of the common people. What the ordinary people find is disillusionment. We find that life is not perfect. Things are inherently flawed. At times, we feel hopeless. There seems to be no use in believing "HIM." We become cynical or atheistic. What is to be done?

Abandoning desires uplifts from greatest despair and becomes greatest gift – Sometimes we all often find ourselves grappling with hopelessness in life. Where does this state of hopelessness originate from? This all is the result of our habit of desiring and craving. We suffer from spree of desires. Like waves in the ocean, one desire is followed by other desire and that one desire is followed by yet another desire and this goes on causing in life misery, unexplainable frustration and stress. While non-fulfillment of desires causes anger, frustration, jealousy, even fulfillment of desires offers its own problems. We feel pride in owning or doing which others do not have or which others have not done. After fulfillment of desires, we start flaunting. So, desiring obfuscates (deliberately makes something unclear) wisdom and deludes our soul. Therefore, the Gita offers the solution. Abandon the desire, the root of stress and frustration and be devoid of pride (i.e. I am this).

One should not go through the erroneous zone - The "**I, My and Mine**" concept within each of us is the greatest erroneous zone. It dupes all very silently. Lord Krishna says that one who abandons desires and sense of "I, My and Mind" concept attains peace. This view gets substantiated by experiences in daily life. The cure of all illness is stored in inner depth of life, the access to which is possible, only when we are at peace. Peace is something that we all know about. Still very few really experience it. Life is all about making the way through this erroneous zone to that distant "**Castle of Eternal Peace**" within each of us. Two very important points in this verse are i) Concept of "I,my and Mine" concept and ii) concept of peace.

"**I, My and Mine**" concept and beyond this – A lot has been said in the previous verses about abandoning desires, which arise due to "I, My and Mine" concept. My and mine are related to "I." Who am I? It is a million dollar question. It has beset the mankind always. The self is an aggregate of i) body with its level of awareness such as breath, mind, intelligence, memory and ego (ego is a constant state of self enhancement to make self more secure or to acquire more material goods, power, prestige and so on) and ii) soul (the most subtlest part of the self, the indestructible essence of Divinity, the Universal Consciousness within each of us). When the experience of life transcends (goes beyond) the physical body, we start realizing the soul and become available to the "Supreme Grace." For getting entitled to this elevation, we have to go to through the gateway of peace i.e. the second important point of the verse.

Concept of Peace - Peace **is** absurdly near, yet it is so distant like the mirage in the desert. It orchestrates the Divine music and sets the stage for "Divine Grace." Being without some of the things that we want is an indispensable part of life. It does not bother us when we are at peace. **We feel the weight of our ignorance in peace interlaced (to weave things together by twisting them over and under each other) with silence.** How do we come from facing hassles of life to experience peace? For this, sages and scriptures prescribe cajoling (gradually persuading) the mind to go inward and wean (gradually stop) it away from perpetual habit of going out i.e. persuading the mind to go beyond limits of desiring and not remaining confined to "I, My and Mine." When locus shifts from desiring to "giving and meditation," one seeks silence in and around. Silence is the oasis of pace. It is most eloquent language. Peace whispers in silence. It is the mighty weapon to counter the vicissitudes of life. Uncertainty, in the flow of life, is but inevitable. The more we acknowledge this, the more the reality of here and now dawns. This is not an ordinary experience. This releases the mind from the illusion of doer-ship and involvement with "I, My and Mine" and the constant involvement of or thoughts about the past and the future. Therefore, from desiring and flaunting (showing pride) en route silence (within and around), we have to move to the point where we are at peace.

Peace accords the turn towards contemplation, self-enquiry and realization – "Peace and grace" set in the stage for contemplation and the final journey begins. For this, we have to enquire within and realize the futility of the sense of individual volition or doer-ship. **The source and power behind everything is only "Consciousness."** As mentioned earlier, it is necessary at this point to surrender and submit to the "Divine will." To will what the divine will is wisdom. So, **we all have to increase our capacity to be still** (i.e. without moving but with intense awareness) abandoning the domination of "I, My and Mine" concept. Controlling desires and relieving ourselves of the feeling of "I. My and Mine" leads us to the condition called peace, in which we accept even the worst with ease. In peace, we remain divinely intoxicated in only thinking about "HIM" or any of "HIS" attributes. In peace, mighty forces come to our aid with things of continuing and stimulating values. **Peace speaks in universal language of silence. It explodes in huge gigantic waves of bliss, because in peace we are uncovering deeper layers of truth. In peace, we follow our own inner guidance. In peace, we come to know our own "True Nature."** The surface of life is always changing. The depth of life changes little, if at all it changes. We realize it only in peace. In peace, we realize that it does not matter, where we came from. We are all united at the deepest level. There is something startlingly common among us (living beings) somewhere very deep within us. This is the greatest truth. "Going beyond knowing and becoming aware of this fact only" takes us to the highest point of our spiritual growth. Being in desire is misery. Being in peace is bliss. Life was given to us primarily for living. We start knowing it first. Live life first. Feel it fully to the extent of gaining its full awareness. Knowledge will flow in. Our sequencing requires improvement. We try to gain knowledge first postponing living. Living cannot be postponed or substituted. Life has to be lived first with 100 % awareness and involvement. Knowledge is bound to flow in. One suffers in the vicissitudes of desires. One suffers in remaining confined to "I, My and Mine."

This verse mentions of abandoning desires. It also warns of the concept of "I, My and Mine." All this indeed is not very easy. But from the water weeds, the lotus blooms. Following quotation of Marcus Aurelius aptly describes this point:

"Thou must be like promontory (a high long narrow piece of land which goes out into the sea) against which the wave beat continuously. Yet, it stands itself and about it are those swelling waves stilled and quieted."

72. In this last verse of this chapter, Lord tells Arjuna about the final goal of *Vedanta* (end result of the Divine Knowledge of the Vedas) or *Brahmi Sthiti* (State of oneness with the Supreme Being, Ultimate Absolute Truth).

एषा ब्राह्मी स्थितिः पार्थ नैनां प्राप्य विमुह्यति ।
स्थित्वास्यामन्तकालेऽपि ब्रह्मनिर्वाणमृच्छति ॥ २- ७२ ॥

esa brahmi sthitih partha nainam prapya vimuhyati
sthitvasyam anta-kale 'pi brahma-nirvanam rcchati 2.72

esa--this; *brahmi*—relating to Supreme or spiritual; *sthitih*-- state; *partha*--O son of Prtha (Arjuna); *na*--not; *enam*--this; *prapya*—having attained; *vimuhyati*--bewilders; *sthitva*--being established; *asyam*—in this; *anta-kale*--at the end of life; *api*--also; *brahma-nirvanam*—oneness with the Supreme or state of self realization or transcendental experience beyond the limits of human experience and understanding (kingdom of God, as it is called); *rcchati*—(one) attains.

"This, O Son of Pritha (Arjuna), is brahmi sthiti (state of oneness with the Supreme Being). After having attained this, none remains deluded. Being established therein, even at the end of one's life, one attains oneness with The Brahma (The Supreme)." II 2-72 II

Each word spoken by the Lord is a beauty and substance. The verse reads as follows:

i) *esa (this)* - In this verse use of this world 'this' is very important. Arjuna asked questions about an individual with steadfast wisdom in verse 54. Lord answered these questions in verses 55 to 71.

Here the word 'this (or esa)' points to that, which has formed the subject of discussion in the verses 55 to 71. Therefore this refers to the state in which an individual shows the following characteristics:

a) Abandons all desires and controls the pull of the sense-objects and the ego.

b) Develops freedom from craving, attachment, fear, anger and feeling of "I, My and Mine."

c) Maintains equanimity (evenness) for both (a) good and evil and (b) favorable and unfavorable circumstances.

d) Remains constantly and unshakably absorbed in the Divine.

ii) esa brahmi sthiti partha – O son of Pritha (Arjuna)! This is the state of self-realization or attaining oneness with the "Infinite Truth."

iii) na enam prapya vimuhyati – After having attained this stage, a man is not bewildered i.e. once you achieve this, never again can delusion overpower you.

iv) sthitva asyam antakale api brahma nirvanam rcchati – Having established in this (explained at beginning of the discussion of this verse) even at the time of death, one attains oneness with the Brahma or one attains the absolute state of liberation.

Certain words used in this verse require detailed discussion:

Brahmn – It is the "Ultimate Reality," the amalgam of truth, consciousness and bliss. It is limitless ever continuing knowledge and limitless self renewing joy. That, from which the origin, sustenance and dissolution of the universe is derived, is called **Brahmn. Brahmn** is the substance or the material and the efficient cause of the universe. It is rather underlying cause or ultimate truth of everything in the Universe. It is also referred to as the "Unified Field," the Supreme Spirit, the Divinity, **Param Purush**, "**The Total Consciousness**" that is responsible for awarness in all living beings by functioning through mind and intellect.

> **Brahmi Sthitih** - This is the stage in which finality is achieved. This is the stage of submersion of self in the "Omnipresent Consciousness" of spirit or soul. This is the stage of permanent blessedness of soul communion. This is the stage of feeling "**anchored-in- the-Infinite State.**" This is the stage of self-realization called "established in **Brahma Sthitih**." Self-realization develops and matures in a distinctive kind of awareness. This is the stage in which one feels charged with a very high degree of supersensitive perception along with a blend of extreme calmness, total contentment and overflowing peace. It has been described in different ways by different "Sages." Some call it "Perception of the Divinity or the Supreme Perfection of the World." Some call it "Cosmic Consciousness." Some call it perception of "The Miraculous." The Miraculous refers to the most extra-ordinary phenomenon in the most common place experience. Absolutely nothing can evoke this special awareness, till very close enough attention has been paid to it. Once perception is disengaged from the domination of the preconceptions and personal interests, the mind is free to experience the world as it is in itself. There, it is able to behold its inherent magnificence. **This true wonder of the world is available everywhere, in the minutest part of the body, in the vast expanse of the cosmos and in the interconnectedness of these and all things.** We are a part of a "Balanced Whole" in which interdependency goes on hand in hand with individualization. At this point one gains an intimate awareness that we are all individuals, but at the same time we are a part of the "Greater Whole" united in something "vast and beautiful beyond description." Perception of the "Miraculous" is the supreme achievement of

mankind. When we get matured in this thinking, we start feeling strange affable happiness of continuing nature. The Universe starts opening doors, where there are walls (lust, anger, attachment etc.). One has to only believe it to experience it. This is the stage in which one transcends the mind and intellect and experiences "eternal unfolding of joy ever renewing itself." The difference between the individual soul and the Supreme Soul exists as long as the stage of illumination or submersion has not reached. After the submersion, the individual soul loses its identity into The Supreme or "The Everlasting Felicity (bliss)." Following lines form an Upnishad beautifully indicate towards the "*Brahmi Sthiti*":

> "By constant practice, the manifested universe gets merged in the "**Universal Self.**" The world of name and from gets merged in the vastness of the void as "**One Homogeneous Whole.**"
> When the void disappears, there is the "**Ineffable (too great or beautiful to describe) Supreme**" alone.
> This, O Brahmin, is the true "*Brahmi Sthiti.*"

Brahamanirvanam – It means nirvana in Brahma (Supreme Truth) or being one with Brahma or getting merged in the felicity (bliss) of Brahmn or getting submerged into the "Super consciousness." The term "*nirvana*" is extensively used by the Buddhist for the state, which is achieved, when desire and its corollary (something which is direct result of something else) have ceased to fuel the psychophysical entity that constitutes an individual and drives it on to further rebirth. It is state associated with deep coolness and peace. Here this term is used to refer to state of merger with "The Supreme Universal Self or Reality" or "Absolute Principle of *Upanishadic* Tradition (hence Vedic) tradition or *Brahmn.*"

This is the concluding verse of this chapter. Lord is summarizing in this verse where all this, discussed in this chapter, is going to lead us to. When one has attained the stage of (Brahmi Sthiti, state of getting established in Supreme Wisdom) befitting an individual with steadfast wisdom (discussed between verses 55 to 71), delusion cannot overpower. One gets relieved of false beliefs about oneself or the situation. "*Brahmi Sthiti*" emerges when, by various disciplines and approaches discussed in detail in subsequent discussions in the Gita, one goes through the roots deep down realizing or effortlessly retouching ever existing connectivity with "The universal." In that *Brahmi Sthiti*, mentioned by the Lord, "the individual I am" attains its perfect end and realizes its freedom of harmony in "The Infinite I am." Only revelation of the Infinite, which is endlessly new and eternally beautiful, accords or gives or unfolds the true nature of the being or the truth of the being or "The Miracle of Oneness." Lord is making it very clear that, even if one attains this stage just before death, one achieves oneness with Brahma (self-realization, *Nirvana, moksha*). By this statement, Lord Krishna has relieved the humanity of great worry. It is never too late to start preparing for this state. Goswami Tulsi Das wrote Ramacharitra Manas when he was quite old (about 90 years). This is a very beautiful verse full of promise. The opportunity is here and now. In this very life, realization of self can be attained. Convert these instructions from verses 55 to 71 into realized practice and the objective of human life will be achieved. Nothing can make it simpler than this. In subsequent discussion in the Gita, Lord has elaborated the issues touched in this second chapter. One, who succeeds, in attaining this stage during life time, is best (perfect) individual. Such an individual enjoys "Brahmi Sthiti" and gets liberated in this very life.

ॐ तत्सदिति श्रीमद्भगवद्गीतासूपनिषत्सु
ब्रह्मविद्यायां योगशास्त्रे श्रीकृष्णार्जुनसंवादे
साङ्ख्ययोगो नाम द्वितीयोऽध्यायः

Iti srimad bhgvadgitasupanisatsu brahmavidyayam yoga satre I
Sri krisnarjuna samvade samkhya yogo nama dvitiyo adhyayah II

This is the second chapter entitled "The Yoga knowledge."

Practical Relevance of 2ⁿᵈ chapter in life

The Lord concludes the second chapter with pragmatic (practical and sensible) and promising note. When sun dawns, darkness disappears. The last verse is like that only. It has made everything calm and clear. Approach has been given. Verses 55 to 71 (attributes of an individual established in universal onesness) only show what an individual has to be like. Final destination (i.e. Supreme Bliss) has also been mentioned i.e. address of destination has been given. By saying *"Brahma Nirvana,"* Lord has pointed out what individual soul has to strive for to get free from cycles of birth and death. The very understanding of this concluding verse culminates in joy and seems exhorting an individual:

"Delusion has been removed. Night of ignorance is long over. Path has been brightened by the glimmer of the sun of knowledge. Move on, you emancipated soul. Your Lord is whispering deep within you words of wisdom. There is light and vibration all around. Only keep moving on immersed in the thoughts of divinity, fully surrendered. That you will meet your destined end, is a proclaimed reality."

With this last verse of the 2ⁿᵈ chapter, let us remember that life is a fragment, a moment between two continuing realities (i.e. the soul and the Supreme). This delusion of two entities remains, till there is merger or self realization. Life moves on in long waves but does not follow a straight line. Sometimes there are setbacks, reverses, dark periods of trial and confusion throwing opportunities for supreme test of courage, endurance and resolve. Life has been influenced by all that has happened. It will influence all that follows. The only way to illumine is to have the right way to view. Why should we not then view it in the Gita's way? Now with all these Gita's clarification in mind and final objective in view (self-realization, clear as day light), let us keep moving on as a grateful enraptured soul with perseverance, patience and determination in the glow of our firm belief in the benevolence and love of the Divinity. The best of life is always ahead, further in the direction just given by the Gita. No one can give us gift of serene mind, a calm and tranquil way of life. It is something that we have to develop for ourselves or earn for ourselves within ourselves practicing the knowledge given in this chapter 2. This chapter 2 tells us the techniques (path of knowledge, path of action and path of devotion) of living life. It gives us the insight to cognize our true potential. It outlines the path of perfection and helps the reader to become perfect person, a realized soul. Let the discussion about the 2ⁿᵈ chapter be concluded with the following lines:

"O, ye, soul, yearning for calm and quietness, let the teachings of the Lord in the second chapter of the Gita drop upon you the petals of divine, peaceful fragrance. Feel it, Abide by it and go with it always in this beautiful interlude (short period of time) called life. Seemingly two entities in life are in reality one only. Gaining first hand awareness of this is the nectar. Drink it and get submerged into ever continuing joy of the Divine with grace and bliss."

This second chapter is the wholesome meal of spirituality. It is complete in itself. It suffices adequately. It is the foundation. It is the root. All other chapters are like leaves, flowers and fruit and gain their vitality in this root only. It contains the basic thoughts and approaches, which have been further taken up for development in other chapters. It is said that 2nd chapter alone can suffice? Lord's reaction to Arjuna's helplessness gives the best answer. Briefly it was:

"First know yourself and your true relationship with everything around you. Your attitude is very important. Abandon your attachment for results. Surrender to the Supreme to get rid of the ego. Be ever linked to the Source of Peace within you and don't ever let the problems of the world disturb the equanimity of the mind."

Everything else will fall in line. The inquisitiveness (asking too many questions) will subside. There will be bliss around you. You will blossom from within radiating your inner happiness all around. **Your chief achievement will be your awareness of what you are.** Life will come to become a triumphant journey towards that "**Unifying Force**" within all.

तृतीयोऽध्यायः (Chapter 3)

कर्मयोगः {Karam (Action) – Yoga}

In this chapter, Lord tells Arjuna in detail about Karam-yoga, which is highly motivational to the common man. Lord's teaching truly unfolds the secret underlying the words "work is worship i.e. how work becomes a medium of establishing connectivity with the object of worship (form or the formless)." Lord explains how even an ordinary act, done with detachment to its reward in the soul-touched wisdom, becomes an offering to the "Supreme Reality." Activity, done in the spirit of karam-yoga, becomes sanctifying (that transforms imperfection into perfection; makes the act holy) and thus spiritually uplifting. Lord tells in this chapter the nitty-gritty (basic or most important details) of "karam-yoga." This chapter underlines the importance of discharge of one's svadharma (activity in line with one's propensities and attributes such as poise, feverishness and indolence or sluggishness) with awareness of the divine dimension within.

1. In verses 49 (yoga buddhi), 50 and 52 of the previous chapter, Lord has declared the superiority of knowledge to action. On the other hand, Lord is also inspiring Arjuna to take up arms and fight the bloody war. Arjuna feels confused and seeks clarification from the Lord.

अर्जुन उवाच ।
ज्यायसी चेत्कर्मणस्ते मता बुद्धिर्जनार्दन ।
तत्किं कर्मणि घोरे मां नियोजयसि केशव ॥ ३- १ ॥

arjuna uvaca
jyayasi cet karmanas te mata buddhir janardana
tat kim karmani ghore mam niyojayasi kesava 3.1

arjunah—Arjuna; *uvaca*—said; *jyayasi*— superior; *cet*— if; *karmanah*—than action ; *te*—by you; *mata*—thought or opinion; *buddhih*-knowledge (i.e. outcome of application of faculty called intelligence); *janardana*—O Krishna; *tat*— then; *kim*—why; *karmani*—in action; *ghore*— terrible; *mam*—me; *niyojayasi*—(you are) engaging me; *kesava*—O Krishna.

Arjuna said:

"If, O Janardana, it is held by you that intelligence is better than work, why then do you, O Kesava, urge me to this terrible action?" II 3-1 II

Here Arjuna has used the word intelligence. This has a reference to the word "Buddhi yoga" of verse 49 of 2nd chapter. What is Buddhi yoga? It is a state in which Buddhi (discriminating faculty), strengthened by yoga [all mental, physical and emotional disciplines to get united with the truth (divine energy) within the soul], controls and guides through mind the sensory organs towards the higher objective of human destiny. It is relevant to understand the actual reason for confusion of

Arjuna. Lord has actually praised "**action**" inspired by intelligence and strengthened by yoga i.e. intelligence rooted in faith. Lord did not talk of mere knowledge and wisdom. Then at the end of the 2nd chapter Lord says that a perfect sage (*muni*) does not work. Arjuna has picked up the two words "knowledge and action" out of context. Arjuna is thinking why he should work (fight here) when the other option knowledge is there. Arjuna at this stage does not does not know about divine knowledge. He does not know that even action (work) can become a medium for achieving highest objective of human existence (i.e.the divine reality within the soul and all that is). He finds Lord's words "intelligence is better than work" confusing. He is not able to find out why Lord is not asking him to go for "Buddhi Yoga" instead of "Karam Yoga" (action, in Arjuna's view at this stage, is an act of massacre or killing of a lot of people). For this reason he shares his doubt with the Lord.

2. In this verse also, Arjuna continues presenting his point of view.

व्यामिश्रेणेव वाक्येन बुद्धिं मोहयसीव मे ।
तदेकं वद निश्चित्य येन श्रेयोऽहमाप्नुयाम् ॥ ३- २ ॥

vyamisreneva vakyena buddhim mohayasiva me
tad ekam vada niscitya yena sreyo 'ham apnuyam 3.2

vyamisrena-- perplexing; *iva*--as; *vakyena*--words; *buddhim*—understanding (of intelligence); *mohayasi*—confusing or bewildering or puzzling; *iva*—as it were; *me*--my; *tat*--that; *ekam*--only one; *vada*--tell; *niscitya*—for certain; *yena*--by which; *sreyah*—the highest good; *aham*--I; *apnuyam*--may attaint.

"With these perplexing words you are, as it were, confusing my understanding; tell me with certainty the path by pursuing which I may get to the highest good." II 3-2 II

The word "*eva*; as if it were" has been used twice in this verse. Actually Lord has not confused Arjuna. Due to his ignorance, Arjuna finds that two paths of jnana and karma are contradictory to each other. With child-like innocence, Arjuna is asking the Lord to tell him the best course of action to be followed by him. The main words used are as follows;

i) *vyamisreneva vakena* (**By confusing words, if it were**) – Actually lord has not used confusing words. In verses 47 and 51 of 2nd chapter, Lord praises selfless and unattached action. Then in verses 55th to 72nd of 2nd chapter, Lord says that perfect sage does not work at all. Arjuna finds it confusing.

ii) *Buddhim mohaysiva me* (**you are confusing my mind**) - The conflict is not in Krishna's words but it is in mind of Arjuna. Arjuna is not able to reconcile Krishna's teaching with the deep rooted popular beliefs of Hinduism of those days. He is confused by such words as svadharma, dharma, naishkarmayam (action-less-ness) used in 2nd chapter. Any one new to the Gita finds it difficult to understand meaning of these words.

iii) *tad ekam vad nischitya* (**tell me for certain that one path**) – Ajuna has not yet grasped the unique combination of path of jnana and path of action. He does not know that path of action culminates in jnana. He wants to follow either the path of knowledge or path of action.

iv) *yena sreyo 'ham anupyam* (**by which I can attain my best interest**) – This is Arjuna's request. He wants to know for certain what course will be the best for him to attain the highest (supreme felicity. Arjuna so far is not clear about the highest good for him). Brahman-Sthiti (being into the highest bliss of the Supreme Being or the Divinity manifested in all) is the highest state achievable by a human being. It is also called bliss or *moksh* (absolute liberation).

3. Lord answers Arjuna and tells him two phases of liberation.

श्रीभगवानुवाच ।
लोकेऽस्मिन् द्विविधा निष्ठा पुरा प्रोक्ता मयानघ ।
ज्ञानयोगेन साङ्ख्यानां कर्मयोगेन योगिनाम् ॥ ३- ३ ॥

sri-bhagavan uvaca
loke 'smin dvi-vidha nistha pura prokta mayanagha
jnana-yogena sankhyanam karma-yogena yoginam 3.3

sri-bhagavan uvaca--the incarnation of Supreme Truth, Lord Krishna said; *loke*--in world; *asmin*—in this; *dvi-vidha*--two fold or twofold course of spiritual discipline; *nistha*—path or faith; *pura*--priviously; *prokta*—(were) said; *maya*--by Me; *anagha*--O sinless one (Arjuna); *jnana-yogena*—path of knowledge; *sankhyanam*—for those who are followers of Sankhya (Self-knowledge) having discerning mind and empirical philosophers; *karma-yogena*—path of action *yoginam*—for karam-yogins i.e. who perform action as a matter of duty and devotion without attachment to fruit of action.

Blessed Lord said:

"O Sinless (blameless) One! The twofold path was given by me to this world at the beginning of the creation – the path of knowledge for men of contemplation who can discriminate and path of works for men of action." II 3-3 II

Basically, the twofold path was given by the Lord in the beginning of the creation to attain the highest good (supreme facility or happiness). The word "twofold path" stands for two phases of the seeking made for evolving spiritually i.e. path (phase) of intelligence and path (phase) of work. These paths (phases) are not exclusive but complementary. Each individual has got his own particular combination of gunas (attributes of nature – sattva, rajas and tamas) resulting in his or her own particular disposition (tendencies and thought pattern). Each individual is free to choose path (phase) conducive to his or her individual frame of mind. There is no compulsion. Any imposition adversely affects the desired results. The Gita mentions so many yogas (paths). All of them can be brought under these two main divisions- Jnana Yoga and Karam Yoga.

Jnana yoga (path of knowledge i.e. self application of soul by which it enters into Brahmic state, elaborated in detail in the earlier chapter) - Some are born with intellectual frame of mind. Jnana-yoga (path of knowledge) is for those who have got intellectual frame of mind, who like to make enquiry into the self (who am I? Where did I come from? Where will I go after this life?). What is jnana? It is that by which you discriminate between truth and untruth, between **prakriti** (nature) and **atma** (purusha; Individualized Divinity covered in the veil of ignorance). It is jnana (divine knowledge) which helps you to transcend the limitations imposed by prakriti (nature). It is jnana (divine knowledge), which makes you aware that the divinity within you is immortal. It is jnana that makes you aware that body, mind and intellect are modifications of nature. The Divinity within is immortal and it is different from body, mind and intellect. The seeker on this path (path of jnana) practices those particular spiritual techniques by which you cease working. Still you are in a calm and steady state of mind. You do a lot of work, yet you do not feel it. You carry so little burden even after doing immense work. That is wonderful merit of the jnana-yoga. Through path of knowledge, action finds its completion in jnana in its pursuit to repose (to be put to rest) in the "bliss of atma" (i.e. immortal joy of being established in the divinity within covered with ego). This path is for those whose inner being has the tendency to get lapsed (gradually come to a stop for a brief period of time) into deep spiritual contemplation i.e. those who are introverts and keep thinking instinctively about the truth of that "Reality" which defies (refuses to obey) to be confined to specifications but validates its ever continuing presence within by emanating ripples of joy. Jnana is a *nivritimarg* (path of renunciation i.e. renunciation not from activities but from reward of activities). It suits the introverts. Jnana Marg (Path of knowledge) is that in which one reaps the benefits of inaction even in the middle of action by developing a particular attitude of mind.

Karam-Yoga – This path is also a means of liberation quite as efficient as path of knowledge. It is for those who have practical temperament i.e. who naturally love action. Those, who are possessed of the intellect, which is agitated by objects of the senses, are qualified for Karam Yoga. In this path focus is on action. A Karam-Yogi tames the senses to avoid such impediments as desire, anger, lust, hatred, ego etc. and seeks harmony with his own true nature, abandoning self-sense (being ego-centered) and attachment to fruit of action. Karam-yoga is for energetic personalities with love for action (for extroverts). *Karam-Yoga is a Pravriti marg* [i.e. based on particular combination of gunas or attributes of nature (sattva, rajas and tamas) in individual or natural propensities].

What is the inter-relationship of the two paths (knowledge and action) mentioned above? True understanding of this question is necessary. It is perhaps futile to attempt to find difference in path of knowledge and path of action. There is only one path i.e. gaining **"supreme happiness typical to being lodged in the divinity within the soul."** Intellectuals go through the phase of knowledge and those having a lot of physical energy go through the phase of action. Both the modes are complementary to each other. How do we come to this conclusion? Lord says in this verse that the *nishtha* (spiritual discipline) aimed at achieving sreyas (spiritual felicity or happiness) is twofold. Lord uses singular number i.e. *nishtha dvividha*. The pursuit is just one. Those with pure mind do **nishkama-Karma** (action without attachment). Knowledge comes after renunciation of all works. When work is done with attachment for fruit of action, a seeker in the end is left with hankering for results. Some feeling of incompleteness, often, overwhelms an individual. An action normally is a cause of bondage. When one gains the skill in the form of absence of hankering for results (i.e. when one gets into this attitude of detachment or this particular mode of self-less-thinking), action becomes source of liberation, through purification of mind and awakening of knowledge within. Always, an external activity has to begin. Subsequently, the seeking gains maturity and refinement. The seeking, then, becomes knowledge-attuned. The same individual in the same seeking may pass through the two phases. Arjunna's apprehension that sankhya pursuit (path of knowledge) is opposed to karma-pursuit (path of action) is out of place. That is the focal point. It should be taken like this. A river at the source may be very small. Gradually when it proceeds on its journey towards sea, it undergoes so many changes. The distance between its two banks keeps on changing at different points before it merges the sea. This distance between two banks at different points indicates different phases (jnana, action, meditation, devotion) with different shades. Destination is the same for all. All phases (not only knowledge and action but also devotion and meditation) lead to the same destination (supreme happiness of being lodged in the felicity within the soul) at their completion. The object always remains to experience the divine secret within the soul. That is the journey, which is like a river. With any one of the phases (knowledge, jnana and also devotion and meditation) as dominant, anyone can go across to that far end where human limitations, for final rest, recede (go further and further away) into submission to the **"Ever Continuing, Glimmering, Expanded Awareness with Extreme Purity, with Supreme Peace and Eternal wisdom."**

4. In this verse Lord tells Arjuna that avoiding action either by non-starting an activity or by abandoning an activity does not lead to fulfillment at the level of conscience (that part of consciousness within which tells whether what one is doing is morally right or wrong).

न कर्मणामनारम्भान्नैष्कर्म्यं पुरुषोऽश्नुते ।
न च संन्यसनादेव सिद्धिं समधिगच्छति ॥ ३- ४ ॥

na karmanam anarambhan naiskarmyam puruso asnute
na ca sannyasanad eva siddhim samadhigacchati 3.4

na-- not; *karmanam*—of actions; *anarambhat*—from nonperformance; *naiskarmyam*—action-less-ness i.e. freedom from reaction; *purusah*--man; *asnute*--achieve; *na*--not; *ca*--and; *sannyasanat*--by abandoning action and thus attaining action-less-ness; *eva*--only; *siddhim*--success; *samadhigacchati*--attains.

"No man gains 'action-less-ness' by 'abstaining from activity'; nor does he rise to perfection by mere 'renunciation; abandoning work'. " II 3-4 II

These words used by the Lord are like neon signs sparkling in the darkness. Their understanding will add profusely to wisdom (divine knowledge).

i) *Na karmnam anarambhat naiskarmyam purushah anusyate* (a man does not attain **action-less-ness** by **abstaining from action**) – True "action-less-ness" cannot be attained by "non-performance" of action. Words used by Lord are as follows:

a) *Naiskarmyam* (Action-less-ness) – By use of this word, Lord is referring to a state where one remains unaffected by work whereas the activity goes on. It is that perfectly peaceful state where all the different levels of existence are in perfect harmony so much so that the seeker experiences "inaction in action" i.e. action goes on with supreme skill without causing overload, strain and mismatch anywhere. *Naiskarmyam* is the highest form of spiritual attainment. Naiskarmyam is a state of awakening within one's own divine nature. Experiencing action-less-ness is almost end (ultimate) state of Karam-Yoga. Normally actions follow desires. Normal state of functioning is not the state of *naiskarmyam* (action-less-ness). This term refers to a state of one's **self-fullness within,**" which wipes away all desires. Mind becomes clear and cheerful i.e. completely devoid of confusion and dualities. Action goes on like the car in fifth gear with no noise or disturbance whatsoever. When the car is going on at the peak of efficiency, you are able to listen to radio or you are able to talk as if you were not driving at all. Car still goes on smoothly. This is the stage in which different levels of controls within an individual take over leaving the driver relaxed as though no activity was going on. Inaction (perception of supremely relaxed state with awareness in total control) is experienced even when action goes on. This is real Karam-Yoga. This state is evidence of efficiency in the discharge of action. In this state, mind becomes transparent. Mind is face to face with the "Still-Soul" being aware of discharge of activity at the same time. Due to awareness of divine dimension within, an individual experiences "that extra perception (ability to notice quickly)" which helps the individual to oversee "self and work" simultaneously. In that state, the individual gradually starts offering work towards divinity within the soul. The activity becomes a yajna, in which work is offered to the Divinity within. How does it happen? *Naiskarmya* does not mean physical negation or escape from activity by either non-starting the activity or by abandonment of activity. It simply means accomplishment of action in such a way that you are able to taste the "relaxation and bliss of inaction even while doing action." At this moment (naiskarmya), you are free from ego "i.e. I do it; I enjoy it; I suffer from it." Whenever doer-ship goes away and one starts slipping into the divine zone within with full awareness of discharge of function, divinity starts manifesting through work done. Feeling-of-not-doing even while doing is *naiskarmya*. This is particular state of **spiritual maturity** and reflects that while doing action some inner-connectivity with the divine component has got established. It results in skillful discharge of activity and "abandoned-after-effects of action." *Naiskaramya* is discharge of activity at supreme level of efficiency so much so that even in doing activity one feels relaxation of inactivity. In *naiskarmya*, feeling of relaxation is due to dawn of renunciation and absence of feeling of doer-ship (ego). *Naiskarmya* results in seeking enlightenment while doing activity. *Naiskarmya* is a state of fruition of **jnana** and this does not involve stopping of an activity **in any manner whatsoever.**

Naiskarmya can be interpreted in another way also. An individual is a combination of i) prakriti (nature) and Purusha (soul). Prakriti (nature) is ever active. Nature does the work and Purusha (soul), remaining in its serenity and poise, mutely witnesses over the work of prakriti without getting affected by nature's work. Naiskarmya refers to soul's naiskarmya (i.e. harmony of nature and purusha or the divine existence) which remains unaffected by current of activities of nature. At this stage, one experiences "calm void within" even when the work goes on at peak.

b) *Anarambhat* **(without beginning a work i.e. by abstention from work or non-performance of action)**- *Arambha* means starting something or beginning something. *Anarambha* means not starting an activity in view of its after-effects (i.e. troubles and binding or capturing effects). It has been a considered opinion of some school of thoughts that action binds resulting in transmigration (rebirth of the soul in different body after death due to lingering effects of impact of karmas; this thought has been taken for granted by Indo Aryans and the Gita also). To prevent impact of action (binding effect of action or cause of transmigration), they advocated "*Sanyas* i.e. abandonment of action." This tendency to escape active involvement, in view of the capturing nature of karmas, is referred to here as "*anarambhat*" in this verse i.e. avoiding the physical action by not starting the work. Not starting an action considering the associated troubles due to binding nature of action is not *naishkarma* (action-lees-ness). Not starting a work speaks of physical negation of activity i.e. non-performance of activity. *Naiskarmya* is a state of feeling of relaxation of "inactivity" while performing the activity. *Anarambha* is negation of physical activity. Anarambha can never lead to state of naiskarmya.

c) **Sanyas (Ababdonment)** – It is a very beautiful word used by the Lord. The abandonment can be of two types i.e. i) renunciation of action and ii) renunciation of rewards of action.

i) **Abandonment of action** involves avoiding physical activity apprehending problems. This is precisely Arjuna's position. The war had been declared after a lot of deliberations. The warriors had reached the battle fields. The practice of blowing the conches signaling the commencement of war had been observed. At this stage, the action of starting a war had been initiated. When Arjuna saw paternal uncles, grand fathers, teachers, material uncles, cousins, sons, grandsons, comrades and father-in-law ready to fight from the opposite camps, Arjuna experienced a violent, sensational and physical crisis. He refused to fight. He was ready to leave the scene to embrace non-active, ascetic life. This type of abandoning of work is inappropriate and does not lead to spiritual perfection. The Bhagavad Gita abhors abandonment of this type of action and advocates renunciation of fruit of action. Therefore Lord Krishna advises Arjuna to opt neither non-beginning nor abandonment of work (i.e. beginning an act and then giving it up without completing it). The detail of renunciation of fruit of action (i.e. inner rejection of desire and egoism) has been taken up by the Lord in detail subsequently.

This discussion should not give the impression that "Sanyas i.e. abandoning physical activity" is an invalid concept. Actually "*Sanyas*" is a very difficult concept. It is relevant to mention here that one cannot abandon obligatory actions. Even when we are not doing a physical activity, we may be thinking. That is also an action. Actually Sanyas is for those who have achieved a particular level of maturity i.e. a stage where an individual gets established in the self. At this stage, abandoning external actions may help in spiritual evolution. It becomes a need due to spiritual maturity. Therefore, Sanyas is not for all tom dick and harry or common man. It is only for those selected ones who have already developed themselves spiritually. For ordinary individual, renunciation of physical engagement in work is not recommended.

d) *Siddhim samgacchati* [**Nor does he attain perfection (in abandoning action)**] - What is this '*Siddhim;* spiritual perfection'? It is the accomplishment of aim of discipline through yoga. It means achieving the ultimate purpose of pursuit. When an individual gets to the state referred to as "Siddhim" by the Lord, the impact of one's actions, which becomes the basis of one's behavior even in future, does not attach to (or capture) the individual any more i.e. one gets freedom from impact of actions. It also means that in this state an individual gets established into the peace akin (very similar to) to true divine nature within. "Inaction and simply witnessing" are the characteristics of the Divinity within the soul. Action is the characteristic of nature (mind, intelligence and ego). What is it that happens when one reaches state of siddhi? In this state, one sees inaction in action. One experiences fullness with serenity within. One goes beyond mind, intelligence and ego. In this state soul is at peace (being established within) and witnesses the operations of nature or *maya* (mind, intelligence and ego, off- shoots of nature). It is a state which reflects manifestation of connectivity with divinity with in soul or it speaks of onset of absolute freedom beyond human experience and understanding.

Now after understanding the four terms used, Lord's message comes out beautifully. Experiencing action-less-ness (naiskarmya) is a spiritual achievement. It is different from abandoning or escaping action (sannyas) or non-starting an action. Only the spiritually awakened can take to sanyas (from fruit of action) which is a step ahead in spiritual growth or rather it is an advanced version of sadhna. If sanyas had been that easy, all in ochre clothes might have attained the highest spiritual achievement. Even in that state (Sanyas), one cannot do away with obligatory work (even while meditating the activity of digestion is going on within). State of self- fulfillment through work cannot be achieved by avoiding physical engagement in the form of non-starting an activity or abandoning an activity.

This verse points out at hub (most important zone) of karam-yoga. Both inaction and attachment to fruit of action have to be avoided for "naishkarma" i.e. a state of one's perfection which emphasizes not renunciation of work but renunciation of selfish desires. It means **both giving up of life (i.e. involvement in work) and work (renunciation from reward of action) is indispensable for movement towards liberation on path of action.**

5. Lord is about to let out a great secret in this verse i.e. fundamental reason why an individual behaves in a particular manner.

न हि कश्चित्क्षणमपि जातु तिष्ठत्यकर्मकृत् ।
कार्यते ह्यवशः कर्म सर्वः प्रकृतिजैर्गुणैः ॥ ३- ५ ॥

na hi kascit ksanam api jatu tisthaty akarma-krt
karyate hy avasah karma sarvah prakrti-jair gunaih 3,5

na-hi—not; *kascit*--anyone; *ksanam*--even a moment; *api*--even; *jatu*--ever; *tisthati*-- remains; *akarma-krt*--without performing something; *karyate*—is made; *hi*-- forcertainly; *avasah*--helplessly; *karma*-- action; *sarvah*-- all; *prakrti-jaih*—born of *prakriti* (nature) i.e. the modes of nature; *gunaih*--by the qualities.

"Verily (really) none can ever remain for even a moment without performing action; for everyone is made to act helplessly indeed by qualities (*gunas* i.e. *sattva, rajas and tamas*) of nature." II 3. 5 II

No one can remain inactive even for a second. Some or the other activity is always going on within an individual. It is indeed impossible for an individual to completely abandon action through thought, word and deed. What is it that compels an individual to act? It is not will of the individual as many will say. Will of an individual is also a result of something, which prompts an individual to act. What is it? An individual acts due to a particular composition gunas (attributes of nature). There is no being, either on earth or in the heaven or among the Devas (not fully liberated but sufficiently graced to be in the service of the Lord), who is free from the three gunas (attributes of nature), the material nature. This knowledge about the reasons of behavioral pattern of an individual can immensely help an individual in spiritual growth.

Here comes the role of nature. Nature is the aggregate of the five primordial elements (earth, water, fire, air and space) and known (gravitation, photosynthesis) and unknown (black) laws of nature. Nature takes just everything under its sway (influence) due to gunas (attributes of nature) of nature. There are three "gunas" or basic characteristic qualities of nature i.e. sattva, rajas and tamas. Sattva manifests taint-less-ness, brilliance, knowledge and happiness. Rajas manifests in activity, desire and attachment. Tamas is the reason for ignorance, delusion, laziness and sleep. Just none can avoid the influence of this nature. Nothing in this world can remain inactive even for a moment. Earth and planets are constantly revolving. Sun shines without break. Air just keeps blowing all the time. Even in an atom, incessant activities of elementary particles are going on. Think of an individual. An individual's body, mind and other organs are always active or else there is deformity or lacunae. Nourishment will be distributed when the blood is circulating. Life thrives when the breathing process and thought process is going on. Where does it all lead us to? We all carry a particular composition of sattva, rajas and tamas with dominance of one particular attribute more than others. This constitutes our nature. Our body, our mind, our intellect are all manifestation of nature. So long as we are in the realm of body, mind, intellect and ego, we are captive of nature. We are not the master of nature (For gaining that mastery we will have to go beyond body, mind and ego complex through yoga). That gunas of nature will influence our behavior, is law of nature. It is futile not to accept this as law of nature. Acceptance of this law gives us the space, wisdom, strength and opportunity to evolve spiritually. Even the incarnation like shiva, and the sage like Narada could not escape influence of nature. It is as per nature to act and be bound. It is by yoga that one transcends the three Gunas. Any effort to avoid action on any ground whatsoever is reflection of ignorance. First accept that activity cannot be shunned. Attachment or not allowing attachment to activity is our choice. There lies the escape from the problem. This is the message of this verse. To control one's reactionary response is not immediately possible. What is the reason for that? We control our mind through intelligence. Intelligence is also an instrument of nature. Where from does it get feed for discrimination? Here we get the clue. Soul travels from one birth to another with a sort of baggage of impressions of past actions. It is this baggage which is primarily responsible for our behavior. Intelligence can be brought round but the accumulated impressions of past karmas are very powerful. To erase the memory of the impressions of past karmas, meditation offers the solution but it requires patience and time. It requires participation of organs of action in the mode of *Karam-Yoga* i.e. non attachment with rewards of action, organs of action fully absorbed in doing action for *Loksangraha* (cosmic benefit). Intelligence can be brought round but controlling restlessness of *prana* (subtle life force) due to accumulated past impression in soul takes time. Salvation does not lie in avoiding action. Salvation is in action through yoga.

The purpose of this verse is simple. We should lead life with the perception of this great cosmic action (impact of gunas). One should not try to stop it. One should try to go beyond it or transcend it. This perception arises with consciousness of eternal activity and power of this cosmic energy. This acceptance (a being is helplessly driven to action by the gunas of nature) is not the end. This acceptance (action is inevitable, inescapable and destiny of a being due to impact of gunas till a level of spiritual maturity is achieved) leads to wisdom which Lord describes elsewhere afterwards. This acceptance means one should always be active in serving the Lord by various means of one's choosing. One should never be without work because an empty mind is devil's workshop. Performing action till death with a desire-less (without attachment to fruit of action) state of mind is better than abandoning work and leading the life of an ascetic, who cannot escape the impulse of action (eating, sleeping, breathing, beating of heart are always karmas which none can stop). One should not become a hypocrite. Even a thought of doing an action is an action. Everything is an action here in this world. Our living is an act of movement of nature (only Divinity remains in action-less-ness and none else can in this universe).

6. In this verse Lord criticizes those who abandon work externally but remain thinking about objects of senses.

कर्मेन्द्रियाणि संयम्य य आस्ते मनसा स्मरन् ।
इन्द्रियार्थान्विमूढात्मा मिथ्याचारः स उच्यते ॥ ३- ६ ॥

karmendriyani samyamya ya aste manasa smaran
indriyarthan vimudhatma mithyacarah sa ucyate 3.6

karma-indriyani--the five working sense-organs (refer to chart in introduction); *samyamya*--restraiing; *yah*-- who; *aste*—sits; *manasa*--by mind; *smaran*-- remembering; *indriya-arthan*-sense-objects; *vimudha*- deluded understanding; *atma*- soul; *mithya-acarah*—hypocrite or pretender; *sah*--he; *ucyate*--is called.

"An individual, who merely restraints senses of action (namely the tongue, the hand, the foot and the organs of procreation and excretion) but feasts his or her imagination on sensuous pleasures is a hypocrite i.e. an individual of false conduct." II 3-6 II

Lord in this verse criticizes renunciation of "external sense objects but internal or mental association with objects of senses." Such an individual is a hypocrite. Such pretension (a claim to have a particular quality) of action-less-ness is dangerous and must be eschewed (deliberately avoided). Why does this desire to pretend abandoning action arise? It is again a result of ignorance. *Karmas* or works do not mean physical movements or activities alone. Our thoughts are great complex actions. Actually these are thoughts which trigger actions. Actually these thoughts represent the restless energy which take an individual astray (to get stolen or lost). It is inappropriate to avoid action but retain its cause in the form of thought. Such pretentious people develop false notion of self satisfaction by avoiding external actions whereas their mental association remains with the sense objects. One gains nothing by repressing action while retaining cause of action within, at mental level. This is the hypocrisy or false conduct.

A very good question arises here. Why does an individual feel prompted to work at all? This is due to past actions. Impressions of past actions travel with the soul and remain with the soul till matching effect of those actions is gone through. Till an individual develops divine knowledge, the potency of scars of past karmas remains and compels the individual to work. For this reason, a situation arises in which the individual abandons external action but internally gunas compel him to work. An individual is always in doubt (on the horns of dilemma) in these moments and thus becomes responsible for false conduct. To be inactive is a high ideal. To pretend to be inactive is degrading. For this reason, this verse contains a sort of warning to those who renounce action before gaining spiritual maturity, enough to make the individual conscious of Divinity within.

To explain this thought, Sri Ramakrisna cites a beautiful example of a sanyasi (one who has taken to renunciation i.e. abandoned actions and remains away from active participation in society) and a prostitute. The Sanyasi had outwardly renounced the world but spent his time in keeping an account of all the customers frequenting the prostitute's house. The prostitute on the other hand, while physically carrying on her sordid (immoral) trade, employed her private hours in intense prayers for a pardon from God for her sin. As a result, the Sanyasi was doomed to hell and the prostitute was awarded the celestial bliss of heaven.

7. Lord Krishna does not want Arjuna to be a mithyachari (man of false conduct). Therefore, this verse offers the solution.

यस्त्विन्द्रियाणि मनसा नियम्यारभतेऽर्जुन ।
कर्मेन्द्रियैः कर्मयोगमसक्तः स विशिष्यते ॥ ३- ७ ॥

yas tv indriyani manasa niyamyarabhate 'rjuna
karmendriyaih karma-yogam asaktah sa visisyate 3.7

yah-whose; *tu*-- but; *indriyani*--senses; *manasa*--by the mind; *niyamya*-- controlling; *arabhate*--begins; *arjuna*--O Arjuna; *karma-indriyaih*—organs of actions; *karma-yogam*—yoga of action i.e. that path in which action is the medium of seeking union with the Supreme; *asaktah*--without attachment; *sah*--he; *visisyate*-- excels.

"The one, who controls the senses by (trained and purified) mind and, without attachment, engages the organs of actions to "Karam-yoga," is far superior." II 3-7 II

This verse deals with pravratiti (based on behavior) marg or path of work. This verse makes direct reference to *karmendriyas* (organs of actions). This verse also states that the sense organs should be controlled by mind. This verse also makes a reference to jnanendriyas. What are these karmendriyas and jnanaendriyas? Karmendriyas (organs of action) are: hands with which we grasp; the feet with which we walk; mouth with which we talk; genitals with which we procreate and the excretory organs with which we evacuate. Jnanendriyas are: eyes with which we see forms; ears with which we hear; tongue with which we taste things; nose with which we smell things; skin with which we touch things. Sight, hearing, taste, smell and skin are main gates of knowledge for an individual.

In preceding verse, Lord clarified to Arjuna that abandoning of action is not possible so long as an individual is alive. Gunas of nature (sattva, rajas and tamas) drive an individual to action and individual runs towards the target like the bloody hound towards the prey. Therefore it is futile to try abandoning action. It is equivalent to combating (fighting against) mighty force of nature because so long as life is there, impact of gunas is there. What should be done then? Lord comes out with an answer as follows:

i) *Yah tu mansa indriyani niyamya* (but whosoever restrains the senses by the mind) – Now Lord is coming out with a solution. The seeker will have to control the senses. It is called disciplining the body and mind. This is possible only after engaging the ever active senses on things nobler and more elevating in nature than things which are ordinary and vulgar. Here we are not following objects of senses. We are giving different direction to senses to be busy with.

ii) *Arabhate karmendriyaih karamyogam* [(he or she) is busy in "yoga of action" with sense organs of action) – Such a person performs action with "karam-yoga." What is this "karam-yoga"? It is different from working with ordinary worldly intelligence i.e. working for fruit of actions alone. It means action in disciplined mode with intelligence focused on the unity of the individual self with universal self. The word Karam-yoga emphasizes that medium is action and finale is union of individual self and universal self. Here intelligence will guide the actions not towards results of actions alone but towards an aim higher than mere rewards of actions. In Karam yoga, soul-touched-intelligence, which gets awakened by physical disciplines and meditation with consciousness of divinity within, guides the individual to perform action as if it were an offering in the fire of thoughts of the Supreme. Done with karam-yoga (disciplined manner, non-attachment with fruits of action and final objective higher than mere tangible reward i.e. soul felicity or unending happiness of soul), an ordinary activity becomes a yajna. An offering primarily with devotional intensity or the internal touch from "the core" (inside of an individual), turns even an ordinary activity into soul satisfying *Yajna*. The impact of doing action gets burnt, when work is done in yajna-mode. The action does not bind. It becomes a liberating activity instead of a binding activity i.e. ordinary action becomes a "spiritually elevating action." When an action is done in this mode, mind is not attached to fruit of actions. The mind, guided by spiritual introspection, adds magic of Karama-Yoga to an activity. In this state, an action does not interfere with the process of doing an action. It rather helps in discharge of action effectively.

Lord first mentions about control of senses. Then there is immediate reference to participation of organs of action through Karam-yoga. What is it due to? To control one's "reactionary response" is not immediately possible. We control our mind through intelligence. Intelligence is also an instrument of nature. Where from does it get feed for discrimination? Here we get the clue. Deluded Soul travels from one birth to another (Supreme is immovable; that soul with a sort of baggage of impressions of past actions is moving in ignorance). It is this baggage (of sattva, rajas and tamas) which is primarily responsible for our behavior. Intelligence can be brought round but the accumulated impressions of past karmas are very powerful. To erase the memory of the impressions of past karmas, meditation offers the solution but it requires patience and time. It requires participation of organs of action in the mode of Karam-Yoga i.e. non attachment with rewards of action, organs of action fully absorbed in doing action for Loksangraha (cosmic benefit) and divine consciousness within i.e. surrender to the will of the Supreme. Intelligence can be brought round but controlling "restlessness of prana (subtle life force) due to accumulated past impression in soul" takes time, effort and determination. For this reason Lord has used two words very boldly i.e. i) control of senses with mind ii) initiating participation in action through Karam-yoga. By use of the word Karam-yoga, lord is adding spiritual dimension to mode of working. Salvation does not lie in avoiding action. Salvation is in action through yoga i.e. will with divine dimension facilitates control of senses as well.

iii *Asaktah se visisyate* (such an unattached person is excellent) – Such a person achieves excellence. This particular verse is the best description of excellence in yoga. The work of such an individual manifests excellence and results in sublime spiritual growth. How does it happen? The discriminating mind restrains the senses so that they are not overwhelmed by the objects. This happens not by negation but by persuasion. This word *asaktah* (unattached to rewards of action.) is very important. Attachment is two-fold: i) attachment with fruit of action and ii) attachment to being the doer of the action. The senses of knowledge are controlled by dispassion or *vairagya*. This process is called sama. The mind is subdued by purification or absence of desires. This process is called *uprati*. Thus controlling the mind and senses, a Karam-Yogi discharges all obligatory functions in spirit of dispassion or detachment through the senses of actions, which are merely servants obeying the commands of the mind. Such a yogi takes the quality of discharge of action to such a height that he or she sees inaction in action. This is a fairly good level of spiritual experience and manifests seeker's excellence in work.

This verse beautifully clarifies the difference between indulgence in an action and doing an action in Karam-Yoga. Discharge of function in self control for the service of the Lord (for cosmic benefit) culminates (reaching highest point) in self-fulfillment. Abandoning of action is not possible due to drive of attributes of nature (sattva, rajas and tamas) within. Action through Karam-Yoga relieves the individual of restlessness of prana (due to accumulated impressions of past karmas) and tames the organs for spiritual evolution. Restlessness of prana does not have intelligence. It simply is. It is a feeling of incompleteness without apparent reasons, which does not lend itself to explanation. It is due to past impressions stored in some unknown corner or chamber within. The focus of the verse is to differentiate: i) mere action i.e. reactionary response based on accumulated impression of past karmas stored within and ii) Karma in the mode of karam-yoga i.e. with divine consciousness, for common benefit and in spirit of surrender to the Supreme. After making a commitment with cosmic benefit in view (Arjuna had committed to the war to relieve the society from unrighteousness), discharging work with equanimity, without attachment to fruit of action, is Karam-Yoga. This is the essence which sublimates (better utilization of energy involved in) the ordinary action to liberating action in Karam-Yoga. If this distinction between ordinary action and liberating action through Karam-Yoga is properly understood, the individual far excels in life. Life becomes self-satisfying. Life becomes a celebration of the Divinity within. Why is it so? 'The awareness of the divine connectivity within' blossoms through the medium of work done in the mode of Karam-Yoga. In the preceding verse Lord condemns mere outer renunciation (i.e. abandoning of action). In this verse, Lord commends the true and self-elevating spirit of inward detachment, which means keeping a justifiable space for introspection, review, contemplation and recharging for spiritual growth. It helps to discriminate between truth and untruth. This distinction of vital importance is possible only through detachment from the rewards of action. It essentially does not mean abandoning relationship with, people, objects and situations.

The term "Karam-yoga," used in this verse, is not an ordinary term. Its understanding can change the whole life of an individual. It requires a) prior commitment i.e. both tangible and intangible impact of the work have been taken into account and work is being done with some intangible benefit or cosmic benefit definitely. Looting a bank may have been done very efficiently but this activity cannot be said to have been done in spirit of karam yoga. "Soul participation or that extra inordinate power from within" is not possible without at least intangible considerations in form of cosmic benefit, b) once a commitment has been made, there should be no attachment with the results. This is very important component of karma-yoga. It is here that "intangible considerations or cosmic benefit" save the seeker form feeling discouraged. Fear cannot be a cause of fear to a karam-yogi. A karam-yogi rushes into zone of fearlessness and c) offering the work to the Supreme makes the individual to go into that "zone within" where "Higher Divine Potential Within" participates in the accomplishment of the objective. Karam-yoga changes an ordinary individual into a "karam-yogi" i.e. doing work without attachment to the results as an offering to the supreme for cosmic benefit.

8. In the first verse of this chapter, Arjuna asked Lord why he was being urged to take such a dreadful act as war. Then Lord explained that taking action was better than not taking action at all. In this verse Lord warns Arjuna to be careful about inaction.

नियतं कुरु कर्म त्वं कर्म ज्यायो ह्यकर्मणः ।
शरीरयात्रापि च ते न प्रसिद्ध्येदकर्मणः ॥ ३- ८ ॥

niyatam kuru karma tvam karma jyayo hy akarmanah
sarira-yatrapi ca te na prasiddhyed akarmanah3.8

niyatam—prescribed or bounden; *kuru*-- perform; *karma*--duties; *tvam*--you; *karma*--action; *jyayah*- superior; *hi*-- for; *akarmanah*—than inaction; *sarira--yatra*—maintenance of the body; *api*--even; *ca*--and; *te*--your; *na*--not; *prasiddhyet*—would be possible; *akarmanah*—by inaction.

"Perform your obligatory duties because working is better than sitting idle (or not working); even maintenance of physical body will not be possible without work." II 3-8 II

Lord explains to Arjuna that action is better than inaction. Divine knowledge does not advocate for renunciation of karma i.e. abandoning action. By renunciation, the Gita advocates renunciation of fruit of action which culminates to equanimity within and non-attachment to desire and objects of senses. As desired by Arjuna, Lord comes out with a decisive reply in this verse as follows:

i) *Niyatam kuru karma tvam* [**Whatever obligatory (prescribed, allotted] actions have to be done, do them well**] – It means that whatever actions have to be done should be done well. What should be the meaning of *niytam karma*? *Niyatam karma* means bounden duties. In first category the actions laid down in scriptures are the bounden duties of an individual. In all fairness and considering the universality of the Gita's message, it will present very great difficulty to interpret these words as actions laid down in scriptures alone or some other external rule. An individual is a multi dimensional entity having social, moral and personal obligations. Actions in conformity to *svadharma* (actions complying with your basic innate nature i.e. composition of your attributes or a particular mixture of sattva, rajas and tamas) have also to be done for spiritual evolution. Therefore, "*niyatam karma*" should not be interpreted as actions fixed by some external rule. Best course should be to do those actions which fall in the category of desire-less actions controlled by liberated buddhi (intelligence steeped in divine proximity and matured enough to discriminate between the real and the unreal). Therefore, "*niyatam karam*" should mean those actions which are in conformity to both the obligations (bounden duties) as well as the wisdom enriched by divine knowledge. In brief, whatever actions have to be done should be done well. Niyatam Karma should be taken to mean obligatory work and interpretation of "niyatam karmas; obligatory work" should be left to awakened budhi. Obligation may be maintenance of body i.e. breathing, drinking and eating. Obligation may be according to dictates of an individual's attributes. Obligation may be work of cosmic welfare. Therefore whatever is to be done (i.e. bounden duty) has to be first properly ascertained. Then it should be attempted with total involvement. If one determines one's bounden action in the light of one's awareness of spiritual dimension, then it is the best idea. Till one has achieved that spiritual maturity, laid down actions should be determined in the light of scriptures or Guru or spiritual master. If a broad view is taken then an individual will include in it all duties in personal, social and national life. Of course this view should be taken by Yoga-Buddhi, intelligence nurtured by inner connectivity and awakened by yoga.

ii) *Jyayo hy akarmani* (**because action is superior to inaction**) – Spirituality does not mean laziness. Action is superior or more praise worthy or more meaningful keeping in view the total objective of life.

iii) *sarirayatra pi ca te na prasiddhyed akarmanah* (**even the maintenance of mere body will not be possible**) – Now Lord is giving a sort of warning to Arjuna. If undue renunciation from work (i.e. abandoning the work completely) is taken, then even taking care of body will present difficulty. To carry on this body as living entity, something has got to be done. One should throw away all external considerations and work industriously based on one's awareness of inner strength. Lord's focus is on intense efforts and inner efforts. That is what matters. Mostly people get what they strive for. Sometimes results may not be in tune with expectations. That is no reason why someone should give up the effort and the activity. Activity done with 100% dedication is in itself a reward, a blessing, an uplifting phenomenon in life, which otherwise becomes dull and boring. The increased work may increase the chances of bondage but the spiritual turn that you give to the work by yoga-attitude makes work done another offering in the divine fire for spiritual growth. That is what Lord wants to communicate to Arjun by saying "You perform your bounden duty."

It is a very good verse. Lord has given a sort of mantra (string of words having miraculous impact) to Arjuna and all i.e. **"Niyatam kuru karma twam**; do your bounden duty." Each one, in one's own field, has to do work, more work, as much work as possible, to justify one's awareness to one's own divinity within, and to give meaning to one's own understanding of spiritual pursuit. Without work, mind cannot be purified. Self realization is not possible. Even physical existence becomes impossible by inaction.

9. Lord has amply clarified that action is superior to inaction. Now Lord deals in detail about the method by which even an ordinary action can be transformed into a liberating action. In this verse lord asks Arjuna to do the work in the spirit of yajna.

यज्ञार्थात्कर्मणोऽन्यत्र लोकोऽयं कर्मबन्धनः ।
तदर्थं कर्म कौन्तेय मुक्तसङ्गः समाचर ॥ ३- ९ ॥

yajnarthat karmano anyatra loko 'yam karma-bandhanah
tad-artham karma kaunteya mukta-sangah samacara 3.9

yajna-arthat--only for the sake of Yajna (sacrifice); *karmanah*—of action; *anyatra*--otherwise; *lokah*--the world; *ayam*--this; *karma-bandhanah*— (is)bound by its own action; *tad- artham*--for that sake; *karma*-- action; *kaunteya*--O son of Kunti (Arjuna); *mukta-sangah*—free from attachment; *samacara*-- perform.

"The world is bound by actions other than those performed for the sake of yajnas. Therefore, O Arjuna, do perform for yajna (i.e. that action which facilitates liberation, mukti) free from attachment to fruit of action. II 3-9 II

This verse focuses on the word yajna. What is Yajna? First of all this term (yajna-concept) has been dealt with in detail.

Yajna (as concept, it is different from laid down rituals) – This term has been extensively used in the Gita. There is no equivalent English word for this. Normally it is taken to be ceremonious sacrificial fire, in which some thing is offered to a deity (symbol of Divinity). Yajna is an offering (sacrifice) with intense devotion towards the object of reverence with or without rituals. Sacrifice can be of material, time, effort and wisdom. Seen in this context, "Putreshti Yajna" performed as per ritual laid down in Vedas, is yajna. Looking at it from the expansive vision, Mother Tarrasa was performing yajna in the gutters of Calcutta. Similarly, Swami Vivekananda was also performing a yajna while making his address in Chicago. This concept requires to be elaborated:

Any act or ritual can be a '*Yajna*', if it satisfies the following conditions;

a) it should be a means of making sacrifice. Some amount of sacrifice is essential in *yajna*. It can be a sacrifice of time, means, desires, actions or something tangible.

b)*Yajna* is always an oblation (gift offered to deity i.e. symbolic version of Gods or God) from the one doing it to the 'Supreme Lord' directly or through His or Her creation or symbolic version (Intermediate Gods).

c) It should be done for common welfare except in case of laid down rituals.

d) It assumes self dedication and veneration or else it will remain a ritual (sacrificial act for a particular purpose) only like "Putreshthi yajna; yajna for being blessed with a son."

As per common understanding, *Yajna* is a ritual, in which some material (sesame, rice, animal* etc.) is offered to sacrificial fire to propitiate the deity (demi gods, anything offered even to demi gods reaches the Supreme Universal Self) with the words " This is for such and such deity and not for me." This only tells about one particular ritual and not the term *Yagna*. This is not sufficient to understand Gita. *Yajna* is something more than ritual of sacrificial fire only, as it is understood in common parlance.

Keeping above mentioned four points under consideration, Yagna means sacrifice, selfless service (seva), unselfish work, meritorious deeds giving away something to others and religious rites in which oblation is offered to demi gods through the mouth of fire. Keeping this in view, dedicating oneself to spiritual life is *yajna*. Waging a war against wickedness to protect righteousness is *Yajna*. Increasing the wealth of nation, not for self benefit but common benefit, is *Yajna*. Anything, which is done with sweat of brow for the service of Lord, becomes *Yajna* with attributes of sacrifice, self dedication, common welfare and offering to the Lord. Mother Teresa was doing *Yajna* near the gutters of Calcutta, when she was serving the poorest of the poor as a personification of humility and compassion. Swami Vivekananda was doing *yagjna* when he spoke in Chicago in that religious conference.

Yajna, therefore, can be with rituals and without rituals. Ritual is not as material as the feeling i.e. **intense internal touch from the core inside of an individual**. It is primarily the devotional intensity or the internal touch from the core inside of an individual, which can turn even an ordinary activity into soul satisfying *Yajna*. Divinity reveals itself when *Yajna* takes place. That *Yajna* is 'Vishnu' (Lord in Hindu mythology), is a Upnishadic statement. Performance of *Yajna* essentially elevates an individual on spiritual path. In short, any action which is done with pure frame of mind for common good with above mentioned attributes, is *Yajna*. One should so live life that all activities become entitled to be graded as Yajna like mother Teresa Vivekananda and Christ. Now the discussion about *vajna* can be summed up. Life requires performance of action (*yajna*). The performers of yajna fall in two categories: i) those who go through life in the manner prescribed by the sastras (religious treatise) with desire of reward i.e. the orthodox ritualists ii) those who go through life with a desire-less frame of mind and perform action merely as duty or offering towards the Supreme. Pure orthodox ritualists obtain non-permanent fruit in shape of heaven. Those falling in the remaining category obtain reward in the form of release from the cycle of birth and death. The yajnas of the orthodox ritualists require compliance to a laid down procedure. The best objective should be to fall in the category of individual whose every action is categorized as *yajna*. The Gita is not confined to ritualistic meaning of yajna. The Gita follows expansive, self elevating, self defining and spiritually uplifting meaning of yajna. Yajna is an offering to the Divinity for an aim higher than individual benefit, loosening the knot of ego and finally arriving at soul-freedom. In yajna, the act is done "God-wards" raising it by self dedication and offering to high psychological and spiritual truth.

Different people have different *sanskaras* (physical habits and mental tendencies due to a particular

---

* Some people start the futile discussion about the justification of animal offering in Yagna. It will be good to pause here a little. What was the intake of man in the primitive age? Even at that time, man suffered from a foreboding fear (for lack of knowledge) about the Unknown Supreme Reality governing this vast cosmos. It offered what it took. Even the Bible talks of animal killing as an offering to the Supreme. Our intake changed with time and knowledge and it still continues to be so. This ever continuing change reflects in our practices. Important thing to be noted is that even in primitive times offering was made to the Supreme. Practice of Yagna is as old as the Creation. Only the practices and not the principles have undergone changes. Therefore, it will be relatively more meritorious to offer animal tendencies like desires and anger into the fire of mental control instead of animals. In Yajna the stress is on offering with dedication and reverence for common good. Lord Krishna tells Arjuna (Chapter 10.25) in the Gita "From among the Yajna, I am Jap Yajna (Constant recitation of Divine names and attributes)."

way of looking at the things). Accordingly, they perform different yajnas. Some specific *yajnas* mentioned in the Gita are:

i) **Dravya-yajna**- Under this form of *yajna*, wealth is offered to the deserving persons for benevolent purposes as form of sacrifice.

ii) **Tapo- yajna**- Under this form of yajna, body and senses are subjected to severe austerities by vows of fasting, silence etc. A very simple life is lead with very few things to make it comfortable or enjoyable. Sacrifice is of desire for pump and show for spiritual growth.

iii) **Yoga-yajna**- Under this form, breath control is observed. Breath- control is the form of sacrifice.

iv) **Svadhyay-yajna**- This involves study and recitation of scriptures (holy books of different religions for spiritual growth i.e. the Ramayana, the Bible and the Quran etc.) for self-development. Time spent on the study of different texts is the form of sacrifice

v) **Jnana-yajna**- Under this method, imparting the divine knowledge is the form of sacrifice.

With this expansive concept of the Yajna in view, the verse is taken up as follows:

i) *yajnarthat karmano anyatra loko ayam karma bandhanah* **(the world is bound by action other than those performed for the sake of yajna)** – The world is bound by actions which are not performed as yajna. If the actions are done in the spirit of yajna (i.e. without attachment to fruit of actions; for cosmic benefit; with feeling of surrender to the Supreme or symbolic version of the Supreme), these actions become cause of liberation. Then there will be no bondage. The Yajna-mode of working is necessary to get rid of capturing nature of actions. The stress of the Lord is on spirit of sacrifice, the spirit of giving, which in its expansive (covering a large amount of space) state transforms into spirit of worship. State of worship is a state in which one is clinging (to hold something tightly) to those unclear, clattered, utterly soothing, immensely and intimately personal thoughts of the Divine, disposed (feel willing) for profusely giving and totally surrendering to the divine within or its symbolic version. From this spirit emanates the idea of service to family, society, country and humanity at large at large. Important point is to keep thought of yajna (as elaborated in the beginning of the verse and not just ritual for laid down objective) in mind at the time of discharge of action. Very simplistically and in terms of activities, yajna means sacrifice, selfless service, unselfish work, *seva* (service; an action in which one soul offers to some other soul something, tangible or intangible, good enough to restore spiritual connectivity at some level; this offer is irrevocable without any sort of expectation whatsoever), meritorious deeds, giving away something to others and a religious rite in which oblation is offered to Demigods (Intermediate Gods) through the mouth of fire. Adna butcher used to sell meat. He earned spiritual merit even in this work by doing this work with the attitude of yajna. Lord emphasizes that the world is bound by actions other than those performed for the sake of yajna.

What is the important point here? Work done with attachment binds. Same work done without attachment liberates. Work performed as service to mankind and dedicated to God liberates. Thus there is nothing evil as such in work. Evil lies in the personal motive behind it. It is the desire for rewards and enjoyment which creates binding effects in actions. If this thing is kept in mind, then actions can be performed in the spirit of sacrifice.

ii) *tad artham Karma, O kauntey, muktasangah samacar* (Therefore, perform, O Son of Kunti, all your duties without attachment) - Divine knowledge has been given. The nitty-gritty of yajna has been explained in full details. Now lord again exhorts Arjuna to perform action (warfare) without attachment to rewards of action (without consideration of gains coming out of it) . Lord is not asking Arjuna to do just any action. Very specific words have been used i.e. "mukta sangah samachar; perorm (that action) which is free from attachment." It means that Lord wants Arjuna to perform only that action which conforms (agree to) to essentials of yajna. That is liberating action. That action is done without attachment to rewards. That action is done without ego. That action is done for lokasangraha (cosmic benefit; common good) with awareness of divine dimension within i.e. awareness of self and through self all. Last condition is also very important. Till this awareness is there, one will not understand the true import (meaning) of "work for *lokasangraha* or cosmic benefit." This awareness unites the individual with the divinity i.e. ever ensuing blessedness, ever expanding joy, ever continuing consciousness. This essential condition enlivens the individual to universal interconnectedness. This condition accords individual spirit to expand without limitation to original state of immanence (present everywhere), indestructibility, eternity, inexhaustibility, without beginning or end. It is compliance to this condition that entitles the individual for divine grace, which is essential to transcend the limitations of this world. This meaning prominently comes out when the two words used by Lord are considered together i.e. **yajnarth** (done for yajna) and **muktasangah** (free from attachment). It is extremely important to understand that meaning of sacrifice in the context of the Gita is not confined to ceremonious sacrifice in rituals (distinction between Vedas and Vedanta or practice and knowledge is relevant here). The Gita's concept of the sacrifice embraces the work done for the Divine. All beings and all actions of prakriti are for the divine. From here we get the clue how the yajna-act proceeds, how the yajna-act endures (i.e. bearing without complaint the sufferings of the act being done, not for the self but for all beings of the Divine) and how this divine-angle (this attitude of doing for divinity) gives direction to the act. Ego is the knot of bondage. When we work for the Divine (for cosmic benefit) we loosen this knot of ego and set ourselves acting on the eternal path of truth. This yajna-attitude transforms a simple act into a psychological and spiritual truth demonstrating how soul's inherent divine nature is developed out of the imperfect human nature by this yajna-attitude. At this point mortal is made immortal through action.

The Gita's interpretation of yajna takes it beyond the limits of karam-kanda of Vedas i.e. rituals for specific purposes and specific Gods. According to the Gita, any offering, for cosmic benefit without focus on the reward and with awareness of divine consciousness within, is yajna. Radha's intense longing for Krishna or Radha's seeking strength and fulfillment through mute but strength-giving, suffusing (to spread all over and through) thoughts of Krishna and still not interfering with activities of Krishna for cosmic benefit, is yajna of the highest order. It is this yajna-spirit of half of Krishna (radha-component) which rejuvenates the other half of Krishna (Krishna-component) to continue with the work of world's welfare.

Now the message is clear. The world is bound by those actions which are not out of the spirit of yajna. Do that which is free from attachment. Do that which is liberating in nature. Do that which is for the benefit of cosmos. For Arjuna that action is fighting a war to restore righteousness in the society. The Divinity reveals best when yajna takes place.

10. Lord informs in this verse that concept of yajna (an offering with non-attachment; cosmic benefit; surrender to the supreme with awareness of the Divine consciousness) was an integral part of the cosmic plan.

सहयज्ञाः प्रजाः सृष्ट्वा पुरोवाच प्रजापतिः ।
अनेन प्रसविष्यध्वमेष वोऽस्त्विष्टकामधुक् ॥ ३- १० ॥

saha-yajnah prajah srstva purovaca prajapatih
anena prasavisyadhvam esa vo astv ista-kama-dhuk 3.10

saha--yajnah—together with sacrifices; *prajah*-- mankind; *srstva*—having created; *pura*—in the beginning; *uvaca*--said; *praja-patih*--the Lord of creatures; *anena*--by this; *prasavisyadhvam*—shall ye propagate; *esah*-- thiscertainly; *vah*--your; *astu*-- let it be; *ista--kama-dhuk*—milchcow of desires or giver of desired enjoyments..

"In ancient days the Lord of creatures (Prajapati or Brahmna) created creatures and said "By this you shall bring forth (cause to bring about fruit or off-springs; producing a child for adding to lineage is a yajna; that is how the Aryan culture saw this) or propagate (produce) or multiply; this shall be the milch cow (Kamdhenu or wish-fulfilling cow) of your desires]." II 3-10 II

A lot of importance has been given to yajna-concept in the Gita. It is not related to human experience on earth alone. It has cosmic dimension. The whole cosmos is based on yajna-concept. While emphasizing this fact Lord has used different terms or words as follows:

i) *Prajapati* **(or Brahama; one of the Trinity i.e. Brahma, Vishnu Mahesh)**– The term "Prajapati" is used to refer to the aspect of the **creative force of nature**. As there are different executives handling different specific different portfolios, that aspect of nature (considered a specific God, Intermediate God i.e. one who depends on the Supreme Universal Reality) which handles the function of creation (word used in Sanskrit is srashti i.e. projecting out of self the universe) in universe is called Prajapati. Prajapati governs and guides the creation of different species in the universe. Prajapati is one who in the beginning imaged the creation of this universe. The same Prajapati who created the Universe projected the yajna (an act of sacrifice for the cosmic benefit without vested interest as humble instrument of the Supreme Self) in order to maintain this universe i.e. after creation of universe the sustenance aspect of the universe is to be taken care of by Yajna i.e. spirit of sacrifice (offering) of the self or self interest for the overall benefit of the universe. In the beginning, Prajapati projected the Universe as well as yajna out of self and made three important statements "i) O yajna! You may be a great blessing to all these beings; ii) may you be prosperous iii) Let this be the Kamdhenu to all of you." The spirit of sacrifice was inbuilt or integral part of the cosmic plan is clear. The yajna and the universe were projected out of self (Prajapati).

ii) *Kamdhenu* **(wish-fulfilling cow referred to in Indian mythology)** – At the time of churning of oceans by Devas (Intermediate Gods) and Demons, a cow came out. It is referred to, in Indian mythology, as the wish-fulfilling-cow. So this name "kamdhenu" is from Indian mythology. Kamdhenu, the celestial cow in heaven, is supposed to yield all enjoyments and fulfill all desires. *Prajapati* said "Let this be the *Kamdhenu* to all of you." This means that by yajna one will get whatever one wishes, as the cow *Kamdhenu* fulfils the wishes. This metaphor is used to emphasize that one should not underestimate the wish-fulfilling potential of *yajna*. Allegorically, it is that aspect of the Divinity which grants fulfillment of wishes. What Lord Krishna wants to say is simple. **Yajna is wish-fulfilling like *Kamdhenu*.** The understanding and implementation of yajna-concept has the potential to be wish-fulfilling. This is what Lord wants to say.

iii) *Sahyajna prajah srstva purovaca prajapatih* **[having projected this universe (out of self) along with yajna]** – It means that concept of yajna is as old as creation. It is the integral part of the cosmic plan, which ensures the sustainability of the universe. The universe and yajna came out of Prajapati. That means it is so important that sustainability of the whole universe is based on "yajna-concept." This aspect of this concept of yajna is reflected in the universe also. All movable or immovable species are doing something for the sustenance of the universe. Even earth worm has a role to play. Its existence is for some cosmic benefit. Even vultures have a role to play. Their existence serves a purpose. This all is to emphasize how important it is to work with concept of yajna in view. Life will serve its purpose if all our actions are in agreement with the "essentials of yajna" elaborated in the beginning.

iv) Anena prasavisyadhvam (May you prosper with the help of yajna)- The performance of acts in the spirit of yajna ensures prosperity. What does it mean? With the help of yajna one will add to the lineage i.e. increase in number. This (producing a child exclusively to add to lineage and not for indulgence) is considered sacred act. Manu underwent long tapas to gain the capacity to produce child. This sanctity of yajna in the form of adding to lineage is at variance with the western thinking. The intention is very important. Producing a child exclusively for adding to lineage and not for indulgence is yajna, a very sacred act as per ancient Indian thinking. Father and mother make the sacrifice for producing the child and thus perform a sort of yajna for cosmic expansion. The intention behind an act determines whether an act is of capturing nature or of liberating nature. An act of producing a child with yajna concept at the core becomes a spiritually liberating act. As per Indian thinking, married life (grastha ashram) is a yajna. Most of the narrators and listeners of Upnishads (ancient scriptures dealing with Truth), with few exceptions, were married rishi (advanced yogis with spiritual enlightenment). Understanding and assimilating these thoughts requires purity at the core (central part of something) within with awareness of divine consciousness or universal inter-connectedness.

v) Esa vo' istvistakamdhuk (Let this be Kamadhenu to all of you) - Lord wants to say that Yajna is a wish fulfilling concept. This is to strengthen and propagate (spread an idea) the spirit of yajna.

A society will be strong and people will be progressive, if the "Yajna-concept" becomes the core concept behind all actions. Non-attachment with the results of action, offering the activity to the Supreme and awareness of the divine consciousness along with surrender should be at the heart of every action. If an action is done with the yajna-concept at the core (central part of something) it will lose its capturing impact. Action will not cause any bondage. Every action will become spiritually up-lifting. Yajna is like *Kamdhenu* in fulfilling the material and spiritual desires of the seekers. This is the basic idea of this verse.

11. In this verse also the Lord continues the discussion about yajna.

देवान्भावयतानेन ते देवा भावयन्तु वः ।
परस्परं भावयन्तः श्रेयः परमवाप्स्यथ ॥ ३- ११ ॥

devan bhavayatanena te deva bhavayantu vah
parasparam bhavayantah sreyah param avapsyatha 3.11

devan—demigods or intermediate gods (refer to discussion in introduction); *bhavayata*— nourish (ye); *anena*—with this; *te*--those; *devah*--the demigods; *bhavayantu*—may nourish; *vah*--you; *parasparam*—mutual or one and other; *bhavayantah*--nourishing; *sreyah*-- good; *param*—the highest; *avapsyatha*—shall attain.

"May you propitiate (to make someone more friendly) the Gods with this; and may the Gods in return gratify (please and satisfy) you; thus, mutually satisfying each other, you attain the highest good." II 11 II

Lord has used the word Devas (Gods). When this term "God" is used in plural, reference is to Intermediate Gods i.e. Gods who are known by names, forms and methods of worshipping or the Gods who depend on the grace of the Supreme. When this term is used in singular, reference is to the Supreme Reality or Param Purush or the Formless Eternal Infinite Energy which alone exists either through form or without form. The Gods are the ruling powers or cosmic forces or the cosmic executives of the universe. Deva means a deity, demigod, a celestial person, the agent of god who fulfills the desires and protects. One should always remember in this context that it is the Supreme Lord who appears in the form of different Devas (shining ones) embodying the multifarious powers of the "One ruler of the Universe" i.e. with form or the Formless are the same.

Lord says that Devas (Shining ones or Gods or cosmic forces with name and form) can be pleased by yajna (sacrifice for cosmic benefit, offering of activity to the Supreme with feeling of surrender). In turn Devas also gratify the worshippers. Why is it necessary to propitiate the Devas? If the Devas (Gods with a particular name and form) are favorably disposed, all elements or rather whole nature will be conducive to the welfare and the prosperity of the worshipper. How do the Devas respond to the yajna-efforts? The concerned individual will not only attain worldly prosperity but will also be awarded the joys of heaven in terms of peace, contentment and happiness. It is important to know what it is that makes the Gods happy. It is spirit of yajna (non-attachment, cosmic benefit, offering to the deity with feeling of surrender and divine awareness). The wise seek to serve themselves in the service of others while the ignorant serve themselves at the cost of others.

Lord says "Propitiate the Gods." Is it possible to propitiate the Gods? It is a very good question. Yes one can propitiate gods. The one with form is propitiated with food and offerings. The one who lives in the heart is propitiated by the sacrifice of thoughts. The one who lives in the subtle life force is propitiated by the sacrifice of each breath with HIS thoughts. These Gods are propitiated by sacrifice of thoughts, life-breaths and intense remembering at the level of consciousness. Material offerings in Yajna are symbolic sacrifices reminiscent (which remind of) of the intensity of the feelings within. It is longing within, the restlessness at the level of prana (consciousness) for the deity and the purity in thoughts, words and deeds which finally pleases the Devas.

How does material offering in the fire of yajna satisfy the Gods? Material offerings are offered in the fire in yajna. Its exterior gets burnt but everything that is material has divinity within. Everything that exists has a divine component. The fire cannot extinguish that divinity within the material-offerings put in yajna. It is that divinity which feeds the Devas and establishes divine connectivity. It is this divinity (i.e. divinity of material offered and burnt in fire in the name of a particular God) which sanctifies (to make holy) the whole process of yajna and divinely connects the worshipper and the Devas.

The concept of yajna is in-built in the universe. 'The life-less kingdom (mountains; rocks)' sacrifices itself or destroys itself to become parts of trees and plants (or plant kingdom). Trees and plants sacrifice themselves to become parts of animal kingdom. Animals sacrifice themselves to find place inside the humans. Humans sacrifice to become devas. 'The Devas' make sacrifices to go higher in the spiritual evolution. The whole process of evolution is based on the spirit of yajna. That is why Lord asks Arjuna to propitiate the Gods through yajna concept (or fight with yajna spirit i.e. not for self indulgence but for restoring righteousness in society). The spirit of sacrifice is central to spiritual growth. A seed sacrifices or destroys its existence to bring about a blooming tree. The whole sustenance of the universe is based on this spirit of sacrifice (spirit of yajna). That is the idea of Lord Krishna.

The word used by Lord is supreme good. It may mean anything starting from heavenly pleasures to knowledge of Brahmna. It does not mean worldly happiness of transitory (existing for a short time) nature i.e. wife, wine and wealth. It means that reward or response of the Devas will not be in terms of material alone. The supreme good is that peace that happiness and that contentment which continues or lingers on even after death in the realm of uncertainty or the spiritual realm. Therefore, the supreme good may turn out in terms of Indra's Heaven with its ethereal (so delicate and light that it does not seem to be real) pleasures, meals of ambrosia (that tastes and smells extremely good) and dances with *apsaras* (celestial maidens) etc. The supreme good may also turn out in terms *Brahamn Nirvana* or eternal bliss with final freedom from bonds of birth and death.

What is the message of this verse? Helping others (not only human beings but everything living or non-living) with Yajna-concept is the best meritorious deed one can do.

12. In this verse Lord explains what happens to the individual who makes no sacrifice but appropriates everything to his or her own self.

इष्टान्भोगान्हि वो देवा दास्यन्ते यज्ञभाविताः ।
तैर्दत्तानप्रदायैभ्यो यो भुङ्क्ते स्तेन एव सः ॥ ३- १२ ॥

istan bhogan hi vo deva dasyante yajna-bhavitah
tair dattan apradayaibhyo yo bhunkte stena eva sah 3.12

istan--desired; *bhogan*- objects; *hi*—so; *vah* -- to you; *devah*--the gods; *dasyante*—will give or award; *yajna-bhavitah*- nourished by sacrifice; *taih*--by them; *dattan*—(things) given; *apradaya*--without offering; *ebhyah*--to them; *yah*--who; *bhunkte*--enjoys; *stenah*--thief; *eva*--verilyly; *sah*--is he.

"Nourished by Yajna, the Devas favor you with your cherished enjoyments; a thief is he who enjoys what is given by them without offering to them (anything in return) is a thief." II 3-12 II

The concept of yajna is based on idea of sacrifice, giving or offering with devotion for the pleasure of giving and not for return. An individual's actions become yajna in proportion to their utility to all (cosmic utility). The words used by the Lord are as follows:

i) Istan bhogan hi vo deva dasyante yajnabhavita (Nature's Devas, propitiated by offerings, will give you back desired for objects) – Lord has used a very beautiful word here "yajnabhavita; propitiated by the offerings in yajna." What is it that happens when we offer something to Devas in yajna? They get satisfied. They get disposed (approving of) towards you i.e. whenever we give something to nature (cosmic Gods; Devas), nature gives back good things. Now two points arise here. How do we give to nature? How does nature give back to us?

How do we give to nature? Nature is to us what a mother is to the child. It is our obligation to give something back to nature in whatever we do. In ancient Indian thinking a lot of importance is given to yajna. According to Hindu tradition, performance of the five Mahayajnas (five great sacrifices) is obligatory for each dwija (twice born). A day passed bereft of yajna is a day gone waste. Traditionally, we perform five types of yajnas (*Panch Maha Yajna*) to give to nature:

Dev yajna **(the worship of the Lord)** – The day starts with worship of some Deity and in that something is offered to the Deity. That is why this worship becomes a yajna. This is done devoutly and to the best of one's knowledge. In villages, it is still performed scrupulously in one form and other. It undergoes changes according to rituals, individual tastes and also the pressure of daily life especially in urban areas. The debts to *devas* (Gods i.e. rain God, sun God etc.) are traditionally discharged as per rituals in Vedas, by libation (offering wines as per local practices), by offering fruit, water and ghee along with hymns, rituals and instruments. All mantras (strings of holy words for recitation for spiritual effect), tantras (some method of worship by not very enlightened persons) and yantras (instruments) are used for this purpose.

Rishi Yajna **(the adoration of the enlightened)** – The realized souls are always adored and respected. The enlightened people do not die by death. They survive death by the work done by them in the form of scriptures and sacred books or through some other work done by them. For example a devoted study of Ramayana in a particular group in a particular spell of time is a yajna. In this yajna, expounding (talking about in detail) the scriptures with devotional attitude is the offering. Prasad (the remnants which are distributed to all after propitiating the Deity) is always there and it is offered to all. Remembering the ancestors and thinking daily holy and auspicious thoughts for the departed ancestors and serving the society with that memory is also a yajna.

Pitru Yajna (Service to the living and offerings to the ancestors)- Parents are the living Gods as per the ancient Indian thinking. A good care is to be taken of the living parents. In India, there is a period called "*Sraddhya*" when offerings are formally made in the memory of the ancestors. Our ancestors gave us the gift of life, gift of what we are, gift of our existence. We are indebted to these ancestors to pass on this legacy of passing on the gift of life strictly not for indulgence but to repay the debt of our ancestors with regards and with respectful, fond memories. This can be done in two ways. This debt to ancestors is discharged by making offerings of food and other things with memory of the departed souls of the ancestors. Secondly this debt is discharged by begetting a son (according to Indian traditions, only linearly descendent son can offer water to the departed souls). In non-traditional way, the same objective can be attained by opening hospitals for weaker sections, by starting blind schools, by constructing *Dharamshalas* (rest houses) and by establishing temples of knowledge etc.

Nara yajna (service of the mankind) – Devoted services rendered to mankind come under this yajna. The feeding of the hungry and the guests falls under this category. This should be done without expectations of any kind. If someone distributes food articles in clusters of the weaker sections and advertises this act, the whole sanctity of this act goes away. *Nar-seva* (service of man) is service to *Narayan* (Supreme Universal Eternal Reality) seva. Divinity exists in all. With this attitude and without consideration, service should be rendered for mankind "awakening the self to the divinity inherent in all." Have the experience to feed without asking an emancipated individual with big round eyes balls coming out and each bone protruding, who has not eaten for days. See the sparkle in his or her eyes when he or she looks at you after getting the hunger quenched. It will give you an awareness of what is meant by words "awakening the self to the divinity inherent in all." Debt to human beings is also discharged by performing one's duty of hospitality.

Bhuta Yajna (Rendering service to sub-human species) – This involves feeding or taking due care of sub-human species i.e. any living beings, be it animal, bird or trees. It is an old practice in Indian house hold to take something out for cow, crow, and dog. Many people start hospitals for birds and animals. Having empathy for any suffering being and doing something accordingly without expectations of any kind comes under this category.

How do devas (cosmic forces of nature) give back to us? This was the next question. Devas (cosmic forces) respond to the offerings made to them by gratifying (satisfying desire) the worshipper. Always remember that cosmic forces cannot relieve anyone from the cycles of birth and death. For that grace of Supreme Infinite Formless Reality is required. Cosmic forces (Devas including the local deities) can give you all the pleasures of life i.e. wife, children, cattle, health wealth and longevity i.e. bliss of heaven even. The response of Devas depends on your own level of spirituality. They give you or guide you if what you demand is beyond their purview (each Deva is having a particular portfolio and a certain limitation).

ii) *Tairdattan apradayaibhyo yo bhunkte* (**if you enjoy, what they have given to you without returning to them their share**) – When Gods give us the enjoyments that we seek in life, it becomes obligatory on our part to give something back in return as token of gratitude or as acknowledgement of their magnanimity. Suppose God blesses us with good rains. There is good crop. We should not forget to acknowledge the magnanimity of the God ever. What is it that happens? Lord replies in the remaining words.

iii) Stena eva sah (such a person is only a thief) – If someone does not give back what is due to nature and nature's Gods, the Gita calls such a person thief i.e. someone who steals without using violence. A thief is he who grabs everything but gives nothing. A thief is always punished. Are we not thief with regard to environment? Indiscriminate use of something without feeling gratitude and without offering something back is inappropriate and deserves to be punished. Natural calamities, water pollution are Gods' ways of responding to indiscriminate use of resources of nature. Practices of yajna i.e. "offerings to Devas back" maintain the sustainability of the universe.

What is the conclusion? No one is entitled to eat or drink (food or rain; gifts of the Gods) unless he or she has sacrificed something to the bhutas (beings), pitris (ancestors), rishis (enlightened persons like Tulsidass) and Devas. It can be a sacrifice of wealth, knowledge, comfort or labor. Non-traditionally, offering mentally our strengths, perfection, limitations to the Gods earnestly and consistently is also yajna. Making our selves instruments of HIS graciousness to the world is also yajna. Spending time in thinking of the Gods earnestly and feeling happy and grateful to the Gods consistently for their grace is also yajna. "Sharing divine knowledge, divine sports and divine actions with due devotion and without expectation" is yajna. Yajna is not necessarily an action. Yajna is an attitude of accepting the favor with gratitude and reciprocating it with magnanimity with celebration with awareness of the connectivity with the Gods at the level of consciousness. True performance of Yajna will essentially culminate in joy within due to its sanctity. Yagna-conept will make you feel "inactivity" in activity. If someone does not perform yajna even after getting all enjoyments, favor of nature, he or she is, as per the Gita, a thief of the property of God (The Supreme).

13. In this verse, Lord tells Arjuna how performance of yajna washes away sins. Then HE informs the plight of those who do not perform yajna in life.

यज्ञशिष्टाशिनः सन्तो मुच्यन्ते सर्वकिल्बिषैः ।
भुञ्जते ते त्वघं पापा ये पचन्त्यात्मकारणात् ॥ ३- १३ ॥

yajna-sistasinah santo mucyante sarva-kilbisaih
bhunjate te tv agham papa ye pacanty atma-karanat 3.13

yajna-sista- asinah —who eat the remnants of the sacrifice; *santah*--the righteous; *mucyante*—are freed; *sarva--kilbisaih*-from all sins; *bhunjate*-- eat; *te*--those; *tu*--indeed; *agham*-- sins; *papah*—sinful ones; *ye*-- who; *pacanti*-- cook; *atma-karanat*--for their own sake.

"The righteous individuals, who eat the remnants of the sacrifice, are freed from all sins; but those sinful ones who cook food for their own sake verily eat sin." II 3-13 II

The remnants (the leftover after distribution) of a sacrifice (yajna) are termed *amrita* or nectar. The one who takes it becomes immortal. The sustenance of this whole creation is based on the concept of yajna [without attachment; for cosmic benefit; offering to the Supreme (or the particularly mentioned deity) with awareness of divine consciousness]. By self-sacrifice and by self denial (state of ego-less-ness), one evolves to the state of Divinity. The Divine state is a state of perfect selflessness. Spirituality is a march from selfishness to selflessness. The righteous partake (eat or drink) the remnants of yajna and earn merit for spiritual evolution. The words used by the Lord are as follows:

i) **Yajnasista (remnants of yajna or Prasad, holy food)** – Whatever we eat after a *yajna* i.e. after having propitiated (making someone friendly) the *Devas* is called *yajnasista* i.e. remnants of *yajna* or Prasad. Prasad is holy food i.e. leftover after having served the God or Gods. This thinking holds well in universe and equally in society. In society we have to pay tax and whatever remains is there for us to enjoy legitimately.

ii) **Kilbisha (sin or evil)** – What is a sin or an evil? That, which causes mortification, suffering and suffocation to the deluded-self or individualized self (Exclusive Divinity always remains the same full of bliss, peace and knowledge), is sin. Sin is that which breaks the laid down time-tested most sacred rules of the society and results in extinguishing the life in any form. Life in any form is the light of the Supreme and its extinction, if not for establishing righteousness, is a sin, moral and ethical end of a being. This is not all. The sin is that which causes shaking movement in the deluded-soul (or individualized) self and creates doubt in the mind of perpetrator right at the first stage. There is some component of divinity even in the impure as well. The purity within the perpetrator cries, gives the warning signals in the form of subdued mute intense concern, finds itself in sinking doubts right at the first stage of combat of purity within and the sinful act. Call of the conscience becomes feeble as the perpetrator of the sin continues with the crimes. This is being emphasized to bring round a very important message. Each one of us inadvertently becomes a sinner in any of the following manner:

a) fire-place – Many living beings (small almost invisible insects) may die in fire place without our knowledge. This is especially true in villages.

b) Water – pot – Many living beings may die near the water pots especially earthen pots in the villages.

c) Cutting machine may be responsible for death of many insects.

d) Grinding apparatus may also take life of insects.

e) Brooms are daily used in the morning and many insects may die in the process of using the broom.

Each one of us might have extinguished life inadvertently many times. While adding to lineage of ancestors (not for indulgence) is taken a yajna, extinguishing life is taken a sin. Each one of us should do yajna because even without intention we commit sins in daily life.

iii) yajnasistasinha santo mucyante sarva kilbhisaih (the good people, living on the remnants of yajna, are freed from all sins) – The good people who eat what is left after offering the sacrifice in yajna are released of all sins. How is it? All the sins get washed away by the five sacrifices: i.e. to Gods, to departed souls, to humans, to creatures and to rishis (enlightened yogis). These five sacrifices have been mentioned as *maha yajnas* in *Smiriti* (ancient scriptures) and as nitya karmas (based on eligibility criteria) in Vedas. These sacrifices exert releasing effect and relieve the seeker from the daily sins that might have got committed unknowingly now or in past. In brief, Yajna is the only way to get rid of the impressions of past karmas, which are the causes of present and future sufferings. The one who truly acts based on the yajna-concept i.e. without attachment of rewards of action and offering strictly for benefit of universe stands like rock in the sea (in this world) immovable by the stormy waves (capturing effect of the impressions of past karmas), which threateningly strike and move away for good leaving the rock in the sea majestically standing as the glory of the Lord.

iv) *Bhujante te tvagham papa ye pacantyatmakaranat* (but those sinful ones who cook only for themselves verily only eat sin) Lord has already stated that the sustenance of whole universe is based on the concept of sacrifice (yajna). This principle (concept of Yajna, offering to others or at least sharing with others without expectation or return of any kind) is the will of the God or Gods. Life is a gift of God, an expanse of divine magnanimity, an opportunity for self redemption. 'Divinity within' manifests its fullness only by living life in accordance to the principle of yajna i.e. a life of sacrifice, a life of sharing and caring for others, for humans, for plants for animals for environment (i.e. every action except the obligatory actions for self existence should be for a divine purpose). Those who cook for themselves alone and confine to "I, my and mine i.e. remain ego-centric," verily eat sin i.e. they will remain confined to cycles of birth and death only. The word used by Lord is sin i.e. they do something against the divine will, against the law of nature, against the commandment of the Supreme. They will not get liberation (mukti) from the individualized self. They will remain confined to this world of miseries, dualities and suffering descending further in hierarchy (system) of spiritual evolution. That is the meaning of using the word sin here.

There are certain noticeable points in this verse. i) The one who takes yajnasista (remnants of *yajna* or *Prasad* i.e. holy food available after propitiating the God or Gods) has been called a *sant* i.e. a righteous person; ii) When basic concept of yajna becomes a way of life i.e. every action, except obligatory action like taking food for bare sustenance, becomes a yajna and whatever one eats becomes yajnasista. That is how one should lead life; iii) Yajna-concept of living relieves a seeker of desires. When the entire time one is serving or thinking of the God or Gods, one remains so contended that desires (wants or hopes for something for self-satisfaction only) do not pollute the mind. One gradually starts becoming an instrument of spreading divine grace; iv) If one cooks only for self-satisfaction, the action is no more a worship of the Lord. Action loses sanctity of yajna; and v) cosmic benefit and offering for the Lord are two major components of this concept of yajna. By this small change of attitude, action in life becomes sanctified like fruit offered to the Supreme with devotion.

There is a profound wisdom underlying the statement of the Lord in this verse. Basically there are only two points. The good eat the remnants of Prasad (holy meal for distribution after propitiating the lord). The ones who are self centered or ego-centric eat sin. Lord's emphasis is on doing yajna. Yajna means no attachment with fruit of action and offering to divine with spirit of surrender. In other words lord is emphasizing "establishing connectivity' with the God or Gods through the medium of action. It further means that at the point of doing yajna duality exists (i.e. worshipper and worshipped). In a way, by enlivening us to the spirit of yajna, Lord has guided us towards path of salvation. River has started flowing towards sea. Gradually, the seeker is blessed with the divine knowledge. At later stage the seeker realizes that that separate existence is a myth. Lord alone exits. This is the highest point of self realization. This establishes that action can be a medium of self realization. This is the underlying message of the Lord. This also establishes that all activities can be converted into yajna by the knowing ones. Even the Christian habit of saying grace before partaking of food comes from the same fundamental belief or yajna-concept.

14 & 15. In the next two verses Lord explains the cycle i.e. how yajna can take an individual to the highest good i.e. the highest state of achievement or self-realization or attainment of moksha (liberation).

अन्नाद्भवन्ति भूतानि पर्जन्यादन्नसम्भवः ।
यज्ञाद्भवति पर्जन्यो यज्ञः कर्मसमुद्भवः ॥ ३- १४ ॥

annad bhavanti bhutani parjanyad anna-sambhavah
yajnad bhavati parjanyo yajnah karma-samudbhavah 3.14

annat--from food; *bhavanti*—come forth; *bhutani*—beings or the material bodies; *parjanyat*--from rains; *anna--sambhavah*—production of food grains; *yajnat*--from sacrifice; *bhavati*-- arises; *parjanyah*--rains; *yajnah*—sacrifice; *karma-- samudbhavah*—born of action.

कर्म ब्रह्मोद्भवं विद्धि ब्रह्माक्षरसमुद्भवम् ।
तस्मात्सर्वगतं ब्रह्म नित्यं यज्ञे प्रतिष्ठितम् ॥ ३- १५ ॥

karma brahmodbhavam viddhi brahmaksara-samudbhavam
tasmat sarva-gatam brahma nityam yajne pratisthitam 3.15

karma-- action; *brahma--udbhavam*—arises from the Supreme; *viddhi*--know; *brahma*—the Supreme; *aksara--samudbhavam*—arises from the Imperishable; *tasmat*--therefore; *sarva-gatam*--all-pervading; *brahma*—the Supreme; *nityam*-- ever; *yajne*--in sacrifice; *pratisthitam*—(is) established.

"The living beings are born from food grains; grains are produced by rain; from yajna arises rain; and yajna is born of karma or action." II 3-14 II

"Know karma to have arisen from Vedas; and Vedas from the "Imperishable"; Therefore **Sarvagatam Brahmn** (All Pervading Indestructible Reality) is ever present in Yajna." II 3-15 II

These two verses wonderfully describe the cycle of yajna, i.e. how and why the phenomenon of yajna sanctifies the action from mediocrity to the highest achievement, in the following words:

i) ***Annat bhavati bhutani* (all beings are evolved from food)** - The word food (anna) has been used here in comprehensive sense. It refers to all types of gross and subtle articles of food, which go to nourish the bodies of different beings. The words "all beings are evolved from food" means that food when consumed, digested and assimilated gradually get transformed into sperm and ovum etc. from whose combination all types of beings take birth. It is food again that nourishes the body of beings after birth. This is how all beings are evolved from food i.e. food is cause of birth, growth and nourishment of all beings. Sruti (ancient Indian scripture or the recorded message of the Divine) says "It is from food that these beings take their birth and it is food again on which they live after being born."

ii) ***Parjanyat annasambhavah* (food is produced from rain)** - Production of food depends on water and water comes from rain. This is the meaning of the words "production of food is dependent on rain." How does it come to be? An activity done with right frame of mind gets transformed into yajna. The effect of work which has gone into performing a yajna assumes a "**subtle force**" which in Vedic parlance is called "*apurve.*" The sun converts sea water into vapor. Similarly, rubbish consigned to fire changes itself into carbon dioxide. The force behind all this is called "apurve." Due to "Apurve" plants get food assimilated through leaves. On the same lines, mental force of an individual in yajna is "apurve." The syllables in a mantra (strings of holy words) do not by themselves become Mantra. It is the intensity of thought (deeper pulsations and exhortation) and feeling i.e. "apurve" which becomes a mental force. This is mental force, which finally influences and regulates even the rain fall and the production process in both animal kingdom and plant kingdom. Thus production of grains for food depends on the availability of water caused by rain. This is the meaning of the words " …from rain is food produced." Lord wants to convey that "rightly pursued collective yajna" assumes far greater dimensions. The focus is on the point that there is a definite linkage between the yajna and the rainfall.

iii) ***Yajnad bhavati parjanyo* (rainfall originates from yajna)** – The yajna (sacrifices) or the merit called "apurva," in Vedas parlance, results in rain. Sun rays fall on the sea (a yajna) and vapors are formed, which result into rain. Evaporation of water takes place regularly and formation of cloud is also regular. It is sacrifice somewhere which results into rain. **This unseen, unexplainable definite force behind this phenomenon has been called "Apurve" in Vedas.** There is no doubt about it. *Kairiri* and *Agnihotras* (yajnas, mentioned in karam-kand of Vedas) have long been performed for rains. *Maha Rishi Valmiki*, the author of Ramayana, has vouchsafed (to tell as a privilege) something relevant in this matter. Dandkarnya was a huge desert. When rishi (enlightened yogi) Agastya saw this place, he was moved by its plight. He decided to remain there plunged into his fond austerities. The spiritual vibrations found their response from the sky above. Clouds collected all around and there was a continuous downpour. The whole region became lush green with plants and trees. How is it possible? One wonders. Every form of life in universe is a definite combination of sentient (which feels things through senses) spirit and insentient (which does not feel things through the senses) matter. Sentient spirit exerts its influence on the insentient matter to make it vibrant and creative (apurve, merit of yajna). Immense sincerity and purity is required for all this. By this example of Maharishi Agastya, Valmiki has tried to enlighten the readers to exhort them to seek intervention of subtle higher forces to redress (correct or make fair again) when gross lower nature fails or proves inadequate. There is a definite linkage between the sublimity (high quality causing admiration) of yajna and the cloud formation resulting in rain. The act of yajna exerts influence on the environment. ***Astdhyayi-Kand (Satapada Brahamana)*** in the section containing six questions in the form of dialogue between *Janaka* and *Yajnavakalkya* (Brhadaranyaka Upnishad; chapter four) contains a detailed discussion on how Agnihotra-sacrifice becomes originator of rain. That yajna (sacrifice) results in rain fall is not a matter of understanding by intellect. With intensity of thought-waves and internal purity at soul level (i.e. without clatter of past karmas and burdens of future) one can definitely exercise influence on subtle forces at work in nature. This is a science or art or proficiency of being able to connect the sentient (which can feel) and the insentient (which cannot feel)]. This proficiency has almost become practically lost these days. Yajna was an essential part of daily life those days in *Traita Yuga* and also in *Dvapur Yuga*.

iv) *Yajna Karma Samudbhavan* (*Yajna* is product of *Karma*) - *Yajna* means an action which has been done for cosmic benefit i.e. for the welfare of all around you. In earlier discussion there was a reference to the word "*Apurva*" from Veda terminology. It means the unseen, connecting link which the sacrifice (yajna) takes between the time of performance and the time when the result get manifested. This "*Apurva*; the unseen force; this immediately unexplainable merit of yajna resulting in rain" is the result of activities of one who performs sacrifice (yajna) and the priests engaged in the Yajna. No yajna can be performed without some amount of physical mental activity. Even scriptures have emphatically laid down that no *yajna* can be accomplished without action. This is to emphasize that intensity of thought-waves and purity alone are not enough to perform a yajna. Yajna is a product of action (physical or mental).

v) *Karma Brahmodbhavam vidhi* [**know karma to have arisen from Brahmn** (means Vedas here)] - Action is born from Vedas (the Vedas are the voices of the sages who transcended their consciousness beyond human understanding and experience to live in God). Word "Brahmn" has been used differently in different contexts i.e. for God, for Prakriti, for the creator (Cosmic Force responsible for the function of creation, for Vedas). Here it has been used for Vedas because, immediately after this, Lord says that Brahmn proceeds from Indestructible Infinite Reality (Supreme Self).

vi) Brahmn aksarasamudbhavan [Vedas (Brahmn) are born of Imperishable Parmatama (Universal Eternal Infinite Reality] – It is finally the "The Supreme Universal Eternal Formless Reality" which is underlying all manifestations in all forms. The Supreme is indestructible. It is the cause of all knowledge in the form of Vedas.

vii) *Tasmat Sarvagatam Brahama nityam yajne pratisthitam* (Therefore know that Supreme Universal Eternal Reality is always established in yajna) - This statement of the Lord supports the view that "All Pervading Reality" is always present whenever a yajna is performed. The "*Apurva*; the unseen and unexplainable force" which is responsible for food and rain evidences that wherever sacrifices are there for the cosmic benefit with thoughts of the Divine, the "The Eternal Presence" is there. What is the purpose of this statement? Lord wants Arjuna (to fight for righteousness) and all to do action with *yajna-thoughts* in view. While ordinary actions are of binding nature, the actions done with *yajna-spirit* are of releasing nature.

Thus Lord in this verse has explained the **"Dharma- Chakra**; Cycle of Righteousness" i.e. from Brahmn to Veda, from Veda to Karma (i.e. those actions which have been sanctioned by Vedas or those actions whose righteousness cannot be in doubt) and from Karma to *Yajna*. This way or that way, Lord is coming to the same "Truth" time and again in different words and different modes. There is some Divinity (that which is indestructible and eternal is divine) in all and thus every act is in some way or the other linked to divinity. One understands this "secret," when one knows the term "Sarvagatam." That is why Lord has laid emphasis on using the word "Sarvagatam i.e. the one who is all-pervading." All actions, except obligatory actions for self-sustenance should be done with *yajna spirit* knowing that "Sarvagatam; All-Pervading" is already there. The Gita is coming to this fundamental fact time and again. Do not ever let go the awareness of that "Divine Connectivity within." Then do the work with *yajna-spirit* for *lokasangraha* (cosmic benefit). This is the surest way to be entitled for spiritual evolution. For everything some price is to be paid. **Yajna is the price that we all must pay for spiritual evolution.** The life itself becomes a yajna when it is directed to the service of the Divine. Do not ever entertain the doubts. The *"Sarvagatam- All pervading"* remains established in *yajna-spirit* i.e. offering in the name of the Divine for service of all. What does the normal man do? A normal individual does for all, whom he or she belongs to by blood and relations. **Lord wants us to bring about slight change in the approach.** "Sarvagatam- All Pervading" is there everywhere. If this meaning is assimilated (fully understood to be able to use), then everything, the whole world (flowers, plants, animals, mountains and all humans) will appear to be our very own, genuinely related to us from "Father's (Supreme's) point of view." **"Essence of universal oneness" is naturally born.** Each living being or even insentient (not able to feel with senses) being has the same "Ultimate Source." With *"Sarvagatam; All Pervading"* in our thoughts, we will gain new perspective of this world and all our actions will imbibe (absorb) the *Yajna-spirit*. Then in everything the *"Sarvagatam- All Pervading"* will cast off the veil of ignorance to bare (uncover) the reality to the seeker as a revelation of "Supreme Joy." Then, with each *yajna-effort* a cosmic force will lift us up smilingly in our spiritual evolution.

16. The Lord talks of "Dharam- Chakra; Cycle of Righteousness; Brahma-Veda-Yajna" in previous verse. In this verse, Lord explains what happens when this cycle is ignored.

एवं प्रवर्तितं चक्रं नानुवर्तयतीह यः ।
अघायुरिन्द्रियारामो मोघं पार्थ स जीवति ॥ ३- १६ ॥

evam pravartitam cakram nanuvartayatiha yah
aghayur indriyaramo mogham partha sa jivati 3.16

evam--thus; *pravartitam*—set revolving ; *cakram*--cycle; *na*-- not; *anuvartayati*-- follows; *iha*--here; *yah*--who; *agha-ayuh*—living in sins; *indriya-aramah*—rejoicing in the senses; *mogham*—in vain; *partha*--O son of Prtha (Arjuna); *sah*-- he; *jivati*--lives.

"O Parth (Arjuna)! the One who does not work in accordance with universal scheme of things (Dharm Chakra; Brahama – Veda- Yajna" is living the life of a sin and being delighted in the senses, he or she lives in vain." II 3-16 II

Lord has already pointed out in the earlier discussion that "concept of yajna" is inbuilt in universal scheme of things for sustenance of the universe. Life i.e. manifestation of Divinity in form, means some action in one form or the other. Life manifests itself in action whether it is for mere sustenance or for preparing for release from cycle of birth and death, the highest aim for human existence. Voluntary action for sacrifice (life of caring, sharing and life of self giving in the form of divine knowledge or through self-less action as service to Lord) with focus on the welfare of universe (as an offering to divine) becomes a yajna, an activity releasing from all limitations and up-lifting in spiritual pursuit. Life confined to "I, my and mine; i.e. ego-centric" or life spent for sense pleasures in eating, drinking, earning and begetting is life of sin i.e. a life which enforces rebirth (sin is that which causes unmatched, emotional upheaval at the level of awareness, which robs individual of divine serenity and necessitates rebirth; sin inevitably results in restlessness or in hankering for peace at the level of awareness). For this reason, the self-centered life of a materialist has been condemned in strongest way in this verse as follows:

i) *evam parvartitam cakram na anuvartayati iha yaha* [**The one who does not follow here (on earth) the wheel thus revolving**] - Lord here again refers to the chakra (Dharam-cakra; Brahma-Veda-Karma- yajna; Cycle of universal interconnectedness). In this universe everything is interconnected with that "Unseen Essence" called "Sarvagatam; All-Pervading" in the previous verse. The whole universe is interwoven with the spirit of sacrifice. A seed sacrifices for flowers, plants and crops. Sustenance of universe is dependent on yajna (sacrifice). Voluntary efforts to forgo self interest and to do something for common welfare is yajna i.e. an act without attachment for the fruit thereof, for cosmic benefit or an act done as an offering to the divine in the spirit of surrender. Efforts made, merely for eating, drinking, earning and begetting, make life one-sided, selfish, self-capturing and self-enslaving exercise of giving oneself to death for rebirth. It is the attitude that makes a difference. Same acts can be a yajna (self releasing, spiritually up-lifting) in one situation and spiritually self-capturing in the other situation. For example an individual is blessed with a son. Child is brought up with a lot of love and care. Now the son grows up and is blessed with a son and in the old age the individual is still suffering and getting worried and extremely tied down with the uncertainty associated with the new born child. Bringing up the son means repaying debt. In terms of ancient thinking, we are repaying for effect of past karmas and past associations. It is not an act of yajna. Getting tied down and feeling helpless in old age with the uncertainties of son's son is like tying ourselves to the cycle of birth and death and not utilizing the opportunity of human birth for obtaining release from cycle of birth and death. On the other hand, the individual brings up his own son making him a responsible individual and at the same time takes on the responsibility to bring up an orphan making him also responsible citizen and whenever individual gets recess he actively remains busy with the responsibility of taking care of weaker sections of society, philanthropic projects [i.e. projects of, *seva (service), sadhna (preparing the self for divine grace through yoga), satsang, svadhyaya,* self-introspection and meditation). The life in the first case will be self-capturing i.e. the individual will remain tied down with cycle of birth and death and in the second case the life will be self-releasing and spiritually up-lifting, a yajna. The idea is that the individual should not remain confined to merely eating, drinking, earning and begetting. Even an animal does the same. After having been born as humans, we are duty-bound to spend life, after doing obligatory work, for cosmic benefit, for protection of environment for social awareness. Those who are actively alive to social responsibility and to the Lord's creation are aware of social inter-connectedness. They are preparing for life beyond limitations. They are aware of the universal chakra, mentioned by Lord Krishna. They are investing life spiritually and those who are self-centered are spending life to remain tied down to cycles of birth and death. They are postponing for preparing for redemption in the life to come. "**Being conscious of universal Chakra**" is equivalent to being aware of our "**Universal Inter-Connectedness.**" Awareness will automatically guide us towards activities of spiritual promise and growth.

ii) *Aghayuh Indriyaramoh mogham Parth sa jivati* [**(such a person) lives a life of sin and being delighted in the senses, O son of Pratha! – he or she lives in vain**] - In these words, Lord sheds light on the life of an individual who ignores the Dharam Chakra. Such an individual lives the life of sin or evil. Ayuh means life. Agha means sin or evil. Sin means doing something immoral which ties down the individual to cycle of birth and death. Sin necessitates future life to undergo the impact of having committed the sin. This is based on the universal principle as we sow so shall we reap. It cannot be otherwise. The precious opportunity of human life for doing something for *Moksha* (liberation from all limitations) goes waste. Such a person becomes *indriyarama* i.e. one who delights only in sense-pleasures. They remain always after fleeting pleasures, which delight only for a short time. Their life is not useful (spiritually) for themselves or to others. Their lives become waste spiritually. They live life like animals, reptiles, worms and germs, a life of routine existence devoid of spiritual worth. Lord has used the term *moghum* (in vain). They live a meaningless life, a life bereft of spiritual significance. Human birth is a chance to get rid of cycle of birth and death. It is in human birth only that an individual can prepare for life to come. This awareness for life to come is missing in animals, plants and in individual living routine life of sense pleasures. Those, committed to sense pleasures only, lead life like beasts of burden, shocked by wail of woes, of misery, of degradation, of child-birth. Time passes, death urges, knells (death knell) call, hell threatens but those committed to sense pleasures do nothing to justify their human birth for spiritual development.

What is the message of this verse? For spiritual elevation, it will be necessary to change the direction of flow of life i.e. from sense pleasures to divine bliss. A change of attitude is necessary to make life spiritually worthwhile. When an individual refuses to be a part of the divine scheme of things (or individual ignores the "yajna-concept" dominating the sustenance of the universe), **he or she becomes a discordant note (or out of tune) in the divine symphony**. Human being must realize the "Universal Interconnectedness" to play individual role in the universal scheme of things. If this objective of human life is not achieved, life becomes a waste or life becomes an opportunity lost. Then individual will always miss the eternal love, the highest bliss that an individual can attain to. It is through this eternal love alone that an individual will truly know that he or she is more than just himself or herself and that he or she is one with all. That is the purpose of giving reference to Daram-Chakra in this verse.

The Gita puts in one category the hypocrites, the thieves and the parasites. One thing is common in them all. They do not want to work. They just consume life (divine favor) given to them and do not utilize the chance for spiritual evolvement by use of "**yajna-concept; exclusive giving spirit**" with or without limitations." Lord is guiding towards coming in action mode with "yajna-concept" i.e. offering with full dedication for the "**right to live to uplift spiritually**" in this great fair and celebration called "human life."

17. In this verse Lord extols (praises very much) the self-knower and the self-knowledge. In other words Lord is bringing out clearly what one should do.

यस्त्वात्मरतिरेव स्यादात्मतृप्तश्च मानवः ।
आत्मन्येव च सन्तुष्टस्तस्य कार्यं न विद्यते ॥ ३- १७ ॥

yas tv atma-ratir eva syad atma-trptas ca manavah
atmany eva ca santustas tasya karyam na vidyate 3.17

yah--who; *tu*--but; *atma-ratih*—rejoices in the self; *eva*--only; *syat*—may be; *atma-trptah*—satisfied in the self; *ca*--and; *manavah*--a man; *atmani*--in the self; *eva*--only; *ca*--and; *santustah*-- contended; *tasya*--his; *karyam*-work to be done; *na*-- not; *vidyate*-- is.

"But the individual who rejoices in the self, who is satisfied with the self and who is contended in the self - for such an individual verily (really) there is no obligatory duty" II 3-17 II

The meaning of this verse will be easy to understand if one fundamental fact is kept in view. Each being has got two components i.e prakriti (nature; five primordial elements, three gunas and known and unknown laws of nature) and soul (Divinity covered in the veil of ignorance). Prakriti is restless. Our mind in reality is a phase of nature. It is always active. So many thoughts are going on in mind all the time. Mind has got one peculiarity. When it is busy with the external world, it is always busy with activities. Its activities increase. When mind focuses on the self (Divinity within), its activities automatically diminish. When it persistently goes on pursuing self, it gets established in the self. Self is action-less. Self is reservoir of bliss knowledge and consciousness. When mind reaches self and gets established there, it reaches the state of absolute completion. The river meets the sea. There is no movement of the river after it merges in the sea. The one who knows the *Brahmn* (the Supreme), the Truth, The all-conscious, and the infinite as hidden in the soul, enjoys all objects of desire in union with the all-knowing Brahmn (the Supreme). The resting of the mind in the self is the finale of all activities. The Lord gives this knowledge in the following words:

i) *Yastu atmaratireva syat atmatrptasca manavah atman yeva ca santustah* (But the individual who rejoices in the atman, who is contended in the atman and who finds joy in atma alone …) – Lord is talking about the individual who "atmaratireva syat" rejoices in the self. How does it happen? That "divine essence" within the soul of all of us, is actually joy unlimited, knowledge unlimited and consciousness unlimited. It is peculiar characteristic of that divine essence that even its small fraction is equal to its whole and whole remains whole even when a part is taken out of it. That divine content within is ocean of joy. "Getting connected" with that divine component within means being in the ocean of joy. *Rati* in Sanskrit actually means sex delight. But sex delight cannot match the ever continuing, immensely satisfying and suffusing (spread all over and through) experience of divine bliss. Taittiriya Upnishad says "all types of human pleasures are only a fraction of "atmananda; bliss of *atman*." The second word used by Lord is "atmatrptasca manavah." It means that the human, being referred here, remains contended or satisfied. One cannot be in touch with the divinity without being pure to the highest degree physically, mentally and emotionally. After having achieved so much of purity one feels contented with in soul (*atma*). The third word used by the Lord is "atmanyeva ca santustah" i.e. one finds delight in *atman* only. Use of these three words emphasizes the self-knowledge. The Upnishads say "Know thou the soul; it is the bridge leading to immortal being."

ii) **tasya karyam na vidyate** (he or she has no obligatory duties to perform) – The seeker of the self is not to seek anything from the world outside. When one realizes the atman (soul), mind does not go out for sensory satisfaction. There is no action as there is no desire. We do actions only after getting impelled by desires.

What is the message of this verse? An individual has no duty to be performed if that individual has attained fulfillment, contentment and joy within. How does it happen? All our egoistic impulses, all our selfish desires obscure our true vision of the soul. When we are conscious of the soul, we perceive the inner being that transcends our ego. It helps us to gain deeper affinity with the "All." When focus is on the inner self, our imperfections (in the forms of desires, doubts, dualities and limitations) recede (move away from us), human soul transcends the limit of the self reaching across the threshold of the Infinite, where fulfillment, contentment, joy and knowledge eternally overflow. What is the reason? Lord was talking about Yajna and actions and then immediately changed the discussion to focus on the self. What is the central message? Know your own soul. Be connected and established in the self. Then you will realize the "one great principle of unity" that there is in every man. Thereafter, there is no work that needs to be done by you. Every action will become a yajna and individual will assimilate (understand so much that you can use it) the meaning of eternal love. If the focus is on the divine self within, action will itself be taken care of. Lord is talking about something which transforms an individual completely. By changing the discussion from yajna to self, Lord is telling us how we should live life. What is our sequence? Normally we do (act) and then think about self and God as well. What will happen if we get established in the self first? It is the greatest worship. Be connected with the self. Be happy in the self. Be established in the self. Then whatever we do will become a yajna. Action will lose its sting. There is no duty thereafter. Life will become a medium of spreading divine fragrance within through action. The self-knowledge, self-contentment and joy-in-self manifest an individual's inward enrichment and sublimation.

When an individual is satisfied with the employment of the self in the self, the individual feels contended. Then one ceases to return constantly to own desires. The self-offering (application of yajna –concept) grows more and more intense. Then there is completion. Then there is joy and awakened powers cry for "unlimited fulfillment" even in animal, plant, leaf, flower, fruit and just everything.

18. Now a thought may come to the mind why an individual should think of getting established in the self. Lord elaborately answers this question in this verse.

नैव तस्य कृतेनार्थो नाकृतेनेह कश्चन ।
न चास्य सर्वभूतेषु कश्चिदर्थव्यपाश्रयः ॥ ३- १८ ॥

naiva tasya krtenartho nakrteneha kascana
na casya sarva-bhutesu kascid artha-vyapasrayah 3.18

na--not; *eva*--even; *tasya*--his; *krtena*—by action; *arthah*-- concern; *na*--not; *akrtena*—by action not done; *iha*-- here; *kascana*-- any; *na*--not; *ca*--and; *asya*--of this man; *sarva-bhutesu*--in all beings; *kascit*--any; *artha-vyapasrayah*—depending for any object.

"Such an individual has no object to gain in this world by doing an action; nor is there any loss by not doing an action; nor has he to depend on anybody for anything." II 3-18 II

We all pass through different phases in life. When we are children the key words that we hear are "Work hard; achieve something; make your place in life." Children respond to these calls by earning money and achieving different targets in life. Is earning and achieving targets all in life? Carl Jung of Zurich says "Whoever carries over into the afternoon law of morning i.e. whoever goes against the law of nature must pay for so doing with damages to the soul." Achievement is great but personality enrichment, in terms of ever continuing joy at the level of consciousness, is greater than that. It is very important to serve the purpose of human existence. This message has been passed on by the Lord in the following words:

i) **Naiva tasya krtenartho na akrtenaha kascana** (neither by doing nor by non-doing he or she is going to gain anything) – Based on the discussion in verse 17, the reference here is to an individual who is delighted, satisfied and established in atma (soul) alone. In such an individual there can be no feeling of any kind of want or absence. "Doing and not doing" lose relevance for such an individual. What does this mean? "Doing" means satisfying a desire. Such an individual goes beyond desires. He or She concentrates on self-enrichment, self-sublimation i.e. Brahamavastha or Brahama-jnana (divine knowledge about the self). For this reason doing loses relevance for such an individual. Such an individual loses relevance for inactivity also. How is it? Inactivity is degrading (physically and mentally) for an ordinary individual. For such an individual even inactivity is irrelevant. He or she remains inactive only physically. His or her mind is all the time absorbed in divine thoughts which are inspiring and energy-generating. Such an individual sees inaction in action and action in inaction. This is an advanced state of self-absorption. Such an individual is very clear in thinking. Everything for which one has to depend on others leads to sorrow. Everything that depends on oneself alone leads to happiness. The Budha said in dying breath "Do not depend on others. Seek no other refuge than yourself."

ii) na ca sya sarvabhutesu kascid arthavyapasrayah (nor has he to depend on anybody for anything) – The discussion is about the individual who knows self, who revels in self and who remains established in the self. Such an individual become Brahma-jnani (knower of Truth). Such and individual has nothing to seek from anybody, be it individual or one of the Gods. Such an individual exists only in the peace of the Supreme self and in the divine bliss. The liberated individual has nothing to gain by action and nothing to gain by inaction as well. Such an individual does not make his or her choice based on personal objects. The realization of the *Parmataman* (Supreme Soul) within our *antaratman*, our inner individual soul, is a state of absolute completion. There is a very good message in these lines. We all have deep within us "that" where time and space cease to rule and where links of the evolution are merged into unity. Lord is referring us to that "island of tranquility ' within each of us. After reaching that space within us, there remains no need to depend on anyone for anything. Reaching "that space within us" is the epitome of spiritual journey. Reaching "That Space" within us, one attains *Brahmavasta* or state of *Brahmn-jnani*. Action and inaction lose their relevance for such an individual. That is the focus of the Lord here. Key to cosmic-consciousness and God- consciousness is in consciousness of the soul. Such an individual takes rebirth from blind envelopment in the self to the freedom in soul-life. A liberated individual has nothing to gain from either action or inaction. The choices of a liberated individual are not based on personal objects. A liberated individual has no one to depend on except the "self or Truth" within and remains satisfied in the self alone.

19. Lord has told Arjuna about yajna and self-realization in earlier discussion. Now Lord commands Arjuna to work without attachment.

तस्मादसक्तः सततं कार्यं कर्म समाचर ।
असक्तो ह्याचरन्कर्म परमाप्नोति पूरुषः ॥ ३- १९ ॥

tasmad asaktah satatam karyam karma samacara
asakto hy acaran karma param apnoti purusah 3.19

tasmat--therefore; *asaktah*--without attachment; *satatam*-- always; *karyam*—which should be done; *karma*- action ; *samacara*--perform; *asaktah*—without attachment; *hi*-- because; *acaran*--performing; *karma*-- action; *param*--the Supreme; *apnoti*-- attains; *purusah*—man.

"Therefore, that work which should be done, do it always without attachment; one who acts without attachment will attain the highest." II 3-19 II

Lord has told Arjuna about yajna and divine knowledge. Now lord exhorts him in following words:

i) *Tasmat asktah satatam karyam karm samacara* (**Therefore, without attachment perform the work that has to be done**) - It is clear from the previous discussion that nature forces an individual to do action. Inaction ordinarily is degrading physically and mentally. Inaction loses its relevance only for those who have developed a particular level of spiritual maturity. Those who have achieved a particular level of spiritual maturity are entitled for mendicant's life for the barest necessities of life.

These people have nothing else to do than resort to devotion for self knowledge. Arjuna is not in that category. He is a warrior. For this reason Lord exhorts Arjuna to work.

For work, two primary conditions must be satisfied i) work should be done without attachment ii) work should be done as prescribed by *sastras* (scriptures) i.e. work should be done taking into consideration varna (categorization based on *gunas*), age, *lokasnagraha* (cosmic benefit) or *sarvabhutahita* (for common good. One should do *nishkam-karma* (action without attachment). Therefore Lord exhorts Arjuna to work always as *karam-yogi* (one adept in *Karam-yoga*) without attachment.

ii) asakto hy acarankarma param apnoti purusah (by performing action without attachment a human being obtains the Supreme) – One who performs action in spirit of detachment will achieve the highest realization in this life itself. This is the main teaching of the Gita. One should do whatever one has to do in life with detachment (without focus on the reward) with zest and devotion. Lord lays special emphasis on Karam-yoga (action in divine light and mind focused on the "Eternal Existence within") for Arjuna for it is the most natural path of spiritual evolution for majority of mankind. This option was in conformity with Arjuna's svadharma (duty according to one's combination of natural attributes, heritage, social status as well as mission of existence).

This verse states how the work should be done. Secondly, Lord also states what one is going to "get" after doing work in the spirit of karam-yoga. The second clarification is very important. The work should be done without attachment to fruit thereof. What is it that happens? Lord replies beautifully. Individual attains the Supreme, the Sovereign Truth i.e. one attains "The Highest." How is this term Highest to be decoded? By doing the work in the spirit of detachment i.e. without focus on the reward, one will finally reach the Supreme i.e. state of peace, state of bliss, state of knowledge, state of self-blossoming, state of self-fulfillment, state of "Universal Oneness." Thereafter there remains nothing for the individual to gain either by performing or abstaining from action. He or she then performs action without attachment as naturally as sun rises, river flows or night follows the day.

20. In this verse, Lord cites king Jankas's example to emphasize that focus in life should be primarily on the well being of the world on the protection of the people.

कर्मणैव हि संसिद्धिमास्थिता जनकादयः ।
लोकसंग्रहमेवापि सम्पश्यन्कर्तुमर्हसि ॥ ३- २० ॥

karmanaiva hi samsiddhim asthita janakadayah
loka-sangraham evapi sampasyan kartum arhasi 3.20

karmana--by action; *eva*--only; *hi*--verily; *samsiddhim*--perfection; *asthitah*-- attained; *janaka-adayah*--Janaka and others; *loka-sangraham*—for protection of the people or cosmic benefit; *eva*--also; *api*-- only; *sampasyan*—having in view; *kartum*--to perform; *arhasi*—(you) ought.

"Janaka and others attained perfection verily (really) by action only; even with a view to **lokasangraha** (maintenance of world order; protection of the masses) you should take to action." II 3-20 II

The main focus of this verse is on "**Lokasangraha**" i.e. welfare of the world and all creatures in it. This should be the guiding principle when one is about to act. All actions (except the obligatory duties) should focus on this point only to make whole life a yajna. Lord explains this in the following words:

i) **karmanai 'va samsiddhim asthita jankadayah** (king Janak and others attained perfection by action) - Lord has illustrated, by example of Janaka and others, the principle that a human being attains liberation from nishkama-karma (actions without attachment of fruit thereof). Words used by Lord are as follows:

Karmani **(by action alone)** – King Janaka once wanted to be sanyasi (mendicant; member of religious group who live by asking people for money and food) but finally resolved to continue to be king to discharge his kingly duties for *lokasangraha or sarvabhutahita* (for maintenance, welfare and guidance of the world). He got his release (liberation from cycle of birth and death) finally. It is important to understand what this word stands for. It does not refer merely to janaka's religious and philosophical justification of social service, cosmopolitan and humanitarian efforts and his numerous social schemes. So many politicians do that. That is not what Janaka is famous for. Janaka is famous for his **spiritual unity with the truth within and with the world of beings around him**. It was not his principle to subordinate the individual to society and humanity. His principle was to make the individual (self or other) aware of the "divine truth" within and to sacrifice the ego on the altar of all embracing divinity. Action alone is not important. Whatever action is done with this internal change is important. Activities and projects mentioned above will undergo change if this "change at the center within" is taken care of.

Samsiddhimasthita **(attained perfection)** – What is the meaning of this perfection? It means balancing the attitude and not allowing personal prejudices and motives to influence the work for maintenance and benefit of the society. Most of the politicians prejudice the activities and the projects with personal biases which corrupt the activities from becoming a yajna for welfare of the society. Janaka attained perfection. It means he did not allow his activities to be victim of personal biases and personal interests. India will be immensely relieved if its politicians understand and value this perfection. If this purity in balancing the motives while doing activity is taken care of, activity will be taken care of by itself. Our motives corrupt our activities and society suffers. Only those who have high standard of morality, character and awareness of "**internal connectivity**" are able to generate this perfection, which Lord is talking of here. This *samsiddhim* (perfection) results from the energy which accrues when the work is done with knowledge of soul (atman). Janaka and other had this perfection in action.

Janakadaya (men like janaka) – King Janaka and Asvapati etc. were able to gain this perfection in their actions. Lord mentioned the name of Janaka to convince him that work done without attachment to results thereof will lead to perfection and the achievement of the supreme state. Janaka was king of Mithla and father of Sita. His life was a long yajna. He carried out his pressing royal duties along with listening to enlightening discourses. Once he was listening to the discourse of Suka along with other poor Brahmins. One day Janak got late and Suka did not start the discourse. He waited for the king to come. This did not pass on a good message to poor brahamins who had nothing else to do. A little after there was a fire in Mithla. All the Brahmins ran away to save their petty things from fire. When all other pupils had gone, Suka told the king "Janaka, we should better stop here. Mithla is in flames." Janka replied "What does Janak lose if Mithla burns? Nothing that is really valuable for Janaka is in Mithla or in any place outside him. Pray continue and conclude the soul-enthralling discourse." This shows what king Janaka was like. He used to work with total dedication without attachment. Janaka was intensely aware of his soul connection. Janaka really worked for *Loksangraha* and *sarvabhutahita* (maintenance, welfare and guidance of the world).

ii) *lokasangraham eva api sampasyankartum arhasi* **(Having an eye on the maintenance and welfare of the world, you should perform action)** - Even after attaining such a state (as king Janaka had), one should continue to carry on worldly duties, not for one's personal-self but for the welfare and well-being of the world at large. Special emphasis is on *lokasangraha*.

Lokasangraha (maintenance, welfare and guidance of the world) – This is the key word in karam-yoga. The action should be for *lokasangraha* i.e. for maintenance, welfare and guidance of the world at large. Action done for *lokasangraha* loses its capturing tendencies and becomes liberating in nature. Consideration is not for human beings alone but the whole world i.e. welfare of all the living, the non-living and the environment. It is very important thought of the Gita (Lord Krishna) and it is completely in tune with spirit of Vedas. It involves taking of the masses along the path by one's own example. The focus is on unison of mind, thought and actions. *Lokasangraha* (welfare of the masses; cosmic benefit) should be the thought underlying all our actions. Then action transforms into *karam-yoga*. What is the central message of this word Lokasangraha in context of karam-yoga? It means our concern has to extend beyond land, human beings to environment including animal kingdom and plant kingdom etc. Wake up and work for the welfare of universe and everything in it. If *loksangraha* is the underlying thought of all our actions, life will become a yajna, an offering to the Supreme for the common good and welfare. If the message of this word (*lokasangraha*) is truly assimilated and implimented at all levels, not one stomach will starve and despair and not even one body will go unclothed and bare.

This verse beautifully explains what one is to do to transform an action into karam-yoga. Be like Janaka. There is no joy in this world or in the next equal to doing work for the world's welfare. Do not lose the opportunity of getting such a joy in this life. Be Like clouds which rain for the welfare of the world. Be like earth which gives crop to him who digs it. Be like a tree who gives shade to him who cuts it with an axe, whose handle is made from its own branch. Be like the earthworm that enriches the soil for him who treads it. This is the message of the Gita in line with Puranas (scriptures). There is very beautiful story in Panchtantra which explains the relevance of this thought very nicely. There once lived a "two headed bird." The heads were in opposing direction but it had one body and one stomach. One day one of the head got some honey and was about to eat it. The other head asked a part of it but was refused with the remark "I got it. I have the legal right to consume the whole of it. Why should I give you a bit of it?" The other head was utterly depressed on seeing the whole of the honey being eaten by the sister head. The other head decided to take revenge. It searched for and got some deadly poison. It swallowed it. The poison entered the common stomach and soon killed the bird and with it both its heads. Common stomach in this story is the Divine essence. If spirit of *lokasangraha* (cosmic benefit; common welfare) is not observed who will suffer? Some one less fortunate, someone needier will suffer? Someone having the same divine essence will suffer. The final impact of all is on the common stomach (in the story) i.e. the Divine Essence in all of us. This sensitivity of other's suffering is necessary for spiritual growth. By spirit of yajna, this aspect is automatically taken care of.

Lord has cited the example of Janaka and others who achieved self-realization through action with focus on *lokasngraha* (cosmic benefit and common welfare). Lord is passing a message to turn even an ordinary life into a life of depth, meaning and substance. To know the divinity within in this life is to know the "Truth." Not to know that "Truth" is the desolation (feeling of being very lonely and unhappy) of death or rebirth. How is that "Truth" to be known? This is possible by realizing that "Truth" in each and all. Not only in nature but in the family, in the society, in the state and in the environment, the more we realize the world-consciousness (divine reality) in all, the better it is for us. Failing to realize this, we turn to destruction. What is the way out? Act and continue to act with focus on *lokasangraha*. This is the message of the Lord. Self-gratification, insatiable greed and the pride of possession are stilling shroud (something that covers something) of death. Salvation lies in awakening soul by working for "*lokasnagraha*; cosmic benefit" in line with the message of this verse.

21 In this verse, Lord exhorts Arjuna to set a good example as a "leading warrior" so that others may follow him.

यद्यदाचरति श्रेष्ठस्तत्तदेवेतरो जनः ।
स यत्प्रमाणं कुरुते लोकस्तदनुवर्तते ॥ ३- २१ ॥

yad yad acarati sresthas tat tad evetaro janah
sa yat pramanam kurute lokas tad anuvartate 3.21

yad—yat- whatsoever; *acarati—*does ; *sresthah—*the best; *tat— tat—* that ; *eva—*only; *itarah—*the other; *janah—*people; *sah—*he; *yat—*what; *pramanam—* standard; *kurute—*does *lokah—* the world; *tat—*that; *anuvartate—*follows.

"Whatever a superior person does that is followed by others; what standard he or she demonstrates by action, people follow that." II 3-21 II

Arjuna was the most famous warrior of his time, a role model for the people of his time. He had skill, humility and strength of character. Still he was suffering from indecision. To pull Arjuna out of this state of desperation and to make him recall his inherent strength, Lord wants him to be conscious of his reputation in the society as a famous warrior. This is always one of the very important considerations in human life to propel (to push forward) an individual to make him or her conscious of his or her obligation in a particular situation. Still this is only one of the considerations because most important consideration is the shrill voice from within of the individual, which comes after considerable silence, introspection and meditation, for which Arjuna did not have time in the battle field. This also shows that dignified people respect their reputation in society. To make Arjuna conscious of his reputation as a warrior, Lord uses the following wording:

i) **Yad-yat acarati sresthah tattadevetaro janh (Whatever a great man does is followed by others)** - Being eminent with virtues is a rare gift of the divine. Arjuna had the rare distinction of being the foremost warrior of his time. Almost all knew Arjuna as a warrior in his times. Such an individual is taken as a model in society. People try to emulate such a leader in society. The word used by the lord is srestha i.e. one holding a high position (in any field). It can be any field. Arjuna was acknowledged as a warrior. The one, acknowledged as a leader, holds a responsibility of setting good example because people follow him or her. Lord is reminding Arjuna that he was not an ordinary man that he was Arjuna known for his valor all over the world those days. He was therefore expected to set good example.

Setting good example requires sacrifice, a little personal suffering, a commitment to character, but it never goes waste. This can be explained by the example of father of Ramakrishna. His name was Kshudhiram Chattergee. One day he was asked by a zamindar (a landlord) to give a false statement in his favor in the court of law. Ramakrishna's father replied "Sorry. I cannot. I know it is wrong. I cannot give a false witness." That landlord was a wicked man. He said "Then you will have to suffer." Ramakrishna's father replied "I do not mind. I will speak the truth only." Because of this, Ramakrishna's father was sent out of the village by the landlord with a small bundle of possessions, two children and Ramakrishna's mother. After some distance, another good landlord was coming. He recognized Kshudhiram Chatergee and told him "You come to my village Kamarpukur. I will give you a piece of land." There in that little known village Kamarpukur, Kshudhiram was blessed with a son as illustrious as Ramakrishna. This is what happens if one sacrifices to set an example following the inner call. Lord is exhorting Arjuna to set example for others to follow by his valor in the war for restoring righteousness in the society.

ii) *Sa yat pramanam kurute lokastat anuvartate* (what standard he or she demonstrate by action, people follow that) - Other people follow the path that the *srestha* (one whose eminent virtue has been acknowledged) takes. Whatever standard is set by the acknowledged great, other people follow it. To be an acknowledged leader in society is not easy. One has to set high standard for that by actions.

Lord's focus in this verse is on *srestha* (one holding a high position). This Sanskrit word has got a special appeal. Arjuna was already a known warrior. Lord is not pointing to this feature alone. Based on the Gita discussion so far, a srestha (one holding high position in the society) is one who has exalted oneself out of lower imperfect prakriti (nature) into unity with the divine being, consciousness and nature. By getting to this point alone (awareness of divinity within), an individual will set example for the generations to follow. Awareness of divinity within brings perfect harmony among the various levels of an individual's existence (body, mind, intellect, memory and ego) and generates within an individual that extra bit of efficiency which makes him an example to be followed by others in society. One has to go beyond one's physical-self to be entitled to set example for others by action. By worldly attributes alone one cannot do this. Arjuna was already famous. Now Lord wanted him to be conscious to the spiritual call to his perfect self-development (for self development, reputation in society is also important consideration) by means of waging a war, not for lower distinction of sin and virtue but for restoring the righteous-ness in the society. Lord wanted Arjuna to do a yajna (by waging a war) not for self development or self-satisfaction but for the welfare of the world, for restoring righteousness in the society. This aspect of the word "srestha" becomes clear when Lord gives His own example in coming verse. Therefore, key word in this verse is "srestha" which matures an individual for the divine grace when the physical achievement is coordinated with spiritual maturity to make an action a yajna, an offering in terms of action for the common good with the memory of the supreme in thoughts with a smile. This verse is extremely important for the "acknowledged leaders" In the society. Their role has to be in line with their reputation. One, who works but is selfless, who acts un-urged by others, who teaches all by his or her example, sticking to the path of righteousness, is followed by all. Arjuna falls in this category. This is a sort of implied warning being given to Arjuna. His reputation in society as a leading warrior is at stake by his decision to withdraw from war.

22. In this verse, Lord cites His own example to Arjuna to pass on the message that one should, in all situations, continue to work for the common good and world's welfare.

न मे पार्थास्ति कर्तव्यं त्रिषु लोकेषु किञ्चन ।
नानवाप्तमवाप्तव्यं वर्त एव च कर्मणि ॥ ३- २२ ॥

na me parthasti kartavyam trisu lokesu kincana
nanavaptam avaptavyam varta eva ca karmani 3.22

na--not; *me*--Mine; *partha*--O son of Prtha (Arjuna); *asti*--is; *kartavyam*—to be done (duty); *trisu*--in the three; *lokesu*—worlds; *kincana*--anything; *na*--not; *anavaptam*--un-attained; *avaptavyam*--to be attained; *varte*-- am; *eva*--also; *ca*--and; *karmani*--in action duty.

"O Partha (son of Pritha; Arjuna)! There is no duty for me to do in the three worlds (Gods, men and other beings). There is nothing unattained or to be attained by me. And yet I am also engaged in work." II 3-22 II

Lord Krishna represents the Supreme Universal Eternal Reality. He is in all the worlds and all the worlds are in Him. Therefore from an ordinary individual's point of view there is nothing that he has to work for. Lord cites His own example to tell Arjuna that He is practicing what He is preaching. There is nothing unattained for the Lord. Still Lord continues to work for the welfare of the world i.e. for its generation, sustenance and destruction of the world. Actually this statement has been made by the Lord to warn the people against complacency (feeling of satisfaction which one develops and which makes one stop from trying to improve). This is a tendency. There always remains a danger of becoming complacent after a little progress. For this reason this warning is very relevant. Lord Krishna is a sovereign Lord. He is omniscient (knows everything). There is nothing un-acquired for "Him'. Still Lord is continuously busy working for the world's welfare. Action represents what is hidden in life (due to past karmas) and what is about to come as a result of union between the individual and his or her perception of the society with or without awareness of divinity within. Inaction is temporary departure from life, from inner connectivity while physical existence continues. Action for the cosmic benefit means life with awareness of the divinity within. Inaction stands for temporary disconnection between the individual and the divinity within which always prompts an individual to press forward to improve spiritual worth. Wrong action stands for suppression of divinity or strangulation (killing by pressing some part of the body to death) of the self due to illusion of the world.

The message of the verse is simple. No individual should give up action under the false notion that since he or she has no attachment for enjoyments nor requires anything for his own self or herself as fruit of actions, he or she has no reason to work. Some people nurture the wrong notion that after attaining the supreme state there is no reason to work. Lord has put all these wrong notions to rest in this verse. One should continue to work at least in the interest of the world order. Continuity of action for world welfare saves an individual from those "intermittent, threatening spells of inaction" which bring an inevitable split between the individual and the divinity, which practically is a loss of life from the spiritual point of view. What is the message? Lord seems to say in this verse "Continue to work for the common good however difficult, pressing and desperate the situation may come to be. Look at me. I am always there. I am always working." In brief, inactivity is disastrous and is against the providential (verdict of the force that controls the life) commands. Let the welfare of the world be the sole reason for our actions following the Lord. Then the life will uncover its true meaning, its real beauty, the fragrance of divinity within and the blossoming of the individual's inherent true nature.

23. Lord told Arjuna in the last verse that even after being the Lord of three worlds (God, men and other beings) "He" abides (accepts and follows) the path of action. In this verse Lord tells Arjuna what will happen if He does not engage in action.

यदि ह्यहं न वर्तेयं जातु कर्मण्यतन्द्रितः ।
मम वर्त्मानुवर्तन्ते मनुष्याः पार्थ सर्वशः ॥ ३- २३ ॥

yadi hy aham na varteyam jatu karmany atandritah
mama vartmanuvartante manusyah partha sarvasah 3.23

yadi--if; *hi*-- surely; *aham*--I; *na*--not; *varteyam*—engage in action; *jatu*--ever; *karmani*--in action; *atandritah*- unwearied; *mama*--My; *vartma*--path; *anuvartante*-- follow; *manusyah*--men; *partha*--O son of Prtha (Arjuna); *sarvasah*--in all respects.

"For, should I not engage myself in action unwearied (without feeling weaker), O! Partha, men and women in every way follow my example." II 3-23 II

Lord has used the world "I." What does it refer to? It refers to not only Krishna, son of Vasudeva, sitting and talking to Arjuna in the battle field in the chariot, but also to the "Eternal Force," which is omnipresent (present everywhere), omniscient (knowing everything) and omnipotent (most powerful in every situation everywhere). It is this force which grants our existence validity of life. With it, we are alive, existing. Without it, we are not there. There cannot be any existence without it. It is the same power to which we address our prayers and thoughts in different words, in different modes [style of living, behaving and doing due to different beliefs (such as religions) and local influences all over the world] and different manners, when our strength give in and we are utterly desolate (feeling sad and lonely) due to weariness, having no strength and alternative to turn to.

If the Lord ever remains inactive, people will imitate and keep quiet. They will all become tamsic [guna of nature responsible for anger, indolence (makes lazy, luxurious, not wanting to work) and sleep] and pass into state of inertia. Following three words have been beautifully used by the Lord:

Atandritah (**without weariness**) - How does the Lord perform cosmic functions of creation, sustenance and dissolution? In Lord's way of doing things, there is no hurry or worry or disinclination. Lord's will is carried out by nature. Sun and moon ever remain in service. Child is born and nature simultaneously makes arrangement for its intake. There is never a delay. Everything is taken care of with precision and startling accuracy. What is the purpose of using this word? Lord wants to bring our attention to attributes of promptness, accuracy and reliability. Human beings delay due to fatigue, procrastination but this capacity to continue to bear can be increased with yoga (inaction in action). Human beings can also learn to work without weariness and disinclination with yoga i.e. physical, mental, emotional and spiritual disciplines to gain unity with truth of our nature.

Anuvartante (**follow**) – Men and women have a tendency to imitate the ever present, ever active force within all of us. Staunch adherence to the good and devotion to duty are the characteristics of the spiritually advanced achievers. Ordinary people emulate the characteristics of the acknowledged greats. Sri Krishna or that Eternal and Infinite Force which He represents sets the example which the people follow. In all doings, the Lord is the model of mankind. All through the life, Lord Krishna adhered to scriptures. Many of His actions are beyond the understanding of the common individual. For examples i) on his way to Hastinapur in the company of Narda and other sages Lord offers His twilight prayers to the sun, ii) He explains to Vidura the purpose of his mission though He knew that war was inevitable and iii) his childhood pranks are the most misunderstood mysteries. His play of "*Cheer-haran*, stripping the cow-herd-maidens of their clothes while bathing" was a play requiring extremely high level of spiritual understanding. Actually Lord wanted to communicate to the *Gopis* (maidens of *Vrindaban*) that the Divine cannot be obtained till the worshipper goes beyond the physical level, level of forms and names. Those Gopis were not ordinary physical women. They were all devotees of highest level whose love was far beyond the domains of human infatuation. Radha's (the play-mate of Krishna in childhood) lifelong aching silence, her feeling of fullness even in separation, her intense ever fresh love without ever having any complaints for Krishna and her inhuman determination just not to disturb "her Krishna" from undertaking the work of world-welfare was a tapas (austerity) so extraordinary, so celestial (relating to sky or heaven i.e. not worldly) that it has never been repeated in annals of world history. Krishna cannot be understood by worldly understanding alone. Krishna's childhood pranks are most mystical i.e. He demonstrated to his mother Yashoda the whole universe in His mouth; He killed Putna and so many demons even while he was a child; a child fought with an elephant; a child lifted the mountain on a finger. Except his childhood pranks requiring very high level of spiritual maturity to be understood, all his actions, especially his acumen as a politician, the divine knowledge given through the Gita and his devotion to welfare of others are role models for the world.

Jatu (always)- The Lord is always intensely aware of his role for the welfare of mankind. Our scriptures say "negligence is death." Lord wants us all to be with our awareness all the time to be ever constructively and effectively busy for the welfare of the world.

What is the message of this verse? Be alert. Always be wakeful in the contemplation of the self. Briefly, be in the present moment to experience "inaction in action" like Lord Krishna.

24. What will be the final impact if the Lord stops working? This verse answers this question.

उत्सीदेयुरिमे लोका न कुर्यां कर्म चेदहम् ।
सङ्करस्य च कर्ता स्यामुपहन्यामिमाः प्रजाः ॥ ३- २४ ॥

utsideyur ime loka na kuryam karma ced aham
sankarasya ca karta syam upahanyam imah prajah 3.24

utsideyuh- would perish; *ime*--these; *lokah*--worlds; *na*--not; *kuryam*—would do; *karma*-- action; *cet*--if; *aham*--I; *sankarasya*--of confusion of castes; *ca*--and; *karta*—author or creator; *syam*--shall be; *upahanyam*—would destroy; *imah*--these; *prajah*—beings or living entities.

"These worlds would perish if I did not do action; I shall be responsible for the confusion of species and destruction of people." II 3-24 II

There is only "One Truth" (Supreme Divine Universal Energy) that does not need anything else in this world. It is the only "One" without second. Rest all need something else for existence. It is this "only One" that smiles as source of life beneath each single diverse manifestation in this whole universe. A tree takes its nourishment through roots. How do all living and non-living entities sustain their existences? There is only one single, primary, eternal, ever-present and indestructible "Force," which is the primary cause of all existences. By using the pronoun "I" in this verse, Lord is referring to this "One Truth" as Krishna. A man is standing on a dais. If the dais suddenly breaks down, what will happen to the man standing on it? Similarly, if the propelling, sustaining, potent-divine-energy source is not there even for a split of a second, it will cause unimaginable havoc in the universe. This is what Lord wants to clarify in this verse. Catastrophe (terrible event causing extreme destruction) will happen. Universe, consisting of untold millions of worlds, will perish, if the Lord (fundamental divine energy source, which presence of Lord Krishna symbolizes) is not there. The virtuous will be destroyed by the wicked. There will be annihilation of lives, total destruction and complete extinction of any order, if there is even pause by this particular "One" in the form of Lord Krishna . This is the main thought which Lord emphasizes using following very good words:

i) **Utsideyuh (will perish)** - What is the meaning of perish here? If the Lord renounced action, people will also do likewise. A downward course of nature will set in i.e. people will become selfish, corrupt and immoral. They will take to worldly enjoyments (wealth, women and wine). Giving no heed to what others are going through, they would begin to indulge in sinful acts prohibited by scriptures and detrimental to individual's spiritual growth. As a result of this they will be deprived of the fruit of human existence and they will be thrown into wombs of lower species or into hell. This is how spiraling (moving continuous drive), perishing trend sets in.

ii) **Samkarasya (confusion of categories)** – This word has appeared second time in the Gita. First, Arjuna used this word in the first chapter with a little difference. Arjuna said there using the term **varnasamkarah** (intermingling of castes) - " ... ... by the prevalence of impiety (lack of respect for religion and Universal Truth), the women of the family will become immoral, mixing of castes (intermingling of castes) will result." There is difference in intermingling of castes and intermingling of categories. Castes, in the Gita, means a specific categorization based on natural attributes (Gunas) i.e. Brahmins, kshetriya, vaisyas and sudras. Here Lord is talking not of castes (only one category) but categories.

How does intermingling of category take place? There is a hierarchy (system or order which may be downward or upward based on merit) in the universe. For example, if an individual's actions do not qualify him or her to be born as human being, then he or she may be born as a snake or a dog or a bird etc. based on merit in each case. If an individual is born as different type of human being again, it is case of intermingling of caste. If an individual is born as different species, it is a case of intermingling of categories.

Lord's emphasis is that in an individual's evolution a downward trend will set in i.e. instead of being born as better human being, he or she will be born in lower species in the order of evolution. This downward trend will put the whole universe in utter confusion. Downward trend can be interpreted differently. An individual may become very selfish in the next birth to be confined only to physical enjoyments only. Tyranny may become the order of the day. World may be visited by natural calamities such as epidemics, draught, floods, famines, fire, earthquakes etc. This is what the Lord means by saying " …these people will sink to destruction, if I (i.e. Krishna or Supreme Force through nature) did not work.."

This verse passes on a good message. There is an order in this universe. There is no escape from it for even the Gods (Intermediate Gods or cosmic forces which sustain on the grace of the Supreme). It is not based on someone's whims and fancy. Merit (i.e. judging something exclusively on how good it is without considering anything else) and discipline (method of training mind and behavior) are inbuilt universal considerations. That is why Lord is talking about what will happen if there is a slip anywhere even at the highest order. We are the creators of the destiny (as you sow, so shall you reap). We should do something to be entitled for "**the light of the soul**" and not for "**the darkness around the soul**" right today. Improve the nature of quality of action and the thinking behind it. We should stir our vision by the divine wisdom of the words of the Lord who is inspiring us to look into the direction of "The Unknown," who knows everything. The incessant activities of the Lord preserve the world and prevent it from falling back into non-existence.

25. Lord uses a beautiful simile to say that the enlightened should also work with intensity like the unenlightened working with attachment.

सक्ताः कर्मण्यविद्वांसो यथा कुर्वन्ति भारत ।
कुर्याद्विद्वांस्तथासक्तश्चिकीर्षुर्लोकसंग्रहम् ॥ ३- २५ ॥

saktah karmany avidvamso yatha kurvanti bharata
kuryad vidvams tathasaktas cikirsur loka-sangraham 3.25

saktah-- attached; *karmani*—to action; *avidvamsah*-- the ignorant; *yatha*--as; *kurvanti*-- act; *bharata*--O descendant of Bharata (Arjuna); *kuryat*—should act; *vidvan*--the wise; *tatha*--so; *asaktah*-- unattached; *cikirsuh*--desiring to; *loka-sangraham*—for benefit of the people in general or cosmic benefit.

"The manner in which the unenlightened (those who do not know) act from attachment to action, O Son of Bharata Dynasty (Arjuna), in the same manner should the enlightened (those who know) act without attachment desirous of guiding the well-being of the world." II 3-25 II

This verse has something infinitely useful with regard to practical living and functioning in life. What is Lord talking about? Most of us are following a rut (living in a situation that never changes)

called the routine of life. See the enthusiasm with which we work to earn name, fame and money in life. We do all this with fervor (very strong belief or feeling), with a particularly distinct enthusiasm i.e. we follow only that which is doomed to be no more one day. We always ignore the truth which is perennially with us in us from the beginning. We work unmindful of the divine aspect of life. Suppose we show the same enthusiasm in working, after gaining awareness about our divine consciousness, for world-welfare. A sea change will be there in our production, productivity and spiritual growth. This happens as our awareness improves. We common people nurture a wrong notion. We feel that spirituality is the domain for idlers who have lived life. That is not correct. The term "the unenlightened" has been used for those lacking spiritual awareness and working for sense satisfaction for worldly pleasures. The term "the enlightened" has been used for those who are aware of divine consciousness and work for the welfare of the whole world. From the Gita's point of view, a billionaire bereft of awareness of soul bliss is a poor individual. Even a worldly poor man, who is conscious of individual's divine consciousness and is ready to share even last loaf with the poorer man, is a rich individual. There will be a difference in the level of enthusiasm and intensity with which people in these two categories approach life. There will be definite and distinct positive change if the individual in the second category starts working in life with the enthusiasm of the individual in the first category mentioned above. This is the brief message mentioned in the following words:

i) *saktah karmanyavidvamso yatha kurvanti* (**as the unenlightened, attached to work, acts**) - Two words have been used in this verse i.e. *a-vidvan* and *vidvan*. A-vidvan means the unenlightened i.e. who are confined to life of "eat, drink and be merry" or life of sense pleasures. These people are too occupied with the routine of existence to spare time towards divine awareness and well being of the world. They completely lack awareness of the life beyond and the relevance of the work done for welfare of the world (*lokasamgraha*). They revel in worldly life and their focus is on attachment to oneself, one's pleasures and one's comfort. Their whole world centers round "I, my and mine." All that they do is to please or flatten them-selves or the people immediately related to them. They intensely work for the fulfillment of personal desires (sense pleasures) with full attachment for fruit of their actions. This is one approach of life followed by those confined to satisfaction of sense-pleasures. This approach brings soul-bondage. These people feel darkness, fear and uncertainty around their soul. They are never in a position to be aware of the **"Transcendent Core (beyond limitations of human understanding and experience a central part), like space"** deep within each one of us which does not at any time get involved or affected the least. These people even do not know what bliss they miss due to this ignorance. Soul has no practical relevance for these people.

ii) *kuryat vidvan tatha asaktah cikirsuh loksamgraha* (**so should the enlightened act but without attachment, desirous of the well being of the world**) – Vidvan are those who are aware of divine consciousness. They very well understand the relevance of the work done for the *lokasamgraha* (cosmic benefit) for spiritual growth. These people work for the happiness and welfare of the world. *Loksamgraha* becomes the key word in their life. They know the stability, strength, spiritual difference and insight (of the divine connection), which work done for welfare of the world, brings about in life. They know that work done for welfare of the world without attachment yields spiritual motivation. This is another contrasting approach of life. These people are fully aware of the **"Transcendent Core (beyond limitations of human understanding and experience a central part), like space,"** deep within each one of us, which does not at any time get involved or affected the least. These people are fully conscious of the sure effect which this awareness exerts on the mind of the seeker.

"The ignorant" act eagerly from attachment for results with desire to fulfill their own interests and dreams. The wise should also eagerly do the acts with the same intensity, without attachment, for cosmic benefit or common welfare of the world. The focus in the second approach is on *loksamgraha* (world welfare or common good).

    iii) *Lokasamgraha* **(world welfare or cosmic benefit)** – Again Lord is emphasizing the world welfare by use of the word *lokasamgraha*. This is the spirit of karam-yoga. Actually an action entitles to be included in the category of karam-yoga, when it is for cosmic benefit, for common good. How does it happen? With attitude for world welfare, selfishness goes away. Love for the whole world fosters. This paves way for the "**feel of universal connectivity, eternal love**." One feels expansion, a feeling of release within. Bondage gives way to freedom. The wisdom of "impersonal soul" whispers within the secret of self release (*Moksha*) due to attitude of "world welfare." We think of *lokasamgraha* when we see beyond the limitations of self interest, beyond the bounds of ego. This is where divine connectivity emerges and guides us in its mute language towards that "eternal love" which is the sunshine of each soul, divine content of each soul. That is why the wise perform actions aiming at the well-being of the world. This prayer " …May my heart be thine.." cannot be actualized till internal change takes place, till we open ourselves to divinity in the work done for the common good, for others. Till this thought resonates at soul level that "**work done for cosmic benefit is my work**," transformation of human being into the divine will continue to elude. The moment one starts offering oneself and losing oneself to the Divine through the work done for the "well being of the world," the ever restless "I" disappears. The work done for the common good becomes the bridge to lead to "The Immortality." What should then be our attitude in karam-yoga? **A woodcutter's axe begged for its handle from the tree. The tree gave it.** The concept of "*lokasamgraha*" helps an individual to perform true worship of the Divine through the medium of action. Here offering is the work done for the common good. Each and everything in the universe is the divine fire having divinity within. Simply selfishness and self gratification should not be there in the work done. One can remove the self imposed barricades placed all around in life by reposing in continuing peace through the work done for others for common good. **Life is given to us. We earn it by giving**. That is *lokasamgraha*. What we are, we do not see. What we see is shadow. Lord is explaining all this by one single word "*Loksamgraha*." It will never do the least good to attempt the realization of the Infinite apart from the world of action (for common good). That is why the Upnishad says "**In the midst of activity (for common good) alone will thou desire to live for hundred years**."

    iv) Asaktah (unattached) – This is another good word used by the Lord. It means that the seeker should remain unattached to the fruit of action. For the ignorant, deluded in their thinking and ways, attachment is natural. Only with attachment, they (ignorant) can derive their motivation for working. For the wise, it is not so. The wise remain active and efficient. In place of ignorance and delusion, it is the wisdom of the soul that will motivate them. They unite themselves to the wisdom of the soul through the actions done for world's welfare naturally i.e. without pump and show. Wisdom has the power to remove attachment and identification. **Non-attachment shows the want (***swartha***, interest) of another self to be the inherent want of own self**. This requires a lot of introspection. When we gain this awareness, our activities get regulated. Action, then, is not goaded on by want but it gets stimulated by the satisfaction of the soul. Then activity gets inspired by "The One" who is pervaded by eternal peace, knowledge and joy.

    Therefore, one should work with full vigor for *loksamgraha* (for the well being of the world) without attachment to help the world to attain peace, harmony, purity of heart, divine light and knowledge. The wise people mentioned in this verse are like village-medicinal herbs in full growth i.e. these people are alive to the social responsibility and to the obligation of being enlightened human beings. They work not for themselves but for the world's benefit.

    26. In this verse, Lord tells Arjuna that the wise should never confuse (by unsettling) the ignorant.

न बुद्धिभेदं जनयेदज्ञानां कर्मसङ्गिनाम् ।
जोषयेत्सर्वकर्माणि विद्वान्युक्तः समाचरन् ॥ ३- २६ ॥

na buddhi-bhedam janayed ajnanam karma-sanginam
josayet sarva-karmani vidvan yuktah samacaran 3.26

na--not; *buddhi-bhedam*—unsettlement in the mind; *janayet*—should produce ; *ajnanam*--of the ignorant ; *karma-sanginam*—of the person attached to action; *josayet*—should engage; *sarva*--all; *karmani*--actions; *vidvan*—the wise; *yuktah*-- balanced; *samacaran*-- performing.

"Let no wise individual unsettle the minds of the ignorant who are attached to actions. The enlightened individual, steadily working in balanced manner (i.e. in yoga-spirit), should engage the ignorant also in all actions." II 3-26 II

It is possible to make the ignorant bewildered by speaking to them something that they are not prepared for. The wise should take care not to breed confusion in the minds of the people in general. What do the people in general do? Initially, they take recourse to austerities, charities and going to pilgrimages with a view to attain happiness here and here after (life beyond). The enlightened (with divine knowledge) should never discourage them by telling that the divinity is within them, that there is no need to go to Varanasi, Ujjain and Rameswaram and that the austerities and the charities are promoted by the people to serve their own ends. The best course is to take them along lovingly on the path of righteousness and make them realize how it feels to set a high personal example. Practicing righteousness along with them is better than giving them a sermon about the righteousness. This is the idea of the Lord in the following words:

i) *na budhi bhedam janayed ajnanam karam sanginam* (**Let not the wise individual unsettle the mind of the ignorant people attached to actions**) Doing duty for the sake of performing duty alone without desire, is an exalted state of an enlightened mind (aware of divine consciousness). This state dawns after observing various physical, mental, emotional and spiritual disciplines. The ordinary individual gets stuck up at the initial level of asanas (physical exercises). How can such an individual have the feel of someone adept in pranayam (breathing exercises), Pratyahara (witnessing the outgoing tendencies of the mind; gathering it), Dharna (fixing the mind on some location, thought or idea; or concentrating on that space of the mind which is not identified with any thought), Dhyan (gaining state of thoughtlessness by just not doing anything with awareness; continuing holding the mind in suspension; it is "not doing" with awareness and Samadhi (state of total absorption in the object; reaching the end of duality). The ignorant want to avoid exertion on one plea or the other. There is no point in goading them. To work for results is far better than being given to laziness born of inertia. Do not let the doubt arise in the mind of the ignorant people. Doubt is a great enemy. Neither this world nor the next is for the man who doubts. If we condemn an ignorant man's charity to one and all including the able bodied, his charity itself may stop.

ii) *josayet sarva karmanividvan yukta samacharan* (by doing work persistently and steadily in yoga-spirit the enlightened one should engage the ignorant also in all work) - Lord tells in these lines what the enlightened ones should do. A good teacher is one who comes to the level of the student and then lifts him or her up. The *vidvan*, the enlightened one should do what they are doing taking the ignorant along with them to induce them (the ignorant) to be aware of how it feels to work without attachment and for the common good. Lord has used a beautiful word "yukta; balanced." This state comes when work is done in yoga-state of mind i.e. there is no hurry, no worry about the results of action, no hankering for completion at a speed which disrupts the inner rhythm. If the work is performed by the enlightened in yoga-state taking the ignorant along with them, then it will be possible to involve the ignorant not by precept (rules about how to behave or how to think) but by the experience gained them. A true teacher is one who comes down to the level of students. **A true teacher is able to transfer his or her soul to the student's soul.** He or she is able to be aware of the experience from students' eyes, ears and minds. In brief the enlightened ones should take the un-enlightened ones along with them to instill in them desire of higher knowledge. If the enlightened ones (ones with knowledge) unsettle the minds of the unenlightened ones (ones without knowledge), they (ones without knowledge) will give up even what they are doing in their enthusiasm and attachment and then they will become victim of inertia, degeneration (becoming worse). What then is the advice of the Lord in brief? The wise ones should bring round the minds of the ignorant ones by giving those people gradual instructions and a little exposure of karam-yoga (yoga of selfless and desire-less actions) and its benefits i.e. purification of the heart that leads to attainment of self knowledge through work done for well being of the world.

Jalaluddin Rumi narrates a beautiful story to enforce this point of the Lord. Moses (from Bible era) saw a poor shepherd worshipping fervently and saying "O Master, where are you so that I, your humble servant, may sew your shoes, comb your hair, wash your robes and give you the sweet milk of your goats? Where are you so that I may kiss your hand and feet and sweep your bed-room for you?" Moses was scandalized (behavior that is shocking and not at all acceptable) at this and scolded the shepherd for his blasphemy telling him that God had no body and needed no clothing or nourishment. The shepherd could not conceive of a God without body and was stunned by the reproaches of Moses. The shepherd got dejected and desisted from all worship of God thereafter. God spoke to Moses and said "You have driven my servant away from me by unsettling his mind. I have commissioned you to draw the people to me and not to wean (to make them stop doing) them away. Words are nothing to me. I only regard the heart. If that is true what does the expression matter? Love is the true substance of the heart. Words are the outer garb. Hereafter, do not unsettle the mind of the ignorant with your superior knowledge."

What is the message of the verse? The all-knowing wise (i.e. those who have realized the self, knowing which one knows everything) should not confuse the minds of the imperfect dullards (those who are attached to body, mind and senses and are individuals thoroughly confined to worldly knowledge of cause, time and space) by preaching them sermons (talks for spiritual elevation) which are far beyond their understanding and attainment. Practical living in divine consciousness needs no arguments. When we come across a realized one, who exudes peace and blessedness by very presence, all doubts come to rest. The seeker experiences a state of mind which is conducive to affirmation of truth. Setting an example and taking someone along is better than establishing mastery over spirituality and making someone too conscious of his or her limitations. Setting a person to spirituality involves taking a person along with you, step by step and exposing him or her gradually and naturally to the awareness of individual's higher nature, touching individual's belief, requiring change, very slowly, very softly and very carefully.

27. In this verse Lord explains why the people do as they do.

प्रकृतेः क्रियमाणानि गुणैः कर्माणि सर्वशः ।
अहङ्कारविमूढात्मा कर्ताहमिति मन्यते ॥ ३- २७ ॥

prakrteh kriyamanani gunaih karmani sarvasah
ahankara-vimudhatma kartaham iti manyate 3.27

prakrteh—of nature; *kriyamanani*—are performed; *gunaih*--by the qualities (attributes i.e. sattva, rajas and tamas); *karmani*--activities; *sarvasah*--all ; *ahankara-vimudha*—one whose mind is bewildered by egoism; *atma*—soul (individualized eternal existence); *karta*--doer; *aham*--I; *iti*--thus; *manyate*--thinks.

"The gunas (attributes) of prakriti (nature) perform all karmas (actons). With the understanding deluded (t o believe that which is not true) by egoism, an individual thinks "I am the doer." II 3-27 II

Why do we do as we do? Anger, lust, pride, greed and hatred are not the essential characteristics of human nature. They are the modifications, which are observed like waves on the surface of human nature. They come and go away. Essential human nature is like depth of ocean full of peace, bliss, knowledge and consciousness. Why does human nature get obscured and modifications are always there? This is due to attributes (*gunas*) of nature i.e. *rajas* (mode of passion born of unlimited desires and longings causing feverishness, restlessness), *tamas* (delusion or false belief born of ignorance causing insanity, indolence or not wanting to work and sleep) and *sattva* (luminosity causing health, happiness and knowledge). These are modified into four elements (*manas, buddhi, chitta and ahamkar*), five subtle elements, five organs of action (those of speaking, grasping and moving about, procreation and evacuation) five organs of perception (tasting, hearing, smelling, seeing and touching) and five objects of senses. These are thus twenty three constituents of nature (maya). Any action by any human being is an outcome of the interplay of these constituents of nature. Atman (divine component within which is eternal, indestructible) within an individual is the "real self." The real self is a mute witness, which perennially observes the body, the internal and external organs and the modifications of the mind. Ignorant individual identifies with the body by saying "I am the doer." This false notion (ego) binds the individual to the cycles of birth and death and causes endless suffering, pain and sorrow.

That "constituents of the nature i.e. combination of rajas, tamas and sattva" are the doer, is an important component of divine knowledge (Brahaman Jnana). The deluded (the one whose discriminations has been clouded) individual, having identified himself or herself with the body, thinks that he or she is the doer. To take upon oneself the responsibility for the actions performed by the body is not wisdom. Wisdom lies in knowing that he or she is not the body. Body is simply a vehicle. He or she is the self (indestructible and eternal). He or she is not the doer. He or she is not subject to the binding power of actions.

Ordinarily, we all are subject to the forces of lower nature (identifying with the body). We have to go beyond this notion, not with sense of ego and arrogance, but by being aware of the truth within, by being aware of our own infinite nature. Nature compels to act. Egoistic approach is the attitude of a foolish person. There is no point in fighting with nature. Remedy lies in being aware of the self, the divine component within. This is a very slow process and has to be attempted very diplomatically.

The secret of Karam-yoga lies in knowing how actions are performed and with what power they are performed. What is the driving force behind the actions? One should know this first. Identification with the body i.e. "Dehatma Buddhi; intelligence based on physical existence" is the root cause of the problem. Lord has called such an individual "ahamkar vimudhatma; one whose mind has been deluded by egoism." The wise individual knows that he or she is the blissful self, the divine component within and not the body. Wisdom requires one to know that our actions get influenced due to "impact of attributes i.e. rajas, tamas amd sattva." The combination of attributes is driving the "individualized self; egoistic self" to do as he or she is doing. To bring about the remedy "shift in focus" is required from the doer to the causes "driving the doer" i.e. attributes of nature. Divine knowledge is a great help here. The real self is different from the doer. The doer is doing as he or she is doing due to gunas. Problem arises because a normal individual takes "the non-self as the self." The "deluded self" attributes the acts of prakriti (maya or non-self) to itself. This is the focal point of this verse.

28. Every individual is a combination of lower nature (body, mind, intelligence, ego etc. and three constituents of gunas i.e. sattva, rajas and tamas etc.) and higher nature (the divine component within; the infinite; the indestructible). Lack of this knowledge (distinction between the seer and the seen) is the cause of individual's sufferings. The knower of the truth looks at the divine content within (the seer) and not the "seen" (nature or *maya* or that which changes).

तत्त्वविन्तु महाबाहो गुणकर्मविभागयोः ।
गुणा गुणेषु वर्तन्त इति मत्वा न सज्जते ॥ ३- २८ ॥

tattva-vit tu maha-baho guna-karma-vibhagayoh
guna gunesu vartanta iti matva na sajjate 3.28

tattva-vit--the knower of the Absolute Truth; *tu*--but; *maha-baho*--O mighty-armed one (Arjuna); *guna-karma-- vibhagayoh*- of the dividions of qualities and functions; *gunah*-- qualities (in the shape of senses; *gunesu*—amidst the qualities (in the shape of objects; *vartante*-- remain; *iti*--thus; *matva*--knowing; *na*--not; *sajjate*--becomes attached.

"But he who knows (has the true insight) the truth, O mighty-armed (Arjuna), about the divisions of qualities and divisions of functions, holding that these are gunas (in the shape of the senses i.e. mind, intellect etc.) that move among the gunas (objects of perception), does not get attached to them." II 28 II

The wise (individuals adept in divine knowledge) know that each being is composed of two natures i.e. lower nature and higher nature. Higher nature is divine component i.e. that which is indestructible and eternal. This is the "real self" in an individual. Lower nature is the result of causal body (past impressions and tendencies). This is represented by the twenty seven divisions (mentioned in the chart in the introduction) emanating from three attributes of nature i.e. sattva, rajas and tamas. These twenty three divisions have been further grouped in two categories i.e. as qualities and as functions. The wise are very clear that the sense-organs work among the sense objects i.e. there is action and reaction relationship amongst the twenty seven elements (refer to the chart in the introduction). The higher nature is truth. It is eternal. The lower nature is always changing. It is just like a dream. The higher nature is all peace, knowledge and consciousness. It is eternal. Real self is higher nature. For this reason, the wise escape attachment saying for each pain and pleasure - "**These are the organs of senses that are occupied with sense objects.**" Thus the wise do not get entangled or attached in action and reaction of qualities and gunas. They remain established in the higher nature as a witness to changes in lower nature. The wise know that "**nature itself is the cause and nature itself is the result.**" This knowledge helps an individual to develop an attitude of renunciation towards interlay play of **qualities and functions of nature** i.e. towards pain and pleasure, success and failure. Lord gives this knowledge in the following words:

i) *tattvavid* (knower of truth) – Tattvavid is one who intuitively knows (i.e. knowing with feelings) the truth about i) the self (higher nature) and ii) non self or true nature of two divisions of the gunas i.e. constituents of nature and functions of nature. All the twenty seven elements are categorized either as qualities or distinctive features or as functions. The wise know how qualities and functions of nature inter-act each other and they are impermanent or changing in nature being results of sattva, rajas and tamas.

ii) Guna karma vibhagaya (Divisions in the categories i) qualities and ii) functions)- The twenty seven elements (verses 5 and 6 of chapter 13th) resulting from gunas, are classified as qualities and functions. Gunas are forces of nature (characteristics of nature). Action (Karma) means activities or functions. How do we understand these functions and activities of Gunas (attributes of nature)? There are three attributes of nature i.e. sattva, rajas and tamas. In the company of divine content within, these attributes start acting and reacting. There is a close relationship between senses and sense-objects. They are both constituted of the same elements and emanate from sattva, rajas and tamas. This can be explained by examples. Senses are evolutes of guna of nature in the company of Divine component within (body, senses mind and intellect etc. are evolutes of nature). Everything in the universe is an evolution of attributes of nature. When senses face the sense-objects, there happens a natural movement of the organs of senses. For example, eyes see the objects. Similarly ears hear i.e. respective functions of senses take place. It means one should first know how three Gunas become 23 constituents of gunas and how various sense organs start functioning. This is covered by the term "guna karma vibhaga."

iii) Guna guneshu vartante (gunas work among gunas) – Twenty three constituents detailed earlier are all product of nature (sattva, rajas and tamas). When eyes see an object, say a beautiful jumping, smiling and extremely energetic toddler, what is the result? It passes on a message to mind. The message is processed by the intellect. As a result, the individual expresses love for the child either by kiss, or touch or smiling gesture of the eye. Senses are evolutes of nature. Child is also an evolution of gunas of nature. It means all actions or reactions happen among the evolutes of nature only. This is what is meant by words "gunas work among the gunas." In other words, gunas as senses abide by (to accept or obey) gunas as objects (This is law or rule of nature). Getting lost in this or getting too emotional about it or getting too involved in (or confined to) this game of action and reaction is worldliness. Everything involved in this so enchanting play is temporary, imminent to perish. For this reason a wise man looks at it smilingly (knowing its ultimate result) as a witness i.e. without getting unduly involved in it. The wise individual witnesses this drama of life without attachment and escapes the consequential emotional onslaught due to attitude of detachment.

iv) Iti mattva na sajjate [having known this (the wise) do not get attached] - Everything involved in this so enchanting play of this world is temporary, imminent to perish. For this reason, a wise man looks at it smilingly (knowing its ultimate result) as a witness i.e. without getting unduly involved in it. The wise individual witnesses this drama of life without attachment and escapes the consequential emotional onslaught due to attitude of detachment.

It is a wonderful verse and contains a lot for the daily life. We get depressed unduly forgetting the great wisdom " …even this will pass away." Nature is constantly changing. The awareness of this truth generates inclination towards detachment. We look at what is constantly changing. We do not look at what is ever the same, our essential divine nature. That is why we lose our poise. We get into the grip of ailments, sufferings, innumerable problems. We lose the grip of the greatest providential gift (an opportunity to live as a human) and pass life as prisoners of fate. If our focus is on the divinity within, the difficulties of life (which are bound to be there due to force of heredity, pressure of environment and laws of nature i.e. impact of gunas, will not unduly affect us. Modes of nature (senses) are acting on the modes of nature (objects of senses) as the result of operation of causes (attributes of nature).

Lord wants Arjuna to know that organs of senses are occupied with the objects of senses. Thus knowing the truth, escape attachment with the "**ever changing**" and be established in the "**never changing**." When one takes the attention off from the body, one starts identifying with the self.

29. Lord has clarified the distinction between the outlooks of the ignorant and the wise in the

previous verse. Now Lord again advises Arjuna that the men of wisdom should not unsettle the mind of the mediocre or the imperfect.

प्रकृतेर्गुणसम्मूढाः सज्जन्ते गुणकर्मसु ।
तानकृत्स्नविदो मन्दान्कृत्स्नविन्न विचालयेत् ॥ ३- २९ ॥

prakrter guna-sammudhah sajjante guna-karmasu
tan akrtsna-vido mandan krtsna-vin na vicalayet 3.29

prakrteh—of nature; *guna-sammudhah*—persons deluded by gunas (attributes); *sajjante*—are attached; *guna-karmasu*—in the functions of the qualities; *tan*—all; *akrtsna-vidah*—of improper knowledge; *mandan*—the foolish; *krtsna-vit*—man of perfect knowledge; *na-* not; *vicalayet*—should unsettle.

"Those who are misled by the attributes of nature are attached to works produced by them. Those, knowing the whole (the men of wisdom), should not unsettle the mind of the ignorant, who know only the part." II 3-29 II

By now, it is clear that actions arise due to actions and reactions of attributes of nature in different forms and different ways among themselves. The wise men know it. For this reason, they remain established in their divine nature within them. On the contrary, those who do not have perfect knowledge work under the impulsion of nature i.e. natural propensities and susceptibilities or that which influences them and not under the awareness of the pure wisdom. Deluded by the gunas, these worldly-minded people with imperfect knowledge (referred to in verse 26 also) remain attached to the gunas and actions. The wise should not unsettle the minds of those having imperfect knowledge. The wise should give proper lessons to the imperfect taking into consideration their mental standards and requirements. If this fact is not taken care of, the people with imperfect knowledge will stop doing whatever little they are doing with their imperfect knowledge. This message has been given in following words:

i) **prakrter guna sammuddha sajjante guna karmesu** i.e. those who are deluded by gunas of nature are attached to activities dictated by gunas. Why is it so? When awareness of divine presence is not there, attachment is bound to be there. A deluded human being remains confined to one's personal self i.e. physical existence. When the focus is not on truth, the focus will be on untruth and consequent attachment is bound to ensue.

ii) tan akrtsnavido mandan krsnavin na vicalayet [the people of perfect knowledge (full understanding)] should not disturb the people of small understanding] – Three words used by the lord are relevant here:

a) *akrtsnavido* (people of imperfect knowledge) – This word explains why people of imperfect knowledge get attached. They are not ignorant completely. At the same time they are not fully alive to the bliss of the divine essence within. For example they may do ritual laid down in Vedas for specific purposes invoking specific God (one of the intermediate Gods). If someone with perfect divine knowledge starts giving sermon on the limitations of rituals with attachment, then this message will not go well with the individual having imperfect knowledge. Besides, the one with imperfect knowledge may not even do whatever they are doing. It only hampers the spiritual progress of the individual with imperfect knowledge.

b) *Mandan* (**dullards**) i.e. those who do not understand divine knowledge (all-pervading atman or cosmic force) fully and remain attached to whatever little they know.

C) *krtsnavit* **(people of perfect knowledge)** – these are the people having perfect knowledge consisting of realization of self (all-pervading atman) who is the true self, who is the detached witness within one's own self. They know that one can befool the world but to escape from this 'Reality' is impossible.

What is the message of this verse? No attempt should be made to belittle the faith of any one however imperfect he or she may appear to be. Proper respect should be given to belief of even those having imperfect knowledge. Even in an imperfect approach, they are thinking of the "Supreme." It will be sheer ignorance to undermine this fact. The perfect should induce the imperfect by setting good example. The imperfect should be made to feel (not by verbal lectures alone) that attachment or involvement is there only outwardly at the physical level. At the deeper level, in the vicinity of that vibrant space within, no involvement, no attachment can ever be. This wisdom should be imparted gradually taking into consideration the maturity level and background of the imperfect seeker. Instead of getting the imperfect confused, he or she should be induced gradually to get anchored deep in the divine within, where there is no restlessness, no illness and no anxiety. The wise should make the things very clear to the imperfect. Everything may be threatening and breaking down to them due to attachment. Still there will appear luminous and calm, piercing through the clouds, dispelling the shadows, emerging still greater and stronger from ruins of self-made destruction, the infinite peace and beatitude of our within. In that direction, the wise should induce (persuade or influence) the imperfect along with them.

30 Lord is talking about karam-yoga. There is a difference in just working and working under karam-yoga. For Karam-yoga a particular attitude is required. A different approach is required to be free from attachment to action and its fruits while working. This is discussed in this verse.

मयि सर्वाणि कर्माणि संन्यस्याध्यात्मचेतसा ।
निराशीर्निर्ममो भूत्वा युध्यस्व विगतज्वरः ॥ ३- ३० ॥

mayi sarvani karmani sannyasya adhyatma-cetasa
nirasir nirmamo bhutva yudhyasva vigata-jvarah 3.30

mayi—in Me; *sarvani*--all ; *karmani*--actions; *sannyasya*- - renouncing; *adhyatma--cetasa*-awakened with the knowledge of the self (discussed by the Lord in the second chapter); *nirasih*—free from hope; *nirmamah*—free from ownership; *bhutva*—having become; *yudhyasva*—fight (thou); *vigata-jvarah*—free from mental fever.

"Surrender all your thoughts to "Me." With your thoughts centered on the self and without having any desire or thought of "Me and Mine," put off your feverishness and engage in battle." II 3-30 II

There is an omnipotent (most powerful), omnipresent (present everywhere) and omniscient (knowing everything) universal force underneath all the changes that we see in this universe. There is a sovereign force. Time and again Lord Krishna is trying to awake the awareness towards this Reality (either directly as formless or through its symbolic form Krishna) in all situations. This awareness is the first thing and very important as well. There is a divine pure luminous power. It is boundless love, unmixed peace and endless bliss of Infinite knowledge. Lord is telling the "supreme way" to work in this verse. What do we do in ordinary life? We start working and then grappling with the work wasting enormous time and energy and find ourselves feeling, worrying and run-down in the end. That is not the right way. That is the egoistic way of doing. We should start working with feeling of surrender to the Supreme. Lord has detailed in terms of activities how one should work in karam-yoga as follows:

i) Mayi sarvani karmani sanyasa (renouncing all actions to me) - What does an individual normally do for doing anything? An individual starts working putting pressure on all the individual faculties to achieve the result. That is where the attachment arises. First thing in doing anything is to come in divine mode of surrender. Be aware of the divine component within. Think of the one called "life of the life or light of our being" (either as formless or as Krishna as symbol of the Supreme) and then let the activities be an offerings to the Supreme. This is called surrender i.e. you are working for the Supreme. This releases the individual from the inherent "uncalled for concern" that one shares for the activity. This particular act of offering the work to the Lord helps an individual to go beyond the range of mind and intellect keeping the discharge of activity still continuing. This is the way to get rid of ego. This is the way to get rid of the attachment to fruit of actions. This approach will relieve the individual from the feverishness of actions. We renounce attachment for fruit of actions by surrender i.e. by doing work as an offering to the Lord. This should be the start of working in Karam-yoga (rather first step). Lord is asking Arjuna to offer even this act of fighting as an offering, because even this heinous (shocking and immoral looking) activity will become an act of worship because fighting was to restore righteousness or to finish those who were a party in stripping off a women in the open court or those who connived (worked secretly to achieve something wrong) gambling. It was not a call to fight in the war for self interest. Till this implicit loyalty to the 'Universal force or Me or Krishna here' grips the seeker, yoga-part of "karam-yoga" will not ensue (begin). This will dissolve doer-ship in the seeker. If this surrender part is complete without reservations, the mind of the seeker will be peaceful and intelligence will be clear like the sky without trace of clouds.

Lord is using the word "Me." Lord is gradually unfolding his "supreme identity," because war situation demands immediate action and Arjuna is not able to fully grasp the divine wisdom. Lord says "Surrender to Me." This is a call to initiate the activity with consciousness of Divinity. This is a call to all those who want to work in mode of Karam-yoga.

ii) *Adhyatmacetsa, Nirasih, nirmamah buhtvah* (mind established in the self; without craving for personal interest; becoming free "I" and "mine") – These are three more conditions to be complied with by one who want to convert an act into karam-yoga:

a) *Adhyatmacetsa* (mind established in the self) – There are two aspects of any individual i.e. divine aspect and worldly aspect or physical aspect. Normally we all remain confined to the physical aspect only. That is why we remain bound to cycles of birth and death. Lord wants Arjuna to be aware of our divine aspect within as well while doing any activity i.e. spiritual human excellence or divine loftiness within should never be forgotten or lost sight of. This divine aspect within is a formidable dimension of human personality. It is an "unfathomable ocean of excellence." The difficulty is that we remain confined to physical aspect alone. Lord wants Arjuna to get connected to the divine energy within by getting established within. This is the next point given in this verse to convert "Karma" (act) into "*karam-yoga*." Physical human limits cannot be exceeded till "divine connectivity" is established within by taking refuge in the Divinity.

b) *Nirasih* (without personal interest) – It has been pointed out earlier as well that in Karam-yoga work is done without attachment to personal interest or hope of any kind for self gratification. If work is not being done for "*lokasamgraha*; Cosmic benefit" in some measure, it does not get entitled to be categorized as an act of "*karam-yoga*." It is the offering without self interest for "common good" with focus on the "eternal existence" that differentiates the activity in the "*karam-yoga*" from the ordinary activity. In karam-yoga even work for bare self-sustenance is also a part of "*karam-yoga*" because the instrument of service is being kept ready for the service of the "Supreme." Thus we notice that it is the attitude that is important in "*karam-yoga*." Activity should be bereft of "personal interest" alone.

c) *Nirmamo* (free from egoism) – What was Arjuna's problem? He was baffled because his thinking was based on ego i.e. "if I kill, my relatives, my grand-sire, my teacher … ….." In the discharge of an action, ego (separate or individual self) automatically comes in i.e. my function, my interest, my view etc. For karam-yoga, ego-centered approach is not allowed. With ego in domination, one is not able to connect to divine potential within or the unlimited and inexhaustible source of energy within. When we are conscious that the senses and the objects of senses are both perishable (*guna guneshu vartante*; attributes of gunas act and react upon each other) being the output of attributes of nature, then doer-ship does not bother. The barrier called ego evaporates and one comes face to face with one's pristine glory, one's essential nature, the conglomeration of peace, knowledge and consciousness. Rather one gets connected to the source of "Supreme power." When this state is reached duality ends and "That One" alone manifests in and out of self. This aspect of "*Karam-yoga*" unites the seeker with the Supreme.

iii) *Yudhyasva vigatjvarah* [fight, free from feverishness (mental)] – This word fight, used by the Lord in the battle field has to be properly understood. Does it mean that Lord is instigating Arjuna to murder his relatives in the battle field? No. All channels of communication to bring about reconciliation between the *Kauravas* and the *Pandavas* have been exhausted. Now war is the only solution left to relieve the earth of the burden of the "perpetrators of unrighteousness (recall condition of Draupdi in the open court; the connived gambling and attack on the messenger in the court of Kaurvas)." By asking to fight, Lord is exhorting Arjuna to do duty (*svadharma*, bounded duty) of *Kshetriya*-warrior in restoring righteousness in the society. In this situation, Lord is not asking Arjuna to fight. Lord is asking Arjuna to perform a "*yajna*" in which Arjuna is to put to risk (or sacrifice) his honor, his soft feelings for his kith and kin, his skill, his whole life. This risk is going to be offering of Arjuna in this yajna i.e. war in this situation. The sole purpose for motivating for the war is removal of unrighteousness from the society. The use of the word "fight" emphasizes another ingredient of *Karam-yoga* i.e. action. Action is necessary to translate the thought into a reality. The **Yajna** of karam-yoga remains incomplete without offering of action.

Free from feverishness - Where does the feverishness come from? Feverishness, which gripped Arjuna arises when one works with ego with focus on rewards. When conditions described in a), b) and c) above have been complied with, the individual will be at peace, conscious of divine nature and committed to do work of "*Lokasamgraha*; cosmic benefit." Then there will be no restlessness, no hurry. The soul gets drenched with the thoughts of the Supreme in self surrender. One can manage to smile even in battle field like Lord Krishna due to strength of yoga. In these moments one yearns to become a musical note of an instrument in the universal orchestra in the divine symphony offered to the Supreme for the common good. In karam-yoga divine consciousness, to which work is offered, is necessary. Those thoughts will rejuvenate the seeker while putting the feverishness (uncalled for anxiety) to rest. Thus Lord offers another ingredient of "*Karam-yoga*" i.e. freedom from feverishness or uncalled for anxiety. In *karam-yoga,* work is performed, not out of feverishness but out of internal harmony, based on internal connectivity, based on that power which surpasses the individual human efforts. How should the work be done then in Karam-yoga? At operation level, all senses should work fully. Let the work being done be an offering to the "Supreme" or for the benefit of "His" creation. Mind should be free from undue attachment for fruit of action. The whole thing should be done feeling the inner calm and divine connectivity. That is the crux (most important part) of this verse.

What is the message of this verse? The highest good lies in surrendering to the Lord and acting without desire. Most important point of this verse is surrender. The ultimate knowledge about the self and the nature may not immediately help in initial stages. It takes time. Therefore Lord advises principle of surrender to "The Ultimate Refuge; Use of word 'Me' here." This establishes the spiritual link and sets in motion the especial divine grace. The space vacated by ego gets filled with an unspeakable joy which springs from the "Measureless Divine Love" within. The effect of process of "karam-yoga" starts ensuing (happening).

31. Lord in this verse assures that, if "this advice" given in the preceding verse is followed, the seeker will get released from bondage of work done.

ये मे मतमिदं नित्यमनुतिष्ठन्ति मानवाः ।
श्रद्धावन्तोऽनसूयन्तो मुच्यन्ते तेऽपि कर्मभिः ॥ ३- ३१ ॥

ye me matam idam nityam anutisthanti manavah
sraddhavanto 'nasuyanto mucyante te 'pi karmabhih 3.31

ye--those; *me*--My; *matam*—injunctions (teaching); *idam*--this; *nityam*—constantly; *anutisthanti*—follow or practice; *manavah*-- men; *sraddha-vantah*—full of *sraddha* (faith + awe+ reverence + desire to get some knowledge) ; *anasuyantah*--without caviling (making unnecessary complaints); *mucyante*--become free; *te*--all; *api*--even; *karmabhih*--from the bondage of action.

"Those, who follow my 'this teaching' with 'sradha' and without trusting their critical intelligence, they too are released from action." II 3-31 II

In preceding verse Lord discussed the essentials of "karam-yoga." In this verse, Lord assures that those, who follow Lord's lesson, are also released from capturing impact of action (the reason for an individual's bondage with cycles of birth and death) provided conditions laid down in this regard are complied with as follows:

i) *ye me matam idam nityam anutisthanti manvah* (those individuals who constantly follow this teaching of mine) – Lord is talking about those people who follow this teaching always. Certain words used by Lord require elaboration:

a) *matam idam* (this message) – What in brief is the spirit of this message that Lord is talking about? This message, elaborated in the previous verses, is about essential conditions of karam-yoga i.e. 1) First there should be an action appropriate to the faculties of the seeker i.e. even conceiving a potential and workable plan for betterment of ecosystem is an action; even fighting in a war for restoring righteousness is an action; even "inaction with awareness" for a greater and noble cause is an action; 2) action should be done without ego, without feverishness, without attachment to fruit of action for *lokasamgraha* (i.e. for the welfare of the world and it may include even little acts of service and little deeds of kindness for men, women, animals, birds, plants and their environment; 3) established in one's own divine consciousness (i.e. with awareness of divine components within; only a human being can be aware of this consciousness) the work should be done as an offering to the "Supreme Power being represented by Krishna here"; After this mental-offering of the activity to the "Eternal Infinite Force; Krishna here," undue-capturing relationship with the activity goes away and one feels released within. This, in brief, is the message of the Lord to convert any action into "Karam-yoga." What is the difference between Karam (an action) and Karam-yoga? In action, one may tap one's own physical and mental potential for self interest as well. One may feel fatigued and worried also. In karam-yoga, work is done for *lokasangraha* (welfare of the world) and besides one's physical and mental energy, one uses one's spiritual energy to go beyond the limits of human knowledge and experience. In karam-yoga one often feels rejuvenated (to feel young and strong) after using one's total potential optimally for a common cause or for world's welfare. Work done in the mode of

"Karam-Yoga" instills (gradually makes to feel, think or behave) joy, energy, peace and contentment instead of fatigue and helplessness. Work done in "karam-yoga," makes the seeker feel expansion, elevation, integration (in different levels within) sublimation and fullness.

b) *nityam* (always) – The use of this word means that this principle of "*Karam-yoga*" should be followed always without break as a way of life. The emphasis is to tell that use of these principles of "*karam-yoga*" should become our second nature to be practiced at every moment of life.

ii) *sraddhavante ansuyanto te pi karambhi* [(they) who work with sraddha and without cavil (to make unnecessary complaints about something), also get freed from bondage of action] – The seeker gets freed from bondage (capturing effects of action) provided following conditions are complied with:

a) *srddhavanto* [(reverence + awe + belief + some amount of uncertainty + expectation)] – Action should be done with "*sraddha*." First meaning of *sraddha* should be understood. There is no English synonym for this word. One who has sraddha shows a lot of respect and admiration for the one in whom *sraddha* is reposed. Awe denotes overwhelming admiration (wow-feeling) for one being adored with *sraddha*. The one having *sraddha* always carries a feeling of belief in one in whom *sraddha* is reposed. This happens even without specific reasons. When we develop *sraddha* for someone, we know some aspects and some aspects of that personality we do not know as well. This unknown aspect with belief increases *sraddha*. *Sraddha* develops when some favor, some grace, something even unknown is expected. Faith alone is not *sraddha*. Someone may be having faith in one's intellectual competence and physical endurance and this faith may become a cause for an action and success in that line. This is faith and not *sraddha*. While faith may lead to worldly success, *sraddha* is ennobling experience which matures the seeker spiritually and procures guru grace (divine grace) for journey beyond. *Sraddha* fosters (grants paternal care to) seeker's inherent potential, which may not be visibly noticeable. *Sraddha* is that source of strength, that glue, that connecting element, which helps the seeker to have something "extra and very special" to go beyond the limits of human knowledge and experience to the "sphere of eternally unfolding joy and immortal satisfaction." The seeker should have *sradhha* for the principles of karam-*yoga*, for the inner divine propensities and for the master who guides to work in the spirit of *karam-yoga*.

b) *Anasuyanto* (not caviling; caviling means making unnecessary complaints) – An individual's critical intelligence may hamper spiritual progress by playing negative roles. A true seeker trusts his or her critical intelligence and does not allow it to play negative roles. Caviling only creates doubts. It is indication of unripe mind and intelligence. A seeker should shun uncalled for caviling (unnecessary complaints) by faculty of intelligence. One requires peace to be in tune with the positive interplay of the cosmic forces.

iii) *muchayante te pi karambhi* (they too are released by action and through action) – Those who follow the advice of Krishna as above on *karam-yoga* also get released by work and through work (*karambhi*). What does it mean? First the action keeps the things moving in the desired direction. Action exerts numerous internal and external influences. Action alone cannot liberate an individual. It is non-attachment or attitude with which works are performed, that liberates or creates that something extra, which works.

This verse asserts that by working in the spirit of *karam-yoga* one can get rid of bondage aspect (capturing aspect responsible for cycles of birth and death) of action. This message is music to the soul. One must realize that one's "individuality i.e. I am" is not the highest truth. There is within an individual, which is universal, which is immortal, which is eternal, which is immeasurable. *Karam-yoga* unites with "**That Within**." This principle of *karam-yoga* is not to be viewed in isolation. It is not something apart from us. The universal power, which this spirit of **karam-yoga** touches, is one with "our power." This power thwarts us when we are small, when we are against the current. This power helps when we work with expansive spirit of **karam-yoga** working for all and for the welfare of all. This spirit of **karam-yoga** helps to achieve "*the Universal*" in physical aspect.

32. In this Lord tells Arjuna the consequences of not following the teaching relating to **karam-yoga,** discussed earlier.

ये त्वेतदभ्यसूयन्तो नानुतिष्ठन्ति मे मतम् ।
सर्वज्ञानविमूढांस्तान्विद्धि नष्टानचेतसः ॥ ३- ३२ ॥

ye tv etad abhyasuyanto nanutisthanti me matam
sarva-jnana-vimudhams tan viddhi nastan acetasah 3.32

ye--those; *tu*-- but; *etat*--this; *abhyasuyantah*—c arping (complaining at continuously); *na*--not; *anutisthanti*—follow or practice; *me*--My; *matam*—teaching or injunction; *sarva-jnana-- vimudhan*-deluded in all knowledge; *tan*--they are; *viddhi*--know; *nastan*--ruined; *acetasah*—devoid of discrimination.

"There are those, who carp (criticize continuously) and cavil (make unnecessary comments) at my teaching continuously and do not follow or practice it; know them to be deluded in all knowledge, devoid of discrimination and doomed to destruction." II 3-32 II

Now Lord talks of those who criticize unnecessarily this teaching about **karam-yoga**. Lord describes them in following words:

i) *ye tv etad abhyasuyanto na anutisthanti me matam* **(but those who carp and do not practice my this teaching)** – There are all types of people in this world. They are confined to worldly life driven by desires, haunted by hopes and fears and blasted by frustration. They find it difficult to understand the abstract discussion about the secrets of divine existence and its approach. They do not understand the discussion on **karam-yoga**, which is an effective approach to gain **moksha** (liberation from limitations of human knowledge and experience). Lord has described these people by using two words a) **abhyasuyanto** and b) **nanutisthanti**. "*Abhyasuyanto*" means decrying i.e. they publicly do not approve of this teaching about **karam-yoga** and continuously criticize it or find fault with it [due to heresy (statements contradicting the accepted facts) or faithlessness]. Second word used by the Lord is "*anutisthanti*." It means that these people do not follow or practice the teachings of Lord Krishna relating to **karam-yoga**. It means Lord is talking about those who criticize the knowledge given by the Lord and do not follow it.

ii) *saravjnanavimudhanstan vidhi nastanacetasah* (know them to be devoid of all knowledge and destined to be destroyed) – The higher truths (discussions about divine knowledge; about **purusa** and nature; about supreme truth) starts appealing only when an individual starts getting the "feel of living at the level of consciousness." Understanding higher truths means a transition from animal existence to divine existence. It is not easy. It requires **nigrah** or **samyam** (control with right use and right guidance). If this knowledge is given to those who are not ready (matured enough) to take it, it becomes a sort of "violence done to nature by will." They, inspired by jealousy, disregard this teaching and do not apply it in daily life. They may use words against this divine knowledge. Therefore, Lord says that they are to be considered ignorant of all knowledge (divine knowledge), without discrimination. Such people remain deprived of achievable human ends. Their whole life will be wasteful however resourceful they may otherwise be (in terms of worldly existence).

When mind is confined to the gross objects and discrimination is confused, one wanders in the perishable world tired, weary and restless. Such men are lost. They have no discrimination, no faith. Those, who live by desire, find it difficult to understand the discussion on "**living beyond desire.**" Lord says this so that we may not put the pressure of efforts inappropriately. Lord Krishna wants to give "**a method,**" by which all can be free. But, Lord wants us to know that some people, like rats in the trap, will not understand it. They keep running and running in the trap only. That is why Lord wants these people to be known as ruined and "**acetsah; not alive to their consciousness.**"

In this verse, Lord makes a negative statement to pass on a positive message. By not following the teaching on *Karam-yoga*, one will be ruined and lost to his or her consciousness. What does Lord want to say here? By following the teaching on *Karam-yoga*, a new awakening will be experienced by the individual and he or she will become alive to one's higher nature, one's spiritual self, one's divinity within. All one requires doing for that is orientation of mind, cultivation of divine wisdom within, establishing a mute link with the Ultimate Reality within, which is beyond all articulation. This objective can be achieved by working truly in the "**mode of karam-yoga**" discussed in detail by the Lord before this verse. Nature is in the hold of entire world at all the times without any exception. Therefore, we have to understand nature's true nature and the extent of its hold. We have to understand who we really are. Then we have to live and move in tune with nature, witnessing it without being confined to it and considering it as an inseparable companion to life. We cannot gain this practical wisdom (of karam-yoga) until we learn to follow the "**eternal rhythm and touch of the fundamental unity**" at every step. For this we have to have "**separation, balanced in beauty (eternal beauty) and strength (pull of *maya*).**" That is yoga.

33. In this verse Lord says that one has to follow one's nature. This is one inescapable truth. This inevitability has to be accepted first. Everything else (which Lord deals afterwards) will follow. Actually this verse can be fully understood, only if it is read in context with the coming verses.

सदृशं चेष्टते स्वस्याः प्रकृतेर्ज्ञानवानपि ।
प्रकृतिं यान्ति भूतानि निग्रहः किं करिष्यति ॥ ३- ३३ ॥

sadrsam cestate svasyah prakrter jnanavan api
prakrtim yanti bhutani nigrahah kim karisyati 3.33

sadrsam—in accordance; *cestate*-- acts; *svasyah*—of his own; *prakrteh*—of nature; *jnana-van-* a wise man; *api*-- even; *prakrtim*--nature; *yanti*-- follow; *bhutani*—beings or all living entities; *nigrahah*--restraint; *kim*--what; *karisyati*-- will do.

"Even wise individual acts in accordance with his or her nature; the beings follow their nature; what can suppression (or restraint) do?" II 33 II

The message of this verse has to be understood carefully and in the light of the verses that are about to follow. Does it mean that Lord is talking about the assertion of the omnipotence (capability to do just anything) of nature over the sovereignty of the Supreme? No. The Lord is giving a lesson to escape an unwanted confrontation or unwanted aggression, which will otherwise waste one's capability, one's potential. The whole world is a composition of the "**never changing and the ever changing.**" In our zeal for the 'never changing; the Infinite', we cannot ignore even a bit the 'ever changing; the nature'. One has to follow one's nature. This is to be accepted. This is providential command. Everything else (efforts for the "never changing") will fall in place gradually. It will amount to arrogance to ignore nature. Accept it first and then do anything else (discussed subsequently). This point can be explained as follows. Suppose the present course of flow of a particular river is not in public interest. Now it is not that we cannot do anything about it. We can change the course of the river if we accept that water flows downward. In this verse, Lord is only saying that we have to fundamentally accept first the vital fact and then it can be made best use of subsequently. This is the brief message in the following words:

i) **sadrsam cetsah svasyah prakrteh jnanavan api** [One's own nature shall dictate how one shall act; even a jnani (one adept in knowledge) is carried away by forces of nature] – One's behavior is dictated by the hue (kind of color) of impact of a peculiar combination of rajas, tamas and sattava in one's behavior. The environment in which one grows also exerts its influence. Each one of us has a peculiar combination of these attributes molding our behavior. Each one has to act taking into account one's peculiar nature (svabhav), distinctly traceable impact of particular combination of three gunas. What is one's nature? It is the distinctive nature (svabhava) of an individual representing sum total of tendencies of actions done in the past in the previous lives stored in the mind and also what one is born of plus what one has grown with. One's nature is the natural tendency of an individual based on his or her own particular body-sense-mind complex, one's psyche. Outwardly, it is reflected by impulses of one's sensory system going out into the external world. This natural reaction can be handled in two ways. First, the natural reaction can be suppressed or coerced (forcing someone to do something that he or she does not want to do). Secondly, it can be controlled by right use, right guidance and foresight. First alternative depresses an individual and sub-utilizes one's natural potential. Second alternative is the control of lower nature by higher nature. It results in efficiency (**yogah karmsu kaushlam;** yogah engenders efficiency). Lord is asking in this verse to accept the particular individual nature. Lord talks of its use and guidance afterwards in the verses yet to come. We can elaborate it a little further. Desire and anger are two attributes. One should accept one's nature first. If this point has been accepted, then afterwards, one can desire for self realization. If one has to be angry, one can be angry with one's slow spiritual progress. That is the Lord's point. Accept the nature and its mighty influence. This acceptance will help optimum utilization of self potential. Some plants grow tall and slender while others are shrubby and stout. Some fruits are sweet while others are bitter. The nature of these fruits cannot be changed but it can be augmented and enriched and its new applications can be found out. Similarly, each one of us is a peculiar combination of gunas having shares of sattva, rajas and tamas in different measures. Arjuna was warrior first. *Rajas* (feverishness, being restless for the target) was his dominating attribute. It was a part of his nature to fight for the cause of righteousness. That is what Lord was trying to make him realize. We should know our nature first i.e. dominant characteristics of it. Some naturally feel restless to do something. Some naturally feel lazy. Some by nature are introspective, reflective and meditative. Identify your nature first to make best use of your own nature. That is the point of the Lord. Even those who are wise follow their natural instincts.

ii) **prakrtim yanti bhutani nigrah kim karishyati** (Beings follow nature, what can mere suppression do?) – It is natural to follow impulsion of nature, most dominant abrupt behavioral pattern. Suppression causes depression and sub-utilization of an individual's potential. What is message of the Lord? Animal follow nature mutely. Nature can be sattava-dominated, rajas-dominated or tamas-dominated. What should an individual do? Lord is making this statement from a different perspective. First identify the distinctive characteristics of your nature. This alone is the message in this verse. Lord is making this statement with a different perspective in view. Each human being has lower nature or higher nature. First identify your true nature (Lord ends here in this verse). Then it can be sublimated (to use energy for something else) in the light of divine consciousness (this has been taken up afterwards). Even negative emotions can be used optimally for positive purposes. What will suppression do? Suppression will only result in lower utilization of individual's innate potential. Lord is simply asking not to ignore natural propensities, which cannot be changed but can be optimally utilized. That is all.

Lord is asking not to waste our potential in suppressing our natural instincts. Therefore, do not confront nature. It will exhaust you unnecessarily. Nature is extremely powerful. It is Lord's kinetic energy. By surrender to the Lord, it can be handled effectively. Your own nature (including such negative emotions as desire and anger) can be positively sublimated towards the higher ends. Ashram may be the same. Teacher may be the same. Divine component (in the soul) may be the same. Still all the recipients may have different nature and purposes. Some, given to valor, may take up control of society, its administration. Some with ascetic tendencies may take to austere (plain, simple without decoration) life. Some, with tamasic tendencies, may become notorious. Still all may seek self realization. Ravana deliberately chose the path of war for gaining highest "after-death life." Lord wants all to follow their own promptings, which should be first identified. "Failure to identify your true nature in terms of natural tendencies, propensities and unmixed spontaneous behavior" causes stress and makes life a prison, a tale of suppressions and longings. First one has to idientify these moorings (ropes, chains, anchors of one's behavior) to help us to manifest the real meaning of the self. Therein is life's revelation (divine message). If we do not accept our true nature (in terms of impact of attributes of nature) we will have in life frustration, unhappiness, disappointment and heartaches. After identifying our individual peculiar nature and after sublimating it in the light of divine consciousness, we feel utterly fulfilled. Nothing will be able to disturb us or shake us or dislodge us from being established in our own nature, an abode of peace, contentment and consciousness. Best way to tame the senses or to overcome the negative aspects of our dominant nature is to render service (offer to be useful without conditions and without self interest) for the welfare of the world. Effort to suppress the natural instinct is not recommended. Effort to sublimate the natural instinct offers the solution.

Prakriti (nature) is the mental equipment (or laws) with which one is born as a result of past acts and tendencies. It is law of our being. It is that which brought the being in existence. One has to understand the law (nature) relating to "truth of being." This law is very effective. This law (associated rules; impact of attributes) must take its course. It only ordains that past deeds must produce their natural effects. One should identify one's "true being; eternal existence" and then one should express it in compatibility with one's nature (impact of one's composition of sattva, rajas and tamas). We cannot suppress it even if we desire. Violated nature runs its course against the individual efforts causing sufferings, suffocation, diseases and afflictions. The accumulated stress due to "violated nature or disobeyed nature" turns life (a cause for celebration) into drudgery (hard boring work).

34. This verse passes on a simple but meaningful message "Beware of the enemies within you." Who are these enemies? What are they doing? Lord discusses this in this verse. This verse also answers the point raised in the previous verse i.e. whether we should follow dominant characteristics of individual nature (desire and anger) indiscriminately (without thought).

इन्द्रियस्येन्द्रियस्यार्थे रागद्वेषौ व्यवस्थितौ ।
तयोर्न वशमागच्छेत्तौ ह्यस्य परिपन्थिनौ ॥ ३- ३४ ॥

indriyasyendriyasyarthe raga-dvesau vyavasthitau
tayor na vasam agacchet tau hy asya paripanthinau 3.34

indriyasya—to the senses; *indriyasya arthe*—of the sense-objects; *raga*--attachment; *dvesau*--aversion; *vyavasthitau*-- seated; *tayoh*--of these; *na*--not; *vasam*--control; *agacchet*—should come under; *tau*—those (two); *hi*-- verily; *asya*--his; *paripanthinau*—foes.

"Attraction and repulsion (likes or dislikes) are rooted in between each sense of perception and its object. They are the stumbling blocks or enemies in the way of one's spiritual progress. One should not be enslaved by them." II 3-34 II

There is a natural relationship between each sense (indriya) and its sense-object (indriyasyarthe). These two are related to each other as a consequence of *rajas, tamas* and *sattva*. Let us take the earlier example once again. Suppose you are going. A lady passes by you with a toddler in her lap. The toddler is very handsome, very smart, bubbly (cheerful, friendly) and jumping with energy. Your eyes look at the child. You smile and at the same time wink the eyes abruptly and mischievously. The toddler responds to your smile with a twinkle in his or her eye. The mother does not even know it. What does it all mean? There is an action and reaction relationship in each sense and sense object. There is nothing good and bad about it. It is, as Lord described, "*guna guneshu vartante*; gunas of nature act according to their own rules and regulations in front of sense-objects." This action and reaction relationship between senses and sense-objects is inescapable. It is a very important message. If you bring ghee near the fire, it is bound to change in liquid form. This verse talks of attachment and repulsion. This attachment and repulsion and their intensity is the impact of our perception and understanding and it profoundly exerts its influence on action and reaction relationship of gunas. This action and reaction relationship turns into love and hatred due to inbuilt tendencies (favorable and unfavorable) about how we view the things. Someone may become attached and attracted to the extent of becoming a victim, restless. Some other fellow may develop aversion. Still some other fellow may simply laugh away the situation saying "guna guneshu vartante; gunas of nature act according to their own rules and regulations in front of sense-objects ". Attachment (raga) and repulsion (dvesha) are rooted under the senses and color action and reaction relationship of senses and sense objects. Lord brings round this message with an advice as follows:

i) ***indriyasye indriyasyarthe ragadvesau vyavasthitau*** [senses and sense-objects are related to each other, *raga* and *dvesha* remain established (in the senses, in the human system)] – First the meaning of these two terms should be discussed. *Raga* can be defined as the desire and attachment to experience sensual pleasures again and again i.e. raga is called stubborn continuing desire. What is *dvesha*? It is aversion or dislike for the unpleasant. These are two emotions mentioned here. If the attraction is favorable, one feels attachment. If one feels unfavorably, one experiences dvesha (repulsion). *Raga* and *dvesha* remain in the senses or in human system to influence the action and reaction of senses and sense objects. The focus of the Lord is to suggest that action and reaction relationship of senses and sense-objects gets influenced by our likes and dislikes which also exist in our senses in human system.

ii) ***tayor na vasamagacchet*** (don't get into their clutches) – Why does Lord use these words? These emotions are like highway-robbers, who come to loot whatever you have. We have to take appropriate measures. This is a sort of warning by the Lord that full care should be taken. One has to be alert to save from the influence of these emotions already existing in the human system. In brief caution is necessary. These robbers (emotions) may suddenly become strong even in the middle of the night to make mess of the altar that you have reserved only for the lord. The idea is to accept the danger from these "dangerous emotions" without whimper (weak crying noise).

iii) ***tau hi asya paripanthinau*** (they are known as one's highway robbers) – These *raga* and *dvesha* have been described as highway robbers. What do they do? They rob us of our knowledge, our wisdom, our discrimination, our restraint and resolve. They remain hidden giving impression as everything had been normal, calm and quiet. Then suddenly like robbers in the middle of dark nights in a lonely hamlet (small village), they become violent and corrupt what is sacrosanct (so important that nothing can criticize it) in life. Then we feel pain and cry.

Lord states that *raga* and *dvesa* remain in human system (senses) and manifest as such coloring the action and reaction relationship of senses and sense objects. These emotions are like enemies. What is the underlying message of the Lord? An emotion is either a surge (to move quickly up) of energy or a loss of energy (consequential depression). What is the root causing this upheaval (big change causing problems) of energy? It is all due to desire. Desire is not a problem. How we react to it decides whether it is good or bad. With proper control of mind, we can control both frequency of desires and channelizing of desires i.e. with proper attitude we can have mastery over likes and dislikes, raga and dvesa. The necessity is to have a frame of mind which either makes desire a luxury which we can ill afford or channelize the desire. For example, if we have intense desire for spiritual evolution, it will have profound impact on the consequential emotions like *raga* and *dvesa*. Those, who have knowledge, detachment and devotion, have neither likes nor dislikes for any worldly object, person or work. This is the chapter on **karam-yoga**. If the work is done in true spirit of **karam-yoga** for the welfare of the world, it will bring about startling changes. The raga and dvesa are destroyed in a sattavika (noble) person due to jnana (divine knowledge) and vairagya (or detachment). Raga and dvesa are two obstacles on the path of perfection. Those who have come over raga and dvesa become free individuals and attain moksha (complete freedom from all limitations of human knowledge and experience). By use of two simple words (*raga* and *dvesa*) Lord has guided us towards a path, which is free from all fears, which can help us to realize the truth of soul (unmixed and eternal joy, knowledge, contentment and consciousness). What does it all mean? We all have a dual set of desires in our beings. It should be our endeavor to bring a harmony in the two sets. Wishes of our palate often run counter to what our stomach can allow and that is the root cause of the problem. We must break all illusions that encase the divinity in our soul. One should properly use **viveka** (discrimination) in the matter relating to raga and dvesa so that sensory interactions and mental reactions are properly oriented and balanced by the rational intelligence. The grace of discrimination will facilitate "**composite integrated development**" of the individual.

35. In this verse Lord states the importance of doing one's duty, which is conducive to one's natural tendencies or propensities or attributes.

श्रेयान्स्वधर्मो विगुणः परधर्मात्स्वनुष्ठितात् ।
स्वधर्मे निधनं श्रेयः परधर्मो भयावहः ॥ ३- ३५ ॥

sreyan sva-dharmo vigunah para-dharmat svanusthitat
sva-dharme nidhanam sreyah para-dharmo bhayavahah 3.35

sreyan--better; *sva-dharmah*--one's own duty; *vigunah*- devoid of merit or even faulty; *para-dharmat*—than the duty of another; *svanusthitat*— well discharged; *sva-dharme*--in one's own duty; *nidhanam*--destruction; *sreyah*--better; *para-dharmah*--duties prescribed for others; *bhaya-avahah*—fraught with fear.

"It is better to follow *svadharmah* (one's own law of being, based on one's natural propensities, heritage, cultural background and one's social status), however imperfect or without merit it may happen to be, than to follow *paradharmah* (alien duty based on someone else's law of being) well discharged; death in following one's own law of being is better than following alien law based on someone else's law of being is perilous (very dangerous, fraught with fear)." II 3-35 II

It is a very famous verse and a great wisdom is being passed on by the Lord in these words as follows:

i) sreyan svadharmo vigunah paradharmat svanusthitat (it is better to follow svadharma, even though it is not of high quality than to follow para-dharma (alien duty based on someone else's law of being) well discharged. Three beautiful and meaningful words have been used by the Lord:

Sreya - *Sreya*, in Sanskrit, means that which augurs (sign of what will happen) merit, good future.

Svadharma – The term "*Svadharma*" has also been used in second chapter as well. It is different from "dharma; divine universal code of conduct, not only for human beings but for all beings." One's action and thinking cannot manifest the spirit of the Gita, till important terms are experienced like live wire. Svadharma is one important term like this. What is Savdharma? "Svadarma" is one's duty, which complies with three conditions: i) one's individual natural tendencies and propensities as a result of peculiar impact of three gunas of nature i.e. sattva (manifests through purity, luminosity, health etc.), rajas (manifests through unlimited desires, longings) and tamas (manifests through darkness, lethargy, ignorance etc.) and cumulative effect of past karmas; ii) what an individual is born of i.e. parentage or lineage and cultural heritage and iii) social rules, norms, one's standing in the society and the values that one has grown with. Now first point requires to be elaborated. How is an individual peculiarly influenced by three gunas? The proportion of three gunas is unique in each individual case. Different species of animals and plants show almost common characteristics in different members of species. Svadharma of tiger, fire and storm is all most identical in all cases except extent of ferocity and timing. Case of human being is different. Each individual has intelligent will, *buddhi*. *Svadharma* of each individual will be different. Each individual is influenced differently by different measures of sattvik, rajasik and tamasic components in his or her nature. In brief, all human beings are governed by unique, individual, cumulative impact of gunas differently. The impact of gunas leads to a peculiar and different psychic individuality in each case. This psychic individuality is based on bent of mind, attitude, reactions, likes and dislikes, cumulative impact of past karmas, one's cultural heritage and upbringing etc. Some like to go walking uphill professionally. Some people follow the artistic path even though they are not able to satisfy basic family needs. Some lead a simple life by limiting unnecessary luxuries and developing a hobby for seva to balance the spiritual and material needs of life. Svadharma should be identified cognizing the most dominant characteristic or natural attributes relating to an individual such as poise (calm and in control of feelings), feverishness and sluggishness or indolence. How should we go about deciphering the natural attributes? If an individual shows maturity, introspection, patience and attitude of renunciation, it means "sattva" is dominant. If an individual is passionate and determined feverishly about what he or she wants to do even at the cost of life, that indicates that rajas is dominant. If an individual eats too much like a glutton, takes lot of rest, shows frequent tantrums, it means tamas is the dominant factor. These gunas are the **unseen strings by which the imperishable soul is bound to the body**. If actions are in conformity to these dominant characteristics (natural attributes of an individual i.e. svadharma) then it will improve the efficiency of an individual in journey both in this world and beyond this world. Lord's point can be explained by two examples. Winston S Churchill, the war minister of the Great Britain failed thrice in the third standard. Then one of his father's friend one day identified his hidden flair (instinct; natural ability to do something) for war-games. He was immediately shifted to military school and then the boy who miserably failed in the third standard became world leader in the world war. Lata Mangeshkar, called the nightingale of India, attempted acting as well at the outset of her carrier. She soon recognized her flair (natural instincts) for singing only and she became one of the immortal playback singers of this century. That is why Lord wants Arjuna to understand "svadharma; that action which weaves well or integrates well or suits well or gels (works well) with natural propensities (inbuilt flair) of the individual. This is the meaning of the term "svadharma." Arjuna's svadharma was to fight for restoring righteousness and he was talking like an individual with dominant sattva at a very inappropriate time. That is why discussion of the Gita started.

What does Lord want to say? Identify your "svadharma" first and then act accordingly i.e. distinctly know whether you have inherent poise, feverishness or sluggishness. The focus should be to determine the dominant natural attribute or else it will amount to fitting the square pegs in the round holes. Determination of svadharma is not easy and requires use of intelligent will (buddhi). This is exactly the mistake that Arjuna was doing. He was a kshatriya (warrior) who was known for waging wars to ensure fairness and judiciousness in the society. It was in his blood to fight for righteousness. Arjuna's fault was that he ignored basic dominant characteristics of his individuality, which physically defined Arjuna and started talking like a jnani (wise man), which he was not. That is why Krishna smiled in the chariot in the battle field, seeing the mighty warrior, like Arjuna, stooping (bending) to ignorance right at the beginning of the war by sermonizing about righteousness and sins like a yogi. Krishna wanted him to use his fighting instincts for restoring righteousness. That is why Lord Krishna kept on goading him to fight. Lord Krishna did not want war. He wanted righteousness to be restored because opposing forces were not amenable (willing to listen) to reasoning and Arjuna was the mainstay (one who does the most important work) of the Pandvas.

"Paradharma" is another term used by the Lord. What is this? What is the relevance of this term at this point of discussion? It means alien duty which does not match with the natural propensities (natural flair) of an individual i.e. not being according to one's dominant characteristics such as purity, passion and ignorance. When Arjuna's chariot was placed between two armies ready to fight, he saw his uncles, grandfathers, teachers, brothers, sons, grandsons and comrades in the opposite camps ready to fight, ready to take life of the members of the Pandva's camps. Now for the first time, Arjuna actually felt the "weight of the reality of war" in his mind though he too had come to fight in the war willingly. He lost his poise. At that moment, Arjuna was not the warrior that he was known to be. Compassion overtook him. Weakness dominated his behavior. Overwhelmed by emotions, he forgot the purpose of war. The pandvas did not take the decision to wage a war to take revenge. They suffered a lot. They had the strength to claim their princely rights, but they observed reticence and patience. They tolerated to live in a jungle but did not perpetuate the issue to take proportions of war. They (Pandvas) came to war, after tolerating a lot and after very long deliberations, to rid the society of the vagabonds who were ready to outrage the modesty of a lady in the open court and who deceived others treacherously in the name of a game. Arjuna was the known warrior of that era. He forgot all this and started saying that he was ready to be slaughtered by the sons of Dhritarashtra in the battle, unarmed and unresisting. This behavior, utterly influenced by controllable emotions, was not in line with the "svadharam" of Arjuna. He started talking like an ordinary man overwhelmed by emotions by saying in the beginning of the Gita discussion "It would be better, indeed, to live on alms in this world than to slay these noble gurus, because by killing them I would enjoy wealth and pleasures stained with blood." This (living on alms) was only an emotional outburst of Arjuna and his expression at that moment was antithesis (exact opposite of something) of his original nature of a warrior. This meek and weak behavior was "para-dharma" for Arjuna, unknown to his basic, valiant (very brave) nature. Similarly, the most judicious and the greatest warrior Bhishma remained silent when in an open court his own daughter-in-law was being stripped off. This behavior was "para-dharma" for

Bhishma. Sometimes it becomes very difficult to identify "svadharma and paradharma" but correct interpretation is of paramount importance for achieving the mission of life. This can be explained by an example. In Ramayana, Ravana forcibly took away Sita from jungle while she was alone. Ravana had inkling (slight idea about something) that Rama was not an ordinary man and that he was "Supreme Divinity" in human form. Ravana wanted to see Rama (if he was divinity in human form) before him at the time of his death to experience the best possible "after life experience." There were two options available to him: i) following self-releasing activities such as seva (connecting with the divinity in others by offering one's service selflessly), sadhna (physical, mental, emotional and spiritual disciplines), satsasng (enjoying with those sharing truth) and svaddhyaya (study and introspection about truth within and around) based on sattvik disposition and ii) following path of war. Ravana was a demon of tamasic nature. He found it difficult to follow "self releasing activities mentioned above" as they were opposed to his natural tendencies. Therefore, he deliberately chose the path of war and did not choose the self releasing activities based on sattva. Self-releasing activities (seva, satsang and svadhyay) were falling in the category of "para-dharma" for him (Ravana).

A question may arise as to why the Lord started talking about "svadharama" and "paradharma" at this point of discussion. Arjuna was in agony of confusion in the beginning and he became Lord's disciple when he used the words "My heart stricken by compassion; my mind, perplexed, does not know where my duty lies; and so I ask you. Tell me for certain which is better between waging a war and becoming victim to emotions. Teach me, for I am your disciple and seek refuge in you." Now in this verse, Lord is clarifying the this point to him and answering to his prayer to help him understand his *svadharma* in that utterly confusing situation.

Now half of Lord's statement becomes clear. It is far better to do *svadharma* (action matching with natural propensities or cumulative impact of natural attributes of the individual), even though faultily (or not high in quality; vigunah), than to follow *paradharma* (action distinctly not matching with individual's natural propensities). Identifying "svadharma" amounts to identifying in full measure one's own dominant human characteristics i.e. identifying those characteristics which make an individual distinct in human race or identifying oneself in terms of poise, passion and sluggishness (habit of reacting very slowly). Determining *"svadharma"* will amount to decoding an individual's personality in terms of attributes of nature or characteristics or psychological disposition or one's likes and dislikes.

ii) **Svadharme nidhanam sreyah paradgarmo bhayavaha** [better it is to die in svadharma (one's own law of being) or duty in conformity with natural propensities; perilous or fraught with fear than to follow alien duty (i.e. duty not matching with one's own natural propensities)] - A natural singer is not likely to be a distinctly known fighter. A natural fighter is not likely to be a distinctly known singer. Lord concludes that death or destruction in course of performing one's duty is better than engaging in alien duties (i.e. duties not matching with the natural flair of an individual). Why does Lord say this? Performing "svadharma" will mean some satisfaction, some smooth performance somewhere irrespective of the result (at least one's efficiency i.e. "output per unit of input" is very high in following "svadharma"). Performing "paradharma" means undergoing stress and sub-utilization or burial of one's innate potential. Efficiency (i.e. output per unit of input) is very low in paradharma. It is dangerous and full of fear and uncertainty to be engaged in paradharma (duties not matching with natural propensities of the individual).

Let us review Lord's statement that death following "svadharma" is better than following paradharma (alien duties not matching with one's innate disposition) and becoming slave to uncalled for limitations. What does it mean? If an individual dies in "yoga-sadhna," he or she does not perish (it has been discussed in second chapter already). He or she will attain to higher world and would come to act again in human body to continue unfinished work. By following duties alien to one's nature, one lowers quality of one's performance as an individual and one only prolongs one's bondage with cycles of birth and death. That is what Lord means by using the word "death" in this context.

What is the message of this verse? When pure necessity drives an individual to work (alien work), the outcome is like a make shift arrangement i.e. quality deserts and leaves the results to be in ruins. When work is a joy (i.e. work done is in conformity with one's psychological individuality or according to svadharma or the work done is an outcome of harmony in different levels of existence or an outcome is according to one's fundamental nature), the work done takes the form of immortality. "Work done" imparts to an individual "unmatched quality" of permanence. One blossoms through work. "The invisible personality of the individual; the invincible within an individual, the indestructible giant within the individual, that mighty force in us which surpasses everything else in this world" manifests itself through the work done, if work is done in accordance with one's natural propensities and in karam-yoga mode. That is what the Lord is focusing at in this verse. When one acts in accordance with the deepest silence whispering within reminding one of one's true nature (svadharma), one realizes the futility of "seeking" based on others' dharma. One comes in contact with the "Unbroken Perfection" in the universe and one experiences the "Joy Unalloyed, Ever Flowing filling" in every nook and corner of the Universe.

36. In preceding verse Lord advises to work according to one's "svadharma; one's natural propensities or impact of gunas." Now Arjuna puts a question. He wants to know why, then, an individual commits a sin, if there is no fault in following one's propensities.

अर्जुन उवाच ।
अथ केन प्रयुक्तोऽयं पापं चरति पूरुषः ।
अनिच्छन्नपि वार्ष्णेय बलादिव नियोजितः ॥ ३- ३६ ॥

arjuna uvaca atha kena prayukto ayam papam carati purusah
anicchann api varsneya balad iva niyojitah 3.36

arjunah uvaca—Arjuna said; *atha*- now; *kena*—by what; *prayuktah*—impelled; *ayam*- this; *papam*—sin; *carati*—acts or does or happens; *purusah*—man; *anicchan*—without desiring or unwillingly; *api*— even; *varsneya*—O descendant of Vrsni (Krishna); *balat*—by force; *iva*—as it were; *niyojitah*— driven or constrained.

Arjuna said:

"O descendent of Varshni (Krishna, the descendent of Varshni clan)! By What an individual is compelled to commit sin, even though unwillingly, as if engaged by force?" II 3-36 II

This is a very common question that often props up (comes to) in the mind. On one side Lord is asking to follow natural instincts. On the other side there are people who commit sins. Arjuna wants to know what it is that impels an individual to commit sin. First we will take up what a sin is.

A sin is that act whose memory, when it is realized sometime or the other, suffocates us, makes us feel miserable, haunts our life and disturbs our "inner rhythm; symbolizing our connectivity with the Supreme" even when the act has been done ostensibly (seeming to be true but this is not the case) without being noticed by anybody long time back. There is a slight difference in evil and sin. Evil is something wrong done to us to make us feel miserable and unpleasant. Sin is the result of **resident evil within**" whose memory haunts an individual, shatters one's right to be happy and at peace and causes indescribable sufferings at the level of consciousness. Dushasan was pulling the sari (long piece of cloth to cover the body of ladies) of Draupadi in an open court with full contempt for righteousness. Could he have tolerated the same treatment being given to his daughter? A sinner is one drowned in passion and totally lost to reasoning, righteousness and feeling of others. Sin is that which pierces one's "individualized-soul" (no change or impact can be brought about in soul or exclusive divinity or eternal existence within) and commits, both to the victim and the perpetrator (sooner or later), intense, immense and indescribable sufferings. The Hindus, traditionally, have been terribly conscious of baleful (expressing anger and hatred) effects of sins. Arjuna asks this question to get the explicit and concise reply of causes of sins so that he may exert himself and exterminate (finish those causes so that they no longer exist) them.

An individual is fundamentally good i.e. original nature of a human being, without influence of passions and worldly impact, is good. It is divine (eternal, indestructible, immanent capable of creating both wonders and thunders). This is fundamental premise (idea forming basis) of any thinking relating to righteousness and unrighteousness anywhere in the world. What is it, then, which impels an individual to commit sin? This is precisely the dilemma of Arjuna. In many cases, sinners are appalled (show horror and disgust) and sometimes surprised over what they have done. They feel that, at the spur of the moment, they were driven, unwillingly as if by force, to do the sin by something. What is this something? What is it that makes even sinners feel that they were the victims, whereas sinners perpetrate (to commit crime) sin? This is a common experience that happens in life when in weak moments (i.e. when self control is missing) an individual commits an act which he or she may not even like to recall before anybody (not to talk of daughter and son) due to agony and suffering, not inflicted by any outsiders but experienced in unfathomable (not capable of being measured) depths in the vibrating zone of one's inner silence and peace even without provocation. Arjuna seeks this clarification from the Lord when Lord advises him to follow "svadharma; action in conformity with one's innate natural propensities."

A storm still seeks its end in peace, when it strikes against peace with all its might. But, where does the storm come from in the human life? That is the anxiety of Arjuna.

37. Lord answers why an individual commits sin.

श्रीभगवानुवाच ।
काम एष क्रोध एष रजोगुणसमुद्भवः ।
महाशनो महापाप्मा विद्ध्येनमिह वैरिणम् ॥ ३- ३७ ॥

sri-bhagavan uvaca
kama esa krodha esa rajo-guna-samudbhavah
mahasano maha-papma viddhy enam iha vairinam 3.37

sri-bhagavan uvaca—Krishna, the incarnation of the Supreme Reality, said; kamah—lust, intense desire, blinding desire; esah-- this; krodhah-- anger; esah-- this; rajah-guna—born of rajo-guna i.e. tendency of feverishness or the mode of passion; samudbhavah--born of; maha-asanah--all-devouring or all-consuming; maha-papma—all-sinful; viddhi--know; enam--this; iha—this (in the material world); vairinam-- the enemy.

Blessed Lord said:

"It is due to desire (sensual desire) and anger, which are born of or begotten by "rajo-guna; feverishness, unlimited desires and longing"; all-consuming, all sinful; know this as foe here on this earth." II 37 II

Desire here means "sensual desire" i.e. wishing something very strongly for personal satisfaction, completely disregarding feeling of others. Desires change character due to attribute that impels desires. "Desire to construct a big charitable hospital for welfare of the poor" is a desire born of *sattva*. "Desire to victimize for sensual satisfaction" is born of rajas. Desire to annihilate the masses, as terrorists do, is born of tamas. Lord here is referring to desires for sensual satisfaction. They create intense restlessness to gain sensual pleasure. If that is not possible or if it is obstructed, it changes into anger, which is a strong feeling of wanting to harm someone. The origin of sensual-desire is from *rajas* (attribute of nature causing feverishness, unlimited desires and longing). 'Rajoguna' is the absence of mental equilibrium leading to rigorous activity to achieve the desired result. The desire (intense) due to 'rajoguna' is called in Sanskrit "kama," desire for sensual and material pleasures. Kama becomes anger (fierce rage) if it is not fulfilled.

If the mind becomes affected by desire, wrath, and other passions, it turns towards sin and sin forces an individual to dwell in painful regions. For this reason, the Lord says that lust and anger, born of "*rajo guna*" are the mighty enemies. They are the off springs of sensual desires, "the resident evil within, the Satan within, the destructive force within," born of rajas and tamas. They lead an individual to commit sins. They delude an individual to turn astray from the path of righteousness, self-realization, ultimate destination or supreme goal of human life. When we truly accept this phenomenon (that evils are coming out of the resident evils within us due to food-intake, thinking, life pattern and past karmas) with living awareness, then we are able to find its solution with karam-yoga as well i.e. the "Gita's specific approach; Karam-Yoga" of doing work as an offering to the Supreme for world-welfare with detachment for fruit of action, with divine consciousness and surrender.

The practical advantage of reply of the Lord (in this verse) can be materialized, only when this reply is viewed in completion i.e. with regard to its meaning, reference and context (related situation, event and information). By this reply, Lord tells Arjuna: i) All worldly experiences are impact of actions and reactions of gunas i.e. justification of the earlier statement made by the Lord which Arjuna found difficult to believe due to a question in his mind; ii) consequential reactions such as lust, anger and their associates (jealousy, greed, delusion and pride or arrogance) are also results of *gunas* only i.e. the message of this verse; iii) This chapter is about karam-yoga; When action is done in this mode as a revelation (surprising fact about something) of the Infinite which is endlessly new and eternally beautiful in us, the consequential reactions of gunas (lust and anger and their other associates as well) are also taken care of i.e. obstructions of the worldly existence do not block the channelizing of energy in the right path of spiritual evolution. Mere intellectual understanding of the root cause and the havoc played by *kama* (lust) and *krodha*)" will not be sufficient to overcome their influence in life. Our roots must go deep down into the universal truth within us, if we are to blossom to our full human potential. Present discussion i.e. work done through karam-yoga mode is one approach to go in "That Eternal Direction." "These thoughts of the Gita" transform (change) our existence into "living alive with spirituality" (i.e. with focus on the journey through the world and beyond the world simultaneously, as a witness).

In the Ramayana, we get a very good example to support this point (intense, feverish, maddening desire victimizes the human existence). Sita, wife of Lord Rama, spotted the golden deer in the proximity of her hut in the jungle. Initial fondness for the deer that grew in Sita's mind, swelled overwhelmingly, leading to her abduction by Ravana, full scale war and loss of numerous lives.

To conclude the message of the verse, we can say that consequences of emotions (lust and anger), due to attributes of nature, hide the '**imprisoned divine splendor within; the divine essence validating the human existence**'.

38. In this verse Lord tells Arjuna with similes how desire clouds an individual's understanding.

धूमेनाव्रियते वह्निर्यथादर्शो मलेन च ।
यथोल्बेनावृतो गर्भस्तथा तेनेदमावृतम् ॥ ३- ३८ ॥

dhumenavriyate vahnir yathadarso malena ca
yatholbenavrto garbhas tatha tenedam avrtam 3.38

dhumena--by smoke; *avriyate*—is enveloped or covered; *vahnih*--fire; *yatha*-- as; *adarsah*--mirror; *malena*--by dust; *ca*--and; *yatha*-- as; *ulbena*--by the amnion (a sort of liquid in womb); *avrtah*--is covered; *garbhah*--embryo; *tatha*--so; *tena*--by it (that lust); *idam*—this (knowledge); *avrtam*--is covered.

"As fire is enveloped by smoke, as a mirror by dust and as embryo by the amnion (liquid in pregnant woman's womb), similarly "this; divine knowledge; brahama jnana or knowledge relating to Supreme Energy in form and formlessness" is enveloped by that (passion; kama)." II 38 II

This is a dialogue going on between Arjuna and Krishna. Many words used were taken for granted, as both of them were accomplished personalities of that era. Lord concludes this verse with the words "tene idam avrtam; this is covered by it." What do "*edam*; this" and "*ten*; that" in this verse stand for? The word "This" stands for divine knowledge. It becomes clear from the word "jnanam," used in the next verse. Actually both these verses read together give the complete meaning. "Ten; that" in this verse stands for sensual desires, about which discussion is going on in these verses.

The Lord is referring to divine knowledge, which is as good as referring to "Supreme Universal Eternal Reality." It requires some thought and it is not something small. The Rig Veda and many verses of the Gita clarify that "*Pragnanam Brahma*; God is supreme knowledge." We all beings carry a divine spark of the Supreme Reality within us. This is the resplendent, divine component within the individualized soul (soul i.e. divine component within + ego + accumulated impressions of past life). Our soul remains veiled by corresponding component of three gunas. The divinity within the soul is like fire enveloped from all sides by smoke. Discrimination by enlightened (or awakened) intellect drives out the thin clouds out of sattvik-desire and reveals "divine component within soul in its full splendor," as it is, spotless, blemishless without limitations, without a trace of worldliness. Rajasic desire requires strenuous efforts, as the dust on the mirror requires efforts to be removed. Some amount of dusting has to be done to take the dust off the surface of the mirror. Lastly, tamasik desire is like amnion (liquid in the womb of a pregnant woman) which covers embryo from all sides in the darkness of the womb. Time, care and "regulated living" help the embryo to develop and be delivered as a newly born baby.

What does Lord want to say in this verse in brief? Truth (which, defies influence of time; which was there, which is there, which will always be there, which is naturally present everywhere) and untruth (which ever keeps changing) combine to facilitate existence. The influence of untruth (originating from attributes of nature i.e. lust, anger and their associates) creates delusion (false belief) and makes it difficult to see the truth, the vital essence, the ever continuing reality. Imprisoned in its own web, incapacitated by its own helplessness, the 'divine essence within' yearns for release (moksha), to be restored to its original nature of purity, splendor and unmixed divinity. This verse stops after saying that one gets entrapped in life by attributes of nature.

Due to imprisonment of Divinity within, one is unable to take a whole view of the reality. What is the result? One suffers from suffocation and incompleteness. A sort of mystery surrounds the "reality;

truth and the whole phenomenon." "The entrapped one; the lost one; the Divinity within" only keeps crying in its imprisoned, suppressed state throughout life in silent murmur " …release me .. release me and make me see aright…"

In this verse, higher nature is compared to fire and lower nature is compared to smoke. By conquering the lower nature, as directed in 2.61, an individual can remain constantly in higher knowledge.

39. In this verse also Lord continues discussion on the irrefutable (which cannot be disproved and must be accepted) influence of sensual desires in an individual.

आवृतं ज्ञानमेतेन ज्ञानिनो नित्यवैरिणा ।
कामरूपेण कौन्तेय दुष्पूरेणानलेन च ॥ ३- ३९ ॥

*avrtam jnanam etena jnanino nitya-vairina
kama-rupena kaunteya duspurenanalena ca 3.39*

avrtam— enveloped or covered; *jnanam*-- wisdom; *etena*--by this (insatiable fire of desire); *jnaninah*--of the wise; *nitya-vairina*--eternal enemy; *kama-rupena*—whose form is lust i.e. intensely alluring; *kaunteya*--O son of Kunti (Arjuna); *duspurena*—unappeasable i.e. it can never be satisfied; *analena*-- as fire; *ca*—and

"O Kaunteya (son of Kunti; Arjuna)! Knowledge remains covered or enveloped by this eternal enemy of the wise in the form of desire which is insatiable like fire." II 3-39 II

Desire remains covered within an individual. When it grows to the stature of greed, it becomes a destructive force of mankind. This message has been passed in the following words:

I) avratam jnanam etna jnanini nityavarina [Divine knowledge remains covered by this constant foe of the wise) – Lord says that knowledge remains covered by this enemy of the wise. What does Lord mean by using the word "tena; this"? The word "this" refers to kama (lust), the associate of the anger and the eternal enemy of the mankind. Lord calls desire the eternal enemy because it appears and reappears, not once or twice, but throughout the life. Desire (along with its associates) hides this jnana. When jnana, the faculty of discrimination is hidden, the individual starts committing all sorts of blunders.

ii) Kamrupena kaunteys duspurena nalena ca [in the form of kama, O Arjuna, (this enemy remains) like an unquenchable fire] – This is the teaching of the Gita that lust is the cause of the origin of the crime. When *rajas* and *tamas* predominate in life, crime and similar problems arise. Lord is not talking of the solution in this verse. Lord's focus in this verse is to bring out only this fact that this enemy of mankind (desire) remains hidden within nearer than we think. It is a sort of warning about the enemy hidden right within us. In sin, an individual takes part with the finite against the infinite that is in him or her while the root cause of this sin, i.e. desire, also remains in him or her. Where is it hidden within? Lord replies in the next verse.

40. Lord has told clearly in the preceding verse that that divine knowledge remains covered by insatiable desire of "*kama*-lust." Where does *kama* remain hidden in human personality? Lord answers in this verse.

इन्द्रियाणि मनो बुद्धिरस्याधिष्ठानमुच्यते ।
एतैर्विमोहयत्येष ज्ञानमावृत्य देहिनम् ॥ ३- ४० ॥

indriyani mano buddhir asyadhisthanam ucyate
etair vimohayaty esa jnanam avrtya dehinam 3.40

indriyani--the senses; *manah*--the mind; *buddhih*--the intelliect; *asya*— its (desire) ; *adhisthanam*--seat; *ucyate*--called; *etaih*--by these (use of senses) ; *vimohayati*--bewilders; *esah*--of this (desire); *jnanam*-- (his) wisdom; *avrtya*—by veiling or covering; *dehinam*--the embodied (soul).

"The senses, the mind and the intellect are said to be the seats of "kama-lust"; Kama, with the help of the senses, deludes an individual by veiling jnana (divine-knowledge)." II 3-40 II

It is clear from the preceding discussion that desire is the root cause of all ailments and miseries. Where does the desire remain entrenched or established in the body? Lord answers this question in following words:

i) **indriyani mano budhir asya adhisthanam ucyate** (the senses, the mind and the intellect are said to be "its" seat) – Lord has used the word "it" in this verse. What is this that Lord is talking about? Lord is talking about desire, the mother of lust, anger and their associate i.e. pride, greed and capturing, captivating and incapacitating infatuation (unreasonable strong feeling of love). First the identification of location of enemy is necessary before laying down the siege (to be surrounded by army from all sides) to it. There within all of us is a space vibrating with divinity. Identifying this and being established in that space is the life-mission of the wise, the enlightened and the ones blessed with divine grace. This space is subtler than body, mind, intellect, memory and ego (complex). On route to this "vibrating divine space within" are other levels of existence. Desire remains obscured (prevented from being seen and heard), hidden within, at these points i.e. senses, mind and intellect like robbers and thieves in the forest. They suddenly attack in the darkness of ignorance and sometime in the middle of night and become violent polluting the route to the divinity. Then we find that, at the "altar within" exclusively reserved for the Supreme, everything is lying scattered, disheveled (untidy) and in utter mess. "The temple of divinity within," where we nurture the life's ambition, has been usurped (to take someone else's power). All we experience is disappointment, surging pain and sense of loss or defeat. The idea is that these weaknesses, originating from desire, are very powerful, effective, swift and stubborn. They attack with ferocity, intensity and precision. The idea is to convey the "location within" vulnerable to the attack of the enemies, again from within only. This knowledge increases our awareness of the impending danger and forewarns us. This enemy in the form of desire, cause of all negative emotions, remains entrenched (strongly established and not likely to change) within the three enclosures namely the senses, the mind and the intellect. Like fog in the extreme winter, the "discriminating faculty within an individual" becomes dull and finds it difficult to make way past these enemies, which take an individual astray bewildered and deceived.

ii) **etair vimohayaty esa jnanamn avrtyadehinam** [These (lust, anger and their associate) delude an individual by veiling his wisdom) – These enemies of an individual (desire and the consequent family of emotions) take hold of an individual's wisdom. What is it that happens then? Perforce, an individual serves his or her base pleasures. Mind is made to go on lustful missions and it cogitates (thinks seriously and carefully) to covetous (strong desire to have something that someone has) concepts. The intellect is made to go for designs that are vulgar, self-defeating and degenerating (to become worse). The instruments, which otherwise would have been used for serving the "life's mission; self-realization for the wise and accomplishment of the objective for the worldly," get used in a silly, careless and sometime immoral way. Lord has used a beautiful word "*vimohayaty*," which means here making the "complex of body, mind and intelligence" victim of manifold illusions by turning it away from the knowledge of its true nature and making it indulge in sensuous experiences.

This verse beautifully describes how ignorance (tamas) prevents an individual from seeing the source of enemies within. "Rajas (feverishness)," then, induces the faculties of an individual to project himself or herself through the medium of senses, mind and intellect. There is a great message in Krishna's statement that kama (lust) reigns the senses, mind and intelligence. It is a sort of warning to discern (to make good judgment after looking at it closely) carefully whether our arguments are eclipsed by any latent desire and preference. At times one should ask from one's own self "Am I arguing to win my point only or seeking to unearth (to find out the truth) right insight in the mist within?" One has to surely ensure that one's intelligence is not under the influence of kama (lust). It amounts to going beyond the "confinement of life of the individual-self (self with ego)." Only after achieving this awareness, we gain the "revelation (surprising secret made known) of completion" in the incomplete. Only then the millions of atoms in the body of an individual will vibrate in tune with the thrill at the touch of the master and perfection will appear dancing in imperfection symbolizing the epitome (perfect example) of spiritual journey. We must understand the divine music inherent in the words of the Lord. These words were not uttered to wage a war only. The message is to unveil the "secret within" by keeping the vision clear of the obstructing elements in the journey of life. Coincidently the objective here is a war for righteousness. Otherwise "this wisdom" can help anyone achieve life's any target, whatsoever it may be.

What is the final message of the verse? The error and delusion will surely come to be faced on the pathway of life, as long as life is there. One has to ensure that one's intelligence is not under the grip of "kama" while enquiring into or reasoning any subject. The awareness of the self (purpose of divine intelligence) alone can save an individual. A child gets its sustenance in mother's womb through the union of its life with the larger life of its mother. Similarly the recognition of "inner kinship; eternal existence within" helps an individual to reconcile conflicts and contradictions (lust and anger) of life. In this state, one goes beyond the life of habits to attain internal harmony and the wholeness of our being.

41. Next three verses are very beautiful. Lord describes how an individual's life can be given direction to move towards the fullest manifestation of the spiritual possibilities lying within, unexplored.

तस्मात्त्वमिन्द्रियाण्यादौ नियम्य भरतर्षभ ।
पाप्मानं प्रजहि ह्येनं ज्ञानविज्ञाननाशनम् ॥ ३- ४१ ॥

tasmat tvam indriyany adau niyamya bharatarsabha
papmanam prajahi hy enam jnana-vijnana-nasanam 3.41

tasmat--therefore; *tvam*--you; *indriyani*- the senses; *adau*--in the beginning; *niyamya*—having control; *bharata-rsabha*--O chief amongst the descendants of Bharata (Arjuna); *papmanam*--the sinful; *prajahi*-- kill; *hi*-- surely; *enam*--this; *jnana*-- *vijnana*-- *nasanam*-- the destroyer of knowledge and wisdom (realization by application and contemplation of knowledge).

"Therefore, O! Best of the Bharatas (Arjuna)! Mastering first the senses; slay it, the sinful, the destroyer of knowledge and realization." II 3-41 II

Control of senses is the first step in the conquest of desire which present the main obstruction in gaining knowledge and wisdom. Lord explains this in the following words:

i) **tasmat tvam indriyani adau niyambh** (first master the senses) – This is the first command in this verse. In the preceding verse, Lord talked of senses i.e. mind and intelligence as the seats of sensual desires. Therefore, Lord wants control of senses i.e. five senses of action, five senses of perception and five pranas), mind and intelligence etc. Lord wants all disciplines (physical, mental, emotional and spiritual) to be observed to bring about sense-control. The idea is that the enemy should be first dislodged from its citadel. Now the question arises how the sense control, referred to by the lord, should be brought about. This requires a lot of practice and culturing and cultivation of mind and intellect. First mind has to be freed from its inherent attraction for the worldly things. For this, one has to develop dispassion i.e. association and involvement devoid of attachment, craze and feverishness. Dispassion automatically ensues, when one takes it to deeper layers of awareness, that 'rajasika-type of joy' and deluding 'tamsik-satisfaction' from sleep and indolence are temporary, perishable and sorrowful. One can experience a change of attitude towards positivity, if one takes to reflect on divine glory, virtues and actions. Practical steps for positivity in modern language means *seva* (service that renders connectivity at soul level among beings not necessarily human beings), *sadhna* (disciplining the body, mind and intellect to receive the divine grace), *satsang* (keeping company with truth by recitation, singing and discourses), *swaddhyay* (study of self by introspection, meditation and study of scriptures etc.) can be effective in bringing about a turn towards positivity, towards truth in life. By adopting all these measures, one can bring under control the complex of senses, mind and intelligence, which can afterwards be used for "achievement of life's mission ranging from attainment of objective to self-realization." Diversion of senses, mind and intelligence towards divinity (that which is eternal, indestructible and immanent) automatically initiates the self-control. Control is better effected not by prevention but by engaging them (senses, mind and intellect) positively.

ii) ***papmanam prajahi hy enam jnanamvijnanam nasanam*** (slay it –the sinful, the destroyer of knowledge and wisdom) – The focus of discussion is on kama (lust). The nature of kama is sin. It is all sinful (*mahapapam*). Desire for lust, gold, position and power has victimized even the best and the wisest the world over. The words used are "papnam prajahi hy enam; this sinner, this criminal within you, slay it." This cause of infection (this sensual desire), this devilish existence within has to be removed so that sensory system is clear of it. This lower nature, this explosion of kinetic side of our behavior for reasons hidden within, revolts and takes grip of our senses, mind and intelligence. Rather it colors mind and intelligence and drags the senses to go unbridled towards sense objects. The impact of desire and its companion anger is all-devouring, all polluting and all-consuming. It limits our search for perfection. We have to slay this to be able to live in calm, clear and luminous state of truth. One forgets "*svadharma*" and the scriptures, if one allows oneself to be swayed by desire and anger.

Why should the source of sinful behavior be destroyed? Lord uses two beautiful words explaining the reasons. It destroys 'jnanam and vijnanam'. Jnanam is divine knowledge i.e. nature of supreme eternal truth and its manifestation all around or say "What is that fundamental truth which validates all existences; which was there always, which is there and which will always be there? How do I trace (understand with awareness) this truth within me and within all? What is it with which we live and without which we die?" Divine knowledge deals with these questions. Its (Divine knowledge) focus is on that which is there but we cannot see it and at the same time its existence cannot be disputed. Nobody knows the extent of its influence, its powers and its limits. The divine knowledge focuses on that "Reality" which is the innermost self of all that which exists. That Reality is seated in the hearts of all. That Reality is the ruler of all. All beings become one with that Reality. Divine knowledge helps to gain the "**expanded vision of unbounded awareness**" of inner and outer purity. After gaining divine knowledge there remains nothing to be known. The rule of this knowledge is that you have to have faith first and then you gain this knowledge. It is direct knowledge i.e. we are able to intuitively feel awareness of this 'Reality', its light, its magnificence, its peace and impact of its proximity in the form of knowledge. What is vijnana (science)? That which helps us to know discernible (which can be known by looking and working at them carefully) laws of nature by relating reasons and consequences is vijnana (science)? In science, we prove first and then we accept it. That which we do not know is much more than that which we know due to science.

For this reason Lord tells Arjuna to discipline (accepting the senses first and then subjecting them to obey the senses i.e. discipline) the sensory system first. Then only it will be possible to be free from infection (infection of sensory pleasures), which will otherwise destroy the jnana (divine knowledge; knowledge relating to the Absolute or the Un-manifest) and vijnana (science; methodology of deciphering the phenomenon of nature by relating reasons and consequences).

"Reality or The Ultimate or Peak Experience of Truth" is the harmony which gives to the component parts of a thing the equilibrium of the whole, the rhythm of the whole, the feel of the whole. Disciplining the senses is the first step in that direction. That is what Lord wants to communicate in this verse to Arjuna and to the world at large.

42. In preceding verses, Lord tells Arjuna to observe sense-control to tame senses, mind and intelligence and the way to be followed. In this verse Lord tells Arjuna the sequence in which one should go about taming senses, mind and body.

इन्द्रियाणि पराण्याहुरिन्द्रियेभ्यः परं मनः ।
मनसस्तु परा बुद्धिर्यो बुद्धेः परतस्तु सः ॥ ३-४२ ॥

indriyani parany ahur indriyebhyah param manah
manasas tu para buddhir yo buddheh paratas tu sah 3.42

indriyani—the senses; *parani*—superior; *ahuh*—they say; *indriyebhyah*—more than the senses; *param*—superior; *manah*—the mind; *manasah*—more than the mind; *tu*— but; *para*—superior; *buddhih*—intelligence; *yah*— who; *buddheh*—more than the intelligence; *paratah*— greater; *tu*—but; *sah*—he (indweller or the soul).

"They say that the senses (organs of senses i.e. ears, eyes etc.) are superior to the gross body or the object of senses; superior to the senses is mind; superior to the mind is the intellect; superior to the intellect is He (sah)." II 3-42 II

Lord has told clearly that kama (sensual pleasure) is the root of all problems. Its locations have been discussed. Thereafter lord has given the final verdict that this enemy (sensual pleasures) has to be controlled. In this verse Lord says in what sequence and in what way one should take up the different layers of human individuality to bring about the "sense-control," "mind-control" and "intelligence –control" to do away with the sway (influence) of kama (lust). This has been done in the following words:

i) indriyani parany ahur indriyebhyha param manah [they say that senses are superior (to sense objects); the mind is superior to sense organs) – The Sanskrit word "para" has been repeatedly used in this verse by the Lord. "Para" means relatively subtler or superior. Subtle means that it is not easy to notice and understand, till you pay very careful and exclusive attention to it. Whatever is subtler compared to gross is superior and higher. Energy in gross is inferior to energy in subtle. Whatever is relatively subtler is more in range, more in power and more in expansion.

Senses (sense organs i.e. hands, legs etc.) are subtler than sense-objects, which can be touched and handled. This is so because sense-organs have more range of activities than sense-objects. Senses can work without sense objects (in controlled mode). There is no relevance of sense objects without senses. Senses make sense objects relevant. For this reason senses are superior to sense-objects. Mind is superior to senses because it has still wider range of activities and endowed with higher powers of generating actions. Senses cannot do anything independently without the help of mind. Mind directs the senses in their operations. Senses do not know the mind. Mind knows all the senses. Each sense knows only its respective sense object. For example ear can listen only; skin knows only touch and eyes can only see. Mind knows the senses, sense objects and limitations of senses as well. Therefore mind is obviously superior to senses.

ii) **manastu para buddhir yo buddhey parastu sah** [superior to mind is intellect and superior to intellect is He (atma)] – Intellect is superior to mind as mind's operations are dictated by intellect. Intelligence is endowed with the faculty of discrimination. When the mind is in doubt, intellect comes to the rescue. Mind does not know why it is running and running all the time, but the intelligence knows it. Mind simply hops towards the sense-objects by the impulsion of senses. It does not know whether it should go or not. Intellect guides the mind. Therefore, the intellect is beyond the mind. Beyond the intellect is … the '"Sah," the self, the "atma." Where is this "Self or Atma"? How is it so relevant to us? The use of this word "Sah" is very meaningful and requires to be dealt with very elaborately, since it has depth. It has range. It has meaning. It focuses something fundamental and of primary importance discussed everywhere in the Gita, sometimes as first person and sometimes as third person. The awareness of "Sah" is necessary (rather pre-requite) to understand the Gita. It indicates towards something eternal, something ever continuing. Some people call it "Atma." Let us start the discussion from "Atma" then. What is "atma"? Atma is divine component within covered by ego and impressions of the past. It takes its genesis (origin) from the merger of "Higher nature" and "Lower nature (refer to the flow chart on page …)." Cosmic intelligence in the divine component initiates individual intelligence (individual intelligence borrows light from the self) but immediately afterwards the cosmic intelligence in an individual goes into oblivion (state of being completely forgotten). All that remains is individual intelligence with ego giving attention to the individualized-self and not to "the witness within" or the divine component within. What is the reason that the people want to get established in the self? The divine component within or the soul is the zone of indestructibility and eternity connected with the cosmic intelligence and Source of all energy and power in the Universe. Actually divine content within or atma covered by ego and memory of past karmas is the "real self." With this we are and without this we are not. Its association with the inidividualized-soul remains till ego and memory last. When no ego and memory remains in the baggage of the individualized soul, divine component merges with the Supreme. Duality (ignorance) ends. Self-realization or moksha (total freedom from all limitations) is achieved. The river merges in the ocean marking the end and the highest point of spiritual journey.

The Lord stops at the point of saying that "Sah" is superior to intelligence. What is this "Sah"? It is the fulcrum (the point, at which the lever turns, balances or is supported) of all the discussions. It is the divine component within the individualized-soul. This component is omnipotent (most powerful), omnipresent (present everywhere) and omniscient (knowing everything). It remains connected to the cosmic intelligence. The moment one goes beyond ego, one gets to that zone of divinity, to that realm of cosmic intelligence, in the proximity of self effulgent Reality, with which we are alive. The Lord is referring to "That" whose presence within us validates our existence. In that zone one gets connected to that unlimited source of energy, unlimited source of power and unlimited source of knowledge. When one gets to that zone, lower instruments get deprived of the usual ramblings (something that is long and does not serve its purpose) in the world of matter. **What is the difference in "Sah" and the individualized soul?** Individualized soul is a combination of three components. First is divine component which Lord is referring here. Second is ego, that is, that which deludes us into the feeling of duality i.e. that cover, which envelopes the "Reality." Third is the past impression, stored in the memory. The highest purpose (one can choose any purpose up to the highest purpose i.e. self realization, in life) is to get in that exclusive first component and get rid of the second and third components relating to an individualized soul. The whole struggle in life is to get rid of the second and third component of the individualized soul. That is what all around us is about. The elimination of this second and third component means "self-realization or the Absorption in the ultimate Absolute i.e. you regain consciousness of your divine nature." At this point of awareness of the self (divinity within the soul), senses, mind and intelligence come to a standstill in their respective positions, intoxicated with the divinity, fully surrendered and tamed. These instruments of existence (senses, mind and intelligence etc.) cannot entangle an individual in the meshes of enjoyment once an individual manages to get to this divine zone within. This zone is zone of bliss. There remains no desire when one gets connected to this zone. Actually Lord is referring to this zone as *atma* (or soul i.e. eternal existence or divinity within). The moment ego and memories of past become zero, one merges into exclusive divinity. There can be no existence without ego and memories of past. By using the word "sah," Lord is referring to the divine component within the individualized soul. The most important thing in the whole Gita is to understand this "Sah." Miracles happen when one touches that zone. This "Sah" (within the soul), in exclusion, is synonym of the "Eternal Universal Reality." It is the same "Reality" which Jesus Christ referred to in his last words when he said at the time of getting crucified "My God, my God, Why did you abandon me?" It is the same Reality which divided the red sea to save Moses and the other Israelites as they went into the sea on the dry ground with walls of water on both the sides (the sea split to give them the way with walls of water on both the sides) and the Egyptians could do no harm to them. It is the same Reality which saved Draupadi when her modesty was about to be outraged in the open court and none of her mighty husbands could come to save her. It is the same "Reality" which each individual in the universe stumbles (walking unpleasantly and almost falling) to search for, at one point of time or another, when all is bleak in all directions. Darkness abounds. At times there happens to be no one to come to the rescue and the shore still seems to be far away lost somewhere in the four directions. Even richness of faith, the only cause of one's existence in that particular condition, seems getting emaciated (extremely thin due to lack of food, nourishment and illness). Yes, this reality (sah) was. It is. It will always be. Lord is referring to this Reality by using the word "Sah." The most pleasant and startling thing is that it is the same "*Sah*," which Lord is referring elsewhere in the Gita while promising … "Setting aside all else, just completely surrender to my will. I shall liberate you from all sins (capturing and enslaving bondages of karmas). Do not grieve." It is "One" only, imprisoned in the individual self with ego or intermingled all around in everything else in the universe at the same time, as the cause of everything that is. It is blessedness to be aware of this "Sah."

By these words "superior to *buddhi* is That," Lord has pointed out the way to conquer the senses, mind and *buddhi*. How is it? We do not have to descend to lower planes of senses. We have to ascend to "*Atma*," to that vibrant zone within, which is rich with bliss, peace and cosmic intelligence. That is the injunction (command by some authority) of the Lord. Lord's message is clear. We are not body. We are not mind. We are not intelligence. We are blessed "*atma*," the divine component within. This component is pure, perfect, infinite and ever blissful. The more one goes nearer to the divine zone within or the soul, the more senses lose power or sway over the individual. Lord just wants to make it clear that there is nothing superior to this Reality, to this "Sah." All questions crumble. Desires fade away. Even the shackles of illness and limitations give in when one truly touches that zone of "Sah; The Supreme Reality" even in thoughts. Lord beautifully concludes this chapter indicating towards "Sah" that is the ultimate solution for all the ailments under the sun and even beyond in other galaxies. By referring to "Sah," lord has given an indication that there is only one way and no two ways finally to get rid of lack of sense-control, mind-control and control of intellect (to get rid of sensual desires). Arjuna asked for cause of sin. Lord told him about "Sah" the cause of everything that is.

43. Lord has now told Arjuna about karam-yoga in detail. While concluding this chapter, Lord gives the panacea (something that, people think, will make everything better and solve all the problems) for all ailments, afflictions and limitations.

एवं बुद्धेः परं बुद्ध्वा संस्तभ्यात्मानमात्मना ।
जहि शत्रुं महाबाहो कामरूपं दुरासदम् ॥ ३- ४३ ॥

evam buddheh param buddhva samstabhyatmanam atmana
jahi satrum maha-baho kama-rupam durasadam 3.43

evam--thus; *buddheh*—than the intellect; *param*--superior; *buddhva*—having known; *samstabhya*—by restraining or steadying; *atmanam*—(in) the self (atman individualized eternal existence) ; *atmana*—(by) the self (indweller of the soul i.e. Supreme Self or original cause of everything i.e. realization); *jahi*-- slay; *satrum*--the enemies (in the form of lust, anger avarice etc.); *maha-baho*--O mighty-armed one (Arjuna); *kama-rupam*—in the form of desire (lust); *durasadam*—hard to overcome or formidable.

"Thus knowing that "Reality (referred to as Sah in the preceding verse)," which is superior to the buddhi (intelligence) and restraining self by the self, destroy, O mighty armed (Arjuna), that enemy, hard indeed to overcome, in the form of *kama* or unrestrained sensual desire." II 3-43 II

In this concluding verse, Lord gives an ultimate solution in the following words:

i) *evam buddhey param buddhva* [thus knowing "That" (referred to as Sah in the preceding verse) which is superior to intelligence) – Lord beautifully uses the words. The verse has been started with the words "thus knowing." What does it mean? It means that first one has to come in that state of awakening which comes by gaining the awareness of "The Highest; The Indestructible; The *Sah*; The divine component in the soul." It was talked about in detail in the previous verse. This divine component within or soul is superior to buddhi, which is discerning (ability to make good judgement) and liberating in nature. It liberates by getting rid of veil of ignorance and uncovers the "Truth" within. In brief, first focus should be on divine consciousness within.

ii) *Samstabhya atmanam atmana* (restraining the self by the self) – Who is the self? This is the crux (most important part) of the remedy given by the Lord in this verse. What does it actually mean? How does it come to be like that? This requires to be dealt with elaborately.

A common individual [i.e. without divine knowledge; Arjuna, the mighty warrior, also behaved like a common man with his emotional outbursts in the beginning of the Gita; he lost his poise and spoke words unbecoming of a warrior of his genre (or his type having certain proven characteristics)] considers egoistic self as the "real self; truth within an individual; eternal existence within" and thus relates to egoistic self when there is any talk about the self (atma). This was the case of Arjuna who did not bother about truth (which remains the same in past, present and future) or untruth while speaking at the beginning of the Gita. In other words, an individual without divine knowledge remains associating with the "un-truth" only. This egoistic self is very deluding and association with egoistic self means desire (sensual desire; the arch enemy of mankind) will automatically come. Rather "egoistic self" harbors (to protect and hide criminals) the desires and its associates in its realm (area of knowledge and thoughts).

As a result of this, an ordinary individual always remains chained to cycles of birth, death and this world which is not real (Real is only that which was, which is, which will always be). When an individual is blessed with divine knowledge, he or she first understands the real and unreal components relating to an individual. An individual with divine wisdom always associates with divine component whenever there is a talk of self. Divine component means "real self," eternal self, ever continuing self. Divine component always remain associated with cosmic intelligence. When one gets established in divine component, one comes in contact with cosmic intelligence. There remains nothing to be known for such an individual. Such an individual is free from desires or any sort of limitations. Lord stops at the point of saying "know the one superior to the buddhi." The buddhi (divine intelligence) makes one realize that beyond ego is the self (atma or soul). An inidividual has a choice to concentrate on either the "divine component" or "the egoistic self." If one associates with "divine component" or the self (atma), one gets inclination towards divine characteristics and one remains in the midst of divine fragrance. Nothing outward disturbs the individual and one gets peace, knowledge and contentment. If one associates with "egoistic self" within, one is unduly influenced by food intake, mental impressions, memory and one's dominant characteristic like tamas and rajas etc. Here one makes resolve to avoid sensual desires but stumbles in the mire of maya (nature) again and again. When one focuses at the divine content within the soul, one escapes the "egoistic region" within, which is germinating ground of sensual desires.

Lord is telling Arjuna to control the lower self (the ever changing within an individual; all that which is influenced by nature) by the higher self (the never changing or the real self or soul). Normally an individual outrightly starts controlling sensual desires and keeps grappling with it throughout life. Why is it so? It is difficult to conquer sensual desire because it is of very complex nature. When one keeps associated with egoistic self, one faces a lot of difficulty. Nature is restless and nature keeps disturbing. In divine zone, sensual desires do not disturb and very naturally one bypasses the point of origin of desires i.e. ego. For this reason, Lord says "restrain the self [body, mind, intellect and ego i.e. physical body, subtle body (ego, intelligence, mind etc.) and causal body (past impressions and tendencies); everything except divine component is nature and therefore perishable and changing]" by the self i.e. by the "higher self or the Atma" or divine component within, which cannot be polluted by sensual desires and which remains connected with the cosmic intelligence (the divine component i.e. all divine characteristics of Supreme Reality).

Lord becomes silent after saying "knowing that (Reality or atma) superior to intelligence ...." But this silence is speaking volumes. This individualized-self has two poles. One pole is egoistic self, where one always feels the gravitational pull of the sense-objects. The other pole is the divine reality within. Even the whole weight of universe cannot crush this divine component of atma in the individual (Arjuna here). In this zone an individual is small in appearance but great in reality. In this zone, one holds its own against the forces that rob it of its distinction (features of divinity i.e. eternity, indestructibility and immanence) and make it one even with the dust. In this zone one gains by its loss and rises by its surrender. What should one (here Arjuna) do then? Sufficient clue has been given by the Lord by statement "restraint the self (body, mind, intelligence, memory and ego, relevant due to egoistic self or the lower nature) by the self (the divinity within; the indestructible; the awareness of universal oneness kindled by divine knowledge; zone of unlimited love and joy or the higher nature)."

iii) **jahi satrum mahabaho kamarupam durasadam** (slay, O mighty armed, the enemy in the form of desire, difficult to overcome) – The knowledge has been given. Sufficient clue has been given. Now comes the command to slay the enemy in the form of desire, which is indeed difficult to be dealt with. Still one thing is there. If enemy is difficult to be dealt with, the divinity within is invincible, in-crushable, beyond decay and not subject to even small diminution (reduction).

This chapter concludes here. Lord has told *Arjuna* the *Karam-yoga* (action for welfare of the world; non-attachment with the results of action; action as an offering to the Supreme; action done with divine consciousness with the feeling of surrender). Last verse highlights the most important point even in karam-yoga. "Atma-bodham" (divine consciousness; awareness of that which is superior to buddhi;) has to be awakened. When work is done with divine consciousness within, base desires (primarily relating to sensual objects) automatically disappear. The little self (the egoistic self) dwindles (becomes too thin due to lack of nourishment) and "real self; divine component within" emerges in its divine splendor, in full glory. The enemy in the form of desire is difficult to be tamed by direct efforts. The trick is to bypass the "egoistic self." The simplest way to win the battle of life is to keep the thoughts of "divine component within" foremost in our consciousness even in the midst of intense activity of karam-yoga (i.e. maintain connectivity with the divinity within even while performing work). It means that karam-yoga is brought about to the fore (to the front) only when you get steeped (to put something into something) into divinity operating for world welfare, not from emotions but from deeper state of inner quietude. In very brief, final message is "Be anchored deep into the divine component within the soul and then be busy in performing karam-yoga for welfare of the world to give direction, meaning and substance to life." Therefore, life in Karam-yoga should be a life of awareness of our own hidden, indestructible, eternal element combined with action for cosmic welfare. It is not enough to examine the action and the motive behind it (to remain detached from). We must examine the "examiner within" simultaneously.

ॐ तत्सदिति श्रीमद्भगवद्गीतासूपनिषत्सु
ब्रह्मविद्यायां योगशास्त्रे श्रीकृष्णार्जुनसंवादे
कर्मयोगो नाम तृतीयोऽध्यायः

In the Upnishad of the Bhagavad Gita, the knowledge of Brahmn (The Absolute;
The Supreme), the science of yoga and the dialogue between Sri Krishna and
Arjuna, this is the third discourse designated "The Yoga of Action"

Practical Relevance of 3rd chapter in life

What is the crux of the message in this chapter? One does not gain by action-less-ness, by abstaining from activity, nor does one rise to perfection by mere renunciation. One should work in the mode of "karam-yoga." One should not spoil oneself by indulging in pleasures of senses. One, who can control the senses, can control the whole world and can achieve success in all endeavors, in all walks of life. Passions cannot be eliminated but passions can be sublimated (to use the sudden rush of energy flow for higher causes) by jnana (divine knowledge). Setting a higher goal like "realizing self by self in the self" prevents the senses like mind and intellect from being tainted by the distractions of sensual pleasures. It facilitates "karam-yoga."

चतुर्थोऽध्यायः (Chapter 4)

ज्ञानकर्मसंन्यासयोगः (The yoga of knowledge or Renunciation of Action in Knowledge)

Some important terms of this chapter – Title of this chapter is "The Yoga of Knowledge." Knowledge is divided in two parts i.e. mundane knowledge and divine knowledge. First it is necessary to deal with frequently used terms in the chapter.

Mundane knowledge is ordinary knowledge (or worldly knowledge or knowledge considering space, time, reasons and consequences) relating to perishable existential phenomenon. Mundane knowledge is gained by sensation, perception, understanding based on reasons and consequences (vijnana) and insight or intuitive knowledge (prajnana). All these subdivisions are progressive developments. A new born baby lives in a world of sensations. An illiterate adult largely remains in the world of perceptions. An educated individual remains in the world of understanding. Intuitive knowledge (knowledge obtained by feelings) is a prelude (that which happens before) to divine knowledge. This is the reason why some of the sages of yore were able to recognize Ram and Krishna as *avtars* (incarnation). What is divine knowledge?

Divine knowledge is knowledge about the self, about the Supreme Truth, about that which is eternal, indestructible, immeasurable, immanent (present everywhere all the time) and most fundamental. It is knowledge about that "Truth" which alone exists and which is un-manifest, inconceivable (in totality) and immutable (not changing). Self-knowledge is the most tremendous of all mysteries. It is the highest secret and it is prime focus of the Gita as well. It is divine knowledge that unfolds or gives a feel to an individual of the secret of the "Universal Ideal of Perfection within the Soul," its divine birth and divine action. It is divine knowledge that gives the feel of attaining divine being, divine nature (madbhavam) and divine work (which is free or without limitations, un-egoistic, disinterested, impersonal, universal, full of divine power and divine love). Divine knowledge can be truly deciphered (to find meaning of something) in the light of soul only or by soul-touched approach. Mere human intellect is not enough to take a full measure of the expanse of divine knowledge. Divine grace is also necessary for divine knowledge.

Lord was telling Arjuna about "Karam Yoga" in third chapter. What is the relevance of change of discussion to divine knowledge? Third chapter was about karma yoga, which stipulates: i) right action i.e. for common good or cosmic welfare, ii) without attachment to fruit of action surrendering the action to "the Supreme Infinite Reality." Very determination of action presents difficulty. How is one to select among action, inaction, wrong action, knowledge-less-action (action based on pravriti or one's nature or accumulated habits) or action based on knowledge {i.e. that action in which there is no attachment to fruit of action and which is performed with supreme release or moksha as the objective (action performed with absolute liberation or moksha in view is always for common good and cosmic welfare)}? Absolute release (moksha; freedom from all possible limitations, physical, mental, emotional and spiritual) cannot be gained except by divine knowledge.

This chapter has also been called renunciation of action in knowledge. What does it mean? It means that divine knowledge is necessary even for Karam-Yoga, which was the subject of the previous chapter. Thus it becomes yoga of sacrifice of work i.e. work for cosmic benefit with memory of the Lord and self surrender with divine knowledge. In this yoga i.e. yoga of renunciation of work with divine knowledge, yoga of work and divine knowledge combine for union with the Infinite. **What is renunciation? Abandoning attachment with fruit of action is true renunciation i.e. "being with it without being of it or maintaining some space form the point of attachment."** Due to renunciation, one sees "inaction in action and action in inaction." It is that quality which brings an individual in state of contentment, being supremely satisfied with the present and active at the same time for cosmic benefit without being passionate (unduly attached) about past or future. Divine light (or awareness of truth or life of everything everywhere) bestows its grace only on an individual, who is endowed with contentment through renunciation.

This knowledge (this divine knowledge which is transcendental i.e. which takes an individual beyond the limits of human knowledge, experience and reasons) is very old and Lord starts this chapter telling Arjuna how this divine knowledge has been passing through the generations.

1. The blessed Lord starts this chapter telling Arjuna how this knowledge passed on from generation to generations.

श्रीभगवानुवाच ।
इमं विवस्वते योगं प्रोक्तवानहमव्ययम् ।
विवस्वान्मनवे प्राह मनुरिक्ष्वाकवेऽब्रवीत् ॥ ४- १ ॥

sri-bhagavan uvaca
imam vivasvate yogam proktavan aham avyayam
vivasvan manave praha manur iksvakave abravit 4.1

sri-bhagavan uvaca—Sri Krishna, the incarnation of the Supreme Reality, said; *imam*--this; *vivasvate*—to Vivasvate, the sun-god; *yogam*—yoga i.e. disciplines (physical, mental, emotional and spiritual) to unite with the Supreme Reality; *proktavan*-- taught; *aham*--I; *avyayam*--imperishable; *vivasvan*--Vivasvat (the sun-god's name); *manave*-- to Manu, known for his Smiriti, the code of conduct; *praha*--told; *manuh*-- Manu; *iksvakave*—to King Iksvaku, first among the solar dynasty; *abravit*--said.

The blessed Lord said:

"I (Lord Krishna, incarnation of the Supreme Universal Eternal Reality) taught this (the philosophy discussed in two preceding chapters) imperishable yoga to Vivasavan (Sun); Vivasvat (Sun) taught it to Manu; Manu taught it to Ikshvaku." II 4-1 II

The use of this word "I" in this verse emphasizes that Lord Krishna, the charioteer of Arjunja talking to him in the battlefield, is the incarnation of the "Eternal Indestructible and Immanent Reality." On one hand, this Reality in the form of lord Krishna, is before Arjuna in the battlefield and on the other hand the same Reality taught this knowledge to Vivasvat (Sun-God). This further shows that this Reality incarnates whenever there is diminution of righteousness and growth of unrighteousness.

Eternal Yoga - The Yoga of the Gita is yoga-sastra, as it calls itself. The synthesis of the Gita transcends Karm-yoga, Gyan-yoga or Bhakti Yoga. It combines all of them in "Supreme yoga" to make the seeker master of sacrifice, fountain of knowledge and Lord of Love. It is eternal yoga, as it is eternally true (eternally connects to divinity) and it leads to eternal bliss by immortalizing the mortals by divine knowledge, work (which knows no self interest, which is for cosmic benefit) and divine love (that love which knows no limitations, no reasons or no pre-conditions; this love is that relationship, which has always existed and continues to exist for all the time to come, undiminished and unaffected; a lamp lights another lamp without diminishing its ability to lighten; similarly divine love expands undiminished forever). Under all circumstances desire-less action culminating in divine knowledge (action in the spirit of sacrifice for common good or cosmic benefit removes all sins and renders self-knowledge possible) is the law of spiritual life. Therefore, the Gita's yoga-sastra is the eternal yoga, always relevant as "direct and sure path" to spiritual evolution.

Vivasvan to Manu and Manu to Ikshvaku- This knowledge was first of all taught to Vivasvan (Sun-God) by the "The Supreme Eternal Infinite Reality" in the beginning of the creation. The Sun-God is the giver of physical life to the world. Lord taught the Sun-God the spiritual truth through the yoga of the Gita. The Sun is the father of the present Manu (vaivasvata) the ancestor of the solar dynasty of kings. Ikshvaku was the first king of solar dynasty. It should be noted that royal sages (raj rishis and not the brahman rishis or brahman sages) were the first recipients and transmitters of this knowledge. The Brahman sages concentrated on "Absolute Brahmn," whereas royal sages worked for loksangraha (for good of all or cosmic benefit). This must have been the reason why Gita Gospel of unattached action was first taught to ever active Kshatriya sages and not the Brahman sages who were bent upon achieving perfect freedom from all actions.

2. This knowledge passed from generation to generation from father to son through Royal sages.

एवं परम्पराप्राप्तमिमं राजर्षयो विदुः ।
स कालेनेह महता योगो नष्टः परन्तप ॥ ४- २ ॥

evam parampara-praptam imam rajarsayo viduh
sa kaleneha mahata yogo nastah parantapa 4.2

evam--thus; *parampara--praptam*- handed down in regular succession; *imam*—this (yoga); *raja-rsayah*--the royal sages; *viduh*-- knew; *sah*--that (knowledge of yoga); *kalena*--in the course of time; *iha*-- here; *mahata*--by long; *yogah*—yoga (the science of rekindling one's immortal relationship with the Supreme); *nastah*-- destroyed; *parantapa*--O Arjuna, scorcher of the enemies.

"This handed down thus in regular succession. The royal sages knew it. This yoga, by long lapse of time, has been lost here, O Parantap (burner of enemies)." II 4-2 II

With lapse of time this doctrine perished- The great kings of solar dynasty, like Ikshavaku, Raghu, Dilipa, Aja, Dashratha and lord Rama, could control their senses and do selfless work for the good of the world in spirit of dedication and self surrender to the "Eternal and Infinite." These were royal sages i.e. they were kings and sages at the same time. Afterwards the kings of this dynasty could not maintain that level of dedication and selfless work for which the solar dynasty was famous and consequently this doctrine (this yoga, discussed in chapter two and three) perished in course of time.

Arjuna called Parantap- Arjuna could burn or harass his foes like the sun by the heat of his velour and power. For this reason Lord called him Parantap.

3. Lord shares the same old supreme knowledge with Arjuna.

स एवायं मया तेऽद्य योगः प्रोक्तः पुरातनः ।
भक्तोऽसि मे सखा चेति रहस्यं ह्येतदुत्तमम् ॥ ४- ३ ॥

sa evayam maya te 'dya yogah proktah puratanah
bhakto 'si me sakha ceti rahasyam hy etad uttamam 4.3

sah—that (same ancient yoga); *eva*— even; *ayam*—this; *maya*—by Me; *te*—to thee; *adya*—today; *yogah*— yoga; *proktah*—spoken; *puratanah*— ancient; *bhaktah*—devotee; *asi*—you are; *me*—My; *sakha*—friend; *ca*—also; *iti*—therefore; *rahasyam*— secret; *hi*—for; *etat*—this; *uttamam*—supreme (secret).

"The same ancient yoga has this day been imparted to you by Me, because you are My devotee and friend; and this secret is supreme indeed." II 4-3 II

Secrecy is maintained in regard to many things because of selfishness or because of their being harmful, if misused. The science of yoga remains a secret not for these reasons. The science of yoga remains a secret because of incompetence of man to pursue it properly. This knowledge becomes obscure when right type of people (people with dedication, discipline and devotion) become rare in society. It remains a secret because people with very high moral, dedication, discipline and commitment become the recipients of this knowledge.

Lord calls this yoga the highest secret. This is the yoga of sacrifice of works with divine knowledge i.e. with full awareness about its character. This yoga is capable of uniting with Supreme Infinite Reality which is eternal, indestructible and immanent (present everywhere at all times). In this yoga, work is done in knowledge and both work done as well as knowledge is offered to the Supreme Reality, Supreme Divinity (Purushottama), which becomes manifest within us as the Supreme Truth, resplendent and full with bliss and peace. Lord Krishna declares that this was the ancient and original yoga which was given to Vivasvan (Sun God) at the time of creation and now it was being given to Arjuna. It is considered superior to all other forms of yoga. Other yogas lead to impersonal Brahmn or a personal Deity. This yoga is transcendental yoga i.e. one which takes beyond human knowledge, understanding and experience.

This one statement of Lord Krishna is very important and points out so many aspects all at once. Firstly, this knowledge is supreme secret and it is given only to those who deserve it or entitled (or qualified) to know it. Secondly, the Sun-God, Manu and Iksvaku appeared very early at the dawn of creation. Lord Krishna manifested as late as towards the close of Dvapara Age. How can this be then believed that Lord Krishna taught this yoga to the most ancient Sun-God? This indicates about the divine descent (Avtars). Whenever righteousness suffers and unrighteousness grows, the Supreme Divine takes form (Avtar or incarnation) to re-establish the righteousness. Thirdly, this knowledge is given only to those who are entitled for it. Lord imparts this knowledge to Arjuna who is a bhakta as well as a friend? Who is a bhkta or a devotee? Bhakta or devotee is one who is intensely aware of the "connectivity with the Supreme or desired deity." A true devotee revels (to enjoy something very much) in this connectivity and feels agony for the loss of "this connectivity" even for a short while. Bhakti is highest love and confers immortal bliss finally. Arjuna is a bhakta (devotee) and friend of Lord Krishna.

4. The facts in the statement given by Lord Krishna (in preceding verses) were beyond the worldly understanding of Arjuna. Sun-God, Manu and Iksvaku appeared at the dawn of creation. Lord was talking to Arjuna at the close of Dvapara Age i.e. after thousands and thousands of years. Lord

also says that HE (the world ME has been used by the Lord) taught this yoga to Sun God. Arjuna is confused. He seeks a clarification from Lord Krishna in this verse.

अर्जुन उवाच ।
अपरं भवतो जन्म परं जन्म विवस्वतः ।
कथमेतद्विजानीयां त्वमादौ प्रोक्तवानिति ॥ ४- ४ ॥

arjuna uvaca
aparam bhavato janma param janma vivasvatah
katham etad vijaniyam tvam adau proktavan iti 4.4

arjunah uvaca—Arjuna said; *aparam*— later; *bhavatah*—Your; *janma*—birth; *param*— prior; *janma*—birth; *vivasvatah*—of the sun-god; *katham*—how; *etat*—this; *vijaniyam*—shall I understand; *tvam*—You; *adau*—in the beginning; *proktavan*—instructed; *iti*-thus (science of yoga).

Arjuna said:

"Later was your birth and earlier (thousands and thousands years before) was the birth of Vivasvan (Sun-God). How then am I to understand that you told it to him (Vivasvan) in the beginning?" II 4-4 II

The practical intelligence (worldly understanding) of Arjuna is baffled by the assertion of Lord Krishna that it was HE (Lord Krishna), who in ancient times revealed this yoga to Vivasvan (Sun-God). Since it is lost with efflux of time, HE (Lord Krishna) is again revealing it to Arjuna. How can a man (Lord Krishna), born centuries afterwards, teach an ancient individual (Sun- God)? This is precisely Arjuna's question. This question provokes inquisitiveness about the oft- quoted discussion about the avtars (incarnation).

To the modern mind habituated to logical thinking, incarnation (the act of the Supreme Infinite Energy to appear in human form or in any other form) is the most difficult concept, which is streaming from the East to the rationalized human consciousness. The "Ever Unborn Creator" cannot be the creature born into the world. 'Appearance of the Infinite as the finite' has been a topic of great interest at many different places:

i) The Buddha claimed to have been the teacher of countless Bodhisattvas in bygone ages (Saddharmapundarika XV).

ii) Mr. Johnson has reproduced the following passage from Bible in his Gita:

"your father, Abraham, rejoiced to see my day, he saw it and was glad" said Jesus.
Then said the Jews unto him "Thou art not fifty years old, and hast thou seen Abraham"?
"Jesus said unto them 'Verily, verily, I say unto you, before Abraham was I."
The same discussion appears in the Gospel according to John viii 58 as follows:
"I am telling you the truth," Jesus replied. "Before Abraham was born, 'I am'.

The theory of re-birth and transmigration, as old as Hindu civilization, is affirmed here. The spirit is old, always anew, afresh, ever the same. The exterior is new. The same thought of transmigration (soul passing different bodies after death) was explained by Krishna in chapter two.

Coming back to Arjuna's concern, the "Eternal Universal Infinite Reality or the Reality that Lord Krishna represented" has been before any man, being timeless and limitless. All men (including physical body of Lord Krishna) are subject to time and space. Lord thus clarifies Arjuna on this issue.

5. Lord explains to Arjuna that all incarnations are personifications (to represent objects or qualities as human beings) of the "Supreme Eternal Universal Reality."

श्रीभगवानुवाच ।
बहूनि मे व्यतीतानि जन्मानि तव चार्जुन ।
तान्यहं वेद सर्वाणि न त्वं वेत्थ परन्तप ॥ ४- ५ ॥

sri-bhagavan uvaca
bahuni me vyatitani janmani tava carjuna
tany aham veda sarvani na tvam vettha parantapa 4.5

sri-bhagavan uvaca—Shri Krishna, the incarnation of the Supre Reality, said; *bahuni*--many; *me*--of Mine; *vyatitani*--have passed; *janmani*--births; *tava*--of yours; *ca*--and also; *arjuna*--O Arjuna; *tani*-- them; *aham*--I; *veda*-- know; *sarvani*--all; *na*--not; *tvam*-- thou; *vettha*--know; *parantapa*--O scorcher of the enemy.

"Many are the births that have been passed through by me and by you, O! Arjuna; I know them all, while you do not know, O Parantap (scorcher of foes)." II 4-5 II

Lord unfolds a divine mystery by this answer. Arjuna is a *jivatman* or a soul i.e. an individual in whom the divinity has got individualized due to ignorance. The Divinity is infinite, but due to cover of ego (ignorance of truth and taking feeling of separation to be real) it (divinity) gets individualized and the divine becomes mortal by becoming, individual, jivataman or soul. The struggle of an individual starts here. Individual or jivatman (divinity with cover of ignorance) remembers present birth only. This is due to universal law of nature. With birth memory of past lives goes away from mind of an individual but impressions of impact of past actions travels with the soul. Lord Krishna is "Parmatman" or Supreme Soul or "Supreme Universal Eternal Reality." The Infinite also manifests as jiva for specific divine purposes, time and again, as the situation demands. Lord Krishna represents the "Infinite," who remembers that both (Arjuna and Krishna) have lived several births. This is the first statement of Lord Krishna in which limitedness of jiva and unlimited-ness of the Infinite is highlighted. What is the difference between jivatman and parmatman? Jivatman is one who has limitations. Parmatman (Supreme Self or the Supreme Universal Eternal Reality) is one who has no limitations whatsoever. When a jivatman or individual overcomes or transcends limitations, laid down for it by nature, it becomes Parmatman (the Infinite Reality, the transcendental Universal Force). Arjuna does not know about past lives because his power of vision is limited. Lord knows about the secret of Divinity (eternal, indestructible, immanent, beyond any limitation of time and space), because HE is omniscient (knowing everything). That message of Vivekananda is very relevant here and helps to understand the reply of Lord Krishna "Each soul is potentially divine. The goal is to manifest the divinity (or remove the cover of ignorance) within by controlling nature (mixture of impact of ignorance and negative impressions of actions like lust, anger, hatred, feeling of separateness or "doer-ship" etc. which is not our true nature; true nature is love, knowledge and consciousness), external and internal. To understand the "limitations of an individual" divine knowledge (and not intellectual understanding) is required. That (divine knowledge) is exactly what Lord Krishna is passing on to Arjuna. This is the first verse in that direction.

6. In this verse also, Lord continues clarifying Arjuna's dilemma as to how Lord Krishna taught this eternal yoga to Vivasan (Sun- God) who appeared thousands and thousands years before birth of Lord Krishna. In this verse, Lord explains how an incarnation is different from an ordinary birth.

अजोऽपि सन्नव्ययात्मा भूतानामीश्वरोऽपि सन् ।
प्रकृतिं स्वामधिष्ठाय सम्भवाम्यात्ममायया ॥ ४- ६ ॥

ajo api sann avyayatma bhutanam isvaro api san
prakrtim svam adhisthaya sambhavamy atma-mayaya 4.6

ajah--unborn; *api*-- also; *san*--being; *avyayaatma*—imperishable nature; *bhutanam*—beings i.e. all those who are born; *isvarah*--the Supreme Lord; *api*—also; *san*--being; *prakrtim*—nature (Lord's divine power, beginning-less and endless; subordinate only to the Supreme); *svam*—My own; *adhisthaya*-- ruling; *sambhavami*—come into being; *atma-mayaya*--by My own maya (divine energy, which is Lord's very own power, beyond common understanding and capable of rendering the impossible as actual; refer to introduction)

"Though I am unborn, imperishable and Lord of beings (all those who exist), yet, subjugating my own nature (prakriti), I come into being by my own maya (divine and illusive power)." II 4-6 II

Lord told Arjuna in preceding verse, that he does not remember his previous birth while Lord (actual word used by Lord is "I") remembers everything. Lord clarifies this point in this verse. For understanding this reply three points are required: i) What is nature? ii) Difference between appearance of a being (ordinary birth) and the appearance of Lord of beings i.e. Supreme Eternal Universal Reality, Fundamental Cause of everything that is or avtar (incarnation); And iii) What is maya (divine illusive power)?

i) What is nature? Nature remains with the Lord as much as shadow remains with the individual. It comes out of the Lord at the time of creation and remains as main instrument of the Lord in discharging universal functions of creation, sustenance and destruction. The intermingling effect of three Gunas (sat, rajas and tamas) and all the known laws (gravity, photosynthesis etc.) and unknown laws (black hole etc.) come under the nature. When one is born, one has to face nature for birth, sustenance and destruction. One may say that nature is universal software which exerts its influence on birth, sustenance and death of a being. This world is like a divine play. A being is born with individualized divinity i.e. with no knowledge of its divinity. The existence of individualized divinity means that every being has potential for spiritual evolution. In human birth, a being gets a chance for full blossoming of its spiritual potential i.e. merger of the self with the Supreme, which is the supreme success of a being. Nature, the divine software, always either helps or tests or even challenges the individual in spiritual growth. All laws are fixed and apply equally to all. It allows no laxity, no wrong play. No one can gain exemption from nature (divine software, extremely powerful and simply too effective) except the Lord or the ones who have been bestowed the grace of the Lord. Expressing it very simplistically, nature represents the divine rules for the divine play of the Lord in which Lord allows the divine functions of creation, sustenance and destruction to be discharged intermittently.

ii) This incarnation is the most difficult concept for the modern mind. Perfect being (spiritually most evolved fit for merger with the Supreme) merges with the Supreme. Imperfect beings (i.e. those not fully blossomed spiritually) remain chained to cycles of birth and death. Birth means another chance to experience the impact of actions done by the individual based on laws of nature to evolve spiritually. Birth of a being means appearance is due to laws of nature and entitlement of a being. Incarnation is not due to laws of nature. Nature is subordinate to the Supreme. The Supreme appears in form when unrighteousness grows and righteousness suffers. The laws of nature are not limitations to the Supreme. That is why Lord has used the words- "standing upon my own nature, I am born of my *Maya*." Therefore, if birth is according to laws of nature and according to dictates of nature, it is

305

ordinary birth. When birth is imposed even on nature by the Supreme, it is incarnation i.e. divine appearance for a divine purpose in the overall interest of the cosmos. Incarnation means divine birth which may not necessarily be according to laws of nature. Incarnation is according to situation and divine purpose. In incarnation, Lord exerts divine authority over nature, which is subordinate only to Lord. In ordinary birth, nature becomes mechanical (i.e. laws of nature work routinely). Multitude of creatures is held helpless before laws of nature. On the contrary, in case of incarnation, the indwelling divine spirit stands upon and over the nature. The Divine is not helplessly driven by nature through ignorance. Nature, full with divine light and divine will, helps in the case of incarnation (divine appearance). There is more than ordinary in a divine birth. Ordinary birth is a birth into ignorance i.e. the being completely forgets the divinity within due to cover of ignorance. Divine birth is not a physical phenomenon alone in conformity with rules of nature. It is birth of knowledge, a conspicuous revelation of divinity. It is manifestation of "Self Existent Being," controlling consciously it's becoming even at the point of subjugating the ordinary rules of nature (birth in the form of mixture of human body and a lion). This assumption of imperfection by the "Perfect" is the most mystic phenomenon. It is always for a divine purpose. It is called incarnation. Lord's appearance as Krishna is incarnation i.e. appearance of Supreme Universal Eternal Reality in Form. For this reason, Lord remembers previous births but Arjuna, ordinary mortal, does not remember previous births at all.

iii) My Maya- Lord is using two words i.e. i) My own nature and ii) My self-Maya. What is the difference between the two? My nature is the reference to set routine rules of universe, mechanism, which automatically takes care of the worldly phenomenon such as law of gravitation, law of photosynthesis, law of reprocreation, law of attraction of the opposites. This nature is subordinate to Lord and emphatically none else. But Lord at times, according to exigency of situations, subjugates its own "Prakriti (Nature) i.e. ordinary set of laws" by a forceful downward extra pressure of "Divine Illusive Power or *Maya-Sakti*." The second term refers to extra, inordinate use of illusive power of the Lord which comes to play only in exceptional circumstances to overcome the influence of the ordinary laws of nature. Lord showed Arjuna the Universal Form. Similarly, Lord showed Yashoda all the worlds in his mouth when Yashoda opened baby Krishna's mouth to take out mud put by him into it. Thus, this second category i.e."My self-Maya" includes such miraculous events as are beyond human comprehension and logic such as human birth without procreation; birth of Karan in Mahabharta and Lord Christ; lengthening of cloth (*sari*) covering the physical body of Droupdi in Mahabharta when her modesty was threatened to be outraged in the open court and finding herself helpless, even in the middle of the mightiest of the family members, she cried for help from the Supreme; Coming out as mixture of lion and human body from the pillar to save *Prahalad, a* devotee. This was all possible due to "Divine Illusive Power or *Maya Sakti*," which is used only in exceptional circumstances.

Lord is not an ordinary being. Lord mentions here three cardinal (important or basic) characteristics of appearance of Immortality:

i) Lord is not born. Birth and death are relevant for body only i.e. for worldly existence. Birth and death are result of time, space and causes. The Supreme is beyond these limitations. The existence of a being means that "supreme eternal presence" is already there (of course under the cover of ignorance). Therefore, Lord is not born. Appearance of Lord is not necessarily according to laws of nature. Nature, being subordinate to Lord, supports the appearance of the Lord. Incarnation is assumption of imperfection by the "Supremely Perfect." In a birth, a being forgets the past. In incarnation i.e. appearance of the Supreme Self, past is not forgotten. Ordinary birth is due to Karmas i.e. for undergoing the impact of having committed to a particular act (general theory- for every action matching impact has to be gone through, if not in this life then in next life or lives) or a desire at the time of death. The divine birth is due to Lord's free will riding over the His Nature (Ordinary divine scheme of laws for running the universe). Neither heredity nor environment, affect a divine birth, as they do in case of an ordinary birth. That is why Lord remembers all past lives. Incarnation should, better, be worded as mystical change of form by Lord for a divine cause. The divine appearance becomes conspicuous for the wise. The seven wise people immediately recognized the birth of Christ due to a particular star-formation.

ii) Lord is imperishable i.e. beyond decay. What is Divine? It is divine only if it is eternal, indestructible and immanent (present everywhere). How can the eternal, indestructible and immanent reality be perished? It can never be. It alone exists.

iii) The Supreme Being (The Supreme Truth) is the Lord of all beings. It is subordinate to none. It has no limitations or rules. What it wills, is the rule. The exterior may be looking ordinary but the Lord has within inner innate divine dimension, which makes it conspicuously different from the ordinary.

This is a very important verse of the Gita. Lord wants to explain to Arjuna why HE (Lord Krishna) remembers all past lives i.e. Lord Krishna, the charioteer sitting before Arjuna, is an incarnation. The Supreme Infinite Reality is unborn. It exists already in all beings. At times, it appears, conspicuous by use of its divine, illusive powers for a divine purpose. This Reality is master of all beings. It is subordinate to none. It is beyond any limitations. It exerts its own authority to facilitate its divine play. As Krishna is incarnation, representing the Supreme Eternal Universal Reality, HE remembers past lives. Past, present and future is a worldly phenomenon. Time, space and cause present no limitation for the "Eternal Being," which Lord Krishna is.

7. At this point of discussion, a thought comes to mind as to why the "Infinite" takes to become finite. Lord answers this point in this verse.

यदा यदा हि धर्मस्य ग्लानिर्भवति भारत ।
अभ्युत्थानमधर्मस्य तदात्मानं सृजाम्यहम् ॥ ४- ७ ॥

yada yada hi dharmasya glanir bhavati bharata
abhyutthanam adharmasya tadatmanam srjamy aham 4.7

yada—yada—wherever; *hi*— surely; *dharmasya*—righteousness as per laws of nature; righteousness as per soul-touched wisdom; righteousness as contemplated and confirmed in the deeper layers in silence within, in the proximity of soul; (it is) felt (universally) in one's consciousness and is not based on mere written and spoken words; *glanih*— decline; *bhavati*—is; *bharata*—O descendant of Bharata (Arjuna); *abhyutthanam*—rise or predominance; *adharmasya*— contrary to righteousness; *tada*— then; *atmanam*— myelf; *srjami*—manifest; *aham*—I.

"Whenever there is a decay of *Dharma* and rise of *adharma*, I embody Myself, O Bharata (Arjuna)." II 4-7II

This is one of the most famous verses of the Gita. Lord has used a peculiar word here i.e. Dharma. It has been extensively used in the Gita. There is no synonym to this word in English dictionary. It is essential to understand the meaning of the word Dharma to be able to live life in conformity with the Gita. This term has been very extensively dealt with below as the very assimilation of this term can capitulate one's understanding of the Gita to open doors to awareness of the Gita.

Dharma- What is Dharma? Dharma is righteousness (unbiased, truthful compliance of divine code of conduct) as per the law of nature or as per the yardstick of the Supreme Creator. It is essential nature of a being (one who exists) which should mould behavior of a being. It means compliance to rules of nature (not man-made rules or the rules based on an individual's assessment or interpretation of the situation). This correctness to conformity to nature is not judged by intellectual assessment. It is based on the awareness of conscience of a being (one in existence not necessarily human). Non-compliance to Dharma is felt as agony of soul, very deep into the personality of an individual beyond the range of mind and intellect in the vicinity of soul in the form of "tearing silence or turbulence or extreme uneasiness or self suffocating burden." Dharma is universal. It is never man-made. It is the same to an Indian or an American or a Palestine. It is based on blood, soul, and coexistence of a being with environment **and nature strictly in conformity with the wishes of the creator**. Its application is not limited to humans alone. It applies to nature, animals and birds equally. Dharma does not have a language. Its dictates come in the form shudder at the level of conscience or cry of the soul. It communicates its message even to strangers not related with language. Dharma is "Creator's inbuilt, Universal Communication" to soul through silence about the infringement of rules of the Creator. Dharma is interpretation at the level of soul or consciousness. It is mute whispering of the soul of a being (or the voice of the Supreme at the level of awareness in the region of soul and not intellect). It directs the being (one in existence) towards spiritual evolution, towards most natural course available at the spur of the moment. The Infinite wants to communicate about non-compliance of rules of nature to the finite based on Dharma- "Unwritten, inbuilt, universal code of conduct to behave in conformity with the nature's Divine wisdom."

For this reason, it is said that Dharma is that, which holds the individual, family, society, country and the whole world together. There can be no conflict, where there is Dharma. For Dharma enables a life of peace, harmony, truth and justice. A few days back there was, in newspaper, a photo of a bitch (female dog) milking a new born baby monkey, whose mother had died. Who was it, who told the female dog to milk the orphan, newly born, baby-monkey? A newly born child was left in jungle and a snake came to protect it from all dangers with its hood, which the snake used to bite others. When the help for the child came, the snake silently went away. How does this communication at soul level in so contrasting entities take place? It is Dharma, Universal Code of Conduct, inbuilt near the conscience of a being (one who exists) to judge compliance or otherwise to the will of the creator. It is "Universal, Inbuilt, Divine Mechanism" in all beings which makes a being feel at the level of conscience that all is not well or well. In very short, **Cosmic Intelligence, which embodies itself in a being, as a matter of course, is Dharma.** Dharma upholds the cosmic and moral order considering the whole universe as one unit and represents the will of the Creator of the Universe everywhere and in all circumstances.

What is religion then? Dharma's interpretation by someone in human form is religion. A religion may have human bias, but Dharma is pure feeling at the level of awareness (consciousness) reflecting in the form of experience (awareness through conscience) whether or not divine will is being followed. Religions may differ somewhere at times due to human bias but Dharma remains the same as the leave of a banyan tree of a particular type remains the same throughout the world. Hinduism, Christianity, Islam are only interpretations of Dharma, religions, outpouring of some soul's experience, translating the code of conduct, interpreting the righteousness as per 'The Divinity'.

Dharma is "Divine Universal Wisdom or Unwritten, inbuilt Code of Conduct for all Beings." Lack of awareness of Dharma, due to cover of ignorance, is one fundamental reason for all evils and conflicts in this world. This divine wisdom comes in silence in the proximity of soul through awareness at the level of conscience. The discussion is of paramount importance and it will not be complete if ways to improve sensitivity to Dharma are not discussed. Therefore it is essential to further prolong the discussion to mention in very brief how sensitivity to Dharma can be improved:

i) *Brahamcharya* (celibacy) i.e. self control to conserve (protect) the essential life-force for the good of cosmos and essentially not for luxury of indulgence; ii) *Satya* (truth) - What is truth? Truth is that which does not change with time or truth alone defies the influence of time. Every being in this universe has a "bit of truth within" because there cannot be any existence without truth. Falling in line with that "Internal Existence within a being" is satya and the wordless language of that *Satya* is Dharma; Untruthfulness is *adharma* (or lack of Dharma) iii) *Tapasya*- Natural instinct of senses is to go out for satisfaction. An extra effort and denial of luxury or satisfaction at level of senses is required to divert the senses inwardly. This extra effort and denial of even routine sense satisfaction for spiritual growth is *tapasya*; iv) Charity constitutes sharing a part of your income (without pump and show and for the satisfaction of the soul only) with those who are less fortunate than you; v) Niyama (Discipline)- It is the practice of making obey rules and orders to follow a regulated life. Discipline helps to enhance body, mind and intellect; vi) Forgiveness- Anybody can commit mistake. It is necessary to understand, tolerate and reform by resorting to forgiveness. It is necessary at all levels i.e. family, society and country; vii) Non-violence- It constitutes not inflicting injury on another by violence, which only triggers reaction and ignites more violence; viii) Tranquility- A proper decision can be taken only by a calm mind. Tranquility harmonizes the internal levels of existence to take right decision; ix) Austerity- it means being simple and allowing no luxury or comforts. This quality is necessary to remain focused on the objective of life and keeps the individual's life clear of uncalled-for disturbances in life; x) Love all- It is most important (highest Dharma) to love all profusely without condition and without reservation.

When an adjective is used with Dharma, it swiftly changes meaning, for example, *sva-dharma, kshetriya dharma* or *rashriya dharma* etc.

What is then sum and substance of this verse? This verse explains the purpose of incarnation i.e. why the Supreme Reality, which is beyond any specific form or limitation, appears in forms in this world of limitations. The Supreme Reality embodies or takes form (any form i.e. fish, boar, human being or lion and human being, just any form), whenever there is decay of Dharma i.e. whenever people start going against the "Divine Consciousness" present partly in all beings as "share of cosmic intelligence." During this period (i.e. when serious tension prevails in lives; all-pervasive materialism invade the human souls; the righteous, the innocent, the weak, the pious and the spiritual are exploited), people show distinct disregard to "awareness to call of conscience" and wrong doing (actions which cause deep pain, utter disappointment, sense of helplessness and burden on souls in victims) tends to predominate. Moral values are lost and upsurge of unrighteousness prevails The focus of divine manifestation in form remains to check *adharma* (impact of the evil forces, i.e. forces of ignorance and selfishness, in terms of actions contrary to righteousness, not as per laid down rules alone but also as per awareness of self-conscious people) by compelling the evil forces to recede into comparative powerlessness. The Supreme Reality manifests or appears, not as per the normal natural ways but in its own peculiar way according to demand of the situation enforcing its divine illusive power. The idea is that Lord is not subordinate to nature. The "Supreme Reality" forces its "Divine illusive power, *Maya*" on nature as well. Normal seen and unseen laws of nature present no limitations to the Lord. This verse also points out that the "Supreme Eternal Universal Reality" upholds Dharma (i.e. being with essential nature of a being) and comes down in some form to overturn the forces of evils and selfishness.

"I embody myself"- Lord's selection of the word is very important. Lord is not born. The Supreme Self exists through all beings as the "Eternal, Universal, and Indestructible Reality under the cover of ignorance." The terms birth and death are relevant for the finite (chained to cycles of birth and death) and not the Infinite. Lord appears, based on divine illusive powers (exceptional force more effective than ordinary rules of nature), in a particular form, as if it were a form (in actuality Lord does not have a particular form; it is not born; Lord appears in conformity to Lord's own will for a divine purpose). This happens always for the good of the cosmos under certain compelling circumstances. This is called *avtar* or incarnation or **"specific bold appearance in a particular form"** for a particular divine purpose. Why is it so? Nature is subordinate to Lord and it is not necessary for the Lord to abide by the laws of nature. The form of the Lord is always so peculiar, so powerful, so effective and so inordinate at times that divine appearance automatically becomes conspicuous (very easy to notice) for the spiritually matured. Lord embodied as fish, boar, short-statured *brahmin* etc. and all forms were peculiar due to action, power, ferocity, effectiveness and astuteness (understanding behavior correctly and quickly) that was far different from the ordinary level of existence. Even in Krishna *avtar* (incarnation), Lord's childish pranks were all different from the ordinary. Nothing comes and nothing goes in this world. Lord alone exists. This mystery unfolds only with the grace of the Lord and at that time knower only laughs away this discussion, because it is not subject of mind. It is a matter relating to awareness of soul for which one has to meditate, introspect and dive within self, besides disciplining the body and serving the cosmos selflessly as the expansion of divine grace.

8. Having described the fact of incarnation in the preceding verse, the Lord in this verse deals with the purpose of incarnation.

परित्राणाय साधूनां विनाशाय च दुष्कृताम् ।
धर्मसंस्थापनार्थाय सम्भवामि युगे युगे ॥ ४- ८ ॥

paritranaya sadhunam vinasaya ca duskrtam
dharma-samsthapanarthaya sambhavami yuge yuge 4.8

paritranaya—for the protection or for the deliverance; *sadhunam*--of the good; *vinasaya*--for the destruction; *ca*--also; *duskrtam*--of the wicked; *dharma*—righteousness as mentioned earlier; *samsthapana-arthaya*--to re-establish; *sambhavami*--I distinctly appear or manifest (in worldly language, Born) ; *yuge--yuge*—in every age.

"For the protection of the good (the virtuous), for the destruction of the wicked and for establishment of Dharma, I 'facilitate my conspicuous appearance or incarnate' age after age." II 4-8 II

In this verse Lord explains to Arjuna that the 'conspicuous divine appearance' (incarnation), age after age (rather in every age), takes place for three reasons (these three reasons are also three vows of the Lord or assurances of the Lord in the event of an incarnation) :

i) For the protection of the good- One purpose of 'conspicuous divine presence' or incarnation is to protect the good. The word '*sadhunam*' has been used for those good men, who are naturally inclined for the good of others. One purpose of Divinity is to keep the world going on lines of righteousness. The good nurture righteousness, human values and world order. It is the promise of the lord that the good are always protected. Lord has used the word '*sadhus*'. It is not limited to *sanyasis* (ascetics) only. It refers to all who are righteous, whatever their caste or position and occupation may be.

ii) For the destruction of the wicked- This is the second vow of the Lord. Lord destroys the wicked, the evil-doers and the sinners, how much ever powerful they might have been. An incarnate uncompromisingly crushes the *adharma* (unrighteousness) and the wicked. In all ages it has been like that. The Lord appeared as Rama expressly to prevent the cry of distress anywhere. Evil doers are those who lead life of unrighteousness, who break the laws of the society, who are vain, dishonest and greedy, who injure others, who take property of others by force and who commit atrocious crimes.

Lord is disinterested friend of all beings. Lord is not against even the wicked. Lord is against the wicked actions, wrong doing, which harm the society and the wicked as well in the long run. Lord destroys the wicked to do the good to the world and as well as to those wicked persons.

iii) For establishment of righteousness- There is only one sin in this universe and this is lack of awareness. All evils emanate due to lack of awareness only. This may happen due to ignorance or arrogance. There is only one virtue in this world and this is awareness. All positive attributes emanate due to one's awareness to one's deep shrill, leaning within, near the soul. Awakening one's sensitivity to one's awareness, deep within, is the first step towards establishment of Dharma. Why is it so? Dharma is not an output of intellectual exercise. It is one's sensitivity to one's awareness at the level of soul. An Incarnate (Conspicuous Divine Appearance for a divine purpose), in an effort to restore Dharma, may resort to preaching (sermons by Lord Christ; Gospel of the Gita to Arjuna), propagating selfless performance (being a role model like Lord Rama) or taking a direct action, if things are beyond control, with full might annihilating (destroying) the bane (something that causes trouble and makes people unhappy) of contention as was done in case of Hyrnakashyapu, father of Prahalada. Developing sensitivity to one's awareness is the "real education" and all else (i.e. sensitivity to ethical, humanistic values and universe) comes afterwards automatically. In all ages, all incarnations (conspicuous Divine Forms) have primarily sensitized the people to call of conscience, and force has always been used as the last resort. It is from here that restoration of righteousness sets in the society. An individual sensitive to one's awareness knows the due demands of the self, neighbors, society, country and universe. If there are individuals like Ravana in the age of Lord Rama, who take to unrighteousness as a matter of strategy or consciously, Lord imposes might on them to enforce them to surrender. In nut shell, an Incarnate (Conspicuous Divine Appearance) ensures that righteousness i.e. compliance to natural order is naturally established, how much ever difficult it may happen to be. This is the promise of the Lord and great assurance to all beings. The words "naturally established" have got special relevance. **Dharma mostly blossoms from within the beings like blossoming of the flower in the spring i.e. naturally.**

After giving the three assurances, Lord makes another revelation (fact that has been a secret and surprise) in this verse:

Sambhavami yuge yuge (facilitate the Divine incarnation ages after ages)- The Supreme Universal Eternal Reality (represented by Lord Krishna here) facilitates divine incarnation age after age (rather in all ages) . Why does it happen? Is it not possible for the omnipotent (all-powerful) Lord to protect the good, destroy the wicked and establish righteousness without Divine Manifestation? The Lord manifests Himself as an incarnate (conspicuous divine appearance) to shower His special grace on the beings. Lord stages the drama of human life in such a manner that it conduces them (multitude of followers) to be devoted to Him (and naturally thus receptive to natural order or *Dharma*). Lord's presence is unique. It sets in motion an overwhelming current of love, compassion, tolerance and understanding. His very presence decimates (destroys to large extent) the negativity. There is a divine spark in all beings, which shines a little bit in twinkles but this brightness of divinity within comes alive, shinning in brilliance, in the presence of the Divine personality or an Incarnate. During His incarnation, His vision, touch talk etc. and later on practice of hearing, thinking, chanting and reliving His messages lead the people to salvation. The appearance of the birth-less symbolizes the revelation of mystery in the soul of a being. It is not anything ordinary. It rings a message to the world to evolve spiritually. This is to restore Dharma (a being's receptivity to eternal values stored within a soul). Dharma alone can protect on a continuous basis. Dharma alone can give peace, prosperity (richness of soul), tolerance and contentment. Lord has to manifest Himself again and again in all ages to save

Dharma in order to prevent universe from falling to pieces. Lord's presence sets the decaying Dharma on the right track and assures the devotees that the "Divine Love" is steering the universe all the time. The incarnation also gives a message to people that whoever defies "Dharma," is the foe of the Lord and will be destroyed by the Lord.

9. In this verse, Lord tells Arjuna that those who know the mystery of divine birth and work have no birth. In divine birth, a birth is with some exceptional divine powers and purposes.

जन्म कर्म च मे दिव्यमेवं यो वेत्ति तत्त्वतः ।
त्यक्त्वा देहं पुनर्जन्म नैति मामेति सोऽर्जुन ॥ ४- ९ ॥

janma karma ca me divyam evam yo vetti tattvatah
tyaktva deham punar janma naiti mam eti so arjuna 4.9

janma--birth; *karma*-- action; *ca*--also; *me*-- my; *divyam*—divine (having attributes of indestructibility, eternity an immanence or present everywhere); *evam*-- this; *yah*--who; *vetti*--knows; *tattvatah*--in reality; *tyaktva*--leaving aside; *deham*--this body; *punah*--again; *janma*--birth; *na*--not; *eti*-- gets; *mam*- to Me; *eti*-- comes; *sah*—he (the knower of divine birth and action); *arjuna*--O Arjuna.

"O Arjuna! One who thus knows, in essence or in its right principles, my divine birth and work, after leaving the body, is not born again; and he or she attains to me." II 4-9 II

The focus of this verse is on the difference of divine birth (or incarnation) and ordinary birth. An ordinary birth is based on time, space, and cause-effect relationship. A divine birth is divine's conspicuous appearance, in which Lord subjugates 'ordinary nature (dealt with in detail in preceding paragraph)' to conform to divine appearance and divine will. In divine birth, secret soul comes out of its secrecy as "Lord of the nature in body" for a divine purpose. A Divine birth is with some exceptional divine powers. It is more of the nature of appearance than birth. While 'divine eternal force' routinely exists in a being in an ordinary birth undercover of ignorance, in case of divine birth, this force is extremely conspicuous and active. It does not allow itself to be driven here and there by laws of nature mechanically. It subjugates the laws of nature to comply with the divine will. Nature, being subordinate to the Absolute Divine, only cooperates. The prison doors opened at the birth of Krishna. The Guards took no notice of the birth. The flooded Yamuna water receded to allow to Vasudeva, father of baby Krishna, to take baby Krishna to Gokul. In Bible, Moses was near the red sea and the Egyptian army was following them. Israelites were frightened. Moses prayed and Lord said "Lift up your stick and hold it over the sea. The water (of red sea) will divide and the Israelites will be able to walk through the sea on the dry ground." It happened and the Egyptian army could not catch the Israelites. There is uniqueness in divine birth and divine work. Both birth and work in case of divine birth are divine i.e. super natural, impossible to be accomplished by others (ordinary beings) and exceptional. Only those, who have some spiritual development, recognize in reality the divinity in birth and work of an Incarnate. Divine birth is an illusion. It is aprakrita (beyond the range of ordinary phenomenon of nature). It is divine. It is peculiar to the Lord. Lord manifest in human form but His body is *chinmayamnanda* (i.e. full of consciousness, not inert matter as are human bodies composed of five elements. In divine birth, in Rama avtar (incarnation), many sages could not recognize Lord Rama's divinity. In the same age, there were sages like Vishwamittra, who went to king Dashratha (Lord Rama's father) to ask for Lord Rama's help in order to get rid of demons, creating havoc for those practicing spirituality. Lord Krishna, even in his childhood, lifted the whole mountain (Goverdhan) to protect his village folks and animals from the havoc of the incessant rain. Thus, the mystery of divine work is always beyond the mental and physical reach of common humanity. Those who recognize the divine birth and divine work are blessed souls. Without some spiritual merit, it is not possible to take notice of the inherent perceptible spiritual change in divine birth and divine work. It is not possible to see spirituality with ego and arrogance. For this reason, Lord says that those, who come to know the essence of divine birth and divine work, do not take to rebirth i.e. after abandoning their bodies they go to the abode of the Supreme, beyond cycles of birth and death, beyond any limitations whatsoever. It means that they get enlightened and become divine themselves taking active part in divine processes of creation, sustenance and destruction in whatever form they may happen to be (i.e. before death or after death).

This verse emphasizes that Lord's birth-less-ness (i.e. Lord is unborn or Lord appears rather than taking the normal route of birth) is not to be taken as emptiness or nothingness. This reaction, at times, is the result of human limitations or incapacity to envision the Infinite. The Divine Manifestation should be taken as one particular appearance of "positive state of perfection and blessedness" for cosmic good. With body, mind and intelligence, it is not possible to envision a state beyond this mortal plane. **The unity of life with the "Supreme Eternal Universal Reality" stands for life at all levels** i.e. i) at level of existence in mortal world as one among the many seeking perfection and ii) as inseparable and integral part of a "Conscious Perfect Whole" as eternal existence.

Having abandoned the body- Lord has used these words to emphasize that the enlightened one will not have to go for rebirth after death, for death is imminent for the embodied being. This does not at all mean that death is pre-condition for enlightenment. Those, who are called "Jivan mukta i.e. liberated while alive" gain enlightenment before death and continue working for the common good or cosmic benefit. King Janak or Ramakrishna Param Hans were "*Jivan Muktas* or liberated souls" who continued their good work even after gaining enlightenment.

Essence (*tattvatah*) of divine birth and divine work- This word "essence" has been very carefully used by the Lord. It emphasizes a Vedic truth i.e. "One who knows Brahmn (The Supreme Eternal Universal Reality) becomes That." This knowing is something beyond logical argument or intellectual conclusion. "This knowing" amounts to awakening of one's awareness to principles of universal existence at the level of conscience. Without awakening to self, this "essence" cannot be known, because this knowing means experiencing with feeling directly or "being through the whole process of creation, sustenance and destruction at the level of one's consciousness." Suppose it is said "This wire is a good conductor of electricity." Now it goes without saying that electricity has definitely gone through the wire to come to the conclusion that it is a good conductor of electricity. "Knowing this essence" means that one has had the direct conscious experience, like actual tasting of water, of that "Divine Eternal Universal Elixir," "that Unexplainable, Untouchable, Un-discernable, All-pervading Reality, Repository of all energy ", which validates all existences, remains in all existences and keeps all existences moving towards the chosen end in the total scheme of universal existence.

The message of the verse is simple. One, who knows the mystery of the divine birth (Divine Conspicuously Manifest in a being) and the divine work, attains union with the supreme i.e. one reaches to that point where there remains no difference between the seeker and the sought-after-reality.

10. Descent of the "Divine in Form or *Avtar*" stands for "realizing the glory of the divine birth and divine work." This is one aspect of the divine knowledge. The other aspect of divine knowledge is culmination (finally reaching the highest point) of mortal being to the point of immortality.

वीतरागभयक्रोधा मन्मया मामुपाश्रिताः ।
बहवो ज्ञानतपसा पूता मद्भावमागताः ॥ ४- १० ॥

vita-raga-bhaya-krodha man-maya mam upasritah
bahavo jnana-tapasa puta mad-bhavam agatah 4.10

vita-- raga-- bhaya-- krodhah—freed from attachment, fear, and anger; *mat-maya*—intensely absorbed in Me so much so that one starts cognizing divine licker in everything and everywhere (i.e. the stage Lord is talking about); *mam*--unto *upasritah*—having taken refuge in the Supreme alone and not anything else whatsoever; *bahavah*--many; *jnana-- tapasa-- putah*—purified by the warmth (of fire) of knowledge (divine knowledge here); *mat-bhavam-- agatah*-- (many) become one with my being (i.e. attains eternity, indestructibility and immanence or mortal becomes immortal or river merges into the ocean and becomes ocean) .

"Free from passion, fear and anger, absorbed in Me, taking refuge in Me, purified by the knowledge, many have attained to my Being." II 4-10 II

This chapter is about divine knowledge. What is divine knowledge? Understanding by awareness the divine mystery i.e. divine birth, divine work and divine objective (new creation, sustenance and pruning by destruction; after every autumn new leaves sprout ringing out the new message of the Divinity) is divine wisdom or divine knowledge. The state of "Self Realization (*Brahmnlina or brahmnnishta* or absorption of self into the life sustaining Reality or Truth of the universe)" is not possible without being through and through with the creation, sustenance and destruction. There are twofold aspects of the divine wisdom. Firstly, it unfolds the secret of the divine birth, and the divine work. Secondly, it provides an opportunity to the mortal beings to evolve spiritually to become an integral part of the "Universal Divinity at its never ending flow." This verse specifically describes the merits of divine knowledge. What are the hall marks of the divine wisdom? Lord gives point-wise description:

i) **Freedom from attachment, fear and anger (*vita raga bhaya krodha*)**- When one gets divine wisdom, attachment to sense objects ceases. How does it come to be? One comes to understand the short-term relationship of senses and sense objects. Truth will finally outlive the veil of ignorance. When one realizes the truth of worldly relationship, one starts yearning for the "immortality" to get rid of the cycles of birth and death, the reasons for unceasing worry and afflictions. When one realizes that one is fundamentally constant, indestructible and eternal self, one becomes desire-less, fearless and calm. That is how one feels delivered from passion (lust or unquenchable desire), fear and anger with divine knowledge. How does it happen? When the mind ceases to exist due to yoga (yoga is the control of impulses or urges, modifications of tendencies arising out of mind-stuff), self is realized and when self is realized mind ceases to exist. An individual becomes one with the pure consciousness that does not change.

ii) **Full with Me or absorbed in Me (*manmayah*)** - With divine knowledge, one realizes one's true nature (one's eternal, indestructible and immanent nature, one's unchanging nature, One's real ever 'continuing Truth within'). It means one has gained consciousness about that vital "**Divine Eternal Infinite Essence Within**" which defies death. It means realizing that Vedic proclamation "That I am." One daily sees the body in the mirror. One has gained no divine wisdom, if one does not feel this conviction at basic level that our real self is different from the body. On realizing the "Divine Eternal Existence Within," one lives a fearless life. Then one is not afraid of death. Then, one confidently and resolutely seeks deathlessness in death. One manifests divine nature in human nature. One may rest or work but, somewhere within, one is always conscious of inherent divinity, as a tree always remains green, if its roots remain connected with water source below the earth. As live wire is full with electricity passing through it, a "*manmaya* or absorbed-in" individual is always loaded with consciousness about the "Supreme Divine Existence Within."

iii) **Mam Upasritah** (Takes refuge in ME) - The individual with divine knowledge takes refuge in the "Supreme Divine Existence Within." How does it happen? The individual with divine knowledge views the things in "Universal Oneness" and desists separation (egoistic tendency) in any form whatsoever. Such an individual truly lives the statement of Kabir- "When I am, God is not. When God is, I am not." How does taking refuge effectively help finally? An individual with divine knowledge ignores individual imperfections. Differences in capabilities, capacities and competences are like individual details of scenery, that, when put together, makes the scenery beautiful, unmatched and unforgettable creation of the Supreme Master. Such an individual blissfully integrates the differences in his or her state of divine intoxication and utilizes the synergy (additional energy) for achieving the results, all with the Divine Grace again … … automatically. While an ordinary individual, in the testing moments of life, leans towards husband, wife, son, parents, superiors, the seeker with divine knowledge, knowing the fragile nature of worldly relations, commits himself or herself solely to the resolute, unshakable and enduring faith in the will of the "Supreme Divine." Perfect surrender to the will of the "Supreme Reality" completely drives away the fear and doubt and makes "dependence on the Lord" the crowning glory of life.

What is it that happens when an individual shows the hall marks of divine knowledge? The individual becomes (Lord uses extremely beautiful words):

Jnana Tapasa Puta {i.e. purified by the penance (willing action to suffer) for knowledge}- The flattened cakes of floor (*chapaties*) become good for eating after going through the heat treatment in an oven or on a hot plate. Similarly an individual gets purified in the fire of knowledge. What is jnana tapasa or baked or matured with the pangs for divine knowledge? Anything worthwhile in this universe requires, constant efforts, sacrifice of comforts, disciplining of body, mind and emotions. "Stumbling again and again in the darkness of ignorance, bruised thoroughly but still rising, hoping consummately (completely and perfectly) against all the odds, suffering immensely still yearning and continuing for divine knowledge" is divine tapas. It is the warmth of going near the fire of divine knowledge. It matures the individual for acceptance of the divine grace. The divine knowledge perfects the mind confused by *ajnana* (ignorance). With divine knowledge, mind becomes crystal clear to facilitate the glimpses of the Divine Reality or Truth (that which defies impact of time) within a being. *Jnana Tapas* is fire of divine knowledge. Just as fire burns cotton, so also this "jnana tapas or warmth of fire of divine knowledge" burns all latent tendencies (vasanas), cravings (trishnas), mental impressions (samskaras), sins and all actions and purifies the seeker. Penance (willing action to suffer) through fire of knowledge, matures a seeker for the divine grace.

After the seeker is purified in knowledge, what is it that happens? Lord again uses beautiful word:

Bahavo madbhavam agatah (many have attained to state of nature of my being (Purshottama)- Many seekers, after having attained the divine knowledge, attain to the state of "**madbhavam**; nature of the Supreme Being." What is the state of "nature of the Supreme Being"? It is eternal conscious state with eternal love, eternal joy, eternal peace, limitless blessedness and all the divine features such as eternity, indestructibility, omnipresence (presence everywhere) and omnipotence (power to do just anything in the universe). It amounts to saying "O man! Only follow my rules and thou shall be my-self." What is the meaning of these words "thou shall be my-self"? If the wick of a "not-burning-candle" is brought near to the wick of a burning candle, what will happen? Now both the candles will start dispelling darkness. Similarly, when the seeker matured in divine knowledge enters the "Exclusive Zone of the Supreme Divine Reality Beyond limitations," the seeker also becomes "effulgent with divinity" to bestow divine blessedness to all who seek. The river merges in the ocean extinguishing its separate existence. This is the state of supreme blessedness, utterly peaceful and full with bliss and consciousness, which the lord is referring by the term "*madbhavam* (transcendental state of perfection) or state of nature of Supreme Being.**"

How does one who has attained the state of "Madbhavam agatah" look like? This will start a beautiful discussion. Before this, it is necessary to recapitulate the terms, Devas, Gods and "Supreme Universal Eternal Reality." These terms always appear in discussion.

Devas, Gods and Supreme Universal Eternal Reality- Devas are those blessed souls, which have not attained total absorption in the "Supreme Universal Eternal Omnipresent Essence." They are souls awakened to Absolute Divinity and committed to the divine work. They are just like working executives with some limited powers in an organization. They remain serving and guiding the true seekers. Their forms and way of worship is according to traditions. For example lord Hanuman. They help and relieve the seekers but they cannot get the seeker relief from cycles of birth and death. Gods are perceived divinities i.e. incarnations like Lord Rama, Lord Krishna (They fully represent the Divinity). The form and way of worship is again according to traditions. People may differ about the Gods due to religious bias. They represent "Absolute Divinity" in form. They surpass the general rules of nature. They are "The Formless in Form," incarnations. The "Supreme Universal Reality" is that Universal Truth, which surpasses the limitations of time, space and causes. Actually, it is the ever continuing, ever blissful, ever peaceful, ever conscious, ever the same and the 'Ultimate Source of Divine knowledge'. If ever anywhere in the universe any being feels unprotected, lonely, suffering and tormented deep within and cries for redemption (being saved) from the levels of consciousness, it is this "Energy Source" that responds either in form or even without form. It is actually this 'Energy Source' that works even through devas and Gods. It alone is. Nothing else exists without it. It is the "Greatest Mystery of the Universe." It does not have a form. It cannot be seen in entirety but there can be no dispute about the existence of the Supreme Truth or Reality or the Divine Infinite Consciousness. It is smaller than the smallest and bigger than the biggest. It walks without legs, speaks without mouth, hears without ears, works without hands. It is omnipresent, omnipotent and omniscient (knowing everything). It is the "Source" and the "Fundamental Reason" of generation, operation and destruction (for renewal) of the universe. Actually, it is this "Divine Infinite Energy" which responds to all invocations to even Devas and Gods. Reference to this Reality, this Truth does not require adherence to any religion (laid down code of conduct for leading life by some good soul in human form with detailed description keeping this Absolute Divinity in mind is religion). It is there always whether in form or without form. Nothing (not even *Devtas* and Gods) can work without grace of this Reality. This Reality is unborn, eternal, indestructible, omnipresent (present everywhere), omnipotent (having power to do just anything in the universe) and omniscient. It is this Reality which takes form (incarnation) to serve a divine purpose. It is equally effective in form or without form. Everything is with it. There can be nothing without it. Lord Krishna in the Gita represents this "Energy Source in Human Form."

How does one who has attained the state of **"*Madbhavam*, mentioned by Lord Krishna"** look like? This question refers to four concepts of salvation (based on the thinking of the Hindus). First is the category of **salokyas i.e.** these devotees inhabit the same worlds as Gods (Gods are perceived divinities in line with or without traditions, representing the Infinite Formless) and never deviates to any other place. The second category of **Sammepya i.e.** those devotees who are always near God and they never go away from God's side. The third category is of **Sarupyas i.e.** those devotees who take on the form like God's i.e. bright and effulgent. The fourth category is of **Saujyas i.e.** those devotees who enter the state of nature of "Supreme Universal Eternal Infinite reality" and is merged therein, as a river in the sea, losing their own separate forms altogether. This is the highest final stage.

Now the meaning of the verse becomes very clear. There are innumerable souls who reach the state of nature of the Supreme Being (referred to by the words "*Madbhavam*"). They are all matured in divine knowledge (baked in the fire of divine knowledge). They all have certain common features i.e. i) they are free from attachment fear and anger; ii) Their minds are always fresh with the divine fragrance (or their minds are always full with thoughts of the Supreme); iii) They consider the Supreme as their only resort at the most basic level or based on their personal convictions.

11. In the preceding verse, Lord has mentioned that the devotees attain HIM? Now question arises how they attain Him. Lord answers this question in this verse.

ये यथा मां प्रपद्यन्ते तांस्तथैव भजाम्यहम् ।
मम वर्त्मानुवर्तन्ते मनुष्याः पार्थ सर्वशः ॥ ४- ११ ॥

ye yatha mam prapadyante tams tathaiva bhajamy aham
mama vartmanuvartante manusyah partha sarvasah 4.11

ye--all of them; *yatha*--as; *mam*--unto Me; *prapadyante*--surrender; *tan*--unto them; *tatha*--so; *eva*--certainly; *bhajami*--do I reward; *aham*--I; *mama*--My; *vartma*--path; *anuvartante*--do follow; *manusyah*--all men; *partha*--O son of Prtha; *sarvasah*--in all respects.

"O Partha (Son of Pritha or Arjuna)! As the people go for Me (towards Me), so do I accept them to my divine love or my divine existence (bhajami); human beings follow my path in every path." II 4-11 II

In this verse, Lord Krishna, as an *avtar* (an incarnate) or descent of the Divine in human form makes very bold statement bringing out wide variety and universal relevance of the Gita's thoughts. Certain words are very simple to look at but they are having very profound and deep meaning. These are discussed below:

i) "**As the people go for Me (i.e. move towards Me or proceed towards me), so do I accept them to my divine love (bhajami)**" – Life of an individual passes through different phases. Sometimes "pain, pressure, sufferings, afflictions, ignorance" so constrain (to force) an individual that the individual finds no alternative but to surrender according to relevant faith to the power far stronger than one's own capacity. Ordinary individuals demand material gains. Other individuals who have understood the inevitable phenomenon of change in this ever changing universe due to spiritual maturity seeks "strong consciousness of one's own possession of the truth, the whole truth and nothing but the truth." This surrender, either for relief from the present predicament in mortal existence or for self realization, in most of the cases, is to "a **particular Form or to the Formless**" based on traditions, local faith and spiritual maturity of the devotee. Different people from different places proceed to connect themselves to mute whispering of the soul-touched message within differently (i.e. with different concepts, perceptions, inclinations, different notions and different traditions). The "Supreme Universal Eternal Reality" whom Lord Krishna represents here, responds to them respecting their concepts, perceptions, inclinations and traditions and takes them in its divine fold based on their spiritual merits. Lord has used beautiful words "*bhajami aham*." What do these words "Lord worships the devotees" mean? It means that the "Infinite Eternal Reality" takes them in the reassuring, generous divine nature of the Supreme or makes them integral part of the divine process of creation, sustenance and destruction or causes them to be one with the "Infinite Eternal Activity of the Universe" or the seeker becomes a part of the exercise of the activity of the "Universal, Unbiased, Unmatched Goodness" or the seeker is rewarded either in material terms or blessed with immortality. What are these forms, concepts and traditions based on which Lord takes the devotees in the divine fold? This requires further detailed discussion.

The Form and the Formless – Proper assimilation of the words "The Form and The Formless" is very important. There is an inexpressible "Impulse throughout the Universe" to which an individual naturally addresses at the time of either mortal suffering or spiritual darkness. Worshipping or addressing the power stronger than self "in Form" is for those feeble in divine knowledge. The seekers spiritually advanced and with some divine knowledge seek the "Formless, the Ultimate and Eternal Cause, behind every change (change of being and change of one being worshipped is." It is just like addressing the grievances either to the king directly or through an appointed executive. Worshipping the form and the formless i.e. worshipping the tree or the eternal existence which keeps the race of tree alive is the same finally from the point of view of one being worshipped. Those worshipping the form may worship, local deity, Hanuman Ji, Sai Baba or Mother Mary based on concept of duality (i.e. the idea that one is worshipping and the other is being worshipped). Even those who worship Vedic deities with sacrifices and with expectations of reward, find what they seek by the grace of the Supreme. Worshipping the Formless means worshipping one who validates all Forms whatsoever. It is like addressing the king and not any one in between.

The "Form" worshipped by devotees may be different in case of different devotees based on individual temperament, family traditions, local practices and level of spiritual maturity. Different devotees worship the idol of their worship in different forms i.e. Hanuman ji or Sai Baba or Mother Mary and that most sensitive "Divine Reality existing everywhere at every moment, whom Lord Krishna represents here in this discussion" responds to the surrender (or act of worship) in the same form i.e. as Sai Baba or Hanuman ji or Mother Mary i.e. the Supreme reveals "Himself" to them in the same form.

Some devotees seek the "Unknown Universal Magnanimous Reality" to appear to them in different forms i.e. as son, as friend, as master, as lover, as guide etc. The Divinity responds to act of surrender or act of worship as son, as friend, as master, as lover and as guide etc.

The Supreme Universal Eternal Reality or the Universal Eternal Consciousness or the embodiment of Universal Dharma is the same everywhere at every point of the universe. Gods (Perceived Divinities based on local traditions and customs or Intermediate Gods) are different in forms based on different religions (interpretations of Dharma and the Divine). Reference to a particular God is reference through duality i.e. one is the seeker and the other is the sought in the act of seeking. The same Supreme Reality responds through different Gods (Intermediate Divinities). Worshipping the "Formless" means worshipping based on knowledge that the "Divine One" is the same within and out in everything else. This is based on concept of Universal Oneness or non-Duality. Final dispenser is the same whether path of duality (the seeker and sought are different) or non-duality (the seeker and the sought are the same considering the inherent Divinity in all) has been followed.

What are these different paths? A path is a particular religion, an interpretation of Dharma and the Divine by some in human form. The Supreme Universal Reality (the Absolute Divinity whom Lord Krishna represents through *avtar* or incarnation) is the same for the entire humanity or all beings. HE rewards all (even devotees of other deities) just in the same way in which they seek Him. To the ordinary human beings, HE gives material joys and good things of the world. Those, who worship Vedic deities with sacrifices and with expectations of reward, find what they seek by the Divine Grace. To a yogi, who wants Brahamn Nirvana {Salvation (or total liberation from all possible limitations) by merger in the Supreme Divinity), Lord grants *moksha* or total liberation.

ii) Human beings follow Lord's path (my path) in every way or in every path- What are these different paths? A path is a particular religion (like Hinduism, Christianity or Islam etc.), an interpretation of the Dharma and the Divine by someone in human form. These words boldly ring the divine message of the Gita having universal relevance. The devotee's choice of manner of approaching or worshipping (Worshipping is offering one's sacred feelings at deepest level to Lord based on rituals, traditions or through meditation and Samadhi) are at times marked by local concepts and approaches i.e. traditional ways of worship i.e. Hinduism, Christianity or Islam, Jainism, Buddhism and Sikhism etc. These different religions (paths), apparently manifesting different concepts and approaches (i.e. Hinduism, Christianity and Islam etc), have been laid down keeping the same "Ultimate Universal Eternal Reality" in view. Every religion is basically an effort to identify the "Indestructible Eternal Reality" within and to understand (at the level of consciousness) the relationship of a human being with the "Underlying Eternal Reality" which defies influence of time and all possible limitations. Every religion seeks the same "Truth." A well i.e. deep hole in the ground from which people take water, may have a path on all the four sides. Finally one will get the same water. Ramakrishna Paramhans worshipped through different religions and final got the same divine experience. The difference in concepts and approaches (i.e. in religions) is an evidence of lack of far-sightedness. In certain cases, uncalled-for attachment of some people to their creed makes them blind to universal oneness. This is the result of egoism in the domain of religious ideas. The Truth (the Divine elixir or eternal substance subsisting in all, everywhere at all times) finally is the same whatever path (Hinduism or Christianity or Islam etc,) has been resorted to. It is the immovable faith deep within "having attention of the soul" that matters. Rest all is immaterial. Whatever path or religion an individual follows is Lord's path, because all religions follow the same "Eternal Truth," same "Inherent Divine Blessedness." The Gita therefore affirms, that, though the religious practices may be many and different, the spiritual realization or awakening of one's consciousness or awareness, to which they necessarily relate to, is the same.

What is then sum and substance of the verse? The common individual demands from the Lord worldly satisfaction or relief in present predicament. The individual who has understood the inevitable phenomenon of change in this ever changing universe due to spiritual maturity seeks "strong consciousness of one's own possession of the truth, the whole truth and nothing but the truth" i.e. that which is eternal, indestructible and immanent i.e. present everywhere. Lord declares in this verse that reward for human beings, who worship, will be strictly in accordance to their object of worship and level of complete mental faith connected with the soul. What then are the striking points of the verse? Lord favors or reciprocates to the devotees in the manner desired by them (devotees). Lord reveals Himself to the devotee in the manner desired by them. Lord respects any religious practice (religion) followed, as all religion focus the same "Truth." Differences of caste, creed or religion all over the world, emanating due to egoistic religious bias, exert no influence on the generosity of the Supreme, who alone exists in all everywhere, validating all existences.

12. In foregoing verse Lord makes extremely bold statement "whoever, in whatever manner according to their inclinations, take refuge in Me, I favor them in the same manner as desired by them." What else is required? Why do the people then worship the different Gods? The Lord answers this question in this verse.

काङ्क्षन्तः कर्मणां सिद्धिं यजन्त इह देवताः ।
क्षिप्रं हि मानुषे लोके सिद्धिर्भवति कर्मजा ॥ ४- १२ ॥

kanksantah karmanam siddhim yajanta iha devatah
ksipram hi manuse loke siddhir bhavati karma-ja 4.12

kanksantah—intensely desiring or longing for; *karmanam*--of actions; *siddhim*-- success; *yajante*-- by sacrifices; *iha*--in this world; *devatah*—gods (refer to God and Gods in introduction); *ksipram*--quickly; *hi*--because; *manuse*—in the human; *loke*--in the world; *siddhih* (success); *bhavati*— is attained ; *karma-ja*—born of action.

"Those, who desire the fulfillment of their works (worldly success) on earth, sacrifice (worship through different rituals of yajnas or traditions) to Gods (various forms and personalities) here, for in this world of human beings such works bear (or lead to) fruit quickly." II 4-12 II

We are sometime saying God. Sometime we are saying Gods. What is the meaning? What is God? Where does it all lead us to? The words used by the Lord are taken up below as follows:

"**Gods here**"- God in human form of lord Krishna was talking to Arjuna. Still Lord **is using the words** "Gods here." What does it mean? Literal meaning of terms "Universal Eternal Reality" and God has already been dealt with in verse? How do we recognize whether we are thinking about The Supreme or the "Intermediate Gods"? Many use the term God for Lord Krishna also. How do we use these terms relatively?

Devas, **Gods and Supreme Universal Eternal Reality**- *Devas* are those blessed souls, which have not attained total absorption in the "Supreme, Universal, Eternal, Omnipresent, Omnipotent, Omniscient Essence." They are souls awakened to Absolute Divinity and committed to the divine work. They are just like working executives with some limited powers in an organization. They remain serving and guiding the true seekers. Their forms and way of worship is according to traditions. For example lord Hanuman. They help and relieve the seekers but they cannot get the seeker relief from cycles of birth and death. Gods are perceived divinities i.e. incarnations like Lord Rama, Lord Krishna (They fully represent the Divinity). The form and way of worship is again according to traditions. People may differ about the Gods due to religious bias. They represent "Absolute Divinity" in form. They surpass the general rules of nature. They are "The Formless in Form," incarnations. The "Supreme Universal Reality" is that Universal Truth, which surpasses the limitations of time, space and causes. Actually, it is the ever continuing, ever blissful, ever peaceful, ever conscious, ever the same and the 'Ultimate Source of Divine knowledge'. If ever anywhere in the universe any being feels unprotected, lonely, suffering and tormented deep within and cries for redemption (being saved) from the levels of consciousness, it is this "Energy Source" that responds either in form or even without form. It is actually this 'Energy Source' that works even through *devas* and Gods. It alone is. Nothing else exists without it. It is the "Greatest Mystery of the Universe." It does not have a form. It cannot be seen in entirety but there can be no dispute about the existence of the Supreme Truth or Reality or the Divine Infinite Consciousness. It is smaller than the smallest and bigger than the biggest. It walks without legs, speaks without mouth, hears without ears, works without hands. It is omnipresent, omnipotent and omniscient (knowing everything). It is the "Source" and the "Fundamental Reason" of generation, operation and destruction (for renewal) of the universe. Actually, it is this "Divine Infinite Energy" which responds to all invocations to even Devas and Gods. Reference to this Reality, this Truth does not require adherence to any religion (laid down code of conduct for leading life by some good soul in human form with detailed description keeping this Absolute Divinity in mind is religion). It is there always whether in form or without form. Nothing (not even *Devtas* and Gods) can work without grace of this Reality. This Reality is unborn, eternal, indestructible, omnipresent (present everywhere), omnipotent (having power to do just anything in the universe) and omniscient. It is this Reality which takes form (incarnation) to serve a divine purpose. It is equally effective in form or without form. Everything is with it. There can be nothing without it. Lord Krishna in the Gita represents this "Energy Source in Human Form."

There is one "Supreme Universal Eternal Reality or Truth" that alone exists and validates the existence of other beings. It is formless. It exists in all. Rather it alone exists in this universe. It manifests in three ways i.e. i) routine manifestation because nothing can exist without usual quota of divinity; in this manifestation limitations of time and space are respected; the whole world is made up of this manifestation though the measure of content and capacity of awareness of divinity differs; for example extent of capacity to understand divinity differs in stone, tree, animal and human beings; ii) Some souls are graced with special powers of divinity (i.e. significantly more than entities in 1st category). These are called Devas, Deities and specific Gods with form and name; Their purpose is to help the devotees come out of hurdles (physical, mental, emotional and spiritual) in routine existence (within routine laws of nature); These souls are not deathless (considering the cosmic cycles) and they are like executives of the "Supreme Divinity" with limited powers and defined missions; Devas, Deities, Local Gods and 'Gods with defined forms and names i.e. Indra, Agni Sun etc.' all come in this category; Their glaring limitation is that they cannot relieve a being from cycles of birth and death; iii) Supreme Universal Eternal Reality is formless; It alone exists; **Ekam Sat Viprah Bahuda Vadanti** (i.e. This alone is truth, the wise call this one God by different names; It incarnates for cosmic benefit; all incarnations come in this category; If the seeker is resorting to God in form and with name, he or she is thinking about "Intermediate Gods or Gods with limitations"; If the seeker is seeking higher divine power without form and name, reference is to either the Supreme Energy or the Incarnation having divine birth, divine actions and the mystical powers to subjugate the laws of nature (Lengthening of *saree* (cloth covering the body) in open court to prevent Draupdi from getting strip off; lifting of a mountain on a finger to save the town from torrential rains and anger of Lord Indra; the water in the Red sea got divided and Moses and other Israelites could walk through the sea on dry ground). Here Lord Krishna is referring to "Intermediate Gods with limited powers" by the words "Gods here."

Those who hanker after the fruit of actions (in the form of sons, cattle, food wealth etc.) in this mortal world and worship various Gods (Intermediate Gods with limited powers like Lord Indira) will speedily reap the results of actions here. Why do these people go to other Gods (leaving the Supreme Reality represented by Lord Krishna)? The worldly people lack discernment of divine knowledge. Their focus is not on final objective of human existence i.e. absolute liberation or *mukti*. They forget that after one desire is satisfied the other desire will arise to bother in this mortal world due to *sanskaras* (tendencies). They lack the absorption in thoughts of Supreme alone or purification by divine knowledge or true *Karamyoga* (action without attachment to fruit of action for cosmic benefit with feeling of surrender to Supreme) i.e. all points discussed by Lord earlier in this chapter. There is another reason for this. The worldly people suffer from domination of rajas and tama (two attributes of nature). A seeker seeks the transcendental knowledge (that is the knowledge which takes beyond all limitations) when there is domination of *sattva* (attribute of nature) which arises by meditation and work without attachment to fruit of action. Worldly people do not seek absolute liberation (*moksha*) which can be gained only on having discrimination, dispassion (non-attachment from fruit of action), longing for liberation and six-fold virtues (control of mind, control of senses, endurance, turning away from the objects of the world, faith and tranquility). Fulfillment of work for attachment by propitiating other Gods (i.e. Intermediate Gods or Gods who work based on the grace of the Supreme Universal Reality) is swift and easy.

The worldly people only seek sense-objects, which are easily available. These worldly people cannot enjoy "*Madbhavam*, state of nature of Supreme Being, referred to in preceding verse." This is the emphasis of this verse.

13. Lord Krishna told Arjuna in verse 10 how it is possible to go into state of nature of Supreme

"*Madbhavam.*" Still some people go for fulfillment of worldly desires. Why is it so? What is that one factor which perfects the path of karam-yoga? Lord answers these questions in this verse.

चातुर्वर्ण्यं मया सृष्टं गुणकर्मविभागशः ।
तस्य कर्तारमपि मां विद्ध्यकर्तारमव्ययम् ॥ ४- १३ ॥

catur-varnyam maya srstam guna-karma-vibhagasah
tasya kartaram api mam viddhy akartaram avyayam 4.13

catuh-varnyam--the four divisions of human society based on inherent attributes; *maya*--by Me; *srstam*—has been created; *guna--karma--vibhagasah*—according to differentiation of gunas (attributes) and Karma (actions); *tasya*—thereof; *kartaram*--the author; *api*-- even; *mam*--Me; *viddhi*--know; *akartaram*-- non-doer or action-less; *avyayam*— immutable or changeless.

"The four-fold order (or social order) was created by Me according to gunas (attributes of nature i.e. sattva, rajas and tamas) of prakriti inherent in them and the actions, for which they have a natural aptitude. Though I am the creator of this system of the division of labour (Varnashram Dharma), Know Me as non-doer, eternal (i.e. doer and yet a non-doer)." II 4-13 II

This is the most controversial verse of the Gita. Lord's statement is clear. Many people have simply misunderstood it. We should take up this verse as follows; i) what does Lord want to say in this verse? ii) Why does Lord say this? iii) Four Varnas or social orders, purpose and misunderstood part of it.

What does Lord want to say in this verse? Human society has been divided in four varnas (four-fold caste-hood, chaturvaranas) based on classification of *gunas* (attributes, natural propensities). From empirical (based on experience rather than ideas) point of view, Lord is the creator of those four castes. From real point of view, Lord is a doer and still a non-doer. What does it mean? Dividing the society in *chaturvarnas* (which has been taken up in detail afterwards) is an act of the Lord but Lord remains completely detached (claiming no doer-ship) i.e. doer and yet a non-doer. Focus of the Lord in this verse is to teach the lesson of "working with detachment for the welfare of the society." One can do better work, more creative work, when the doer is not claiming the doer-ship or mind is detached. For this Lord has cited an example. *Chaturvarna* is an activity done for social welfare for which Lord neither acts nor changes.

Why does Lord say this? Lord says in verse 10 that purified by the fire of divine knowledge a seeker can attain the divine nature (*madbhavam*) of the "Supreme Being." In verse 12, success in working (without divine knowledge) for material gains comes quickly. In verse 13, Lord by an example informs divine way of working i.e. being a doer and yet a non-doer of this act of "*chaturvarnayam*; creating four-fold-classification for social order." That is the lesson of working with detachment (renunciation). Renunciation is one characteristic that uplifts the quality of working to a higher dimension to help the seeker to transcend limitations in spiritual evolution. This detachment (renunciation) is necessary for higher development of human beings. Lord is giving a sort of key to turn worldly way of working into "Karma-yoga." Lord is the doer of works, who acts not, "*kartaram akartaram.*" This is the focal point of this verse. Creation of four-fold divisions in society is an example of an act for which Lord is a doer and yet a not doer.

Four Varnas or social orders, purpose and misunderstood part of it - As per the original concept of the Lord, four types of people (a universal truth) exist in any and every society based on their i) inclinations (feeling that makes you want to do something) or inborn quality and ii) quality of action or self-expressive functions. It is summarized in the table given below:

Dominant Guna (attributes of nature)	Symptoms	Functions
Sattva (Purity)	Serene and self restraint	Tapas (austerity) and self control, natural interest in divine Knowledge, meditation and divine discourses
Rajas (Passion) Sattva subordinates	Great skill at doing, daring chivalrous attitude (behaving with honor) towards women	Domination, war, kingship, extremely committed, help others
Rajas (dominates) and Tamas (dullness) subordinates	Shows great skill in negotiation investment and trade	Business and agriculture
Tamas (dullness and ignorance)	Predominance towards following habits, Self-gratification and sense-gratification	Labor and service

This natural categorization is based on mental disposition (inclination of their minds) and self expressive actions. In any society, people will fall in any of these categories. If the people show tendencies to take up jobs according to inherent mental and physical characteristics, the objective of individual and society will be best served. This shows the freedom and choice available to an individual. This natural categorization is based on mental disposition (inclination of their minds) and self expressive actions. In any society, people will fall in any of these categories. If the people show tendencies to take up jobs according to inherent mental and physical characteristics, the objective of individual and society will be best served. This shows the freedom and choice available to an individual to optimize individual output or contribution. Based on these considerations, Valmiki who was a *sudra* initially became a *brahmn-rishi* (a sage having divine knowledge). No one is forced into a classification. This classification is for self-guidance, self benefit and the benefit of the society at large. In original scheme of things, the higher you go the less becomes your remuneration. *Vaisyas* earned maximum remuneration. *Kshatriyas* cared for honor more than money. Brahmin was the simple priest. No specific privilege was allowed to anyone. No one in earlier days was denied food, shelter. This classification envisages freedom to choose what you like and freedom to change your classification. This classification is essentially not based on birth. Lord has used the word *varna*, which is different from English word caste. Caste reminds us of inheritance while *varna* reminds us of dominating attribute.

This natural categorization of "chatuvarna" is based on mental disposition (inclination of their minds) and self expressive actions. In any society, people will fall in any of these categories. If the people show tendencies to take up jobs according to inherent mental and physical characteristics, the objective of individual and society will be best served. This shows the freedom and choice available to an individual to optimize individual output or contribution. Based on these considerations, *Valmiki* who was a *sudra* initially became a *brahmn-rishi* (a sage having divine knowledge). No one is forced into a classification. This classification is for self-guidance, self benefit and the benefit of the society at large. In original scheme of things, the higher you go the less becomes your remuneration. *Vaisyas* earned maximum remuneration. *Kshatriyas* cared for honor more than money. Brahmin was the simple priest. No specific privilege was allowed to anyone. No one in earlier days was denied food, shelter. This classification envisages freedom to choose what you like and freedom to change your classification. This classification is essentially not based on birth. Lord has used the word *varna*, which is different from English word caste. Caste reminds us of inheritance while *varna* reminds us of dominating attribute.

Purpose of *chaturvarna* was to help an individual to optimize individual output or contribution to society. An individual those days always had chance to uplift the categorization. Based on these considerations, *Valmiki* who was a *sudra* initially became a *brahmn-rishi* (a sage having divine knowledge). No one is forced into a classification. This classification is for self-guidance, self benefit and the benefit of the society at large. In original scheme of things, the higher you go the less becomes your remuneration. *Vaisyas* earned maximum remuneration. *Kshatriyas* cared for honor more than money. Brahmin was the simple priest. No specific privilege was allowed to anyone. No one in earlier days was denied food, shelter. This classification envisages freedom to choose what you like and freedom to change your classification. This classification is essentially not based on birth. Lord has used the word *varna*, which is different from English word caste. Caste reminds us of inheritance while varna reminds us of dominating attribute.

It is relevant to mention here that castes envisaged by the Lord here are not hereditary. The people claiming to be Brahman must have *gunas* (attributes) of Brahman. Lord Krishna says in the *Anusasanaparva* of Mahabharta that the devotee of the Lord can never be Sudra, that every devotee is a Vipra (Brahman) and that every individual who is not a devotee of the Lord is a Sudra whichever caste that individual belongs to.

In India, the problem arose when this Caste-classification became hereditary instead being based on attributes (*gunas*), inherent mental and physical traits. More privileges were given to some and fewer privileges were given to others. This caste-classification based on inheritance became an evil when special privileges were given to one group over the others. Caste-classification in India does not follow the Gita's thinking. For this reason, caste-classification in India is taking a menacing (threatening proportions). This is the misunderstood part of thinking of the Gita relating to "*Caturvarna*; four-fold castes." Lord's "*caturvarna*-classification" starts on natural division based on attributes (*gunas, sttava, rajas and tamas*). This will optimize the results due to harmony in activities and natural (mental and physical) tendency to do those activities. Bringing inheritance and special privilege for selected groups has brought about chaos, confusion and dissatisfaction in caste-divisions in India.

14. Lord's "doer and yet not a doer" approach; *kartaram akartaram*" discussed in the preceding verse adds normal worldly working the essence of *karam*-yoga i.e. renunciation and dispassion. What is the unique advantage of renunciation or dispassion? Lord answers in the present verse.

न मां कर्माणि लिम्पन्ति न मे कर्मफले स्पृहा ।
इति मां योऽभिजानाति कर्मभिर्न स बध्यते ॥ ४- १४ ॥

na mam karmani limpanti na me karma-phale sprha
iti mam yo abhijanati karmabhir na sa badhyate 4.14

na--not; *mam*-- Me; *karmani*-- actions; *limpanti*—affect or taint; *na*--not; *me*--My; *karma-phale-* -in the fruit of action; *sprha*-- desire; *iti*--thus; *mam*-- Me; *yah*-- who; *abhijanati*-- knows; *karmabhih-* -by actions of such work; *na*--not; *sah*--he; *badhyate*—is bound by actions or becomes entangled.

"Works (or actions) do not bind (contaminate) me, because I have no desire for fruit of actions; the one who thus knows Me (this truth) is not bound by karma." II 4-14 II

Actions do not taint or contaminate or pollute the Lord because Lord does not have attachment to fruit of actions. What does it mean? Every action, good or bad, exerts impact, which has to be experienced by the being either in this birth or in next births. The distinction of Gods (Intermediate Gods or blessed souls who keep doing work for the common good) and men and rebirth is due to good or bad action of created beings. A being in this world has got a natural tendency (attachment) for fruit of actions. Springing from attachment to fruit of actions, embodied selves or created beings are endowed with bodies and organs at the time of creation. "The desire for results of actions and for the results of creation" (wealth, women, wine and fame) have a capturing or inviting or alluring tendency. These reasons necessitate rebirth or cause of another journey into this mortal word of pain and pleasure (both pain and pleasure are to be ignored for exalted spiritual status). This is a phenomenon which represents the fundamental traditional thinking of Hinduism. One comes to identify this phenomenon by awareness also by a process of discrimination between the acquired and the inherent characteristics of the being i.e. by the fundamental difference between the finite and the infinite. The varied actions of nature i.e. creation, sustenance and destruction do not bind the Lord, as Lord is not attached to fruit of actions.

One who "thus knows the Lord" (the truth) is not bound by actions. What is the underlying truth or universal message behind this statement "thus knows"? **This truth** or the phenomenon, referred here, requires to be discussed further. The Lord (the Divinity in exclusion or other than nature) is only the operative cause (fundamental cause, **the divine essence** which gives validity to existence) in the creation of beings. That from which the creative forces spring is the material cause. If a being is without material cause, it will continue to remain an integral part of the "formless divinity." A being is led into condition in which it is by material causes. Material cause includes the potentiality in the form of previous karmas of the selves to be created. One's own actions are responsible for one's birth. Therefore, a being should refrain (keep away) from attachment to fruit of action (following the Lord) by renunciation or dispassion. Action without attachment does not bind the soul. That is the message.

When one understands this truth (besides exclusive divine essence, material causes are required for creation or detachment keeps Lord untainted from actions), one keeps away from the attachment to fruit of action. Due to attitude of renunciation such an individual is not bound by actions. Such an individual becomes "a doer yet a non-doer." Emergence of this attitude "i.e. being a doer and yet a non-doer" is a mark of **divine knowledge**. Such an individual works without attachment, without egoism, without expectation of fruit, without developing bondage with the work. Such an attitude takes a seeker towards enlightenment towards state of "*madbhavam,* supreme nature of the Divine." Such an individual becomes free from birth and death or any conceivable limitation. The emulation (to be like someone else) of the great is the way of the elite.

15. Lord describes the divine character of divine actions. This divine character of actions arises from non-attachment to fruit of actions. In this verse, Lord advises Arjuna to work without attachment to fruit of actions like the ancient seekers of liberation.

एवं ज्ञात्वा कृतं कर्म पूर्वैरपि मुमुक्षुभिः ।
कुरु कर्मैव तस्मात्त्वं पूर्वैः पूर्वतरं कृतम् ॥ ४- १५ ॥

evam jnatva krtam karma purvair api mumuksubhih
kuru karmaiva tasmat tvam purvaih purvataram krtam 4.15

evam--thus; *jnatva*--knowing well; *krtam*--performed; *karma*--work; *purvaih*--by past authorities; *api*--although; *mumuksubhih*--who attained liberation; *kuru*--just perform; *karma*--prescribed duty; *eva*--certainly; *tasmat*--therefore; *tvam*--you; *purvaih*--by the predecessors; *purva-taram*--ancient predecessors; *krtam*--as performed.

"Having known this, ancient seekers for liberation performed actions (karmas); do therefore, thou also perform action as did the ancient in days of yore." II 4-15 II

Working with renunciation i.e. without attachment to fruit of action, an individual is not bound by the capturing tendency of karmas. Thus comprehending truth about karma (work done with renunciation does not bind), the seekers of liberation (salvation) in ancient days have discharged their legitimate worldly duties from time immemorial. Lord Krishna exhorts Arjuna to follow the example of ancestors and tread the well tried path. This will ensure safe arrival at final destination (*madbhava*; state of nature of the Supreme).

Lord is emphasizing (or giving knowledge about) the "divine aspect" of *Karamyoga*. This is renunciation i.e. non attachment to fruit of actions. It is non-attachment of fruit of action which unites an individual to the Supreme even while performing action. Renunciation helps an individual to identify divinity in doing. Even in doing, one can gain freedom from birth and death by assuming right attitude of renunciation. That is the message of this verse. Lord is telling Arjuna the divine aspect of doing (renunciation). Renunciation fills the consciousness of the individual with thoughts of divine at the time of even doing work. That invokes the divine dimension to doing and replaces the individual's thoughts of insufficiency of human will, human fear, wrath and passion with thoughts of the Divine. Doing work with renunciation, one can access the zone of divine power and divine love and divine knowledge where The Divine accepts, loves and takes the individual into the fold of divine bliss. This knowledge, thus imparted, is precious. An ignorant working earnestly without attachment will get the discipline of *nishksma- karma* (working without focus on fruit thereof). Those, knowing truth but working without attachment to fruit of action, will do well for welfare of masses like Janaka.

There are two parts of the term "*Karam*-yoga." Karam (action) should be for the world benefit. Yoga part is for the benefit of the self i.e. union with the Supreme. Doing work becomes yoga when renunciation is exercised in doing work. Even our forefathers have been doing work like this for time immemorial.

Life cannot go on without work. Work is essential. Therefore Lord tells Arjuna "Therefore, you do work all the time, but with this attitude (spirit of renunciation; no attachment with fruit of action)."

16. It is clear now that one should work with no focus on fruit thereof. What is work? What is not work? In this verse, Lord proceeds to explain to Arjuna truth about action i.e. philosophy relating to action.

किं कर्म किमकर्मेति कवयोऽप्यत्र मोहिताः ।
तत्ते कर्म प्रवक्ष्यामि यज्ज्ञात्वा मोक्ष्यसेऽशुभात् ॥ ४- १६ ॥

kim karma kim akarmeti kavayo apy atra mohitah
tat te karma pravaksyami yaj jnatva moksyase asubhat 4.16

kim--what; *karma*--action; *kim*--what; *akarma*--inaction; *iti*--thus; *kavayah*—the wise; *api*--also; *atra*--in this; *mohitah*— deluded or bewildered; *tat*--that; *te*--unto you; *karma*--work; *pravaksyami*—(I) shall teach or explain; *yat*--which; *jnatva*—having known; *moksyase*—(thou) be liberated; *asubhat*—from (binding effect of) evil or ill-fortune.

"What is action? What is inaction (or not action or non-action)? Even sages are perplexed about it? Therefore, I shall tell you that action (i.e. truth about action or philosophy of action or the action having knowledge within itself) knowing which you shall be freed from evil." II 4-16 II

Arjuna or common man thinks that work means movement of the body. No-work means absence of it and that is all. This is not enough. What is action? What is inaction? Even the sages are deluded about this subject. Lord seeks to convey that mystery of action is extremely difficult to unravel. Most important thing is to understand the motive with which an action has been either done or renounced. It is the motive of an action, which leads to either rebirth or salvation. After knowing this truth in reality, one keeps away from action or reaction likely to lead to bondage and becomes free from bondage (capturing effect) of karma.

17. Lord emphasizes in this verse that for knowing the nature of action or inaction, one has to go deeper into the truth.

कर्मणो ह्यपि बोद्धव्यं बोद्धव्यं च विकर्मणः ।
अकर्मणश्च बोद्धव्यं गहना कर्मणो गतिः ॥ ४- १७ ॥

karmano hy api boddhavyam boddhavyam ca vikarmanah
akarmanas ca boddhavyam gahana karmano gatih 4.17

karmanah—of actions; *hi*-- for; *api*--also; *boddhavyam*--should be known; *boddhavyam*--should be known; *ca*--also; *vikarmanah*—(of the) forbidden work; *akarmanah*-- inaction; *ca*--also; *boddhavyam*--should be known; *gahana*—deep or mysterious; *karmanah*—of action; *gatih*—the path or way.

"For there is something to be known even about action, something to be known about prohibited action and something to be known about inaction; hard to understand is the path of work." II 4-17 II

The true nature (truth) about action (enjoined by the scriptures), inaction (sitting idly or quietly and doing nothing) and wrong action (prohibited action) is difficult to understand. The accepted ideas of our time tested by traditions, influence of thinking changed by time and prick of conscience confuse a seeker. This is where the knowledge is required. Knowledge helps to identify 'right action' capable of taking the individual towards release, towards freedom.

18. In this verse, lord explains the truth of action and inaction.

कर्मण्यकर्म यः पश्येदकर्मणि च कर्म यः ।
स बुद्धिमान्मनुष्येषु स युक्तः कृत्स्नकर्मकृत् ॥ ४- १८ ॥

karmany akarma yah pasyed akarmani ca karma yah
sa buddhiman manusyesu sa yuktah krtsna-karma-krt 4.18

karmani--in action; *akarma*-- inaction; *yah*--one who; *pasyet*—sees or observes; *akarmani*--in inaction; *ca*--also; *karma*-- action; *yah*--who; *sah*-- who; *buddhi-man*-- wise; *manusyesu*—in men; *sah*--he; *yuktah*—yogi (one who has entitled to the Supreme-Knowledge by strictly observing relevant disciplines); *krtsna-karma-krt*- performer of all actions.

"One, who sees inaction in action and action in inaction, is individual of true reason and discernment; he is a yogi and accomplisher of all actions." II 4-18 II

In this verse, Lord is adding dimension of divine knowledge to discussion on karma yoga. An individual is a combination of i) individualized divinity; it is under the cover of ignorance but ever the same, eternal full of inherent bliss and knowledge and ii) the nature, along with its hardware (tree, animal etc.) and software (Divinity within), is always restless, always changing, always moving forward and backward. In atman (soul) there is no action. There is no rest in the body even when it is at rest. Digestive activity is going on in the body even when body is at rest. This aspect has to be kept in mind for understanding this verse.

Inactivity in activity- When an individual works, all the change is at physical level. Body, mind and intellect work, but deep within the "Divine Spectator or Divine essence within" is mutely watching, unperturbed, undisturbed supremely serene as ever. If an enlightened individual is at work, the movement of the activity will be at physical level, but the soul will be in union with the Divine. An ordinary individual will notice activity at physical level only. A wise onlooker will notice inactivity (serenity of soul in union with the Lord) at the level of spiritual existence and activity at physical level only. This is what is meant by seeing inactivity in activity. This means that when you are aware of the divine knowledge, only then you see the divinity within (soul in yoga with Divine) and movement due to activity at physical level only. That is what is meant by the words "inactivity in activity." One cannot perceive like this without divine knowledge about the composition of individual in two parts i.e. i) divinity within soul under cover of ignorance and ii) nature with its hardware and software, ever active and restless. Only spiritually advanced individuals are able to view things like this. Lord Krishna in battle field is the embodiment of inaction in action. Action there belongs to prakriti (nature) to physical body driving the chariot. Atma embodied as Krishna is ever established in inaction. This perception of "inactivity in activity" cannot come without our being conscious about the Divinity within.

Activity in inactivity – Imagine a man sitting under a tree thinking and doing nothing. For an ordinary man, the man sitting under the tree is doing nothing, because body and sense organs are apparently at rest. For an enlightened observer, the cessation of work due to idle body and sense organs is not inactivity. Mind of the man, sitting under the tree, may be racing all over the world. The inherent *sansakaras* (tendencies) may play havoc with the mind stuff. The latent and acquired tendencies of mind are the root cause of birth and death. Therefore, an observer with divine knowledge will notice in this case "activity in inactivity." Nature is always at work even in stone, keeping unimpaired her hold. We are acting even when we sit quiet without an outward action. Sri Ramakrishna seemed all inaction externally but the greatest of all actions, the quest of the Infinite was going on within him always. It is an example of activity in inactivity.

An activity takes dimension of karam-yoga only when it is looked at with spiritual knowledge. Activity is at physical level. Soul is in union with the divine. Then there is no doer-ship or ego. There is no attachment with fruit of action. The work done becomes an offering to the Supreme.

For this reason, one who sees "inaction in action and action in inaction" is a yogi (i.e. one who is in constant communion with the self, with the fundamental source at spiritual level; or *yuktah*). Such an individual is the performer of all actions. Such an individual remains detached, free from all limitations. Such an individual gains transcendental position (beyond ordinary level of human thinking and experience). Lord in this verse is telling Arjuna the path of gaining immortality through the medium of work.

This is a wonderful verse with this very high level thought. This can help an individual to get into the best possible mode of working in this worldly existence. An individual is composed of two essential 'natures' i.e. higher nature and lower nature. Higher nature means being calm, quiet and serene. Lower nature is active, ever restless, ever moving forward and backward. A worldly individual always remains in lower nature, oblivious (forgetful) of the higher nature within. By these words "inactivity in activity and activity in inactivity," Lord is emphasizing us to first perceive the exclusive divine presence within and its relationship with anything else. First come in 'connecting mode with the Divinity' and then make activity a medium to send the offering of your efforts and emotions to the Supreme. What is "inactivity" in Lord's statement in this verse? This "inactivity" is Divinity, the supreme reservoir of peace and wisdom within an individual. If you focus this "inactivity" with all the activities of the body going on, you will be able to grasp "inactivity in activity." Again, as already mentioned, if you focus this particular "inactivity" and recall life of Sri Ramakrishna with no particular activity in day long routine, you will find "upheaval of thousands waves of restlessness seeking proximity to Mother Divine." That is activity in "inactivity." Lord wants us to understand "this inactivity," "this fundamental ground within us," "this calm and quiet higher nature," whose presence validates our lower nature to carry on all activities uninterruptedly, smoothly. This is the secret of "inactivity in activity and activity in inactivity." Once we are conscious of this truth and start our activity in the background of this thinking, then there will be no hurry, no worry, no clinging to uncalled for concerns distracting attention. 'All the work done' will be an offering to the Supreme. In the absence of attachment to fruit of action, an individual will remain free from the "capturing tendency of actions or reactionary elements of actions." One will automatically come in "equanimity-mode" which is highest yoga, a state of being in highest divine consciousness, a state of ever continuing blessedness. Such an individual becomes an individual of knowledge with divine wisdom and uncanny (strange and difficult to explain) discernment (ability to show good judgment.

19. In this verse, Lord describes wise man (having divine knowledge and working with divine consciousness), who sees inaction in action and action in inaction.

यस्य सर्वे समारम्भाः कामसङ्कल्पवर्जिताः ।
ज्ञानाग्निदग्धकर्माणं तमाहुः पण्डितं बुधाः ॥ ४- १९ ॥

yasya sarve samarambhah kama-sankalpa-varjitah
jnanagni-dagdha-karmanam tam ahuh panditam budhah 4.19

yasya-- whose; *sarve*--all; *samarambhah*—all undertakings; *kama*-- *sankalpa*--*varjitah*- (are) devoid of desire and purpose; *jnana*--*agni*--*dagdha*--*karmanam*- whose actions have been burnt up (become devoid of impurities to be called pure) in (the fire of) knowledge; *tam*--him; *ahuh*—call or declare; *panditam*—a sage (knower of truth); *budhah*—the wise.

"An individual, whose all undertakings (doings or works) are free from selfish desires and sankalpas (mental motive to do something) and whose all karmas are burnt up (screened) in the fire of knowledge, is called a sage by the wise." II 4-19 II

In the preceding verse Lord talked about the person who can see "inaction in action and action in inaction." Lord continues this discussion. Therefore it is to be taken that the undertakings or works, mentioned here, are for *lokasangraha* (common good or cosmic benefit) or for bare maintenance of body and the persons doing them are free from attachment to fruit of action or feeling of doer-ship. Why is it so? Lord has used the word "*samarambh*; not arambh or beginning" i.e. Lord is referring to the beginnings of those undertakings or works which have a potential of spiritual merit.

Free from desires and *sankalpas*- What are desires and *sankalpas*? When sense organs meet sense objects, they develop a sort of association with sense objects. This association gives rise to a wish for that sense objects. It is desire. When this desire gains intensity, it is called "*kama*." Kama generates mental resolve to gain the desired objective i.e. feeling like "I will do this or I will get it'. This is called *sankalpa* (mental resolve to do or to get something). Desires represent attachment to objective. Sankalpa characterizes doer-ship. For this reason the undertakings of an individual who sees "inaction in action and action in inaction" lack desires and *sankalpas* (mental resolves). The existence of desires and *sankalpas* mean the individual is not being guided by soul-touched wisdom. Desire and *sankalpa* (mental resolve) are two factors responsible for transmigration (passing of soul after death into another body). When an individual becomes conscious of the divinity within and gets connected to the "wisdom of the soul," the individual becomes the instrument of the "Divine Will." All activities are done as an offering to the Supreme in the light of soul-touched wisdom.

Jnanaagnidagdhkarmanam – Lord is talking of the work of a man whose all karmas (actions) have been burnt in fire of divine knowledge. What is the meaning of this? Divine knowledge (*brahmn-jnana*) leads to realization of "inaction in action and action in inaction." Divine knowledge (*brahmn-jnana*) is mighty spiritual fire which burns all reactions to work or capturing residual impact of work, whether it is good work or bad work. "***Jnanaagnidagdhkarmanam***" means those undertakings which have been screened for entitlement to divine results in the soul-touched wisdom i.e. the wisdom, which one gains after being centered in spirit or which has approved the selection of these actions. That means selection of activities has taken care of such factors as i) non attachment to fruit of actions, ii) the actions are for either cosmic benefit or bare maintenance of body, iii) activities are free from personal egoism of the doer.

Such an individual is called a sage (i.e. a person who leads a life of perfect renunciation; does only what is required either for bare maintenance of body or cosmic benefit; does work without a trace of egoism; remains calm in the silent poise of the soul) by the wise (i.e. who discern in the light of soul-touched wisdom; who perceive the divine knowledge).

The wise confer the title of the sage on that individual whose actions are not prompted by seeds of desires and mental resolves and whose residual impact of karmas (actions) are all burnt up in the fire of divine knowledge. What is the conclusion? There is a very important role of divine knowledge in Karam-yoga. Divine Knowledge sows the seed for flowering of consciousness in the soil of unconsciousness within an individual.

20 Lord describes in this verse how a wise individual gets established in "inaction in action and action in inaction" mode.

त्यक्त्वा कर्मफलासङ्गं नित्यतृप्तो निराश्रयः ।
कर्मण्यभिप्रवृत्तोऽपि नैव किञ्चित्करोति सः ॥ ४- २० ॥

tyaktva karma-phalasangam nitya-trpto nirasrayah
karmany abhipravrtto 'pi naiva kincit karoti sah 4.20

tyaktva--having given up; *karma-phala-asangam*-- attachment to fruits of actions; *nitya--trptah-* ever content; *nirasrayah*-depending on nothing; *karmani*—(though) in action; *abhipravrttah*— engaged (fully); *api*-- even; *na*-- not; *eva*-- verily; *kincit*--anything; *karoti*--does; *sah*--he.

"Having given up attachment to the results of action, the individual (whom Lord is describing and who is able to see inaction in action and action n inaction), who is ever contended, dependent on nothing, does not do anything though engaged in activity." II 4-20 II

The basic concept of "inaction in action" is emphasized here again to describe how such an individual (divinely awakened) works. Lord stepwise narrates some signs of such an individual (who is a jevan-*mukta* i.e. one who has attained exalted state of spirituality but still works for cosmic benefit and bare necessities of existence):

Abandoning attachment to fruit of action- This is the cardinal (most important) trait of a divine worker. The individual in this category is desire-less. For this reason that unnecessary drive or overemphasis, which results in craze, is not there. Where does this non-attachment for fruit of action come from? This happens when one is conscious of the Divinity within. One assumes this attitude in existence when one works as an instrument of the divine. The worry (nagging feeling for unpleasant things that might happen) for material, actions and results of actions is not there. Due concern is always there. This attitude saves the vital energy from getting dissipated unnecessarily. Actually this attitude adds divine dimension to activity, releases the pent up energy of working and turns normal working towards karam-yoga.

Eternally satisfied in the self - Such an individual experiences perfect inner joy and peace i.e. soul-touched joy and peace. This joy and peace does not come from external factors. It emanates from source within. Such an individual is not driven to the activity. Such an individual responds to the activity naturally, harmoniously. Again, spiritual awareness is the cause of this eternal satisfaction in the self. Such an individual remains satisfied in the present (life is in the present moment; past is dead; future is unborn) considering this as the blessing. Object of senses do not attract such an individual due to awareness of divinity. Such an individual gains perfection of non-action (nature of divinity within) and remains supremely satisfied being with what he or she naturally is. Such an individual enjoys holiday in work. That is the result of attitude of adding divine dimension to working.

Nirashraya **(not depending on anything)** – None can have this attitude without being spiritually aware. People depend on wife, husband, children, relatives etc. This is worldly understanding. An ordinary man depends on outward things. This results in worry, anger and passion. One who is connected to the Divine source within is ever satisfied without any kind of dependence. The trees, whose roots are connected to the water within the earth, do not require water from external source for survival. This attitude should better be described as a sort of natural relaxation due to firm faith in connection with the Divinity.

Does not do anything though engaged in work – All these characteristics are emanating from divine awareness. One who is not spiritually aware will find it difficult to understand how it can happen that an individual does not do anything (good or bad) though engaged in work. This requires an understanding that an individual is a composition of lower nature and higher. Higher nature (Domain of exclusive Divinity) does not do anything. Nature is never at rest, always at work. Spiritually an individual is higher nature (truth of an individual which does not die). "Body, mind and intellect etc." are always at work. That is why it is said that a divinely conscious individual does not do anything though he or she remains engaged in work. This is divine nature. One has to desist from not doing. Physical body has to work to the progress of an individual from the lower to higher nature, from the apparent un-divine to the conscious Divine. These words "does not do anything though engaged in work" simply mean that individual is spiritually aware. The individual remains established in the "exclusive domain of Divinity within" in the bliss radiating from soul while body (mind, intellect and other organs) remain engaged in working for spiritual evolution.

Thus Lord describes three attributes of divinely awakened individual in this verse. Only such an individual can understand "inaction in action and action in inaction." It is very important to note that each of these three attributes sprouts from divine consciousness alone. It therefore becomes further clear that "Karam-yoga" is not a mechanical exercise followed routinely by renunciation and surrender. Even renunciation and surrender will remain farce (events and situations that do not happen) without that soft awareness of the proximity to light of soul, which alone defies (refuses to obey) all that is untruth. The most important thing is to remain connected to one's spiritual dimension within.

21. In this verse also Lord describes three more attributes (mental make-up) of divine worker i.e. one who sees "inaction in action and action in inaction" or one who is awakened to spiritual dimension within.

निराशीर्यतचित्तात्मा त्यक्तसर्वपरिग्रहः ।
शारीरं केवलं कर्म कुर्वन्नाप्नोति किल्बिषम् ॥ ४- २१ ॥

nirasir yata-cittatma tyakta-sarva-parigrahah
sariram kevalam karma kurvan napnoti kilbisam 4.21

nirasih--without hope; *yata--citta-atma*— (one) who has subdued mind and senses, being freed from attraction and repulsion, are not influenced by contact with the objects of senses and body is also amenable to his control; *tyakta--sarva--parigrahah*—having abandoned proprietorship over all possessions; *sariram*-- bodily; *kevalam*--only; *karma*—action; *kurvan*-- doing; *na*--not; *apnoti*--obtains; *kilbisam*—sin.

"An individual (whom Lord is describing) who nurtures hopes for nothing, controls consciousness and self (soul), does not receive at all gifts and possession from others and performs merely bodily actions, does not get sin." II 4-21 II

A *jivan-muktah* (liberated man), who is being described by the Lord, shows certain attributes as follows:

"*Nirasih* (without hope)" – This literal translation of "*nirasih*" does not give the correct meaning. Normally an individual without hope is desperate. An individual of the category discussed here can never be desperate. Such an individual does not nurture hope because hope means some attachment. Such an individual is deep rooted at the level of consciousness. Goal-less-ness is the natural way of living of such an individual. How does an individual remain in this state of "*nirasih*"? "Potential of seeking of a divine individual" goes for moksha i.e. release from limitations, which restrict from absorption in the eternal consciousness, bliss and knowledge within each individual. Hope of any kind whatsoever is too trivial for an individual committed for moksha.

Yatchittaatma (controlling chittah and soul) – The literal english translation again does not correctly reflect intention of the Lord. Atma cannot be controlled. In Sanskrit chittah is called mind, intellect and ego (antahkaran, internal controls). The control of mind, intellect and ego stimulate the psychic energy of the individual to transcend the cover of ignorance on soul shortening its association with cycles of birth and death. This interpretation appeals the words used by the Lord. An individual under this category exercises all disciplines (physical, mental, emotional and spiritual) to facilitate moksha (absolute freedom for soul from all conceivable limitations or self realization).

Tyakatva sarva prigraha (**non-receiving of gifts and favors**) – Non-receiving of gifts and favors is considered a very important discipline for the seekers. Receiving gifts and favors essentially weakens the spiritual stand of the seeker and consequently seeker's suitability for *moksha* (absolute freedom). A seeker who accepts gifts and favors cannot escape karmic effect (capturing effect of actions) of the individual giving gifts and favors.

Thus, in this verse also Lord has mentioned the three divine attributes which essentially improve spiritual worth of an individual. Such an individual does not get sin. What is a sin? It is an act which causes extreme (tormenting) misery at the level of consciousness (at one point of time or other) and intuits impending (sure to come) spiritual doom. A sin essentially prolongs a soul's cycles of birth and death. An individual, nurturing no hope of any kind, exercising internal controls to relieve soul from cover of ignorance, not welcoming gifts and favors, does not attract sin and thus expedites his or her spiritual evolution.

22. Lord describes three more divine traits due to which an individual is not bound by what he or she does.

यदृच्छालाभसन्तुष्टो द्वन्द्वातीतो विमत्सरः ।
समः सिद्धावसिद्धौ च कृत्वापि न निबध्यते ॥ ४- २२ ॥

yadrccha-labha-santusto dvandvatito vimatsarah
samah siddhav asiddhau ca krtvapi na nibadhyate 4,22

yadrccha--labha--santustah- satisfied with what comes to him out of its own accord; *dvandva-atitah-*-surpassed; *vimatsarah*--free from envy; *samah*—even minded; *siddhau*--in success; *asiddhau*—in failure; *ca*--and; *krtva*-- acting; *api*--even; *na*--not; *nibadhyate*--is bound or affected (by his actions).

"An individual (whom Lord is describing), content with whatever comes naturally (i.e. without action by own will but by divine will), unaffected by dualities, free from envy, equipoise in success and failure, is not bound by action though engaged in work." II 4-22 II

Each of this attribute is discussed below:

Yadrcchalabhasantushto (satisfied with whatever comes by chance) – This attitude comes only after gaining spiritual maturity. The individual in this category does not arrange for things to be brought to him or her. This type of individual does not bother even for things necessary for maintenance of body and remains content with whatever he or she gets unasked or by mere dignified begging (permitted by scriptures). In these cases the seeker is so overwhelmingly absorbed in the thoughts of the Divinity that bare requirement even for body is too trivial to be asked for. Ramakrishna Paramhansa did not ask the Divine mother even for cure of cancer. These individuals remain so much confined in their "divine domain within" that requirements of body get neglected. This trait is not result of arrogance. It is the result of absorption in divinity.

Dvanda tito (free from dualities) - Good or bad, happiness or misery, heat and cold, pleasure and pain and success and failure are dualities. Dualities in life reflect ignorance. Shadow of ignorance cannot exist before the sunshine of divine knowledge. The divine worker does not at all remain in dualities at all as he or she remains in his or her essential nature i.e. "existence–knowledge–bliss absolute."

Vimatsarha (**free from envy**) – Such and individual is jealous of none in this world. Matsara means desire for own excellence with non-tolerance of excellence of others.

Smah sidhau asidhau (equal-minded in success and failure) - Such an individual is equipoise or having equanimity in success and failure. Such an individual is not elated on success and depressed on failure.

An individual having above mentioned attributes does not become bound by his or her actions. What is the reason? This cosmos is a manifestation of the Supreme. What binds an individual is not act but selfish or egoistic attitude to work. This attitude is the result of ignorance and ego (feeling of separateness). It manifests dissatisfaction, dualities, envy and lack of equanimity. The divine worker is free from this attitude and does not become bound for his or her actions. Thus this verse describes why an individual while acting is not bound by action.

23. Seeds germinate but roasted seeds do not germinate. Now Lord is describing in this verse how an individual can destroy "capturing or binding effect of actions" i.e. lord is telling the way how reasons causing cycles of birth and death can be dealt with effectively. In other words ignorance can be caused to cease to exist and Supreme Truth can be realized.

गतसङ्गस्य मुक्तस्य ज्ञानावस्थितचेतसः ।
यज्ञायाचरतः कर्म समग्रं प्रविलीयते ॥ ४- २३ ॥

gata-sangasya muktasya jnanavasthita-cetasah
yajnayacaratah karma samagram praviliyate 4,23

gata-sangasya—one devoid of attachment; *muktasya*—liberated (freedom from all limitations); *jnana-avasthita--cetasah*—(with) mind established in knowledge (divine knowledge or knowledge of the self); *yajnaya*--for sacrifice (Yajna); *acaratah*— acting; *karma*-- action; *samagram*—the totality of action; *praviliyate*—melts away.

"The whole work of an individual, whose attachments are gone, who is liberated, whose mind is established in knowledge (divine) and whose actions are for performing **yajna** alone, dissolves (here it means loses potential to exert residual impact causing birth again), away." II 4-23 II

It is indeed a beautiful verse. Actions exert residual impact in an individual and this residual impact at the level of consciousness (which continues to remain till matching effect is experienced in this life or in future) results in cycle of birth and death. If this residual impact of karmas is removed from consciousness, one goes beyond the three gunas (*tamas, rajas and sattva*; refer to notes after chart in introduction) and the individualized divinity loses its separateness merging into calm, immortal, eternal universal consciousness (conceivably highest state of achievement for a human being). Lord in this verse summarizes some traits of the individual who reaches to this sublime state:

Gatasangasya (whose *sanga* or attachment is gone) – It has already been mentioned that an individual in this category does not attach to fruit of action. For an individual in this category all thoughts of "I and Mine" are gone. Divine motive inspires the individual in this category. The soul of such individual becomes the silent channels that cognizes and communicates the actions likely to serve the *loksangraha* (good for all or cosmic benefit). Focus here is on divine consciousness {inalienable (which cannot be taken away) purity within} without which the reasons to lean in this direction will not arise. Maya or deluding power of the Lord will attract the mind towards worldly possessions only.

Muktasya **(totally free from all limitations)** - Total freedom is the state of desire-less-ness. Such an individual experiences calmness even in the rush of activities due to his or her inseparable connectivity with the "Ultimate Source" within. Vital link is the "Connectivity within," feel of "Divine Presence within." No freedom is possible without this divine connectivity. Divine connectivity sprouts the causes leading to consequences towards unlimited freedom.

Jnanavasthitchetsah {mind is established in the knowledge (divine knowledge)} – An individual, whom Lord is describing remains established in divine knowledge i.e. this individual remains in the state of knowing divine birth and divine work. First one should be aware of one's divine consciousness and universal inter-connectedness i.e. one sees divinity within and divinity outside. When one reaches this state of spiritual maturity, one starts seeing divinity all around. One realizes that bondage is the creation of one's own mind. It is not the effect of the reasons outside. This awareness is experienced when one has realized the original freedom of one's own self. After gaining the awareness of this 'Reality', one finds all actions as the waves on the ocean of consciousness, rising, falling, disappearing for all the time to come and signifying nothing. This results in a state of renunciation. Mind reposes in ocean of silence within, rich with proximity of soul. Mind gets established (does not run here and there) there because there is no desire for personal enjoyment and no feeling of doer-ship. All one sees is the light and expanse of one's own self. In this state, actions performed as offerings to divine do not bind.

Yagya 'acharatah (work is done like offering in yajana) – What is a yajna? In common parlance it means offering in to a particular God (perceived Divinity as per traditions). Yajnas of this type are performed based on rituals as per procedure laid down by traditions. When something (material, thoughts, one's strength and one's weaknesses) is offered in the fire of divine knowledge to the "Supreme Infinite Eternal Reality or the Lord of the Lords" with full "*nishtha*' (immovable faith in the unknown) and without attachment to fruit thereof, it is yajna. It means any sacrifice for "common good and cosmic welfare" with divine knowledge, without attachment and with *nishtha*, is yajna. Only those actions, which are performed as yajna i.e. as offering to the Supreme with no attachment to fruit thereof, have this liberating nature. Action of an individual who performs action in the spirit of performing yajna is not bound by his or her action. Lord is telling the spiritual seeker to perform actions in the spirit of yajna to get rid of the capturing impact of actions.

Karam samagram praviliyate (all actions are dissolved) – All actions of the individual, whom Lord is describing, get dissolved. What is the meaning of this "actions getting dissolved"? A seed loses its tendency to sprout, if it is roasted. Similarly the actions of an individual, having traits described above, lose tendency to prolong individual's cycle of birth and death. One gets rid of all karmas (prarabdh karma, agama karma and sanchit karma) i.e. one becomes ready for moksha (total liberation from all limitations). It is necessary to explain these words used here. Prarbdha Karmas are those actions of previous birth for which matching effect has not been experienced so far, but it has started maturing. Sanchit karmas are the actions for which matching effect has to be experienced. Agma karmas are those karmas which one is likely to perform in future. Sanchit and agama karmas are destroyed (or become ineffective to exert influence to enhance cycle of birth and death) in divine knowledge i.e. understanding with feeling of divine birth and divine action. Prarabdha Karmas remain as along as body lives and when the body falls, it is all over. The individual's mind gets established in the self. When there is no mind, there is no thought. When there is no thought, there is no action. When there is no action, there is no rebirth.

Lord does not talk of renouncing actions. Actions should be performed in such way that their potency of lengthening cycles of birth and death is no more. Four points described in this verse are i) non attachment to fruit of action, ii) freedom from desire and its results i.e. hatred, attraction and repulsion, iii) absorption in the self (divine knowledge) and iv) work should be performed in the spirit of performing yajna (sacrifice for the supreme with absolute faith and spirit of surrender). It is a wonderful idea. If every action is done in spirit of performing *yajna*, our life will blossom divinely surrendering our imperfections, our poverty, our sufferings, and our limitations to the "Being who manifests One Essence in a multiplicity of forms" and silently keeps watching us from within and from all directions.

24. The preceding verse made it amply clear that one gets rid of capturing nature of "impact of actions" if actions are performed in the spirit of performing *yajna*. How is this spirit (spirit of yajna) to be developed and nurtured? This again requires a particular attitude, knowledge in which the liberated individual has to perform works of sacrifice. Lord answers this point in this verse.

ब्रह्मार्पणं ब्रह्म हविर्ब्रह्माग्नौ ब्रह्मणा हुतम् ।
ब्रह्मैव तेन गन्तव्यं ब्रह्मकर्मसमाधिना ॥ ४- २४ ॥

brahmarpanam brahma havir brahmagnau brahmana hutam
brahmaiva tena gantavyam brahma-karma-samadhina 4,24

brahma--arpanam—(act of offering the gift or act of making contribution or oblation (*in yajana to Brahmn or specific Gods)*); *brahma*--the Supreme (Eternal Universal Reality); *havih*—butter (clarified); *brahma— agnau*--in the fire of Brahman; *brahma*--by the Supremet soul; *hutam*--offered; *brahma*—the Supreme; *eva*--only; *tena*--by him; *gantavyam*--to be reached; *brahma-- karma*—the man who is absorbed in action, which is *Brahmn*. [the act of offering, that which is being offered, that in which offering is made and one, who is offering, is Supreme Reality only; That alone is the underlying truth; That alone exists; that one 'Universal Energy and vital cause of all causes' alone passes through all, connects all and final remains; one gains this true realization in Samadhi (awakened consciousness in total absorption) only].

"The act of offering is Brahman. The offerings are Brahman. By Brahman it is offered into the Brahaman –fire. Brahman is that which is obtained by Samadhi in Brhman-action." II 4-24 II

Lord is imparting the highest wisdom. What is the basic thought being emphasized here? The "Eternal, Universal, Infinite, Energy, represented by Lord Krishna in this discussion" is at play or underlying everything (whatsoever) and in all aspects. In the Gita's words thought is "Vasudev *Sarvam – Vasudeva* (The Supreme, Eternal, and Infinite Spirit, represented by Lord Krishna here) is all that is." Nothing else exists. Everything is its manifestation. This is to be grasped with feeling. Lord passes on this message by example of an act of sacrifice (yajna) whose all aspects (i.e. actions, subject, object, universe, everything) converge on one focal point i.e. the "Supreme Infinite Eternal Energy Source, represented by Lord Krishna here." If the work is done with this spirit i.e. perceiving the Supreme in its various aspects of action (i.e. in action, in seeker, in objective of action), then all actions get transformed into inaction like the mist on sunshine and one does not suffer the capturing impact of performing actions. One lives in the spirit of "inaction in action and action in inaction'. The doer only becomes an instrument facilitating the divine will. Lord explains that perceiving the Supreme in everything everywhere is not a concept but a reality, a living experience. This is done by discussing in detail various aspect of *yajna* as follows:

Brahma 'rpanam (Act of offering is Brahmn) – Act of offering is important in sacrifice (yajna). While performing yajna, it should be borne in mind that this act of sacrifice is divine grace. Then the doer will get relieved of the feeling "I am doing yajna" i.e. egoism. The ladle (the spoon with a long handle) by which an offering is being made is "material-creation of nature or effect of Brahman through nature being the fundamental cause." It is made up of lord's material-nature. For a common individual it is ladle. For an enlightened individual it is Brahmn. The induction of this thought that yajna should be performed is Lord's grace to the individual. Therefore, act of offering or means through which offering is made or the process of offering is Brahman only.. Divine will.

***Brahma Havir* (offering is Brahman)** – In *yajna* with rituals some offering in the form of clarified butter (ghee) other material rice etc. is made with thoughts of the Supreme Reality (represented by Lord Krishna here) or some specific deity. The offering is also Brahman. Where does the rice and ghee etc. come from? It is nature or the partly manifested form of the "Eternal Un-manifested Reality." *Yajnas* are not by rituals alone. Someone sitting and offering all thoughts in the fire of knowledge of the Supreme is also doing *yajna*. In this case, where do the thoughts of the Supreme come from? It is the grace of the Lord or divine dimension within the seeker. That again is Brahman alone. All offerings in a yajna is Brahman.

Brahmagnau (the fire in which something is offered) - In *yajnas* with rituals, something (ghee and rice etc.) is offered in fire. In mental *yajnas*, offering is of thoughts to the fire of the Divinity or Divine Knowledge. Where does the fire come from? It is one of the primordial (existing at the beginning of the time or the earth) elements of nature, which is integral outgrowth of the Lord (Supreme Reality) only. Similarly all divine thoughts in an individual emanate from consciousness of one's divine dimension. Therefore, the fire in which offering is made is nothing but the Brahman, the Supreme Reality, the "Fundamental Cause" of everything that is.

***Brahman Hutam* (one who offers is also Brahman)** – The seeker is also Brahman. Can there be existence without the Divine Essence within? The one who conducts *yajna* purifies himself or herself by mantras or extreme resolve of mind. He or she becomes one with the Divine. All manifestations are on the seedbed of divine consciousness. Therefore, the one who is offering is also Brahman.

Karam samagram praviliyate (all actions are dissolved) – All actions of the individual, whom Lord is describing, get dissolved. What is the meaning of this "actions getting dissolved"? A seed loses its tendency to sprout, if it is roasted. Similarly the actions of an individual, having traits described above, lose tendency to prolong individual's cycle of birth and death. One gets rid of all karmas (*prarabdh karma, agama karma* and *sanchit karma*) i.e. one becomes ready for *moksha* (total liberation from all limitations). It is necessary to explain these words used here. *Prarbdha* Karmas are those actions of previous birth for which matching effect has not been experienced so far, but it has started maturing. *Sanchit* (accumulated) karmas are the actions for which matching effect has to be experienced. Agma karmas are those karmas which one is likely to perform in future. *Sanchit* and *agama* karmas are destroyed (or become ineffective to exert influence to enhance cycle of birth and death) in divine knowledge i.e. understanding with feeling of divine birth and divine action. *Prarabdha Karmas* remain as along as body lives and when the body falls, it is all over. The individual's mind gets established in the self. When there is no mind, there is no thought. When there is no thought, there is no action. When there is no action, there is no rebirth.

Brahman karma samadhina (whose Samadhi is in *Brahmn-karma*) - What is **Samadhi**? It is a spiritual state in which Chittah (combination of internal levels of existence or mind, intelligence and ego), devoid of its modifications, gets completely absorbed (submerged) in the object of Samadhi i.e. getting in absorption after achieving "mo-mind state." *Brahman-karmas* are those acts which are for common good or cosmic benefit (with nothing personal). The seeker being discussed here seeks total absorption in "Brahman-karma or acts related to cosmic benefit without attachment" i.e. seeker gets so thoroughly consumed (mentally, physically, and emotionally) with the activity that all remaining with the seeker is only joy of feeling "oneness" with the Supreme, that soft bewitching presence of Eternal Infinite Reality (whom lord Krishna represents in form), which sweeps away all that "separateness of an individual; ego" is. In that state of utter delight, the seeker sees only the Supreme everywhere. Lord has used a very good word "*karam-samadhi*." Lord is not talking of '*Dhyan-Samadhi*' (absorption through meditation) here. Lord is talking of '*Karma-samadhi*'. In '*karam-Samadhi*' the seeker identifies with the objective (the Supreme Being) not through meditation but through the action (action for cosmic benefit), not ordinary action but consummate action (i.e. action having total absorption of all faculties of the seeker leaving absolutely nothing called "of the seeker"). In this state, action becomes the medium through which one seeks identification with the "Innate Nature or Divine Nature or Never-changing of the Self." In this state (*Karam-yoga*) also, the divine secret within an individual blossoms fully. Lord here is telling another route i.e. with *karam-samadhi* also one can reach the highest state (submersion in the Supreme) that one gets in '*dhyan Samadhi*'. Again let us recall meaning of *Karam-Samadhi* i.e. cessation of all modification of chitta (mind, memory and ego) by absorption in the feeling of proximity with the supreme with all the available human faculties totally engaged in divine activity. Therefore, this phrase "***Brahman karma samadhina***" means realization of the "Supreme Divine Truth" is achieved through "*karam-samadhi - cessation of modification of chittah in divine activity feeling full with awareness of Divinity within.*"

What is the central idea of the verse? Dhyan-yoga is not the only approach for realization of the "Supreme Divine Secret-Awareness of One's Own Real Nature," as is understood by many. Even work can be a direct means for the "vision of the self," if the work is done in the true spirit of "*karam-yoga* i.e. divine activity, divine knowledge, *Karam-samadhi*, awareness of divine dimension within." A mother reveals her "true nature- her inherent divinity in motherhood" in service of the children. So our freedom (*mukti*) is not from action but in action {i.e. work through the Lord (medium of action), for the Lord (object) and by the Lord (subject)}. That is true *Karam-Yoga*. When we so work for the Lord (in the manner stated by the Lord above), that we are left with just nothing except the exclusive, mute, overwhelming joy of being in the Lord (all around above and below), then it is Karam-Yoga (union with the Lord through path of action), a medium in which karma (action) takes form of knowledge (divine knowledge) unfolding the "Supreme Secret."

25. After having told Arjuna the path of self-realization through action, Lord now explains various kinds of karam-yogas.

दैवमेवापरे यज्ञं योगिनः पर्युपासते ।
ब्रह्माग्नावपरे यज्ञं यज्ञेनैवोपजुह्वति ॥ ४- २५ ॥

daivam evapare yajnam yoginah paryupasate
brahmagnav apare yajnam yajnenaivopajuhvati 4.25

daivam—gods (refer to God and Gods in introduction); *eva*-- only; *apare*--some; *yajnam*--sacrifices; *yoginah*—yogis (committed to yoga for self-realization); *paryupasate*-- perform; *brahma--agnau*--in the fire of the knowledge of the Supreme; *apare*--others; *yajnam*—sacrifice in the shape of self i.e. sacrifice of superimposed limiting adjuncts mind, intellect and body by their appropriate use and through this sacrifice of individualized-self (to the Supreme Self); *yajnena--eva*- only through sacrifice known as perception of identity i.e. thought of the Supreme *upajuhvati*—offer as sacrifice.

"Some yogins perform sacrifice (yajnas) relating to Gods only. While others offer 'yajna itself' as offering to fire of Brahman by performing yajna (of self-knowledge)." II 4-25 II

Now Lord highlights to Arjuna the difference between the '*yajna*-practice' of some lacking perfect divine knowledge and '*jnana*-practice' of those endowed with divine wisdom. Some words should be dealt with first:

Yogins – In previous verse Lord described '*yajnas*' of those who see Brahman the Supreme Divinity or Truth everywhere. Here Lord wants the attention to be brought to those aspirants who perform yajnas (rituals with offerings and without attachment considering it as duty) as per laid down practices (in scriptures such as Vedas) to propitiate various deities (such as Indra, Brahama, Sakti, Ganesha etc). These yogis may be termed as *karam-yogis* or *bhakti yogis*.

Daivam eva yajnam (yajnas for propitiating Gods and Goddesses)- Gods and goddesses here mean "Intermediate Gods." These Gods and Goddesses with different forms and names are worshiped in different places as per local customs and traditions. They also fulfill the expectations of the seeker (within their limitations) by the grace of the "Universal Unified Consciousness." However they cannot get the liberation from cycle of birth and death. The *Yajnans* mentioned in Vedas such as Darsa, *Purnamasa, Jyotistoma* etc. fall in this category. These *yajnans* are performed in a particular way for a particular Deity and for a particular purpose and all these details are mentioned during performance of yajnans.

Yajnam yajnena upjuhvati {Offer 'yajna itself' as offering to fire of Brahman by performing yajna (of self-knowledge} – In these words Lord is talking about *jnana-yajna* or the wisdom sacrifice by those who are devoted to *jnana-yoga*. First let us understand the words "*yajna* itself i.e. *jnana-yajna*" which is offered as sacrifice. There is one 'Unified Eternal Universal Consciousness'. It alone exists manifesting itself diversely. Name and form cannot change the nature of the original divine substance. Name and form creates ignorance. Suppose you are going in the forest in late evening in dark. You take the movement of the rope as snake. This is due to delusion of eye. In the sunlight of the day, rope is seen and known as the rope. Similarly when an individual sees in the divine light, the delusion of ignorance (i.e. feeling of separateness or ego) is cleared, mind gets clarified. Then one realizes that name and form has been super imposed by the delusion of mind and the senses on the "exclusive divine essence- Brahman" within. When ignorance goes away and mind gets crystallized, everything is seen and known as Brahman. The sage knows this truth. Everything that we see, feel and think is Brahman. Remaining in this thinking is wisdom (divine knowledge). It is this thinking (*jnana-yajna*) that is represented here by the word "*yajna-itself*." This thinking (*jnana-yajna* or "*yajnan with Brahman-jnana* or divine knowledge as offering" i.e. performing yajna by offering of ego to The Supreme Consciousness) is offered as oblation (offering) to fire of Divine Knowledge (again Brahman). Thus in this *jnana-yajna*, offering is "wisdom discussed above." Fire is Brahman. Sacrifice is Brahman. The act of sacrifice is Brahman. Remaining in this mode of thinking, an individual realizes the Brahman (the Supreme Reality) everywhere, all the time.

Preceding verse highlights a methodology by which all work can be transformed into Brahman. When all work is done with all physical, mental and emotional faculties, keeping the "inner-connectivity with the 'Divine Dimension' within intact, ever fresh and blossoming," work melts into Brahman. Work, thus, loses its capturing or binding power i.e. one is relieved of the impact of doing the activity and the work done assumes a divine, spiritual and liberating quality. On the same lines of "*Karam-Yoga*," when "Divine knowledge" is offered as oblation, it becomes a *jnana-yajna*. Cognizing the limitation of "individualized divinity- soul," a jana-yogi, disassociates the self from the objective world and focuses on Supreme Eternal universal Reality. This "*mental-yajnan* or yajna with mind" is of great importance. Knowledge considered as sacrifice is greater than a sacrifice requiring materials. Any action (devoid of attachment to its fruit, for cosmic benefit, performed with consciousness of pure divinity within) can be *yajnan*. It is background feeling which determines whether an activity is *yajnan* or not. Knowledge of self is also *yajnan*, if it satisfies the above mentioned conditions with emphasis on non-attachment to fruit of actions and non-doer-ship.

This is a wonderful verse where the distinction between *karma* and *jnana* is, thus, eliminated and Brahman alone is realized in all that an individual thinks and does. This verse shows the path to

"Brahman-Jnana." Any individual doing any activity, anywhere in any kind of work can practice this method and reach the goal. This perhaps is the reason why **Adana Kasaaee** (butcher); an individual who slaughtered the goats and sold meat" was considered a holy man. The individuals in this category are *jnana-yogis*. The mind keeps inquiring the underlying real divine nature at work in all situations. The aspirant offers pure jnana (*Brhaman-jnana*) as the offering. Now the meaning of the second half of the verse i.e. "offering the self by the self in fire of knowledge" becomes clear. Knowing the conditioned self (individualized divinity) as the "unconditioned self-Supreme eternal Universal Reality" is to sacrifice the self to Brahman (The Supreme). This thinking is *yajnan* (sacrifice). This sacrifice (*yajnan*) is possible only by those who are steady (regular, not changing, uninterrupted) in their knowledge of the identity of the self with Brahman (Supreme Reality).

This verse thus discusses i) *karam-yogis* worshipping "Intermediate God and Goddesses" and ii) pure *jnana-yogis* offering "through Brahman jnana separate entity-ego" to the Supreme i.e. yajna through yajnan.

26. Hitherto Lord has explained two yajnans i.e. karam-yajnan and jnana-yajnan. Different people perform different types of yajnans based on their levels of wisdom. In this verse Lord expresses two more diametrically opposite yajnans (sacrifices). One makes the senses ineffective. The other makes the senses super effective.

श्रोत्रादीनीन्द्रियाण्यन्ये संयमाग्निषु जुह्वति ।
शब्दादीन्विषयानन्य इन्द्रियाग्निषु जुह्वति ॥ ४- २६ ॥

srotradinindriyany anye samyamagnisu juhvati
sabdadin visayan anya indriyagnisu juhvati 4.26

srotra-adini-indriyani—organs of hearing and other sense; *anye*--others; *samyama--agnisu*--in the fire restraint; *juhvati*—sacrifice or offer offers; *sabda-adin--visayan*—sense objects such as sound etc.; *anye*--others; *indriya-- agnisu*--in the fir of senses; *juhvati*--sacrifice.

"Some offer hearing and other senses as sacrifice in the fire of restraint, while others sound and other sense objects as sacrifice in the fire of senses." II 4-26 II

Fire transforms the nature of things consigned into it. It is definitely used in ritualistic *yajnans*. In *jnana-yajnan*, it is used symbolically. As mentioned earlier Lord is talking about two opposite *yajnans* as follows:

'Yajnans' that make the senses ineffective – Some people offer the senses (such as hearing and other senses) as sacrifice in the fire of self-control. This is how they control the sensory system. They light a different type of fire i.e. a fire of self-control (*atma sanyam yogagni*). This involves an effort to restrain the senses, like ear and the rest, to keep them away from the respective sense-objectives, which please them. Sense control is first of all spiritual disciplines. By following several vows, rules and regulation of the conduct, the seeker gets the senses under control. Sense control leads to mind-control. Mind-contol leads to liberation. This sense-control is mentioned here as *yajnan* (sacrifice). This involves a psychological sacrifice (*yajnan*) and results in self control and self-discipline. The emphasis is on senses, which are so disciplined that they avoid falling prey to sense-objects.

'Yagnans' that make senses super effective – In the second type of *yajnan*, mentioned in the second half of the verse, the senses are allowed to move freely in the objective world experiencing pain and pleasure in pleasant and unpleasant objectives. In this approach, emphasis is on rejecting the sense-objects by very deeply examining them and understanding how painful and worthless they are. Mind is disturbed when the senses rush towards the sense objects and bring the mind in state of noisy confusion and excitement. When by discipline senses do not rush out towards the sense objects, mind is calm. Therefore second yajnan (mentioned in this verse) involves sacrificing the objects of senses in the fire of several senses. In second approach seeker regards it a sacrifice (yajnan) to direct their senses only to un-forbidden objects of senses.

This verse refers to internal sacrifices, which are of the nature of 'yajnans'. These 'internal sacrifices' are explained as sama (what one should not do; non-killing, truthfulness, non-stealing, conserving the energy and non-receiving of gifts and favors) and Dama (what one should do; purity cleanliness, contentment, tapah or austerities, self-study, surrender to the Supreme) by Rishi Patanjali under the head "Ashtang-yoga." These internal controls are processes of discipline, mental purification and elimination of desire.

How do the aspirants referred to in this verse behave? They hear scriptures not scandals. They speak to teach knowledge to pupils but not for gossips. They go to see temples, mountains, rivers but not the women. They inhale fresh air but not scent.

27. In this verse, discussion deals with the culmination (highest point) of internal controls.

सर्वाणीन्द्रियकर्माणि प्राणकर्माणि चापरे ।
आत्मसंयमयोगाग्नौ जुह्वति ज्ञानदीपिते ॥ ४- २७ ॥

sarvanindriya-karmani prana-karmani capare
atma-samyama-yogagnau juhvati jnana-dipit 4.27

sarvani--all; *indriya--armani*—functions of senses; *prana-karmani*--functions of the life-breath (vital energy); *ca*--also; *apare*--others; *atma-samyama-- agnau*--in the fire of yoga of self restarint; *juhvati*—sacrifice or offer; *jnana-dipite*—kindled by knowledge.

"Yet others sacrifice all actions of senses and the function of life energy as a sacrifice in the fire of self control kindled by knowledge." II 4-27 II

Mind is the link between the "divinity within" and the external words. What is it that feeds tendencies in mind or gives color to the crystal called mind? This is all due to: i) All activities of senses and ii) functions of breath. If impact of these two factors is neutralized, mind will become pure like crystal to reflect the true divine nature of the being. Therefore, these two should be taken up in detail as follows:

Sarva indriyakarmani (All functions of senses) – First, it is necessary to understand how our own senses create impediments (something that delays) in self-realization. Senses produce bio-impulses (stimulus), which result into urges, modifications and tendencies in mind stuff. The word "Mind-stuff" is used for the unconscious mind, subconscious mind and domain of memory or mind, intelligence and memory. Mind is like a crystal. Crystal reflects the color of the cloth placed near it. Crystal has no color of its own. It only reflects. Similarly mind works according to stimulus given by senses. All the senses, described below, always keep the mind up with some stimulus. The result is that mind is never in crystal-like-state, which is its natural state. Due to the influence of senses, mind is not able to see beyond the domain of ego and an individual always remains deprived of the knowledge of the self. In brief these senses and their influences can be classified in three categories i.e. i) the organs (senses) of perception are those of tasting, hearing, smelling, seeing and touching; ii) the organs (senses) of actions are those of speaking, grasping, moving about, procreating and evacuating; iii) internal controls are mind (thinking) and intelligence (discriminating and deciding).

The effort of an individual is to put to rest all urges, modifications and tendencies of mind so that mind goes beyond ego (its limitation) to realize real nature, divine nature of the individual.

Prana karmani (**actions of the vital force**) - What is the meaning of this word "prana" mentioned by the Lord? Oxygen simply nurtures the body. When an individual dies, oxygen will still be there, but prana will not be there. In Sanskrit prana means life. Anything that moves, functions depends on its prana (vital force). Prana is nothing but the vital force in all of us. It is prana (vital force) that keeps us alive. Entire living process depends on this vital force called prana. An individual is so long as prana (vital force) is there. Entire living process depends on this vital force called prana. Prana is not a thing which can be isolated from the cosmic existence. Miracles can happen by controlling of the motion of exhalation and inhalation. This is what Lord is coming to. This control of exhalation and inhalation is possible through *pranayam*. Regulating exhalation and inhalation by breath control is *pranayam*. It is subject in itself and requires specialized guidance. Given below are the "five vital breaths" and their functions which lord has talked about by above mentioned words:

Five vital forces (*pranas*) are i) *prana*, ii) *apana*, iii) *vyana*, iv) *samana* and v) *udana*. The functions are i) leading out, ii) leading downward, iii) contracting and spreading, iv) digestion of what is eaten and drunk and v) leading upwards.

All these functions vital force are necessary for us. We all know what happens when there is indigestion.

Atmasamyama yogagnau juhavati (**sacrifice in the fire of yoga of self restraint**) – Whenever you want to control a tendency, you oppose it. This is exactly what lord is asking to do. Offer actions of senses and functions of vital forces into the fire of yoga of knowledge (identification of mind with atma is referred to here as fire of self control). What does this word "offer" refer to? Lord is referring to a discipline, that unites an individual to individual's essential nature (divine nature; nature which does not change or get destroyed or ever continues). For this reason the word yoga has been used by the Lord. After this yoga of self restraint (i.e. controlling the disturbed impressions by the rise of impressions of control) a state is achieved where objects of sense-perception, activities of senses and functions of vital force do not disturb the mind. Senses themselves become pure fire of sacrifice i.e. get disciplined. This is the state which stills (calms) the senses. Mind becomes pure like crystal with no trace of influence of anything whatsoever. Then mind goes beyond its limitation i.e. domain of ego and sees the panorama (vide view) of purity of soul, 'Divinity' in full grandeur (great and impressive), calm, tranquil, resplendent (emitting self brightness), expanse of silence, which whispers wisdom without use of words. This happens when actions of senses and functions of vital breath are offered as sacrifice in the fire of yoga of self-restraint.

Jnanadipite (**Kindled by knowledge**) – This is like dropping the seed in the soil. All else will come of itself. This all offering, mentioned above, should be made with consciousness of divine dimension within (i.e. with awareness of divine connection with pure consciousness within). This last addition in the verse is very important failing which offering of actions of senses and breath control (pranayam) will become mechanical exercise bereft of divine fervor. This can be explained by an example. One man was brought to Swami Ranganthanada of Advait Ashram. That man used to do *pranayam* (practice of regulating exhalation and inhalation) daily. Also, regularly and everyday he used to beat his wife. Ranganathananda was teaching pranayam. The people wanted the *pranayam* to be stopped quoting the habit of that man. It was explained to them that without love, without *jnana*, physical exercise was mere ritual activity. To make these offerings a 'yajnan' (sacrifice), awareness of divine consciousness within was necessary. 'The absorption with the self' within awakens an individual to clarity, sensitivity, love and truth. The seekers with divine knowledge sublimate (direct) their energies for spiritual evolution by disciplines mentioned above.

Thus in this verse, Lord Krishna mentions about a *yajnan*, which leads an individual to higher-self and self-knowledge or to the 'atmic-state' with absolute fullness of light, knowledge and bliss. In brief it markedly sanctifies (makes holy) the performer. For working it out actually, one requires a Sadguru (Spiritual master). The *"Atmasamyama yogagnau-* fire of yoga of self control" should attract special attention. It is strengthened by spiritual knowledge enquiry and spiritual knowledge.

28. In preceding verse, Lord mentions how performer of *yajna* (an act of offering with sublime spirit of detachment leaving ego and sense of possessiveness) becomes *Brahmn* (re-enlivens own divine features like eternity, indestructibility and immanence i.e. present everywhere) by the sacrifice of senses and vital-life-energy. It sanctifies (makes holy) the performer. Now Lord is telling about some more Yajnans (purifying acts which add to spiritual dimension of the performer) in this verse.

द्रव्ययज्ञास्तपोयज्ञा योगयज्ञास्तथापरे ।
स्वाध्यायज्ञानयज्ञाश्च यतयः संशितव्रताः ॥ ४- २८ ॥

dravya-yajnas tapo-yajna yoga-yajnas tathapare
svadhyaya-jnana-yajnas ca yatayah samsita-vratah 4.28

dravya-yajnah—those who offer wealth as scrifice; *tapah-yajnah*—who offer austerity (plain and simple living) as sacrifice; *yoga-yajnah*—those who offer yoga (eight-fold) as sacrifice; *tatha--* again; *apare--*others; *svadhyaya*—contemplation about the self as sacrifice; *jnana-yajnah*—offer study and knowledge as sacrifice; *ca--*and; *yatayah*—striving souls or earnest seekers; *samsita--vratah*—persons of rigid vows.

"Some offer wealth, austerity and yoga as sacrifice, while some ascetics of self-restraint and hard vows offer study of scriptures and knowledge as sacrifice." II 4-28 II

Lord in this verse mentions different *yajnas* (acts of spiritual content for cosmic benefit) as follows:

Dravya-yajnas (yajnas in which wealth is offered as sacrifice) – In these *yajnas*, wealth is distributed among the deserving as charity. It involves completely giving up of ownership of things. These yajnas are performed as per laid down practices (in scriptures) and traditions. Indian *smrities* (ancient scriptures) mention works like *Purta* and *Dutta*. Purta includes such acts as excavation of ponds, wells and tanks, construction of temples of Gods (mostly Intermediate Gods with name, form and traditional method of worship), distribution of food, building rest-houses for the pilgrims. Dutta includes such acts protecting those who take refuge (resettling the homeless and the devastated, the orphans, arranging marriage of the poorest of the poor) and giving charity outside the sacrificial ground. These acts definitely add to spiritual worth of the performer. Some people sacrifice for *Ishta* (Specific Gods with specific traditional worship). This worship also comes in this category. Lord Mahavira gave his whole wealth to the deserving.

Tapo-yajnas (yajnas in which austerity is offered as sacrifice) – What is tapa (in sanskrit)? It is austerity i.e. being simple without decoration and allowing no luxury that gives pleasure and comfort with whole life-energy devoted to sole focus on nurturing "divine connectivity within." Well-known yajnas in this category are: i) *Krchha* and ii) *Chandrayana*. Krchha involves body mortification. *Chandrayana* involves increasing and decreasing morsel of one's food in accordance with phases of moon. People opt for yajnas according to their understanding and spiritual maturity. This is only an account of different yajnas.

Yoga-yajnas (yajnas in which eight limbs of ashtang-yoga are offered as sacrifice – Some seekers offer their yoga practices as offering in the fire of thoughts of enlivening connectivity with the supreme. Yoga does not mean asanas (physical postures) alone. What all is included in yoga? Rishi Patanjali describes it in Ashtang yoga i.e. i) *yama* (what all one should not do), *niyama* (what all one should do), asanas (physical postures), *pranayam* (regulating exhalation and inhalationa), *Pratyahara* (withdrawing the mind from all thoughts; it is like telling the mind not to mind; it is like telling the mind to hold on and not to behave like the mind or monkey), *Dharna* (It is holding the mind on to something i.e. giving the mind something to mind; between the two thoughts there is space and holding the mind in that thoughtless, idealess, impression-less, image-less space is dharna), *Dhyana* (unbroken flow of holding the mind on to something; incessant flow of mental substance on object of meditation; *Dyana* {continuation of holding the mind on to something (object of meditation) is meditation; Due to continuous holding of mind at the object of meditation, it does not go after thoughts; there is no flow of mental substance in Dhyan; mind becomes free from both mental activity and inactivity; concentration (no flow, no movement) results; mind gets tamed and forgets its nature to move; Dharna is not concentration as flow of mental substance is there at the stage of dharna; concentration (or continuance to stick to one point) results from dhyana}; *Samadhi* (concentrated mind penetrates through object of meditation and gets absorbed there resulting in Samadhi; at the highest stage of smadhi, individual realizes his or her true divine nature; only object of meditation remains, the individual virtually loses consciousness of self; mind at the last stage of samadhi assumes the form of object of meditation). First five i.e. yama, niyama, asana, pranayam and pratyahara are external limbs. Last three i.e. Dharna, Dhyan and Samadhi are internal limbs. The last three are collectively known as '*samyama*' i.e. effective control over the tendency to hold or to let-go. Going all through these routines and making offering of pratyahara, dharna, dhyam etc. with divine consciousness in view are parts of yoga-yajna.

Svadhyaya jnana yajna yatayah samsitvratah (Some striving souls, who are well disciplined and austere severe vows, offer as sacrifice self study and knowledge in *svadhyay* or *jnana yajna*) – Svadhyaya is self- knowledge (when this knowledge is experienced at the level of awareness, it becomes self-realization). Svadhyaya (self-study) is attempted through study of scriptures (celebrated time tested books dealing with divine birth and divine action) and introspection (careful examination of own thoughts). The scriptures {like the Gita, the Ramayana, the Vedas, the Bible, and the Quran etc … Lord's message is universal, eternal and not for a sect or a group; for its true meaning, it should be seen from broad spectrum (range) of views} deal with imparting knowledge about divine consciousness, divine birth and divine actions. An individual is imparted exposure to Reality which is eternal, indestructible and immanent or present everywhere. The study of these texts for self-study and achieving divine knowledge (and removing other's spiritual ignorance) becomes a yajna (*svadhyay jnana yajna*). These yajnas are performed by those whose vows are very severe i.e. they treat their vows (*ahimsa, truth, yama, niyama etc.*) also as sacrifices.

One thing very good comes out of this verse. Any act, with sublime spirit of detachment, for cosmic benefit and done dispossessing the performer of ego, becomes a yajna, a process of exchanging ideas and feelings or "establishing connectivity" between the performer and the Divine Reality (Truth). Lord is giving different choices to different people of different disposition (natural qualities) to attempt spiritual evolution. What is the hub (central and most important part) of the point? Energy of the soul (divinity within) should be directed towards higher aim like cosmic benefit instead of spending it in satisfying mundane (ordinary and uninteresting) desires. Any activity, done right in the spirit of yajna, becomes a *yajna*. Why is it so? Any activity, which an individual devotedly and earnestly contributes for welfare of others, multiplies his or her own spiritual worth in geometrical proportions. This is the universal experience and essence of all religions. Of course, even this fact should be forgotten while doing an act of *yajna*.

29. Having described different yajnas in preceding verse, Lord in this verse describes how some people perform yajna by yogic-actions (explained below).

अपाने जुह्वति प्राणं प्राणेऽपानं तथापरे ।
प्राणापानगती रुद्ध्वा प्राणायामपरायणाः ॥ ४- २९ ॥
अपरे नियताहाराः प्राणान्प्राणेषु जुह्वति ।

apane juhvati pranam prane apanam tathapare
pranapana-gati ruddhva pranayama-parayanah
apare niyataharah pranan pranesu juhvati 4.29

apane—in the outgoing breath; *juhvati*—sacrifice or offer; *pranam*—incoming breath; *prane*—in the incoming breath; *apanam*—outgoing breath; *tatha*—thus; *apare*--others; *prana--apana-* courses of incoming and outgoing breath; *gati*--movement; *ruddhva*--retaining; *prana-ayama-parayanah*—solely absorbed in regulating the breath; *apare*--others; *niyata--aharah*—regulated food; *pranan--pranesu*—life breaths in the life-breaths; *juhvati*--sacrifices.

"Others, solely absorbed in the restraint of the breath (*pranayam*), pour as sacrifice "prana into apana and *apana* into *prana*" having restrained the *prana* (the outgoing breath) and the *apana* (incoming breath)." II 4-29 II

This verse contains extremely useful information for individuals on spiritual path. There exists a very close relationship between mental state and the flow of breath. When we are angry, we breathe very fast. When we are relaxed, we breathe differently. We can regulate the entire human organism, by controlling or regulating motion of inhalation and exhalation (*pranayam*). This vese is based on this basic thinking. To understand the language used by the Lord, some terms have to be discussed first:

Prana is outgoing breath (*prana* is also subtle life force in an individual). *Apana* is incoming breath. *Pranayam* is controlling motion of inhalation and exhalation. A *pranayam* involves three types of motions:

i) **Rechaka** means emptying or breathing out the internal airs through nostrils and mouth. There obviously occurs in *rechaka* stoppage or sacrifice of *apana* (incoming breath).

ii) **Puraka** means filling in the external air into the body. There obviously occurs in *Puraka* the stoppage or sacrifice of *prana* (outgoing breath).

iii) *Kumbhak* means holding the breath. Both the movements of prana and apana are stopped or sacrificed in *Kumbhak*. *Kumbhak* is done in two parts: a) Internal *Kumbhak* is when stoppage or sacrifice of inhalation and exhalation is practiced after drawing in the air according to one's capacity; b) External Kumbhak is stoppage or sacrifice of inhalation and exhalation is practiced after expelling all the air in accordance to one's capacity.

Rectum is declared to be the seat of vital air known as "Apana." Heart is declared to be the seat of vital air known as "Prana"

Regulation of pranayam means changing the distance, time and number of breath.

Therefore a pranayam will be in four phases: i) Puraka (filling in) sacrificing prana, ii) Internal Kumbhaka (stoppage or sacrifice of apana and prana) after drawing in, iii) Rechaka (exhalation) sacrificing apana, iv) External Kumbhak (stoppage or sacrifice of apana and prana) after expelling all air according to capacity.

It should be noted that pranayam is often accompanied by sound of such mantras as "OM" or "SOHAM." Pranayam is capable of taking an individual to super conscious state or breathless state of

Samadhi by gradually mastering the breathing process. Since in all the phases of pranayam sacrifice is involved and any kind of sacrifice leads an individual towards immortality, *pranayam* is considered a great yajna.

A question may arise as to how pranayam is a yajna. In pranayam, an individual gives time and attention to divinity keeping aloof (detachment) from worldly activities. Prana (outgoing breath) is sacrificed into Apana (incoming brath) and apana is sacrificed in *parana*. In Kumbhak both apana and prana are sacrificed. Therefore breath control is yajna or an act with detachment, with divine consciousness and with offerings. These "practical *yogic kriyas*" are acquired from a realized master (Sadguru) only.

With the details, discussed above, it will now be possible to understand the wording of the Lord.

Prana juhati Apana (**Prana is sacrificed into Apana**) – In purak (in the process filling the breath in), external air is taken in (i.e. apana). The seat of Apana air is located in the lower part of the body (i.e. rectum). Therefore, external air, when drawn into the body, follows a downward course through heart (seat of prana air in the body) towards rectum. In this process the prana air in the heart is sacrificed into the Apana air at the point of rectum. Thus Apana becomes the sacrificial fire and Prana becomes the offering. This phase of pranayam (i.e. Purak) becomes a yajna.

Apana Juhati Prana (**Apana is sacrificed into Prana**)- In Rechaka (the process of breathing out the internal air through nostrils) internal air is taken out (prana air). The seat of the prana air is described to be in the heart. When the aspirant drives out the air within through the nostrils and shuts it out, it is the prana air seated in the heart which comes out first and stays out. Apana air at the rectum rises up due to holding of breath and goes to the point of heart and gets absorbed into it. Here prana air becomes the sacrificial fire and Apana air at the rectum becomes the offering into the Prana i.e. *Apana Juhati Prana*.

Prana Apana Gati rudhva (**Restraining of the course of outgoing breath and incoming breath**) – Here reference is to internal and external Kumbhakas described already. In both the Kumbakhas, both apana and prana are restrained or stopped.

30. Lord is concludes the list of yajnas in this verse, saying that regulation of food and offering life breaths into life breaths is also Yajna.

सर्वेऽप्येते यज्ञविदो यज्ञक्षपितकल्मषाः ॥ ४- ३० ॥

sarve apy ete yajna-vido yajna-ksapita-kalmasah

sarve--all; *api*--also; *ete*-- these; *yajna-vidah*—those conversant with; *yajna-ksapita--kalmasah*—whose sins are destroyed by sacrifice;

"All (others, who regulate their diets, offer life breaths into life breaths, as mentioned in earlier part of this verse) these individuals know what *yajna* is and by virtue of their sacrifice are their sins destroyed." II 4-30 II

In this verse Lord explains three different important facts as follows:

i) *Apre nityataharah pranan praneshu juhati* (**others of regulated food habits offer life breaths into life breaths; this part of this was added with previous verse also**)- In this verse Lord declares the importance of regulating of food habits. There exists a close connection between food and spiritual attainments. A spiritual aspirant has to be very careful about the food failing which all efforts in spiritual direction are likely to come to a naught. One has to keep away from over-eating, under-eating and eating at odd times in all places all types of food from all types of persons. It is food that turns into physical energy. Physical energy turns into mental energy. Mental energy leads to spiritual illumination. Success in yoga is achieved by those, who are disciplined and spiritually inclined, consider eating carefully selected food and dieting a yajna, in which they offer quality food (food that suits spiritual temperament) in right measure and at due intervals in the fire of Brahman, which is in stomach. Eating is not merely for satisfaction. It gives the life-energy. Taittriya Upnishad (Upnishad is enquiry into the nature of Brahmn) begins with the statement "*annam brahameti vyajanat*; consider food as Brahmn." Good food (purity, moderation, righteous earning, offering to "The Supreme," timeliness) curbs impudence of senses and facilitates to have discipline in life.

The discipline of food helps the spiritual aspirant to offer "**life-breaths into life breaths.**" What is the meaning of "offering life breaths into life breaths"? Lord has used the word breaths (i.e. in plural). The air within the body has been classified in five categories i.e. the prana (located in heart), the apana (located in rectum), the smana (located in the navel), the udana (located in the throat) and the vyana is believed to spread all over the body. These five types of air are jointly known as "pancha-pranas." By using the word prana in plural, Lord is referring to practice of controlling and suspending the functions of all the five airs. This offering of "panch pranas" gains the character of yajna in which fire and clarified butter both are represented by the pranas. In this yajna, there is no offering of prana and apana. The functions of five airs are suspended at their very seat of existence. This practice is called "Kevala Kumbhaka; Absolute Pause."

ii) *Sarve apy ete yajnavido* (all these are knowers of sacrifice) - Lord has mentioned twelve specific yajnas so far. Those performing these yajnas are knowers of Yajna. They know what yajna is? What do they know who know Yajna? Yajna is not a particular ritual only. Any act (physical or mental), can be yajna, if it satisfies certain conditions i.e. sublime spirit of detachment should grace one's mind while pursuing the activity; the individual should feel dispossessed of feeling of doer-ship completely; activity should be an offering to the Supreme in true spirit of dedication like a flower placed for good on the altar (raised platform or table serving as symbol of divinity) in the name of divinity i.e. act should be performed with consciousness of feeling of divine connectivity within. Last condition is most essential condition i.e. act should be performed with consciousness of feeling of "divine connectivity" within. Even "inaction" may be a yajna. In World War II, Hitler was asking on telephone "Is Paris burning"? If the commander In-charge does not fire or refuses to carry out the order to save genocide (deliberate murder of masses) taking risk of his own life, then it is yajna. In Mahabharta War, Lord was urging Arjuna to fight (or to commit genocide to restore righteousness in society). Lord was actually asking Arjuna to perform a yajna. It is indeed very difficult to know the subtle, touching and ever continuing aspects of Yajna, full of substance, depth and meaning. If one truly understands Lord's concept of yajna, then one's only desire in life will be just to convert each activity into yajna performed in the memory of one, who speaks without speaking, sees without seeing and appears nowhere still dwelling in each heart, ever blissfully smiling, still doing nothing.

Yajnak Sapita Kalmsah (By virtue of their sacrifice are their sins get destroyed) - Lord has spoken so much about yajnas. Why should anybody do Yajnas? Lord answers it here. By performing yajnas, all sins get destroyed. What are sins? Sins are those acts committed without remorse with utter contempt to sufferings of the victim. The victimization is of such magnitude that it causes constant uneasiness at the level of awareness and it exerts the effect of prolonging soul's eternal journey. Sins save wounds and scars in the store of consciousness. Yajna removes the wounds and scars stored on the level of consciousness of an individual. Yajna (performed by killing the kith and kin perpetuating extreme un-righteousness) is the solution to Arjuna's difficulty. In a yajna every act, every thought, every emotion, every word used, play of senses, mind and intelligence is surrendered to the Supreme in true spirit of dedication and surrender. The result is self-purification. All the disciplines in the form of yajnas, enumerated by the Lord, are extremely effective and free the performer of the sacrifice (Yajna) from capturing impact of past actions and rebirth. "Purity within" leads the seeker towards spiritual enlightenment.

Lord is giving a beautiful lesson on how an individual should live life to blossom inherent divine potential fully.

Lord has mentioned twelve yajnas from verse 24 to verse 30 as follows:

1) *Brahmn Yajna* (in an action, all aspects i.e. doer, process of action, offerings are all taken (or worshipped) as Brahmn) (verse 25)

2) *Bhagavad rupa darshan or Daiva yajna* {Conceiving Divine in various forms and performing all consecrated (declared holy) rites for Divine itself}. (verse 25)

3) *Sense control Yajna* (verse 26)

4) *Rejection of sense objects Yajna* (verse 26)

5) *Mind Control Yajna* (verse 27)

6 *Dravya yajna* (Utilizing all wealth and material for cosmic benefit in selfless service). (verse 28)

7) *Tapo yajna*- (Observing austerity, bearing with difficulties with patience, happily enjoying the spirit of pain, identifying true spirit in suffering and scarcity with silence that speaks and contentment that dances). (verse 28)

8) *Yoga Yajna* (Facing success and failure and favorable and unfavorable circumstances with equanimity observing all the eight limbs of *Ashtang Yoga* in pursuit of spiritual realization or enlightenment). (verse 28)

9) *Svadhyay Yajna* (verse 28)

10) *Jnana Yajna* (verse 28)

11) *Pranayam Yajna*- (Observing Puruka, Rechaka, internal and external Kumbhaka with divine consciousness). (verse 29)

12) *Niyataahara Yajna* (verse 30)

What is the conclusion on this long discussion on Yajna (from verse 24 to verse 30)? Identify the Divine Truth in all situations everywhere (in me, in you and in others). Keep on surrendering the lower impulses to higher aim making all actions in life a "Yajna," a consecrated (made holy with intense thoughts of Divine) act of offering with humility, devotion and intensely felt longing for *lokasangraha* (cosmic benefit). Make every existence a symbol of divine presence (whether with blossomed divinity or divinity covered) and every act an act of worship (utter submission, utter humility and utter dedication). Everything is divine. If experience sounds different even a little, offer another yajna to blossom the covered Divinity. Living for the Divine, feeling for the divine, thinking for the Divine and working for the Divine is Yajna and nothing else. Yajna is that which unites the individual with the Divine annihilating the ego imparting on the limited individual the wholeness of "eternity, indestructibility an immanence (present everywhere)."

31. Lord has talked so much and so good about yajna. Naturally a question may come to mind. What is the use of yajna? Lord answers this question in this verse.

यज्ञशिष्टामृतभुजो यान्ति ब्रह्म सनातनम् ।
नायं लोकोऽस्त्ययज्ञस्य कुतोऽन्यः कुरुसत्तम ॥ ४- ३१ ॥

yajna-sistamrta-bhujo yanti brahma sanatanam
nayam loko asty ayajnasya kuto 'nyah kuru-sattama 4.31

yajna-sista—amrta-bhujah—eaters of the nectar of remnants of the sacrifice; *yanti*—go; *brahma*—the supreme; *sanatanam*—eternal; *na*—never; *ayam*—this; *lokah*—planet; *asti*—is; *ayajnasya*—of the non-sacrificer; *kutah*— how; *anyah*—the other; *kuru-sat-tama*—O best amongst the Kurus.

"The eaters of the nectar in the form of remnants of yajna go to the eternal Brahman. This world is not for the non-performer of yajna, how, then, any other world, O Best of the Kurus?" II 4-31 II

Why should anyone perform Yajna? Lord answers beautifully stepwise as follows:

i) *Yajnasistamrta bhjo yanti brahma sanatana* {**eating the nectar of remnant of yajna, (such people) reach the eternal Brahman**} - Remnant (a small part of something offered in yajna after the rest has been used) is called *Prasada*. Lord calls it nectar (drink of the Gods) or ambrosia. Those who take this ambrosia reach the eternal Brahman. Is Lord referring to remaining sweets and food stuff only? If so what is it that remains after Tapoyajna, Yogayajna or Pranayam Yajna? Therefore "ambrosia that is left over after the yajna" should be taken to mean "not easily excited or irritated, calm, contended and peaceful" state after performing yajna. That experience is more important than the material left over in the form of banana or sweet. It is this experience (psychological satisfaction of having performed for the Divine and having shared with those having same Divinity) which lingers on at the level of conscience and helps the individual to attain the eternal Brahman. "This prasada (remnants of yajna)," which Lord is referring, is not bananas and sweets alone. It (ambrosial food) is that experience of richness within, that expansion, that unspeakable feeling of freedom, that contentment of having done the due, which naturally become the possession of one who has performed a *yajna* in its true spirit. It is this experience of freedom, which is "the kinetic energy of yajna" that pushes the seeker to transcend (to go beyond) limitations towards the supreme end (moksha).

What is this eternal Brahman? Does the term Brahman mean Brahman with attributes or Brahman without attributes? Actually "Brahman with form and name" and "Brahman without form and name" are not two entities. The difference between Saguna (with form and name) and Nirguna (without form and name) are due to spiritual maturity of the individual. A child never uses aid after it once learns to walk. Initially the devotion for Nirguna Brahman presents difficulty. When you start to learn driving, you are so particular that accelerator is on right side and the brake is on the left side. When you get adept in driving everything is taken care of automatically. You are able to sing and talk while driving. "The Eternal Universal and Infinite Energy Source or Ultimate Principle of Exiatence" always remains the same and responds whether you are worshipping for saguna or nirguna i.e. the same energy responds even when you are worshipping the "Intermediate Gods and Goddesses." When Eternal Brahman (The Supreme Secret or Ever Continuing Eternal Truth" is realized, all differences cease. True performance of yajna can take an individual to the Eternal Brahman, the zenith (highest point) of spirituality. Eternal Brahman (Absolute Immortality) is that which manifests in diversity all around without losing its own wholeness, its eternal silence, its perfect peace, its joy unlimited, its love divine {divine love is that love which only gives, which only expands, which purifies the impure, which suffers no penury (state of being very poor) come what may}.

ii) *Na ayam loko asti* {**not this world is (for non performers of yajna)**} - Those who perform no yajna will not be able to achieve even human ends which are associated with the material world and are called by the names of virtue, wealth and worldly satisfaction.

iii) *A-yajnasysa Kuto Anyah* - **How can there be the other world for one who does not perform Yajna?**- The Lord has already said that those who do not perform Yajna (Offering; spirit of detachment; cosmic benefit; total surrender to the Divinity) do not achieve the richness of this world (i.e. wife, children, wealth, honor, fame, prestige and other means of fleeting-happiness sought after in this world). How can there be, for the non-performer of yajna, the other world that is available through special disciplines only? The use of other world has got a special meaning here. By the words "other world," Lord means the supreme end of human existence, called Muksha (absolute freedom; merger in the Infinite Divine Essence; a state in which subject, object and the act become one). Lord has also used the words "this world" which means the material world.

This verse contains volume for the people of worldly thinking. The one who does not perform Yajna (i.e. does not abide by traditional rites; does not work without detachment; does not work for cosmic benefit; does not work with divine awareness as mentioned above or does not perform the twelve *yajnas* already discussed) is referred to in this verse as "*a-yajnas*" here. Of all the created beings human being alone is able to follow these practices. The one who neglects these practices not only gets deprived of liberation from bondage but even heavenly enjoyments are withheld from such an individual. Peace eludes. Sufferings victimize. The individual gets consumed by worries and anxieties of various kinds. Lord has clarified in verse 3.13 "The righteous, eating remnants of *yajna*, are freed from all sins but the wicked people who cook food only for themselves (for existing-self and those emanating there from or blood and matrimonial relations) verily eat sin (i.e. activity which is soul suffocating and tormenting at the level of conscience." *Yajna* in this discussion is not confined to rites of lighting a fire and putting ghee and other kinds of food grain into it. *Yajna* is being used in this discussion in a very wider sense of the term. Whatever we do, we should do it in the spirit of yajna {detachment; cosmic benefit; awareness of divine dimension* (perceiving ever present "Still Divinity; Ever Constant Mute Witness" in everything)}. The people will then evolve spiritual awareness, spiritual strength and spiritual qualities. With Yajna-attitude one can learn to live life, celebrate it opening infinite possibility of perfection and still making this life an eternal unfolding of joy.

32. In 16th verse Lord promised Arjuna to explain the "truth of action." Then Lord told Arjuna that action should be done in such a way that one should experience "inaction in action and action in inaction." Having described all this Lord concludes the discussion in the present verse emphasizing that action should be performed keeping in view the truth of action.

एवं बहुविधा यज्ञा वितता ब्रह्मणो मुखे ।
कर्मजान्विद्धि तान्सर्वानेवं ज्ञात्वा विमोक्ष्यसे ॥ ४- ३२ ॥

evam bahu-vidha yajna vitata brahmano mukhe
karma-jan viddhi tan sarvan evam jnatva vimoksyase 4.32

evam--thus; *bahu-vidhah*-- manifold; *yajnah*--sacrifices; *vitatah*—are spread; *brahmanah*--of the Vedas; *mukhe*--in the face of; *karma-jan*--born of action; *viddhi*—know (thou); *tan*--them; *sarvan*--all; *evam*--thus; *jnatva*—having known; *vimoksyase*—shall be liberated.

"Thus various yajnas, like the yajnas discussed above, are spread out before the mouth of Brahman (the mouth of fire which receives the offerings or lie scattered in Vedas). Know them all to be born of karma (action); and thus having known thou shall be free." II 4-32 II

***Evam bahuvidha yajna vitata brahmano mukhe* - (many yajnas of this type lie scattered in Vedas; The words Brahman Mukhe has been used for Vedas because Vedas are considered voice of the Lord)** – Lord has mentioned twelve yajnas between verse 24 to verse 30. Many Yajnas, like the above, have been laid down in Vedas as a means gaining self-realization i.e. in no way this is the

---

* Awareness of divine dimension is essential attribute. When this is not there, we need benevolence, compassion, justice and righteousness to guide our actions and behavior. When divine dimension is there, everything is automatically taken care of.

exhaustive list. There are different sections of Vedas. *Karam-Kand* of Vedas deals with rituals to be performed for specific Gods in specific manner for specific purposes. For example *karam-kanda* of Vedas mentions about "*Putreshthi yajna*" for obtaining son. The Vedas have knowledge portion (Vedic texts, sruti and smriti) besides Karam-Kand, which contains a lot of knowledge for self realization. For example, Vedas impart this knowledge through such passages as "we sacrifice prana in speech." The usage of this knowledge becomes *yajna* if this knowledge is used with Yajna-attitude. It should suffice to say that there are innumerable ways of performing *Yajna*. Therefore, focus of the individual should be on Yajna-attitude to make every act of life a *yajna*, an offering to the one who is "Source of all Things." One more point also emerges out of this. Vedas, which are considered the ancient, authentic, and celebrated repository of divine knowledge, advocate performance of *Yajnas*.

Karamajan vidihi tan sarvan (**Know them all to be born of *karmas* or actions**) - Know them all (all *yajnas*) to be born of actions. *Yajnas* are all different modes of actions. Action can be performed through speech, through thought, through work, through body and through senses. Individual effort is required in performance of *yajna*. There can be no yajna without action. Inaction is irrelevant in the context of performance of *yajna*. The seeker has to essentially use one of his or her faculties (speech, thought, work, body and senses) in performance of yajna. Actions performed with yajna-attitude (Offering; spirit of detachment; cosmic benefit; total surrender to the Divinity) leads to highest fruit in the form of liberation (absolute freedom).

Evam jnatva vimokshayse (**thus knowing you shall be liberated**) – These words "thus knowing" are very important. What is the Lord referring in these words? Thus knowing stands for "knowing the truth of action" i.e. an action becomes a *yajna* (medium of union with the "Nameless and Formless One," source of all that is) if it is done with sense of detachment, for cosmic benefit, with awareness of divine dimension, within total surrender to the Supreme Reality. An action, done with this yoga-attitude assumes a divine character, which can lead an ordinary mortal to the lofty height of immortality. Working with this yajna-attitude, one can achieve freedom right in this life in the midst of the work that we do. One can gain freedom from cycle of life and death right here. This knowledge about the yoga-attitude is the key, knowing which one can transform the whole life into yajna. Even as murderous act as waging a war at the cost of one's life becomes a yajna, a liberating exercise, a spiritually up-lifting phenomenon, if it is done with the sole aim of restoring righteousness in the society. Lord's Yajna-attitude unfolds unique universal principles of life i.e. "Managing work of detached actions unlocks the doors to inner hidden source of energy" or "Those who do not dwell on success (but concentrate only on doing the best for cosmic benefit) never go away" or "Those who do not exist for themselves can last forever" or "Confining to existing self is no more without danger" or "You live life when you give life."

Lord says that having understood that (i.e. *yajna-attitude*) one becomes free. What is the meaning of this freedom? This freedom means experiencing that relief which is possible only by self-knowledge or Brahmanic–consciousness i.e. gaining a realization that individual-self or existing-self is not the highest meaning of our being, that in us we have the World-Being who is immortal, who looks upon pain as the other side of joy, who eternally endures as silent witness in all of us remaining in the perfect state of equanimity. This Yajna-attitude generates infinite possibility of perfection, eternal unfolding of joy, and strengthening an individual to transcend any limitations. That is what Lord means by use of words "vimoksyase i.e. becomes free."

Now, **Yajna-attitude of Lord Krishna can be summed up as "Give, Give, Give; Give with rituals; Give without rituals; Give to those you love; Give to those whom you do not love; Give to the unfortunate and the deprived; Give to those whom you do not want to give; In giving you are born to eternal life."**

Don't let the *yagna-attitude* of Lord Krishna be lost in the clatter (loud unpleasant noise) of religions. Prophet Mohammad said "A man's true wealth is the good he does in this world to his fellow men. When he dies, people will say "what property he has left behind him? But the angel will ask "what good deed has he sent before him?"

This verse, thus, adds "knowledge-dimension" to the routine of Yajna and makes this routine gain spiritual energy. Without this knowledge component (i.e. yajna-attitude), a yajna will remain like gold bars on a mule's back.

33. After having described yajna in full detail, Lord now explains in this verse how liberation ensues.

श्रेयान्द्रव्यमयाद्यज्ञाज्ज्ञानयज्ञः परन्तप ।
सर्वं कर्माखिलं पार्थ ज्ञाने परिसमाप्यते ॥ ४- ३३ ॥

sreyan dravya-mayad yajnaj jnana-yajnah parantapa
sarvam karmakhilam partha jnane parisamapyate 4.33

sreyan--greater; *dravya-mayat*—with objects; *yajnat*—tha sacrifice; *jnana-yajnah*--sacrifice in knowledge; *parantapa*--O chastiser of the enemy (Arjuna); *sarvam*--all; *karma*-- actions; *akhilam*--in its entirety; *partha*--O son of Prtha (Arjuna); *jnane*--in knowledge; *parisamapyate*—(is) culminated.

"O Scorcher of enemy (Arjuna)! Jnana-yajna (Knowledge-Sacrifice) is superior to Dravya-Yajna (Material-sacrifice). Knowledge is that in which all action (whether relating to lower knowledge or the highest divine knowledge) culminates." II 4-33 II

Lord starts this verse comparing Jnana-Yajna and Dravya-Yajna. First the two terms should be dealt with.

Dravya-Yajna is that which is performed by use of money and material. You need wood for fire. You need clarified butter (ghee) besides sugar, curd, milk, camphor, incense, sesamum seeds, barley and fragrant herbs etc. to be offered in fire. This is not all. Some people get involved in such activities as distributing suitable gifts to the poor and the destitute, constructing wells and rest houses for the pilgrims, offering of morsels of cooked food before meals to Gods, birds, animals and ancestors. All these acts, done without self interest to help others, come in the category of Dravya-Yajna and Daiva-Yajna. Something is arranged from outside. That is the peculiarity of these Yajnas. Dravya-Yajna leads to liberation only when it is done with full insight into the truth about yajna, renouncing the feelings of possession, attachment or desire for fruit or else it will lead to bondage.

Jnana-Yajna (Knowledge-Yajna), in contrast to above, is that which involves the use of discrimination and spiritual insight. In this yajna nothing is required from outside. Life keeps moving as it is. Change is brought inside. Change is brought in attitude. One does not require anything external in this sacrifice. The Infinite Absolute, its birth, life and actions become the focal point. For the attainment of the true knowledge, proper mental attitude is the only requirement.

Lord declares that sacrifice of jnana is definitely superior to sacrifice of materials.

Sarvam Karmakhilam Parthe jnane parisamapyate (O Arjuna! all karmas eventually get dissolved into jnana)- All actions, without exceptions, culminate in knowledge. Knowledge here means divine knowledge, an insight into one's own divine nature, divine birth and divine actions. Divine knowledge embellishes a seeker's personality, helps to discern between self and non-self and leads the seeker beyond all limitations towards enlightenment and liberation.

Jnana and Jnana-Yoga - In this verse, both the terms jnana and jnan-yoga are used. Relatively speaking, Jnana is the object. Jnana-yoga is the action. An action gains complete fulfillment in knowledge. Jnana is the divine light which annihilates the ignorance and propels the individual to go beyond limitations. Jnana fosters (encourages) the awareness that the self is not body. The self is atman. When this jnana dawns, ignorance evaporates like the mist after the sun rise. An action terminates in knowledge. What does it mean? An action, done in the spirit of yoga, finds its fulfillment in divine knowledge. A seed turns into a plant. A seed finishes itself to bring about a plant. A seed is no more after the plant emerges. An action is no more after the dawn of divine knowledge. Thereafter Divine Knowledge alone guides the seeker to move towards self-realization.

34. Lord has told in the preceding verse that knowledge-sacrifice is better than the material sacrifice. In this verse Lord explains how and from whom this knowledge is to be obtained.

तद्विद्धि प्रणिपातेन परिप्रश्नेन सेवया ।
उपदेक्ष्यन्ति ते ज्ञानं ज्ञानिनस्तत्त्वदर्शिनः ॥ ४- ३४ ॥

tad viddhi pranipatena pariprasnena sevaya
upadeksyanti te jnanam jnaninas tattva-darsinah 4,.34

tat—that (knowledge of different sacrifices); *viddhi*--know; *pranipatena*--by long prostration (before a spiritual master); *pariprasnena*--by questions; *sevaya*--by the rendering of service; *upadeksyanti*—initiate instruct; *te*--to you; *jnanam*--knowledge; *jnaninah*—the wise; *tattva--darsinah*—those who have realized the truth.

"Know that by long prostration, by questions and by service; the wise who have realized the truth will instruct thee in that knowledge." II 4-34 II

Lord is telling Arjuna how from whom such knowledge is to be obtained.

i) *Tad viddhi pranipaten, pariprsena sevaya* (**Know that by long prostration, by questions and by service**)- Lord is asking Arjuna to know that (divine-knowledge). In preceding verse Lord mentioned **the** relative excellence of jnana. Now Lord is urging Arjuna to know the divine knowledge. This only explains the supremacy of the divine knowledge. Brahaman Jnana is superior to everything else in this world. Lord explains what all a seeker should do for it.

Pranipaten (**by long prostration**)- A seeker should go to a guru and humbly lay prostrate before the guru (sad guru here) to impart divine knowledge. If one has to know the cause of bondage and the difference between divine knowledge and the worldly knowledge, one must cultivate humility (quality of not thinking that you are better than others). Prostrating is traditional way of showing respect to a teacher.

Pariprasnena (**by question**)- Divine knowledge is not easy. Questions should be asked from the Guru seeking clarifications of doubts. Lord is saying that questions should be asked for clarification constantly. Only truth can stand questioning. Common questions are: Who am I? What is this world? What is the cause of bondage? What is salvation? Questioning shows eagerness or seriousness of the seeker to acquire knowledge. The idea is that seeker should satisfy his or her curiosity and gain knowledge from the preceptor.

Sevaya (**through the service of the teacher**) – The disciple must serve the enlightened teacher fondly and attentively. *Brahamn-vidya* (Divine knowledge) is not ordinary exchange of dialogue or set of instructions. It requires soul communication to facilitate depth and fullness of divine knowledge. By rendering *seva* (service) the disciple must earn close proximity of the teacher by serving him and his causes in all possible ways. Close association with the teacher is indispensable for this reason. It should be kept in mind that the *Master* (enlightened teacher) is not in need of it. Service should be rendered as an act of devotion.

When the seeker fulfills these conditions, the Master out of mercy imparts *Brahman-vidya* (divine knowledge) upon the disciple. Lord expresses this by using certain penetrating words.

Upadeksyanti te jnanam **(they will instruct you in this jnana)**- They communicate the seeker the Brahman-jnana. Who are they? They are those who have the jnana or those who have realized the tattvam (Brahman; the Divine Truth; the Fundamental Cause).

Jnannis Tattva Darsinnah **(the sage of wisdom who realized the truth)**- Divine knowledge cannot be learnt from just anybody. It can be learnt only from the Master (Sad-guru) who has directly perceived the truth. The teacher should be one who has realized the self and transcended all doubts. Why is it so? Brahaman Vidya (Divine knowledge) cannot be taught by lectures alone. The master passes the "divine current" to the disciple to initiate him or her on the spiritual path. This is not possible by a teacher who has not had firsthand experience of perceiving the divine knowledge. The Lord uses the word "*tattva darsinnah*; knower of truth" to distinguish the enlightened master from others who have learnt from the books alone. Truth is not anything external. The "Other Shore" is not far. No oceans have to be crossed. It is right within. Actual experience may be like **"returning to stunning simplicity laden with very effective language of silence markedly amazing in a zone of suffusing bliss with everything agog with life-current."** "Being in this experience" amounts to losing self within in the "valley of joy." It is essential that the master should have the actual experience of passage of this divine current. Perceiving Truth amounts to awakening the self. Awakening oneself awakens the whole world. The master should be one who has had firsthand experience of the passage of the divine current of divine knowledge. Even finding a Sadguru (the Divine Guide or the Master) is not a problem. If the seeker is having the right amount of eagerness to know the "Divine Secret," the restlessness of knowing the divine truth will draw the master from the unknown regions of the earth.

35. Lord told Arjuna that the "Truth of Divine Knowledge" should be obtained from an enlightened master who has had firsthand experience of it. In this verse Lord explains how one feels after experiencing the "Divine Truth" or "enlightenment."

यज्ज्ञात्वा न पुनर्मोहमेवं यास्यसि पाण्डव ।
येन भूतान्यशेषेण द्रक्ष्यस्यात्मन्यथो मयि ॥ ४- ३५ ॥

yaj jnatva na punar moham evam yasyasi pandava
yena bhutany asesani draksyasy atmany atho mayi 4.35

yat--which; *jnatva*—having known; *na*--not; *punah*--again; *moham*-- delusion; *evam*-- thus; *yasyasi*--(you)) shall get; *pandava*--O son of Pandu (Arjuna); *yena*--by this; *bhutani*--all living entities; *asesani*--totally; *draksyasi*--you will see; *atmani*--in thy self; *atho*-- also; *mayi*--in Me.

"O Arjuna! Having known this, you will not fall again into this delusion (mind's ignorance) like this; for by this you shall see all existences without exception in the self and then in me." II 4-35 II

Lord has told Arjuna how divine knowledge is to be obtained. This divine knowledge is not an ordinary possession. Now Lord explains this verse how and what sea changes come with the divine knowledge.

Yat jnatva **(knowing this)** – What is this that Lord is referring to? Lord is referring to "truth of Divine Knowledge." Divine knowledge brings about some fundamental awareness as to: Who am I?

What is this world? What is maya (ignorance of mind)? What is Brahman (the supreme secret; Mystery of the mysteries; which is there yet still remains as if it were not there)?

Na punar moham evam yasyasi **(this kind of delusion which has come upon you will not ever come like this)**- Lord is telling Arjuna about the trait of divine knowledge. Divine Knowledge takes the seeker beyond the possibility of delusion [mental confusion i.e. dilemma whether action (mental or physical) is right or wrong]. Remarkable point is that it destroys not only delusion but even the **"possibility of delusion"** as well. Lord is also referring to the present dilemma of Arjuna by use of the word "*evam*- like this." Arjuna had come to the battle field ready to fight. Now at the spur of the moment, he was in utter confusion as to whether his decision to kill his own relatives and seniors was correct. This is a common experience. This situation comes in everybody's life and is responsible for wastage of utter potential of an individual. An individual already on the path of action finds himself or herself unable to use his or her own potentials for the committed cause. "Moments of inaction due to dilemma about the decision" adversely and substantially exert influence in our daily life. Lord is giving permanent solution. First thing for an individual should be awareness about divine dimension, divine knowledge. Then action should follow its course. We reverse the order and get into the problems of life. A strong foundation assures sustainability.

Yena bhutany asesena draksyasy atmany atho mayi **[by this you will see all existences (the whole of the creation) in the self and in Me]** – Divine knowledge destroys all mental and physical barriers. That is the special trait of divine knowledge. After gaining the awareness of divine knowledge, one sees the whole world in one's self (atman or soul) as also in the Supreme Reality (in Me; Vasudeva Krishna; in the Divine Infinite Eternal Existence). These words of the Lord contain the crux of the Divine Knowledge the truth about "The Truth." What is it behind these words? What is the meaning of seeing the whole world in the self and also in the Supreme? It is not easy to grasp it initially.

What is divine knowledge? It is the experience, at the level of consciousness, that the Supreme Reality (represented by Lord Krishna; the Infinite, Universal, Un-manifested Reality with such features as eternity, indestructibility, immanent or present everywhere) alone exists in diversified forms. It is the only "Truth" rather "truth of the Truth." It is Un-changing Reality. Rest all changes including our existential self, our body. Hence rest all is un-truth.

This divine knowledge is a state of perception of awakened consciousness, beyond ego. This knowledge is realization, awareness, an awakening about the "Divine Eternal Divine Presence" within. This knowledge cannot come by own efforts or reading the books. Some enlightened Sadguru initiates the seeker into Divine knowledge. A flame of a burning lamp alone is required to light the flame of another lamp. An action reaches its fulfillment after this divine knowledge. Divine knowledge is such that an "action becomes inaction and inaction becomes action" after this knowledge. It takes some time to grasp this phenomenon.

This divine knowledge is not an intellectual achievement or intellectual acceptance. It is an experience. What does it mean? Suppose you are sitting at some pleasantly secluded place meditating. Someone comes and touches you softly with a finger. Your heart starts pounding, you look wide eyed astonished. It takes you sometime to regain your composure. You can now well imagine what happens when someone enlightened touches you. Swami Vivekananda could not forget the touch of his Guru in his life time. Janaka experienced unique sense of freedom immediately after listening to the words of Ashtavakra. With the divine touch of the *Sadguru* (that teacher who has himself experienced truth and is competent to impart divine knowledge to others), physically or through words, there is immediate change in you at the level of awareness. You go beyond your limitations, beyond the world of ego, beyond the world of duality. Your ignorance crushes. You are face to face with the "Divine Reality" within you. You are struck dumb with amazement. That divine component which was covered under the veil of ignorance, beyond your mind, is before you. Immediately, your divine consciousness starts expanding taking hold of you rather taking full grip of you. You are face to face with your true nature (eternal, indestructible immanent i.e. present everywhere). Then you realize that you are not the body (covering of the self) only. Then you really come to realize that Vedic statement **"That I am."** Then, you feel that the divine component that you are, is in all existences. You feel that you are there everywhere. You have no limitations. A plant bears so many flowers, which may be so many in numbers. Actually it is the extension or outgrowth the same plant. Each flower is related to the plant same way. Similarly diversity is the outgrowth of this divinity only. Rather it is manifested divinity. You find in these moments every existence is your own growth, manifestation of your own Divinity. Your individuality vanishes completely. All beings in the whole universe start becoming manifestations of the divinity within you. Then you feel so akin to all. Love-unlimited starts flowing for all from within you. Bliss becomes your nature and your consciousness encompasses the whole universe. You feel connected to everything or every being in this universe. This is the moment when you **"see all in self"** (awakened, due to grace of Sadguru, to the divine nature within). This is the moment when river merges into the ocean losing its separate entity completely. This is because existential self becomes irrelevant for the enlightened individual. Duality ends. All that remain is "That One" only. There exists nothing else for the enlightened individual.

"… … **and in Me"** – Here, Lord's reference is to the Universal Self (the Supreme Universal Eternal Unlimited Reality, the Fundamental Cause of all that is; represented by Lord Krishna here). Reference is to both the "Un-manifested Supreme Truth" and the Avatar, known as Krishna, *Purshottama*. Everything is happening is this reality.

36. After discussing divine knowledge in detail, Lord in this verse deals with merits and usefulness of knowledge.

अपि चेदसि पापेभ्यः सर्वेभ्यः पापकृत्तमः ।
सर्वं ज्ञानप्लवेनैव वृजिनं सन्तरिष्यसि ॥ ४- ३६ ॥

api ced asi papebhyah sarvebhyah papa-krttamah
sarvam jnana-plavenaiva vrjinam santarisyasi 4.36

api--even; *cet*--if; *asi*—(you) are; *papebhyah*-- than sinners; *sarvebhyah*--of all; *papa-krttamah*—the most sinful; *sarvam*--all; *jnana-plavena*--by the raft of knowledge(divine knowledge) ; *eva*-- alone; *vrjinam*—sin; *santarisyasi*—(you) will cross completely.

"Even if you are the most sinful of all sinners, you will cross over all your transgressions (crookedness of evil; all that is against the moral behavior) by the raft (a flat floating structure made of pieces of wood tied together to be used as boat) of this divine knowledge." II 4-36 II

A sin is a physical, mental or immoral act, which, even after having been committed leads to unpleasantness, suffocation and burden at the level of conscience and results in lengthening the cycles of birth and death of the soul. Thinking mind wanders and doubts. Feeling of sin, emergence of doubts and enquiries are from mind and intelligence. The response to redress (correct) them also comes from the same internal source. Divine knowledge alone has the power to resolve all doubts and dissolve all sins. Thus, one trait of divine knowledge is that it succeeds in the task of redemption (state of being freed from power of evil). Divine knowledge lifts an individual from the dungeon (underground prison) of internal turmoil and sufferings and liberates him or her into unity, peace and joy of divine existence. This verse offers a great relief to all. It is said that there is no saint without a past and no sinner without a future. In view of this verse there is no need for even the sinner to despair. All most all are sinner at one point of the time or other. Divine knowledge offers a charter (a statement of principles and duties) to all to cross over all evils in the boat of divine wisdom. The life of Rishi Valmiki illustrates this point. He lived the life of a dacoit in the beginning, but, when the wisdom dawned on him, he (the sinner) became a saint.

37. In last verse, Lord mentions that in boat of divine knowledge (knowledge about self), you can cross even the ocean of sin. In this verse Lord tell Arjuna the purifying effect of the divine knowledge.

यथैधांसि समिद्धोऽग्निर्भस्मसात्कुरुतेऽर्जुन ।
ज्ञानाग्निः सर्वकर्माणि भस्मसात्कुरुते तथा ॥ ४- ३७ ॥

yathaidhamsi samiddho agnir bhasmasat kurute arjuna
jnanagnih sarva-karmani bhasmasat kurute tatha 4.37

yatha--just as; *edhamsi*--firewood; *samiddhah*--blazing; *agnih*--fire; *bhasmasat*--turns into ashes; *kurute*--so does; *arjuna*--O Arjuna; *jnana-agnih*--the fire of knowledge; *sarva-karmani*--all reactions to material activities; *bhasmasat*--to ashes; *kurute*--it so does; *tatha*--similarly.

"As the blazing fire reduces the fuel to ashes, O Arjuna, similarly fire of Brahman-jnana (Divine knowledge; Self knowledge) reduces all karmas to ashes." II 4-37 II

It has already appeared in earlier discussion that actions are of capturing or binding nature. Every action exerts a good or bad impact (i.e. good or bad reaction of having done that action) which has to be gone through by a being in this life or lives to come. Rather actions are the reasons for the cycles of birth and death. Our causal body (our soul; individual divinity under the cover of ignorance) travels from one life to another life with a sort of complete account (or say a sort of baggage) of actions for which matching effect has not been gone through. The cycles of birth and death continue till there is some memory of action with the causal body. This is the ancient thinking. All the yajnas and divine knowledge, explained by the Lord, are for helping an individual to neutralize and make potentially ineffective the contents of the bag (store of memory of actions) with the causal body (soul). A question arises as to how the impact of action is taken care of by the divine knowledge.

Karmas (actions) are divided in three categories i.e. i) Agami Karma or Kriyamana, ii) Sanchit Karma and iii) Prarabdh Karma. Agami Karmas are actions performed in the course of this life to be credited to one's accumulated account of actions at the end of the present life. This is that accumulated stock of all actions in the past lives for which the matching reaction has not been gone through by the individual. Prarabdha are those actions done in past lives, which have matured and whose reaction has to be gone through in present life. Reason for a particular birth is to undergo the reaction of Prarabdha (actions which have now matured and have to be reaped in the present life).

What is the relevance of this discussion here? Divine knowledge (self knowledge) relieves an individual from impact of all these actions so that cause of next birth (transmigration or passing of soul to next birth after death) does not remain there. This happens as follows: i) divine knowledge helps to do work without attachment so that actions in present life become as good as inactions i.e. actions done in present life lose potentiality of causing capturing impact or actions in present life will have no future. In other words they will not be credited to accumulated account at the end of life. An individual gets relieved of *agami* actions. ii) Past karmas are stocked in the subconscious memory of the causal body (soul) in the form of vasanas (tendencies) subtle seeds of desires. Divine knowledge makes an individual aware of cosmic consciousness and divine bliss. After that an individual does not after worldly desires as he or she knows well the consequences thereof. Therefore the individual does not stoop low to worldly desires. The vasanas (tendencies) then resemble fried seeds, which cannot germinate. Therefore even past karmas (Sanchit Karmas) become incapable of germinating desires due to maturity in divine knowledge; iii) Prarabdha (Portion of Sanchit Karma due for maturity in this life) can be destroyed by enjoying or suffering it out. Prarabdha is like an arrow let loose and cannot therefore be recalled. Egoistic relationship with the body vanishes, when divine knowledge dawns. One is not unduly attached with the body. Body continues to function impelled by its prarabdha (which has to be suffered), but undue effect is not there. It is for this that saints like Shankara, Ramakrishna and Ramana had to suffer from incurable body diseases. These saints do not give prarabdha more importance than a shadow due to divine maturity. Those virtues and vices, which are responsible for present body (i.e. prarabdha), in which knowledge emerges get destroyed with the body itself due to impact of divine knowledge.

Thus this verse deals in detail how divine knowledge helps an individual in getting relieved from impact of *agama karma* and *sanchit karmas* and in facing *prarabdha*. This is precisely how fire of divine knowledge burns to ashes all reactions to material activities.

38. Lord has told Arjuna about the merits of the Divine knowledge. In this verse Lord informs one more dimension of divine knowledge.

न हि ज्ञानेन सदृशं पवित्रमिह विद्यते ।
तत्स्वयं योगसंसिद्धः कालेनात्मनि विन्दति ॥ ४- ३८ ॥

na hi jnanena sadrsam pavitram iha vidyate
tat svayam yoga-samsiddhah kalenatmani vindati 4.38

na--not; hi--verily; jnanena-- to knowledge (divine knowledge); sadrsam-- like; pavitram-- pure; iha—here (in this world); vidyate- is; tat--that; svayam-- oneself *yoga--samsiddhah*—perfected in yoga; kalena--in course of time; atmani--in the self; vindati-- finds.

"Verily there is no purifier in this world like knowledge (divine knowledge; truth about the Supreme Truth); the individual, who has perfected in yoga, finds it of himself or herself in the self by the course of time." II 4-38 II

The focus is again is on divine knowledge, which is the expanded vision of the "Unbounded Awareness," which purifies an individual both internally and externally. There is nothing more purifier than the lively awareness of this eternal wisdom. The words used by the Lord are as follows:

***Na hi jnanena sadrsam pavitram iha vindyate* (there is nothing so purifying in this world as jnana (divine knowledge)** – One can wash the clothes and body with soap and water. For the human system, for cleansing both internally and externally, there is no better purifying agent than divine knowledge in the whole world. Whatever is different from knowledge cannot dispel ignorance, which is extremely deluding and confusing. How does jnana work? Suppose an individual has had a horrible dream. You have to break the continuity of the dream to bring him or her to wakefulness. In this example wakefulness is the purifier of self imposed ignorance. Similarly divine knowledge cleanses the individual's delusion about the birth and death, about the truth of the Divinity within and all around. This divine knowledge places an individual in his or her true state of blessedness, true nature, un-changing state.

***Yogasiiddhaha* (perfected in yogah)** – This divine knowledge is not a prerogative of tom dick and harry. Only those who have perfected in yoga i.e. in various disciplines laid down in Ashtang-Yoga attain this knowledge. The proper practice of various phases of yoga (Yama, niyama, asanas, pratyahara, dharana Dhyan and Samadhi) transform the life of the seeker into jnana-yajna. These phases culminate or enliven *jnana* (divine knowledge). Mind becomes purified and the yogi becomes competent for self-knowledge. One should not remain in a fool's paradise. *Sadhna* (un-relented, continuous persistence of sincere efforts for all phases of yoga) is absolutely necessary. By use of this word, Lord has told what all has to be necessarily done for divine knowledge. One has to achieve that state where one becomes established in yoga. The roots of the worldly knowledge which an individual laboriously gathers by the senses, takes time to go off from the mind. With *sadhna* (persistent disciplines), it is possible to make the mind clear like crystal. That is the state in which the divine knowledge descends to an individual. To gain this knowledge which is self-existent, intuitive, self-revealing, self-experiencing, it is necessary to have self control, faith and persistence of *sadhana*. That is what is meant by gaining perfection in yoga.

Tat svam kakena atmani vindati [(when one has perfected in yoga as discussed above) one realizes it in one's own self in course of time] – The divine knowledge does not come from outside. When the precondition has been complied with, divine knowledge descends from within as the sun rises gradually in the morning. Divine knowledge does not come from outside. It blossoms in one's own self. It comes to an individual from within because it is individual's true nature. It is blossoming from inside. Kalena Atamni vindati or you will enjoy it yourself in the course of time. The knowledge of the Ultimate Reality comes from within. All knowledge, all perfection is already there. Only veil of ignorance requires to be removed by gaining perfection in yoga. Blossoming of self knowledge is a slow process. First the individual grows into desire-less-ness and devotion to divine.

This verse is of immense importance and takes one to a point where divine knowledge and devotion appear to be the same. We all go to long distances, crossing mountains and oceans, in search of a divine knowledge. Where is it actually lodged? It is lodged within one's own soul. Experiencing divine knowledge is the transformation taking place within one's soul. It is not an external experience. Remove the ego and make mind devoid of all impressions of worldly knowledge. Make the activity in hand a medium of communication to the Supreme of your resolve to realize the Divinity. That is all. This divine knowledge which Lord is talking about here is not anything which intelligence has clarified to or brought to you from outside. It is not a resolve. It is an awakened state of realization within of the existence of "truth of the Supreme Truth." There is no difference in jnana and devotion at this point. This jnana is experience of awareness of the pure divine content within, divine consciousness within. It does not happen in haste. It is a state that happens in course of time within. What is the object of divine knowledge? What is the object of bhakti (devotion)? It is the same. At this state, there is no difference between jnana and devotion. In this awakened state of awareness, an individual simply loses trace of the existential self. In this super charged and perfected state of yoga, one sees the whole diversification in the universe as the outgrowth of the divinity within, the same Reality. This divine knowledge is the transformation within the soul and makes one extremely conscious and at the same time humble to surrender without reservation to the same Self-Revealing-Divine.

39. In preceding verses, Lord told Arjuna about the merits of divine Knowledge. Now Lord tells Arjuna who achieves knowledge.

श्रद्धावाँल्लभते ज्ञानं तत्परः संयतेन्द्रियः ।
ज्ञानं लब्ध्वा परां शान्तिमचिरेणाधिगच्छति ॥ ४- ३९ ॥

sraddhaval labhate jnanam tat-parah samyatendriyah
jnanam labdhva param santim acirenadhigacchati 4.39

sraddha-van—a man with *sraddha* (faith + awe + reverence + need for knowledge); *labhate*—obtains; *jnanam*—knowledge; *tat-parah*— devoted; *samyata—indriyah*—one who has subdued the senses; *jnanam*—knowledge; *labdhva*—having achieved; *param*- supreme;- *santim*- peace (this state is not absence of noise; it is an expanse in silence within, in the proximity of sou,l with intense awareness, knowledge and joy ever flowing in unending cascades); *acirena*- at once;- *adhigacchati*- -attains.

"The individual, who has sraddha, who has knowledge as the supreme goal, and who has subdued senses, after having gained wisdom, attains quickly supreme peace." II 4-39 II

In this verse three qualities are mentioned for gaining divine knowledge:

i) **Sraddha** (Faith) – This English translation of this word does not properly explain this word. Sraddha is not mere faith. It is combination of faith (strong belief without knowing fully the target), reverence (feeling of great respect), expectation and awe (feeling impressive). We have faith when we know what it is all about. A scientist has got some logic and faith. When we have *sraddha* we nurture strong belief even without knowing very well. This sraddha for divine knowledge is a sort of aspiration or itching or soft restlessness of the soul to gain wisdom. *Sradddha* also implies that seeker is having reverence for divine knowledge. *Sraddha* also means that seeker wants to know about the supreme Secret. At the same time the seeker is having awe (feeling of respect) about the divine knowledge. There is no spiritual progress without sraddha. Faith develops due to some reasons. *Sraddha's* development means that there already exists a seed of divine knowledge in the seeker. *Sraddha* is not an intellectual desire. Seeker is having *sraddha* for divine knowledge means seeker is having love, reverence for divine knowledge and is very impressive about it. It is not pure emotion. It is a sort of awakening of love, reverence for divine knowledge. *Sraddha* for divine knowledge is very strong, intense, and deep. When we have sraddha for something we start living with it in our thoughts, in our actions in our spirit. "Our purity inside" nurtures our *sraddha* for divine knowledge. *Sraddah* is an indication of strong belief. It is a capacity for longing for something meaningful, something divine for something of continuing nature. *Sraddha* for divine knowledge means expectation for something which is attainable by nothing except total, immersing (making completely involved) devotion.

ii) **Tat parah** (single minded devotion) - For gaining divine knowledge one should have single minded devotion (combination of great love, care and support for this) to experience truth. You cannot rise to the level of gaining divine knowledge till you fully control all sensory energies for this. Single minded devotion is necessary for gaining control of senses. Here the effort is to turn mind inward. With this control, senses become subdued or powerless and do not cause disturbance to the mind in the spiritual journey inward.

iii) **Samyatendriyah** (having control and discipline over the sensory system) – This control facilitates new mastery over life. It becomes a pleasure to live life. With this control, individual is no more confined to remain a creature of circumstances. Internal turmoil within does not direct the sensory system. Discipline and control brings about even flow of *prana* (subtle life force) in the body resulting in peace. One feels getting established in the self. This causes the dawn of inner wisdom. Gradually an individual goes beyond the doubts, beyond the dualities and beyond the miseries.

Jnanam lbdhava Param Shantim acirena adhigacchati (Having obtained the divine knowledge, the individual promptly attains Peace Supreme)- After having these qualities, an individual promptly experiences dawn of divine knowledge, an awakening which intensifies the extra sensory perception to identify truth within and around. This awakening is like sunrise which completely wipes out the ignorance. This wisdom is not learnt from books or lectures. It grows within as an outgrowth of various spiritual disciplines. It is realization of an inherent connection with something, some energy which is beyond mentionable reasons and tangible proofs. The first realization is the difference between the truth (i.e. divine essence which is eternal, indestructible and presents everywhere) and untruth (nature i.e. primordial elements, impact of gunas or attributes and known and un-known laws of nature). This difference dawns internally as a matter of experience gradually in due course. Experience is that individual is not body. Truth of the self is divinity (exclusive individualized combination of attributes like eternity, consciousness and knowledge within) i.e. energy which continues forever till realization takes place. With this internalized change the ignorance that self is body goes away resulting in a state of desire-less-ness.

Supreme peace- The divine knowledge leads to Supreme Peace. **What is this peace?** It is not an absence of noise alone. It is not peace of sensory level or psychological level. There are disturbances at these levels. It is the peace at the divine level or the deepest level of human personality. This peace is experienced only when one touches the deepest core in one's own being i.e. all within one's own self. There remains nothing to be achieved after this peace. This Supreme Peace is the reward of having achieved the highest level, achievable by a living entity. No words are exchanged in this state. It is a state of experience only, experience not at sensory level but at the level of conscience. It is a state of contentment. It is a state of bliss. In this state there is no desire, no duality no misery. Your awareness is at peak, but you just do not need anything anymore. You were two when you started. What is this that happens in this spell of Supreme Peace? You alone are there now in this zone of peace and you are the cause of everything. "Everything that you turn your attention to" simply seems belonging to you, your own outgrowth, your own extension and your own very self. This Supreme Peace is a fruit of divine knowledge. It is a state, an abode of the Supreme, an island right within you, which your Divine Knowledge established you in. This Peace is not an ordinary peace. It is a soothing feel of the Divinity. It is a state of self realization. It is the end result of spiritual *sadhna*. *Sadhna* (pursuit of spiritual disciplines) reaches its culmination (highest point here) and *sadhak* realizes here what the supreme grace of the Lord is. The *sadhak* feels astonished, amazed, completely at loss for the words. The subject and object so intermingle in this vast expanse of silence in this zone that subject becomes the object which was always followed thus far. This peace is overwhelmingly drenched with bliss and marked awareness of consciousness. It is a point where being becomes the source of beings. A being is not there anymore. Only a mute divine existence remains with no end, utterly expansive, making you pivot in the cosmic drama to just keep witnessing eternally. Now neither you can do nor you can undo and you are still there, blissful, conscious utterly contended. Divine knowledge picked you as an ordinary being and places in this "Supreme Peace" to make you an immortal being. In a way this "Supreme Peace" is a state of self-effacing (making something disappear i.e. existential self with ego is no more). At the same time it is intuitive (known by feeling rather than considering the facts) state of self-experiencing, self-revealing and self-rewarding. This "Supreme Peace" is indeed the empirical (based more on experience than ideas) self of the divine wisdom that remains always in the fathomless (too deep to be measured) depths of our own being.

The path suggested by the Lord in this verse is straight and simple. Discover divine wisdom through *sraddha*, single minded devotion and control of senses. Then you will quickly attain "Supreme Peace" akin (similar) to self realization or rather self-realization in the form of "Supreme Peace" (a state in which everything is so intensely alive yet so markedly mute and self-communicating, self-revealing, self-suffusing.

40. In the preceding verses Lord talks about those with divine knowledge and *Sraddha* (explained earlier) etc. In this verse lord describes the fate of those who lack *Sraddah* and divine knowledge.

अज्ञश्चाश्रद्दधानश्च संशयात्मा विनश्यति ।
नायं लोकोऽस्ति न परो न सुखं संशयात्मनः ॥ ४- ४० ॥

ajnas casraddadhanas ca samsayatma vinasyati
nayam loko asti na paro na sukham samsayatmanah 4.40

ajnah-- theignorants; *ca*--and; *asraddadhanah*—without sraddha (faith + awe + reverence+ desire for some grace in some form); *ca*--and; *samsaya--atma*—a doubting self; *vinasyati*—goes to destruction; *na*--not; *ayam*--this; *lokah*—world (refer to 14 lokas in introduction; *asti*--is; *na*--not; *parah*— other world; *na*--not; *sukham*--happiness; *samsaya--atmanah*—for the doubting self.

"An individual, lacking divine knowledge, *sraddha*, with tendency to doubt everything everywhere, perishes. Neither this world, nor the world beyond, nor happiness is for the individual who doubts." II 4-40 II

In earlier verses, Lord made positive declaration assuring "Supreme Peace; Salvation" for those having *sraddha* and divine knowledge. This verse is a negative assertion condemning those without sraddaha and divine knowledge. A focus on the fate of unbelievers will only reinforce the relative merits of being with divine knowledge and *sraddha*. Each word used by the lord is touching, passes on the divine current:

i) *Ajna* (lacking divine knowledge) – In the Gita, knowledge means divine knowledge i.e. awareness of divine existence of the self. Worldly knowledge remains confined to finding our relationship between reasons and consequences in the framework of time, space and tangible and intangible laws of nature. Divine knowledge transcends (goes beyond) this limitation. Here Lord is referring to those who cannot discriminate between the truth (which exists eternally) and the untruth (which perishes with lapse time). The individuals in these categories can be called the ignorant i.e. those who take the objective world as real and go for pleasure and fortune in it. The same reasons of pleasures and fortune become the cause of pain, suffering and duality. We are born again and again, going through the immense ordeals of birth and death. We let go of the human life, an opportunity for salvation, an opportunity to get reestablished in our divinity, true nature. We bargain the supreme bliss with ephemeral (important only for a short time) pleasure of senses devoid of divine knowledge. The *ajna* (ignorant) does not know the true self, the "Divine Reality Within."

ii) *Asraddhanas* (those lacking sraddha) – Here Lord is referring to those who lack belief, respect for divine knowledge, own self, scriptures and the Guru. Here Lord strongly condemns "*asraddha*; lack of *sraddha*" in spiritual pursuits. Lord warns Arjuna. It is extremely degrading, destructive and self defeating to be inattentive to divine knowledge or to foster doubts repeatedly about the divine knowledge. It is unfortunate to lack *sradhha* (belief, respect and love) for divine knowledge. An individual in this category seals all the indoors to divine knowledge in life. Such an individual remains involved in unending arguments with all on why we should repose faith in something which defies even logic. Logic or intellectual argumentation deprives such individuals of blessedness of knowing the distinction between truth and untruth. The personality of such an individual starts disintegrating gradually and they start disbelieving all. It becomes their second nature to doubt. They doubt wisdom. They doubt Guru. They doubt Truth (Eternal Universal Existence). It is a sort of disease in an individual which deprives him or her of "life (combination of bliss, contentment and awareness of divine dimension) in life."

iii) **Samsayatma** (One who doubts or doubting Thomas) – Those who doubt presume out rightly that something is not true or unlikely. It is a sort of mental disease. People in this category doubt everything i.e. divine knowledge (i.e. each existing entity is a sort of reflection on the level of divine consciousness, which alone exists), universal connectivity, scriptures and the Guru. The people in this category try to be aware of the divine truth based on logic or worldly knowledge. Divinity is not a subject to be approached based on logic. Divine Realities have reasons which reasons (reasons of human knowledge, knowledge based on facts and logic) do not know. This is precisely the difference between the divinity and science. In science, we prove and then we believe. In divinity, we believe with so much intensity and devotion that our very belief gets transformed into the Reality, which is self evident, self revealing, and self illuminating. Only one caution should be taken care of. The belief should be nurtured under the guidance of Sadguru (i.e. a Spiritual Master who has had a spiritual experience of self realization).

iv) **Na ayam loko asti na paro na sukhamsamsayatmanah** (a doubting person can win neither this world, nor the next, nor happiness) – An individual in doubt does not get on well with other people in society. It is difficult for the people in this category to make friends with others. The habit of doubting precludes (prevents) them from enjoying company of other people. Neither this world (earthly pleasures), nor the supreme world (celestial or heavenly pleasure), nor happiness is for the soul full of doubt.

Therefore, now three good points emerge out of this verse for all spiritual seekers i) Have divine consciousness, ii) Have full faith in self, in Guru and in divine knowledge and iii) Do not ever be doubting Thomas (one who doubts everything without seeing proofs).

41. In this verse, Lord has brought out relationship of true work, divine awareness and self discipline.

योगसंन्यस्तकर्माणं ज्ञानसञ्छिन्नसंशयम् ।
आत्मवन्तं न कर्माणि निबध्नन्ति धनञ्जय ॥ ४- ४१ ॥

yoga-sannyasta-karmanam jnana-sanchinna-samsayam
atmavantam na karmani nibadhnanti dhananjaya 4,41

yoga--devotional service in *karma-yoga*; *sannyasta*--renounced; *karmanam*--of the performers; *jnana*--knowledge; *sanchinna*--cut by the advancement of knowledge; *samsayam*--doubts; *atma-vantam*--situated in the self; *na*--never; *karmani*--work; *nibadhnanti*--do bind up; *dhananjaya*--O conqueror of riches.

"With work renounced by yoga and doubts destroyed by divine knowledge, O Dnanjay (Arjuna), actions do not bind one who is in full possession of the self or established in the self." II 4-41 II

In this verse Lord mentions merits of divine knowledge and working without attachment to fruit of work. Again Lord has used penetrating words as follows:

i) Yogasanyastakarmanam (one who has renounced all actions in yoga) – What is the meaning of renouncing all actions in yoga? It does not mean avoiding work or running away from work (i.e. leaving town; going to jungle or telling everybody that renunciation of work has been taken as spiritual sadhna). It means doing work with a particular attitude of detachment from fruit of action. When you are doing actions for cosmic benefit without attachment to fruit of action as an offering to Supreme, the work done becomes a yajna, a ritual in which the work done is offered in the fire of *Brahaman* (The Supreme Divine). Here the word yoga is used as yoga of the Gita in general and *karam-yoga* or *nishkama-yoga* in particular. All the capturing tendencies of the work get burnt and work-done becomes an offering to the Supreme, a song sung in the memory of the Supreme. This is called the yoga-mode of doing the work. Work is being done but for the cosmic benefit and without attachment to fruit of actions. Fire of knowledge burns all action to ashes. It does not mean cessation (pause or stop) of work. It means that the individual in state of yoga and knowledge is not bound by action done in yoga-mode. The renunciation of such a yogi is not from action but from fruit of action. For this reason, Lord is mentioning of one who has renounced actions i.e. attachment for fruit of action is not there and actions are for cosmic benefit and are done as an offering to the Supreme. Lord is talking of actions done in yoga-mode. Actions of such an individual are like offerings dropped by the ladle in the fire.

ii) *Jnana sam chhinna sansayam* **(who has destroyed all doubts through jnana)** - Such a person destroys doubts through jnana. How is it? The distinction of such a person is his or her awareness of divine dimensions. There is no confusion as to who he or she is. There is no confusion as to why he or she is doing the work. When body is unreal, what is the point of getting unduly attached to the body and relations emanating from physical existence? Such an individual does not neglect. Such an individual only remains with divine consciousness, which results in his or her clarity and yoga-mode of doing work as *yajna*. The *jnana* results in yoga attitude and consequent skill in work. This *jnana* and yoga finally take the individual to such a charged state of awareness that doubt is not possible. How can there be darkness when sunlight is there. What is the point of focus? *Jnana* is the light of divine-knowledge to annihilate the darkness of ignorance of one who is

iii) *Atmavantam* (who is fully established in the self) – What is the meaning of this? Who is an atmavan (self established)? *Atmavan* is one who thinks that atman (soul) alone is real because atma is everything and everything is atman. *Atmavan* is one who has realized the self, whose atman is a free soul. What is the difference in a free soul and a soul? A soul is an individualized divinity with ego. Free soul of an *atmavan* has no ego. Free soul is self-conscious, self-realized state of awareness beyond body, breath, mind, intelligence, memory and ego. Once we are possessed of the self or the free soul (like an *atmavan*), we are in possession of all things. An *atmavan* is a master of the body and senses. Atmavan does not lose hold on the self even in his or her pursuit of good for the others. Atmavan remains thoroughly drenched (extremely wet) in the elixir (magical liquid that is supped to cure all illness and make people young) of being in the proximity of the free-self (liberated soul) and, from out of this, he or she regains the strength to come out alive (rededicated to living with enthusiasm and smile). Atmavan does not use the body and senses for sense pleasures like an ordinary individual. An atmavan directs the body and senses and the divine essence of a being towards Supreme Bliss, a state in which feeling of proximity of self is all and all-providing. Free soul adequately suffices. The whole nature follows an *atmavan*. An *atmavan* has got complete control of senses. Different levels of existence of such an individual (body, breath, mind, intelligence, memory, ego and self, mentioned above) are in perfect harmony. One, who works with worldly knowledge, occasionally develops doubts and skepticism (not believing without proof). One who is established in the self, who is in the midst of higher knowledge simply laughs away the problems and does not face the stumbling blocks of doubts and skepticism. The secret of the individual referred here is not his balancing between truth and untruth. The constantly progressing realization of revealed truth is the light and strength of the person who is established in the self. Such a person does not have to prove anything to anybody. An individual established in the self lives truth within, of which he or she is always conscious. The work of a self established person constantly reflects the perfection and precision of the Greater Reality in which we all have to grow, in which we all have to seek meaning and purpose of life. That is the reason why the one who is established in the self is always smiling.

iv) *Na karmani nibhadhanti Dhanamjay* (**O Arjuna! no actions can bind such a person**) – Now comes out the secret in the form of an assurance. No action can bind the individual, who is established in the self and whose doubts have been destroyed by the divine knowledge. This is why all should go for divine knowledge and getting established in the self. If action is not capturing or binding an individual, individual is blessed. There will be no desire, no hatred and no jealousy. An individual will realize the meaning and purpose of human birth, the highest state achievable by a living being.

Why did the Gita start? Arjuna threw away the weapons and refused to fight giving arguments based on worldly wisdom of reasons and consequences. Arjuna was afraid of sin (an act which is wrong according to moral standards) of murdering his own relatives, grand sire and teacher though the action of war was chosen as last alternative to restore righteousness in society, where attempt was made to strip off a woman in the open court after refusing the legitimately due share to the princes of the dynasty. Now Lord is telling Arjuna that actions do not bind. Capturing effect of an action is not a must. Work can be performed in such a way that the work will not lead to capturing effect. Lord is exhorting Arjuna to act (fight) after knowing the "yoga-mode" of doing the work i.e. one should remain in divine consciousness; one should not harbor doubts and one should work without attachment to fruit of work or as an offering to the Supreme.

42. In this last verse, Lord exhorts (try very hard to persuade someone to do something) Arjuna to stand up and act in the true spirit of self-realization.

तस्माद्ज्ञानसम्भूतं हृत्स्थं ज्ञानासिनात्मनः ।
छित्त्वैनं संशयं योगमातिष्ठोत्तिष्ठ भारत ॥ ४- ४२ ॥

tasmad ajnana-sambhutam hrt-stham jnanasinatmanah
chittvainam samsayam yogam atisthottistha bharata 4,42

tasmat--therefore; *ajnana-sambhutam*-- outcome of ignorance; *hrt-stham*—residing in the heart; *jnana-asina*--by the sword of knowledge; *atmanah*--of the self; *chittva*—having cut; *enam*--this; *samsayam*--doubt; *yogam*-- *atistha*--take refuge in yoga (to save from the impact of modifications of mind in present); *uttistha*--stand up or arise (alive to the call of the hour i.e. to fight to do away with the rampant unrighteous); *bharata*--O descendant of Bharata.

"Therefore, with the sword of knowledge cleave (cut something in separate parts) asunder the doubt born of ignorance about the self, dwelling in the heart, be established in yoga. Stand up, O Bharta (Arjuna)!" II 4-42 II

Now in this last verse of this chapter, Lord again comes back to the original issue underlying discussion in the Gita. At the start of the discussion of the Gita, Arjuna is sunk in the depth of despair and doubts about his duty (whether to fight or not) at that particular moment. He was seeing the situation from worldly point of view without knowing the "eternal truth." What is the significance of these fleeting (which will pass away) relationships of the world in the context of the objective of human life? Our whole perspective of life under goes a change when we realize that we are not body alone. The Truth within us is eternally alive, ever anew. For this reason, Lord taught Arjuna the secret about the "Supreme Self; Divine Universal Essence alone is in one and all." This self-existent Reality might have been self-evident as well if there had not been the influence of the evil power of ignorance. Our doubts and perplexities arise from ignorance which prevents us from accepting and following the truth. The ignorance has to be cut away by sword of knowledge. See how intimately and beautifully Lord exhorts Arjuna in the following words:

i) *Tasmad ajnanasambhutam hrtstaham* (therefore, born out of ignorance and residing in the heart) - Lord's reference is to doubt, uncertainty, or vacillation (changing of opinon) which is born of ignorance i.e. spiritual blindness. Doubts and perplexities of life prevent us from accepting and following the truth within all of us. The main cause of their origin is spiritual blindness i.e. our incapacity to perceive the divinity in the self and in all. This spiritual blindness subsists in the heart and clouds our vision and precludes (make something impossible) the clear view of the 'Divine Reality Within'. 'The moment the divine knowledge' dawns, the spiritual incapacity to have awareness of self goes away like darkness after the sunshine. The spell of evil impact of ignorance goes away after divine knowledge and it is difficult to question the existence of Higher Reality or the Divine Component within. Arjuna's doubt, whether it is better to fight or abstain was the result of spiritual blindness. The only remedy for spiritual blindness is divine knowledge. Arjuna did not know the truth of path of action i.e. even action to fight (to restore righteousness) can be *yajna* and redeemer (capable of making free from evil impact of action).

ii) *Jnanasina atmanah chittvai samsayam* (with the sword of the knowledge of the self, cut the ignorance-born doubt about the self) - Doubt, arising out of ignorance creates a great deal of mental torment. Therefore Lord is exhorting Arjuna to make sword of knowledge about the self (i.e. divine knowledge or strong conviction with no doubts about the self, the divinity within and its manifestation in all) and kill ruthlessly this evil in the form of ignorance-born doubt. First of all, Lord wants Arjuna to be aware of divine dimension within. That is perhaps the right way of starting just anything good because everything good follows thereafter. Experiencing continuously divine existence within is not anything ordinary. Divine knowledge is like a weapon sharp and effective, good enough to put to rest the evil of ignorance and consequential doubts arising there from.

iii) *Yogam atisto uttista Bharat* [be established in yoga, stand up. O Bharta (Arjuna)] – At the start of discussion of the Gita, Arjuna was in utter dilemma about whether he should fight or not. Lord does not want Arjuna to follow anyone blindly. Lord wants to rekindle Arjunas's original nature. He was a fighter to the core. For this reason, Lord has told him about divine knowledge about the self (individualized self and free-self) and also about yoga. Now Lord is exhorting Arjuna to stand up, not like an ordinary man with inertia of spiritual blindness but like an individual established in yoga i.e. one who has complete control of senses and who is able to unite with inner "Ever Fresh Source of Knowledge and Strength" which defies (refuses) running out. Lord is concluding the chapter repeating the clarion (strong and direct) call of Kathopnishad "Arise.. awake … …." The word "arise" has been used to call Arjuna out of the inertia of ignorance. At the start of the discussion, Arjuna was looking from the perspective of an ordinary man confined to think in terms of relationships arising due to physical body. He did not know about righteousness. He did not know about divine knowledge. He did not know that mere action can be yajna connecting the individual to the "Eternal Source of Divine Energy." Now Arjuna is equipped with insight about all these aspects. He must collect himself (body, mind intelligence at one single point) to restore the old doubting self to "real nature of Arjuna, a warrior who depicted pure beauty and excellence in war-fare." Arjuna now has to get up to be out of this inertia of spiritual slackness. Lord is using the next word "awake" i.e. Arjuna should be fully awake i.e. he should be up with full cognizance (understanding of) of divine consciousness and his absorption in the objective before him i.e. he was to wage war to restore righteousness, a divine purpose of immensely continuing nature in terms of cosmic benefit. Arjuna has to be awake i.e. enlivened to the present moment, its delicacy, its far reaching consequences, its impact on the future of the world at large. Lord wanted Arjuna to do a yajna, an activity of self-offering in the fire of cosmic benefit ("disregard to Dharma" was to be annihilated, finished). That is why Lord wanted him to be fully awake i.e. fully conscious, fully understanding the present moment. All this goading (to make someone to do something) was necessary to get Arjuna out of soul-killing doubt, which necessitated the Gita discussion.

इति श्रीमद्भगवद्गीतासूपनिषत्सु
ब्रह्मविद्यायां योगशास्त्रे श्रीकृष्णार्जुनसंवादे
ज्ञानकर्मसंन्यासयोगो नाम चतुर्थोऽध्यायः ॥ ४ ॥

Thus ends the fourth chapter entitled
"The yoga of knowledge or Renunciation of Action in Knowledge"
In the Upnishad of the Bhagavad Gita, the science of God, the scripture of yoga
The divine-dialogue between Sri Krishna and Arjuna.

Practical Relevance of 4ᵗʰ chapter in life

This chapter emphasizes the sacrifice of action in the light of divine knowledge (knowledge relating to all aspects of the form and the Formless). What is it that happens when yoga and divine knowledge become one? Divine knowledge guides, sets the course and takes the seeker towards the purpose of existence (Supreme Universal Eternal reality; *Purshottama*). The yoga discussed in this chapter is superior to all other forms of yoga. Those other yogas may take the seeker to impersonal Brahmin (Supreme universal Reality) or to a personal deity (one of the perceived Gods (refer to introduction for God and Gods) or liberation (*moksha*) in action-less knowledge. The yoga discussed in this chapter unfolds the highest secret, the whole secret, the sovereign secret in its most sublime form. The result is divine peace, divine work or divine knowledge. Then, one undergoes the experience that this creation is the manifestation of the 'Divine-joy' (joy of the Supreme Master, the indweller sitting in all). This creation is sustained by that 'Divine-joy' only. It progresses towards that 'Divine-joy'. That 'Divine-joy' alone is its final abode. This chapter guides towards the fullness of that 'Divine-joy'.

Key Knowledge-points discussed so far in this volume and view beyond

1. The discussion in the Bhagavad Gita starts with knowledge (11ᵗʰ verse of 2ⁿᵈ chapter). The term knowledge has different connotations (additional meanings in addition to main meaning). Knowledge, in the Bhagavad Gita, means knowledge about the self, about the "Never Changing Aspect" within a being (one in existence) or divine knowledge. This is the eternal, indestructible and immanent aspect of a being. It is the "Truth" or Reality of a being or "Un-manifested Eternal Existence" relating to a being. Knowing this "truth" amounts to realizing "Universal Principle of Unity" that there is in every being, animate or inanimate, and even beyond this too i.e. un-manifested state. It is the realm of inner stillness, an ever continuing peace and joy that is inseparable from a being. It is true fundamental nature of being, an amalgam of *Sat* (Truth), *chit* (consciousness) and *anand* (bliss). When it is under the cover of ego within, it is called "Individualized soul or the soul under the cover of Ignorance." When this cover of ignorance is removed by divine knowledge, then the self, whose brilliance shines the whole Universe, majestically appears in full glory. Then one realizes the main source of the being. Lord explains in subsequent chapter that it is a very great achievement. The knots of the heart are broken. All doubts are cut. Karma and its effects cease to exist when the self is realized. It (this self) is different from the entity that one sees in the mirror i.e. the ever changing aspect of a being. In the

Bhagavad Gita's parlance, it is called *Atma* (soul) or *Purusha or* the self or inner energy or spirutal field within the body or doorway to the deeper affinity with "The All." In the parlance of the Bhagavad Gita, knowledge about this "never changing universal eternal and immanent aspect" is called "*Sankhya*-Knowledge or *Upnishadic* Interpretation of the Soul or yoga of Divine Knowledge or wisdom (which one attains by application of right intelligence in the right way) ". Lord Krishna starts talking about this aspect from verse 11 of the 2nd chapter and leaves its advanced aspect i.e. universal aspect for the subsequent chapters.

2. This "Never Changing Aspect" of a being is not a subject to be understood by mind. For realizing this, one needs to get to the "inner sky of one's consciousness." This can be realized only by resolute, one pointed disciplined intelligence. For this reason, Lord uses the term "Buddhir-Yoga; Yoga of Intelligence" in 39th verse of second chapter. The word yoga is being continuously used with all discussions. It means perfecting all disciplines (physical, mental, emotional and spiritual) for uniting "the deluded individual eternal existence" with the "Universal Eternal Principle" that there is in a being, animate, inanimate or beyond i.e. in an un-manifested state as well. Cosmic consciousness is in the consciousness of soul. Getting to "cosmic consciousness and getting established there" is the ultimate focal point of yogas (various paths of disciplines) discussed by the Lord Krishna in the Bhagavad Gita.

3. Developing a "resolute, one-pointed, disciplined or cultured intelligence" is not possible without action. Therefore, Lord introduces another term in the 2nd chapter i.e. "Karam-Yoga; action done with awakened awareness, for cosmic benefit and full surrender."

4. Arjuna, an accomplished warrior of his era, is in an extremely agitated state of mind. He is utterly dejected and he has lost touch with his discriminatory faculty. This is the state of a common man. All achievements appear transitory and devoid of substance in this state. Each individual is carrying some burden somewhere inside due to human afflictions (illness, bereavements, failure resulting from ignorance). Arjuna asks from the Lord description of one, who has steady wisdom and who is in super-conscious state. Lord answers this question in detail. In a way this also explains why a common individual from any background should read the Bhagavad Gita. An individual with steady wisdom is not shaken by adversity. He is free from attachment fear and anger i.e. this individual is free from three afflictions i) arising from diseases or disorders in one's own body, ii) arising from thunder, lightening, storm and flood and iii) arising from scorpions, cobras tigers etc. Such an individual remains self-controlled, moving among the objects with senses under restraint, free from attraction and repulsion. Such an individual enjoys the peace (suffusing, enchanting, enthralling) of "The Eternal." Such an individual gets the *Brahmic* state (eternal state without any trace of any limitation of any type) or the true fundamental eternal, unchanging nature of a being.

5. In 3rd chapter, lord elaborates "Karam- Yoga" by explaining action, inaction and wrong action. Then Lord adds new dimensions to this discussion about "karam-yoga" by introducing such thoughts as "predominance of modes (sattva, rajas and tamas; refer to introduction for detailed discussion) of *Prakriti* (nature) in the performance of action of a being," "Yajna (Sacrifice)-concept," "*Lokasangrah*; cosmic-benefit," performing work without attachment to fruit of action and surrendering to the "Supreme." Lord beautifully concludes this chapter by highlighting the hierarchy (system showing the order of different levels) of elements [both ever changing (all except Eternal Existence) and never changing (Exclusive Eternal Existence) within a being]. Lord says "..the senses are superior (to the body); superior to senses is the mind; superior to the mind is the intellect; one who is superior to the intellect is He (the self; the never changing; eternal indweller within)." Therefore, knowledge of the self (..thus knowing Him as superior to intellect) is the last word of the Lord in this chapter "Karam-Yoga;

yoga of action." Knowledge is the foundation of the karma-Yoga. Nishkama Karam (action detached from fruit of action) leads to jnana (knowledge) and jnana makes nishkama-karam possible. Therefore, yoga of knowledge is the 4th chapter.

6. To work and yet to be free from the effects of work requires subtle understanding of the secret of work. For this reason Lord deals in detail with "Jnana-Yoga" in the 4th chapter with such knowledge as "inaction in action," "action in inaction," abandoning attachment to fruit of action, action for the sake of sacrifice (Yajna, the spirit of sacrifice, which facilitates the universal cycle) and remaining connected with the eternal existence within in all situations. Thus there is sufficient discussion so far to take a seeker to "Sankhya-knowledge." Is that all? No. The seeker has to go still beyond with the divine knowledge towards the "Soul of all the Souls." For this one needs renunciation. Therefore, in the 5th chapter, Lord now discusses "Yoga of renunciation" which matures a person to get rid of ever capturing tendencies of action.

7. The basic target of human existence has been given by the Lord i.e. being established in the knowledge (divine) and attaining oneness with the Supreme or "Centering the awareness and entering the Divinity." For this, there are basically two yogas (disciplines) i.e. yoga of knowledge and yoga of action. All other paths are combinations or refinements according to the attributes of the seeker or the intermediate stage of spiritual development of the seeker. Now Lord will deal in detail about the "The ever changing aspect" of a being i.e. manifested nature or *Prakriti* or that which is influenced by time, cause and effect or tendencies like illumination, activity and dullness.

8. Thus, in the rest of the chapters, lord elaborates on various facets of this "Supreme Secret," which is more secret than secrecy itself. The main focus will be on the Supreme Lord who dwells in the heart of all beings. Final advice of Lord Krishna will be "Take refuge in 'Him' in every way of thy being and by His grace thou shall come to the 'Supreme Peace' and 'Eternal Status'." Following the words of lord Krishna one experiences the "Unbounded Spirit of the universe" in one's own soul. Consciousness of "That Holy Presence" helps the individual to transcend surely failure, grief and despair.

9. The words of Lord Krishna will continue to help in experiencing "Timeless and Soundless Sound" or the "Eternal Universal Excellence" within and around. "That ever beckoning light" will save from the snare of deception and even beyond.

Note: Let there be pause in continuity. Further discussion about the "words of lord Krishna" will be resumed in the second volume due to paucity of space.

Parting Note

Dear Reader,

If intensity, depth and substance of the words of Lord Krishna have touched the chord within you somewhere and it makes you feel serene, composed and radiantly sure of the road ahead, then do pass on a message to all your friends and relatives on social media to refer to the following link:

https://feelthebhagwadgeeta.wordpress.com

About the Author

Vijay Kumar Saxena is a postgraduate in commerce and a fellow of the Institute of Cost and Works Accountants of India. He retired from Bharat Heavy Electricals as Deputy General Manager. He has written several books on cost accounting, financial accounting, management accounting, cost audit, and management audit.

Printed in the United States
By Bookmasters